D0897910

ATHENS ON TRIAL

ATHENS ON TRIAL

THE ANTIDEMOCRATIC
TRADITION IN WESTERN THOUGHT

JENNIFER TOLBERT ROBERTS

PRINCETON UNIVERSITY PRESS

PRINCETON, NEW JERSEY

The citation from the *Aeneid* is from *The Aeneid of Virgil* by Allen Mandelbaum. Translation copyright © 1971 by Allen Mandelbaum. Used by permission of Bantam Books, a division of Bantam Doubleday Dell Publishing Group.

Citations from Homer's *Iliad* and Euripides' *Suppliants* appear courtesy of University of Chicago Press, from *The Iliad of Homer*, translated by Richmond Lattimore, copyright © 1951 by the University of Chicago, and the translation of *Suppliants* by F. W. Jones in *The Complete Greek Tragedies*, ed. Richmond Lattimore and David Grene, copyright © 1958 by the University of Chicago.

Excerpts from *The First and Second Discourses* by Jean-Jacques Rousseau, translated, edited, and annotated by Victor Gourevitch, copyright © 1986 by Victor Gourevitch, reprinted by permission of HarperCollins Publishers.

Citations from *The Politics of Aristotle* translated by Ernest Barker (Oxford, 1946) appear by permission of Oxford University Press.

Citations on pp. 112–15, from *Plutarch's Lives*, collected in *The Rise and Fall of Athens* and translated by Ian Scott-Kilvert (Penguin Classics, 1960), copyright © 1960 by Ian Scott-Kilvert, reproduced by permission of Penguin Books Ltd.

Library of Congress Cataloging-in-Publication Data

Roberts, Jennifer Tolbert, 1947–
Athens on trial : the antidemocratic tradition in Western thought /
Jennifer Tolbert Roberts.
p.   cm.
Includes bibliographical references and index.

ISBN 0-691-05697-8 (CL)
1. Democracy—Greece—Athens—History.   2. Democracy—History.
3. Political science—History.   I. Title.
JC79.A8R63   1994
321.8'0938'5—dc20   93-24553

For Bob . . .

Whence comes it, this universal big, black Democracy?
—Thomas Carlyle

CONTENTS

PREFACE AND ACKNOWLEDGMENTS

D RAWING ON Nietzsche's *Gay Science*, Foucault identified truth as "undoubtedly the sort of error that cannot be refuted because it was hardened into an unalterable form in the long baking process of history." It is a very long baking process indeed that I seek to undo in this book.

For centuries Athens has enjoyed a reputation as the unrivaled artistic and intellectual center of the Greek world. Bearing in mind Pericles' description of his city as the "school of Hellas," many a modern metropolis has sought to exalt itself by posing as the cultural heir of the Athenians. Renaissance Florentines styled their city-state a second Athens, and Wittenberg cast itself as "Athens on the Elbe"; Edinburgh has claimed to be a new Athens; Bogotá dubs itself the Athens of Latin America; and in the United States, Boston has put itself forward as the Athens of the Northeast, Transylvania College of Kentucky has purported to be the Athens of the West, and both Atlanta and Nashville have claimed the name of Athens of the South (though only Nashville has built its own Parthenon.) To appropriate the mantle of the "school of Hellas," however, is not to support the Athenians' unusual form of government either as a phenomenon unique in time and place or as an example to be followed in other times and places. Throughout most of Western history, Athenian democracy per se has been in bad odor. It is important to remember this in a world in which democracy has, in the words of political scientist John Dunn, become "the moral Esperanto of the present nation-state system, the language in which all Nations are truly united." Once democratic principles became synonymous with legitimacy in government, the democracy of the Athenians was accorded a place of great honor in the pantheon of political regimes. It should not be imagined, however, that Athenian government served as the inspiration for the democratic movement that gathered force in modern Europe and America in the age of revolution. Now regarded as a legitimizing ancestor, classical Athens was for centuries excluded from the company of respectable governments. Modern democracies, of course, are given to putting themselves forward as the Athenians' heirs, rather like the usurpers who became emperors of Rome through military coups and then piously adopted themselves into the families of their predecessors. The reality is quite different. It would be too simple to suggest that modern democracies came into being in spite of Athenian democracy rather than because of it. In reality, much of the important political thinking of the West derived from thinkers like Plato and Aristotle who, though fundamentally opposed to Athenian democracy, were nonetheless very much its products. But prior to the age of revolution there was little in the reputation of Athenian government that was likely to inspire emulation. Rather, Athens served as a foil the better to set off the virtues of governments that accorded far less power to the untutored masses.

The hostile tradition about Athenian democracy, which has its roots in ancient Athens itself, forms the subject matter of this book. Why, I have asked, has Athenian government been the focus of so much opprobrium? If Athenian government was really not so bad, why should so many people have thought it was; and if it truly was as terrible as it has often been made out to be, why should its critics continue to devote so much time to demonstrating its weaknesses again, and again, and again? Beginning in class bias and developing into an intellectual construct with a life of its own, the anti-Athenian tradition has become a crucial building block of Western political thought. How did this tradition begin, and, once begun, how did it gather strength?

My exploration of these questions has led me to examine a large body of literature written over several centuries and in a variety of languages, and it calls for a few words on methodology. First, there is the question of primary versus secondary sources. The works of twentieth-century scholarship that I cite in the notes have plainly been designated as "references," "authorities" of some kind with which I have interacted in a different way from the way in which I have interacted with the texts I analyze. This designation is, of course, entirely arbitrary; it may and should be discarded by any reader who investigates the origins of these modern texts. My own ability to probe the sources of people's thinking is limited by the same factors Protagoras reputedly identified as preventing certain belief in the gods—the shortness of life and the difficulty of the subject matter. Now if I had written a book on Greek tragedy, I would have made reference to the work of Aeschylus and Sophocles and Euripides, and I would have made reference to the work of Karl Reinhardt and Charles Segal and Helene Foley and Froma Zeitlin, and everyone would understand that I approached these two sets of texts in very different ways. Because I am part of "everyone," I would also understand this myself. But I have not written a book on Greek tragedy. Instead, I have written a book about how people think about Athens and, more broadly, about how they think about politics and society. When an author writes about intellectual genealogy, an ineluctable paradox cuts him or her off from *all others*, for if what Niccolò Machiavelli or James Madison or Benjamin Constant said about Athens needs to be placed in the context of his individual perspective, then of course my own views must be placed in the same context; and how can I cite the wisdom of Mark Hulliung on Machiavelli or Sheldon Wolin on Madison or Stephen Holmes on Constant, as if a birthdate after 1900 somehow guaranteed objectivity and omniscience—something my discussion of recent critiques of Athens in chapters 12 and 13 makes perfectly clear I do not believe? Why should I not busy myself investigating the politics of Mark Hulliung and Sheldon Wolin and Stephen Holmes and then explain *their* way of writing about their subjects as the product of their distinctive approach to the world?

The answer, of course, is that I cannot, because I would find myself delving into the political orientation of the *Dictionary of American Scholars* and the history of higher education in the twentieth century, and pretty soon it would be necessary to get a sabbatical to look into the genesis of the political opinions of people who had written books about higher education, and then . . . A case in point might be Frank Turner's study of *The Greek Heritage in Victorian Britain*, a tremendously thoughtful work I have found to be of enormous assistance in my own project. Readers who find the kind of intellectual history I have traced to be intriguing will certainly want to read Turner's book. Turner's approach to shifting perceptions of Greece differs from mine, and in the future someone may want to write about our work, grounding these differences in fundamental philosophical disagreements. Then Turner and I, who have each set up our texts as the *explicans* of the *explicandum* that is "thinking about Greece" will in turn become someone else's *explicanda*, and that is fine. We can only do our bit to extend the expanding genealogical framework; the next stage will be up to others. Should some scholar wish to suggest in a book or article that my writing about Athenian democracy is colored by my own view of the world, I will be honored to be the object of such discourse. (This promise applies to books and articles *only*. I make no commitment to be honored by such contentions if they appear in hostile book reviews.)

Second, there is the related question of perspective. In the preface to *The Whig Interpretation of History*, Herbert Butterfield lamented the tendency of many historians "to emphasise certain principles of progress in the past and to produce a story which is the ratification if not the glorification of the present." The particular story I have chosen to string together traces a line of development culminating in the thinking of the age in which I live—something that would look to Butterfield suspiciously like "progress." But this is the version of events that, having weighed and rejected alternative hypotheses, I am disposed to endorse. I considered writing a somewhat different book, one that questioned or even denied the existence of the ontological object "Athenian democracy" and refused to discriminate among more and less productive approaches to the state of the ancient Athenians. In the end, however, I determined that this amiable openness would ultimately be insincere. My conviction that ideologies of one kind or another have sometimes inhibited constructive thinking about Athens should not be taken to imply that I see myself as lacking ideology, that I believe that ideology is bad, or that I consider the writing of history to be separable from ideology. Nor do I mean to suggest that the march of civilization automatically facilitates a more thoughtful and open-minded examination of the past. In his unsettling book *Black Athena: The Afroasiatic Roots of Classical Civilization*, Martin Bernal has argued that a significant shift can be identified between 1815 and 1830 in the way people have viewed the contribution of Asian and African civilizations to the growth of Greece. This change, he maintains, resulted in a less accurate assessment of this contribution, one vitiated by racism. Curiously, the years he identifies as pivotal are precisely those years in which attitudes toward Athens underwent the most dramatic transformation.

Third, I would like to say a few words about the scope of this book. On the whole I have avoided examining generalizations about "the Greeks" except where it is plain to me that the Athenians specifically are intended. By the same token I have tried to focus on allegations that distinguished Athens from other ancient states; thus for example I have not examined in much depth the charges that were leveled against the Athenians for their participation in a pre-Christian worldview. I have also tried as much as possible to keep to the question of democracy—seeking, for instance, to organize my discussion of modern interpretations of Athenian gender relations around their political implications. I have not discussed responses to Athenian government in poetry and in the visual arts. Nor was I able to include more than a cursory discussion of contemporary (i.e., ancient) responses to democracy in classical drama. I have rationalized this last decision, which was a difficult one, on the grounds that the political implications of tragedy have not on the whole played much of a role in thinking about the Athenian state until fairly recently, and where comedy is concerned, the political opinions of Aristophanes are somewhat elusive. Some years after publishing his book *The Victorians and Ancient Greece* Richard Jenkyns published a separate book on Greek themes in Victorian art; perhaps the same fate awaits me.

Because I am largely concerned with the era during which Athens was viewed in a fundamentally hostile way, I have dealt in depth largely with the period before 1850, and I have not discussed in any detail the treatment of Athens in the academy of the twentieth century. The limits of time and space have also precluded discussions about debates over Athens among European journalists that might stand alongside my discussion of Athens in the American press. Being an American has given me fairly easy access to materials that would have been difficult to obtain for, say, France or Germany. My slowness in reading modern Greek and Russian as well as my hopeless ignorance of Asian languages also placed obvious limitations on the scope of my work. This is, perforce, very much a book on the Western tradition.

Finally, a few words on my own language: my reference to Athens and "her" government may at first appear to be a strangely sexist usage. This usage is occasioned by the tradition that forms the subject matter of this book. Despite the exclusion of women from the political decision-making process at Athens, for centuries historians have written about Athens as if it were female. In addition, people writing about the relations of the sexes regularly discuss the treatment of women by "the Athenians" as if "the Athenians" were all men. Until the twentieth century, moreover, there is virtually no evidence about what women have thought in looking back on Athenian government (though Greek drama both tragic and comic offers some tantalizing hints about what

Athenian women themselves may have believed). The first text with which I deal that was clearly written by a woman (Jeanne-Marie Roland) dates from the late eighteenth century; it is only during the past half-century or so that a significant number of women have left written records of their opinions about Greek history. Because this book traces the Western tradition, therefore, it has seemed appropriate to me sometimes to refer to Athens as "she" and discuss "her" government, although I myself see no reason to believe that states have gender.

Translations from foreign languages are my own unless otherwise specified. Classical texts are cited according to the standardized format that appears in the *Oxford Classical Dictionary* (Oxford, 1970).

Some of the ideas expressed here were foreshadowed in journal articles published throughout the 1980s. Readers may recognize some of what I have said about British attitudes toward Athens from "Athenians on the Sceptered Isle," *Classical Journal* 84 (1989): 193–205, and portions of "The Teflon Empire: Chester Starr and the Invulnerability of the Delian League," *Ancient History Bulletin* 23 (1988): 9–53 reappear here and there in chapter 12. Parts of chapter 6 appeared in somewhat different form in "Florentine Perceptions of Athenian Democracy," *Medievalia et Humanistica*, n.s. 15 (1987): 25–41.

This book ranges over many centuries and deals with texts in a variety of languages, and it was ten years in the making. During this decade I have acquired more debts than I can begin to reckon up. As my project has taken me farther and farther from my field of expertise, I have relied increasingly on the kindness of scholars who gave generously of their time and employed the greatest of tact in discouraging me from pursuing novel hypotheses whose charm exceeded their defensibility.

Let me begin at the beginning. The premises that inform this book began to take shape around 1970 when I had the privilege of studying at Yale College with two impressive and very different teachers, Eric Havelock and Peter Rose. I am greatly indebted to them both for alerting me to the ideological conflicts that have shaped the study of classical Athens. As a graduate student I was encouraged in my interest in Athenian government by Donald Kagan, and several years later I began work on this book while teaching at Southern Methodist University in Dallas. My colleagues in the Department of History at SMU have been a source of many different kinds of support over these years, and this book owes much to them. It is always precarious to single out individuals, but I would like most particularly to thank Daniel Orlovsky and David Weber for their advice and support during the time they each served as Department Chair; Jeremy Adams for providing continual infusions of energy and insight; Peter Onuf and Edward Countryman for helping to guide me through my investigation of the perilous period of America's foundation; Donald Niewyk for saving me from a variety of embarrassing mistakes; James Hopkins for offering the aid and comfort of his office as Associate Dean for

General Education as well as his friendship as a member of my department; James Breeden for his warmth and wit; Judy Mohraz for her unstinting generosity; Dennis Cordell for asking good questions; Luis Martin for being Luis; and Thomas Knock for a brotherly nurturing and palship of a kind I have never received elsewhere. I also owe a profound personal and professional debt to another member of the department, Kathleen Wellman. Although it is true that she has been willing to take considerable time and trouble discussing the Renaissance and the eighteenth century with me, my chief debt to her is for a sustaining and enduring friendship that has survived over the years despite syncopated leaves of absence that kept one or the other of us away from Dallas for half of the eight years we both taught at SMU.

Colleagues at other institutions whose assistance was invaluable to me are many. Dorothea Wender bears much of the credit for molding a scholar out of the unformed matter she encountered when I first came to teach at Wheaton College in 1975 full of ignorance and enthusiasm. Robert Rowland, Barry Strauss, and Susan Wiltshire provided warmth and wisdom throughout. Among those who were gracious enough to read portions of my work and offer useful suggestions I would particularly like to thank Michael Altschul, Ernst Badian, Jeffrey Barnouw, Stanley Burstein, William Calder, Anthony Molho, Martin Ostwald, Carl Richard, Richard Weigel, and most particularly Kurt Raaflaub, for whose thoughtful and detailed comments on the early chapters I am profoundly grateful. Juliet Floyd was kind enough to share with me her perspectives on Hegel. I have also profited a great deal from participation in various programs with Ward Briggs, Elaine Fantham, Josiah Ober, and Paul Rahe.

Throughout the past ten years, one friend and colleague in particular offered indispensable support as well as precious insight into the issues surrounding Athenian democracy. Just a phone call away, Donald Lateiner was an unstinting source of encouragement and advice as well as of an astonishingly rich and pertinent bibliography. He and Marianne Gabel fielded frequent despairing calls and were always ready to administer stern doses of common sense, and for this I am profoundly grateful.

My friends in the Association of Ancient Historians have always been an important part of my life, and this book owes much to their comradery of many years. I particularly wish to express my thanks to a few members of the Association who took a special interest in this project—Eugene Borza, Jack Cargill, Phyllis Culham, Walter Donlan, Frank Frost, Erich Gruen, Judith Hallett, Jerzy Linderski, Vincent Rosivach, Larry Tritle, Martha Vinson, and Allen Ward. I also benefited a great deal from comments received from colleagues on parts of this work presented not only at meetings of the Association but also at a variety of conferences throughout the United States and in Athens. I am particularly grateful to participants in the 1992 NEH Institute on Athenian Democracy at the University of California at Santa Cruz, at which Charles Hedrick was kind enough to invite me to spend a week as a visiting speaker.

Michael Hudson, Drew Harrington, Eli Sagan, Lowell Edmunds, Mogens Hansen, Daniel Tompkins and Frank Turner were all kind enough to supply me with copies of their own work, either recently completed or in progress, that were of considerable assistance to me, and my research went the faster for their cooperation. I owe a particular debt to Michael Shute, whose manuscript on Benjamin Franklin I had the privilege of reading while it was in progress. My own treatment of the reception of Athenian democracy in eighteenth century America might have proceeded along quite different lines had Mike not died during the summer of 1991 with so many conversations still unfinished.

Peter Euben and Ellen Wood not only read the manuscript for Princeton University Press and offered innumerable helpful suggestions but gave generously of their time in subsequent conversations and correspondence. My debt to them both is enormous. During the years the book was in progress Joanna Hitchcock of the Press gave much-needed encouragement with welcome regularity, and the final stages were made easier by the hard work of Lauren Oppenheim and Lauren Osborne.

This project could never have been completed within a decade without the generous assistance of the American Council of Learned Societies, which provided me with a Grant-in-Aid to conduct research in Florence in the summer of 1984, and the National Endowment for the Humanities, which awarded me a Fellowship for College Teachers for 1985–86. I am also very much indebted to Southern Methodist University for two research leaves and for summer support that enabled me to conduct research in Italy and France and to return to the Institute for Advanced Study in Princeton, where I was a member in 1985. Throughout, the Institute provided a fertile and much-cherished working environment, and I think of it with enormous gratitude and affection. My time there, however, would have been lonely indeed without the warmth and hospitality provided by Christian and Freia Habicht.

Many industrious librarians furthered my research. I would particularly like to thank the kind souls in the rare book room of Princeton's Firestone Library. I am indebted to Matthew Maltzman in Cambridge, Eva Stehle in Maryland, and Rosaria and Eric Munson in Princeton for their hospitality, which afforded me (among other things) much-needed opportunity to do library work. William Harris was gracious enough to arrange for me to use the Columbia University libraries during 1990 and 1991. I also owe much to Mark Randolph and Cathy Alton-Thomas for assistance of various kinds in preparing the final manuscript.

It would have been difficult to complete this project without the sustenance of a number of friends in Dallas, and I would particularly like to express my gratitude to Paul Crabtree, Vicki Hill, Jill Nelson, Mary Read, Martha Satz, and Bonnie Wheeler. Friends and family in other parts helped in many different ways. Chris Roberts allowed himself to be persuaded that the fate of humanity hung on the completion of this book—or so, at least, he led me to believe. Page Tolbert understood the importance of the scallion pancake in fostering the life of the mind. Ingrid and Walter Blanco providing unfailing encouragement when spirits flagged and even let me win at Trivial Pursuit now and again. Stanley Heller was always there to remind me that no book is ever perfect. My parents, Jack and Elinor Tolbert, were happy to open the ancestral home to me during my sabbatical leave in 1990–91 (though informants have suggested to me that they were even happier when I found alternative housing). In the last stages of production, the liveliness and curiosity of my students at the City College of New York was invigorating and inspirational.

The support of Robert Lejeune was indispensable in completing this book. When I first met Bob in the Hunan Balcony at 98th Street and Broadway in Manhattan, this manuscript existed in embryonic form in thirty-nine Word-Star files on thirteen disks in the operating system CP/M. The assistance he rendered me in bringing these scattered documents together went far beyond the ruthlessness with which he upgraded my computer literacy to the level of quasi-respectability. For his insights as a sociologist, his tolerance for my frenetic work habits, and his determination that I would finish this book in spite of myself, I am more grateful than I can adequately express in words.

ABBREVIATIONS

AJA   *American Journal of Archaeology*
AJP   *American Journal of Philology*
CJ   *Classical Journal*
CP   *Classical Philology*
CQ   *Classical Quarterly*
GRBS   *Greek, Roman, and Byzantine Studies*
JHS   *Journal of Hellenic Studies*
QS   *Quaderni di Storia*
REG   *Revue des Études Grecques*
TAPA   *Transactions of the American Philological Association*

ATHENS ON TRIAL

Chapter One

INTRODUCTION

> The search for descent is not the erecting of foundations: on the
> contrary, it disturbs what was previously considered immobile;
> it fragments what was thought unified; it shows the hetero-
> geneity of what was imagined consistent with itself.
> —Michel Foucault, *Nietzsche, Genealogy, History*

DURING THE LONG WAR between Athens and Sparta, the irrever-
ent Athenian aristocrat Alcibiades defected to the enemy because of
serious charges pending against him concerning various kinds of sac-
rilege against the state-supported religion. Once in Sparta, Thucydides maintains, Alcibiades sought acceptance by insisting that his active involvement
in Athenian politics did not really suggest support of Athenian democracy,
which, he contended, was an "acknowledged folly" that all sensible Athenians
recognized as silly.

The accuracy of this claim cannot be proven or disproven. Alcibiades' criteria for good sense must necessarily have been subjective, and even if we could
tell who was sensible and who was not, still we could not poll the dead Athenians to find out what the sensible ones thought. What is plain, however, is
that some of Alcibiades' brightest contemporaries spoke ill of the democratic
government of their native state—Thucydides, for example, Plato, and Alcibiades' teacher Socrates—and that they were supported in this endeavor
after Alcibiades' death by a famous adoptive Athenian, Aristotle (from
Stagira in northern Greece), who became Plato's longtime pupil. Out of their
reservations was born political theory—literally, "looking at the city-state."
As J. S. McClelland has recently pointed out, "It could almost be said that
political theorizing was *invented* to show that democracy, the rule of men by
themselves, necessarily turns into rule by the mob. . . . If there is such a thing
as a western tradition of political thought," McClelland concludes, "it begins
with this profoundly anti-democratic bias."[1] And so in fifth- and fourth-century Athens there began a strange and compelling symbiosis between the democratic body politic and the body of antidemocratic theorizing. This interplay
lived on in thought long after the independent democratic city-state of
Athens had ceased to exist. Parasitic on Athenian democracy, classical political theory kept it alive by its compulsive need to point up its failures again and
again and again.

It is a curious phenomenon that the hostile tradition about Athenian de-mocracy should have sprung from the written word, for in reality Athenian government was the product of a civilization that was oral in essence. Much in politics is always accomplished by politicians talking to one another, but democracy frequently entails some kind of public record of formal debate and decision, something along the lines of the American Congressional Record or the French Archives Parlementaires. For Athens this is completely lacking. Words once spoken in the assembly and the council vanished into the air, and we are left with Thucydides' version of Pericles' funeral oration, Demosthenes' accounts of his own heroism, and parodies of political life such as those in Aristophanes' *Congresswomen* out of which to reconstruct what was really said. An intensely verbal people, the Athenians had little interest in a literal record of sayings and doings. An underdeveloped technology discouraged reg-ular record keeping, and lack of interest discouraged improvements in tech-nology. No real records of government proceedings survive beyond the laws and inscriptions chiseled in stone. Even words, of course, can be cryptic. The vote to send Miltiades out to accomplish good for Athens concealed an expe-dition against the island of Paros, and an impending attack on the Corinthi-ans was encoded in the vote that Corinth should be "safe." People lie about both their intentions and their motives, and the survival of words is no guar-antee that lived reality can be faithfully recaptured. But words are a beginning, and the highly impressionistic nature of the images of Athenian democracy that have come down to us has opened the door to a wide range of interpreta-tions of Athens's government and history.

Despite the secondhand nature of the words that have survived—the speeches "reported" in Thucydides' history, Plato's version of Socrates' trial, Plutarch's moralizing biographies written centuries after the fact—most of those who have sought to recapture the reality of Athenian political life have done so through media that are almost exclusively verbal. Only recently have archaeologists sought to clarify cruxes by seeking out and analyzing evidence of a physical nature. During the Roman republic as well as the French Revolu-tion, in both Renaissance Italy and eighteenth-century Britain, the history of the Athenian democracy was reconstructed by reading the writings of the ancients and the accretion of early modern speculation that was itself based on these writings, as one written word upon another sought to recapture a phe-nomenon that was oral in its origins.

Writing about Athenian democracy began in the fifth century itself. Trag-edy and comedy both were intensely concerned with the nature of the civic bond. Their messages, however, are inscribed in a way that has made the ideology of Attic playwrights singularly obscure. As in the Roman republic, moreover, surviving texts date from a comparatively late period in the state's development, and they are rarely authored by the chief participants. We have not a word from the pen of Cleisthenes, of Themistocles, of Aristides, of Ephialtes; given the uncertainties that surround the speeches in Thucydides' history, we may have nothing from Pericles either, or from Cleon. We have, in short, no equivalent at all of America's federalist papers; we have no diaries of Miltiades, no correspondence between Pericles and Ephialtes in which they map strategy and grope toward ideology. The antidemocratic account of the development of Athenian government in the treatise entitled *The Constitution of the Athenians* sometimes attributed to Aristotle was written about a century after the outbreak of the Peloponnesian War, a century and a half after Xerxes' invasion of Greece. The poetry of Solon aside, the studied verbal tradition about Athens started only after the Persian Wars and began with the tragedies of Aeschylus, followed by Herodotus's casual asides and the debate on government he set in sixth-century Persia. One of the most popular sources from which later civilizations learned about Greek history was the biographies of Plutarch, composed half a millennium after the Peloponnesian War.

Neither Herodotus nor Thucydides deals much with theories of domestic politics, but the picture of Athenian democracy in Thucydides' history has made a deep impression on readers. Thucydides seems to have preferred some form of broad oligarchy, and he consistently portrays the Athenian demos as unreasoning and unreasonable. He connects Athens's loss of the Peloponnesian War with the inadequacies of her democratic system. In Pericles Thucydides saw a dramatic exception to the norms of Athenian political life; for Pericles, he writes, unlike other Athenian politicians, was able to control the multitude rather than being controlled by it, whereas his successors, "more on a par with one another, and each seeking to be foremost, ended by committing even the conduct of public affairs to the whims of the masses," a practice that produced a predictable "host of blunders" (2.65.6). The so-called Old Oligarch (once thought to be Xenophon) depicted democracy as a tyranny of the poor over the beleaguered rich, whereas the real Xenophon was captivated by Sparta and discounted working people as a legitimate force in politics.

During the fourth century, the question of Athenian democracy came to be subsumed by larger questions of political, ethical, and educational theory and the search for the best life in the best state. Plato mocked the amateurism of the democratic system and pilloried the leaders it brought to power, and Plato's Socrates maintained that Pericles was accused of having made the Athenians "idle, cowardly, loquacious, and greedy" by instituting state pay for state service such as jury duty (*Gorgias* 515E). Horrified by the execution of Socrates and pessimistic about the possibility of reforming his native state of Athens, Plato sought refuge in composing ideal constitutions for various (presumably imaginary) elitist states. In his *Republic* he elevated his disapproval of Athenian democracy into a broad theoretical attack on democracy in general, and his intellectual authoritarianism discouraged an open dialogue on the subject with truth as its aim. Meanwhile the other renowned fourth-century educator, Isocrates, cast soulful glances back at the so-called ancestral constitution of bygone days when political privilege was allotted on a sliding scale according to class. In his own century he longed for some overlord such as Philip of Macedon who could lead the Greeks to recover their lost pride in a glorious campaign against the Persians. In the meantime his pupil Theopompus composed a searing attack on the Athenians' choice of leaders.

Taking up political theory where Plato had left it, Aristotle foreshadowed certain schools of twentieth-century thought in advocating apathy as the tamer of democracy. Sharing Xenophon's conviction that the poor simply were not political material, he sought to exclude such people from the decision-making process, arguing on occasion against granting them any share in the state but at other times resting content with the expectation that indifference would deter at least the farmers from bothering themselves with the political life of the city. Only people with a modicum of property, Aristotle writes, can have the leisure that fosters the attainment of goodness, and so ideally "it must be these people and only these who are citizens" since the class of mechanics and shopkeepers lead lives that are "ignoble and inimical to goodness" (*Politics* 1328b–29a [7.8.2]).[2] Specific allegations against Athens are buried in the *Politics* in a theoretical attack on democracy in general, but the shortcomings of Athens in particular come to the fore in the *Constitution of the Athenians* composed in Aristotle's lifetime either by Aristotle himself or by one of his pupils (based perhaps on notes taken during Aristotle's lectures.) There Pericles' institution of state pay for jurors is ascribed solely to his desire to compete with the personal largess of his rival, Cimon, and reference is made to the school that considered this system corrosive. The author emphasizes the decline of Athens after Pericles' death when "a series of men who were the ones most willing to thrust themselves forward and gratify the many with an eye to immediate popularity held the leadership of the people (*demagogian*)" (28.4).[3]

Only democracy made antidemocratic theory possible. Some of this facilitation lay in principles of dialogue and antithesis; as the Yale political scientist Robert Dahl has recently pointed out, "The very notion of democracy has always provided a field day for critics."[4] Some lay in a shared belief in responsible citizenship and the equitable distribution of authority and privilege. Aristotle's concept of the citizen, for example, owed a great deal to the evolution of that ideal in classical Athens. With the building blocks of political thought forged in democratic Athens, Athenian intellectuals constructed an elaborate attack on the very idea of democracy. By the time of the Macedonian conquest, all these blocks were squarely in place: Athenian democracy was a class government that constituted a tyranny of the poor over the rich. Like all tyrannies, this one was conducted according to whim rather than law. The democracy was incapable of conducting foreign policy and hence brought upon itself its grievous defeats first at the hands of Sparta and subsequently at those of Philip. The execution of Socrates was only the most prominent example of the rottenness of the Athenian jury system, which selected jurors largely from the lower classes and even went so far as to pay citizens for their time. The demos was irrational and excessive in its expectations of its leaders and thus treated them harshly and unreasonably. The Athenian system was bound to fail, posited as it was on the erroneous supposition that people of unequal merit should receive equal treatment. People who are not of comparable excellence should not be treated as if they were, and struggling workers cannot hope to attain the wisdom or objectivity accessible to men of leisure and education. A moderate sort of democracy at Athens was perhaps not such a bad thing when some appropriate class distinctions were observed, but at some point in the fifth century these distinctions ceased to be made. Pericles himself may possibly have had some merit, but his successors exploited the potential for demagogy in the rule of an uneducated assembly unfettered by legal precedent, and after his death Athenian political life became debased. Nor were the Athenians always just in their dealings with other city-states. It was no wonder they got their comeuppance at Chaeronea.

There existed an alternate and equally impressionistic tradition, one that could be extracted from the fragments of the pre-Socratic philosophers, from the pages of Herodotus and Demosthenes, from Sophocles and Euripides, and even from speeches reported by the antidemocratic Thucydides and Plato—Pericles' funeral oration delivered in 430 after the first year of the Peloponnesian War, for example, and Protagoras's defense of the democratic system. But it was not this alternate strand that European thinkers picked up and developed, but rather the hostile tradition. Under the Roman republic, Polybius discounted classical Athens as a chaotic state unworthy of serious examination, and Cicero was preoccupied with the ingratitude of the demos toward its leaders, with whose martyrdom he identified passionately. In the early empire, Valerius Maximus underlined the Athenians' mistreatment of their great leaders and Pompeius Trogus stressed the decline of Athens in the fourth century. Livy, though he did not discuss Athens directly, did much to undermine the reputation of classical democracy in the eyes of future centuries by his disparaging treatment of the Roman plebs. Athenian government did not fare much better at the hands of Greek writers than it had at those of Latin ones. Diodorus of Sicily, who relied primarily on the fourth-century world history by Ephorus of Cyme in Asia Minor, was supportive of the Athenians in their foreign policy but extremely critical of their form of government, stressing the emotionalism and ingratitude of the demos in dealing with its leaders and applauding the murder of the democratic reformer Ephialtes. Plutarch, by far the most influential source for ancient Greek history and politics until the nineteenth century, was inclined to view Athenian politics as a series of attempts by unscrupulous demagogues and persecuted statesmen to manipulate a fickle and volatile mob. The second-century orator Aelius Aristides wrote an impassioned attack on Plato's view of Greek democracy, but it represented

such a departure from a comfortingly consistent tradition that future generations chose to disregard it.

Not surprisingly, people in the Middle Ages knew little about Athenian
democracy and cared less. During the Renaissance, classical history was redis-
covered, and because the Renaissance began in Italy, it sparked a certain
amount of interest in the city-state as a political unit. In view of the notorious
obsession of Renaissance men and women with the life of the mind, one might
suppose that the school of Hellas would have captured their imaginations. In
fact, however, other Renaissance preoccupations—stability, for example—
proved dominant, and the writings of Machiavelli, Giannotti, and Guicciardini make clear that it was the armed camp on the Eurotas that was held up as
an ideal to emulate while the city of Athena was put forward as a cautionary
example to avoid.

If Italian republicans had little warmth for Athenian democracy, the great
experiment received a still chillier reception from northern monarchists. In
1576 Jean Bodin published his *Six Books of a Commonwealth*, which was translated into English in 1606 and enjoyed enormous popularity throughout Europe. There Athens is portrayed as the prototype of the popular state, and
Bodin marshals a full panoply of classical citations to demonstrate the evils of
popular government. "If we shall beleeve Plato," he begins, "wee shall find
that he hath blamed a Popular estate, tearming it, A Faire where every thing
is to bee sold. We have the like opinion of Aristotle, saying, That neither
Popular nor Aristocraticall estate is good, using the authorities of Homer. . . .
And the Orator Maximus Tirius holds, That a democraty is pernicious, blaming for this cause the estate of the Athenians, Syracusians, Carthagineans and
Ephesians: for it is impossible (saith Seneca) that he shall please the people,
that honours vertue." "How," Bodin asks, "can a multitude, that is to say, a
Beast with many heads, without iugement, or reason, give any good councel?
To aske councel of a Multitude (as they did in oldtimes in Popular Common-
weals) is to seek for wisdome of a mad man."[5]

Bodin exercised a profound influence on the British royalist Robert Filmer,
who in the 1630s composed his memorable *Patriarca*, subtitled A DEFENCE OF
THE NATURAL POWER OF THE KINGS AGAINST THE UNNATURAL LIBERTY OF THE
PEOPLE. Predictably, Filmer makes use of Athens as an example of the evils of
popular government, and in a pastiche gleaned from Thucydides, pseudo-Xenophon, Livy, Tacitus, Cicero, and Sallust, he assails the shortsightedness and
volatility of the mob, who "are not led by wisdom to judge of anything, but by
violence and rashness."[6] Opposed to Filmer in seventeenth-century England
was a whole school of classical republicans whose writings sparked the contention of Hobbes that there was scarcely anything so conducive to antimon-
archic sedition as the study of classical history.[7] Athens fared rather better in
this climate, but since the cardinal question that exercised these men concerned the contest of republicanism and monarchy, their writings do not al-

ways show fine distinctions among the classical states. To the idealistic martyr Algernon Sidney, governments as diverse as Sparta, Athens, and republican Rome all afforded variations on a single theme: the wondrous excellence of the mixed constitution. James Harrington, however, took a harder look at Athens and concluded that the Athenians had sinned grievously in their aggressive foreign policy, calling it inexcusable to bring one's allies under bondage, "by which means Athens gave occasion of the Peloponnesian War, the wound of which she died stinking."[8]

As the eighteenth century began, the abortive attempts of the British Tories to impeach a handful of Whig ministers spawned a series of remarkable essays on accountability in government, the first of which, the *Discourse of the Contests and Dissentions Between the Nobles and the Commons in Athens and Rome with the Consequences they had upon both those States*, was penned by none other than Jonathan Swift. Swift's tract set a precedent for the intensive mining of Athenian history for use in contemporary political squabbles, and he was promptly answered by several other essayists who harvested antiquity with a glee difficult for twentieth-century minds to comprehend. While some involved in the controversy repeated the accusations of fickleness and ingratitude that it had become customary to make against the Athenians, others held up the rigorous Athenian system of accountability as an exemplary prototype for modern times. Lavish use was also made of the Athenian example by the enemies who hounded Walpole in the 1720s and 1730s, as the collection known as *Cato's Letters* and the journal *The Craftsman* cried out for the need to keep an ever-watchful eye on government expenditure. The name of Pericles was frequently brought forward, and so far from decrying the ingratitude he encountered at the hands of the demos, the opposition to Walpole saw an inspiring example for their own day in the high standards to which the Athenians held him.

Accountability, however, is only one issue in good government, and though toward the beginning of the century Athens found numerous defenders among journalists and pamphleteers, the dominant tradition in eighteenth-century England was markedly hostile, with Hume looking down his nose at the emotional Athenian mob and Montagu frantically warning his compatriots that Britain would soon go the way of Athens if she did not mend her ways. Athenian government fared slightly better in France. To be sure, most French writers of the eighteenth century took a dim view of Athens. It was in France that the first thoroughgoing history of antiquity was published by the schoolmaster Charles Rollin in 1729, preceded by an imprimatur praising Rollin's "endeavours to improve the minds of youth."[9] Specifically, youthful minds were to be improved by learning that "fickleness and inconstancy were the prevailing characteristics of the Athenians" already in the fifth century, and in the fourth (as Tourreil had pointed out in his preface to his French Demosthenes), "the love of ease and pleasure had almost entirely extinguished that of glory, liberty, and independence"—a process begun by Pericles, the "first author of this degeneracy and corruption."[10] Shortly before the revolution, the Abbé Mably decried the capricious multitude of the fifth century in his *Observations on Greek History* and devoted his *Conversations of Phocion* to the degeneracy of the fourth; the *Conversations* stand in the tradition of a widespread cult of Phocion that was predictably hostile to the democracy that put him to death. In the 1780s the Abbé Barthélemy complained of the Athenian masses "insolently substituting their caprices for the laws" and praised Solon's precautions against "the incongruous measures of an ignorant and mad populace."[11] At the same time, however, creative thinkers like Voltaire prized the Athenian state for its patronage of the arts, its eloquence, its liberty, and its commerce, and debunked the received wisdom about the interlocking evils of luxury, decadence, and trade; and the iconoclastic Abbé Cornelius De Pauw defended the Athenians at almost every turn, even arguing that the blame for Philip's success at Chaeronea belonged to Sparta.

Voltaire and De Pauw, however, were considerably ahead of their time in their response to Athens, and given the more customary reputation of the Athenian democracy, it is not surprising that revolutionaries in both France and America made few appeals to Athenian examples. On the whole, America's founders considered Athens to be a negative model. The eventual collapse of all the ancient states was frequently held against them, and among the classical republics, Athens was the one that gave the most offense. Madison complained often of the "turbulence of democracy" in chaotic Athens, and John Adams saw in popular sovereignty an alarming threat to the sanctity of property, which he claimed Athenian democrats had violated. Too busy with the pressing concerns of their own situation to write about antiquity in any sustained way, eighteenth-century Americans reflected in their passing references to Athens an extraordinarily high anxiety level, and when the time came to gather for the remarkable dialogue about government that issued in the constitution, men whom the mobilization of King George's armed forces had not been able to deter from a bloody revolution nonetheless quaked at the Halloween pictures of Athenian democracy that had been painted for them by its detractors from Plato to Rollin, and, like the Florentines, ran scurrying for stability with such haste that the life of the mind was left carelessly behind. They also failed to see the radically different picture of the Athenian democracy that had been painted in Attic tragedy, and neglected to ask what kind of a people would have the appetite for such spectacles and the capacity to understand them. While some creative intellects in France and, most particularly, Germany, were beginning to suspect a connection between Athens's democratic constitution and her cultural achievements, the Americans, for all their supposed revolutionary mentality, followed their anglophone friends and relations in Britain in discounting the Athenian democracy as a scene of disorder and distress.

Insofar as the French appealed to classical precedents for their daring insubordination, they harked back to Sparta and to Rome. The principal Athenian identification discernible in revolutionary France was that of revolutionary heroes and would-be heroes with Athens's most famous martyrs, Phocion and Socrates: Jeanne-Marie Roland, awaiting death in prison, proclaimed herself a victim of injustice in the school of Socrates, Aristides, and Phocion; and her companion Buzot proclaimed that their confrere Brissot had died for the liberty of his country like Phocion and Algernon Sidney. Inevitably this paradigm cast the Athenian democracy in a bad light. Some on both sides of the Atlantic sought to sever ties with the past altogether; the French cast aside their calendar to signal the beginning of a brave new world, and many Americans—Quakers, for example—questioned the utility of classical *exempla* on the new frontier across the sea. Still, for British thinkers in particular, the disturbing developments in France and America served to reinforce the excoriation of the Athenians.

To apprehensive Britons, it looked very much as if Athenian democracy had been resurrected across the channel in all its license and caprice, and in the antidemocratic backlash that followed the revolutions, the pamphleteer Robert Bisset, the historian William Mitford, and the dean of Bristol, Josiah Tucker, all trotted out the Athenians as sobering examples to would-be revolutionaries. The study of Greek history, in Bisset's words, might do much to persuade Englishmen who were "deluded by democratic theories" that in truth "the happiest of all lands is THE LAND WE LIVE IN."[12] The many volumes of Mitford's Greek history were rife with invidious comparisons between Athens and England and punctuated by frightening parallels between Athenian and French democrats. At the same time that modern republican and democratic movements were causing alarm on the political front, however, the resurrection of the Greek aesthetic ideal in Germany was breeding a new respect for Athens. Spartan sculpture, after all, hardly afforded a promising field of study, and Winckelmann himself had identified Athens's democratic institutions as the source of her artistic achievements. In literature, meanwhile, Hölderlin and his mentor, Schiller, waxed romantic about Athens, and Herder had much good to say of the Athenian state in his *Outlines of the Philosophy of Man*. When toward the beginning of the nineteenth century the notion of democracy began to appear less threatening in some quarters and the Greek independence movement fired the minds of many Western Europeans, particularly in England, there was a predictable rise in the stock of Athens, the Greek capital. Most dramatically, the growth of liberalism in Britain led to a gradual rejection of Mitford's view of Greece at the hands of Macaulay and many men less well known. Though James Mill had placed Mitford's *History* in his son's hands, he had also cautioned that son against Mitford's view of Greek politics, and a groundswell of liberal thinking found its voice not only in John Stuart Mill but in Mill's friend George Grote and Grote's friend Connop Thirlwall.

The publication of Grote's *History* in ten volumes beginning in 1846 introduced a potent new strain into the study of Athenian government and society. What Grote saw as the hallmark of the Athenian state was the ability of its citizens meeting in assembly to transcend and override precisely the sorts of particularist interests that he believed stood in the way of social and political progress in Britain. Exalting Athenian democracy as the safeguard not only of liberty but, more surprisingly, of stability as well, Grote called into question such time-honored features of classical historiography as the glorification of Sparta, the contempt for the sophists, and the ridicule of the Athenian demagogues. What for centuries had been good was now bad, and what had been bad was downright heroic. The effect of Grote's work on continental historians was enormous. This impact is attested in an amusing footnote to the second edition of the *Histoire Grecque* of Victor Duruy, a professor at Reims and Paris and the minister of public instruction under Napoleon III from 1863 to 1869. In this note Duruy relates that his idiosyncratic preference for Athens over Sparta in his first edition of 1851 had earned him a severe chastisement from the administration of his university on the subject of his "temerities"; but since the publication a year later of Grote's assessment, he reports, his view has attained respectability.[13]

In Britain itself Grote's mark could be seen not only on numerous Victorians but on many of the eminent Edwardians who followed as well. E. A. Freeman, writing shortly before 1880, was to maintain that the Athenian "mob" in fact "made one of the best governments which the world ever saw," and in 1911 Alfred Zimmern in the footnotes to his study of *The Greek Commonwealth* described Periclean Athens as "the most successful example of social organization known to history."[14] Meanwhile across the Atlantic the ability of the independent American confederation to maintain itself without a king had done much for the reputation of all nonmonarchic governments, and many Americans themselves changed their tune about Athens as numerous southern landholders discovered in the glories of the acropolis hard evidence that slavery and freedom were more than compatible.

The rise of Fascism, Nazism, and Communism in the twentieth century served by and large to reinforce the new tendency to favor Athens over Sparta, as the liabilities of democratic license came to seem far less worrisome than the threat of totalitarianism. The anti-Athenian tradition, however, has continued to thrive, having had grafted onto it important new features missing in antiquity. To be sure, the time-honored strictures are often repeated; thus for example students who learn about ancient history from Tom Jones's *From the Tigris to the Tiber* are taught that "democracy for the Greeks is actually synonymous with ochlocracy, or mob rule" and that Athenian democracy "ended in dismal failure."[15] Just as commonly, however, the Athenians are censured today for oppressing women, slaves, and allies, and the state that was once reproached for being too democratic is now lambasted for not having been democratic enough. Whereas Americans confronted with two world wars had been happy to identify with high-minded Athenians fighting to make the world safe for democracy, ominous echoes of the Sicilian expedition in the wars in Vietnam and the Persian Gulf focused attention on the dangers of imperialism. Meanwhile the Athenians have suffered redoubled attacks on the invasive nature of ancient Greek society as a whole, with its indifference to privacy, emphasis on glory, and preoccupation with politics above all else. More thinkers than ever before are inclined to identify slavery as the fulcrum of the Athenian system, and feminists are not alone in suggesting that so far from the devaluation of women being an anomalous blot on an otherwise exemplary society, in truth the democratic ethos was entirely dependent on the denigration of all outsiders. The poor Athenians, it seems, cannot win. Once censured as crass levelers, they now find themselves under fire as closet aristocrats.

New issues have come to the surface as well, as interest in individual Athenian authors has provoked special kinds of thinking about Athens. The painful wars of the twentieth century have drawn many journalists to reread Thucydides and to see in him a determined defender of a democracy out to destroy itself. Meanwhile the redefinition of the American academy under pressure from marginalized groups (such as women and nonwhites) has moved some more conservative thinkers to reassert the values of Plato, who saw politics as the business of an intellectual elite, and to hold up for imitation an image of ancient Greece radically different from the world of Athenian democracy— lamenting, in the words of Allan Bloom, that philosophy has been "dethroned by political and theoretical democracy."[16] Recoiling in turn from the exaltation of the Platonic worldview at the hands of Bloom and others of the Chicago School founded by Leo Strauss, others have advocated a return to the pre-Platonic roots of Greek democracy. Like their predecessors in Victorian England, many American admirers of ancient Athens wish to bring about the improvement of public education to facilitate more widespread participation in democracy. Taking a broad view of what is political, they often stress the important role of shared civic festivals (such as tragedy) as forces for both unification and instruction. Thus while in eastern Europe the Communist-Socialist alternative to liberal democracy has been crumbling, in North America academics have been squabbling over who will receive custody of the Athenians.

.   .   .   .   .

If it were clear that the Athenian democrats were guilty as charged, the vigor and longevity of the anti-Athenian tradition would occasion little interest. Belief in the Athenians' exclusivity and the significance of this exclusivity for the lives of those who were not excluded—the citizen-voters—seem to me to be solidly grounded in the evidence. So are concerns about the consuming nature of an ethos that privileged politics above private and family concerns and inhibited the free differentiation of individuals among themselves. It is not in the least clear to me, however, that all the attacks on Athens rest on a solid base. A misplaced reverence for authority, I would argue, has shaped thinking about Athens in a double-barreled attack. First, this reverence led to denigration of government by the people; second, it promoted uncritical reading of the antidemocratic texts of classical Athens and early modern Europe.

In a little treatise once cataloged with the works of Xenophon, the fifth-century figure known to English-speaking readers as the "Old Oligarch" analyzed the Athenian democracy as a class government on the part of the demos in its own interest. Countless modern thinkers have agreed, taking demos as meaning, in Roman terms, *plebs* rather than *populus*, as the lower classes rather than as the entire citizenry. It is not obvious why this should have been so in a society like classical Athens in which all citizens, rich and poor, had the same political rights. Most have also seen the Athenian assembly as composed of ignorant, self-interested boors who were in no position to make enlightened decisions about the public good. Why these inadequacies should characterize the citizens of a bustling city-state small enough for everyone to have access to pertinent information is not clear either. In 415 the Athenian envoys to Sicily were duped by the citizens of Egesta into believing that Sicily was in fact wealthier than it was, and the envoys in turn were believed by the Athenian assembly, which voted a huge expedition to Sicily. Because the expedition ended in catastrophe, Thucydides highlights the gullibility and malleability of the *ekklesia* on this occasion. But despite his opposition to the Athenian assembly, which he attacks whenever possible, he is able to provide no other instance in which ignorance of the facts issued in an unwise policy decision. Nor is there any reason to be confident that the Athenians' democratic form of government occasioned Sparta's victory in the Peloponnesian War. It can be argued just as convincingly that it was the misconduct of Athens's aristocrats that led to the loss of the war—the timidity of Nicias, the vacillations of Alcibiades, and the treachery of the men who evidently betrayed the fleet in the battle off Aegospotami that ended the war. The aristocratic tradition—the same one that regards the corn dole at Rome as the beginning of the end—seeks to ground the final collapse of Athens in 338 in the rise of the so-called demagogues, and to the eventual separation, allegedly pernicious, of military from civilian power—and this despite the fact that thinkers writing in this tradition have themselves been loyal citizens of states that have taken such a separation to be axiomatic.

The claim that rich men were excluded from power in Athens and financially exploited by the lower classes rests on weak evidence, as does the conviction that rich people make better citizens than poor people. So does the allegation that the loss of the Peloponnesian War should be ascribed to the

Athenians' democratic form of government and the insistence that the politicians who succeeded Pericles lacked public spirit. Facile distinctions between ochlocracy and democracy, between demagogue and statesman, have informed the study of Athenian history, and historians have on the whole showed little sensitivity to the class bias of those Greeks who had the leisure to write about politics. In addition, oddly simplistic views of historical causation and inevitability seem to have been at work convincing thinkers both ancient and modern that the roots of Athens's two stunning defeats—at the hands of Sparta in 404 and of Philip in 338—can easily be traced to weaknesses in her political system and in fact go back over several decades. (Athenians themselves, of course, were concerned only with the first of these defeats, as little writing about democracy took place in Athens after the second.) Neither of these arguments is impregnable. Tracing the beginning of the end as historians of Athens have perceived it can be an amusing pastime. Many place it after the defeat of 404; some insist it began already during the Decelean War (the middle phase of the Peloponnesian War); for still others it began with the death of Pericles; and several have traced it to the rise of Pericles himself. Some date it to the victory over Persia in 479 or the reforms of Cleisthenes a generation before; Mitford thunders that it was the reforms of Solon—who was normally regarded as a folk hero by democrat and oligarch alike—that paved the way for the final debacle. One is reminded of the search for Tacitus's ultimate verdict on the origins of Roman decline, a search that begins with the death of Tiberius in A.D. 37 and ends with the Twelve Tables (ca. 450 B.C.), which Tacitus pronounces the last piece of equitable legislation passed at Rome.

To some degree, the anti-Athenian tradition of the West arose naturally out of the class biases of the primary sources, and we cannot help wondering what sort of tradition would have sprung up had tracts on Athenian government been handed down from the pens of Pericles or Demosthenes or Sophocles. This, however, is not the whole story, for the dominant Western tradition about Athens became what it did through an ever-growing accretion of literature that systematically ignored dissonant texts challenging the received wisdom. For Plato, one twentieth-century scholar has written, "Democratic equality is . . . not a value among other values, but an attack upon all value, all order," and for many centuries this was a common belief among people who wrote books.[17] This belief hardly encouraged any open-minded examination of how the Athenians achieved what they did, and when praise of Athens was put forward by the minority who always rise above tradition, it generally fell on deaf ears. The lengthy defense of democratic ideology contained in Aelius Aristides' oration attacking Plato's Gorgias was greeted by a conspiracy of silence even on the part of those who cited the sentimental paean to Athens in Aristides' Panathenaic Oration, and the same American revolutionaries who fell so eagerly upon the Whiggish republican ideals expressed in Cato's Letters showed no interest in the defense of Athenian accountability expressed there. De Pauw's thoughtful book on Greece was largely ignored, and no reconsideration about the causes of the disaster at Chaeronea arose from its publication.

It is probably safe to say that all scholars, whether historians or biologists or political scientists, perceive themselves as open-minded and impartial students of their subject matter. (If Tacitus can claim to have written about Tiberius *sine ira et studio*—"without bitterness or partiality"—then anything is possible.) When I suggest, therefore, that I bring to this enterprise an openness and objectivity lacking in some of my predecessors, no reader has any reason to place faith in my claim. It would be dishonest, however, for me to suggest that the daunting obstacles to our understanding have persuaded me that there is no ontological object, however elusive, that is Athens—to put myself forward as a curious student of the human mind who has no particular beliefs about what might constitute a better or worse view of what happened in classical Athens and what it all means. Haskell Fain has likened the situation of a historian to that of the shut-out suitor whom a garden wall separates from his beloved, frustrating him "from ever achieving an epistemological consummation with the object of his intentions." The hapless historian, Fain observes, is reduced to using the occasional piece of trash tossed over the wall to "reconstruct what has taken place in those delightful walled gardens to which he is forever denied access."[18] Were some miracle of modern science to enable me to enter the walled garden that was classical Athens, I might be very much surprised, not to mention embarrassed, by how different it really was from what I have suggested. I do, nonetheless, have some opinions about how things were, some of which must by now be plain to readers—that the government was not unstable, that the citizens were not less knowledgeable or more irrational than the average person, and that the exclusion of outsiders was both economically and psychologically indispensable to the system.

In his book *On History and Philosophers of History*, William H. Dray opened a chapter on presentism by citing two conflicting views of how history must, and can, work.[19] The philosopher and educator John Dewey, he reminds us, insisted that "all history is necessarily written from the standpoint of the present, and is, in an inescapable sense, the history . . . of that which is contemporaneously judged to be important in the present." The historian Herbert Butterfield, however, author of *The Whig Interpretation of History*, roundly condemned this practice, contending that "the study of the past with one eye, so to speak, upon the present, is the source of all sins and sophistries in history." Approximate contemporaries, Dewey and Butterfield stand at opposite poles in their view of what history is for, but historians seeking guidance in the day-to-day practice of their craft will recognize instantly that both men are right. Therein lies a tale, and it is the fraction of this tale that touches on classical Athens that I wish to tell.

People who write about Athens by their own choice and not because they have been compelled to do so by a teacher whom they will remember grimly in adult life inevitably have some stake in this now-dead civilization. (It could even be argued that those constrained to write about the Athenians in order to receive academic degrees will develop such a stake in the course of their forced labor.) Not everyone's stake is the same, and the nature of the stake will shape what is written. There is no innocent and value-free writing about Greece. How could there have been, when Greek men who took up their pens were heavily invested in the political universe that swirled around them? How could there be, when the very choice to do so is remarkable in men and women who live in strikingly different societies with different priorities? As Allan Nevins has observed, moreover, history, unlike the physical sciences, "is violently personal," since "stars and molecules have no loves and hates, while men do."[20] (This observation, made in 1928, would be hard to get away with today as scientists and philosophers—feminists in particular—increasingly question the imagined objectivity of physical science; but that is another story.) Thinkers of the late twentieth century are divided about contentions made by scholars such as Hayden White that even narrative is a profoundly moral phenomenon and that all the tiny decisions, conscious or otherwise, that go into shaping a narrative arise from moral concerns and make moral statements. As part of his argument, White maintains that life does not present itself in story form—that there is no beginning or ending of anything but moral judgment makes it so, and that it is only the demands of the individual narrator for closure that account for the existence of discrete "stories" in history.[21] In this he is supported by Louis Mink, who contends that "particular narratives express their own conceptual presuppositions" and in fact cites the plots of Athenian tragedies as ways of expressing enormously important beliefs that the Athenians did not articulate elsewhere.[22] Mink and White are opposed by William Dray and David Carr, who contend that life frequently presents itself in story form and that many stories do have natural beginnings and ends. The events with which history concerns itself, Carr maintains, "are already narrative in character"; historical stories "are told in being lived" as well as "lived in being told."[23] For Dray, "It is *what* begins and ends, not *that* it begins and ends, which . . . makes the historian's work the conduit of a moral vision of the past."[24] To make his point, Dray contrasts the stories of the use of the stagecoach or the bow and arrow with the stories of the development of freedom and democracy. The story of Athens, plainly, is about freedom and democracy—even when the authors under examination deny that Athenians enjoyed any—and not about the stagecoach or the bow and arrow. Both schools of thought, then, would concede that writing about Athenian government was destined from the start to find itself encrusted in a buildup of moral judgments; and so it has been. These judgments are sometimes evident in nonnarrative formats, as when Plato snipes at democracy in the *Republic* or when Machiavelli cites Athenian *exempla* in the *Discourses*. But they can be extracted from narrative as well, and in fact thinkers whose suppositions are very different from those of Hayden White or Louis Mink have been making just such extractions—though generally at an unconscious level—from narratives about Athens, beginning with Thucydides' "story" of how Athens declined after Pericles' death and lost the Peloponnesian War and continuing with subsequent "stories" about the decay of the fourth century and the failure to guard against the Macedonian takeover.

Similarly the phenomenon of "colligation" identified by W. H. Walsh has played a conspicuous role in shaping what has been written—and thought— about Athens: Athenian history has often been read backward, inferring a coherent line of development when the reality may have been quite different.[25] Again, this is most evident in writing about the defeats at the hands of Sparta and of Philip, which historians and other students of the past have frequently used as organizing principles in telling the "stories" of the Peloponnesian War—which the Athenians nearly won—and of the fourth century, during which, it could just as well be argued, Athenian policy did not disintegrate until the decades immediately prior to the Macedonian takeover. The system that now dates events in relationship to the birth of Christ—surely an egregious example of reading history backward where ancient Greece is concerned!—has also facilitated easy distinctions between the "fifth century" and the "fourth century." Though the watershed has some connection with an important event, the end of the Peloponnesian War, it has nonetheless been reinforced by the accident of history that divides the "story" of Athenian democracy into years that start with four and years that start with three. Some twentieth-century titles of books on the fourth century reveal the story that their authors have imagined: the English translation of a work by the French historian of Greece Claude Mossé, for example, which appeared under the title *Athens in Decline*. Buried even beneath these stories is the schema that sees a complete transformation of Athenian life with the death of Alexander and ignores the restoration of democracy early in the third century.

As Freud was happy to tell us, the part of the dream that the patient omits in the telling is likely to provide the clue to its meaning. What has been left out of writing about Athens itself tells a dramatic tale. In his treatise on Florentine government, Donato Giannotti explains in a sentence that he will omit discussion of the majority of the inhabitants since they lack political power: "About these, lacking as they do any degree whatever of citizenship, it is unnecessary to speak further."[26] The same principle has characterized writing about Greece until the later part of the twentieth century, and it still obtains in many quarters today. It explains the joyous exaltation in the Renaissance and the eighteenth century of the repressive Spartan oligarchy as a "mixed government" whose "democratic" element was provided by the tiny minority of Spartiate warriors, and it explains the striking omission of slavery from the pivotal history of Greece penned just before the American Civil War by George Grote. (Donato Giannotti was a champion of Sparta, and Grote favored the southern states when war broke out in America.) The way in which people have written about the dynamics of the Athenian state makes resoundingly clear that for most people writing about politics has meant writing about people who exercise political power. In the preface to her book *Manhood and Politics: A Feminist Reading in Political Theory*, Wendy Brown tells how those who had heard of her projected feminist study of politics assumed she was planning to write about women.[27] That the marking out of disadvantaged groups is a crucial element in the self-definition of a ruling class seems painfully obvious, but this belief is not universally shared. An account of *The Classical Athenian Democracy* by David Stockton, published in 1990 by Oxford University Press, seems to include only two sentences about women; one states that women were assigned to the demes (neighborhood political units) first of their fathers and then of their husbands, and another discounts modern concern over Pericles' dismissal of women as an anachronism.[28] Even among those who would not dream of disputing the value of studying Athenian women and Athenian slaves, the belief remains common that this study is discrete from the study of politics: though contemporary interest in social history has led more and more scholars to focus their research on Athenian residents who did not vote (women, slaves, the resident aliens known as "metics"), it is not unusual for those who have taken up the mission of describing the dynamics of Athenian political life to limit themselves to voters—that is, free adult males.

Colligation and the organization of discrete historical events into "stories," criteria of relevance, and principles of selection—all this has shaped the history of writing about Athens. Viewed in this light, the Plutarchian belief that the study of history is morally improving—a belief shared by many in the era of America's founding and still popular today—loses its grounding in the actual events of the past: if what young people have been taught as history in reality represents an accretion of values built up by many generations of unwitting interpreters, and if those interpretations are based on conscious or unconscious beliefs shaped in part by the concerns of each individual interpreter, then the improving value possessed by history is no different from the improving value of myth, poetry, and religious texts. This is not to say that the perusal of historical writing may not effect wondrous moral improvement; for all I know, it may from time to time do just that. But it is not clear in what ways its inspirational value differs from that offered by other genres.

Having said this, it is necessary for me to justify my own enterprise. Those who make the writing of history their life's work are in no position to open their books with clever conceits that treat history as a pseudo-legitimate branch of fiction without acknowledging that a certain honor attends on efforts to reconstruct what really happened in history even if in fact those efforts do not succeed. One could fall back on Ernest Nagel's observation that even the most prejudiced of historians stands a chance of hitting on the truth, but such extreme special pleading is not necessary.[29] In reality, of course, historians are constrained by different parameters from those faced by their counterparts in fiction writing. (I have written fiction, and I know the difference.) The paradox is that although there exists an infinite number of ways in which one may write about Athens, just as there is an infinite number of ways in which one can end a novel, there is also an infinite number of ways that are precluded. Many, many choices are open to me in writing about Athens, but I cannot invent a splendid sea battle in which the Athenians win the Peloponnesian War or a new Federalist paper in which Alexander Hamilton, under the pseudonym of Pericles, calls for a government in which the only arbiter of policy is an outdoor assembly of the landless poor. I can and do deny that the mismanagement that led to the Macedonian takeover of Athens had gone on for many years and arose from the decadence of democracy; I might also question the legitimacy of the notion of decadence. I can, though I do not, deny that the Macedonian takeover was a bad thing; and I could, and might, deny that Athenian democracy ended when Macedonian power brought Athenian independence to an end. But try as I may, I cannot make the combined forces of Athens and Thebes defeat the forces of Macedon at Chaeronea. However distorted the "evidence" of the past that comes down to us may be, it places limits on our own writing and even, I believe, lends a certain heroism to our enterprise.

My former teacher Jack Hexter once observed in writing about Garrett Mattingly that "not to be concerned with justice to one or many encountered in the record of the past is to diminish not their human nature but ours."[30] My purpose in telling this "story of the story" about Athens is in part to do justice to what I see as the truth, to do what historians view as "setting the record straight." I hope to acquit the Athenian democrats themselves of peculiar accusations that seem to me to have discreditable origins—class prejudice, excessive reverence for sources, preoccupation with political and moral theory at the expense of historical inquiry, facile confusion between one era and another, and unwarranted pessimism about human potential. But though the traditional accusations against the Athenians have a history of over two millennia, the project of refuting them in the late twentieth century simply in order to do justice to the dead and to the truth would hardly seem a worthwhile undertaking. Many of the traditional charges against the Athenians have fallen into desuetude, and others that still hang on have been answered forcefully by a number of scholars during the past ten or twenty years. A major part of my agenda, therefore, is to track the genealogy of the anti-Athenian tradition with an eye to understanding how it started and how it grew and changed.

Those who have engaged intensely with antiquity have imagined very different cities to which they have given the name "Athens." For Renaissance thinkers the hallmark of Athens was its instability; for the Enlightenment, its decadence in the face of growing commerce. The French created the "bourgeois Athens" that was to be the subject of the long twentieth-century essay of Nicole Loraux and Pierre Vidal-Naquet; in the German mind, Greece as a whole became, in the words of Richard Jenkyns, "a sort of heavenly city, a shimmering fantasy on the far horizon"; the English felt free to fantasize an Athens that had snatched unity from diversity and forged the cohesive pluralistic society that seemed ever to stand just slightly beyond their own Victorian grasp; twentieth-century social critics have seen a "phallocratic" slave society.[31] Each school claims for itself perception, not creation, but outsiders are bound to see things differently.

The recurrent fascination with the Athenian experiment is itself remarkable in view of the very different political structures that characterized the states in which subjects and citizens returned again and again to the Athenian example. There appears to be something surprisingly hardy and haunting in the Athenians' little democracy, something that cries out for response and will not be denied. Much can be learnt from the different angles from which various thinkers throughout Western history have attacked the Athenians, who have been condemned as everything from seditious egalitarians to heartless oppressors of the downtrodden, and also from the bright flash of pro-Athenian feeling that burst forth from Victorian Britain and whose rays continue to illuminate some strands of ancient history in both Europe and America. Some have been content to bask in the glories of the school of Hellas eulogized by Pericles; others have denied even the slenderest hope of redemption to the killers of Socrates. The history of thinking about Athens has much to tell us about the vulnerability of historians to the indoctrination that is pressed upon them by intellectual constructs that take on lives of their own. The tiresome repetitiveness of much anti-Athenian rhetoric testifies to the vigor of hallowed traditions when they are not subjected to creative analysis, while the variations wrung on familiar themes signal the importance of contemporary values as shapers of the imagined past. Where thinking about Athens has remained static, this uniformity bespeaks a sterility of thought that is in itself worthy of note; where it has not, changes in thinking about Athenian democracy have come almost entirely from changes in modern political thought and not from the discovery of new physical or textual evidence for its workings. The debate over Athenian democracy has touched on questions not only of historiography but also of ethics, political science, anthropology, sociology, psychology, philosophy, gender studies, and educational theory. It is worth examining.

PART ONE

CLASSICAL GREECE

Chapter Two

THE ATHENIAN EXPERIMENT

> Some will say that a democracy is neither prudent nor fair, and
> that those who have property are the ones who should rule. But I
> say first that democracy is the name for the whole people, oligarchy
> of only a part of the people, and next that while the wealthy are
> best for guarding property, the wise give the best counsel, and the
> many, having heard things discussed, are the best judges;
> and that these groups, severally and collectively,
> share most equitably in a democracy.
> —Athenagoras of Syracuse, speaking in the pages of Thucydides

IT MAY BE HELPFUL to begin by reviewing the history of the Athenian experiment from its beginnings in the sixth century to the Macedonian conquest of Greece. I have made an effort to offer as impartial an account as I know how, but inevitably my narrative will be shaped by my own perspectives and presuppositions.[1]

Ancient Athenians shared much in common with other Greeks of their day. They lived in a city-state, a polis, that confined citizenship to a narrow kinship group and engaged in frequent warfare with other city-states. Their income derived on the whole more from land than from commerce, and their economy was dependent on the labor of large numbers of unpaid slaves and women. They believed that reverence for the gods was a matter of patriotic duty and hence that religious belief was a legitimate province of public concern, but they had no canonical theological treatises, and religion was largely a matter of rituals. In these rituals the sacrifice of animals played a large part. They had a limited notion of what people today would call privacy, and the idea that the rights of the individual might take precedence over those of the community would have struck them as distinctly strange. Most of them were confident that, as Greeks, they enjoyed intellectual and moral superiority over other peoples they might encounter. The production of legitimate heirs was the primary purpose of marriage, and a considerable age gap generally divided husbands and wives. Political decisions were considered, at least by males, to be the province solely of men. Fundamentally, Athens was a community of households headed by male farmer-soldiers who made the public decisions that were to a considerable degree determined by the need to defend the community against attacks by one or more of the many similar communities that dotted the Greek landscape. In some crucial respects, however, the Athenians were atypical—in the nature of the democratic government they developed, for example, and in the extent of the power they came to wield throughout Greece. For this reason their polis has been the focus of an extraordinary amount of interest both in their own day and subsequently.

It is not surprising that such atypical Greeks as the democratic Athenians should have attracted so much attention. According to most Greeks, accidents of birth and wealth were no accident, and they correlated to a high degree with the possession of civic virtue. Despite this, the Athenians dared to replace the oligarchy that had succeeded iron age kingship throughout Greece with an increasingly radical democracy. Under this democratic regime Athens acquired a far-flung empire and produced one of the more memorable bursts of artistic activity the world has ever seen. Whereas the Spartans cast their singular form of government and way of life as the brainchild of one specific legislator, Lycurgus, Athenian tradition depicted the evolution of democracy and the democratic way of life as a gradual process extending over several centuries.[2]

The Evolution of Democracy at Athens

It was probably toward the beginning of the first millennium B.C. that the free inhabitants of Attica joined together as citizens of the predominant Attic polis of Athens; Greek tradition ascribed this unification to their king Theseus, a friend of Heracles (Hercules) and the slayer of the monstrous Minotaur. Some time afterward the Athenians abolished the kingship and replaced the king with three archons who served life terms. One archon was apparently chosen from the aristocratic family of the Medontids, whereas the other two were elected. At some point during the eighth century the archontate became a ten-year term, and by the middle of the seventh century the term had been cut back to one year and the number of archons increased to nine; the Medontids also lost their special privileges. By the sixth century class conflict had developed that was sufficiently serious to spark an unsuccessful attempt at tyranny by one Cylon, and around 620 Draco was appointed to quell popular unrest by formulating a written law code. The harsh legislation of Draco, later said to have been written not in ink but in blood, failed to put an end to the widespread unrest among the Athenian poor, many of whom were hopelessly in debt to the rich. The problems in Athens were intensified by the existence of a new aristocracy of wealth that had sprung up as a result of the expansion of trade, and this class challenged the traditional aristocracy for a share in the political pie.

Toward the beginning of the sixth century the aristocrat Solon was set up as an arbitrator to mediate among the various classes, particularly between the disaffected peasants and the landed aristocrats to whom they owed a portion of their produce.[3] Solon's solution to the class struggle was to establish in Athens a timocratic system dividing all Athenians into four groups depending on their income. Each group was allotted a different gradation of political privilege. By this system the archontate was available to the highest class, lower offices to the middle two classes, and membership in the assembly to all classes including the very poor fourth class, the thetes. Fine distinctions made between the middle two classes remain obscure. In addition, all four classes were eligible to serve on the new popular juries Solon created, to which citizens might appeal the verdicts of the magistrates. The poor also benefited from Solon's cancellation of debts, a measure in which their creditors acquiesced out of relief that Solon had not sought to heal his country's wounds by a wholesale redistribution of property. It is possible too that Solon created a council of four hundred; though this is uncertain, he did assign the role of guardianship of the laws, protector of the constitution, and supervisor of the magistrates to the Council of the Areopagus, an already existing aristocratic body of uncertain composition that was henceforth to consist of all ex-archons, serving for life.

Although Solon's system remained in force for nearly a century, it did not put an end to party strife in Athens. In 560 Peisistratus, with the help of an armed guard, established himself as *tyrannos* ("tyrant") in the city, following the precedent set already in other city-states such as Corinth, Megara, and Sicyon. (Despite its modern connotations, the Greek word "tyrant" at first simply connoted a strongman who took power outside proper legal channels, and the imputation of harshness and self-interested autocracy did not attach to the word until somewhat later.) The age of Peisistratus was a prosperous one for Athens as the tyrant developed the city into a major cultural center and provided many jobs to the poor. Since Peisistratus left the machinery of the Solonic system largely in place, moreover, the era of increased stability afforded the populace considerable practice in the day-to-day routines of participation in government. As was frequently the case in Greek tyrannies, however, the good feeling Peisistratus had generated did not long outlive him, and considerable tension developed after his son Hipparchus was assassinated in 514 and his other son Hippias driven into exile in 510.

It was at this juncture that a popular reformer arose in the figure of Cleisthenes, a member of the prominent Alcmaeonid family. Cleisthenes sought to replace old tribal loyalties with a new loyalty to the state by dividing Athens into ten brand-new tribes (replacing the four old ones), each tribe divided among three units known as trittyes, each trittys in a different section of Attica. The trittyes were composed of smaller existing units known as demes, cohesive neighborhoods that had the potential to function as religious centers, administrative districts and voting wards; participation in deme affairs would serve to educate Athenians in the daily workings of democracy.[4] Through the reshuffling of old tribes and the geographic fragmentation of new ones, Cleisthenes hoped to break the hold that powerful aristocratic families had exercised in their self-appointed domains. Though scholars have not failed to notice that the tribal reorganization left the Alcmaeonid sphere of influence surprisingly intact, Cleisthenes' tribal reform did by and large advance the weakening of local aristocratic loyalties already begun by Peisistratus. In addition, Cleisthenes established a council known as the *boule* to prepare business for the assembly, consisting of fifty men chosen from each tribe by lot for a total of five hundred.[5] Ten *strategoi*, or generals, were to be elected, one from each tribe. Both the position of councilor and that of general carried one-year terms, but though a man might serve on the council only twice in his life, the terms of the *strategoi* were renewable as long as popularity permitted. The generalship came to be so important in Athens that after the first Persian invasion in 490 the Athenians decided to use a random lot to select not only their councilors but also their archons, a clear statement that the generalship had overtaken the archontate in prestige. Generals were usually chosen from well-to-do candidates, but anyone who owned property in Attica was eligible; the archontate was officially thrown open to the third class in 457, and though it was never formally opened to the lowest class, the thetes, in practice this distinction was probably disregarded. It is likely that most Athenian voters by the time they died had held political office of some kind at least once, if not several times. Although the *strategoi* had the privilege of addressing the assembly before other citizens were allowed to speak, they did not themselves have the power to make decisions beyond the provisional ones that had to be made in the field, and on the whole the responsibility for decision-making lay with the *ekklesia* (assembly) and with the popular courts.[6]

After two stunning defeats (Marathon in 490 and Salamis in 480) and one victory that gained them little (Thermopylae, 480), the Persians were forced to abandon their plans to conquer Greece. The Athenians seem to have taken their success in the Persian Wars as a sign that their unconventional form of government had not incurred divine disapproval for its disregard of the traditional prerogatives of wealth and lineage. They regarded the naval victory at Salamis as decisive in ending the war, and the provocative admiral Themistocles, the architect of that victory, became a national hero—though Athenians and other Greeks enjoyed telling stories that contrasted his deviousness with the sober scrupulousness of his rival Aristides. Inevitably, the pivotal role of the Athenian navy under Themistocles in the Greek victory over Persia provoked a pronounced shift in the balance of power among the Greek city-states. Once viewed as the most powerful state in Greece, Sparta now had to share that position with Athens. A combination of good fortune and Spartan mismanagement had placed the Athenians at the head of the league of islanders and coastal states who sought protection from the Persians and, if possible, vengeance and compensation for the ravages of war in the form of booty from anti-Persian raids. Aristides was charged with assessing the amount of tribute owed by each league member. This league the Athenians gradually converted into their own empire, using military force to demand the participation of some states and prevent the secession of others. Members of the league were frequently pressured into accepting democratic governments, and citizens of allied states had to travel to Athens to have legal cases heard.

The increasing conversion of the league into an Athenian empire sparked fear and anger in the Spartans. The aristocratic *strategos* Cimon, son of the Persian War hero Miltiades, had advocated a strong anti-Persian, pro-Spartan stance at Athens, but in the end his policy was rejected. In addition, the central role of the Athenian navy had increased the political aspirations of the ordinary rower in the fleet (causing Themistocles to be blamed by some for catapulting Athens into democracy). The constitution of Athenian imperial power along naval lines gave special importance to sailors, a class that included many of the truly poor, and led them to believe that they were the basis of Athens's power as much as—or more than—the heavily armed hoplite soldiers who formed the land army and who required at least enough money to furnish a shield and sword in a time when governments did not issue weapons to their conscripts. Led by the democratic and aggressive Ephialtes and his associate, Pericles, an Athenian majority seems to have voted late in the 460s to limit the power of the Council of the Areopagus, composed of former archons, and give much of its jurisdiction over to popular courts.[7] These reforms were strenuously opposed by an outraged minority. A few months later in 461 the requisite number of citizens also voted to send Cimon into exile by the process known as ostracism, whereby a total of six thousand votes against any one man would send him into a nonpunitive exile for ten years. Sometimes attributed to Cleisthenes, and frequently viewed as a safeguard against another tyranny, the process was first used in the 480s as a tool in the party strife that accompanied the departure of the tyrants and the war with the Persians, as the upstart Themistocles vied with the popular Aristides. After the ostracism of Aristides, the procedure continued to be used as a party weapon until it fell into desuetude during the Peloponnesian War.[8]

The ostracism of Cimon brought to a head the underlying tensions between Athens and Sparta, a very different kind of polis. Although bitter civil strife appears to have plagued the Spartans early in their history, the story was current in Greece how their legendary lawgiver Lycurgus had established a political system—indeed, an entire way of life—that had endured with minor revisions for centuries. With their two kings, their five ephors ("overseers"), their council of twenty-eight elders, and their assembly of citizens (the "Equals"), the Spartans were envied by many Greeks for the notorious stability of their government and the concord among their citizens. To be sure, this concord was posited on the fact that the Spartans limited their citizenship to a tiny body of soldiers who were outnumbered about ten to one by state serfs known as helots. These helots provided all the disagreeable manual labor necessary to support the Spartiate citizens in what amounted to a perpetual armed camp. Although modern thinkers are generally alienated by the system of helotry, slavery was commonplace in Greece, and the Spartan system was much admired by contemporaries.[9] Spartan sympathies were particularly common among Athenian aristocrats. Nonetheless, in the end expansionist aspirations proved dominant in Athens, and the departure of Cimon was attended by the outbreak of the so-called First Peloponnesian War, an undeclared war between Athens and Sparta that extended until a peace was signed in 446, and by the rise of Pericles, who after the murder of his associate, Ephialtes, became the leading democratic politician at Athens.[10] Pericles was elected one of the ten *strategoi* nearly every year between the murder of Ephialtes and his own death in 429, and nobody in fifth-century Athens matched him for enduring political prestige. Under his leadership the Athenians strengthened the democratic element in their government, establishing a low state pay for service on juries and on the Council of 500 that would enable more poor people to exercise their legal right to serve, and they also intensified their hold over their allies, moving the league's treasury from Delos to Athens for what they unpersuasively insisted was safekeeping.[11] It was in part the tribute from the league that enabled the Athenians of Pericles' day to carry out numerous building projects, the most famous of which resulted in the Parthenon.

The art forms for which the Periclean age was known included not only sculpture and architecture but also the tragic drama, already flourishing by the middle of the century but perfected during the time of Pericles' ascendancy by his friend Sophocles and Sophocles' slightly younger contemporary, Euripides. Tragedy provided a vital arena for examining the painful questions that beset human existence, and the dramatic format encouraged a capacity to see tricky problems from more than one side, a skill of enormous value in a democracy where citizens were called upon to make difficult decisions. Tragedy failed, however, in one crucial area; for all their efforts, Sophocles and Euripides were unable to instill in their fellow-citizens any radically new view of the human race, which the Athenians, like other Greeks, perceived as clearly divided into various binary groups—free and slave, male and female, Greek and barbarian, citizen and alien. The egalitarianism of the Athenian ethos extended only to free citizen males. Women and slaves had carefully circumscribed rights and played a part in public life primarily by facilitating the leisure of free males, and it was only under extraordinary circumstances that resident aliens might become Athenian citizens. Although their slaveholding and their exclusivity in extending the franchise to aliens were typical of ancient Greeks as a whole, the vehemence of their denial of women's value and capacity set Athenian men somewhat apart from other Hellenes.[12] Pericles himself attracted considerable attention by divorcing his Athenian wife and setting up housekeeping with a cultivated foreign woman, Aspasia, who welcomed celebrated intellectuals into their home. Throughout their history a strong elitist strain marked the thinking of the Athenians, who continued to return rich men to office with great regularity. Affluence was not without its perils, however. The wealthy were regularly assigned public burdens known as liturgies. The variety of possible liturgies reflects the vibrancy of cultural life at Athens; they included not only outfitting warships but also holding banquets and training choruses for dramatic performances. The rich were understandably ambivalent about exercising this sort of "privilege"; noblesse oblige could be very expensive.

The Athenians appear to have been willing to pay some price for their aggressiveness abroad. This price was to come in the form of a deadly war with the Spartans. What the Athenians did not foresee was a protracted conflict that lasted (with some interruptions) for twenty-seven years. Pericles died shortly after the outbreak of the war, though not before delivering the funeral oration for the war dead that stands out so dramatically from the pages of Thucydides' history, and not before being impeached and temporarily removed from office by the disaffected populace. A member of the same distinguished family as Cleisthenes, the Alcmaeonid Pericles played, like his kinsman, the role of the democratic aristocrat in politics, subject, of course, to the will of his constituency.

Pericles had no successor of comparable stature. None of the politicians who came afterward matched him in his firm hold on the popular will, and policy seems often to have been made more by the assembly than by individual statesmen. Other changes were also evident in Athenian politics after Pericles' death. Although positions of importance continued to be held by men from well-to-do families, these families were often part of the new aristocracy of trade wealth rather than of the old aristocracy of land wealth. In addition, preeminence in the assembly came to be accorded to eloquent, assertive men who might never have held the position of *strategos*, and a certain degree of specialization crept into public life, with some men distinguishing themselves in the military sphere alone and others known only for their persuasive powers in the assembly; the word *demagogos* (literally, leader of the people) came to be applied to popular speakers. The *demagogos* about whom the most is known was Cleon, a brash, outspoken politician hated by both the historian Thucydides and the comic dramatist Aristophanes.[13]

The Athenians and the Spartans signed a peace treaty in 421 following the death of the aggressive Cleon on the Athenian side and the successful general Brasidas on the Spartan, but the peace did not last, and it was in the course of the next stage of the war that the Athenians resolved to undertake a huge expedition to assist their Sicilian allies and consolidate Athenian power in the West. In so doing they accepted the arguments of the flamboyant young aristocrat Alcibiades, a relative of Pericles, and rejected the more cautious counsel of the conservative Nicias. The expedition ended in disaster, and soon afterward it was resolved to turn the government over to a smaller group of 400 who in time would yield place to a somewhat more broadly based group of

5000. The short-lived oligarchy was soon overthrown, however, by the democratic navy. The theater of war had shifted from Greece to Sicily to the Hellespont, and there the Athenians had some success; but the use of the rigorous Athenian system of military and political accountability ended in the execution of nearly the whole slate of generals who had been in command in the victorious battle off the Arginusae islands in 406 after which they had failed to retrieve soldiers from the cold Hellespontine waters (dead or live soldiers, depending on which sources are to be believed). The next major engagement against the Spartans—at Aegospotami in Asia Minor—ended in defeat for Athens, evidently because of treachery.

The debacle at Aegospotami was decisive in ending the war. Under the auspices of Sparta, oligarchs once more took control of the Athenian government, but their rule was so bloody that even the Spartan king Pausanias was alienated, and he gave his support to the democratic resistance that overthrew the so-called Thirty Tyrants in 403.[14] Following the reestablishment of the democracy in its most highly developed form—with most office-holders selected by lot and state pay reinstated for state service—the Athenians signed the first recorded amnesty in history. Its provisions prevented anyone from being tried for political misconduct prior to 403, but the democrats sometimes managed to evade the terms of the amnesty by focusing on more recent events, the most famous instance being the trial of Socrates, who had given offense by questioning both traditional and democratic values. Although it is plain that the trial was politically motivated, Socrates' failure to insist on his right to his own beliefs underlines the degree to which the democratic Athenians shared the common Greek assumption that a certain concord—*homonoia*—among citizens in civic and religious matters was indispensable to the community. Democracy in Athens did not imply a principled commitment to the rights of individuals where they might seem to conflict with the needs of the state.

The end of the war also marked the end of the great age of tragedy at Athens. The war itself had become the object of several of Athens's most memorable comedies, however, and the comic dramatist Aristophanes continued to write until his death in the 380s. Toward the end of Aristophanes' life, philosophy came to replace drama as the vehicle for sorting out the complexities of the universe. Shortly after Socrates' death Plato began composing dialogues in which his beloved teacher, Socrates, was generally the principal speaker, and Plato's own pupil Aristotle was born within a year or two of Aristophanes' death. The war had brought about a new state of affairs in Greece as a whole. In general the protracted hostilities had been bad for the economies of the city-states as well as for Greek morale, but within a decade of the Spartan victory at Aegospotami, Sparta's old allies Corinth and Thebes had joined a resurgent Athens in waging war on their former hegemon. Although Sparta won this so-called Corinthian War, her high-handed peacetime tactics alienated many Greeks, and the Athenians soon found it possible to organize another league.

Greek diplomacy becomes somewhat elusive in the fourth century, as it was an era of shifting alliances that lacked the comforting bipolarity of the fifth. Two important features of the fourth century are the failure of the Spartans to hold the loyalty of their allies and the ability of the Athenians to induce Greek states to join a new confederacy under their leadership. Although the attempts of Mausolus of Caria to spark insurrection in the confederacy were thwarted by the death that afforded his wife the occasion to build his renowned memorial, the efforts of Philip of Macedon to subdue not only Athens but all Greece met with success. Thus the political ascendancy in fourth-century Greece was passed on from Sparta to Athens, from Athens to Sparta's old ally Thebes, from Thebes back to Athens and then finally to Macedon.

Response in Athens to the rise of Philip was mixed. The most popular general of the fourth century, Phocion, inclined in many ways toward Macedon, and in a Macedonian hegemony the orator and educator Isocrates saw an opportunity for the Athenians to join with a united Greece in a crusade against Persia. Meanwhile Demosthenes sought to alert his fellow-citizens to the Macedonian threat to Greek liberties. Demosthenes threw intense passion into his efforts to rouse the Athenians to an adequate resistance against Philip, a passion to which his orations bear painful witness. Fighting Philip would have entailed the expenditure of more energy and money than the Athenians were willing to countenance, and Athens failed dismally to rise to the Macedonian challenge. Because of this stunning failure, many Western thinkers have viewed the fourth century as a protracted period of decline that led inevitably to the collapse of the city-state system, both throughout Greece in general and in Athens in particular. Indeed, many have sought to trace the decline back into the fifth century, in some cases to the death of Pericles and in some instances to the ascendancy of Pericles himself, whose institution of state pay for state service has sometimes been seen as planting the seeds of indolence and greed.

RECOVERING THE IDEOLOGY OF THE DEMOCRACY

The halfhearted resistance the Athenians offered to Philip led to their defeat in 338 at the Battle of Chaeronea, and in 322, after Athens's unsuccessful rebellion from Macedon, Alexander's general Antipater dismantled the democratic constitution and imposed a Macedonian garrison. It was not only the eventual collapse of Athens, however, that gave rise to the anti-Athenian position, for the tradition of hostility to the Athenian democracy traces its origins almost to the very foundation of the democracy around the middle of the fifth century. Most Athenians, of course, were not hostile to the city's government. Monarchy need not be popular in order to go on existing, nor tyranny, nor aristocracy, nor oligarchy; but by definition democracy cannot continue in an autonomous Greek polis unless the majority of free males of voting age are amenable to its doing so. Athenian democracy was briefly over-thrown twice, first in the short-lived coup of 411 and again in 404 at the insistence of the Spartan Lysander, who established an oligarchy so distasteful that his countryman King Pausanias assisted Athenian democrats in its over-throw. Aside from these two episodes springing from the strains of a devastat-ing war, no known attempts were made against the democracy from its estab-lishment by Cleisthenes until the defeat of the city-states at the hands of Philip. We are forced to conclude that democracy was extremely popular among adult male citizens in Athens.

The contemporary supporters of democracy, however, have been turned by the passing of time into something of a silent majority. This phenomenon is partly explicable and partly mysterious. One might argue that the most articu-late enthusiasts of democracy were more likely to be out governing than clos-eted in their studies cogitating: thus writing about government was left largely to the disgruntled. One could claim that the merits of popular government were self-evident—or, alternatively, that the idea of democracy was so incen-diary in elite circles that its supporters thought it best to say as little about it as possible. The truth is that it is impossible to be sure why the ideology of democracy was diffused throughout the literature of drama and oratory rather than concentrated in tracts on government, and why the only dialogues in which Athenian democracy puts forward its claims directly and effectively are the modern debates that late twentieth-century thinkers have imaginatively reconstructed to fill the gap.[15] The teachers known to their contemporaries and to posterity as the sophists did sometimes write about political matters, but they have left us next to nothing of their works; most of what we know comes from fragments, isolated quotations, or speeches in dialogues that their rival Plato wrote to discredit them.[16] The relationship between *nomos* (cus-tom, law) and *physis* (nature) was the object of heated controversy among the sophists, and the bearing this dialogue had on the debate concerning the best form of government must have been considerable.[17] Although some scholars have sought to trace this connection, because of their desultory nature the fragmentary snatches of extant pre-Socratic writings must remain by and large a tantalizing reminder of how much has been lost.[18] For all these reasons, some industry is required to determine just what the theory was behind Athenian democracy. There existed no formal democratic manifesto at Athens, no pre-amble to the Athenian constitution, indeed no Athenian constitution; stu-dents whose eyes light on volumes entitled *The Athenian Constitution* will be disappointed to find only a brief essay on the topic filed among the writings of

Xenophon or a longer one classed among those of Aristotle.[19] The genuine article—or articles—existed only in Athenian minds; indeed, Aristotle himself questioned whether they existed at all.

Despite the paucity of texts extolling democracy, however, enough remains to give some sense of what its supporters liked about it, and the passages in praise of democracy that have survived demonstrate that its admirers differed markedly from its critics in what they saw as the cardinal principles of the system. One of the earliest surviving passages in praise of democracy appears in the debate on government set in Persia and inserted into Herodotus's history of the Persian Wars (3.80.1–82.5), composed probably around 435. The dramatic date of the debate is 521, when three of the noblemen who had been involved in the overthrow of the previous rule of the Magi are discussing what sort of government to put in its place. Herodotus's repeated insistence on the reliability of the story and his defense of it against skeptics both here and later (6.131) suggest that he at least did not make it up out of whole cloth. Though many scholars have thought that the debate reveals about as much about Persian political theory as *Hamlet* does about Danish history, still it gives some sense of what Herodotus's contemporaries might have had to say about the different types of government.[20]

All three Persian noblemen, Otanes, Megabyzus and Darius, make strong cases for the forms of government they advocate: the rule of one, the rule of a few, and the rule of the people. The admiration Herodotus manifests throughout his history for the Athenians has led many readers to suppose that he sided in the debate with Otanes, who says: "First of all the rule of the multitude has the most beautiful name of all, *isonomia* [perhaps best translated 'equality before the law' or 'equal opportunity to participate in politics'], and secondly, it works completely differently from monarchy. Offices are assigned by lot, all the magistrates are held accountable for their actions, and all deliberations take place before the common assembly" (3.80.6). The use of the lot and the accountability of magistrates certainly seem to point to the post-Cleisthenic democracy of Athens and not to any government in existence in 521. Herodotus's use of the word *isonomia* instead of the more specific *demokratia* has left open the door to speculation that he was not in fact discussing democracy at all, but it is difficult to imagine what else he would have been thinking of that would constitute the third form of government in the balanced set of which the other two members were monarchy and oligarchy. More decisively, later in book 6 when Herodotus once again insists that the account of the debate is historical, he vents his spleen at those who deny that Otanes advised the Persians to *demokrateesthai* (6.43.3). It would seem that Herodotus was absolutely discussing democracy and that what was later called *demokratia* was at the outset known more often by the less provocative but equally tendentious word *isonomia*.[21]

Herodotus's enthusiasm for Athens permeates his history to such a degree that he has been taken to task for it. To the vigor of the Athenians' form of government Herodotus attributes their resolution in fighting the Persians, and he ascribes the ultimate victory over Persia to their heroism, calling the Athenians the "saviors of Hellas" (7.139). The victory of Greece over Persia, then, is billed as a victory for democracy. Herodotus even goes so far as to insist that after the expulsion of the tyrants the Athenians became the best fighters among the Greeks, an extraordinary claim indeed in view of the fact that as much as eighty years later Pericles, in framing his strategy for the Peloponnesian War, took as axiomatic the improbability of an Athenian victory in a land battle against Sparta.

Because of the enthusiasm—some would say partisanship—Herodotus demonstrates for Athens, it seems likely that he endorsed the sentiments of Otanes, but for the intellectual history of Athenian democracy it hardly matters; what is important is that this debate offers modern readers a small window on the minds of democratic thinkers of the mid–fifth century. What Otanes has to say about democracy certainly does not condemn it surreptitiously as the words of an antidemocrat might.[22] It is significant that neither Megabyzus in his advocacy of oligarchy nor Darius in his case for monarchy brands democracy as a form of class government entailing the oppression of a rich majority by a poor minority. Did this complaint date from the hurt feelings of a later period?

It is important to notice, in Otanes' speech favoring democracy, the word *aneuthynos*, "unaccountable." "What virtue is to be found in monarchy," Otanes asks, "when the ruler can do whatever he wants and not be held to account for it?" Though at first the object of his attack might appear to be simply one-man rule, the context of Greek political life argues against this. Greek oligarchies were no more accountable than monarchies. It was only in democracies that machinery was evolving to hold officials to account, and in fact there is every reason to believe that by the middle of the fifth century *hypeuthynos*, "accountable," had become a democratic catchword. Aristotle, an admirer of the Spartans, nonetheless complains of their failures to hold the ephors accountable (*Politics* 1271a5). The concept of accountability also appears prominently in the writings of two of Herodotus's contemporaries, the playwright Aeschylus and the philosopher Democritus. Predictably, the contrast between accountable and unaccountable politicians is made in Aeschylus's *Persians*, produced in 472. Aeschylus takes much the same approach as Herodotus to the question of the difference between Greeks and Persians, portraying the Persian nobility as well-meaning but deprived—alas—of the advantages of the Greek enlightenment. In a memorable passage, Xerxes' mother announces to the Persian elders that her son, should he succeed, will be greatly admired, but in the event of failure cannot be held *hypeuthynos polei*, "accountable to the city," for his actions (211–13). Clearly this passage was expected to drive home to the Athenian audience the horrors of the Eastern despotism they had so narrowly escaped. Similarly in *Prometheus Bound*, probably composed shortly before Aeschylus's death in 456, the tyranny of Zeus is illustrated by the fact that, in Prometheus's words, he is not *hypeuthynos* (324). The theme of accountability also plays a role in the corpus of Democritean fragments that have come down to us—tiny in comparison with the weighty tomes of Plato and Aristotle but vast in comparison with the snatches that remain of Democritus's contemporaries. Secular, unsentimental, and brooking no nonsense, Democritus the atomist broke his ties with the archaic worldview of the Greek nobility as surely as he broke those with the traditional god-centeredness of scientific thought. Not surprisingly, he had no faith in the automatic virtue of office-holders, since such people have been placed in a position of power by arbitrary human customs and not by any natural superiority. It is fair, he contends, that people remember the mistakes of those who hold office rather than their successes: "For just as those who return a deposit do not deserve praise, whereas those who do not do so deserve blame and punishment, so with the official: he was not elected to make mistakes but to do things well." The emphasis on accountability here strongly suggests that Democritus was thinking of Athenian democracy, and his endorsement of democracy as a form of government is confirmed by his statement that "poverty under a democracy is as much to be preferred to so-called prosperity under an autocracy as freedom to slavery."[23]

The date of Aeschylus's *Persians* is known exactly, that of the *Prometheus Bound*, approximately; Herodotus's debate and Democritus's fragments can be dated only to some time around the outbreak of the Peloponnesian War—probably, but not certainly, to the generation after Aeschylus. Although it would be presumptuous to reconstruct an entire political system to which these three men would happily give their blessing, their writings still give us some idea of the more pleasant associations that were gathering around the idea of democracy in general and Athenian democracy in particular toward the middle of the fifth century. Certainly the subordination of family and religious ties to a formal legal system that seems to be advocated in the *Oresteia* (produced in 458, right after the reforms of Ephialtes) suggests Aeschylus's support of the Athenian democratic state.[24] Affirmations of the value of democracy can also be found in tragedy as the century wears on. Though Sophocles in *Oedipus* reflects some concern about the intellectual restlessness of democratic man and Euripides frequently seems apprehensive about the moral and spiritual consequences of the sophistic acrobatics that had come to form an indispensable part of politics, both playwrights ultimately affirm the joys of democracy. It seems clear that Creon's son Haemon speaks for the playwright in Sophocles' *Antigone* (441) when he takes his autocratic father to task for discounting the will of the people, and Euripides in the *Suppliants* (ca. 422) includes a long and pointed dialogue between the Theban herald and Athens's mythical king Theseus that addresses directly the opposition of democracy and one-man rule and leaves no doubt where the playwright's sympathies lie.

The opening question of the Theban herald at Athens evokes the bewilderment Aeschylus and Herodotus ascribed to the Persians at the Athenians' seemingly masterless government. Who, the herald asks, is the local *tyrannos* to whom he might announce his tidings? This question, of course, has shock value for the Athenian audience in the theater. Theseus loses no time in setting the ignorant herald straight about the way things are done at Athens:

> One moment, stranger.
> Your start was wrong, seeking a master here.
> This city is free, and ruled by no one man.
> The people reign, in annual succession.
> They do not yield the power to the rich;
> The poor man has an equal share in it.
>
> (403–8)

This, of course, is nonsense as it concerns bronze age Athens, but tragedy has never observed chronological niceties. Responding to Theseus's rebuke, the herald expresses his glee in discovering the advantage his native Thebes has over a city with such a pitiful excuse for a government—one swayed by a mob and its self-interested leaders, where decisions are made by poor people with no capacity to understand the public interest. These snide and eminently un-Athenian remarks are designed to set up the paean to democracy that follows immediately. Very well, Theseus replies angrily; as long as you have started this, let me tell you a few things about good government:

> Nothing
> Is worse for a city than an absolute ruler.
> In earliest times, before there are common laws,
> One man has power and makes the laws his own:
> Equality is not yet. With written laws,
> People of few resources and the rich
> Both have the same recourse to justice. Now
> A man of means, if badly spoken of,
> Will have no better standing than the weak;
> And if the lesser is in the right, he wins
> Against the great.

Theseus goes on to cite the formula by which the herald opened the floor to debate in the Athenian assembly of the fifth century:

This is the call of freedom:
"What man has good advice to give the city,
And wishes to make it known?" He who responds
Gains glory; the unwilling may hold their peace.
For the city, what can be more equal than that?

A democracy, Theseus goes on, appreciates talented and valorous youth, whereas a king fears them; even the chastity of virgins is safer in democracy, and Theseus's decision to conclude his speech by expressing alarm at what would happen to his daughters under a monarchy makes clear with what a very heavy brush indeed Euripides has chosen to paint the differences between democracy and autocracy:

Why bring up girls as gentlewomen, fit
For marriage, if tyrants may take them for their joy—
A grief to parents? I would rather die
Than see my children forced to such a union.
These are the darts I shoot at what you say.

$$(430-57)^{25}$$

Democracy, then, is set up by Euripides as the antithesis of both brute force and the rule of wealth. Whereas the herald cites the advantages of one-man rule, Theseus stresses the advantages of democracy over oligarchy as well. His opposition of democracy on the one hand to the ravishing of virgins on the other verges on parody, and it gives us some sense of the ferocity with which Athenian democrats defended their cause.[26] It reminds us too that women were viewed as recipients of the benefits of democracy rather than as active participants in the democratic system.

At about the same time that Sophocles and Euripides were composing tragedies, the sophist Protagoras of Abdera, countryman of Democritus and contemporary (perhaps down to the very year) of Herodotus, was proffering his wares in the imperial city, and in so doing he inevitably attracted the attention of Socrates. The Platonic dialogue that bears Protagoras's name represents a thoroughgoing attack by Plato, in the name of Socrates, on the notion that sophists can educate anybody for anything.[27] In reply to the inquiries of Socrates, who questions that virtue can be taught, Protagoras delivers a long speech in which he advances three related arguments in defense of the thesis that all people possess in some degree the rudiments of civic-mindedness, rudiments categorized at various points as *politike techne* (political wisdom, or the wisdom necessary to live in a city-state), *politike arete* (political excellence, or the excellence appropriate to those seeking to be useful in a city-state), *dikaiosyne* (justice), and *sophrosyne* (sobriety in judgment). These qualities Protagoras sees as originating with the senses of *aidos* (shame, decency) and *dike* (the hardest of these to translate: fairness, even-handedness, equity).

Protagoras begins his discourse with a myth. In earliest times, he claims, though Prometheus had improved the lot of humankind by stealing fire, people were still unable to live together constructively in cities on account of their lack of *politike techne*. Seeing this, Zeus determined to prevent the utter destruction of the species by sending Hermes to bring *aidos* and *dike* to mortals. When Hermes asked Zeus whether these should be distributed to a select few, like the arts of medicine and other *technai* (skills), or rather among everyone, Zeus—and this is the crucial part of the story—bade him give them to all, "for cities cannot be formed if only a few share in these skills as they do in other arts" (322D). It is for this reason, Protagoras tells Socrates, that though many people such as the citizens of Athens (the only polis he mentions by name) consider it the business of just a few to advise in certain technical matters of craftsmanship, nonetheless "when they come together to take counsel on matters in which *politike arete* is relevant, in which it is necessary to be guided in all respects by justice and good sense (*dikaiosyne* and *sophrosyne*), naturally they take advice from everybody, since it is held that everyone should partake of this excellence, or else that states cannot exist" (322E–23E). This myth, then, constitutes Protagoras's first "argument," and it is because of this distribution of the *politike techne*, he says, that the Athenians do right to accept political advice from anyone who is moved to give it.

Protagoras uses the next two "arguments" derived from common sense and human observation to lend credence to this myth. Second, Protagoras explains after he has set forth his myth, when a man who is inadequate in, say, flute playing or some other such skill, insists that he is in point of fact perfectly competent, people are horrified to see him so out of touch with reality, and those close to him scold him for acting crazy; but when justice is involved, the opposite is true: a man would be considered crazy for publicly confessing his injustice, for "they say that everyone should profess to be just, whether he is or not, and whoever does not make such a profession is mad; since it is held that everyone without exception must share in it in some way or other if he is really human" (323B–C). Third, Protagoras points out that lectures, reproofs, and corrective punishments normally attend on those who are found to be unjust, whereas no one in his right mind would dream of reproving anyone for his ugliness or physical infirmity; this distinction, he maintains, shows that people clearly perceive all individuals as having the power to improve their moral physiques in a way that they do not have the power to change their bodily ones. Punishment, Protagoras argues, is only exceptionally undertaken for purposes of vengeance; customarily it is to improve the character of the malefactor, for "he who undertakes to punish according to reason does not take vengeance for a past offence, since he cannot succeed in undoing what has been done; he looks rather to the future, and aims at preventing that particular individual and others who see him punished from doing wrong again" (324B). (Although Protagoras's stress on the rehabilitative purpose of punishment is all very touching, nothing we know about Greek mores suggests that there existed any such consensus on this topic; indeed his contemporaries would probably have found the notion bizarre. Plainly the Athenians did not aim at rehabilitating the victors of Arginusae.)

Though it is advanced in defense of his educational program, Protagoras's contention that all individuals partake in the *politike techne* serves additionally as one of the few theoretical arguments in favor of democracy in general and Athenian democracy in particular that survive from classical times. Indeed, Plato has Protagoras specify that his myth explains not only the teachability of virtue (since everyone by divine dispensation possesses at least a minimal aptitude for learning it) but the rationale behind Athenian democracy as well. Scholars have been understandably skeptical about the attribution of these ideas to Protagoras. Although the exact dates are uncertain, it appears that the Platonic dialogue is an account written around 395 about a speech given around 433 by a man who died around 415. Nearly everyone who had heard the speech was dead by 395. This constellation hardly affords a promising scenario for historical accuracy. The speaker in question, moreover, was diametrically opposed to Plato in his political views; and he was famous for doubting the existence of the gods. Despite all these difficulties, however, it is hard to understand why Plato would have chosen to distort Protagoras's real ideas in this particular direction. How, in other words, would putting this myth in Protagoras's mouth have helped Plato make Protagoras's arguments in favor of democracy look foolish, and what were the far more cogent things Protagoras had actually said that Plato so cleverly suppressed by attaching this plausible tale to his name instead? If the myth did not originate with Protagoras, then where did it come from? All things considered, it seems to me most believable that Protagoras actually said what Plato claims he did.[28]

A similar problem attends on the funeral oration that Thucydides claims Pericles delivered in 430 in honor of the men who died during the first year of the Peloponnesian War (2.35–46), for it seems to me that, on balance and with reservations, Thucydides disapproved of Athenian democracy. The speech ascribed to Pericles, however, was delivered in front of thousands of listeners still alive when Thucydides was writing, and it does not conflict embarrassingly with any other beliefs associated with Pericles. For these reasons most people have found it somewhat easier to accept the reliability of Thucydides' report about Pericles than to be confident about Plato's concerning Protagoras.[29] The funeral oration contains by far the most elaborate contemporary praise of Athenian democracy and explication of the philosophy behind it that has survived from antiquity. Though it cannot be assumed that the arguments Pericles advances were supported by all his democratic contemporaries, it is likely that Pericles chose to express sentiments that would strike responsive chords in his audience. Pericles wisely gauged that what was both most fitting and most strategic on this occasion was a paean to Athens that praised her for being the inverse of Sparta.[30] This is precisely what he delivered.

Pericles addressed his speech in large part to Athenian citizens and allies whom he feared the strains of war might cause to waver in their loyalty to the Athenian way of life, as we know did actually happen not long after the outbreak of the war when some Athenian factions sought to negotiate with the Spartans. Throughout, the speech manifests a defensive tone. What is important to notice about the funeral oration is the sense it conveys of the polis as a cohesive whole in which a wise constitution provides the cornerstone for the good life in all its aspects. To the possible objection that Athens may offer a higher cultural standard while Sparta showed the world a sounder government and better soldiers, Pericles replies in effect that the arts flourish in Athens precisely because of the democracy, and that in fact the democracy produces the best soldiers. The arguments may be summarized as follows:

1. Just because we are called a democracy does not mean we make no distinctions among men of different worth; the point is that we assess worth in terms of ability, not in terms of wealth or class.

2. Although it is true that we are very generous in tolerating eccentricities in people's private lives, in public matters we set a high standard and expect ourselves and others to revere the laws and the magistrates.

3. In military matters we do not need to keep what goes on in our city secret from our enemies, for we rely for our success not on deception but on courage. The fact that we live rich and varied lives instead of confining ourselves within a lifelong military camp does not prevent us from being the equal of the Spartans. Actually, the fact that we can hold our own against them despite their longer years devoted to training is the most solid proof of our greatness.

4. Our love of beauty does not mean we are extravagant, and the fact that we love wisdom does not make us ipso facto weak.

5. Unlike others, we think it is no shame for a man to acknowledge being poor, but we certainly do find it shameful if someone does not do his best to avoid poverty.

6. Athens is the one polis that regards the man who remains aloof from politics as useless rather than as one who minds his own business.

7. In contrast to others one could mention, we consider debate an aid to constructive action rather than a hindrance to it. We have the singular distinction of being outstanding both in action and in reflection.

8. We also differ from others in that we prefer conferring benefits to receiving them.

9. We are, in short, a model polis.

Pericles, in other words, stresses the creative, dynamic power of democracy to unite men of all classes in active participation in the government. (He also observes that the greatest glory of a woman was that she should never be spoken of for either good or evil; plainly he considered women's participation in the polis to be of an entirely different order.) The key feature of the Periclean vision is not the technical legal opportunity offered to each male citizen to participate in government but rather the active solicitation of that participation. What he sees as the value of democracy is not primarily the absence of the injustice that labels individuals according to social class but rather the presence of a positive and vital force drawing each (male) heart and mind into both deliberation and action, a force that lends to that deliberation and action a virtue lacking under other constitutions.

The markedly defensive tone of Pericles' speech points up the kinds of accusations that were leveled in his day against Athenian government, in part by disgruntled Athenian aristocrats themselves: that the worthy and unworthy were treated alike; that democratic "liberty" meant that people were free to live in anarchy, unconstrained by any rules of civilized intercourse; that the Athenian enthusiasm for the arts and the intellect amounted to decadence and softness—*malakia*, by which Greeks also meant "effeminacy" when it was applied to men—and that democratic states spend so much time discussing and debating that they are unable to act as effectively as oligarchic ones.[31] In addition, Pericles uses the word *demokratia* only once, and I suspect that it was a word to which he did not want to draw attention.[32] Though the persistence of class prejudice and rank snobbery enable modern readers to understand at some level the social biases of ancient societies, still it is virtually impossible for a citizen of the twentieth century fully to grasp the terrors that the very word *democracy* could once evoke.

Pericles died soon after delivering the funeral oration, and he bequeathed to his countrymen a war that they lost. Having abandoned Pericles' defensive war strategy and undertaken various land and sea campaigns, the Athenians finally mounted their unsuccessful attack on Sicily in 415. Fifteen years after the delivery of the Periclean funeral oration another democratic orator is reported by Thucydides to have spoken in praise of democracy. Though geography allowed Thucydides more license in rendering the speech of Athenagoras of Syracuse than in reporting that of Pericles of Athens, it is noteworthy that the element of defensiveness in Pericles' speech is carried over into that of the Syracusan. Some, Athenagoras says, "will say that a democracy is neither prudent nor fair, and that those who have property are the ones who should rule. But I say first that democracy is the name for the whole people, oligarchy of only a part of the people, and next that while the wealthy are best for guarding property, the wise give the best counsel, and the many, having heard things discussed, are the best judges; and that these groups, severally and collectively, share most equitably in a democracy" (6.39.1–2).

The Athenians' expedition against Athenagoras's city ended in disaster for them, and withal Athens's conduct of the long war provided still further working matter for her critics. Twice in the late fifth century the democracy was replaced with a pro-Spartan oligarchy, though on both occasions the oligarchy was overthrown by the democrats within a matter of months. In the second instance, as we have seen, democrats and oligarchs signed an amnesty. In the fourth century everybody was careful to be a democrat of one stamp or another, and all fourth-century Athenian orators profess to be eager partisans of the democratic cause. Those who in fact had little sympathy with this cause— Isocrates, for example—were forced to cast their antidemocratic arguments in a prodemocratic mold and to maintain that they sought merely to return to the "true" democracy of Solon and Cleisthenes. Though the pressures of politics and litigation make it difficult to determine what any of the fourth-century orators believed in his heart about anything, the pitch of their rhetoric is a good gauge of what was expected to win votes in an Athenian courtroom.

The extant writings of the orators are consequently our best window on the thinking of the ordinary Athenian voter. Fourth-century rhetoric is a gold mine of democratic cliché. Some of the most striking examples are to be found in Demosthenes' oration against Timocrates, delivered probably in the summer of 353. Timocrates had been dragged into court by Demosthenes' associate Diodorus by the procedure known as the *graphe paranomon*, the indictment for bringing an unconstitutional motion. Since the Athenian legal system operated without a constitution and was not based on precedent, it was difficult for voters to determine just which laws were and were not out of order, and it was not unusual for a politician to find himself accused by *graphe paranomon* either by a vindictive rival or because the demos had repented passing the proposal in question and decided in retrospect that it had been a bad idea. In Timocrates' case, it seems clear that the motion was indeed illegal and its motivation discreditable; but the circle of Timocrates and his friend Androtion had a bitter and ongoing quarrel with Diodorus and his associates.

Some friends of Timocrates, including the prominent politician Androtion, had been required to turn over to the state a large portion of a haul of booty they had seized off the coast of Egypt, which was at war with Athens's then-ally, Persia. Androtion and his associates deployed a variety of procedural maneuvers in their attempt to avoid relinquishing their spoils, and somehow Timocrates had gotten a law carried that would permit debtors to the state to remain at large for some time as long as they gave sureties for their debts. Plainly his friends were planning to run off with their considerable profits. Not surprisingly, Timocrates was indicted on a *graphe paranomon*, and Demosthenes, who had also composed the speech for Diodorus's attack on Androtion on a different *graphe paranomon* in 355, wrote the speech for Diodorus to deliver against Timocrates.

Had there been any real evidence that Timocrates and Androtion were plotting to overthrow the government, Demosthenes would surely have adduced it in his oration. Instead, he simply suggests, repeatedly and at memorable length, that the sort of man who would propose a law at variance with standard procedure is plainly the sort of man who would overthrow democracy and establish tyranny or oligarchy. The laws that Timocrates sought to flout, Demosthenes argues, were not violent or oligarchic but rather prescribed that things be done in a generous and democratic spirit (24). The attempt to alter the laws he casts as *kataluon*, "subverting"—precisely the word used regularly for attempts to overthrow the government, *katalusis tou demou* (31). Having had the clerk read the law declaring the acts of the Thirty to be invalid, Demosthenes points out that doubtless the worst fear of the Athenians is that the state of affairs under the Thirty should ever repeat itself. If it was appropriate to overturn the acts of the Thirty, he maintains, then to allow Timocrates to change a law passed by the democracy would be tantamount to suggesting that the democratic government is no better than that of the Thirty (57–58). What, he requests the jury to ask themselves, "is the real difference between government by law (*nomos*) and oligarchy; and why [do] we regard those who prefer to live under laws as honest, sober-minded persons, and those who submit to oligarchical rule as cowards and slaves?" The outstanding difference, he claims, is that "under oligarchical government everybody is entitled to undo the past, and to prescribe future transactions according to his own pleasure; whereas the laws of a free state prescribe what shall be done in the future, such laws having been enacted by convincing people that they will be beneficial to those who live under them. Timocrates, however, legislating in a democratically governed city, has introduced into his law the characteristic iniquity of oligarchy; and in dealing with past transactions has presumed to claim for himself an authority higher than that of the convicting jury" (75).[33] The bloodiest of the Thirty Tyrants, Critias himself, Demosthenes claims, would have framed just the same sort of statute as Timocrates (90).

In the oration against Timocrates, in other words, Demosthenes bills the self-serving ploy of a some embezzlers in a tight spot as an attempt to overthrow the democracy and replace it with oligarchy in the manner of the Thirty, and he equates *nomos*, "law," with *demokratia*, implying that all other forms of government are unlawful. And not only this: as additional fuel for his argument that the Athenians should not tolerate Timocrates' self-indulgence, he maintains that a further reason the treasonous Timocrates went after the laws was that he had observed that everyone both in public and in private attributes Athens's prosperity to them.

Throughout the fourth century, litigants in Athenian courts sought to suggest whenever possible that a vote against their cause was a vote against democracy and was indeed practically high treason. The fact that no Athenian speaker in his right mind would dare proclaim his opposition to democracy did not prevent Athenian audiences from having their hearts warmed by orators who introduced its praises into their speeches. Though the bipolarity of the fifth century that had informed Pericles' funeral oration was no longer so marked, still oppositions could be made with Sparta, and in his oration *Against Leptines* of 354 Demosthenes compares the free speech of Athens with the lack of it in Sparta (106). Both Demosthenes in his 344 *Second Philippic* (25, 75–76) and Aeschines in his speech *Against Timarchus* in 345 (4–5) suggest that democracy alone constitutes government by law; tyranny, monarchy, and oligarchy have no part in lawful government.

In the schemata of democratic orators, then, democracy is not simply one form of government or even the best form; rather it is the only legitimate form there is. The opposition between Athenian democracy on the one hand and a world of injustice and brute force on the other is dramatically drawn by the author of the funeral oration composed probably around 390 to honor those Athenians who had fallen on the side of Corinth and her allies against Sparta. It was natural, he says, for the Athenians' ancestors to establish a tradition of fighting on the side of justice,

> for the very beginning of their life was just. . . . They were the first and the only people in that time to drive out the ruling classes of their state and to establish a democracy, believing the liberty of all to be the strongest bond of agreement; by sharing with each other the hopes born of their perils they had freedom of soul in their civic life, and used law for honouring the good and punishing the evil. For they deemed that it was the way of wild beasts to be held subject to one another by force, but the duty of men to delimit justice by law, to convince by reason, and to serve these two in act by submitting to the sovereignty of law and the instruction of reason.[34]

To be undemocratic, in other words, was to be—literally—inhuman.

•   •   •   •   •

Without a doubt a number of the Greek intellectuals whose words contribute to our understanding of the ideology of Athenian democracy were hard pressed by rhetorical and political constraints of various kinds. There is no more reason to believe that they were convinced of the truth of everything they said than there is to believe that former U.S. president George Bush really thinks being a member of the American Civil Liberties Union is tantamount to supporting Communism. But their speeches and writings make clear that a significant body of thought in classical Athens rejected the customary paradigm that a community should consist of rulers and ruled. Such a community, many thinkers argued, was no community at all. Rather, the ideal polis involved a kind of active participation on the part of the average citizen that is thoroughly alien to most modern states. Democracy today is perceived largely in negative terms; it is a kind of government in which a minority may not dictate to a majority and in which a minimum of constraints are placed on individual liberty. To have a democracy means to have no monarch, no dictator, no aristocracy, no junta. Apathy, however, is allowed—even, according to many theoreticians, encouraged for the sake of efficiency. This, however, is not the kind of harmless state described by Pericles or Protagoras. Rather, the Athenian democracy was conceived by its supporters as a dynamic entity energized by the combined commitment and capacity of all its male citizens.

Democracy was synonymous with freedom and law not only for Athenians but also for non-Athenian admirers such as Herodotus (and quite possibly the unknown author of the funeral oration of ca. 390, who may have been an alien resident in Athens such as the orator Lysias, in whose corpus the speech has been preserved). The rather tendentious word *isonomia* was used to suggest that democracy was the only equitable form of government. Anything else was a form of tyranny.[35] Jurors in Athenian courts and voters in the Athenian assembly were smug and serene in their conviction that it was democracy that protected them from all manner of terrors lurking in the universe. Often they heard it contrasted with the autocracy of Persia and Macedon on the one hand and the militaristic oligarchy of Sparta on the other. Opposition to democracy was tied in the minds of its champions to traitorous connections with Sparta and Macedon, and particularly in the case of Sparta during the fifth century, the association between antidemocratic ideas and affection for Athens' enemies was a real one and not drawn merely for the sake of rhetorical effect. The democratic Themistocles advocated a strong anti-Spartan stand, whereas the more conservative Cimon advocated friendship with the Spartans. At the end of the Peloponnesian War Sparta made the institution of an oligarchic government at Athens one of the conditions of peace. There is every reason to believe conservative pro-Spartans betrayed the Athenian fleet at Aegospotami in 405, thus ending the Peloponnesian war. Athenians who considered the word *oligarch* to be synonymous with *traitor* were frequently not far wrong. It must be remembered, however, that the aristocratic worldview was endemic in Greek civilization, and it was the egalitarianism of the Athenians that was fundamentally eccentric. Athenian democratic rhetoric struck many Greeks as self-serving propaganda crafted for sinister ends by desperate men— men who had sold their souls by throwing in their lot with that of the coarse sailors and officious shop-keepers who thought that sheer numbers empowered them to rule not only Athens but the Aegean as well. Fully to understand the shock value of Athenian democracy it is necessary to see how deeply elitist values were ingrained in Greek society, and this will form the subject of the chapter that follows.

Chapter Three

THE FIRST ATTACKS ON ATHENIAN DEMOCRACY

> In every country the aristocracy is contrasted to the democracy,
> there being in the best people the least licentiousness and iniquity,
> but the keenest eye for morals; in the people on the other hand we
> find a very high degree of ignorance, disorder, and vileness; for
> poverty more and more leads them in the direction of bad morals,
> thus also the absence of education and in the case of some persons
> the ignorance which is due to the want of money.
> —The anonymous fifth-century author of the
> Constitution of the Athenians

DEMOCRACY MIGHT be *isonomia* to its champions, but to its enemies it was a perversion of justice, an exploitative class government
rationalized by a misunderstanding of the essence of equality. To such
thinkers, Athens's diplomatic setbacks appeared to be the natural outgrowth
of her democratic system, and by the time the Greek city-states lost their
autonomy on the field of Chaeronea in 338, an elaborate multipronged attack
had been mounted on the Athenians and their democracy. There is no need
to reconstruct this attack as one reconstructs democratic theory, from snatches
here and there. Rather, it is splashed unsparingly over the corpus of Greek
literature.

THE CLAIMS OF CLASS

The nature of the attack on Athens varies according to the speaker or writer,
but it is important to remember within what frame of reference Athens's critics operated. A theoretician like Plato might dream of a state basking in the
beatific autocracy of a man wise beyond ordinary mortals, but few Greeks
would have advocated monarchy or tyranny as the best government for classical Athens; it was to defend Hellenism against the horrors of Eastern despotism that the Greeks had united in battle against the Persians. Though the
neat oppositions of Pericles' funeral oration were not always before people's
minds, still the essential question for most contemporaries once the Persian
threat had receded was how Athenian democracy compared not to monarchy
or to tyranny but rather to oligarchy. Except for the members of Athens's own
empire, within which Athens favored governments similar to her own, most

Greek city-states outside Athens were generally governed by some sort of oligarchy. For most Greek thinkers, the alternative to democracy was an aristocracy of either birth or wealth, or some combination of the two. The first complaints against the democracy, consequently, were generally posited on the thesis that people who could boast wealthy or famous ancestors made better citizens—that is, better political decision-makers—than those who could not.

Demokratia was a form of government in which the *kratos*, power, belonged to the demos, people, and throughout Greek history the same ambiguities surrounded the word demos as surround its modern counterparts in European languages today. Skilled democratic rhetoricians like Pericles made a point of taking the demos that was sovereign in Athenian democracy to include every voter, no matter how poor—or how rich. To the enemies of democracy, however, it was clear, first, that *demo-kratia* meant the despotic rule of poor people over rich people, and, second, that rich people made better policy than poor people. In the eyes of Greek antidemocrats, it was not simply a matter of coincidence that majority rule entailed the dominance of poor over rich. This, they thought, was no accident. Rather in democracy they saw a calculated and tyrannical form of class government.

The notion of social class is not, of course, a phenomenon unique to ancient Greece, but, to make use of an appropriately class-oriented phrase, it had in Greece a long pedigree.[1] It first appears as a belief that people from a small number of families were in some way better than people from all other families; in the course of time it is refined to include the possibility that the acquisition of wealth may possibly—but need not necessarily—entitle people from outside the charmed circle to a share in the political pie. Perhaps the first recorded instance of class-consciousness in Greek literature is in the *Iliad* of Homer. Twentieth-century egalitarians are sometimes shocked by Homer's portrait of Thersites, the one commoner of whom we get a glimpse in the intensely aristocratic *Iliad*. To Homer's audience, Thersites was not simply poor and ugly and worthless; he was poor and therefore predictably ugly and worthless. The picture Homer paints is vivid: Thersites is lame, stooped, and sports a straggly clump of wool on top of his pointed head. When Thersites dares speak up in the assembly, he attacks Agamemnon on precisely the grounds Achilles had used earlier. But what is suitable for Achilles is not deemed fitting for Thersites. Homer stresses repeatedly that Thersites' character and behavior violate the laws of order that keep people in their place. He is *ametroepes*, of speech that does not know when to stop; the words in his head are *akosma*, without any organization. The concept of *kosmos*, order, appears again in the next line: Thersites wrangles with princes *ou kata kosmon*, in violation of custom and order. When Odysseus beats Thersites so severely that a welt rises up on his neck and a tear wells up in his eye, the army has a good laugh:

Sorry though the men were they laughed over him happily,
and thus they would speak to each other, each looking at the man next him:
"Come now: Odysseus has done excellent things by thousands,
bringing forward good counsels and ordering armed encounters;
but now this is far the best thing he ever has accomplished
among the Argives, to keep this thrower of words, this braggart,
out of assembly. Never again will his proud heart stir him
up, to wrangle with the princes in words of revilement."

$$(2.270-77)^2$$

These are the words of the *plethys*, the multitude. Of course the men in the army who make up this multitude are not particularly rich or beautiful themselves, but their sense of their place is so strong that they side with Odysseus in restoring the natural social order rather than with Thersites in challenging it. Such is the confrontation Homer chose to recount before the wealthy patrons who supported his artistic endeavors.

A slightly later poet gives us a fuller picture of Greek class-consciousness. The seventh and sixth centuries constituted a period of enormous ferment in Greece, as the traditional aristocracies of birth that were seen ruling in the Homeric poems found themselves struggling to maintain their power in the face of a variety of pressures. Chief among these pressures was the demand of the growing trade aristocracy of wealth for a say in government. With the growth of population, the opening up of commerce, the development of coinage, colonial expansion, and the rise of hoplite warfare came the growth of a new social class whose money was often earned rather than inherited and was more likely to come from trade than from land. One way in which the aristocracy of birth reacted to the demands of this class was by asserting that there existed a special quality in people from certain families that simply could not be developed by any others. This concept of *gnome* plays an important role in the poems of Theognis of Megara, whose class had been ousted by the weaving dynasty of one Theagenes. Writing in the sixth century, Theognis reacted with horror to the phenomenon of social mobility, for in his view certain qualities simply could not be attained; they had to be inborn. "Oh, Kyrnos," he sighs to the young lover to whom all his poetry was dedicated, "this polis is still a polis, but its people are different, people who formerly knew no laws, no settled way of doing things, but wore down goatskins until they were ragged and pastured themselves outside the city like deer. But now these people are [considered] good, son of Polypaus, and those who were once noble are now held to be worthless. Who can bear to look upon this state of affairs?" (53–58). There is irony in Theognis's contention that the erstwhile riffraff are now the *agathoi*, the good, for Theognis does not believe that political virtue can be taught or learned. He explains elsewhere that the nobly born, that is, those who are born into families in which political power has been concentrated for some generations, can lose their *gnome*, their natural inborn virtue and wisdom, through fraternizing with people from families who have not belonged to this charmed circle: "If you mingle with the base (*kakoi*) you will lose what wisdom you already have," he warns (35–36)—but the basely born can never gain it. "No one," he says, "has ever found out a way to make a fool wise or a base man (*kakos*) noble (*esthlos*) . . . you will never make the bad man good by teaching" (430–31, 437–38). Theognis, then, believed in confining political power to an elite consisting of members of certain families who possessed special qualities nonexistent in others. Outside these families, such qualities could not be found even in embryo, to be fostered by the sensitive teacher whom Socrates was to compare to a midwife. One might gamble away one's privileged position in the charmed circle through imprudent associations with people outside it, but the inverse process was impossible.

A large amount of Greek lyric poetry is associated with the name of Theognis, and it is curious that scholars are in doubt whether to attribute various fragments to him or to the Athenian lawgiver Solon, Theognis's approximate contemporary though older than the Megarian by a generation or so. The nature of Solon's reforms at Athens makes clear that Solon could not have shared Theognis's belief that the social order was fixed for all time by a biological law that denied the rudiments of wisdom to all but a select few. Both his reforms and his poetry, however, demonstrate that Solon shared Theognis's view that people fell naturally into classes. In a famous passage Solon wrote: "I gave the demos such privilege as is sufficient to them, neither adding nor taking away; and as for those who had power and were admired for their wealth, I also provided that they should not suffer undue wrong. I stood with a stout shield thrown over both parties, not allowing either one to prevail unjustly over the other" (cited in Plutarch, *Solon* 18.4, and [Aristotle], *The Constitution of the Athenians*, 12). In Latin terminology, he means *demos qua plebs*, not *demos qua populus*, and these lines suggest that Solon viewed the demos as a lobby like any other special interest group, entitled to just so much power and no more. They make it difficult to cast him as a democrat for two reasons. The fact that Solon places limits on the proper sphere of the demos— and sees himself as a hero for doing so—makes it difficult to cast him as a democrat. To be sure, Solon paved the way for fifth- and fourth-century democracy by his replacement of birth with wealth as a determinant of political power and by his creation of the popular courts, and after his death he was acclaimed as an ideological ancestor by more than one Athenian political party. In reality, however, Solon is about as much a democrat as Plato was a Christian—that is, Solon was no democrat.[3]

The differences between Theognis's views about social mobility and those of Solon should not obscure the fact that both men considered it axiomatic that there existed such a thing as class and that some classes had a greater claim on political power than did other classes. The theory of Athenian democracy sought to negate the concept of class. In practice, men from a small number of respected families continued throughout the history of the democracy to be accorded what might seem to modern egalitarians to be a disproportionate amount of power and prestige; and at times the poor majority rode roughshod over the rich minority. Nonetheless, such phenomena played no part in democratic theory—at least not as it was publicly articulated. As Pericles had put it in the Thucydidean funeral oration, in Athens it was *axiosis*, merit, that alone caused some people to be accorded more public honors than others. In the Periclean scheme of things, democracy meant that the polis was to be a joint responsibility and shared delight for all citizens from all classes. The Solonic concept of the demos as a lobby, however, reappears in the first detailed attack on the Athenian democracy that has come down to us—the essay on the Athenian constitution by the man known to English-speakers as the Old Oligarch. Just where the name originated is not certain, though it is first remembered on the lips of the British classicist Gilbert Murray. It seems less confusing than the other name often given the author of the pamphlet, pseudo-Xenophon (based on the long-standing misapprehension that Xenophon was the author of the work), and it will be a convenient label for our purposes; no slight to old age is implied in my use of the epithet, though I suspect some may have been intended in its original adoption.

The fact that we do not know the name of the author of the pamphlet is a minor problem. Somewhat greater difficulties are created by other areas of ignorance. Although most scholars have seen the work as a sincere attack on democracy, others have contended that the author was neither old nor an oligarch and have viewed the work rather as a somewhat squawky exercise in intellectual exhibitionism. Close scholarly examination, moreover, has revealed that the author was certainly not an Athenian citizen and yet definitely a citizen of Athens, and that the work itself was composed neither before the outbreak of hostilities with Sparta in 431 nor, to be sure, during or after the war. Nonetheless, the essay indubitably exists, and it is the first extant account of democracy as the calculated suppression of one class by another.[4]

According to the Old Oligarch, the Athenian democratic naval empire is a carefully calibrated, well-integrated system, though he finds the intrinsic democratic premise unacceptable: "Indeed as to the constitution of the Athenians my opinion is that I do not at all approve of their having chosen this form of constitution because by making this choice they have given the advantage to the vulgar people (*poneroi*) at the expense of the good (*chrestoi*). This is the reason for my disapproval, but what I want to point out is that now that they have adopted this view they in an excellent way back up this form of constitution and manage the other matters, which the other Hellenes think done wrongly by them" (1.1).[5] This last contention appears to refer to the Athenian empire. The Old Oligarch sees the navy, the empire, and the democracy as interconnected. Because it is the poor who man the ships, he argues, it is in some sense *dikaion*, "just," that they should have the most political power; and the revenues from the empire policed by that very navy serve to pay the demos for its participation in politics, as, for example, on juries (1.2, 16).

Like Pericles, in other words, the Old Oligarch views the Athenian polis as a unified whole held together by its democratic constitution, and the opening paragraphs of his essay promise a sociopolitical analysis of the various interlocking parts of the democratic network far more sophisticated than Pericles had provided in his patriotic portrait of his polis. This promise is not fulfilled in its entirety. The author's principal purpose appears to be to reiterate his thesis that the demos is at constant war with the *chrestoi*, the noble, and that the Athenian demos makes a point of making life miserable for the upper classes both at home and abroad in the empire. He does a better job in showing how this works abroad than in showing how it works in Athens itself. In allied cities, the author maintains, the Athenians make false accusations against the *chrestoi*, disfranchise them, take their money away, expel them, and kill them (1.14). In addition, he claims, the demos consolidates its position in the empire by forcing allies to come to Athens for legal proceedings. This practice not only has the advantage of the immediate revenues that accrue from customs duties and from the profits of local innkeepers and other merchants but also sees to it that the allies must pay court not simply to isolated magistrates but to the demos as a whole. In this way, moreover, the Athenians are enabled to side regularly with the demos and against the aristocrats, something prudence might otherwise deter them from doing so far from home.

Whether the facts the author reports are true is difficult to determine, but his line of argument, at all events, is clear and easy to follow. Just how the oppression of the *chrestoi* is carried out in Athens itself is less plain. The author complains that the Athenians *nemousi* (assign, distribute) more to the *poneroi* (base) and *penetes* (the poor in the sense of the working classes) than they do to the *chrestoi*, but he offers no explanation of how this is accomplished (1.4), and in fact the prominent politicians of the Peloponnesian War era generally belonged to reasonably well-to-do families. In trying to explain how clever it is of the Athenians to make sure that the *poneroi* dominate politics, he writes:

> Now one might say that the right thing would be that they did not allow all to speak on an equal footing, nor to have a seat in the council, but only the cleverest and the best. But on this point, too, they have determined on the perfectly right thing by also allowing the vulgar people to speak. For if . . . the aristocracy (*chrestoi*) were allowed to speak and took part in the debate, it would be good for them and their peers, but not to the proletarians. But now that any vulgar person (*poneros*) who wants to may step forward and speak, he will just express that which is good to him and his equals. (1.6–7)

What is striking about this passage is not simply the illogical conclusion that because all may speak, therefore some (e.g., the *chrestoi*) may not, but the assumption that the *chrestoi*, given the chance of which the author claims they are deprived, would in turn govern in *their* sole interest. (The notion that if all may speak then some [the *chrestoi*] may not is sufficiently peculiar that the twentieth-century scholar Hartvig Frisch, whose translation I have used here, amended his rendition to read "For if [only] the aristocracy were allowed to speak." I have removed the bracketed word in my own text in order to highlight the illogic of the original.) Be all this as it may, it is plain that the author views democracy as the oppression of the more deserving people, who are well-to-do, by the less deserving, who are poor. Everywhere, he explains, the aristocracy (*beltistoi*) are characterized by the minimum of licentiousness and iniquity and a maximum of sensitivity to what is good, whereas "in the people on the other hand we find a very high degree of ignorance, disorder, and vileness; for poverty more and more leads them in the direction of bad morals, thus also the absence of education and in the case of some persons the ignorance which is due to the want of money" (1.5). This, to the best of my knowledge, is the first recorded explanation in Western literature of the commonly held belief that poor people make bad citizens: poverty makes people desperate and therefore blunts their judgment, and lack of money sometimes leads to lack of education and knowledge.[6]

Around the same time the Old Oligarch was writing, an attack of a very different nature was being threaded through the strands of Thucydides' history of the Peloponnesian War. Deeply influenced by the new principles of scientific study, Thucydides sought to apply the science of medicine to the art of writing history and thereby to lay bare the workings of historical processes. Convinced as he was that "human nature being what it is, events similar to these are likely to happen again in the future" (1.22.4), he approached his work with a curious blend of clinical detachment and missionary zeal. Tremendous anguish and ambivalence underlie Thucydides' writing. The principal process under scrutiny in his *History* is the progressive decay of his native polis. War is well known to be a stern teacher, and to it Thucydides attributes much of what he perceived as Athens's progressive hardening into a tyrant city that knew no law beyond its own ambition. But he also ascribes Athens's ultimate loss of the war to the inadequacies of the post-Periclean government. In understanding the genesis of Thucydides' view of the Athenians' conduct of their government, we are hampered by not knowing how literally to receive his claim that he wrote up each year as it happened. It seems likely that some revision took place as time passed and that parts of the text reflect the perspective gained as the war progressed; it is certainly true that Thucydides' narrative ends in 411, though he did not die until around 400.[7] The question is of enormous importance to determining to what degree Thucydides' views were molded by the outcome of the war, and the answer seems to be that they were profoundly shaped by what he knew about the war's progress. This uncertainty, however, need not affect our perception of what his views were. Although he nowhere states baldly that democracy is ipso facto a bad thing, he blames both individual leaders and the Athenian demos for ruling badly after Pericles' death, though we do not know whether, for example, his discussion of Pericles' impeachment in 430 suggests that his low esteem for the Athenian demos preceded the death of his hero or was projected backward in the full bitterness of post-Periclean hindsight.

The long Peloponnesian War was rife with high drama. The plague at Athens, the scandal that erupted when it was reported that the mystery religion at Eleusis had been parodied by know-it-all intellectuals (Alcibiades, perhaps), the wholesale desecration of the images of Hermes outside Athenian homes just as the fleet was about to sail for Sicily, the Athenians' annihilation of the people of Melos for refusing to aid them in fighting Sparta—all this it fell to Thucydides to integrate into his history. The war also gave rise to several impeachments, including that of Thucydides himself when he served as general in northern Greece and failed to prevent the key stronghold of Amphipolis from falling into Spartan hands. In every impeachment he discusses, Thucydides sides with the accused *strategoi* and against the Athenian demos, which he portrays consistently as irrational, unreasonable and easily swayed by emotion. When Pericles was returned to office after his deposition in 430, Thucydides writes that the people had changed their minds "as the *homilos* (mob, throng) is fond of doing" (2.65.4); when several years later the demos impeached three generals who had failed to obtain a satisfactory settlement with Athens's Sicilian allies, Thucydides wrote that his fellow citizens at that time "expected to be disappointed in nothing and believed that regardless of the strength of their forces, they could achieve equally what was easy and what was difficult" (4.65.4). Thucydides' own narrative suggests that real policy issues were at stake in the impeachment of Pericles and that the generals in Sicily had done at best a mediocre job, but his editorial remarks take none of this into consideration.

Low esteem for the Athenian assembly is also evident in the debate between Nicias and Cleon concerning military operations at Pylos. Thucydides echoes the language he himself had used of Pericles' impeachment in writing that the assembly encouraged the upstart Cleon in his attack on the seasoned general "as the *ochlos* (mob) is fond of doing" (4.28.3). Most striking of all is his indictment of post-Periclean Athens, in which Pericles' successors "were prepared to entrust even the administration to the whims of the demos, as a result of which many blunders were committed, as is to be expected in a great city possessing an empire" (2.65.10–11). Thucydides attributed the loss of the war in part to the unwisdom of the demos and its post-Periclean leaders. The question remains to what cause Thucydides attributed this unwisdom.

For the mind of the average person Thucydides had little respect. In his discussion of historical methodology and the reliability of sources in book 1, he complains bitterly that ordinary people accept hearsay from one another uncritically and have little interest in establishing the truth (1.20.1, 3). His stress on the *gnome* of both Pericles and Themistocles suggests that this is the quality he seeks in a statesman, and his assertion that it was Pericles' high reputation, integrity, and *gnome* that made it possible for him freely to restrain the demos, leading it rather than being led by it, implies that his ideal statesman needed a special kind of intellect that most people (the people in the assembly and the politicians who succeeded Pericles) did not have. His inclusion of Themistocles among the possessors of *gnome*, however, makes clear that he does not connect *gnome* with membership in a narrow group of families. This is noteworthy in view of the fact that Thucydides came himself from the aristocratic Philaid family, to which had belonged not only Pericles' conservative rival Thucydides, the son of Melesias, but also Cimon and his father, Miltiades, Themistocles' great rival. It is clear that Thucydides had emancipated himself from the philosophy in which he must have been raised sufficiently to bestow on Pericles the consistent praise that he did, stressing in his assessment of Pericles not only that he led Athens wisely during the prewar period but that his plan for winning the war was *prognous*, full of foresight, and that the loss of the war was to be traced to the Athenians' departure from his guidelines, which called for an essentially defensive policy (2.65.5–9). That these lines are themselves defensive and seek to answer charges brought against Pericles concerning the war seems inescapable, and it is likely that those who leveled these charges included members of Thucydides' own family. But though he was neither an anti-Periclean conservative nor a hidebound Theognidian oligarch, Thucydides' estimate of the capacity of the average voter and of the average statesman appears to have been low, and his praise of Pericles also implies a fierce condemnation both of other political leaders and of the Athenian assembly. His contention that Pericles owed his influence to the fact that he was incorruptible, honest, and did not resort to flattery or seek power by dishonest means carries with it the suggestion that Thucydides considered corruption, flattery, and dishonesty to be common attributes of Athenian politicians, and his portrait of Pericles' relationship to the populace is dramatically demeaning to the demos: Pericles, Thucydides writes, "led the multitude [*plethos*] rather than being led by it. . . . Whenever he saw the people were unjustifiably confident and arrogant, he would cow them into fear with his words; on the other hand, when he saw them unreasonably afraid, he would turn them back to hopefulness once more. And so it happened that Athens, though in name a democracy, was coming to be governed in fact by its first citizen" (2.65.8–9). The high marks that Pericles received from Thucydides, in other words, were posited on the low marks the historian accorded to the Athenian demos, which he portrays as highly emotional and extremely malleable, and to other Athenian politicians, whom he depicts as unscrupulous and self-seeking. According to Thucydides, Pericles alone among Athens's war leaders turned this malleability to the advantage of the state; his successors sought only to exploit it for their own ends.

How Thucydides explained the inadequacy of the ordinary run of Athenians, or how he imagined it could be changed, is unclear. It is true that he has words of high praise for the oligarchy of the Five Thousand that succeeded the Four Hundred in 411: it was then, he writes, "that the Athenians appear to have enjoyed the best government that they ever did, at least in my time, for a moderate blending was effected between the few and the many" (8.97.2). Thucydides also describes Antiphon, a well-known oligarch and one of the leaders of the antidemocratic coup, as "one of the best men in my day in Athens" (8.68.1). What made the Five Thousand better decision-makers than the entire demos gathered together in the assembly? Wealth? Birth? Education? Coincidence? Thucydides does not say, but any notion that he saw the traditional criteria of riches or illustrious descent as fair barometers of *gnome* is undermined by his admiration for Themistocles and by his decision to include Pericles' stirring paean to democracy in his account of the war—and at considerable length. Indeed, the funeral oration, by which Thucydides extols Pericles even as Pericles is extolling Athens, makes a statement about the kind of estimable leader the democracy at its best might produce. Probably, too, some approbation of democracy was intended in the nasty speech Thucydides puts in the mouth of Cleon in book 3: even if Thucydides has reproduced Cleon's actual words, which is certainly possible, his decision to highlight the speech in such a position of prominence was plainly a matter of choice. Berating the Athenians for their vacillation in the matter of punishing the Mytileneans, who had rebelled from the empire, Cleon delivers a searing indictment of the Athenians' enthusiasm for both discussion and mercy (3.37–41). The empire, he maintains, is a tyranny, and the Athenians, if they wish to hold on to it, had better learn the ruthless decisiveness of tyrants. Cleon's attack on the virtue of deliberation and debate is so unpleasant that it is hard not to believe that his enemy Thucydides sought, by associating the vulgar Cleon with this swipe at the democratic ethos, to suggest some merit in the system and to identify it with the constructive use of intellect and language.

In the end, we are forced to abandon any search for Thucydides' politics. It is not clear that Thucydides indeed devoted a great deal of thought to constitutional questions; for him, good policy was made by good leaders, and though it may disappoint us, it need not surprise us that in his *History* he did not confront the question of which constitution was most likely to produce such leaders. But his repeated indictment of the volatile Athenian demos was to play a large role in molding the opinion of later thinkers, and Thucydides is also the first source for the notion that Athens declined steadily after Pericles' death—that her post-Periclean leaders were made of sorry stuff, and that the demos itself became progressively coarser and more callous under the strains of war. Though Thucydides appreciated the intelligence of Alcibiades and the integrity of Nicias, he was keenly sensible of the injuries done to Athens by these blue-blooded politicians; though he is often cited as a primary source for the destruction of Athens by rabble-rousing demagogues from the lower classes, in fact he implicates myopic and self-interested aristocrats like Nicias and Alcibiades in the process just as well. Thucydides' *History* may be profitably compared with the essay of the Old Oligarch, for Thucydides seems to mirror his contemporary's position nicely. The Old Oligarch proclaimed that though he did not like democracy he had to admit that the Athenians did a fine job of it; Thucydides suggests that although he is not necessarily opposed to democracy he is certainly appalled at the use the Athenians made of it.[8] Thucydides may also be compared with another contemporary who speaks to us only through the mouth of Plato. Socrates shared Thucydides' contempt for hoi polloi, and he is equally guilty of teasing us unmercifully in his refusal to assume a consistent posture on the question of just what enables people to rise out of the multitude and distinguish themselves.

Conservative Athenian politicians of the fifth century who opposed the march of democracy were for the most part circumspect in voicing their reservations. Cimon was ostracized for his pains, and a generation later his kinsman Thucydides, the son of Melesias (also a relative of the historian), met the same fate after he sought to undermine the position of Pericles by attacks on his use of tribute from the allies to adorn Athens's acropolis, or, in the words used by Plutarch several centuries later, to deck Athena out "like a harlot" (*Pericles* 12.2). The lesson was not lost on Athenian aristocrats, and little is known about antidemocratic sentiment in Athens before the stresses of the Peloponnesian war offered a convenient forum to oligarchs. It was not until the debacle in Sicily had caused Athenian voters to question the efficacy of their form of government that it became common for conservatives publicly to advocate the limitation of the franchise. One speech, however, has been preserved in the corpus of fifth-century literature that offers an ominous harbinger of the bloody civil wars ahead. This speech was given not in the Athenian assembly but rather in the Spartan, and its speaker was Alcibiades. Though the dizzying heights of sophistry the speaker attains may have been amplified somewhat in Thucydides' rendering, the fact that the speech was given, like Pericles' funeral oration, in a public forum suggests that its outlines, at least, are historical.

The speech, which contains Alcibiades' famous dismissal of Athenian democracy as *homologoumene anoia*, or "acknowledged folly," (6.89.6), was delivered on the occasion of Alcibiades' first public appearance at Sparta after his defection from Athens, and though its ostensible purpose was to induce the Spartans to send military aid to Sicily, Alcibiades felt constrained to preface his exhortation with some explanatory remarks about his own history. If this speech is a fair index of his customary lines of argument, it is no wonder some Athenians were incensed against the eccentric philosopher who was credited with teaching him how to reason. Though Thucydides is the last of the Greek historians to be charged with undue mirth (or even due mirth), it is difficult to believe that he was oblivious to the ironies underlying this speech, ironies grim or hilarious depending on one's state of mind, and in part the speech plainly serves to further the historian's character sketch of the wily manipulator. Beginning with allegations that his strong anti-Spartan stand at home was sparked by Spartan slights to his personal honor and was, furthermore, not at all what it seemed, Alcibiades proceeds to a convoluted explanation of his position on democracy. The argument runs something like this:

1. Those of you who harbor resentment against me because I have been inclined toward the demos are offended for no reason.

2. My family, you see, has always fought against tyrants, and people who oppose tyrants are called democrats.

3. Anyhow, given that the government in Athens is democratic, we have to put up with it, don't we?

4. Despite the prevailing license (*akolasia*), we have tried to steer a moderate course.

5. But it is hard to struggle against others, both in earlier times and today, who led the masses into base ways, and it is these individuals who have driven me out.

6. We, however, considering ourselves (unlike others) to be the leaders of the people as a whole, thought we ought to preserve the form of government under which the state had prospered most, even though the connection between the prosperity and the democracy be merely coincidental.

7. Naturally all Athenians of sense have realized how silly democracy is; but that is nothing new, and it seemed unwise to change our form of government when you were about to attack us.

Even passing over the continuation of Alcibiades' speech in which he explains how his defection does not make him a traitor, there is much food for thought here, for several of the themes upon which he touches adumbrate the concerns that were to be articulated by the opponents of democracy during the years that followed. That Alcibiades and his family have only been considered democrats because democracy, a debated good, is the logical opposite of tyranny, an agreed evil, is an ingenious turning of the tables on the democrats who, as we have seen in chapter 2, set up the opposition in the first place. Alcibiades, moreover, co-opts the democratic theory of Pericles to buttress his own antidemocratic position, arguing that his own political group (friends, family, whatever—it is always "we" and not "I") are the truly civic-minded citizens who represent the whole people while their opponents stand only for one particular faction. This, of course, is an unusual variation on the democratic theme; it is now the antidemocrats who stand for the whole people and the democrats who constitute a lobby. Finally, the opposition of moderation to *akolasia*, license, became a common topos in antidemocratic circles. Alcibiades' speech in many ways stands as a blueprint for the rhetorical strategy of the moderates of the late fifth and the fourth centuries who, while demanding a de iure restriction of the franchise and a de facto limit on participation in government by eliminating state pay for public service, maintained that they were the real democrats of Athens, and that the government of Solon and of Cleisthenes was in fact the true democracy that had been perverted by subsequent corrupters (such as Ephialtes and Pericles).

The use of this argument shortly after the defection of Alcibiades and the defeat of Athens's expedition to Sicily is attested in the monograph on the *Constitution of Athens* that was unearthed late in the nineteenth century and is probably connected with the project Aristotle undertook at his school, the Lyceum, to write up the constitutions of 158 city-states; whether the author was Aristotle himself or one of his students is uncertain. Although Thucydides depicts the democrats of 411 using the word *patrioi nomoi* (ancestral laws) (8.76.6) to describe the democracy of their own lifetime and that of their parents, the author of the *Athenaion Politeia* (henceforth *AP*) records that when Pythodoros proposed the initial resolution establishing the oligarchy, "Cleitophon moved an amendment . . . that the commissioners elected should also search out the ancestral laws (*patrioi nomoi*) laid down by Cleisthenes when he was establishing the democracy, in order that they might decide on the best course to advise after hearing these laws also, on the ground that the constitution of Cleisthenes was not popular (*demotiken*) but similar to that of Solon" (29.3). Not a well-known figure today, Cleitophon was apparently an associate of the celebrated moderate Theramenes. The moderates of 411, then, sought to arrogate to themselves traditional democratic watchwords; to set themselves up as the ideological heirs of Cleisthenes; and to associate Cleisthenes and Solon in a single policy, turning Cleisthenes back to face the archaic past rather than the radical future. So far from opening the door to the full-fledged democracy of the fifth century, Cleisthenes is portrayed in moderate mythology as setting the capstone on Solon's class-based constitution.

The call for searching out the laws of Cleisthenes suggests strongly that no one knew precisely what they were; certainly the heated debate that has continued to modern times about whether or not Cleisthenes instituted ostracism lends support to this view.[9] The author of the *Athenaion Politeia* has a penchant for isolating different "constitutions," and he maintains that the Athenian government has moved through precisely eleven of these "constitutional" changes; but identifying the eleven cataracts over which Athenian democracy flowed has not been easy, and the contention of *AP* that there was such a thing as a Cleisthenic constitution is dubious. The actions of the oligarchs of 411, however, make clear what this constitution was perceived to be: it was government based both on limiting the franchise to those who met a basic property requirement and on eliminating state pay for civic service. This constitution, in other words, disfranchised the poor sailors who manned the fleets, and it prevented all the poor, as well as many from the middle class, from participating in government by serving on juries and on the *boule*.

The Cleisthenic constitution was never located; the oligarchic government of 411 was overthrown by a movement initiating in the Athenian fleet moored off Samos; and the democrats sought to reclaim the "ancestral" constitution for themselves, charging that the oligarchs had erred in abolishing the *patrioi nomoi*. It was they, the democrats claimed, who would preserve the ancestral laws and would try to compel the oligarchs to do so as well (8.76.6). The debate over the claim to the ancestral constitution, however, lived on, and it was reawakened in the months of the bloody civil strife in 404/3 when Athenian democrats (and moderates) lay at the mercy of the pro-Spartan "Thirty Tyrants." Both *AP* and the first-century historian Diodorus of Sicily claim that the peace treaty with Sparta included a clause mandating that the Athenians should be governed according to the *patrios politeia*, but the context does not make clear whether the phrase was being used in the democratic or moderate/oligarchic sense, and none of the other sources that list the conditions of peace includes this clause.[10] *AP* lists Cleitophon as a member of the party that was aiming at the ancestral constitution and Theramenes as its leader (34.3). The importance of the call for the return to the ancestral constitution is suggested by the assertion of *AP* that at first the Thirty

> were moderate toward the citizens and pretended to be administering the ancestral form of constitution, and they removed from the Areopagus the laws of Ephialtes and Archestratus [probably an associate of Ephialtes] about the Areopagites, and also such of the ordinances of Solon as were of doubtful purport, and abolished the sovereignty vested in the jurymen, claiming to be rectifying the constitution and removing its uncertainties. . . . But when they got a firmer hold on the state, they kept their hands off none of the citizens, but put to death those of outstanding wealth or birth or reputation . . . and by the end of a brief interval of time they had made away with no less than fifteen hundred. (35)

That the Thirty should have "pretended" to be preserving the ancestral constitution underlines the ambiguity that had come to surround these charged words. It is also quite plain that the democrats as well as the moderates claimed that their program embodied the ancestral constitution. Xenophon, Thucydides' younger contemporary who took up the history of Greece where Thucydides had left it, reports that the democrats when they returned to power were exhorted by Thrasybulus to live according to the ancient laws (*Hellenica* 2.4.42), and the orator Andocides has included in one of his speeches a decree introduced just after the restoration of the democracy that includes a call for a return to the ancestral laws of Solon and Draco; the democratic context of the speech suggests that the name of Solon was invoked to mean not only "the way things used to be" (in the case of moderates) but alternatively (in the case of democrats) "the way things have always been."

Ancient historians are understandably pained by the loss of their guide Thucydides, whose narrative breaks off in the middle of a sentence, after the coup of 411 but before that of 403; but internal politics was not Thucydides' greatest interest, and though his successor Xenophon lacked his analytical mind, Xenophon in some ways tells us more about Athenian politics. It is in the pages of Xenophon that a memorable debate is preserved between the extremist Critias and the moderate Theramenes, whom Critias was in the process of putting to death. Even if Xenophon's account departs considerably from the actual words spoken, it may afford some view into the minds of the camps that opposed each other at this awful hour. Because the confrontation is between a moderate and an oligarch, no specific reference is made to the ancestral constitution—an omission that confirms the suspicion that the squabble over the constitution was limited to the conflict between democrats and moderates. By the different ways in which the two men voice their dislike of democracy, Xenophon illustrates the opposition between shameless self-interest and overt Spartan partisanship on the one hand and, on the other, the desperate balancing act by which Theramenes seeks to distract his audience both from those elements in his thinking that were oligarchic and from those that were democratic.

His efforts to straddle both the popular and the oligarchic camps had earned for Theramenes the nickname "buskin," that is, a shoe that would fit either foot, but the notorious equivocator ended his life in a brief blaze of glory. His admirer Xenophon enjoys telling how Theramenes' vociferous objections to the many bloody executions of the Thirty had frightened Critias into broadening his political base by enrolling three thousand additional citizens to share in the government. Theramenes, however, was in no way placated, but rather continued to rail against the Thirty, ridiculing the idea that the number of worthy citizens in Athens was precisely three thousand, no more and no less (2.3.19); was it in any way likely, he argued, that this exact number should account for all the good citizens, those sometimes called the *kaloi kagathoi* (a common aristocratic expression for their own kind meaning "the beautiful and good" but often tendentiously translated as something like "the party of stout men and true")? When the Thirty then took their new procedure as a redoubled license to murder anyone not on the roll of three thousand, Theramenes redoubled his opposition, and the Thirty plotted to kill him. It is in the meeting that then took place in the Athenian *boule* that Xenophon sets the following dialogue between Theramenes and Critias—a meeting at which young men with daggers had been stationed by the Thirty.

"Members of the *boule*," Critias begins, "if anyone among you thinks that more people than is fitting are being put to death, let that person reflect that where governments are changed this always happens." In Athens, he goes on to explain with chilling sophistry, a new oligarchic government is bound to have the most enemies, both because of its size and because the demos has

been bred up in freedom for the longest time. "Now we," he continues, "believing that for men like us and you democracy is a grievous form of government, and knowing that the demos would never become friendly to our saviors
the Spartans, while the best men (*beltistoi*), would always be faithful to them,
are establishing the present government with Spartan approval" (2.3.24–25).
Critias then proceeds to an attack on Theramenes' chameleon-like history
and adds as a further justification of the Thirty that in putting Theramenes to
death they would only be following the model of the most highly esteemed
constitution in Greece, that of Sparta. "The constitution of the Spartans,"
Critias proclaims, "is, we know, thought to be the best of all constitutions." In
Sparta, he asks, if one of the ephors, instead of yielding to the majority, should
instead undertake to find fault with the government and to oppose what was
being done, "don't you suppose that the entire city would join with the ephors
in deeming him worthy of the severest punishment?" (2.3.34).

Critias, in other words, states openly that his objection to democracy is that
it is grievous (*chalepen*) for men like him and that it is anti-Spartan, and he
seeks to justify the execution of Theramenes by the model of the Spartan
ephorate. (This choice of a model is noteworthy not only for its overt suggestion that Athens should be more like Sparta but for its dubious claim that
Spartan ephors would be punished for resisting the majority of their four colleagues.) Theramenes in response defends some of his past conduct and seeks
to turn the tables on Critias by suggesting that Critias's ignorance of his true
history has arisen because "when these events took place, Critias was establishing a democracy in Thessaly along with Prometheus, and arming the serfs
against their masters. Would that none of the things that he was doing there
should come about here," he adds (2.3.37). Defending his moderation, he
proclaims that he is "forever at war with those who do not think there could
be a good democracy until the slaves and those who would sell the state for
lack of a drachma should share in the government." On the other hand, he is
"forever opposed to those who do not think that a good oligarchy could be
established until the state is brought to the point of being ruled absolutely by
a few." But, he continues, "to direct the government in concert with those
who have the means to be of service, whether with horses or with shields—
this plan I regarded as best in former days and I do not think any differently
now." May he be put to death, he adds, if Critias can discover any instance
where he joined hands with *demagogoi* or *tyrannikoi* to deprive people of their
citizenship (2.3.48–49).

Theramenes, then, seeks to confuse the issue by accusing Critias himself of
democratic agitation in Thessaly, and he seeks as well to condemn the democratic position by suggesting that democrats believe in a government of slaves
and desperate men, the underlying assumption being that the indigent are
therefore by implication treacherous. His own moderate position is portrayed
in such a way as to appear beyond exception. In stressing what he does believe

in—a government of those who can afford to serve with either horses or shields—Theramenes tries to distract attention from his rejection of both the oligarchic program of rule by a few and the democratic program of universal franchise for citizens (a program he has tried to make appear ridiculous by his suggestions that democrats seek to enfranchise slaves and that the poor people they are seeking to enfranchise are ipso facto corrupt). Seeing that the *boule* were inclined toward Theramenes, Critias reminded the assemblage that the Thirty still had power of life and death over those not included on the roll of Three Thousand, and, striking Theramenes' name from the list, he condemned him to death. He then handed Theramenes over to the executioners, explaining to them that he had been condemned "according to the law." As Theramenes was led away through the market place, he continued to cry out against the wrong that was being done, and Xenophon reports that when Satyrus the executioner warned him that he would suffer if he did not keep quiet he inquired whether he would not suffer just as well if he did. He tells, too, how Theramenes toasted Critias's health with the last of his hemlock. (2.3.55–56).

In fact, Theramenes' seemingly innocent proclamation that he supported a government by those who made up the cavalry and infantry constituted a treacherous turning back of the clock by democratic standards. The strongest arm of the Athenian military was, of course, the fleet, landless and indigent members of which had held the franchise for nearly a century and had been enabled to participate fully in Athenian government since the introduction of state pay for state service (i.e., as jurors or in the *boule*) in the time of Pericles. What Theramenes is really saying here is that he supports disfranchisement of the poor. By pairing demagogues with tyrants, he sets off an eddying series of reverberations looking back to allegations against Pericles and ahead to anxious eighteenth-century historians of Greece. In his use of the word *demagogos*, moreover, Theramenes sets himself squarely in the antidemocratic camp; potentially tendentious under any circumstances, the word was especially charged at a time when the leaders of the demos were defending law and order against a bloody sequence of judicial murders. It is no surprise to hear Critias complain (2.3.27) that Theramenes was always the first one to interpose difficulties when he and his crew wanted to put some demagogue out of the way (*ekpodon*, literally, out from underfoot); it is somewhat more interesting to hear Theramenes anxiously asserting his opposition to *demagogoi* and *tyrannikoi* alike. Critias had acknowledged openly his own class-oriented view of government, stating baldly that he opposed democracy because it is bad for "men like him"; Theramenes sought to dissociate himself from those who would govern in the interests of a single group (the tyrant and his friends on the one hand and the demos on the other), but he also places himself in the camp of those who construed democracy as the tyranny of one class over another.

THE ANCESTRAL CONSTITUTION

By the end of the Peloponnesian War, then, assorted Athenian malcontents of various stamps had gone on record maintaining that their democracy was an oppressive class government, conducted foreign policy badly, was irrational and emotional in its treatment of its leaders, gave power to the dregs of society, and was in sum an "acknowledged folly." In addition, the theory was advanced that at some point prior to the end of the war the democracy had fallen away from its true self as realized by Solon and/or Cleisthenes and that only a restoration of "real" democracy could begin to solve the problems of the day, whatever they might be. The exact juncture at which the "debasement" of Athenian democracy began was a topic of heated debate, but the conviction that there had been a falling off from the good old days was frequently voiced— even in comedy, as the chorus of Aristophanes' *Ekklesiazousai* (*Congresswomen*) laments the passing of the good old days when nobody requested payment for public service (304ff.). In an amusing and appropriately laconic speech that purports to have been given in the Spartan assembly, the ephor Sthenelaidas (speaking in the pages of Thucydides) had brusquely summarized the speech of the Athenian ambassadors and dismissed the claim to Spartan goodwill based on Athenian service to Greece during the Persian Wars. If the Athenians' account of their past services is accurate, he points out, then it reflects so much the worse on their bad behavior in recent years, for, he says, they deserve double the punishment for having gone from good to bad (1.86.1). Though the rationale behind it was somewhat different, the notion that the Athenians had indeed gone from good to bad became entrenched in contemporary Greek literature and has been widely believed throughout Western history.

AP itself, composed probably in the 320s with the aid of a variety of sources, is representative of the inconsistency of fourth-century thinking about the decline of Athens. At 27.4, AP reports the allegation of "some critics" that the juries deteriorated as soon as Pericles began the system of state pay for jury service "because ordinary persons always took more care than the respectable (*epieikeis*) to draw lots for the job." AP is not alone among authors who cannot seem to decide whether Pericles marked the end of the good times or the beginning of the bad; Pericles is missing from his list of Athens's best politicians, a list that includes Nicias and Thucydides, the son of Melesias, who he says were not only *kaloi kagathoi* but also servants of the whole state (28.5). After Pericles' death, AP goes on, the demos began choosing as leader someone who was not in good repute with the *epieikeis* (reasonable people? presumably also affluent people), a marked change from previous practice. Listing the various men who had held the leadership of the people and of the wealthy, he lists Cleon as Pericles' successor and names Nicias as the new leader of the others. Cleon, he reports, "is thought to have done the most to corrupt the people by his impetuous outbursts, and was the first person to use bawling and abuse on the platform, and to gird up his cloak before making a public speech" (28.5). He goes on to criticize those who raised payment for public service, and maintains that "from Cleon onward the leadership of the People was handed on in an unbroken line by the men most willing to play a bold part and to gratify the many with an eye to immediate popularity" (28.4).

AP, then, believed that a decline in the quality of Athenian government set in either during Pericles' lifetime or immediately upon his death. Generally an enthusiastic supporter of democracy, even the orator Demosthenes nonetheless alleges a decline in statesmanship at some point after Pericles' death, complaining that Aristides and Pericles have given way to orators who say to the people, "What would you like? What shall I propose? How can I oblige you?" (Olynthiacs 3.22). But it is in the copious orations of Isocrates, delivered over a span of a lifetime that lasted nearly a century, that the theme of a sad falling-off from better days is wrought to its highest pitch.[11] In his early speech the Panegyricus, written to exhort his fellow Athenians to take up the Greek man's burden and unite with the other Hellenes in a campaign against Asia, Isocrates goes on at some length comparing the self-interest, avarice, and recklessness of his contemporaries with the selfless patriotism of the men who raised the generation that defeated the Persians.[12] Citizens of earlier times competed with one another only in vying to serve the state, and he insists that even the secret societies, the gentlemen's clubs known as hetaireiai (which had since become hotbeds of oligarchy), were for the benefit of the many.[13] In his oration On the Peace, written some thirty years later, he complains that it was the Athenians' quest for naval empire that brought an end to the happy demokratia of their ancestors.[14] People will see, he claims, how much better it would be to leave off this quest if they will contrast Athens before and after she acquired this power. The politeia of Athens at the time of the Persian Wars was better than Athens in later times in the same degree that Aristides and Themistocles and Miltiades were better men than Hyperbolus and Cleophon, the democratic politicians of the later Peloponnesian War, and than the current leaders of the demos (75). The Athenians in an earlier time deserved the goodwill of all Athens's allies, whereas during the Peloponnesian War they stooped to pad their navy with mercenaries with whose aid they expelled the beltistoi from their various cities and confiscated their property (79). The inferior leadership of recent generations has been responsible for two oligarchic revolutions, whereas in the old days it remained unshaken and unchanged for many years (122). Pericles he places in a middle position; he took over the state, he claims, when it was "less prudent than it had been before it obtained the supremacy," but still governed it tolerably well, sought no personal fortune, and left only a small estate; to him one must contrast contemporary politicians, and so on and so forth (126–31).[15]

The same themes reappear in his *Areopagiticus*, written around the same time. Composed, in other words, at a time when Athens had just fought a costly war against her rebelling allies, the speech, as its title suggests, blamed Athens's misfortunes on her abandonment of the ancestral constitution and curtailment of the powers of the Areopagus. The earlier democracy, he argued, appreciated the principle of true, that is, proportional equality, by which each held power in proportion to his deserts, a principle the later democracy abandoned (21); and the result of this was that the ancient Athenians had a more democratic (*demotikoteros*) way of choosing magistrates: for, he maintains, under a lottery system such as the one currently in force, there is danger that oligarchic partisans may end up in office, whereas by a system of appointment, the people would have the power to choose those who were most attached to the constitution (23). The rich, he goes on to suggest, will use their offices more honorably than poor men who would be tempted to use it to enrich themselves.

Isocrates goes on to stress the moral element in the early democracy, which, he maintains, saw to it that people acted with propriety and justice in their daily lives, "for when people have laid sound foundations for the conduct of the whole state it follows that in the details of their lives they must reflect the character of their government" (28). Not only were the ancestors morally upright, they were religious: they worshiped the gods properly, discouraged foreign cults, and maintained religious traditions, with the result that divine favor endowed the land with unstinting fertility (30). It is particularly in connection with morality and piety that Isocrates is concerned about the men who led on the youth to gamble and patronize "flute girls" by breaking the power of the Areopagus, which had kept a particularly watchful eye on the character of young and old (37–50). In ancient times, Isocrates contends, there was no need of all the many laws that clogged the Athens of his day, for the moral tone of the Areopagite government obviated any need for elaborate legislation; the Areopagus, he explains, believed that "where there is a multiplicity of specific laws, it is a sign that the state is badly governed" (40). True patriots, he complains, are accused of being oligarchic; but nothing could be farther from the truth. He himself is an enemy of oligarchy and a friend to democracy. What he admires about the Spartans is the democratic element in their government, for it is this, he claims, that explains why the Spartans are "the best governed people in the world" (61).[16]

Decades later, three years before his death, Isocrates in his *Panathenaicus* lambasted the Spartans of the fifth and fourth centuries at some length. He still praised Lycurgus, however, and maintained that he had imitated Athens in framing the mixed constitution of Sparta and had deliberately conferred upon the elders there the same power which he knew that the Council of the Areopagus enjoyed in Athens (153). He also asserts that the Spartans had no skill in warfare before they learned it by copying the Athenians. Where in his speech *On the Peace* he had attacked the Athenians for their first expansion-ism during the fifth century, here at the close of his life he balances the attack on Sparta with a defense of the Athenians' fifth century imperialism that can only be called bizarre. Responding to the evidently common criticisms of Athens for the tribute she had imposed on members of the Delian League, he argues that the members themselves had wished the alliance in order to pre-serve their own democracies; and furthermore, he goes on, as to the cities that were laid waste by the Athenians and the Spartans, "a matter for which cer-tain men reproach the Athenians alone—we shall show that things much more reprehensible were done by those whom these men are never weary of extolling." For, he says, while the Spartans made war on important states such as the home of glorious Agamemnon, who waged war with our hereditary foes in Asia, "it happened that we offended against islets so small and insignificant that many of the Hellenes do not even know of their existence" (70).

This last observation is quite remarkable.

Isocrates' position on the wisdom of Athens's fifth century imperialism was not consistent throughout his long life; while in his speech *On the Peace* he attributes the decline of Athens to her first strivings for naval empire, in the *Panathenaicus* of his old age he defends the first empire even by resorting to the protest that hardly anyone had so much as heard the name of Melos. Nor is it possible to detect an unwavering position as regards Sparta. But Isocrates' view of the democratic government in which he and his father had been raised is unchanging. The reforms of Ephialtes, he believed, had destroyed good gov-ernment. Before the reforms, leaders and followers alike had been patriots of good character; few laws were necessary because of the watchful eye the august body of the Areopagus maintained over the morals of citizens. Even the weather was better in the old days, when the gods who looked after such things were treated with respect.

Isocrates takes great pains to dissociate himself from oligarchy and from philolaconism. Whenever possible, he co-opts democratic rhetoric and ideol-ogy in defense of his program for curtailing democracy. His frequent call for the accountability of magistrates—a key element in democratic ideology—may be sincere, but fourth-century sophistry at its most advanced state is evi-dent in his attack on the use of the lot as opening up the door to oligarchic partisans who might slip by unnoticed and his corresponding praise of the system of appointment for being "more democratic," and his claim that Sparta owed her success to the democratic elements Lycurgus copied from Athens is striking. An enemy of the fully realized democratic system, Isocrates spared no effort in casting himself as the true democrat, upholder of the hallowed princi-ple of proportional equality (though, interestingly, he does not use the expres-sion *patrios politeia* anywhere in his writings).[17] The Athenians did not respond to his many speeches the way Isocrates wanted them to; they were not inclined to mobilize for a massive anti-Persian campaign, and still less were they inclined to turn back the constitutional clock. Apparently the ancestral constitution was an idea whose time had come and gone.

Though Isocrates advocates what amounts to barring the poor from holding office and from participating regularly in the judicial system, he does not fully explain why this is necessary or how the program he proposes will solve Athens's problems. His line of argument in maintaining that democracy has hurt Athens is unclear. Although he sees Athens as more successful in her foreign policy during the Persian Wars than she was later on after the reforms of Ephialtes, he does not show how these reforms contributed to this development, and though he maintains that the Athenians' desire for "the empire of the sea . . . is what plunged us into our present state of disorder and overthrew that democratic government under which our ancestors lived and were the happiest of the Hellenes" (*On the Peace*, 64), the connection between this desire and the constitutional changes of the fifth century is not articulated. (Though a case can be—and has been—made between the Athenians' dependence on the navy and the need fully to enfranchise the indigent rowers, Isocrates fails to make it.) It is uncertain, moreover, how he sees the depravity of contemporary politicians—as the product of the moral decline he is so given to decrying or as the outgrowth of the enfranchisement of the poor. On the whole his laments add up to a rather meandering and unpersuasive *post hoc ergo propter hoc* argument. His speeches do not really explain how the *chrestoi* made better magistrates and citizens than the *poneroi*, and the allegation of moral decline serves here, as so often, to throw a monkey wrench into any intelligible causal analysis. Many post-Periclean statesmen, moreover, came from well-to-do families—Nicias most certainly, and without a doubt the uncouth Cleon, whose father owned a thriving tannery; Solon would certainly have had to allow a Cleon to hold office. On two counts, however, Isocrates' argumentation is clear: wealth in magistrates is a good predictor of integrity, while poverty lays them open to corruptibility—and no oligarchic revolutions troubled Athens before the reforms of Ephialtes.

·   ·   ·   ·   ·

The copious writings in which Isocrates wrestled with the problems confronting his native city demonstrate the close connection between the success of Athens's foreign policy and the popularity of her democratic form of government. The debacle in Sicily, the loss of the Peloponnesian War, and the decrease in prestige Athens experienced during the fourth century drew down new accusations against the democracy on top of those that had always lurked beneath the surface of fifth-century literature. The repercussions of Athens's military and diplomatic setbacks for the esteem in which her government was held were dramatic and unmistakable. The allegations made against Athens were sweeping and included not only politics but religion and morality as well, and the purported decline of Athens as she fell sadly away from what had been best in her heritage would play an important role in Western thinking about classical democracy.

Chapter Four

DEMOCRACY AND THE PHILOSOPHERS

> It could almost be said that political theorizing was *invented* to
> show that democracy, the rule of men by themselves,
> necessarily turns into rule by the mob.
> —J. McClelland, *The Crowd and the Mob: From Plato to Canetti*

MORE A POLITICIAN than a philosopher, Isocrates did not show in his orations much understanding of either politics or philosophy, and the task of properly condemning Athenian democracy was left to his more insightful contemporaries Plato and Aristotle. Like intellectuals in the twentieth century, Plato and Aristotle wrestled with the question of how it could make sense to divide political power equally when people seem so clearly unequal in their capacity to make political decisions—when some are too shortsighted, too selfish, or too ignorant to decide prudently. Unlike their modern counterparts, Plato and Aristotle were not constrained in their thinking by living in a world that taught the equality of all humans as a self-evident constitutional, ethical, and spiritual principle. They bequeathed to posterity a large body of writings in which the weaknesses of Athenian government were inset into an imposing theoretical framework, and of this theoretical construct the natural inequality of individuals formed an important building block. Plato and Aristotle both recur to the fourth-century topos of the two different kinds of equality to support their attack on democracy's pretensions to equity. Measured against the various ideal poleis of Plato's *Republic* and *Laws* and of Aristotle's *Politics*, Athenian democracy was found to violate the natural hierarchy inherent in human associations. Because of this violation of nature, it was deemed both unstable and unjust.[1]

EQUALITY OR JUSTICE?

In the project of lending the sanctity of weighty philosophical argument to the anti-Athenian position, some ground had already been broken by Socrates. Determining the beliefs of the historical Socrates poses serious methodological difficulties, of course, since Socrates, in keeping with his lifelong posture as an intellectual tease, left no writings. (One cannot but wonder whether he would have persisted in his elusive stance had he known what would be put in his mouth in the dialogues Plato so kindly supplied to fill the vacuum.) It seems reasonable to accept the view of the majority of Platonic scholars that the earliest of Plato's dialogues—the *Apology, Crito, Protagoras,* and *Gorgias,* for example—reflect the thinking of Socrates, whereas in the later dialogues written long after Socrates' execution, such as the *Republic* and the *Statesman,* Plato uses Socrates primarily as a mouthpiece for his own opinions. What Plato portrays Socrates as saying in the early dialogues is less hostile to Athenian democracy than what he depicts him as saying in the later dialogues in which he appears and in *The Laws,* a late dialogue in which he is absent, and so it is possible that Socrates was less hostile to Athenian government than was Plato.[2] But the evidence of the dialogues is ambiguous, as is the evidence provided by Socrates' own biography.

Although Socrates does not praise Athenian democracy directly in these dialogues, the paramount importance he ascribes there to unfettered inquiry suggests that in some respects he looked favorably on the government and way of life of Athens, the one state that employed as a synonym of its government *parrhesia,* freedom of speech; Socrates says openly in *Gorgias* (461E) that there was more freedom of speech in Athens than anywhere else in Greece. (Socrates' subsequent fate, of course, endows this observation with heavy irony, but the irony depends for its force on the premise that Socrates and his audience do believe the truth of what he says.) The very notion of Socratic wisdom, that is, the wisdom of recognizing one's own ignorance, is at odds with Plato's suggestion in the *Republic* that there exists an absolute truth to which one may not only aspire but indeed attain: surely the unending dialogue that Socrates advocates in the *Apology* and *Gorgias* is incompatible with the life of public service that the already-perfected Guardians of Plato's *Republic* must live.[3] Though the *Crito* may have a hidden agenda of defending Socrates' patriotism and/or the failure of his friends to spirit him out of prison, still the portrait of Socrates' relationship to Athens there is remarkably warm.[4] The alienation from Athens that is so evident in the *Republic* is lacking in the early dialogues, and nowhere in these dialogues does Socrates state or imply that he has in mind a form of government better than democracy. Despite his manifest distress at the way democracy substituted rule by an ignorant majority for rule by intellectuals, he does not take the occasion of these dialogues to propose helpful criteria whereby the wise minority might be isolated. Although Socrates was critical of the Athenian state on many counts, his focus on its shortcomings can be explained easily enough by his Athenian citizenship and Athenian audience, and it seems likely that he would have directed his criticism toward the government of whatever polis he lived in.

The details of Socrates' life have been adduced as evidence for his political beliefs both by those who see him as a supporter of the democracy and by those who consider him more sympathetic to the oligarchs. His close association with the democratic partisan Chaerephon and the admiration the orator Lysias retained for him after his death have suggested to some that thoughtful people who knew him well did not find his views antidemocratic, something that would have amounted in his day to nothing less than treason. The fact that he never left the city can be also be cited as evidence of his sympathy with the democracy. On the other hand, his proud reminder in the *Apology* that he was unwilling to obey the Thirty when they commanded him to arrest Leon of Salamis implies that he was someone to whom the Thirty felt comfortable giving orders in the first place, and his decision to remain in Athens during the tyranny carries similar implications. We must ask, moreover, how it could be that a prodemocratic Socrates would be executed by a democracy known to be mild (at least to private citizens) but not by an oligarchy known to be murderous.[5]

The truth is that the Socrates of Plato's dialogues exhibited a personality that many have found engaging and endearing, particularly those whose introduction to him came as a result of reading the *Apology* in youth, and that Socrates' perceived charm has combined with his defense of intellectual inquiry to persuade egalitarian twentieth-century readers that nobody who manifests Socrates' humble posture and champions free speech could possibly oppose democracy. Those who themselves oppose democracy have been similarly convinced that no-one as insightful as Socrates could possibly fail to see its patent inadequacy, and much that passes for scholarship on Socrates is actually a series of position papers on democracy. (I except, of course, thinkers who have not succumbed to his charms.)

Regardless of the opinions of the historical Socrates, the criticisms of democracy in general and Athenian democracy in particular that were placed in his mouth by Plato (and, for that matter, by another of his students, Xenophon) have been enshrined in the anti-Athenian tradition. These certainly include the underlying premise of both early and late Platonic dialogues—that most people are ignorant and have incorrect perceptions about right and wrong. Thus for example in the *Crito* Socrates seeks to persuade Crito that public opinion should not be a factor in his decision about whether to escape from prison, since the public is ignorant and its judgments therefore do not command respect (46B–48A). In *Protagoras*, Socrates cleverly manipulates Protagoras' premise that political capacity is a kind of *techne* to highlight the specialization necessary for making sound political "products"; where Protagoras had maintained that this aptitude was diffused throughout the population, Socrates stressed the element of specialization implied by *techne* in a way that looked ahead to the structure of the state in the *Republic*, and in his scheme the very smiths and shoemakers whose *technai* are put forward by Protagoras as models for the *politike techne* wind up excluded from decision making. It is in *Protagoras* that Plato lays the foundations for the antidemocratic argument that would run through his middle and late dialogues. Though the Socrates of the early dialogues does not suggest that rich people are any less likely to be ignorant and incompetent than poor people, still Socrates has understandably been cited as a legitimizing ancestor of antidemocratic theory by virtue of his low esteem for the intellect of the average citizen.

One of the central premises of the *Gorgias*, moreover, seems to imply a grave indictment of the Athenian democracy of the fifth century.[6] In this dialogue, evidently composed in the 390s, the sophist Gorgias tries to convince Socrates of the value of rhetoric as a tool of political persuasion. To counter his argument, Socrates points out the uselessness of persuasion in the absence of the knowledge of what is good, and in so doing calls into question the democratic system whereby power concentrated itself in the hands of the persuasive rather than in those of the wise. Socrates uses the value of rhetoric in a public assembly to undermine the wisdom of the assembly itself: by inquiring whether a doctor or a rhetorician would be a more effective speaker on the topic of medicine, he is able to extract the answer that the rhetorician will be more effective than an expert only if the audience itself is ignorant. Rhetoric, then, is an effective device only in persuading ignorant people (459A–B).

In addition, the Socrates of the *Gorgias* attacks the Athenian democracy specifically in alleging that Athens's most renowned leaders, Pericles, Cimon, Miltiades, and Themistocles, had failed to improve the citizens; indeed, he claims that Pericles made them worse. Claiming to have heard that "Pericles has made the Athenians idle, cowardly, loquacious, and greedy" by initiating the system of state payment for state service, he goes on to argue that Pericles' success as a trainer of men is belied by the Athenians' impeachment of him toward the end of his career. Would a herdsman in charge of donkeys or horses or oxen be considered a good trainer if the creatures of whom he had charge became more ungovernable rather than less so, he asks? And yet Pericles, Cimon, Themistocles, and Miltiades all met similar fates at the hands of the demos they had been charged with improving (515D–516E). In a system based on rhetorical persuasion in open assembly, popular acclaim will attend on the man who tells the people what they wish to hear rather than what truly benefits them. The harm this phenomenon does to the city is as great as the harm that would be done to the body if the true mistresses of health, that is, gymnastics and medicine, were to be shoved aside and replaced with a baker's fine loaves, the cook's tasty dishes, and the vintner's wine (518–19). Underlying the attack on the rhetorician's so-called art is a premise that, although not necessarily antidemocratic in theory, certainly worked to undermine the central dynamic of Athenian government, which made policy on the basis of the public's response to orators in the assembly. Athenian government and society, Socrates argued, was grounded in verbal exercises (both in persuading and in being persuaded) by the intellectually incompetent. In its condemnation of the desultory and superficial educational practices of the Athenians, *Gorgias* looks ahead to Plato's longer *Republic* and *Laws*.

But in reality, much in the *Gorgias* suggests that Socrates saw some merit in the democratic system. For the repeated contention that politicians on whom the demos turns are thereby shown up ipso facto as failed statesmen works to shift the burden here from the demos to its leaders. To attack individual politicians is not necessarily to attack their constituency or the system to which they owed their authority. Though at first glance his reasoning may seem circular, in fact it is astute of Socrates to observe that statesmen who end up in disgrace have by definition failed in their mission of improving their fellow-citizens and hence are genuinely deserving of censure, and this observation certainly calls into question the traditional view of the ingratitude of the demos. Socrates' arrogant challenger Callicles, moreover, refers to Socrates as a *demegoros*, a democratic/demagogic orator (482C, 494D) and complains that Socrates is always talking about cobblers and fullers, cooks and doctors. These allegations certainly cast Socrates as the upholder of the democratic ethos. Like other Platonic dialogues, the *Gorgias* raises the question of the relationship between democracy and tyranny, but the answers it presents are manifold. The rhetorician who is allegedly part and parcel of the democratic system is agreed by Socrates and his interlocutors to be similar to a tyrant in the power he holds. The more the others rejoice in the freedom of restraint that the rhetorician shares with the tyrant, the more Socrates the *demegoros* seeks to show up the men with whom he is speaking as in truth antidemocratic in their preference for oratorical tyranny over an open exploration of issues with a thoughtful and responsive demos capable of thinking for itself.[7]

It may be significant, too, that Socrates chooses the Persians rather than the Athenians as his example of the pitfalls of imperialism. And Socrates fails conspicuously to cast Athens's difficulties in the construct of decline dear to his antidemocratic contemporaries as it has been dear to their most recent successors. In fact, he examines the behavior of the democracy chiefly, if not entirely, during the period before Pericles' death. These departures from conventional anti-Athenian wisdom, combined with Socrates' refusal to join Thucydides in championing Athens's martyred politicians, suggest that the attitude to Athenian government manifested in this presumably antidemocratic early dialogue is complex.

These subtleties, however, have not been incorporated into the tradition about Plato, Socrates, and Athenian democracy, and when the sentiments voiced in Plato's later dialogues and in the *Memorabilia* and *Oeconomicus* of Xenophon were grafted onto the antidemocratic strand in the early Platonic dialogues, the implications for Athens seemed devastating. Throughout the works of both writers there runs an authoritarian strand that led both the dogmatic ideologue and the seasoned military man to believe that mankind divides itself naturally into rulers and ruled—a belief that Plato's student Aristotle was to share. The concept of class, moreover, was an integral part of the thinking of Plato, Xenophon, and Aristotle alike. This stratification, by and large lacking in the early "Socratic" dialogues of Plato, tends inevitably in an antidemocratic direction, stressing as it does the differences among people where democratic theory emphasized what was held in common. A few key passages have traditionally been cited from Xenophon to buttress the notion of the antidemocratic Socrates, but Xenophon, whose intelligence could not rival that of either Plato or Socrates, is not a reliable source for Socrates' opinions, and in any event these passages pale in contrast with the thoroughgoing attack on democracy in Plato's *Republic*, *Statesman*, and *Laws*.

The *Laws* is Plato's longest dialogue. In it Plato seeks to establish a constitution that will stand midway between monarchy and democracy, taking as his point of departure the premise that an "Athenian stranger" is conversing with a Spartan and a Cretan concerning the best constitution for the new Greek city of "Magnesia" that is supposedly being founded on Crete.[8] Criticisms of Athens in specific are apparent at several junctures. Plato's references to the moral depravity of naval states are frequent and pointed. As book 4 opens, the Athenian stranger inquires how far from the sea the new city will be located. Upon being told that it will lie some eighty stades (nine or ten miles) from the shore, he inquires whether it has harbors. To the response that indeed the harbors are excellent, he exclaims, "Dear me! How unfortunate!" (704A–C) and goes on to express concern about the luxury and corruption that are liable to slip in through the port. Such a situation, he concludes, by promoting "foreign merchandise and retail trading," renders the city "faithless and loveless, not to itself only but to the rest of the world as well"; still, one must make the best of things (704–5A). It is good, the stranger remarks, that Magnesia is self-sufficient and will not be located directly on the coast, since a coastal city would need not the constitution he is proposing but rather "a mighty saviour and divine lawgivers, if, with such a character, it was to avoid having a variety of luxurious and depraved habits" (704D). (Aristotle was to express a similar concern at *Politics* 7.6.) The cutting references to Athens are unmistakable.

The Athenian stranger goes on to discuss Athens directly in lamenting its conversion to a naval power when sailors are notoriously cowardly (in comparison with "staunch footsoldiers") and always ready to retreat to their ships to escape danger (706B–C). He also cites that stalwart sailor Odysseus as a source for the bad character of marines, quoting his lines to Agamemnon in book 14 of the *Iliad* to the effect that the Achaeans, if their ships are drawn down to the sea, will withdraw from the heat of battle and take to the water (706D–E), and he goes on to complain that "states dependent upon navies for their power give honours, as rewards for their safety, to a section of their forces that is not the finest; for they owe their safety to the arts of the pilot, the captain, and the rower—men of all kinds and not too respectable—so that it would be impossible to assign the honours to each of them rightly" (707A–B). Plato advances here three separate theses: that some parts of society are more respectable (*spoudaios*) than others; that men who serve in the navy are less respectable than men who serve in the infantry; and that it is more difficult to distinguish the proper recipients of awards in naval engagements than in land engagements. The stranger moves quickly to ask Cleinias the Cretan whether a state unable to determine the proper recipients of honors can be properly regulated, and Cleinias, perhaps more overwhelmed than convinced, agrees that this would be nearly impossible but reminds the Athenian that it was the naval engagement at Salamis that saved Greece during the Persian wars—at least, he adds guardedly, that is what we Cretans say (707B).

After conceding that this is what most Greeks and Persians believe, the Athenian nonetheless puts forward an alternate theory. Along with Megillus the Spartan—whom he co-opts into his belief system in passing—he affirms that it was "the land battle of Marathon which began the salvation of Greece, and that of Plataea which completed it"; and, he adds, "we affirm also that, whereas these battles made the Greeks better, the sea-fights made them worse," presumably in the way he has described, by exalting a disreputable segment of society and by introducing luxury and corruption (707C). Besides, he goes on, our present object is not "mere safety and existence . . . but rather the gaining of all possible goodness and the keeping of it throughout life" (707D). Surely it is reaching to brush aside deliverance from Persian despotism as one of those little things that are ultimately extrinsic to the search for the good life. Altogether the passage is remarkable for its condemnation of naval power and its class-based disparagement of the men who served in the navy—the men who formed the bulk of the Athenian citizenry and of the Athenian assembly. The complaint that naval power makes a state "faithless and loveless, not to itself alone, but to the rest of the world as well" seems also to condemn Athens's foreign policy. Withal, the attack on naval orientation constitutes a serious indictment of the Athenian social, political, and economic structure.[9]

That some people are more respectable than others is axiomatic to Plato's hierarchical view of the world, and it is no wonder the Athenian stranger sees a basic structural weakness in a system that has no sensible plan for distinguishing the more meritorious from the less so. Rehearsing the fourth-century topos of the two equalities (already adumbrated in *Gorgias* 508 and elaborated in the orations of Isocrates), he proclaims that in Magnesia "the selection of officials will form a mean between a monarchic constitution and a democratic; and midway between these our constitution should always stand." For, he goes on, stressing the differences among individuals,

> slaves will never be friends with masters, nor bad men with good, even when they occupy equal positions—for when equality is given to unequal things, the result will be unequal. . . . For there are two kinds of equality. The one of these any State or lawgiver is competent to apply in the assignment of honours . . . by simply employing the lot to give even results in the distributions; but the truest and best form of equality is not an easy thing for everyone to discern. It is in the judgment of Zeus. (756E–57B)

The facile sort of equality, in other words, such as one finds in a democracy, is an ordinary human phenomenon, but "proportional equality" reflects the mind of God. (This view of divinity and equality makes a striking contrast with that of the eighteenth-century Americans who would proclaim in 1776 the self-evident nature of the truth that all men were created equal and endowed by God with inalienable rights.) Plato's proportional equality "dispenses more to the greater and less to the smaller, giving due measure to each according to nature; and with regard to honours also, by granting the greater to those that are greater in goodness, and the less to those of the opposite character in respect of goodness and education, it assigns in proportion what is fitting to each." It is this equality, he explains, at which the founders of his new state will aim—not at "the advantage of a few tyrants, or of one, or of some form of democracy, but justice always; and this consists in what we have just stated, namely, the natural equality given on each occasion to things unequal." Democracy, in other words, is classed with tyranny and oligarchy in their shared opposition to justice. Nonetheless, he goes on, sortition should be used from time to time in selecting officials "on account of the discontent of the masses," on which occasions one must pray to God and Luck for the lot to be guided toward justice. "Thus is it," he concludes, "that necessity compels us to employ both forms of equality; but that form, which needs good luck, we should employ as seldom as possible" (757C–58A). It is only self-preservation in the face of discontent from below, in other words, that impels Plato to co-opt a democratic procedure into the government of his ideal polis. To be sure, a variety of details are adapted from Athenian practice to suit Magnesian needs. The democratically elected examiners, for example, who help call officials to account, recall the Athenians' own *euthynoi*, and the assembly of citizens is divided up into committees that sit separately during different portions of the year as did the Athenian *boule*. The assembly is limited, however, to those who have borne arms; the council itself is chosen in an elaborate multitiered system that makes class distinctions; the assembly and council deal only with a limited agenda, and the guardians of the laws and other high officials appear to be immune from accountability. The fundamental principles of the Magnesian system remain hierarchical and antiegalitarian, and Plato's indictment of the Athenian naval state here is severe and uncompromising.

Plato expresses a still more authoritarian view of the role of law in *The Statesman*, another late dialogue. There he casts the rule of law as a second-best solution to the problem of sovereignty, one that is to be deployed only in the absence of an all-knowing philosopher-ruler. The possibilities of the reign of law, Plato maintains here, are limited and fail to consider the possibility that an exceptional individual would make a wiser government than inflexible laws. Like medical treatment, he claims, a regimen should change in accordance with changes in circumstance. Surely no one would expect a doctor to continue ministering to a patient in the same way despite perceptible alterations in the patient's condition. These sentiments stand at the polar opposite of those voiced by Socrates in the *Crito*, where the philosopher sought to justify his martyrdom on the grounds that no man, however wise, may set his judgment in opposition to the laws—but they continue the theme of the true statesman as a wise doctor that formed the capstone of the *Gorgias*, in which Socrates set himself up as the sole wise physician competent to minister to sick Athens. It is Socrates the governing sage rather than Socrates the law-abiding citizen who lives on in this late dialogue.

Although the *Laws* and the *Statesman* show different faces of the anti-democratic Plato, Plato's position may best be understood through the discussions that fill the *Republic*.[10] Plato's call for a philosopher-king to rule over the less enlightened is well known, as is his second-best solution: the creation of a ruling caste of Guardians, superior in wisdom to the rest, backed up by Auxiliaries who will fight in defense of the state. The Guardians will be both born and bred; intermarriage is used to keep within the fixed group the supreme wisdom that the Guardians will acquire through a carefully designed educational program that has as its culminating experience the perception of the ideal form of the good. There is no point, accordingly, in proffering a watered-down version of this instruction to the masses, since true knowledge is an all-or-nothing proposition to which few intellects may aspire, and strict adherence to the rules of nature, Plato argues, demands that each human "animal" do that for which he or she has the most natural aptitude. Discarding conventional sex roles, he claims that the relegation of females to the traditional tasks of household management fails to maximize their potential for serving the polis. Though he agrees with the bulk of his contemporaries that in most respects the average female is markedly inferior to the average male, he suggests the possibility that an individual bright female might make a better ruler than an individual untalented male. Taking a lesson from the world of the four-footed, Plato points out that often female dogs watch and female horses pull as efficiently as males (451–57). To ensure the continuity of the class structure, each class will mate only within its own ranks, and any unexpected genetic accidents wherein the offspring seem more compatible with another class will be transferred accordingly.[11] To make this structure palatable to the citizens, Plato suggests that a myth be developed concerning the derivation of each class from a different metal. The earth, the citizens will be told, was the common mother of them all, but with this earth gold was mixed to produce guardians, silver to produce auxiliaries, and iron and brass to produce the others (414C).

To this ideal state Plato contrasts some of the shoddy excuses for governments current in his own day—tyranny, oligarchy, democracy, and timocracy. (It is not clear to me just what he means by timocracy—"government by those with most *time*, or honor"—for he acknowledges that striving for honor through virtue is significantly different from seeking honor through riches, and his timocratic state seems to incorporate both elements. The Spartan system may be intended as a model, or it may not.) Though he is unsparing in his criticism of all these forms of government, his attack on democracy is particularly vehement and seems to go beyond what was absolutely required by the framework of his argument. Plato's vivid account of the progressive degeneration of constitutions has had a powerful impact on Western thinkers. Arguing that a flaw in the conduct of his ideal government would lead to timocracy, and that timocracy gives way to oligarchy, oligarchy to democracy, and democracy to tyranny, Plato maintains that a concomitant decline is perceptible at the individual level. Indeed, he argues, these constitutional revolutions are the product of the individual devolution that takes place when the timocratic man produces an oligarchic son, the oligarchic man a democratic son, and the democratic man a tyrannical son. (Explaining how the timocratic man accidentally arises in his ideal state is a tricky proposition, but Plato manages to carry it off.) Democracy, Plato maintains, rises from the ashes of oligarchy, since the precarious condition of a state that makes money the sole criterion of merit will inevitably lead sooner or later to civil war. When the poor are victorious in this conflict, they "kill some of the opposite party, banish others, and grant the rest an equal share in civil rights and government, officials being usually appointed by lot" (557A).[12] Under this type of regime, Plato says, no one has to submit to authority if he does not wish to, no one need fight when his fellow-citizens are at war, and anyone when the fancy strikes him may hold office or sit on juries, even if he has no legal right to do so. The lackadaisical laissez-faire policy of democracy goes so far as to permit condemned or exiled criminals blithely to walk the streets, while "no one takes any more notice than he would of a spirit that walked invisible" (558A). A democracy tramples under foot all the fine principles we have laid down for the training of leaders in founding our commonwealth, Plato complains, and "with a magnificent indifference to the sort of life a man has led before he enters politics, will promote to honor anyone who merely calls himself the people's friend." "Magnificent indeed," Adeimantus replies ironically, and is happy to agree with Socrates in terming democracy "an agreeable form of anarchy with plenty of variety and an equality of a peculiar kind for equals and unequals alike" (558C). As each form of government is typified in Plato's scheme by a certain kind of individual, Plato details the indulgence that will characterize the democratic man. Such a man's life, he concludes, "is subject to no order or restraint, and he has no wish to change an existence which he calls pleasant, free, and happy" (561D).

"That well describes the life of one whose motto is liberty and equality," Adeimantus chimes in.

Plato then provides a convoluted argument to explain how such a government will give way to tyranny. Tyranny will arise, he contends, as a result of the party strife that will come of the democratic anarchy wherein parents fail

to set examples and provide discipline for children. Under these circumstances, children fail to respect their parents; a parallel disintegration over-
takes relations between pupil and teacher, old and young; slaves of both sexes
are quite as free as their masters; freedom and equality characterize interac-
tions between men and women; and even animals fail to defer to humans, as
horses and donkeys feel entitled to walk down the street with all the dignity
of citizens (563C). This excess of liberty, Plato explains, will lead to despotism, for "the truth is that, in the constitution of society, quite as much as in
the weather or in plants and animals, any excess brings about an equally violent reaction" (564A). The plunder of the rich by the poor, he explains in
rather more detail, foments party strife that ends in the masses elevating their
champion to a position of absolute power.

Plato's determination to cast his views about the best state in a broad theoretical framework makes it unclear whether he is describing here what ought
naturally to happen in the tidiest of universes or what has actually happened
in Greek history, but it is plain at any rate that his analysis is gravely vitiated
if in fact the course of history has already proven him wrong. For this reason
it is difficult to understand what genre Plato thinks he is writing in, as a great
deal of what he says is plainly inapplicable to the most well known democracy
of his day, his native city of Athens.[13] Although his complaint about the fine
line that has come to distinguish slaves from free citizens echoes the analogous
complaint of the Old Oligarch, his allegations that proper sex distinctions
have been blurred is peculiar, both from the standpoint of everything we know
about Athenian society, in which both law and custom prescribed very different lives for the two sexes, and in view of his own radical prescription for
women guardians in his ideal state.[14] Altogether the passage is outlandish, and
it is astonishing that so many scholars have been happy to take it at face value.
What on earth can Plato have been thinking in suggesting that citizens of
democracies did not have to fight when their cities were at war or concur
when their cities made peace? As to condemned criminals freely roaming the
streets, Plato knew better than anyone that Socrates was no longer on the
loose at the time the *Republic* was composed. Nor was the alleged natural slide
into tyranny a feature of Athenian life, where the democracy had known a
relatively stable existence for several generations despite two short-lived oligarchic coups. One begins to wonder whether perhaps Plato was thinking of
Syracuse, or even of the insurrection of Cinadon or the insubordination of
Lysander at Sparta, but this line of inquiry seems unproductive in view of the
extreme difficulty of catching Plato's tone in a passage in which he goes so
far as to suggest that even the animals act uppity under a democratic constitution.[15]

Plato had begun the dialogue by posing the question "what is justice?" and
proposing that justice in the state might better be understood by extrapolation
from justice in the individual. Having demonstrated that an individual is just

when all parts of the soul are in harmony, he extends this argument to suggest that the state is justly constituted when all elements are in harmony and that this harmony can arise only when individuals are classed in categories according to their natural aptitudes. Plato's commitment to the concept of ideal forms, moreover, dictates that there should by definition be only one ideal state. It will be timeless, changeless, and beyond criticism. The poets, he says (before expelling them from his ideal state), have erred in portraying the gods as adopting from time to time the guise of mortals; for a god by its very nature is perfect and could not voluntarily exchange its perfection for a lesser condition. Similarly any growth or development on the part of his ideal state is a contradiction in terms. (He is hard put to explain how the degeneration to timocracy could arise, and he resorts to an unpersuasive explanation about careless mistakes in the mating of the guardians.) The openness and fluidity of democracy, consequently, is as far as any government can go in demonstrating its degeneracy. It is in this context that Plato presents his attack on the government of his own state, channeling his condemnation into a high-flown theoretical argument with a questionable basis in historical fact.[16] Inevitably, history is antithetical to his worldview, in which human events function only as distraction from the vision of that frozen reality in which, by definition, nothing good could ever "happen."[17]

The genesis of Plato's thinking about democracy is not clear. His political development is outlined in the famous Seventh Letter, one in a series of epistles that scholars have traditionally ascribed to him. The letter corresponds in all particulars to just what would be expected from a knowledge of Greek history and the Platonic dialogues, and it smacks of a literary exercise in response to a homework assignment, as if the author had sat himself down diligently to compile a list of salient points and reconstructed what such a letter must have contained. But although the bundle is too neatly tied for my taste, the development it traces may well be real.[18] Regardless of the genuineness of the letter, historically speaking Plato's aversion to Athenian democracy probably arose from his observation of it in action and was intensified by the execution of Socrates, which bereft him while still in his twenties of an adored mentor. Whatever its origins, the indictment of democracy that appears in Plato's dialogues both early and late was to become an integral part of the antidemocratic tradition and was to be cited by later writers as evidence of the insufficiency both of Athenian government in particular and of democracy in general.[19] In this tradition, Plato's forceful attacks on oligarchy were generally ignored. From this point of view it matters little to what degree Plato's attack on democracy was aimed at his native city; what is important is that it was subsequently perceived as a firsthand eyewitness indictment of Athenian democracy on the part of one of the most brilliant minds in history. Although it is likely that alienation from the real city of Athens played a large role in the genesis of Plato's antidemocratic position, in the *Republic* these sentiments are cast in an elaborate theoretical framework that seeks to endow them with a timeless relevance. In Plato's construct, the inadequacy of democracy arises from its failure to recognize the differences among individuals and to utilize these differences dynamically by carefully channeling people into the métier in which their skills will enable them to make the greatest contribution to the state. Democracy, Plato believed, by acting if the *politike techne* were diffused (in accordance with the myth of Protagoras) throughout the community, fails to maximize the potential of each individual, for in fact the *politike techne* is confined to a small minority, and it is an inefficient use of manpower (or, as he maintains, personpower) to siphon off the energies of good cobblers and fullers into government while simultaneously wasting the talents of gifted leaders by diverting their energy into cobbling or fulling. As we have seen, the predictable failure of democracy is described at some length in Plato's account of the progressive degeneration of constitutions. In this section of his work, in other words, Plato seeks to test his thesis that specialization is the key to a successful social and political structure, but his constructs do not correspond to the events of Greek history, and his attempt to provide historical validation for his dislike of all existing constitutions is not successful.

Its failure suggests that the origins of his thesis must be sought not simply in the immediate historical background of classical governments but also in his worldview as a whole (to which the history of Greece inevitably contributed in ways that would be difficult to isolate and define). It is easy to see how Plato's beliefs about epistemology and education would lead him to an anti-democratic position, for his vision of wisdom as absolute and therefore attainable only by a small fraction of humanity carries with it a vehement rejection of the Protagorean worldview in which all people share, albeit unequally, in the *politike techne*. The authoritarian nature of Plato's uncompromising truth leads in the same direction. Ironically, despite the presentation of his ideas in dialogue form, Plato rejects the dialectical method of education in his ideal state, in which pupils will be insulated from dialectic until the age of thirty. The continuing dialogue of open debate to which proponents of democracy pointed so proudly held no attraction for Plato; indeed, his own "dialogues" are authoritarian in nature, organized as they are around the desire of the leader to achieve a consensus approving his own thesis (a phenomenon that will be painfully familiar to both students and teachers today). Plato, plainly, knew at the outset where each dialogue was slated to come to rest, and instead of offering a forum for an open-ended search for meaning, the dialogues afford an opportunity artistically to manipulate Socrates' interlocutors into highlighting the ultimate resolution in Platonic "truth."

With this authoritarian element went the persistent drive to impose order on chaos—a drive that is so unrelenting as to invite psychoanalytic explanation, along with Plato's portrayal of constitutional change as a form of Oedipal rebellion. Aversion to change plays a large role in Plato's thinking and is used in book 10 of the *Republic* to justify the expulsion of poets from the ideal state on the grounds that the art they produce entails a transfiguration of ultimate reality that is, by definition, a decline, a falling off; providing wheels within wheels, Plato compounds this argument by alleging that the gods themselves appear degenerate in the writings of the poets because the very stories of divine metamorphoses recounted by the poets portray the gods "changing" their appearance, which no god would do, because change in a perfect being must by definition entail decline. Against this background, Plato's complaint that the existing constitutions of Greece all contain within them the seeds of a revolution that will spark a metamorphosis into another constitution must be seen as representing not only a political opinion but a larger worldview in which truth is perceived as absolute, monolithic, and static. In this universe there can be by definition no history, for history involves growth and change, and for Plato the change of something that is good must entail degeneration. Although Plato's metaphysics bring with them a rejection of all existing forms of government, posited as these governments are on misperceptions of truth that by definition are unreal and therefore decaying already at their inception, they carry the most severe implications for democracy, of which, as Cleon so bitterly complained over the question of Mytilene, change and flexibility are integral parts. Plato's expulsion of the poets from his ideal state must also be seen in the context of the important role played in the education of Athenian citizens by attendance at tragedies. It was tragic drama that afforded Athenians an opportunity to ponder and debate many of the same issues that arose in Plato's dialogues, and it is curious whether Plato wished to expel the poets precisely because he knew the kind of issues that tragedies stirred up in the minds of citizens or because he failed to grasp tragedy's educative power.

The natural diversity that for Pericles had made Athens into a vital, throbbing entity served Plato's state rather as a means of assigning each individual to his or her proper station on the great assembly line of the polis. Relegating to lesser classes the varying talents that produce material goods, Plato frees his guardians from the demands of diversity and endows them with the leisure to become a united front of enlightenment. Although he sees artisans as possessed of a variety of different skills, the *politike techne* appears to him as unvariegated and homogeneous. If a carpenter and a cobbler were to exchange trades, Plato complains, the result would be poor carpenting and cobbling, and the same will happen if a cobbler or other artisan seeks to change roles with a ruler or to add the ruler's function onto his or her own (*Republic* 434A–C). Among the individual crafts, in other words, important distinctions exist, but the *politike techne* is indivisible. Where democratic theorists had seen diversity as the strength of the democratic polis, Plato's ideal state draws its strength rather from the uniformity of vision in its ruling class.

But if Plato's opposition to democracy must be traced in part to his intellectual authoritarianism, it must also be viewed in the context of class prejudice.

Despite Plato's determination to lend an air of abstraction to his work and to cast his wisdom as universal and absolute, knowing no bounds in time or space, his writings nonetheless make plain that he was distinctively a Greek aristocrat who shared numerous traditional convictions with the bulk of his class. These convictions included blithe acceptance of slavery; an inability to see a political structure larger than the polis; a preoccupation with physical beauty (*pace* the high-minded idealism of the *Symposium*); a strong belief in heredity; and a disdain for manual labor that sometimes extended to contempt for any form of earning a living and for all those whom circumstances compelled to support themselves. The last two of these bear directly on Plato's view of democracy, though it is not clear precisely what relation they bear to each other. Beside Plato's insistence that children in his ideal state who are accidentally born into the wrong class will be transferred into the proper station, we must place his conviction that such accidents will be rare, for his careful plan for eugenic intra-class breeding makes clear the expectation that as a rule guardian parents will produce babies who are guardian material, and others will not. Above and beyond the factor of heredity, moreover, Plato stresses the debilitating nature of hard work of a nonintellectual variety. In book 5 of the *Republic*, Plato attacks the sophists by complaining that such men address themselves to the multitude, and "the multitude can never be philosophical. Accordingly it is bound to disapprove of all who pursue wisdom; and so also, of course, are those individuals who associate with the mob and set their hearts on pleasing it" (493E). When men like this corrupt noble natures, he argues, then philosophy, like a maiden deserted by her nearest kin and bereft of her natural protectors, is open to debasement by the unworthy. For, Plato writes (in a passage as jarring to twentieth-century admirers of Greek ideals as the Thersites episode in the *Iliad*), in such cases some "poor creature who has proved his cleverness in some mechanical craft, sees here an opening for a pretentious display of high-sounding words and is glad to break out of the prison of his paltry trade and take sanctuary in the shrine of philosophy," a pursuit that even in its present debased form

> still enjoys a higher prestige, enough to attract a multitude of stunted natures, whose souls a life of drudgery has warped and maimed no less surely than their sedentary crafts have disfigured their bodies. For all the world they are like some little bald-headed tinker, who, having come into some money, has just got out of prison, had a good wash at the baths, and dressed himself up in a new coat as a bridegroom, ready to marry his master's daughter, who has been left poor and friendless. Could the issue of such a match ever be anything but pitiful base-born creatures? (495D–E)

I quote the passage at such length because it has so frequently been passed over by modern readers. The contempt Plato shows for craftsmen here is particularly striking in view of the frequent comparison he makes between God and a craftsman, in particular in the *Timaeus*. Liberated from many of the conventional beliefs of his day such as the hopeless inadequacy of women and the improving effects of reading Homer, Plato was molded by other conventional beliefs, and in his writings he relies on a common disdain for the working man that enables his audience to share his frame of reference and makes possible a scathing analogy such as that of the pathetic tinker whose bald pate so wrenchingly evokes that of Thersites, with his elongated head adorned by its pitiful tuft of wool.

Keeping Out the Banausoi

Plato's contemporaries Xenophon and Aristotle shared this fundamental be-lief in the corrosive nature of what the Greeks called "banausic" labor (liter-ally, work done over a furnace). Xenophon was an oligarchic partisan in 403 and an admirer of kingship and Sparta (though not, as we have seen, of Cri-tias).[20] In his Socratic dialogue the Oeconomicus, a free composition not gener-ally thought to represent the views of Socrates, he has Socrates say: "we have agreed with our states in rejecting those arts that are called 'banausic' because they seem to ruin both the body and the mind, and we have said that an invasion by the enemy would show the wisdom of this if the farmers and artisans were compelled to sit apart and vote separately whether to defend the country or withdraw from the open country and protect the fortresses." In these cases, he predicts, the farmers would vote to defend the land while the craftsmen would vote "for not fighting but rather sitting still, as they have been brought up to do, and not exert themselves or take any risk," and he concludes that husbandry is the best of all occupations for a *kalos kagathos*, for it is liable to endow the body with "the greatest measure of strength and beauty, and to leave to the mind the most leisure for attending to the interests of one's friends and city." The agricultural life, he maintains, has been es-teemed so highly because it seems to produce citizens who are the most loyal to the community (*Oeconomicus* 6. 5–11).

    In the hands of Xenophon, then, the antibanausic prejudice focuses on the arts and on the city and carries within it a snipe at the Periclean war strategy that entailed confining the population of Attica within the city walls—a strat-egy praised by Thucydides, who saw the ultimate Athenian defeat as in part the consequence of departure from that strategy. Xenophon for his part ap-plauds the old-fashioned values of the landed aristocracy while denigrating the efficacy and patriotism of the Athenian democratic system and of Pericles himself. Character, Xenophon maintains, is built by closeness to the land, and in the opposition between the noble countryside and the wicked city, the superior virtue of country-dwellers to that of city-dwellers, he stands toward the beginning of a long Western tradition, articulating with some care the views that had been evident since the days when the Greek landed aristocracy had been compelled against its will to share the reins of government with the new aristocracy of trade wealth.

Squarely within the aristocratic tradition, Aristotle shared Xenophon's contempt for craftsmen and traders and preferred a rural commonwealth to an urban one, but his reasons were strikingly different from Xenophon's.[21] Where Xenophon had seen farmers as superior in wisdom and virtue to city-dwellers, Aristotle argues rather that country people make better citizens because of that benign apathy that discourages them from attending assemblies and meddling in politics.[22] Nonfarming elements of the populace, he complains,

> which form the basis of the other varieties of democracy, are almost without exception of a much poorer stamp. They lead a poor sort of life: and none of the occupations followed by a populace which consists of mechanics, shop-keepers, and day labourers, leaves any room for excellence. Revolving round the market-place and the city centre, people of this class generally find it easy to attend the sessions of the popular assembly—unlike the farmers who, scattered through the country-side, neither meet so often nor feel so much the need for society of this sort. (*Politics* 1319a [6.4.12–13])[23]

A republic of farmers, on the other hand, will be far superior to one of city-dwellers, for the farmers will not gum up the works by exercising their legal rights. Farmers, he says,

> not having any great amount of property, are busily occupied; and they have thus no time for attending the assembly. Not possessing the necessities of life, they stick to their work, and do not covet what does not belong to them; indeed they find more pleasure in work than they do in politics and government. . . . Any craving which the masses may feel for position and power will be satisfied if they are given the right of electing magistrates and calling them to account. (1318b [6.4.2–4])

Maintaining that neither happiness nor wisdom can be maintained except through a life of leisured contemplation, Aristotle insists that the citizens of an ideal state "must have a supply of property" to ensure sufficient leisure for goodness and political activity, and it is to be "these persons who are citizens—they, and they only. The class of mechanics has no share in the state; nor has any other class which is not a 'producer' of goodness" (1329a [7.9.7]). Nor in the best of all possible worlds should farmers be citizens, since a leisure anathema to farming is necessary both for the pursuit of political activity and for growth in goodness; but at least farmers are less likely to exercise what rights they may possess under the law (1328b–29a [7.9.4]). Aware that democracy in Greece is a fact of life, Aristotle seeks to exercise damage control by defusing it as far as possible: if the masses absolutely must have the franchise, let them at least exercise it as rarely as possible. Thus the "virtue" that he ascribes to rustic citizens is the virtue not of greater wisdom but rather of greater indifference.[24] Though his conception of what it means to be a citizen was undoubtedly shaped by the development of the ideals of citizenship current in democratic Athens, he comes to very different conclusions about citizenship from those espoused by the Athenian democrats.

The son of the court physician of Philip of Macedon, Aristotle had received some training in biology from his father, and he had also been trained by Plato himself at the Academy, where he studied for twenty years, beginning in 367 when he was seventeen. Whereas Plato sought to reduce every crux to its lowest common denominator, as befitted a mathematician, Aristotle, as befitted a natural scientist, embraced complexity as the inescapable condition of life. A splitter where Plato had been a lumper, Aristotle was impatient of simplistic answers to social and political questions. He was also impatient of the single-minded laconism of his day. Sharing Plato's glum realization voiced late in his life (in the *Laws*) that Spartans were better trained for war than for peace, he also expresses concern over the inevitable disaffection among the helots, the hereditary nature of the monarchy, and the failure of Lycurgan institutions to maintain proper control over women, who he says have been an increasing source of disorder and decline in the state (1269b–70a [2.9.3–15]).[25] It is important to observe that he attributes the corruption he alleges has taken place among the ephors to the fact that the office is open even to the poor, and such men are notoriously susceptible to bribery. The ephors' importance, moreover, is so great that the kings have been forced to court their favor, moving the government from aristocracy toward democracy. But though Aristotle scoffed at the rapturous idealization of the Spartan state, still he has high words of praise for the system as a whole. A truly prudent constitution, he asserts, lies in a mixture of democratic and oligarchic principles, and "it is a good criterion of a proper mixture of democracy and oligarchy that a mixed constitution should be able to be described indifferently as either. When this can be said, it must obviously be due to the excellence of the mixture. . . . The constitution of Sparta is an example" (1294b [4.9.6–7]).

To the mixture of oligarchy and democracy Aristotle gives the name *politeia*, and he puts forward this winning combination as the ideal government. Non-Greeks have been hard put to discover an appropriate translation for *politeia*. A frequent solution is "constitutional government," a tendentious phrase that imputes unconstitutionality to all other states. Perhaps the best rendering is simply, as some have had it, "polity." This state will be organized along principles of proportional equality, in which Aristotle shared the belief of Isocrates and Plato.[26] Aristotle isolates three common forms of government in Greece: tyranny, oligarchy, and democracy. All three of these systems he condemns as not being directed to the common interest. At several junctures he attacks democracy by aligning it with tyranny. Both tyrannies and democracies, he complains, "encourage feminine influence in the family, in the hope that wives will tell tales of their husbands; and for a similar reason they are both indulgent to slaves. Slaves and women are not likely to plot against tyrants: indeed, as they prosper under them, they are bound to favour their rule—as they will also favour democracies, where the people likes to play the sovereign as much as any tyrant" (1313b [5.11.11]). In an extreme democracy, moreover, popular decrees are sovereign rather than the law, and the government "becomes analogous to the tyrannical form of single-person government. Both show a similar temper; both behave like despots to the better class of citizens; the decrees of the one are like the edicts of the other" (1292a [4.4.27–28]).[27] Oligarchy and democracy, on the other hand, share the common fate of not being able to find enough qualified citizens to govern: democracy produces large numbers of citizens active in politics, but they lack political wisdom; oligarchy finds too few citizens who possess both good birth and merit (1301b–2a [5.1.14]). The proof of this, Aristotle claims, is that neither democracies nor oligarchies long endure. He recommends, therefore, a combination of the two. In Aristotle's ideal state, a moderate-sized body of citizens will share in the course of their lives the duties of soldier (in youth), ruler (in midlife), and priest (in later life). Other duties necessary to the life of the polis such as farming and the production of wares will be relegated to males about whose civic status Aristotle is not consistent. Generally he describes them as partially enfranchised, that is, having the right to vote but not to hold office, but at other times he expresses the wish that these lesser people be excluded even from the ranks of citizens, as in the long discussion in book 3 about whether mechanics may be citizens, wherein he concludes that "the best form of state will not make the mechanic a citizen," and "in states where mechanics *are* admitted to citizenship we shall have to say that the citizen excellence of which we have spoken cannot be attained by every citizen . . . but can only be achieved by those who are free from menial duties" (1278a [3.5.3]). The "freedom" of which Aristotle speaks was crucial in the thinking of all nonslave Greek males of his day. Many—though plainly not all—associated working for someone else (what we could today call having a job) with being a slave. Slaves had no options in their lives, and Aristotle was not alone in asking how people who had no choice in how they spent their time could possibly exercise deliberative capacity in matters affecting the whole state. Although for democrats the distinction between slaves and free men nonetheless loomed large, the opponents of democracy questioned whether the laboring poor were entitled to the perquisites of a freedom they did not seem to possess in any discernible way.

Aristotle's ideal polis, consequently, is self-sufficient only if one takes into account the labor of the majority of inhabitants who are excluded from full citizen rights, perhaps from any citizen rights at all.[28] Quick to identify democracy as the government of the poor majority over the rich minority, Aristotle still considers that he has incorporated the democratic principle into a state that disfranchises nearly all its inhabitants, operating on the Spartan principle that equality among citizens injects an element of democracy into government however exclusive the requirements of citizenship may be. These restrictions obtain in his ideal state despite his well-known departure from Plato in defending the notion that a mass of people who are individually unwise may surpass the wisdom of the few best men "collectively and as a body, although not individually" just as pot-luck dinners may excel those hosted by a single individual. It is for this reason, he maintains, that "the Many are also better judges of music and the writings of poets: some appreciate one part, some another, and all together appreciate all" (ibid., 1281b [3.11.2–3]). (It is unclear how he expects the many to develop these critical faculties, since in book 8 he advocates two different kinds of *mousike* [the Greek equivalent of both literature and music], a challenging one for educable [i.e., not poor] people and a merely entertaining one for audiences "of the baser sort" [ibid., 1342a (8.7.7)].)[29] A large body, moreover, is less vulnerable to corruption. Though he contends that excluding large numbers of inhabitants from office can spark insurrection, he seeks a compromise similar to that of Solon, who conceded to the masses a share in electing magistrates and calling them to account but certainly not the right of holding office.

Aristotle's departure from Plato in the matter of collective wisdom is unquestionably radical. He is inconsistent, however, in applying this liberal philosophy to his political system, for he is unable to make up his mind about the civic rights of tradesmen, artisans, and even farmers. Much can be learned about Aristotle's view of the individuals who make up a community from his remarks concerning consensus in the *Ethics*, which he conceived as the prelude to the longer *Politics*, as well as his opening remarks in the *Politics* on the hierarchic nature of society, in which free rules over slave, and male over female. In a remarkable passage in the *Ethics* he praises the concord that exists among the *epieikeis* but discounts the possibility of such agreement among the *phauloi*. (Predictably, *phaulos* is one of the many pejorative Greek words like *kakos* with a complex of meanings embracing both material poverty and moral worthlessness.) The passage is worth citing at length:

> Now this conception of concord is realized among good men [*epieikeis*], for such are in harmony both with themselves and with one another, having pretty much the same ground to stand upon. For the wishes of good men have a permanent character, and do not ebb and flow like the tides; moreover, they are directed to what is both just and expedient, and it is ends of that nature which they are at one in seeking. But bad men [*phauloi*] are incapable of achieving anything more than a trifling degree of concord as of friendship, since they invariably want more than their share in such advantages as may be going, while at the same time they shirk as much as they can of the trouble and expense of public service. And, while each hopes to secure these advantages for himself, he keeps a critical eye on his neighbour to prevent *him* from getting them. And in fact, unless they do watch one another, the public interest is sacrificed. (9.6.3–4)[30]

The belief that men can readily be divided into *epieikeis* and *phauloi*—civilized folk and riffraff, gentlemen and slobs—is of course hopelessly at odds with the democratic worldview that sees the citizenry made up of a wide spectrum of individuals, some better at one thing, some better at another. In a world in which the *epieikeis* could meaningfully be distinguished from the *phauloi*, democracy might well be a bad idea. And this was the mind-set of Aristotle, who, like Plato, believed it was possible to tell who was who and to allot privilege accordingly.

. . . . .

Socrates, Plato, and Aristotle were all molded by the Athenian democracy in which they lived. From it they derived, and with it they shared, a strong sense that the happiness of the individual was to be located in the just state. The Socrates of the *Apology* (24E) is in complete agreement with his accusers that it is the business of the laws of the city to make the citizens good; this principle would undergird all Plato's writing on government. It was a belief that Athenians shared with other Greek thinkers and was the source of much ancient admiration for Sparta, whose system was believed to inculcate virtue in citizens. The notion voiced by Pericles that the man who has no interest in politics has no place in Athens (Thucydides 2.41) echoes again and again throughout the work of Aristotle, who would become famous for proclaiming that man was a political animal—a creature whose nature it is to live in a polis. Many of the criticisms they offered of Athenian democracy, moreover, were plainly intended to include other Greek polities as well: the concern the philosophers shared for turning people to thoughts of justice rather than honor, to government for peace as well as for war, to the cultivation of the inner person as well as (or more than) the quest for glory—all these appeals were addressed to citizens of democracies and oligarchies alike. For all this, however, the indictment the philosophers crafted of the Athenian democracy was potent. Aristotle, who opened his *Politics* by laying out the basic hierarchies of society, shared with Plato a view of the world that asks the question "Who shall rule?"—a point of departure that presupposes the division of inhabitants into rulers and ruled. To what extent either man derived his authoritarian stance from his perceptions of the most conspicuous democracy of his day it is impossible to know, but whatever the interplay between formulated theory and observed practice, both men cast their opposition to the democracy of the Athenians primarily in the form of theoretical constructs. Despite the interest in tragedy manifested in his famous *Poetics*, Aristotle did not explore in the *Politics* the educative value of either tragedy or other forms of civic life associated with the Athenians, and Plato ignored the obvious parallels between the dialogues of tragedy and those he wrote for pedagogical purposes. Though Aristotle was less squeamish than Plato in referring to the history of the Greek city-states, still he devotes very little space to the actual sins of the Athenians.[31] Indeed, classical Greek literature fails strikingly to show how a different constitution would have made better policy in Athens. The weaknesses of the antidemocratic position, however, did not prevent it from gaining new strength in the centuries that followed when classical Athenian democracy passed into history to become the subject matter for backward glances (through a glass and often very darkly) and the grist for many an ideological mill.

PART TWO
PLAYING WITH THE PAST

THE ATHENIAN ETHOS embraced many opposites. The democracy that put Socrates to death was also the democracy that had facilitated his way of life and of whose restless energy he partook in the most dramatic and demonstrable way. Litigants in courtrooms (and there were many of them, for the Athenians were an extraordinarily litigious people) presented their own wealth as the badge of their integrity while adducing the affluence of their opponents as clear proof of bad character. Pericles insisted that it was merit and not class that determined a man's position in Athens, but the claims of birth were never forgotten by those who were in a position to make them. A varied network of imagery identified democracy with tyranny not only in the minds of antidemocratic thinkers like Plato and Aristotle but also in the rhetoric of democratic politicians like Pericles and Cleon, yet playwrights as different as Aeschylus and Euripides presented democracy and tyranny as opposite poles, a position also developed by Thucydides' Alcibiades in Sparta. Alcibiades' sophistic speech before the Spartans shows the way in which democratic rhetoric could be turned on itself, while the democrats sought to co-opt aristocratic language as well, as Plato's Protagoras insisted that all people of all social classes partook in the previously aristocratic virtue of *aidos*. Antidemocratic thinkers sought to confine political power to the *chrestoi*, the "useful," a term that became ominous under the oligarchic coups of the late fifth century when conservatives sought to establish an "ancestral" government limiting the franchise to those able to make themselves "useful" to the state by providing, say, a horse; but Pericles boasted that the Athenians thought no ill of the poor but only of the *achrestoi*, the useless.

In a famous passage (5.92) Herodotus tells how Periander, tyrant of Corinth, sent an envoy to his fellow autocrat Thrasybulus to seek advice in preserving his position. Thrasybulus, Herodotus relates, said nothing to the messenger but merely took him on a walk through the cornfields, striking off the heads of any stalks so tall that they stood out from the others. The messenger had no comprehension of the coded message, but when he reported Thrasybulus's behavior to Periander, the Corinthian immediately understood what was being communicated to him and he set about eliminating any men who rose above the ordinary lest they prove dangerous. This tyrannical ethos was neatly mirrored in the democratic practice of ostracism, whereby excellence and energy could prove a ten-year liability. One watchword of the democracy was *isegoria* (equal opportunity to speak) and it boasted of its *parrhesia* (freedom of speech), but Anaxagoras was forced into exile because of things he said, Socrates was put to death for his teaching, and fourth-century critics of the democracy watched their language very carefully indeed, as closet oligarchs insisted that all they wanted was to restore a democracy more authentic than the one in power. Whereas writers from Herodotus through Euripides to Demosthenes billed democracy as synonymous with law and order, Xenophon, Plato, and Aristotle all worried about a lawless, unconstitutional tyranny of the majority. The only area in which there seems to have been consensus was the discounting of women and slaves in discussions of political theory; and even there Plato had raised some questions about the natural incapacity of females.

The many paradoxes entailed in the Athenian ethos have made possible a wide spectrum of responses to classical Athens. The chapters that follow, in both part 2 and part 3, will explore the ways in which differences in social, political, and philosophical orientations among individuals and across cultures have worked to shape conflicting perceptions of Athenian democracy, and will demonstrate the continuing vitality of the dialogue that has grown up around the questions the Athenian system inevitably posed.

Chapter Five

ROMAN ADAPTATIONS

> Since it is difficult, or rather impossible, to represent a man's life as
> entirely spotless and free from blame, we should use the best chap-
> ters in it to build up the most complete picture and
> regard this as the true likeness.
> —Plutarch, *Cimon*

THE ANCIENT ROMANS were unique in their relationship to the city-states of classical Greece. Although the Hellenic polis had reached its zenith well before the height of Roman expansion, still to some degree Greek and Roman civilization overlapped. Various points of contact have been alleged between the early Romans and the Greeks, and only a few generations separated the *Graeci* whom the Romans conquered in their Eastern wars from the Greeks who had lived in the heyday of the autonomous city-states. Although a variety of circumstances prompted the Romans to make sharp distinctions between ancient Hellenes and their contemporary descendants, Romans who saw in their own past a living heritage could hardly fail to perceive some measure of unity in Greek civilization. The reforms of Cleisthenes, after all, were dated to almost the same year as the expulsion of the Etruscan kings, and the execution of Socrates postdated the founding of the Roman republic by over a century. Rome's victory over the forces of the Latin League came the year Greece fell before Philip. Though the rivalry of Athens and Sparta lay in the past, that past was neither remote nor mythic.[1] The Romans also differed from subsequent students of Greek civilization in that their relationship with Greece was a two-way street. They had many opinions about the Greeks, but they also cared what the Greeks thought of *them*.[2] Aware of the perceived cultural superiority of Hellas and of their enormous cultural debt to Greeks of earlier centuries, the Romans were constantly seeking to schematize the relationship between Greek and Roman civilization in a way that would place their own culture in a flattering light. For better or worse, what the Romans wrote in their efforts to define this relationship was canonized as primary source material until the nineteenth century, and as such it requires close attention.

GREECE AND ROME: THE ARTICULATION OF DIFFERENCE

The Romans knew what many Greeks thought about them—good for building bridges and highways and other tasks irrelevant to the serious aesthetic
concerns of life; they were well aware that Greeks called them *barbaroi*. For
this reason Romans were quick to denigrate contemporary Greece. Fearful of
being perceived as boorish thugs and anxious about how they measured up
against classical Greece, the Romans hastened to dub Greeks with whom they
came into contact *Graeculi*, "Greeklings," to distinguish them from their illustrious ancestors. By the second century B.C., Romans were well aware of the
glory that had been Greece and were eager to ensure that the effete easterners
they conquered in the Macedonian Wars should not be confused with the
giants who had rubbed shoulders with the likes of Homer and Sophocles.
Keenly sensible that they would never overtake classical Athens in the spheres
of culture and intellect, they took particular pleasure in pointing out the
weaknesses of the Athenian political system in comparison to their own. Centuries later Byron might celebrate "the Isles of Greece" as the place "where
grew the arts of war and peace," but the Romans took care to distinguish arts
on the one hand from war and peace on the other, and Virgil crystallized the
dichotomy in Anchises' famous monition to Aeneas:

> other peoples will, I do not doubt,
> still cast their bronze to breathe with softer features,
> or draw out of the marble living lines,
> plead causes better, trace the ways of heaven
> with wands and tell the rising constellations;
> but yours will be the rulership of nations,
> remember, Roman, these will be your arts:
> to teach the ways of peace to those you conquer,
> to spare defeated peoples, tame the proud.[3]

Centuries before this carefully worded passage was crafted, the earliest Romans lived largely unaware of the Greeks outside Italy and Sicily and referred
to the Hellenes who had colonized southern Italy and Sicily as "Graeci" because of the contingent from the small Boeotian town of Graea that had settled in the Bay of Naples in the Sybil's haunt of Cumae; southern Italy and
Sicily they dubbed "Magna Graecia," "Greater Greece." Though the Romans
came to be convinced that the Cumaean Sybil was the true priestess of Apollo
and would prophesy the destiny of Rome from her cave, this choice of a name
for the Hellenes was entirely coincidental and must have struck the new
"Greeks" themselves as rather amusing. Since the Hellenes, however, had yet
to come up with a name embracing all the "Greeks"—the term *Hellenes* originally referred a single tribe—the label stuck. It is uncertain how or when the

Romans first came into contact with the Greek homeland.[4] Already in the sixth century, Greek vases appear in Rome. Livy wrote that Greek pirates ravaged the coast of Latium in 349 (7.25.4–5, 12–13; 7.26.11–15), and Pliny reported the allegation of the early third-century writer Clitarchus that the Romans sent an embassy to Alexander the Great.[5] Religious links between Greece and Rome appear early in Roman history; the worship of Demeter at Rome (complete with Greek priestesses) is attested at least as early as the fifth century, and Apollo's cult was established in 431. After the famine of 292, the Romans sent for the serpent of Aesculapius in Epidaurus in order to establish a cult of the healing god, and the chilling defeat at Cannae in 216 at the hands of Hannibal prompted the Romans to dispatch a delegation to Delphi to seek advice from Apollo. Rome attracted the attention of Greece by her war with Pyrrhus of Epirus, who championed the cause of southern Italy in the 270s. In 252 Aratus of Sicyon set out for Syria on a Roman ship (Plutarch, *Aratus* 12), and around the same time the freed slave Livius Andronicus began translating the *Odyssey* into Latin and adapting Greek plays for Roman audiences.

It was around this time that the image of *Pistis Rhomaia*, "Roman Faith," appeared on a Locrian coin, and the association of Rome with *pistis*, that is, good faith in the keeping of agreements, is attested in a variety of Greek sources (some of them anti-Romans who accused Rome of insincerity in proclaiming this so-called trustworthiness to the world[6]). But it was another Greek, the hostage Polybius captured in the third Macedonian war in 168, who enshrined in the literature of the Republican period the topos of Roman rectitude outstripping Greek. Polybius became a great admirer of the Romans and made numerous invidious comparisons between them and the Greeks they had conquered, and in one of these instances he maintained that Romans in handling large funds adhered strictly to the oath of good faith, whereas Greeks for their part could not keep faith even when entrusted with a small amount and with numerous copyists, seals, and witnesses to keep watch over them (6.56.13–14).

If a Greek was able to contrast the probity of his fellow Hellenes so embarrassingly with that of the Romans, all the more were the Romans convinced of their own moral superiority. Already before the end of the third century the moral degeneracy of contemporary Greeks had been enshrined in the Latin language with the coining of the word *pergraecare* in Roman comedy; meaning "to live in a loose and lascivious manner," the word appears in four separate comedies of Plautus.[7] When the slaves in the *Stichus* become particularly unruly, Plautus reminds his audience that "such things are allowed in Athens" (*Stichus*, 446–48).

Plautus probably died the year Cato the Elder served as censor. Notorious for his conviction (genuine or affected) that Rome was falling fast and that its impending collapse was directly traceable to the horrors of Greek influence, Cato spared no venom in his attacks on his Hellenic contemporaries, whose turpitude he saw as a serious threat to Roman probity. He ascribed conspicuous consumption and sexual debauchery both homosexual and heterosexual to the undermining of Roman rectitude by Greek decadence, and he was evidently behind the expulsion of Carneades of Athens and his fellow philosophers in 155. Later in the century the orator Lucius Crassus stressed his contempt for Greek learning and Marcus Antonius claimed ignorance of Greek culture.[8] Cicero, from whom we learn about these posturings, quoted his own grandfather as saying that one's moral character degenerated in proportion as one knew Greek (De Oratore 2.265). Again Polybius provides a Greek analogue, decrying as he did Greek licentiousness as a source of corruption to the Romans in the areas of sex and conspicuous spending (31.25.4). Cato for his part made himself the master of a rhetorical mode that required the identification of clear enemies of civilization, and it would be impossible to know how much of his fulminations he really believed. In any case, however, his jeremiads served as an integral building block of a long Roman tradition in which Greece stood for the dangers of decadence.

By the last century of the republic, then, when the Romans began to have a literature of their own, the dissoluteness of contemporary Greeks had become proverbial in Latin speech and writing. At the same time, of course, Greek had become a lingua franca for intellectuals. Cato himself studied Greek, and though he was celebrated for his demand that his son's education be taken out of the hands of a Greek schoolmaster, it is noteworthy that the education of a Cato should have been in such hands in the first place.[9] The disclaimers of Crassus and Antonius were thought to be necessary in view of the time they had spent studying in Athens. Cicero was among those who studied in both Athens and Rhodes, as was his brother, his close friend and correspondent Titus Pomponius surnamed (for this reason) Atticus, and Julius Caesar. Cicero's letters were often thick with Greek words; so were those of Augustus. Though the degeneracy of contemporary Greece had become a stock theme at Rome, moreover, the praises of Greek antiquity were often sung. Cato himself was said to have delivered an oration at Athens expressing his admiration for the virtue of the classical Athenians of yore, though Plutarch questioned whether it was correct that he actually spoke in Greek (Cato 12.4).

REPUBLICAN TOPOI

It is against this background of ambivalence and paradox that we must set Roman attitudes toward the government of classical Athens—Athens the school of Hellas but also the school of Rome. The undisputed primacy of Athens in matters of culture is attested in a variety of Cicero's works, but it receives its first articulation in the oration Cicero delivered in 59 in defense of Flaccus, impeached for misconduct as a provincial governor. The reputation of ancient Athens is so great, Cicero proclaims there, that "the present enfeebled and shattered renown of Greece is sustained by the reputation of this city"—Athens, "where men think civilization, learning, religion, agriculture, justice and laws were born and spread thence into every land."[10]

The way in which Cicero turns the praise of Athens on itself in the *Pro Flacco* is striking.[11] In fact, the praise is inserted to assist Cicero in an elaborate scheme of character assassination directed at the Asiatic Greeks who had testified against his client. In this rhetorical scheme, Cicero defends the wholesale discrediting of the reliability of Asiatics by a pointed contrast between the good Greeks associated with the ancient city-states of Hellas proper and the bad Greeks of Asia Minor who were currently making trouble for his client by accusing him of extortion during his term as propraetor and governor of the province of Asia. Having established this dichotomy, he is happy to generalize about "Greeks"—that is, bad Greeks, who once on the witness stand forget their oaths and are only interested in trouble making and injury—and Romans: "When one of us Romans gives evidence," he says, "what self-restraint he shows, what control over his language, what fear that he may display self-interest or ill-temper, or that he may say too little or too much! Surely," he tells his audience, "you do not view in the same light those men to whom their oath before you is a joke, their evidence to you a game, your opinion of them a worthless nothing; who see in a shameless lie all their chances of honour, profit, influence and favour?" But he will not go on any further, he sighs, since his speech could last forever if he wanted to demonstrate "the untrustworthiness of the whole nation in giving evidence" (12).

Because he makes a special point of praising ancient Athens, moreover, Cicero places himself in a good position to attack Athenian political practice. The resolutions against Flaccus, he maintained, were not based upon considered votes or safeguarded by oaths but were rather "produced by a show of hands and the undisciplined shouting of an inflamed mob" (15), and the dangers of public meetings are in fact demonstrated by the behavior of the ancient Athenian assembly, where "untried men, totally inexperienced . . . would decide on harmful wars, put troublemakers in charge of public affairs and expel from the city the citizens who had served it best. If behaviour like this used to occur regularly in Athens when she outshone not just the rest of Greece but virtually the whole world," Cicero asks indignantly, "what restraint do you think has existed in the public meetings of Phrygians and Mysians? If our own public meetings are often thrown into disorder by men of these nations, what on earth do you think happens when they are by themselves?" It is the corrosive influence of the Greeks, Cicero suggests, that is responsible for the regrettable development at Rome of *contiones*, public meetings, the principal object of contention in the oration (and an issue rather closer to Cicero's heart, one suspects, than the acquittal of Flaccus). To allow decision-making power to lie in *contiones*, Cicero maintains, is to depart from the customs of the ancient Romans:

> Oh, if only we could maintain the fine tradition and discipline that we have inherited from our ancestors! But somehow it is now slipping out of our hands. Those wisest and most upright of our men did not want power to lie in the public meetings. As for what the commons might approve or the people might order, when the meeting had been dismissed and the people distributed in their divisions by centuries and tribes into ranks, classes and age groups, when the proposers of the measure had been heard, when its text had been published well in advance and understood, then they wished the people to give their orders or their prohibitions. In Greece, on the other hand, all public business is conducted by the irresponsibility of a public meeting sitting down. And so—to pass over the modern Greece which has long since been struck down and laid low in its councils—that Greece in ancient times, once so flourishing in its wealth, dominion and glory, fell through this single evil, the excessive liberty and license of its meetings. (15–16)

Cicero's contention that Roman assemblies were more responsible than Greek ones because Romans deliberated standing and Greeks sitting is, as far as I know, unprecedented, and his allegation that the decline of Roman assemblies is traceable to an influx of Asiatic Greeks is improbable.[12] But his argument draws strength from the fulsome praise he includes in his speech of ancient Athens, mother of wisdom and the arts. Would an admirer of Athens such as Cicero malign her to his audience by fabricating weaknesses that did not exist just to score points in a debate about Roman government?

In the *Pro Flacco* of 59, Cicero's allegation that the Athenian democracy expelled the citizens who had served it best gets lost in the general diatribe against popular assemblies, but when Cicero was exiled in the following year by Julius Caesar's henchman Publius Clodius, the orator did not fail to draw the parallel between the sufferings of Athens's unappreciated statesmen and his own misfortune. Though Pompey engineered Cicero's return in 57, the painful episode made an understandable impression on its victim. In his speech for Sestius in 56, Cicero observed that the ingratitude of the people toward Miltiades and Aristides did not deter Themistocles from defending the state, and the later *Brutus* compared Themistocles and the Roman Coriolanus, both billed as great men unjustly exiled by an ungrateful people; altogether Cicero's writings contain over thirty references to Themistocles.[13] An overt comparison between his own situation and that of persecuted Athenian statesmen appears in *De Republica*, a dialogue on government set in 129 in which Scipio Africanus the Younger clearly speaks for Cicero. It is from Athens, Cicero maintains in the preface, that the vice of fickleness and cruelty toward eminent citizens arose and "has overflowed even into our own powerful republic." He cites a variety of attacks on prominent Roman politicians, adding that people "now include my name also, and presumably because they think it was through my counsel and at my risk that their own peaceful life has been preserved to them, they complain even more bitterly and with greater kindness of the treatment I have received" (1.3.5–6).[14]

The dangers of popular government are subsequently set forth in the dialogue that forms the body of the text. Arguing in favor of mixed government, Scipio speaks very generally of the dangers inherent in the three unmixed forms of government: kingship, as in Persia under King Cyrus; aristocracy, as in the Greek city of Massilia (Marseilles) in Gaul; and democracy, as at Athens. He goes on to elaborate on the scheme of the six constitutions originated by Plato and Aristotle and their contemporaries and refined by Polybius: monarchy, aristocracy, and democracy on the one hand and their degenerate forms tyranny, oligarchy, and ochlocracy on the other.[15] Beneath Cyrus, he complains, lies the tyrant Phalaris, known for roasting his victims alive in a hollow metal bull; beneath the aristocracy of Massilia lay the thirty tyrants of Athens; and at Athens, the "absolute power of the Athenian people . . . changed into the fury and license of a mob" (1.18.44). Phalaris, it must be borne in mind, remained the tyrant of Acragas in Sicily and made no effort to take over Persia; the thirty tyrants of Athens made no attempt on Massilia. These examples are merely theoretical. But in Scipio's view the degeneration of the Athenian democracy was a historical fact. Although at first sight Scipio appears to be choosing concrete examples of the flaws of all three unmixed governments, in other words, his reservations about the monarchy of Persia and the aristocracy of Massilia remain on a broad and almost theoretical plane, whereas his complaints about Athens are concrete; because of weakness in monarchy and aristocracy, the door to disaster lay open in Persia and in Massilia, but in Athens, in his view, it was a fact that the democrats walked through these portals. The misfortunes of Persia and Massilia remain hypothetical, while those of Athens are construed as historical and actual. It is amusing to notice as well that Scipio in selecting the Thirty Tyrants as an example of the evils of oligarchy manages to make Athens not only the prototype of the degenerate democracy but host to the latent vice of aristocracy as well. Democracy in general, indeed, is contrasted unfavorably by Scipio with monarchy and aristocracy in respect to the motives of the principals. Kings, Scipio says, seem like fathers to us; aristocrats maintain that they can bring a greater amount of wisdom to government; while the people shout "with a loud voice that they are willing to obey neither one nor a few, that nothing is sweeter than liberty even to wild beasts, and that all who are slaves, whether to a king or to an aristocracy, are deprived of liberty" (1.35.55). Monarchs and aristocrats, in other words, put forward their merits, while the people clamor for their rights, compare themselves to animals, and announce their determination not to have their wishes overridden. There follows a long paraphrase from Plato's *Republic* on the evils of democracy and its proclivity toward tyranny; this disquisition reproduces Plato's allegation that under a democracy even the animals are uppity, but without the slightest trace of the original Platonic playfulness. (It is interesting to note the contrast between Scipio's attack on democracy, so singularly grounded in Athenian history, with that of Plato, in which difficulties are presented in the "degeneracy of constitutions" argument that seem to bear no relation to what actually happened.) Scipio's final conclusion is that the best forms of government are a benevolent monarchy or a mixed state.

Cicero's use of Athenian examples throughout his works demonstrates a complex, then, of three interrelated topoi: the topos of Athens as the cradle of the verbal arts; the topos of the ingratitude of the Athenians toward their leading politicians; and the topos of the unruliness of democratic government. The three themes come together to forge an image of Cicero as the eloquent but unappreciated champion of Roman traditions, Athenian in his intellectual accomplishments but eminently Roman in his antidemocratic orientation, undervalued heir to the mantle of Solon, Peisistratus, Themistocles, and Pericles. By recurring to the superiority of the carefully rigged voting systems of Roman assemblies over Greek free-for-alls, Cicero aligns himself pointedly with the values of the Roman aristocracy into which he was determined to be co-opted. In his eloquent statesmanship he sought to embody what was best in Athenian civilization and set himself firmly against what was worst. He emulates the leaders of the democracy while excoriating the democracy itself. His condemnation of Athenian government is a necessary backdrop to his identification with Athens' scorned statesmen, and his exaltation of Athens as the ancient home of eloquence and the arts lends a certain specious objectivity to his condemnation of the Asiatic Greeks of his own era. To Cicero's early division of Greeks into good (mainland) Greeks and bad (Asiatic) Greeks he added two parallel divisions—one between contemporary and ancient Greeks, and one between Athenian democratic statesmen and the Athenian democratic assembly. These oppositions serve to buttress his own self-proclaimed posture of thanklessly defending good elements from bad in the Rome of his day.

The topos of the Athenians' ingratitude toward their leaders was solidly grounded not only in the works of Thucydides, Plato, and Isocrates but probably in such lost writings as those of Theopompus and Ephorus as well, and it also appears in the biographies composed by Cicero's friend Cornelius Nepos.[16] A correspondent of Cicero as well as an intimate friend of Cicero's crony Atticus, Nepos is the author of the first biographies ever preserved under their author's name. Although his life of Cicero was lost, that of Atticus survives with numerous others in his collection *On Famous Men* comparing celebrated Greek and Roman political figures. Nepos has not as a rule been highly rated as a historian, but his departure from the anti-Athenian tradition is noteworthy and shows if not originality then at least intermittent discrimination in the use of sources.

In writing about the impeachment of Timotheus and Iphicrates during the Social War of the 350s, Nepos characterizes the Athenian people as "emotional, suspicious and on that account changeable, hostile and envious" (*Timothens* 3.5), but this sentence is not of a piece with Nepos's treatment of Athenian impeachment and exile, and in any event the text seems to be corrupt at these lines. Though in his life of Alcibiades he portrays his subject as unwilling to return home to face trial because he was pondering the immoderate license of his fellow citizens and their cruelty to men of high rank (*Alcibiades* 4.4), it is not clear whether Nepos shares the aristocrat's view of Athenian accountability. On the whole, Nepos shows surprising sympathy for the Athenians' readiness to rid themselves of their great men. In discussing the condemnation of Miltiades after his unsuccessful expedition to Paros in the year following his stunning victory at Marathon, he is quick to point out the recency of Peisistratus's tyranny at Athens as well as the fact that Miltiades had borne the name of tyrant while in charge of an Athenian settlement in the Chersonesus on the Black Sea, and he passes no judgment on Miltiades' impeachment (*Miltiades* 7.5–8.4). Similarly in his life of Themistocles, though his admiration for the controversial politician is evident, still he gives an evenhanded treatment to the question of his ostracism and attributes it to "the same apprehension that had led to the condemnation of Miltiades" (*Themistocles* 8.1). Most surprising of all, Nepos in his brief life of Phocion portrays his subject's trial as the natural outgrowth of his own actions. Though the longtime general was to become a martyr in modern European ideology, in Nepos's biography he appears as a man of dubious patriotism and judgment, advocating the exile of his own friend and supporter Demosthenes and failing to defend Piraeus against the Macedonian Nicanor in a crucial hour. Like Alcibiades and Chabrias before him, Phocion is quoted as complaining of the Athenians' treatment of their *clari* (*Phocion* 4.3–4). But whereas this antidemocratic tradition is preserved by Nepos as it lived in the minds of Athenian leaders, Nepos's own position is surprisingly judicious, and when he observes in his life of Chabrias that it is the common flaw in free states that they cannot abide those they see rising above the level of their fellow-citizens (*Chabrias* 3.3), his approach appears more analytical than judgmental.

The biographies of Nepos, then, include many references to the existence of the anti-Athenian tradition, but these references are absorbed in a larger picture in which the Athenian demos appears in a less harsh light.[17] The topos of the Athenians' maltreatment of their leaders reappears, however, in Valerius Maximus's collection of *Memorable Sayings and Doings*, a sanctimonious compendium assembled along topical lines in the reign of the emperor Tiberius, probably in the fourth decade after Christ. In his brief chapter "On Temerity" Valerius condemns the Athenians roundly for their trial and execution of the victors of Arginusae in 406. Accepting the story that the men in the water were no longer alive, Valerius maintains that in executing the generals the Athenians "punished necessity where they should instead have honored bravery" (9.8. *Externa Exempla* 2). The bulk of his censure, however, is reserved for his longer chapter on ingratitude. Beginning with the murder of Romulus in the senate he had himself established, Valerius goes on to list numerous other Roman victims of ingratitude, including five members of the illustrious family of the Cornelii Scipiones. That Valerius portrays them as victims of the "pestilent band" of the popular reformer Tiberius Gracchus and of the "nefarious" supporters of his younger brother Gaius presages no good for his treatment of the Athenian demos, and not surprisingly he is able to round up a good number of Athenian martyrs to the masses as well. These include Theseus, whom Valerius treats as a fully historical personage, and Solon, who he reports died in exile in Cyprus, barred even from the right to be buried in that country he had served so well and from which he had deserved so much. But even such an exile, he goes on, would have been more fitting for Miltiades, the victor of Marathon, than the ignominious death in prison chains that was meted out to him instead. The exile of the just Aristides is duly recorded, as is that of Themistocles (the most celebrated example, Valerius maintains, of those who have experienced the ingratitude of their country). Phocion, predictably, rounds out the list. (The origin of the strange story of Solon's "exile" is unclear, but it continued to pop up throughout the Western tradition. Valerius describes him as living out his old age *profugus*, an exile/refugee in Cyprus. Solon liked to travel; Diogenes Laertius, writing in the third century A.D., reported his death in Cyprus, but no exile was implied.[18])

The unreliability of the Athenian demos and its unreasonable treatment of its most famous sons had its origins, as we have seen, in the writings of Thucydides, Xenophon, and Plato, and it lived on not only in Latin literature but in the writings of the Greek historians who lived in the Roman empire as well. Historians in the Greco-Roman world had access, of course, to numerous sources no longer available. It is a great sorrow that with the exception of Xenophon none of the Greek historians of classical Greece active between Thucydides and Augustus survives in more than fragments or epitomes. For the purposes of Athenian political history, it would be particularly useful to have the entirety of Theopompus's essay *On the Demagogues*, but overall probably the greatest loss is that of Ephorus, a citizen of Cyme on the coast of Asia Minor who had written a universal history in thirty books from the close of the bronze age to the middle of the fourth century. He appears to have consulted a variety of sources, including not only Herodotus and Thucydides but their contemporaries Ctesias, a Greek doctor at the Persian court, and Hellanicus, a historian from Lesbos whose history was slighted by Thucydides for its accuracy (Thucydides 1.97) and by Cicero for its style (*De Oratore* 2.12.53.) It is likely that Nepos consulted Ephorus, and it was apparently Ephorus who served as the principal source for fifth- and fourth-century Greece in the universal history of Diodorus of Sicily.

During the last years of the Roman republic, Diodorus composed his world history in forty books, beginning from the earliest times and continuing to the Gallic Wars of Julius Caesar (54 B.C.). Though Diodorus seems to admire the Athenians for their empire and is generally approving of them in matters of foreign policy, he is highly critical of the democratic system of government as it operated on the domestic front. The only attack on an Athenian leader that Diodorus fails to deplore is the murder of the democratic reformer Ephialtes. This *demagogos*, Diodorus reports, had provoked the multitude (*plethos*) to anger against the Areopagites and had gotten the demos to curtail the powers of the Areopagite council and to overturn their renowned ancestral usages (*ta patria . . . nomima*). Ephialtes, however, so Diodorus tells us, did not escape punishment for this lawless act but rather was murdered by night (11.77.6). Intensely concerned with reminding his readers of the evil fates to which wrongdoers are condemned, Diodorus offers several variations on this theme. The Athenians, he maintained, received the Thirty Tyrants as a punishment for their unjust treatment of the victors of Arginusae in 406; the unfortunate generals' case is stronger in his account even than in that of Xenophon, for Diodorus, like Valerius Maximus, maintains that the sailors whom they failed to pick out of the water were already dead (13.100.40). Similarly, when the democrats at Argos who had put over a thousand wealthy citizens to death then turned on their own demagogues and meted out the same fate to them, Diodorus alleges that these demagogues "were punished in accordance with their transgressions as if at the hands of some avenging divinity, while the people, purged of their mad rage, recovered their senses" (15.58.4). Though he maintains that the murdered Ephialtes got his just deserts, he is consistently critical of the Athenians when they make use of the machinery available to them to discipline political leaders in less final fashion. He labels the Athenians' treatment of Themistocles cruel, finds the accusation against Pericles in 430 to be petty, and calls the allegations against Alcibiades slander. He reveals his view of the Athenian demos in his discussion of Athenian trierarchs, valued public servants who fitted out ships at their own expense: this institutionalized largess Diodorus portrays as indulging the masses. When the Athenians are contemplating the recall of Alcibiades, Diodorus makes a sharp distinction between the motivation of the rich, who expected Alcibiades boldly to oppose the people, and that of the poor, who assumed he would show his support for them by intentionally throwing the city into confusion (13.68.4).[19]

IMPERIAL LENSES

Shortly after Diodorus composed his universal history, another project of similar scope was undertaken by Pompeius Trogus, a historian under the reign of Augustus whose grandfather had received citizenship from Cicero's contemporary Pompey. Pompeius Trogus's work is now lost, but parts are preserved in the epitome assembled around the third century A.D. by a certain Justin. This abbreviated account of early times served as a principal source of knowledge about antiquity during the Middle Ages. Justin coursed through the history of classical Greece at a dizzying pace, but he paused after the death of Epaminondas to reflect on the condition of Athens around the middle of the fourth century B.C. After the death of Epaminondas on the battlefield in 362, he wrote (in a paragraph that was to enjoy considerable popularity in early modern Europe),

> Valor perished among the Athenians. Having lost the man they had learned to imitate, they fell into indolence and sloth. Now the state revenues they had once spent on the army and the fleet were devoted instead to holidays and festivals, and they mingled eagerly with celebrated actors and poets in the theater, preferring the stage to the military camp and praising those who made verses more highly than those who made policy. It was then that the public treasury, which had been used to support the soldiers and sailors, began to be divided among the people in the city. In this way it happened that in a Greece preoccupied with entertainment the previously lowly and obscure name of Macedon was able to emerge.

Presumably Diodorus's work had reflected the ideology of Ephorus and that of Justin the thinking of Pompeius Trogus. Two important sources for imperial history, however, put considerable creative energy into their work. Both the orator Aelius Aristides and the essayist Plutarch made extensive use of a variety of sources when writing about Athens. For all his rhetorical excesses, Aristides was a critical and original thinker. It was Plutarch's more derivative view of Athens, however, that captured the imagination of subsequent generations.

Born in Asia Minor in A.D. 117, Aristides lectured throughout the Greco-Roman world, settling toward the end of his life at Smyrna, where he had studied in his youth. It was probably in the summer of 155 that he delivered the Panathenaic oration in praise of Athens at the festival of the same name.[20] Sensing that the occasion called for an encomium in the grand manner, Aristides praised every aspect of the city from its constitution to its foreign policy. Mistress of the sea, Athens is portrayed in his oration as the liberal benefactress of the Greek world, destined for dominion by some combination of geography, character, and divine right. Those who would question Athenian hegemony are presented as recalcitrant malcontents who do not know when they are well off. If the Athenians' treatment of Mende and Scione was wrong, he claims, then all empires in all regions are wrong; imperialism, he argues, can be opposed only by someone who "is uncompromising about equal rights and prefers to be a sophist rather than to admit the nature of the matter," to wit, that "every empire obviously belongs to the stronger and is contrary to the very law of equality" (1.306).[21] The lack of a clear historical framework makes it possible for Aristides to celebrate the Athenians' openness in extending their citizenship and to conflate the early monarchy, the aristocratic era of Areopagite ascendancy and the period of the unchecked democracy, claiming thereby for the Athenian system the merit of offering elements of all the traditional forms of government. Democracy, however, is given pride of place in Aristides' discussion of the Athenian constitution, as he maintains that a democratic spirit pervaded even the stewardship of kings and councilors (383–92). Addressing the traditional complaints against popular government, moreover, he insists that of all ancient democracies Athens was the least unruly, writing that citizens of all other democratic states "will clearly have been much more unstable and unjust in their wishes and desires, and have not even approached the dignity and glory of those in this city" (389).

Thus far the rhetoric of the Panathenaic oration, predictable in view of its genre except perhaps for the vigor and determination with which its author defends Athenian imperialism. Although the Panathenaic speech was well known in antiquity and came to be imitated by posterity (most notably by Leonardo Bruni, who used it as a model for his praise of Renaissance Florence), Aristides treated the democratic ethos far more hardheadedly in another essay, which, while admired in antiquity, has since been largely ignored. In the early 160s Aristides produced a long piece entitled *To Plato: In Defense of the Four*. The immediate focus of his concern was the defense of Miltiades, Themistocles, Pericles, and Cimon against Plato's attack on them in his *Gorgias*, but more broadly the speech deals with the nature of political life, the function of oratory, and the inadequacy of Plato's worldview in general.

In defending the place of oratory in politics, Aristides unquestionably had a personal agenda. For all that, his vitriolic attack on the central premises of Plato's political universe is thoughtful and engaging. Human life, he argues, is more complex than Plato makes it out to be and is shaped by a wider spectrum of variables. Aristides denies the legitimacy of the expectation that a good statesman should suffer no reverses and leave the entire citizenry better than he found it. Arguing that it is impossible to improve all of the people all of the time, he stresses the role of fortune in determining the vicissitudes of a statesman's career; he also includes a long and merciless disquisition (369–94) on Plato's stunning failure to achieve his goals at the court of Dionysius in Sicily. He defends the legality and procedural propriety of ostracism, though he does not agree with all the individual decisions the Athenians made about their leaders' fates; and at several junctures he is quick to point out that both the virtue and the fate of (the Athenian) Aristides undermine Plato's argument that no noble politicians existed at Athens and that ostracism is proof of a statesman's inadequacy. In praising Aristides in contradistinction to other Athenian leaders, he argues, Plato is attempting to have his cake and eat it too.

Ultimately, however, his argument rests on the nature of political excellence itself. How, he asks, can Plato discount Athens's pivotal role in the Greek victory over the Persians: if this is not statesmanship, then what is? And why should Pericles be lambasted for offering state pay to the poor, an action that in one stroke alleviated suffering, served justice, and discouraged strife (98–113)? State pay, he argues, is hardly unprecedented and appears even in Plato's own *Republic*. Aristides is particularly sarcastic in attacking Plato's denigration of naval power, claiming (in connection with Themistocles' service to Greece) not at all to understand "where the distinction lies, that a land victory is fair, but one at sea is shameful; or that cornel wood and hide [the materials of which spears and shields were made] is valuable, but ship planks and oar wood is worthless; as if someone should remove the sea from the category of real things or should say that it came into existence for no purpose . . ." (290).

Attacking Plato's social prejudices against sailors, his sentimental attachment to the Athenian Aristides, and his central premise that the moral improvement of the citizenry is both possible and necessary for the true statesman, the orator here suggests that the complexity of human psychology and political life make Plato's view of statesmanship both too narrow and too broad. Unlike philosophers, Aristides argues, politicians are forced to make demands on citizens, and consequently it is no wonder that tensions arise. To be sure, his arguments are carried to tiresome lengths and are decked out with mythological trappings that distract from their fundamental thoughtfulness; in his defense of the dignity of sea power, Aristides cites the authority of Poseidon (290), and, alluding to their reported role in fighting the Persians, he also adduces Pan and Heracles as character references for Miltiades (191–92). Nonetheless, beneath the rhetorical reaching and mythological pleading lies a serious sympathy with the dynamics of Athenian political life and a perceptive indictment of Plato's limitations.

It was not to be Aristides, however, who molded the thinking of later ages when it came to classical politics. That honor belongs to Plutarch, who particularly in the Renaissance and the eighteenth century came to be accorded an authority rather surprising in view of the centuries that separated his lifetime from those of many of the politicians he discussed—over half a millennium in the case of Miltiades, Themistocles, Cimon, and Pericles. Despite Plutarch's many weaknesses, however, the access he enjoyed to sources no longer extant makes him an important resource for ancient history. He had read widely, and if he failed to employ a scientific methodology in comparing the value of his sources, at least the sources were there to be evaluated. Where Athens was concerned, they seem to have been primarily Herodotus, Thucydides, Plato, Aristotle, the Aristotelian *Constitution of the Athenians*, and Xenophon, but he also cites lost writers like Theopompus, Idomeneus, Stesimbrotus, and Ephorus, and he made use of the list of Athenian decrees compiled probably during the third century B.C. by the Macedonian Craterus.[22] Except in the case of Herodotus, who dealt only with the early period of Athenian democracy, the antidemocratic stance of the extant writers is well known, and the two treatises on demagogues by Theopompus and Idomeneus seem to have attacked Athenian political leaders as a whole and the system that brought them to prominence. Plutarch's essay on the malice of Herodotus shows that he was certainly aware of possible bias in his sources, but his affable temperament and humane values, combined with his experience under the enlightened imperial government of Trajan, predisposed him to support generous autocracy or aristocracy as circumstances might require, and his preoccupation with character and ethics led him to place his faith not in good institutions but in good men. Although hauteur and arrogance offended him, his concern with great men and their formation focused his attention and his empathy on the significant individual, and the behavior of people in groups—particularly of large numbers of uneducated people in groups—did not excite his intellect; his alleged interest in politics in fact extended only to the behavior of powerful politicians. Like Plato, whom he cites over six hundred times, he saw humanity as divided into rulers and ruled.[23] Only the former held interest for him, and despite his wide reading in Athenian history and politics, the notion of a society in which this dichotomy was not operative was beyond his grasp.[24]

Plutarch took tremendous pride in his Hellenic heritage, and his native Chaeronea afforded easy access to contemporary Athens. A university city as well as the seat of ancient glory, Athens in Plutarch's day was not only a living museum but a bustling one as well; professional guides abounded, and detailed handbooks of antiquities were available to those whose curiosity exceeded that of the ordinary tourist. Unquestionably Plutarch was captivated by the city's mystique, and probably some of the admiration for Athens manifested in his essay *On the Glory of the Athenians* is real and transcended the rhetoric demanded by the occasion. Like Cicero before him and countless others who came later, however, he distinguished the city's cultural achievements from its regrettable form of government, and where politics was concerned he preferred Sparta, whose legendary founder Lycurgus he celebrated in the biography that was to be one of his best-loved works.

Plutarch's treatment of Athenian democracy is enormously important, because his works probably had more impact on the writing of Greek history prior to the nineteenth century than those of any other writer. He is best remembered for the collection of paired biographies in which he coupled Greek and Roman politicians whose careers struck him as roughly comparable, the so-called *Parallel Lives*. The avowed purpose of the biographies was pedagogical and inspirational, moralistic and didactic. Betraying in the bargain some revealing prejudices, Plutarch explains in the preface to his life of Pericles that examples of virtue inspire emulation in a way the accomplishments of, say, sculptors and poets do not. No youth "of good breeding and high ideals," he contends, "feels that he must be a Pheidias or a Polycleitus after seeing the statue of Zeus at Olympia or Hera at Argos, nor does he aspire to be an Anacreon or a Philetus or an Archilochus, because of the pleasure he derives from their poems, for it does not necessarily follow that because a particular work succeeds in charming us its creator also deserves our admiration." Virtue in action, on the other hand, "immediately takes such hold of a man that he no sooner admires a deed than he sets out to follow in the footsteps of the doer"—hence his own perseverance in writing the biographies of great men.[25]

If the preface to the life of Pericles sets forth Plutarch's goals in the *Lives*, the opening of his *Cimon* tells us about his methodology. "When an artist has to paint a face which possesses fair and handsome features," Plutarch writes, "we demand that he should neither exaggerate nor leave out any minor defect he may find in it," since the first would make the portrait ugly and the second invalidate the likeness. By the same token, "since it is difficult, or rather impossible, to represent a man's life as entirely spotless and free from blame, we should use the best chapters in it to build up the most complete picture and regard this as the true likeness. Any errors or crimes, on the other hand, which may tarnish a man's career and may have been committed out of passion or political necessity, we should regard rather as lapses from a particular virtue than as the product of some innate vice" (*Cimon* 2.4–5). Plutarch says nothing about those errors and crimes committed neither out of passion nor out of political necessity, and overall the methodology he outlines does not offer a promising scenario for serious historical writing.

And not only this: Plutarch's indifference to chronology and geography is a minor irritant when compared with his indifference to the social, economic, and political variations that marked the widely disparate eras he treated in his prolific writings and, *a fortiori*, to complex realities within a single generation. He sees no difficulty with championing Demosthenes and Phocion each in his own biography, and he does not hesitate to transplant the conflict between *optimates* and *populares* in the late Roman republic to fifth-century Athens. His treatment of Athenian government and politics consequently suffers from the distortion that so often accompanies cross-cultural models and, befitting the moral and didactic purpose of the *Lives*, casts the complex political machinations of the fifth century as an ongoing duel between sober civil servants trying to maintain ancestral traditions on the one hand and self-seeking demagogues playing up (or down) to an ignorant and volatile populace on the other.

Plutarch's willingness to recount troubling anecdotes only to disown them afterward suggests that his sources disagreed in their assessment of Athens's political leaders. We would like to know more about these sources. Although Plutarch generally adheres to the principle set forth in the life of Cimon and chooses the more flattering rendition—a principle that he adamantly attacks Herodotus for flouting—his inclusion of various slanders in the *Lives* serves as a good guide to the tradition in which he was working. From Plutarch we hear about allegations that Solon leaked word of his projected cancellation of debts to friends who promptly borrowed as much money as they could; rumors that Cimon committed incest with his sister; and accusations against Pericles for crucifying Samian rebels. The life of Themistocles is particularly rich in anecdote, testifying to the existence of a long and lively tradition about the renegade general.[26] Although Plutarch rejects the most damning of the rumors that have come his way and stresses Themistocles' shrewdness and foresight, throughout he portrays him as ambitious and self-seeking, and he loses no opportunity for contrasting him with the selfless Aristides. The opposition between Themistocles' deviousness and Aristides' rectitude is painted with a particularly thick brush in the life of Aristides, where Plutarch reports without confirmation or denial the attempts of "some writers" to trace the rivalry of the pair back to schoolboy games that even in childhood "quickly revealed their respective natures, Themistocles' being resourceful, daring, unscrupulous, and ready to dash impetuously into any undertaking, while Aristides' was founded upon a steadfast character, which was intent on justice and incapable of any falsehood, vulgarity, or trickery even in jest" (*Aristides* 2.1–2).

Plutarch's preference for more conservative statesmen is also manifest in his treatment of the next pair of rivals to appear on the Athenian scene, Cimon and Pericles. Cimon, he reports, "succeeded in arresting and even reducing the encroachments of the people upon the prerogatives of the aristocracy, and in foiling their attempts to concentrate office and power in their own hands" as long as he remained at Athens; but when in 462 he left the city on campaign, the people "broke loose from all control" and, overthrowing "the established order of the constitution and the ancestral customs [*patria nomima*] which they had always observed up to that moment," proceeded to transform the city "into a thorough-going democracy" (*Cimon* 15.1–2). When Cimon returned home, Plutarch continued, and, in disgust at the new developments, tried to restore the Areopagus to its original position and revive the aristocratic regime of Cleisthenes, the "democratic leaders combined to denounce him and tried to stir up the people against him by bringing up all the old scandals about his sister and accusing him of pro-Spartan sympathies" (15.2–3). By linking these two very different sorts of accusations, Plutarch calls into question the appropriateness and legitimacy of the Athenians' concerns about Cimon's stand on a crucial policy issue. As Plutarch concedes in the next chapter, however, Cimon's pro-Spartan sympathies were real and well known, and Plutarch himself tells how Cimon, opposing Ephialtes, recommended that the Athenians grant Sparta's request for aid against the rebelling helots. Upon arrival in Sparta, the Athenians (alone among Sparta's allies) were promptly sent home. Plutarch shows little understanding of political realities in Athens when he reports that the Athenian soldiers who were rejected so unceremoniously at Sparta voted to ostracize Cimon "upon some trifling pretext" in a fit of temper (17.2). All the evidence about Athenian ostracism suggests that it functioned, among other things, as a safety valve by which the demos might choose between two contentious political leaders and their policies. Cimon's support of Sparta had led to a major disgrace for Athens, and his ostracism announced his countrymen's resounding rejection of his policy. But for Plutarch, pettiness and fury alone explain the decision. Plutarch's avowed policy of seeing the best in everyone did not apply to the Athenian demos.

Plutarch's sources did not permit a neat opposition between Cimon the statesman and Pericles the demagogue, for Plutarch respected the judgment of Thucydides, and had not Thucydides stated explicitly that Pericles led the people rather than being led by it? But hundreds of citations demonstrate the influence of the Platonic corpus (particularly the *Gorgias*) on Plutarch's thinking, and the many anecdotes Plutarch slips into his biography attest to the health of the anti-Periclean tradition in his day even outside the sphere of Platonic influence. Plutarch assures us that Pericles did not (as Idomeneus claimed) arrange the assassination of his friend Ephialtes (10) or crucify the rebel Samian captains in their marketplace (as Duris insisted; 28) or (as Stesimbrotus maintained) seduce his daughter-in-law (13), and that those who blamed Pericles for deliberately bringing on the Peloponnesian War to escape from charges leveled against him and his friends were in error. Still, he remains our source for many of these "mistakes."[27]

Plutarch states his dilemma quite plainly at the opening of the ninth chapter:

> Thucydides characterizes Pericles' administration as having been distinctly aristocratic—"democracy in name, but in practice government by the first citizen." But many other writers maintain that it was he who first led on the people into passing such measures as the allotment to Athenians of lands belonging to subject peoples, or the granting of allowances for the public festivals and fees for various public services, and that because of his policy they fell into bad habits and became extravagant and undisciplined instead of frugal and self-sufficient as they once had been.

Let us consider, Plutarch proposes, "in the light of the facts what may account for this change in his policy." But no one had suggested a change in Pericles' policy; the notion of a change is in fact Plutarch's proposal for reconciling his awkwardly disparate data. Torn between admiration of Thucydides and the thriving anti-Periclean tradition, Plutarch adopted a compromise as methodologically unsound as it was rhetorically unconvincing: Pericles started out rotten but ended up good. During his rise to power, Plutarch maintains, Pericles was a self-seeking demagogue. Following the ostracism of Thucydides, the son of Melesias, however, he was no longer so ready to yield to the people's caprices, "which were as shifting and changeable as the winds," and, abandoning the indulgent mode he had practiced previously, "which might be compared to a soft and flowery melody," he "struck instead the firm, high note of an aristocratic, even regal statesmanship" (15.2). Plutarch goes on to praise the unselfishness and incorruptibility Pericles manifested once his power was firmly established.

Whether for a lack of material or out of the conviction that he was beneath contempt, Plutarch did not write the life of Cleon. This is extremely unfortunate. In his life of Nicias, however, he maintains that Cleon's greed and effrontery were so great that even those whom he went out of his way to win over turned to Nicias for leadership instead (*Nicias* 2.3), and he claims too that it was Cleon "who first introduced shouting and abuse into his speeches, as well as the habit of slapping his thigh, throwing open his dress and striding up and down the platform as he spoke." His habits, Plutarch maintains, produced among the politicians an irresponsibility and a disregard for propriety that before long were to throw the affairs of Athens into chaos" (8.3). Plutarch based his life of Nicias primarily on Thucydides, and he echoed Thucydides both in his distress at Nicias's marked pusillanimity and in his censure of the way in which he believed the Athenian demos intimidated its leaders. Though he is himself wary of Nicias's extreme caution, still he alleges that Athenian history afforded "unmistakable examples" of the Athenians' inability to cope with those who truly excelled—in the fining of Pericles, for example, the ostracism of Damon, the distrust of Antiphon that brought about his downfall, and, perhaps most dramatic of all, the case of the *strategos* Paches, who, Plutarch maintains, killed himself while on trial, apparently for actions committed during the sack of Lesbos (6.1–2).[28]

Throughout his fifth-century *Lives* Plutarch recurs to the theme of the Athenian demos' relationship with its leaders, and he attributes the frequent ostracisms and impeachments of Athens's prominent politicians not to policy differences or genuine malfeasance but rather to emotion. The banishment of Aristides is put down to the jealousy of a demos puffed up with pride and exultation after its victory in the Persian wars, and the ostracism of Cimon is ascribed to rage. Plutarch depicts the Athenians after Pericles' impeachment as purged of their anger; Alcibiades, he claims, was impeached because of anger and resentment. Except for a brief period during the ascendancy of Pericles, Plutarch portrays the relationship between the demos and its leaders as an unhealthy and destructive one: the demagogues, he writes, after Pericles' death, increased the tribute in the empire, not so much because of the length and cost of the war as because they themselves had accustomed the people to accepting money for entertainment and for the erection of temples and statues (*Aristides* 24.3).[29]

Plutarch's assessment of Athenian politicians is not consistent: he wants to have it both ways with Pericles, and he is torn as to whether the principal cause of the Sicilian debacle was the Athenian precedent of tough accountability hearings or Nicias's inborn timidity. His treatment of the Athenian demos, however, is uniform. Throughout, he portrays the demos as unreasonable and unreasoning. The rational element in popular decision making is minimized, indeed virtually denied. For Plutarch, as for Plato, the demos is frequently conceived as a nonreasoning entity such as a boat, a musical instrument, a diseased body, or, most commonly, an animal or collection of animals; it is alternately passive and malleable at one extreme or unruly and unmanageable at the other. This is true both in the *Lives* and in the *Precepts of Statecraft* he assembled late in his life.

Along with the degeneracy of the fourth century, Plutarch's concern with the ingratitude of the Athenians forms the unifying theme of his life of Phocion, executed for his pro-Macedonian sympathies in 318. The decadent character of Athenian government during Phocion's lifetime informs the biography at every turn. Phocion himself he pairs with Cato the younger, whose probity was also at odds with the "debased lives and evil customs" characteristic of his day (*Phocion* 3.2). Throughout, Plutarch opposes the wise and virtuous Phocion to the body of the Athenians; indeed, there is scarcely another citizen of Athens of whom he speaks well in the entire biography. The allies and the islanders, Plutarch reports, regarded envoys from Athens conducted by other *strategoi* as enemies; upon the arrival of such visitors they would block their harbors and bring their women, slaves, children, and herds into the city for safekeeping. But those led by Phocion they greeted with garlands and conducted to their own homes (9.1). A similar story is told about Phocion's reputation in Macedon (17.4). The notion of a dichotomy between the wise Phocion and the foolish Athenians was evidently as precious to Phocion as it was to Plutarch. The biography is filled to the brim with Phocion's crabby reminders of his own worth—sayings like "You are fortunate in having a general who knows you since otherwise you would have perished long ago" (9.3; cf. 5.1). Plutarch tells how once when Phocion was speaking to the demos and found that his argument met with general approval, he turned to his friends and asked, "What, did I say something dumb without knowing it?" (8.3).

It is difficult to determine who despised the demos more, Phocion or Plutarch. And it was not the teeming masses alone who drew to themselves the scorn of the crusty old general; much of Phocion's contempt was directed at orators to whom the people hearkened. After the death of Alexander, Plutarch writes, when Hyperides asked Phocion when he would advise the Athenians to go to war, Phocion replied that he would not do so until he saw "the young men willing to stay at their places in the ranks, the rich to make contributions—and the orators to refrain from stealing public funds" (23.2). Plutarch also reports that Phocion after a victory released all his Greek prisoners of war, "being afraid lest the orators of the Athenians persuade the demos to treat them cruelly" (13.4). Phocion was also deeply distressed by the interaction of the *rhetores* and the demos with each other and with the *strategoi*. In a passage that has been cited by dozens of historians, Plutarch wrote:

> Seeing that the public men of his day had divided up as if by lot the work of general and of orator, some of them only speaking in the assembly and proposing decrees, such as Eubulus, Aristophon, Demosthenes, Lycurgus, and Hyperides, and others— men like Diopeithes, Menestheus, Leosthenes, and Chares—advancing themselves by serving as generals and waging war, Phocion wished to resume and restore the political behavior [*politeian*] of Pericles, Aristides, and Solon, which was equally apportioned to both spheres of action. (7.3)

The point of Phocion's famous observation is twofold: that a division had sprung up in Athens between generals and orators, and that this division was a bad thing.

The ingratitude of the Athenian people, the degeneracy of political life in the fourth century, and the destructive division that sprang up after Pericles' death between generals and orators became important themes in the anti-Athenian tradition, and Plutarch's life of Phocion was to serve as an important text in the historiography of Athens. It fits clearly into Plutarch's general schema for Athenian politics. Good Athenian politicians illustrate by their cruel fates the demos's lack of judgment, and bad ones serve to bring out the idleness, volatility, unruliness, and envy inherent in the masses.[30] Such was the message of the man who served as the most common source for Greek history until the nineteenth century. A repository of cautionary tales of all kinds, Plutarch's voluminous writings did incalculable damage to the reputation of a democracy their author did not begin to understand.

. . . . .

The first alien civilization to write extensively about the Greeks, the Romans were intensely anxious about what it meant to be Roman and not Greek. Seeking to appropriate what appeared best in Greek culture and to distance themselves from what seemed worst, Roman writers made extensive use of Greek topoi in their search for self-definition. How much of what they had to say came from the heart and how much was dictated by rhetorical necessity is difficult to determine, but much can be learned from the necessities the Romans perceived as pressing on them.[31] Though shaped by the challenges that defensive Romans faced in discovering and delineating their own identity, however, the silliness of Cato combined with the convert's zeal of Polybius to lay the groundwork for Cicero's arriviste contortions, and in time the affability and stamina of the tireless Plutarch laid the capstone on the anti-Athenian tradition at Rome. (Other Romans contributed to the anti-Athenian tradition in an oblique but crucial way; the dislike of the *plebs* evident in Livy and his connection of popular unrest with the collapse of the Roman republic was to play a large role in shaping the apprehensions of modern thinkers.)

Plutarch was one of the most prolific of the non-Christian writers of antiquity; his extant works, which probably represent only about half his actual output, fill many volumes. During the Renaissance in Italy, during the seventeenth and eighteenth centuries in England and France, and in America during the generations before and after the revolution, Plutarch was by far the most popular classical author. His admiration for republican virtue was so neatly balanced with his warmth for enlightened autocracy that both monarchists and republicans could claim him as their Bible. It was not until the nineteenth century that critical thinkers began to question whether his lively and amiable prose was really a reliable resource for historical and political analysis.[32] When Cato began his grousing about the decadence of Greece, Pericles had been dead over two centuries, Demosthenes a little less. By the time Plutarch sat down at his desk in Chaeronea, the defeat the Athenians had suffered at Philip's hands was nearly half a millennium old. The same time span separated Plutarch from the heyday of Athenian democracy as divides men and women of the late twentieth century from Columbus's voyage to America, and none of us would be taken very seriously as a primary source for the Age of Exploration. Many readers over the past centuries, however, have imagined that Plutarch is just such a source for democratic Athens—partly because he worked from sources no longer available today and because he spoke the same language, but partly because many have shared the belief of American undergraduate students that there existed in antiquity a large island called "ancient civilization" where Plutarch lived in close quarters with Minos, Homer, Sappho, Pericles, Hannibal, Caesar, and Jesus. Because of these beliefs, because of the vast size of Plutarch's surviving output, and because of their preoccupation with the education of the good citizen, reflective thinkers in early modern Europe and America turned frequently to Plutarch as the font of wisdom of all kinds. Until the nineteenth century, Plutarch probably taught people more (or less) about ancient history than all other classical authors combined, and what he had to say about Athenian democracy was not flattering. Combining the specious authenticity of a Greek insider with the equally deceptive objectivity of a Roman outsider, until quite recently Plutarch enjoyed an unparalleled reputation as a source for Greek political history. This reputation would play a crucial part in forming the view of Athens that characterized the Italian Renaissance, the subject of the chapter that follows.

Chapter Six

RECOVERING THE GREEKS

> Among those who have deserved most praise for such a constitution is Lycurgus, who so prepared his laws in Sparta that, giving their shares to the king, to the aristocrats, and to the people, he made a state that lasted more than eight hundred years, with the highest reputation for himself and peace for the city. The opposite happened to Solon, who prepared the laws in Athens, because, organizing there a state governed only by the people, he made it of such short life that before he died he saw arise the tyranny of Peisistratus.
>
> —Machiavelli, *Discourses*

MODERN SCHOLARS are likely to smile at Plutarch's wistful exposition of the difficulties of doing research in little Chaeronea, far from the library resources available in a big city (*Demosthenes* 2.1). His lament rings all too true. It is impossible to know what Plutarch would have made of today's classical scholars sitting at their computers patiently plugging away at their *TLG* databases. It is not difficult, however, to imagine the horror and bewilderment he would have felt at the prospect of an era when the knowledge of Greek would evaporate in the Western empire and the death of Greco-Roman paganism would bring with it loss of interest in the classical system of civic values that unified his intellectual universe.[1]

Looking toward Antiquity

When Augustine's pupil Orosius of Spain (or perhaps modern Portugal) wrote his *Seven Books of History against the Pagans* early in the fourth century, his purpose was not to offer cautionary *exempla* of civic virtue. Rather, he sought to extend beyond the confines of Roman history the thesis of Augustine that as many calamities had attended on humankind before the advent of Christianity as after, thus rebutting the pagans who ascribed the sorry state of late antiquity to the Christians' dereliction of civic and sacral duty. Though Orosius admires the Athenians' resilience under the stress of constant warfare (3.15.4–5) and praises them for learning from their mistakes (2.17.17), he attributes their expedition against Sicily to selfish motives (2.14.7), and though he is somewhat harder on the Spartans' "wicked lust for domination"

(3.2.9–10), he ascribes the failure of the oligarchic revolution of 411/10 at Athens to the "inbred pride and rampant passions" of the race (2.16.1–2; whether of Greeks in general or of Athenians in particular is not clear). All in all, he concludes, Greece, Asia, Persia, Egypt, and Libya carried on such indiscriminate warfare that even were he to list the wars one by one he could not keep track of the thousands of people slaughtered (3.2.10).

Although familiarity with the sufferings of the Greek city-states might be useful to Christian apologists, interest in Greek history faded in the Western empire as knowledge of the Greek language declined precipitously during the fifth and sixth centuries.[2] Even in Byzantium the political history of ancient Greece was reduced to short notices such as that found of Athens in the work of Theodore Metoikites, and the word *demokratia* came to mean a street riot; in the West, interest in the doings of the Greeks focused primarily on the Trojan War.[3] In the twelfth-century *Chronicle of the Two Cities*, Otto the Bishop of Freising gave Greek political history fairly short shrift, incorporating various misreadings of his principal source, Orosius, and eking out his account with a surprising number of quotations from, of all places, Cicero's *De Officiis*.[4]

Ignorance of Greek history would seem to rule out Athenian democracy as an inspiration for the popular communes of thirteenth-century Italy, and though the stirrings of the Italian yearning for antiquity began to be felt in the fourteenth century, generally they moved people only as far as Latin would take them, and Petrarch was known for asking, "What is history but the study of Rome?" Petrarch did, however, encourage his contemporary Boccaccio to learn Greek, and Boccaccio seems to have familiarized himself with some of Aristotle's works. Toward the end of the century, two young Florentines, Roberto Rossi and Jacopo d'Angelo da Scarperia, went to Venice to study with the renowned Greek scholar Manuel Chrysoloras, and it was in large part due to the Florentine chancellor Coluccio Salutati that Chrysoloras was persuaded to come to Florence in 1397 and take up a chair at the University. Though Salutati never managed to learn Greek, Chrysoloras nonetheless educated the first generation of Florentine humanists, the most prominent being Leonardo Bruni, born in Arezzo in 1370, who proclaimed that at Chrysoloras's hands Greek had been resurrected after seven centuries in which no Italian knew the language; as Sandys points out in his history of classical scholarship, Bruni's chronology here is borne out by the date of 690 assigned by Martin Crusius in his *Swiss Annals* to the extinction of Greek in medieval Italy.[5] From Florence and Venice the study of Greek language and civilization spread throughout northern Italy; classical education as a whole began to be put forward as the point of departure for efficacy in public life, and ancient history came to be praised for the models it could provide of behavior to be imitated or avoided.[6]

Classical *exempla* play an important role, for instance, in the two rambling discourses on government composed by the Sienese Francisco Patrizi, Bishop of Gaeta, one around 1460 and another in the 1480s.[7] Assembled from a wide variety of classical sources, Patrizi's discourses were arranged topically for the easy reference of statesmen whose tastes did not run to particularly demanding texts. Their style is chatty and anecdotal; Patrizi especially enjoyed rehearsing the contrast between Nicias's fatally superstitious fear of eclipses and Pericles' matter-of-fact dismissal of such simple phenomena of nature.[8] Though in the earlier *De Institutione Reipublicae* Patrizi recorded with evident approval the strictures of the ancients (Aristotle, Socrates, and the Romans) against artisans and merchants participating in politics, he treats popular government more fully in the later *De Regno*.[9] There he takes over from antiquity the division of government into three good forms and three degenerate ones, and echoes the Greek concern that the popular state can fall into tyranny if the people get "free of the reins" and reject men of outstanding virtue. Significantly, he labels the demos *plebs*, not *populus*. Already in *De Institutione Reipublicae* Patrizi had warned his fellow Sienese against the dangers of envy and had reminded them that many celebrated Athenians had stayed for long periods outside Attica precisely to avoid it. What but envy, Patrizi asks, destroyed Athens?[10] The notion that the fall of Athens was brought about by envy is developed more fully in *De Regno*, where Patrizi rehearses the usual catalog of Athenian martyrs (Socrates, Themistocles, Aristides).[11] It was through envy and ambition, he claims, that Athens fell to the Spartans. Though at first the state was administered by illustrious men, subsequently, as envy and ambition grew, the *plebs* took over by sedition, demanding an accounting from commanders for wartime conduct. It was as a result of this behavior, he asserts, that the Athenians were conquered by Lysander and the Spartans, and in their defeat Patrizi also sees the predictable punishment for their imperialism.[12]

Patrizi's two treatises were designed to offer his readers improving *exempla* in the arts of government. It was in Florence, however, that the relevance of classical history to contemporary Italian politics and diplomacy received its most elaborate articulation. Beginning already with the last generation of the fourteenth century, Florence and Athens were frequently linked together by Florentine writers, sometimes for glory but more frequently in obloquy. While Florence basked in her role as the cultural capital of Italy and vaunted herself the successor to the quondam school of Hellas, the similarities between Florentine government and that of the Athenians became a source of embarrassment and reproach.

ATHENS ON THE ARNO

Undercut by three successive waves of the Black Death and jostled by the Ciompi rebellion of 1378, the Florentine state lived on to face its greatest challenge at the turn of the century, when Gian Galeazzo Visconti, having purchased the title of Duke of Milan in 1395, began his irrepressible march through Umbria and Tuscany. By June of 1402 the chilling news came to Florence that Bologna itself had fallen, and Florentines turned in alarm to Pope Boniface IX as Gian Galeazzo ordered preparations to be made for his coronation in Florence as King of Italy. In September, however, came the astonishing report that Gian Galeazzo had died of a fever. A funeral in Milan replaced the coronation at Florence, and the combined army of Boniface and the Florentines succeeded in driving Gian Galeazzo's widow Caterina back from both Bologna and Umbria.

The terror had passed, but somewhere in the crucible of the Visconti peril was forged the civic humanism associated with the Florentine quattrocento, and around the turn of the century Florentine writers begin to put forward their city politically as the bastion of republican liberty in Italy and culturally as the school of the entire peninsula. It is not likely that the Florentines had any finer definitions of *libertà* than had the Greeks of *autonomia* (autonomy) or *eleutheria* (freedom) or the Romans of *libertas*.[13] A lack of precise definition, however, has never inhibited any catchword from sparking extraordinary passions in the human soul; indeed, a certain vagueness often serves to add fuel to the flames. The Florentines came to see the defeat of the Visconti not simply as a fortuitous deliverance from impending doom but rather as the validation of their form of government, which, however narrow it may seem to twentieth-century democrats, struck the Florentines as quite broadly based. The limited role their own efforts had played in pushing the Visconti out of Tuscany and Umbria, moreover, raised Florence's status in Italy as a whole. The obvious parallel with Athens after Salamis did not pass unnoticed.[14]

Already in 1397 Cino Rinuccini capped his procession of distinguished Florentines with the observation that nothing filled him with more joy than watching there grow up before his eyes "a brigade of magnificent character . . . that would be appropriate in that most literate of cities, Athens."[15] It was probably shortly afterward that Leonardo Bruni produced his *Praise of the City of Florence*, a panegyric based on the *Panathenaicus* of Aelius Aristides.[16] Here Bruni taps the Athenian parallel at a variety of points—in his discussions, for example, of Florence's geographical location, her leadership in the struggle against foreign autocrats, the superior nature of her political institutions, and her cultural primacy. Special emphasis, moreover, is placed on the fact that Florence's Tuscan dialect is a model for the whole peninsula. Like Aristides, Bruni uses both the simile of the moon surrounded by the stars and that of the concentric rings on a buckler to illustrate his city's central geographical location. In a digression on the thirteenth century, Bruni likens the Florentines who left the city after the defeat at Montaperto to the Athenians who fled to preserve their liberty during the Persian War. Patrizi was to suggest that Sparta was the school of Greece, but several echoes of Thucydides' Periclean funeral oration in Bruni's eulogy for Nanni degli Strozzi suggest that Bruni was thinking of Athens. Like Pericles, Bruni took the occasion of a funerary speech to eulogize his city as a whole; like Pericles too, Bruni stressed the liberty and equality of citizens under the exemplary government of a city in which the doors of opportunity—or so he claimed—were open to all men of merit. In a burst of democratic fervor Bruni describes the government of Florence here as a *forma popularis*, though in both the *Praise of the City of Florence* and in his Greek essay *On the Government of the Florentines* he calls the government mixed, an appellation far closer to the truth.[17] It was probably around the same time as Bruni's funeral oration that Gherardi da Prato composed his paean to "that most learned Athens" in the *Paradise of the Alberti*, and the stress Gherardi placed on the Athenians' successful resistance against foreign domination suggests Florentine echoes here.[18]

A sentimental attachment persisted as time wore on. Strong echoes of Pericles' funeral oration appear in Alamanno Rinuccini's 1479 essay *On Liberty*, and early in the sixteenth century Giovanni Corsi is found praising the Florence of Lorenzo de' Medici as a second Athens.[19] The comparison stuck: by later in the century Lorenzo's position was compared to Pericles' in Athens, and both the Periclean and the broader analogy have persisted down to our own time.[20] Whether any solid infrastructure underlay the Florentine affinity for the city of Pericles, however, is another story. The extant writings of the fifteenth century offer little serious discussion of the Athenian political system; even a book with as promising a title as Matteo Palmieri's treatise *On Civic Life* contains few references to Athens to match those to Rome and to Sparta.[21] Early in the sixteenth century came a new wave of interest in antiquity, somewhat less sentimental and contrived than what had been apparent a hundred years before. Political issues began to be discussed analytically and in depth, particularly by the Florentine intellectuals who gathered in the Orti Oricellari to discuss the problems that beset their city and to seek solutions grounded in a proper understanding of antiquity. For all the fascination with liberty and representative government, however, Athens is given fairly short shrift. One Florentine historian, indeed, though singing the praises of *libertà* and lauding the grandeur Athens attained following the expulsion of the Peisistratids, nonetheless manages to get the names of Peisistratus's sons wrong, calling Hippias's brother and fellow-tyrant Diocles rather than Hipparchus.[22] In this he shows reliance on Justin rather than on Thucydides or Herodotus— not a good sign in someone who purports to be a serious student of antiquity.

That historian's name was Niccolò Machiavelli. For him, the Greek *poleis* were of secondary interest to the Roman republic. Where he turns his attention to the Greek world at all it is mostly to princes of the Hellenistic era after the Macedonian conquest or to the great lawgivers—*ordinatori* and *riordinatori*—of earlier days, Theseus, Solon, Romulus, Lycurgus, and Moses, all of whom he treats as fully historical figures.[23] But Solon, Machiavelli observes in his *Discourses*, was less successful in his work than Lycurgus: the mixed government created by Lycurgus lasted eight hundred years without the slightest disturbance, whereas the government of Solon, being merely a democratic state, toppled almost at once.[24] So short-lived was the Solonic state that even in his own lifetime Solon saw the beginnings of the Peisistratid tyranny, and even after the Peisistratids were expelled and the Solonic system revived, still this government lasted less than a hundred years, despite the fact that "a number of laws that had been overlooked by Solon were adopted, to maintain the government against the insolence of the nobles and the license of the populace."[25]

Because of his rejection of contemporary Christian morality, Machiavelli has often been perceived as a dispassionate and objective observer of the drama of history. In fact, Machiavelli (like Thucydides) was a man of painful passions whose emotions were intensely engaged by the political turmoil around him, and his remarks both about contemporary Florence and about ancient government reveal a profound and searing ambivalence.[26] At one moment the people is exalted as the repository of a wide spectrum of virtues, while at another he scorns the volatility and vain ambition of the lower classes. Not surprisingly, classical Athens sparked mixed emotions in Machiavelli.

In the *Discourses* Machiavelli shows some enthusiasm for early Athens, adducing the flourishing of Athens after the expulsion of Peisistratus as evidence of the superiority of popular to monarchic government.[27] In demonstrating the superiority of republics in keeping alliances, he tells how the Athenians rejected the advice of Themistocles to seize or destroy the united Greek fleet: when Aristides maintained that Themistocles' proposal was "highly advantageous but most dishonest," the people "absolutely rejected it; which would not have been done by Philip of Macedon, nor many other princes, who would only have looked to the advantages, and who have gained more by their perfidy than by any other means."[28]

On the other hand, Machiavelli cites Athens as an example in his chapter on "How by the Delusions of Seeming good the people are often misled to desire their own ruin; and how they are Frequently Influenced by Great Hopes and Brave Promises" (1.53). Having offered various examples of this from the Roman republic, he then moves on to Athens, where he pairs Nicias's inability to dissuade the Athenian people from attacking Sicily with an example from Florentine history: "Messer Ercole Bentivogli," he writes, "commander of the Florentine troops, and Antonio Giacomini, after having defeated Bartolommeo d'Alviano at San Vincenti, went to lay siege to Pisa, which enterprise was resolved upon by the people in consequence of the brave promises made by Messer Ercole, although many of the most prudent citizens objected, but could not prevent it." I say then, Machiavelli concludes, "that there is no easier way to ruin a republic, where the people have power, than to involve them in daring enterprises."[29]

Machiavelli's determination to illumine the present by the lights of the past is undermined by his failure adequately to temper his parallels by making appropriate distinctions between one culture and another: what else could explain his bizarre attribution of the short duration of Athenian democracy to the error Solon "had committed in not tempering the power of the people and that of the prince and his nobles"?[30] J.G.A. Pocock has emphasized the way in which Machiavelli and his contemporaries were compelled to wrestle with medieval and Renaissance frameworks that opposed the eternal hierarchies of monarchy and empire with the transitory essence of republics. To affirm the republic, Pocock contends, "was to break up the timeless continuity of the hierarchic universe into particular moments: those periods of history at which republics had existed and which were worthy of attention, and those at which they had not and which consequently afforded nothing of value or authority to the present." Where "affiliation with monarchy . . . was affiliation with the timeless," the republic, on the contrary, "was not timeless, because it did not reflect by simple correspondence the eternal order of nature."[31] In his attempt to distinguish adequately among the different republics that had existed, Machiavelli was frequently pulled back into a generalizing mode that undercut the value of his enterprise.[32] His response to Athens was complicated as well by a haunting ambivalence about the value of popular government. In the words of Mark Hulliung, Machiavelli saw "Athenian democracy, which lit up the skies with glory for a tragically brief moment" as a

> magnificent failure and a warning to Florentine democracy. A popular regime, Athens could arm the people and boast formidable military might; a popular regime, Athens had destroyed her nobility, and in her egalitarian excesses did not permit the rise of a new ruling class. Hence hers was a politics of passion unconstrained, undirected. . . . Similarly, the Florentine empire, insofar as it existed, weakened the city on the Arno, because Florence, too, as the pathetic republican resurgence from 1494 to 1512 attested, was a democracy devoid of leadership. However much a Florence that was the reincarnation of Rome might be Machiavelli's aspiration, a Florence that was the reincarnation of Athens was his reality.[33]

More consistently pessimistic about the capacity of common citizens to form a sound popular government, Machiavelli's friend Guicciardini responded negatively to Athenian democracy. Guicciardini praises Pericles at several junctures but is highly critical of the substructure of Athenian government that underlay Pericles' position as *strategos*; indeed on one occasion his praise of Pericles is accompanied by criticism of the slander that led to his deposition, and though he claims that Pericles used his power for the good of the state, he is disturbed by the demagogic methods he employed and maintains that rising through the senate is superior to ingratiating oneself with the people.[34] His account of the demagogic fawning that brought Pericles to power (followed by genuine statesmanship once his position was secure) points to

Plutarch as a source, a notion reinforced by the detailed contrast between rising by the favor of the people and rising by way of the senate. For it was Plutarch who had reconciled his pro-Periclean and anti-Periclean sources by seeing two discrete phases in Pericles' career, and Plutarch too who imposed the scheme of the Roman republic (which pitted the senate against the popular assemblies) on states such as Athens, to which it did not in fact apply. A similar Roman bias is evident in Guicciardini's contention in the *Dialogue on the Government of Florence* that in the ancient Greek and Roman republics many tumults and indeed disasters were caused by bringing matters of importance before those popular assemblies "that the ancients called *conzione*," an Italian word made from the Latin *contio*, a notion that in turn was thoroughly alien to Greek thinking.[35] Though Cicero might voice fervid anxieties about the horrors of "Greek-style" assemblies, in fact a *contio* was a uniquely Roman event.

In the commentary he wrote on Machiavelli's own *Discourses* on Livy, Guicciardini took issue with his friend's contention that it was because nobody since the expulsion of the Tarquins had sought to deprive the Romans of their liberty that the Romans had been less suspicious of their leading citizens than had the Athenians. Citing the tyranny of the fifth-century decemvirs, Guicciardini argues that Machiavelli is in error. The true explanation, he maintains, may lie in the nature of the Romans, who were not given to the levity of the Athenians but rather conformed to the propriety of the other Greeks; but it is more likely to lie in the popular nature of Athenian government, which enabled ambitious citizens to rise more easily. The mixed nature of Roman government in general and the prominent role played by the Roman senate in particular gave Rome an advantage over Athens, making Roman government "more sober, more temperate, and more prudent than that of the Athenians," which was, he states twice, "merely democratic."[36] He cites the exiles of Alcibiades and Themistocles as evidence that the people should not hear accusations.[37] Nor does Guicciardini overlook what he sees as a positively pernicious parallel between Athens and Florence. It is plain, he argues in his *Discourse of Logrogno*, that laws that are "guided by the appetite of the multitude" are almost always either harmful or pointless, and as evidence for this he cites the "great disorder" that arose from popular input into policy in the ancient states and "most of all in Athens," where much ruin was brought upon the state in this way. From contemporary history he goes on to cite the instance already adduced by Machiavelli in his chapter on "How by the Delusions of Seeming good the people are often misled to desire their own ruin; and how they are Frequently Influenced by Great Hopes and Brave Promises"—the unsuccessful campaign against Pisa in 1505. In his own time, he writes, we see the example of Piero Soderini's proposal concerning the campaign against Pisa: disapproved by the aristocrats and the *dieci della guerra*, the expedition was approved by the people "against the advice of all the wise men in the city." The unsuccessful expedition, Guicciardini complains, brought with it "both harm and shame."[38] It is in the same essay that Guicciardini refers admiringly to the knife with which Lycurgus surgically removed all possible decadence from his fatherland, and he goes on to revel at some length in Lycurgus's glory; the praise of the Spartan founder also appears in the commentary on Machiavelli's *Discourses*, and in the *Dialogue on the Government of Florence* the ordinances of Lycurgus are billed as "those holy laws."[39]

A similar pattern appears in the work of Donato Giannotti, another habitué of the Orti Oricellari who takes up the question of Athenian persecution of their leaders, writing in his *Discourse on the Form of the Florentine Republic* that here Athens is an example to be studiously avoided by the Florentines: it was because the Athenian state was badly balanced, he maintains, that those who acquired distinction generally became overbearing and required ostracism "to bridle their insolence." In a well-ordered state, he contends, such ambition does not pose a threat, and he cites as evidence for this Sparta and Venice, where the sole attempts at tyranny made by Pausanias and by Marino Falerio were quashed with dispatch. A pointed contrast is provided with Florence, where the disorder of the Republic gave rise to the tyranny of Cosimo de' Medici.[40] Though Giannotti mentions both Solon and Romulus as *ordinatori*, moreover, it is of Lycurgus that we hear the most. In a passage evocative of Machiavelli, the Spartans are praised for living for a long time with the same laws and without the slightest alteration, while off in Athens people lived "in continual travail."[41] Giannotti goes on to contend that the Roman republic [sic] while under the kings did not undergo the slightest alteration and achieved great conquests that would enable it to conquer Italy and indeed the whole world—whereas when the regal power was abolished the state fell apart because of the conflicts among ambitious citizens seeking the consulship.

OLIGARCHY, SERENITY, AND THE GOVERNO MISTO

There was, however, one government that did appeal to Giannotti: that most serene republic, Venice, to which he devoted his laudatory *Book of the Republic of the Venetians*.[42] His enthusiasm was shared by Machiavelli, who in the *Discourses* coupled Venice and Sparta as stable mixed republics, and by Guicciardini, who ended his discussion of the superiority of mixed polities with a paean to Venice. A legend in its own time, Venice managed to exert an extraordinary influence on political thought in Italy and was generally held to preserve the balance of a mixed government upon the foundation of an exceptionally broad base. Though the titular executive, the Doge, was elected for life, a majority of councillors could act without him, whereas he himself could not act except in concert with at least four of them. Hedged about by a wide variety of councils and colleges, the Doge had to undergo a regular redefinition of his powers at the hands of a committee of the Grand Council. In this Council, which met several times a month, sat all male patricians whose families were listed in the Venetian Libro d'Oro—a total of 1,843, for example, in the year 1581, for which statistics exist. This Council, in the eyes of admiring contemporaries, provided the democratic element in a beautifully balanced constitution. Twentieth-century scholars have seen things differently, one contending that "with an eye on the 133,047 who had no share in the government, there would be few today who would not unhesitatingly pronounce the Venetian republic a close oligarchy."[43] Renaissance thinkers, however, had their own views: Guicciardini, Machiavelli, Giannotti—all three Florentines saw the Venetian state as the finest example of government and the distillation of what had been best in ancient polities.[44]

Despite the frequency with which its name was invoked by political thinkers of the fifteenth and sixteenth centuries, during the Renaissance Venice itself stood somewhat removed from the eddying currents of humanism. The very stability that drew the awe of their contemporaries militated against any desire on the part of Venetians to turn back their eyes to a time when the city on the lagoon had not yet risen from the marshes. Convinced that they enjoyed the best of all possible worlds under the best of all possible constitutions, Venetians had no reason to hanker nostalgically after the Greco-Roman past. They were, however, willing to indulge themselves in happy comparisons with classical government at its best. Both Cardinal Gasparo Contarini, himself descended from a family that could boast eight Doges, and Trajano Boccalini, whose works became quite popular in England when they were translated shortly after his death, maintained that Venice surpassed all ancient governments.[45] This opinion was shared by Paolo Paruta, the renowned Venetian political theorist, who stressed the improvements Venice had made over the dangerous democratic tendencies that had brought down the ancient republics. But if Venice represented an improvement on antiquity, Florence served as a sober reminder of the dangers of democracy, and in this she was associated with classical Athens.

Although Paruta's view of the superiority of Venice to all other governments ancient and modern is also expounded in his *History of Venice*, it is in his *Political Discourses* and his treatise *On Political Perfection* that he offers the strongest indictments of other states.[46] To be sure, Paruta followed in the Florentines' footsteps in admiring Sparta for her long endurance and praising Lycurgus for instituting such a well-balanced system; he also credits Sparta with protecting Greece from the immoderate ambition of the Athenians.[47] But even Sparta, he complains, had become too democratic by virtue of the addition of the board of five ephors under king Theopompus, and good government was destroyed in Rome when the ambition of the Gracchi brothers led to excessive power falling into the hands of the people, or, as Paruta would have it, "a dissolute democratic license." Likewise, he goes on, too much power was accorded to the Athenian people by Aristides and Pericles, whom he labels "too enamored of liberty—or perhaps eager to maintain their high status by means of the people's favor."[48] This excessive democratic liberty, he suggests, was responsible for the rule of the Thirty Tyrants. Similarly he maintains that it was because Solon had made her too democratic that Athens had fallen under the power of Peisistratus.[49] Solon, Paruta writes, was so severely criticized for his laws that he was compelled to flee his ungrateful country.[50] He also censures the Athenians for ostracizing or impeaching so many outstanding leaders.[51] Athens, he maintains, provides an ancient example of the dangerous instabilities of governments in which there is a substantial democratic element, while of modern states, Florence in her instability demonstrates this same danger, offering too easy an opportunity to men (e.g., the Medici) who wish to oppress the city and take away her liberty by ingratiating themselves with the crowd. But Venice, he reminds us, "on the contrary, by virtue of the excellent form of its government, which, though mixed, retains nonetheless very little of a democratic element and much of an aristocratic one, . . . has been able to retain the very same constitution for the very longest time."[52]

Renaissance Italians, then, preferred the governments of Venice and Sparta to those of Florence and Athens, and the reasons they alleged were fairly consistent: Venetian and Spartan stability were preferable to the constant mutations of Florentine and Athenian government, and a mixed constitution was inherently more durable than one in which the supreme power is vested in the people. The preference for Sparta over Athens was well grounded in ancient sources. Bruni in the first flowering of civic humanism lit upon two of the only ancient texts to praise Athenian political institutions unambiguously and at length—the Thucydidean funeral oration of Pericles and the *Panathenaicus* of Aelius Aristides. (Concerning Aristides' much more thoughtful discussion of Athens in his oration *To Plato: On the Four*, Bruni sustained the conspiracy of silence that has ignored Aristides' analytical essay to this day.) Hostile texts were far more abundant, and among these the political philosophers held pride of place. Though they might be—and indeed were—fair game in other regards, Plato and Aristotle were revered by thinkers of the Italian Renaissance when it came to politics and political theory; it remained for Jean Bodin to approach the political ideas of these luminaries with irreverence. Pietro Vettori's commentary on Aristotle's *Politics* is a case in point: after an introduction that discusses the governments of Rome, Sparta, and Carthage, makes only the most cursory reference to Athens, and includes an impassioned eulogy of Lycurgus, Vettori goes on to comment on the text without ever suggesting that Aristotle's way of looking at political life could possibly have been improved upon in any particular. The examples could be multiplied at length. Even Bartolomeo Cavalcanti, who in 1555 produced his *Treatise on the Best Governments of the Ancient and Modern Republics* comparing the political theories of Plato, Aristotle, and Polybius, contents himself with collating and contrasting the ancient authors' views on a series of topics, refraining conspicuously from offering any opinions of his own—"leaving," as he says, "the judgment of such things to those more intelligent and judicious than I."[53]

Plato and Aristotle had both drawn tight connections between democracy and tyranny, suggesting both that the first gave rise to the second and that the two were in fact quite similar. The repeated contention that democracy in Florence had opened the door to ambitious despots demonstrates both Florentine reality and Greek theory; whether it reflects Athenian reality is another story. In truth the tyranny of Peisistratus opened the door to democracy at Athens, which subsequently was never overthrown from within; two oligarchic (not despotic) coups were quelled within months, as they had insufficient support to take root. The strongman who brought popular sovereignty to an end in Athens was nurtured not in the atmosphere of democracy but rather among Macedonian mores of monarchy and murder. Like many who would follow in their footsteps, the Florentines looked more closely at Greek political theory and at the history of their own civilization than they did at the actual course of Athenian political life.

It is important that we notice among the *ordinatori* praised by Machiavelli and Giannotti the name of Theseus, who appears as a fully historical figure beside Moses, Cyrus, Solon (and of course Lycurgus, to all appearances the least controversial character in all of ancient history). The cheerful acceptance of Theseus's historicity may be ascribed in part to the generally uncritical attitude of the age toward the ancient sources and in part to the Machiavellian preoccupation with founders in general; but in part at least we are surely entitled to see here the fine hand of Plutarch. The veritable obsession with Plutarch during the Renaissance was both symptom and cause of an attitude toward Greek civilization that stressed the role of the great man in history, exalted anecdote over analysis, substituted moralizing for an honest effort to determine what happened, deployed the history of the city-states in the form of cautionary tales penned to make pithy points about human nature, and, last but not least, viewed Greece through Roman eyes.

Hungrily indeed did the civic humanists with their preoccupation with the education of the good citizen fall upon the writings of Plutarch, for in these they found precisely the attitude toward history to which they were most receptive. In this receptivity lay also the source of the virtual canonization of Lycurgus, for if ever a man was associated with the moral formation of citizens, Lycurgus was that man: though Athens might vaunt herself the school of Hellas, the nature of the Athenian *paideia* was less well defined than the legendary Spartan *agoge* that so fired the minds of the Renaissance. Bruni himself praised history as a store of moral *exempla* and identified it as providing to citizens and monarchs alike "lessons of incitement or of warning in the ordering of public policy."[54] Though Machiavelli was not the best audience for sententious Plutarchian moralizing, the two men shared a marked enthusiasm for the notion of glorious leaders.

It is not surprising, then, that Renaissance texts often throw off clearly audible echoes of the Plutarchian view of Athenian democracy. Guicciardini, as we have seen, followed closely Plutarch's picture of Pericles' conversion from "demagogue" to "statesman," and implicitly in so doing accepted the very concept of demagogy so dear to Plutarch's heart. Plutarch probably lurked as well behind Machiavelli's assertion in the proem to his *Florentine History* that political factions in Florence were far more complicated than those in Rome and Athens, since in those two cities, Machiavelli maintains, only two political groups contended for power; for one of Plutarch's signal weaknesses as a historian of classical Athens is his failure to distinguish her complex machinations from those of republican Rome, where a bipartite optimate-popular division did actually correspond to reality.[55] Philip Ralph is particularly acute in assessing the damage done to Machiavelli's analysis of his own society by undue reliance on simplistic Roman models. Machiavelli, he writes,

> fell wide of the mark in appraising social forces. Instead of making a serious attempt to analyze the society of Florence, he fell back on formulas extracted from antiquity. While the Tuscan republic was openly and proudly proclaiming itself a city of merchants and artisans—though in fact it was in the grip of an upper bourgeois elite—Machiavelli continued to think in terms of the traditional opposition between nobles and commoners, which he equated with the struggle between patricians and plebeians in early republican Rome.[56]

The Plutarchian model of ancient society, in other words, seems to have distorted Machiavelli's thinking not only about Athens but, more surprisingly, about Florence as well.

An uncritical attitude toward ancient sources, then, coupled with a hearty appetite for the moral formation of citizens and a corresponding predilection for the writings of Plutarch in particular, helped shape the Renaissance disdain for Athenian statecraft and its concomitant reverence for Sparta.[57] The implications of this unimaginative approach toward the sources are broad and wide-ranging, for in the elitism of the ancient writers Renaissance thinkers found a mind-set that was eminently congenial to their own way of looking at the world. In the study of Greek history, no attention was paid to slavery, imperialism, and the status of women—all topics of considerable interest to later generations; in an age in which the constant rallying cry was to *libertà*, Renaissance writers nonetheless complained only of the excessive liberty at Athens and had not a word to say about those who were deprived of their freedom. Political alchemists seeking the magic formula for stability and immunity from foreign interference, Renaissance theorists exalted endurance at the expense of all else. Their uncritical attitude toward the sources not only blinded them to the weaknesses of the Spartan system, which was transmogrified in Renaissance mythology into the utopian *governo misto*, but, by leading them to accept the historicity of Lycurgus and all his works, led them to exaggerate the length of time the Spartan state endured unchanged as well. Perhaps the finest emblem of traditional classicism during the Renaissance is to be found in a passage on the first page of Giannotti's discourse on the form of the Florentine government. A confirmed republican, Giannotti admired what he saw as the broadly based government of Venice and often reiterated that though a mixed government was best, still if a government had to incline toward the nobles or the people it was safer for it to incline toward the people. Giannotti nonetheless begins his work by announcing that the poor of Florence who make up the mass of the people need not be discussed in his treatise on the government, as they lack citizenship: "About these, lacking as they do any degree whatever of citizenship, it is unnecessary to speak further."[58]

That such a notion of the body politic can be so cavalierly put forward in passing reveals much. Underneath all the ostentatious parading of the ideals of republicanism there lurked the profoundest mistrust of any real attempt to establish a government more broadly based than oligarchy. To be sure, a number of Italian city-states had flirted with democratic governments during the thirteenth and fourteenth centuries; some of the best known experiments in popular sovereignty were tried in Florence itself. Much of the chaos and turbulence that attended on these regimes was the product not so much of their inherent weaknesses as of the continuing competition among wealthy families, a rivalry that often took the form of overextension on the part of ambitious banking houses such as that of the Bardi; disastrous bank failures in turn threw the state into disarray. (The last of the great houses to collapse, the Bardi itself finally fell staggering in 1346.) Rabid imperialism drew Florence into increasingly unpayable debt. Larger guilds, lesser guilds, Guelphs, Ghibellines, wool-workers, friends and enemies of the papacy, disaffected aristocrats, artisans, farmers, magnates—the bitter and often physically violent strife among its factions that marked the bustling commercial city on the Arno might to more thoughtful minds have made Athens look like a peaceable agrarian community in comparison. Determined to hang the instability of this era on the weaknesses of popular government, however, the city-states of fifteenth-century Italy settled down by and large into oligarchies of one kind or another.

Venice was a stable aristocracy, and the many vicissitudes through which the Florentine government passed in the fifteenth and sixteenth century did not include democracy; indeed the dominance of wealthy patrician families had caused the political base to shrink considerably from what it had been in the fourteenth century before the arrival of the much-touted civic humanism. Though democracy seemed to have some prospects at Florence during the middle of the fourteenth century, by careful scrutiny of the lists of citizens eligible for office a few determined families managed to retain power in their

own hands until the period of ferment had safely passed. The highest proportion of enfranchised citizens in any Italian state during the Renaissance was
evidently Bologna, where 12 percent of inhabitants had the franchise—and
this in the fourteenth century.[59] After 1400, only states that combined pretensions of equity with realities of oligarchy could really strike a responsive chord
in Renaissance Italy. The oligarchic bent of contemporaries is made plain by
the promiscuous use of the term "democracy" to describe not only the thirteenth-century Florentine commune and the popular regime of the fourteenth
but also the much more narrowly restricted governments of the fifteenth and
sixteenth centuries. Of the ancient states, therefore, first republican Rome and
then Sparta appealed; of the modern states, Venice. Zera Fink rightly calls
attention to the role assigned to ancient models in the Renaissance oversimplification of class conflict and political life, pointing out that Machiavelli, for
example, had those exaggerated notions of the length of time mixed states
lasted without material alteration "which are a notable characteristic of the
theory of mixed polities in the period. Sparta, we are told, lasted eight hundred years 'in the most perfect tranquillity.' By seeming to provide actual examples, notions of this sort afforded powerful support to the idea that mixed
states attained a stability denied to other forms of government."[60] The rough
edges have been trimmed away; the narrow oligarchy that the Roman optimates were willing to destroy the republic in order to preserve and the domination of Spartiate over helot that many twentieth-century scholars have
viewed as a blight on all antiquity are lost in the Renaissance exaltation of the
governo misto, and the Athenians who were to be attacked in our own day for
their slave-holding and their imperialism appear in Renaissance writings only
as men who allowed altogether too much freedom to the untutored masses.
Behind the humanists' cry for civil government lay principally an opposition
to despotism; the government of Athens the humanists found very uncivil
indeed.

Comparatively little attention was paid to the Greek city-states as a whole
by the Florentines. With the exception of Bruni's *Commentary on Greek Affairs*—in essence a *precis* of Xenophon's *Hellenica*—no work of the Italian
Renaissance that has come my way deals in its entirety with Greek history as
so many writings did with Roman. Rather, Greek history was trotted out on an
anecdotal basis to demonstrate what to choose and what to avoid.[61] Never
studied earnestly for its own sake or on its own terms, it fell victim to the
oversimplifications of eager theorists who cried out for relevance like any
hard-nosed college student, and if the Athenians could not be held up as
models to emulate, at least they could be thrust forward as warnings for subversive egalitarians. The uses to which Greek history was put during the Italian
Renaissance reflects an ambivalence about the past that characterizes the age
as a whole. This ambivalence extended, *mutatis mutandis*, to other forms of
history as well and has made it possible for two distinguished North American

scholars to conclude within a couple of years of one another that, according to one (Paul Grendler), "the Italian reader accepted the Renaissance belief that history was useful to the active life because it taught political lessons," and according to another (Felix Gilbert), "in the Renaissance, knowledge of the past was not believed to be of primary significance" and "history was not highly esteemed."[62] Renaissance Italians were very hungry for history, but they were not hungry for very much of it.

.   .   .   .   .

The early Italian enthusiasm for the Athenian state that manifested itself in the first sproutings of Florentine humanism was neither profound nor carefully thought through. Though Corsi in his life of Ficino labels the Florence of Lorenzo as "the other Athens," his first observations liken the city to Rome under Augustus and Maecenas—surely a horse of a very different color. Gherardi da Prato, who waxed so eloquent about the "innumerable triumphs of the glorious Athenian people," nonetheless climaxes his account of Greek history with paeans to Demosthenes and to Macedon in virtually a single breath— certainly not a sign of a coherent political philosophy. And even Bruni, perhaps the greatest Italian Hellenist of his day, makes errors about Greek civilization, twice indeed confusing the world of Homer with that of classical Athens. A journey through Bruni's letters reveals a man who plainly viewed the Greeks as of far more peripheral interest than the Romans, who are— again and again—*nostri*.[63] As C. C. Bayley has observed, Bruni in his essay *De Militia* ascribes a line to Homer on the relative appropriateness of *taciturnitas* to males and females that actually derives from line 293 of Sophocles' *Ajax*. The citation presumably derives from Aristotle's *Politics*, where it is cited at 1.13.1260a: *gynaiki kosmon he sige pherei*, "a woman's silence adorns her."[64] Though Aristotle cites the author only as "the poet," still the meter should have made clear to Bruni that it could not be Homer. More strikingly still, in the *Praise of the City of Florence* Bruni maintains that one ought not to judge the law-abidingness of the Romans too harshly because of the corruption of Verres or the bravery of the Athenians too severely on account of the cowardice of—Thersites, the crude Achaean commoner who presumes to criticize Agamemnon in book 2 of the *Iliad*! The errors, I would suggest, arose from a combination of simple carelessness with a sentimental presupposition that somehow Greek and Athenian culture are synonymous. That Italians should have thought along these lines should occasion no surprise; even twentieth-century English speakers generally find that the study of Roman civilization and Latin literature demands less energy than that of Greek, if for no other reason than that Greek was written in an alien alphabet, and the distinction must have been far sharper for people born on the Italian peninsula and taught to speak a language derivative of Latin at their parents' knees. In sharing this

Roman orientation, at least, Bruni continued a tradition from earlier decades, when, for example, Domenico d'Arezzo had praised the Florentine Coluccio Salutati by asking:

> Who would blush to be thought inferior to you? Empedocles expressed himself in songs, Plato in dialogues, Socrates in hymns, Epicharmus in music, Xenophon in history, Xenocrates in satires. Or, *if these smack too strongly of antiquity or seem to be examples taken from foreign peoples and rusty with age, listen to these later ones of Roman origin* [italics mine]. Vergil was lacking in prose, and so was Ovid, while Livy, Valerius, and Cicero were destitute of poetry.[65]

For all the egalitarian rhetoric of the *Praise of the City of Florence*, moreover, it is his Florentine history that reveals Bruni's real political orientation. There, in the well-chosen words of Eric Cochrane written from a twentieth-century perspective, Bruni "consistently defined as the government of the people what was actually oligarchy of an increasingly small number of old, established families, and he showed not the slightest interest in the vast majority of the population."[66] Bruni is particularly unimaginative in his inability to see any substantive issues at stake in the rebellion led by the guild of the wool workers known as the Ciompi, whom he regards as beneath contempt: he cautions the Florentine patriciate to take the uprising as a warning never to let the masses have arms at their disposal or to have any opportunity to make trouble: for they cannot be held back from murder and confiscation once they have gotten a taste of power—nor, he maintains, "were there any controls on the unbridled wills of *poor and criminal individuals* [*hominum egentium et facinorosorum*; italics mine]."[67] The coupling of "the poor" with "criminals" is reminiscent, of course, of the Greek *kakos*, which, as we have seen in chapter 3, was regularly used to mean both "indigent" and "bad" in a world in which the stock figure of Thersites provided a living example of the conflation of poverty, ugliness, and warped thinking.

From the start, the Renaissance affinity for Athens—discernible primarily in Florence—was founded on sentiment and rhetoric, neither of which would withstand a sober consideration of anything that had actually transpired in the school of Hellas. When Athenian civilization was subjected to slightly more critical examination, it was found wanting; but a truly serious study of what had happened never took place. No lessons were drawn from the comparative cultural fertility of Athens and Sparta, and superficial similarities between Florence and Athens—cities of high culture, thriving commerce and imperialist proclivities—came to obscure the vital differences between the two cities and the essential stability of Athenian government. As Droysen has observed, the evidence can at best answer the questions that are put to it, and the focus of Renaissance thinkers on the stability of their own city-states led them to ask rather narrow questions of Greek history. As for Athens the school of Hellas, Patrizi maintained that the Spartans were commonly agreed in their day to be "the Preceptors of all the Greeks" as they were teachers of courage and military skills.[68] That Athens should have had to defend her title even as the school of all Greece is an index of how low her stock stood in Italy at the time of the Renaissance.

With the passing of time, ways of looking at Athenian democracy would multiply. But the anxieties of the Italian Renaissance would remain an important building block in the anti-Athenian tradition, as the topos of democratic instability came to eclipse that of democratic injustice to the well-to-do. Unflattering and ahistorical parallels between Florence and Athens became frequent in the works of Jean Bodin, whose thought enjoyed enormous prestige in early modern Europe, and the classical republicans of seventeenth-century England carried forward the happy association of Venice with Sparta. Deeply disturbed by the disorder in the Italian peninsula and more sensitive to the similarities that seemed to link them with antiquity than to the differences that set them apart, Renaissance writers set the stage for much facile and unhelpful thinking about classical Athens.

Chapter Seven

MONARCHISTS AND REPUBLICANS

> Athens and the other cities of Greece, when they had abandoned
> kings and concluded to live as it were in a commonalty which
> abusively they called equality, how long time did any of them con-
> tinue in peace? Yea what vacation had they from the wars, or what
> noble man had they which advanced the honour and weal of their
> city, whom they did not banish or slay in prison?
> —Thomas Elyot, *The Boke Named the Governour*

> No People upon Earth were more grateful to their good Citizens
> than the *Greeks* and *Romans* were, or encouraged Virtue more, or
> rewarded it better: Nor did they scarce ever banish any Man till he
> became terrible to them; and then it was Time. . . . It is better that
> one Man, however innocent, should suffer, than a whole People be
> ruined, or even hurt, if not by him, yet by his Example. . . . Even in
> *England*, the hanging of two or three Great Men among the many
> guilty, once in a Reign or two, would have prevented much Evil,
> and many Dangers and Oppressions, and saved
> this Nation many Millions.
> —Thomas Gordon and John Trenchard, *Cato's Letters*

AS THE DEBATE over the best form of government moved north, it
changed its shape to accommodate different social, economic, and
political conditions, and after 1519 it was necessary for it to accommodate a new religious diversity as well. The concerns that exercised northern
political scientists of the early modern era and led them to mine antiquity for
evidence to support their varied claims came to a head in the conflict between
monarchists and republicans in seventeenth-century England. In this clash
considerable violence was done to ancient history, as the developments of
antiquity were pulled this way and that to buttress all permutations and com-
binations of political argumentation. Beginning with the so-called Paper War,
moreover, classical examples were dredged up relentlessly for use as ammunition in the increasingly bitter party strife that marked the first third of the
eighteenth century as well.

ATHENIANS AND ELIZABETHANS

Britons paid little attention to classical Greece before the seventeenth century, and before the sixteenth even access to classical texts was limited.[1] The sixteenth-century Cambridge printer John Siberch was the first to use Greek type in England; the works he published included an edition of Galen's *De Temperamentis* by Thomas Linacre, who founded the College of Physicians in 1518 and had studied Greek in Italy under the eminent Chalcondyles. During his two and a half years in England between 1511 and 1514, Erasmus offered informal instruction in Greek, and in 1516 Bishop Fox in founding Corpus Christi College at Oxford provided for instruction in both Latin and Greek; in 1518 Wolsey founded a lectureship of Greek.

Around the same time, Thomas More, who not only learned Greek but saw to it that his daughters were instructed in it, incorporated Hellenic elements into both the structure and the vocabulary of his *Utopia*: his *phylarches*, each of whom presided over thirty families, were named after Athenian tribal officials, and the rotation of his *syphograuntes* in the council of the chief *phylarches* is reminiscent of the Athenian *boule*. The notion of rotation, however, may well have been derived from Venetian practice, and certainly the selection of a prince who served for life was eminently un-Athenian, as was the provision that all matters had to be debated for a full three days before being decided. Classical examples were rife in Thomas Elyot's 1531 *Boke Named the Governour*, in which the author advocated the study of Greek for even young children.[2] Elyot sees the best hope for good government in a properly educated prince surrounded by properly educated magistrates, and in chapter 2 of book 1, where he depicts the pitfalls of popular government, he portrays the Athenian state as a "monster with many heads," unstable and ungrateful.[3] Both Greece and Rome, he argues, were destroyed by the license and audacity of the encroaching masses; in Athens and the rest of Greece, popular government led to endless wars and frequent exiles and executions of worthy leaders.[4] (Florence and Genoa, he adds, suffered from similar problems.) Elyot refers the reader to Plutarch as a source for the unfortunate fates of Athenian statesmen, but he seems to have forgotten this lament in Chapter 14, where he encourages the study of the classics on the grounds that it may lead to "a public weal equivalent to the Greeks or Romans."[5] A different tack is taken by another monarchist, John Poynet, in his *Shorte Treatise of politike power and of the true Obedience which subiectes owe to kynges and other ciuile Gouernours* (1556). Poynet argues in his preface that all ancient governments, including those of the Greeks, the Romans, and—*mirabile dictu*—the Assyrians, were limited by the delusion that reason itself was a sufficient principle of government, as ancient peoples had not yet come to recognize that the one God who ruled all had prescribed for man "how he should behaue him self, what he should doo, and what he maye not doo." He goes on, however, to insist that in the people as a whole lay the power to supervise in some degree the government of the king.

In 1565 Elizabeth's minister Sir Thomas Smith completed his essay *De Republica Anglorum*, written, despite its title, in English and dotted from the start with Greek terminology—distinguishing, for example, between *politeia* on the one hand and, on the other, *Demokratia hapanton*, "the usurping of the popular or rascall and viler sort, because they be more in number."[6] Inevitably Athens is brought forth as an example.[7] By the middle of the sixteenth century, interest in things Hellenic had obtained a strong foothold in England, and Roger Ascham in his *Scholemaster* gives a vivid picture of the Greek studies of Elizabeth, whom he served as tutor both before and after her accession to the throne.[8] In 1600 the little-known Thomas Floyd produced his tract *The Picture of a perfit Common wealth, describing aswell the offices of Princes and inferiour Magistrates ouer their subiects, as also the duties of subiects toward their Gouernours.* Though the title page goes on to maintain that the work had been *Gathered forth of many Authors, aswel humane, as diuine, by Thomas Floyd, master in the Artes*, in fact the author's reading was anything but wide. The treatise is derived principally from Elyot's *Governour*, and the collection of parallel passages assembled by D. S. Starnes in 1931 demonstrates that the patterning was at times on the level of paraphrase.[9] Listing the three possible types of government, Floyd opts for monarchy; for the sins of democracy he cites Switzerland, Florence, and Athens, "in which Democratie aforesaid the seede of rashnes and laweless lust held the superioritie."[10] The "weatherlike vulgar," he warns, "are prone to admire every thing, & ready to turne as often as the tide. Wherefore they are rightly accounted to resemble the ugly Hydra, which is sayd, no sooner to lose one head, then immediatly another groweth. Herehence," he continues, concluding the familiar trope, "they are called the monsterous beast of many heads."[11] While the prudence of Lycurgus led Sparta to flourish over five hundred years, the democracy of Athens brought ruin on itself by condemning wise counselors like Solon and Phocion.[12]

In Tudor England, then, the bright flash of *Utopia* was followed by conventional treatments of governance that exalted monarchy as its best form and put Athens forward as proof of the wickedness of democracy. Elyot put his faith in the proper education of princes and magistrates, Poynet dismissed the possibility for sound government without acknowledgment of the one sovereign God, and Smith insisted that the bad character of the common man would ruin a democratic state in short order. In France, meanwhile, sixteenth-century political thought bore its richest fruit in the works of Jean Bodin, who affirmed that sovereignty was by its very nature indivisible and sought in his writings to counter "the rooted error of the mixed state."

Bodin broke new ground in the field of political science in his treatise entitled (with undue optimism) *The Method for the Easy Comprehension of History*, written in Latin and first published in 1566.[13] Indifferent to canonical texts of any variety, Bodin questioned the wisdom of Plato and Aristotle persistently, comfortably labeling many of their notions about government untenable and in some cases flatly absurd. He accepts, however, the classical schema (that he ascribes to Aristotle) of the three good forms of government and their three debased variants. The tyranny of one he labels the least pernicious of the debased forms; the tyranny of oligarchy ranks second; and "worst, finally, is that dominion of the mob, released from all law, which the Greeks called ochlocracy."[14] Popular government, he complains, would not even merit the slightest discussion were it not for the fact that it was supported by numerous writers, including Machiavelli, who, he maintains, thought it was the best of all forms of government. He goes on to remark upon the ambivalence in Machiavelli we have already observed in chapter 6.[15] Though he cites classical authors regularly to bolster his arguments, Bodin reflects distress at the excessive dependence on the ancients that he discerned in other writers, who, he complains, fail to understand that "it is necessary to show by reason why anything is so, not by authority."[16]

Bodin takes a dim view of all ancient republican governments, insisting that not only Athens but Rome as well was ruined by democracy, and he expresses particular concern about the trend toward popular government following great military victories. This phenomenon, he claims, can be seen in Athens, where the Athenians established popular government after the victory at Salamis but handed power over to "the four hundred optimates" after the defeat at Syracuse.[17] The reason for this contrast, Bodin claims, is obvious: the plebs, like an untamed beast, rejoice in prosperity and are suddenly cast down by adverse fortunes, while the "optimates," on the other hand, "who are nearer to the danger, take the helm as in a tempest." In a democracy each ambitious man buys the plebs with banquets and spectacles, and anyone who attempts to intervene meets an unfortunate fate, as did Aristides and Thucydides (the ostracized son of Melesias) at Athens.[18] (A later passage in the *Six Books* makes clear that Bodin conflated this Thucydides, the rival of Pericles, with Pericles' admirer Thucydides, the historian.[19]) Bodin also stresses the role of Aristides in extending political participation to Athens's lower classes, but he sees Pericles as the pivotal corrupter of the Athenians because of his curtailment of the powers of the Areopagus and his institution of state pay for public service.

Although the *Method* was reprinted several times during Bodin's lifetime, Bodin's work came to be known in England chiefly through his later *Six livres de la République,* with which British readers became familiar in its French and Latin versions and then, after 1606, through the English translation made by Richard Knolles from a text painstakingly conflated from the original French text of the 1570s and Bodin's own Latin version of 1586. In the *Six Books* (which somehow seem like more), Bodin plods across much of the ground already covered quite adequately in the *Method.*

Bodin had recurred frequently in the *Method* to the topos of the animal-like nature of the demos, portraying the Florentine plebs stampeding about like a shepherdless flock and comparing Florence under popular to a mindless body.[20] (The truth was that angry Florentines, unsure of their future in a chaotic and frustrating world, did sometimes stampede; angry Athenians, secure in their sovereignty, did not. Bodin, however, failed to make this distinction.) The topos of the demos as a wild animal needing to be tamed reappears in book 4 of the *Six Books,* where Bodin describes Pericles as using distributions of grain and money to tame "this beast with many heads, one while by the eyes, another while by the eares, and sometimes by the bellie," thereby making it possible to promulgate sound laws.[21] The whole panoply of nature is mobilized in Bodin's attempts to demonstrate the inadequacy of popular government, as metaphors are mixed pell-mell. Democratic peoples are compared to those in the grip of "a phrensie, which causeth them to skip and daunce without ceasing," and cannot be cured unless a skillful musician should "tune his instrument vnto their mad manner and fashion, to draw them vnto his owne . . . untill that they be so againe made more quiet and tractable"; in such a way the wise magistrate, seeing the people gone mad, should begin by accommodating himself "vnto their disordered appetite, that so he may afterwards by little and little induce them to hearken vnto reason: and so by yeelding at first vnto the tempest, at length put into the desired hauen." Controlling an angry multitude, he says, "is no other thing than as if a man should by maine strength seeke to stay the force and course of an headie streame, most violently falling from the high and steepe rockes."[22] And so on and on. Predictably, Bodin criticizes the choice of arithmetical equality over the geometrical or "harmonical."

Bodin maintains that it was because of the superiority of one-man rule that such states as Athens and Rome drove out their inadequate republican regimes and replaced them with monarchies.[23] He suggests, however, that some changes in government are due to the fickleness inherent in some national characters such as that of the Athenians, the Florentines, and the Swiss. This "phantasticall disease," he maintains, most commonly afflicts popular states, since there the subjects are "too wise and of too subtill spirits," everyone thinking he is worthy to command.[24] Parallels between Athens and Florence that work to the detriment of both are frequent in the *Six Books.* In book 4 Bodin compares the machinations of Savonarola with the parallel campaign of Ephialtes, accomplished "by the setting on of Pericles by his seditious orations."[25] The same parallels underlie his protracted discussion of democracy in book 6, chapter 4, a long purple passage that weaves together the standard themes of the Athenians' injustice to their leaders (Aristides, Themistocles, Miltiades), the martyrdom of Phocion, and the foundering of the leaderless ship of state, adducing authority upon authority.

Though an independent thinker in many respects, in his analogies between Florence and Athens Bodin followed the lead of Machiavelli, Guicciardini, and Giannotti (all of whom he cites), and his attacks on the evils of Athenian democracy are the conventional ones. His work came to be so influential in Britain during the period of the civil wars that during the first half of the seventeenth century no author was cited more frequently or more favorably. Between their first appearance in 1576 and the end of the seventeenth century, the *Six Books* appeared in twenty-two French editions, nine Latin editions, and Knolles's English edition of 1606.

Elizabeth Tudor died seven years after Bodin, and with her death came the fall of her friend Sir Walter Ralegh. Convinced that Ralegh had been opposed to his succession, James I had him seized and imprisoned, and before Ralegh was finally released in 1616 he had begun his multivolume *History of the World*. Whereas Bodin had been intrigued by psychology, geography, numerology, and other camp schemata for the ordering of human experience, Ralegh leaned instead to a moralistic orientation. The ancient Athenians earned his disapproval mightily, and though he blames both Athens and Sparta for drawing all their followers into a cruel war, the Spartans fare far better at Ralegh's hands than do the Athenians.[26] While the Spartans lived "Utopian-like," the "rascal multitude" in Athens were constantly incurring divine punishment for their insolency.[27] The military disaster in Egypt in the 450s was the Athenians' reward for their "vanity and indiscretion"; the defeat of the Sicilian expedition must not be ascribed to Athena or fortune but rather was the Athenians' deserved punishment for their wickedness in exiling the generals Pythodorus and Sophocles (not the playwright but another man by the same name) after their expedition to Sicily, for it was this decision that explained the extreme caution of Nicias a decade later. Though Ralegh concedes that Nicias should not have yielded to his fear of public opinion and was wrong to be so fearful of an eclipse that he could not fight, still the episode demonstrates that God, "who ordinarily works by a concatenation of means, deprives the governors of understanding when he intends evil to the multitude; and . . . the wickedness of unjust men is the ready mean to weaken the virtue of those who might have done them good."[28] The Thirty Tyrants, Ralegh contends, represented the gods' just retribution for the execution of the victors of Arginusae.[29]

The Fears of Hobbes

It was with this kind of heritage that British thinkers entered on the era of revolution. Predictably, classical topoi were trotted out by a variety of political theorists to buttress assorted arguments during this time of bitter division, and within half a century of the death of Elizabeth Tudor, Thomas Hobbes was to complain that there was nothing so provocative of sedition as the reading of classical texts.[30] The connection Hobbes draws between republicanism and the study of the classics is amusing in view of his own passion for the work of Thucydides, which he translated in the 1620s. Though his reasoning was different from Ralegh's, Hobbes came to equally disparaging conclusions about Athenian democracy; in his autobiography he reports that from his earliest acquaintance with the classics Thucydides had been his favorite subject because of Thucydides' contempt for democratic government. Hobbes makes his opinion of Athenian democracy clear in the introduction to his translation, where he wrote that in Athens

> such men only swayed the assemblies, and were esteemed wise and good common-wealth's men, as did put [the Athenians] upon the most dangerous and desperate enterprizes. Whereas he that gave them temperate and discreet advice, was thought a coward, or not to understand, or else to malign their power. . . . By this means it came to pass amongst the Athenians, who thought they were able to do anything, that wicked men and flatterers drave them headlong into those actions that were to ruin them; and the good men either durst not oppose, or if they did, undid themselves.

It was for these reasons, Hobbes maintained, that Thucydides sought to abstain from public life.[31]

If the study of ancient history had failed to make a republican of Hobbes, still more had it failed to make one of his contemporary Robert Filmer, whose theory of patriarchal monarchic supremacy Peter Laslett has labeled "the most refuted theory of politics in the [English] language."[32] Some of the most dramatic seventeenth-century appeals to ancient examples both positive (biblical) and negative (classical) came from this monarchist par excellence, the first draft of whose treatise *Patriarca* was penned in the late 1630s. The title of the work bespoke its thesis: according to Filmer, the establishment of Adam as sovereign of all creation betokened God's intention that sovereignty should be by its very nature in each and every case absolute and indivisible. (Filmer maintains in another essay that this thesis is not only supported by such thinkers as Grotius, Selden, Hobbes, and Ascham but indeed "evident and affirmed by Aristotle," whom one can only suppose he sees as being a superior authority on the subject of creation because of having lived closer to the event.[33] This orientation represents a dramatic throwback from the mentality Pocock identifies as evolving during the Renaissance, when, he contends, "Thought was approaching the . . . central discovery of the historical intellect that 'generations are equidistant from eternity'—that each of the phenomena of history existed in its own time, in its own right and in its own way."[34]) Drawing heavily on Bodin, Filmer managed to make laughable a thesis that in Bodin's hands had commanded considerable respect. Filmer's chapter headings give some indication of his view of democracy in general: 16, "Imperfections of Democracies"; 17, "Democracies not Invented to Bridle Tyrants, but Came in by Stealth"; 18, "Democracies vilified by their own historians"; and 19, "Popular Government more Bloody than a Tyranny." Under "Imperfections of Democracies," he points out that the most flourishing democracy the world had ever known, to wit, Rome [sic], had lasted a paltry 480 years, and states his preference for the stability of the 1200-year Assyrian monarchy.[35]

Hobbes and Filmer, then, though they read widely in classical texts, had no trouble resisting the seductions of classical republicanism. At the same time, the most radical of British dissidents, the egalitarian Levellers and Diggers, took no heed of the classics, grounding their call for the elimination of political privilege not in ancient precedent but in the self-evident rights of human beings to equality before the law. There was, however, a school of classical republicanism that seemed to bear out Hobbes's apprehensions about the study of the classics. Two writers of the 1650s, Marchamont Nedham, editor of the journals *Mercurius Britannicus* and *Mercurius Politicus*, and James Harrington, author of the Utopian *Oceana*, recurred periodically to classical *exempla* to fortify their arguments. (That their political sentiments had actually been inspired by classical reading seems unlikely, but it is easy to see how things might have looked to an anxious observer.) Although both Nedham and Harrington saw much virtue in Athenian government, however, they also saw much to reject.

Harrington's ideas about Athens are evident both in *Oceana*, which appeared in 1656, and in his other political tracts. In seeking to incorporate the best of all previously existing governments into his ideal Britain, Harrington gives Athens serious consideration, affording as it did an example of power divided between a large assembly and a rotating council selected by lot. Englishmen, he writes, will be horrified at the notion of a popular assembly, but they must understand that such an assembly is like the touchstone in a goldsmith's shop—dull in its own right, but essential to the workings of the whole.[36] Defending the Athenians' decision to ostracize Aristides, he sanctions the institution of ostracism as a matter of public security and, as on dozens of other occasions, cites Machiavelli approvingly, this time for his contention that popular governments are less ungrateful than princes.[37]

Still, Athens violated several of Harrington's cardinal principles for the proper mixed state, and ultimately he rejected the Athenian model, contending that Athens was lost through the want of a good aristocracy. How, he asks, can you compare mechanic commonwealths (i.e., commonwealths run by the ordinary man, such as Athens, Switzerland, and Holland) to Sparta, Rome, and Venice, "plumed with their aristocracies"? For "mechanics, until they have first feathered their nests—like the fowls of the air, whose sole employ-ment is to seek their food—are so busied in their private concernments that they have no leisure" to study politics and cannot safely be trusted with gov-ernment.[38] Drawing also upon the ship of state imagery found already in classi-cal authors, Harrington maintains that no man is faithfully embarked on this kind of ship unless he has a share in the freight. No, far better a government like Sparta or Venice, where a genuine aristocracy is balanced against an as-sembly that votes but assuredly does not debate. Citing the contention of Cicero in *Pro Flacco* that the Greek states were all undermined by the "intem-perance of their comitia," that is, assemblies of the people, Harrington insists that no commonwealth in which the people in their political capacity are talkative, will ever see half the days of Sparta or Venice, but rather "being carried away by vainglorious men (that, as Overbury says, piss more than they drink) [will] swim down the sink, as did Athens, the most prating of these dames, when that same ranting fellow Alcibiades fell on demagoguing for the Sicilian War."[39] As for foreign policy, he complains that Athenian aggression brought down Greek civilization, and this development he sets up as a warn-ing to his contemporaries: the Athenians "brought their confederates under bondage; by which means Athens gave occasion of the Peloponnesian War, the wound of which she died stinking, when Lacedaemon, taking the same infection from her carcass, soon followed. Wherefore my lords," Harrington exhorts his readers, "let these be warnings to you not to make that liberty which God hath given you a snare to others in using this kind of enlargement of yourselves."[40]

Harrington, then, though dogged in his determination to convert his reluc-tant countrymen to the cause of popular assemblies, saw the existence of a continuing aristocracy as essential to the stability of government, and so, de-spite much promise, Athens offered primarily a negative example to the archi-tect of *Oceana*. Other seventeenth-century republicans, however, viewed things differently. Nedham in his pointedly titled study of *The Excellencie of a Free State* expressed a view of Athens far rosier at most points than that of Harrington, and although he seems to have admired an Athens that never existed, the Athens he condemned at certain junctures had not existed either.

It is Nedham's purpose to demonstrate to the divided English the superior-ity of government by free election and popular consent.[41] He finds Solon's determination to concentrate power in the hands of the assembly entirely praiseworthy and proclaims that Solon has been recognized by all posterity as having left the only workable pattern for a free state to follow. Bringing for-ward Machiavelli and Guicciardini as exponents of free states, he notes the amazing rise of Athens after the expulsion of Peisistratus. He plays on the terror that the Levellers had struck in the hearts of the British establishment and pleads earnestly that "kings and all standing powers are the levellers," citing the example of Louis XI and his successors in France ("the greatest levellers in Christendom"). Warning that the same thing has been happening in England as "kings began to worm the people out of their share in government, by discontinuing of parliaments," he also cites the example of Athenian "levellers"—not the people meeting in their assemblies, but rather the Thirty Tyrants of 404/3, "which were a sort of levellers more rank than all the rest."[42]

Nedham repeatedly extols the Athenian system of rigorous accountability.[43] Though some, he notes, have censured free states for impeaching their statesmen so frequently, Nedham inclines rather to the view of those who argue that such vigilance is the mark of a healthy and vigorous state. What provoked the impeachments of such men as Alcibiades, Themistocles, Phocion, and Miltiades, Nedham asserts, was "their own lofty and unwary carriage," an interpretation he claims originated with Plutarch.[44] Though he waxes eloquent about the glories of Athens when the machinery of democracy was well lubricated and running smoothly, Nedham's account of Athens's less shining moments is incoherent and puzzling. Mentioning few names or dates, he compares the brief rule of the Thirty Tyrants with the long ascendancy of Peisistratus. Repeated references to the government of the Thirty treat it not as a short-lived accident of circumstance but rather as a predictable development of Athens's rise to power. Athens, Nedham maintains,

> whilst it remained free in the people's hands, was adorned with such governors as gave themselves up to a serious, abstemious, severe course of life; so that whilst Temperance and Liberty walked hand in hand, they improved the points of valour and prudence so high, that in a short time they became the only arbitrators of all affairs in Greece. But being at the height, then (after the common fate of all worldly powers), they began to decline . . . [and] permitting some men to greaten themselves by continuing long in power and authority, they soon lost their pure principles of severity and liberty: for, up started those thirty grandees. . . . Such also was the condition of that state, when at another time (as in the days of Peisistratus) it was usurp'd in the hands of a single tyrant.[45]

The Athenians, he maintains later on, "lost their liberty when they suffered certain of the senators to over-top the rest in power; which occasioned that multiplied tyranny, made famous by the name of the thirty tyrants: at another time, when by the same error they were constrained, through the power of Peisistratus, to stoop until his single tyranny."[46]

What is meant here? Who are the "senators" of Athens? Who are these "governors" who "gave themselves up to a serious, abstemious, severe course of life"? Aristides, perhaps, but surely not Themistocles or Cimon. Pericles, possibly, who cut himself off from social life on his accession to power—but who other than Pericles can be meant by men permitted "to greaten themselves, by continuing long in power and authority"? When was this glorious era? Athenian impeachments are defended as early as Themistocles and as late as Phocion. It was the era of Ephialtes and Pericles that was most associated with the auditing of Areopagites, a system that Nedham praises, but this era was also the age of Athens's greatest expansion, which he cites as the natural cause of its decline. Was decline the inevitable result of expansion, or of Athens's allotting undue influence to powerful individuals? Which individuals? The loss of the war and the problems of the fourth century have often been ascirbed to the Athenians' failure to secure continuous leadership after Pericles' death; for Nedham, the opposite seems to be true. Nedham, it would seem, sought, like Plutarch in his life of Pericles, to integrate two different traditions, the slender strand of the glories of freedom derived from Sallust (cited in the introduction) and Machiavelli, and the thicker and more venerable strand of the collapse of democracy found in the bulk of the sources. Though Nedham insists that Athens fell not because of the intrinsic weaknesses of democracy but rather as a result of departures from the democratic system, allotting too much power to ambitious individuals, his account of when and how this took place is too incoherent to carry much weight. It is striking, however, that the attempt should have been made.

Nedham also included in his collection of editorials an essay on the theme "The Originall of All Just Power is in the People," in which he attempts to refute Filmer's patriarchalism by references not only to modern history but to the Old Testament as well. A quarter-century later *Patriarca* was reprinted with dramatic consequences. Its reappearance set in motion a chain of events that eventually led the republican Algernon Sidney to the scaffold on 7 December 1683. For Sidney was moved to such an impassioned assault on Filmer's simplistic constructions that he found himself accused of disloyalty to the crown.

Sidney's opening attack on Filmer makes clear his apoplectic exasperation with the patriarchal school of thought: "I have been sometimes apt to wonder," he writes, "how things of this nature could enter into the head of any man; or if no wickedness or folly be so great, but some may fall into it," he goes on in bewilderment, "I could not well conceive why they should publish it to the world."[47] Agreeing with Harrington that mixed governments are best, Sidney nonetheless maintained that Athens was just such a government, with its archons, its assembly, and its Areopagite council, whose fall in the mid–fifth-century he ignores. Sidney accuses Filmer of abusing the ancient sources in his attack on Athens and claims that he has "abominably prevaricated, and advanced things he knows to be either impertinent or false."[48] Xenophon, he argues (i.e., pseudo-Xenophon), was criticizing democracy not in contrast to Filmer's beloved monarchy, which did not exist in Greece, but rather in contrast to aristocracy.[49] Sidney defends ostracism, maintaining that it entailed no

hurt or dishonor, and though he concedes that some were put to death unjustly, he argues—ironically, in view of his fate—that Socrates, for example,
died because the people were deceived by false witnesses, against whom neither the laws of God nor those of man have ever prescribed a sufficient defense.[50] In any event, he insists, there must be remedies against unjust magistrates who place themselves above the law. This, he stresses, is needed in
England, and he cautions his readers to remember that Parliament derives its
power from the people.[51]

For shame or glory, then, the name of Athens was put forward by seventeenth-century writers on the British constitution caught up in the debate
between monarchists and republicans. For all his jeremiads about the anti-
monarchic bias instilled in readers of classical history, Hobbes found the study
of the ancient world to support his monarchic views. To the single-minded
Filmer, Athens was an unremitting evil; for the hardheaded Harrington, it was
a model from which only selected elements could be extracted with profit; for
Nedham and the ill-fated Sidney, it was an inspiration, as it was to John
Milton, who named his *Areopagitica* after its Areopagite council and spoke
warmly in *Paradise Regained* of the school of Hellas and even of the fulminating orators whose "resistless eloquence / Wielded at will that fierce Democraty."[52]

Thus far political theory. During the first third of the eighteenth century,
exempla from Greek history were dredged up to support agendas that were
increasingly partisan and personal. Although Rome claimed the lion's share of
attention, Athenian history was also harvested for what fruit it might bear.
The use of ancient history to score points in contemporary politics is particularly evident in the diatribes that capped the so-called Paper War of the turn
of the century and in the opposition journals that hounded Walpole in the
1720s and 1730s.

ATHENS AND ACCOUNTABILITY

Bitter partisan conflict gripped England at the end of the seventeenth century,
with Whigs and Tories at each other's throats and engaged to boot in strange
role reversals, as Tories insisted on the primacy of Parliament and Whigs not
only undermined the House of Commons but defended the divine right of
kings in the bargain. By 1699 it became clear that the Tories intended to
impeach several Whig ministers. In November, the Tory Charles Davenant
published his massive *Discourse upon Grants and Resumptions*, a tome of over
four hundred pages devoted to searching out parliamentary precedents for impeaching ministers who had procured for themselves grants of crown estates.
Conveniently, the beleaguered Whig ministers were suspected of having secured forfeited crown lands for themselves in Ireland. The search for ancient

precedents for impeachment did not come until somewhat later, but when it did, it engaged several minds quite intensely.

By the end of 1701 the impeachments had fizzled, leaving a considerable residue of rage on both sides. It was during that summer that Jonathan Swift decided to make a name for himself by utilizing ancient history to demonstrate the evils of impeachment in his *Discourse of the Contests and Dissentions Between the Nobles and the Commons in Athens and Rome with the Consequences they had upon both those States.*[53] In this elaborate allegory, the ministers under attack—Edward Russell, John Summers, Charles Montagu, and William Bentinck—appeared as Miltiades, Themistocles, Aristides, Pericles, Alcibiades, and Phocion. Four does not equal six, and Swift is careful not to make the correspondences too neat; Sir Walter Scott in his edition of Swift's works saw both Miltiades and Themistocles as representing Edward Russell and Montagu as indicated by both Pericles and Alcibiades, whereas Frank Ellis, the twentieth-century editor of the *Discourse*, sees both Russell and Montagu in Alcibiades.[54] Swift portrays all charges against the impeached Athenian statesmen as false or trivial. These impeachments did no good to anyone, he argues; rather, through them the most powerful state in Greece was "utterly destroyed by that rash, jealous, and inconstant humour of the people, which was never satisfied to see a General either Victorious or Unfortunate." The power of the Athenian people, he claims, "was the rankest Encroachment imaginable, and the grossest Degeneracy from the Form that Solon left them. In short, their Government was grown into a *Dominatio plebis*, or Tyranny of the People, who by degrees had broke and overthrown the Balance which that Legislator had very well fixed and provided for."[55] Similar arguments are made about Rome. Just such evils may fall upon his countrymen, Swift maintains, if they place too much power in popular bodies.[56]

Swift was answered in several works. In 1702 James Drake published his *History of the Last Parliament*, in which he upheld the value of impeachment in preserving liberty in both Greece and Rome.[57] Arguing that the Athenians' watchfulness afforded their state vital security, he discusses some specific cases "because of a fancy'd Similitude" that some of his contemporaries believe they have identified in the political conflicts of their own day—though, Drake maintains with mock bewilderment, he himself "can't yet discover wherein lies the parallel."[58] Themistocles, he claims, was unduly ambitious. Aristides sought to gather too much of the administration of justice into his own hands. Phocion had gone over to Macedon. Profligate in spending public money, Pericles pursued preferment and grandeur by intrigue; knowing the fondness of the Athenians for pomp, he entertained them with plays and "descended to Court the Common People" (those same common people whose political wisdom Drake defends). On balance, Drake argues, the responsibility for frequent impeachments lay not with the Athenian people but with the misconduct of their politicians whose harsh fates he ascribes to their own "Immoderate Ambitions."[59] If Athenian tribunals were this fair, Drake concludes triumphantly, English ones can be expected to be fairer still.[60] In the following year the anonymous author of *The Source of Our Present Fears Discovered* also responded to Swift's discourse, which he believed to have been written by the controversial Bishop Gilbert Burnet.[61] (Burnet apparently had to disown the discourse publicly in order to avoid being impeached in the House of Commons himself.) "Burnet," the author complains, lays "the gret Body of our Legislators upon an unmannerly level, with the Mob of Athens and Rome," and advocates for England "the most Arbitrary Despotick Government in the World."[62] The author characterizes Swift's discussion of the few versus the many as one of the "Learned Fits" of a man who "rakes up all the Enormities that he can find in the ancient Roman and Greek Histories, to have been committed by any number of Confederated Usurpers, and endeavours by Application, to draw an odious Parallel between those Usurpers and our House of Commons."[63] Frustrated by the turn the government was taking, he writes, the Athenians established the Council of Four Hundred, and when that did not work, they dissolved it again. This flexibility the author compares happily to that of English Kings in putting the treasury into commission instead of creating a Lord Treasurer, and reverting to the original system when the new one proved inadequate.[64]

The habit of using ancient history to illustrate the proper relationship of a people to its ministers subsided briefly after the accession of Queen Anne, but it returned in the flurry of opposition that hounded Sir Robert Walpole in the 1720s and 1730s.[65] It was in 1719 that Sir John Trenchard and his protégé Thomas Gordon published *The Character of an Independent Whig*, in which they articulated the general outlines of their political philosophy, one that entailed—in addition to strong opposition about standing armies and the status of Protestant dissenters—a fierce commitment to accountability in government.[66] Beginning in January 1720, *The Independent Whig* began to appear weekly, and later that year a series of letters composed chiefly by Trenchard and Gordon first made their appearance in *The London Journal* under the name of "Cato," idolized in the pages of the *Journal* as a republican martyr who chose death rather than accept autocratic rule at Rome:

> How bright the shining Patriot stands confest.
> Great Cato's soul informs his generous breast!
> 'Gainst power usurp'd, he points his God-like Rage,
> And deals out Freedom to a future Age.[67]

The letters made plain the apprehension with which many Englishmen responded to the increased concentration of power in the hands of one minister—not an entirely unprecedented development, but nonetheless cause for alarm. In addition to more general concerns about lack of accountability, "Cato" and his associates considered the Walpole ministry venal and corrupt.

"Cato" was intensely concerned with virtue in public life, the importance of unfettered free speech, and accountability in government, all of which he derived from the blessings of liberty. So intense and unrelenting was the attack by "Cato" on corruption in government that within three years Walpole had staged a takeover of the *Journal*, and the voice of "Cato" was not heard there again.

The letters continued to be published, however, and although their title makes clear the Roman bias of *Cato's Letters*, still Athenian *exempla* pop up from time to time. The purpose of these examples was principally to demonstrate the dangers of runaway ministers and the need to hold public men accountable. Because of the dangers posed to the state by bad ministers (like Pericles, who "lavished away the publick Money, to buy Creatures" and brought on the Peloponnesian War to divert the Athenians' attention from his peculation), Trenchard and Gordon defend vehemently the machinery of accountability in classical Athens.[68] Loud echoes of Machiavelli are audible in the letters of March 1722 bearing the rubric "Free States vindicated from the common Imputation of Ingratitude."[69] In reality, the letters argue, this frequent accusation is false, as free states are considerably more grateful than "arbitrary princes."[70] The source of conflict between a people and its ministers, they maintain, is the common tendency of ambitious politicians to overrate their own merits and consequently the adulation to which they feel entitled. When the people refuse to become slaves to their own servants and presume to distinguish protection from oppression, they are tagged as ungrateful.[71] In this vein, the authors defend the impeachment of Alcibiades.[72]

Thus far the letter of 2 March; the 9 March epistle begins with the assertion that "no People upon Earth were more grateful to their good Citizens than the *Greeks* and *Romans* were, or encouraged Virtue more, or rewarded it better: Nor did they scarce ever banish any Man till he became terrible to them; and then it was Time."[73] "Cato" goes on to enumerate the honors the Athenians lavished upon their leaders and to uphold the utility of ostracism, contending that it was acceptable for an occasional innocent man to suffer if his example might prevent an entire people from being ruined "if not by him, yet by his Example." The periodic hanging of two or three great men in England, they contend, "would have prevented much Evil, and many Dangers and Oppressions, and saved this Nation many Millions."[74]

In the preface to the collection entitled *Cato's Letters*, Gordon insisted with an air of injured innocence that no analogues to contemporary history were intended in the epistles. "In answer to those deep Politicians, who have been puzzled to know who were meant by *Cicero* and *Brutus*," Gordon wrote, "I assure them, that *Cicero* and *Brutus* were meant; that I know no present Characters or Story that will fit theirs; that these Letters were translated for the Service of Liberty in General; and that neither Reproof nor Praise was intended by them to any Man living. . . . There was nothing in those letters analogous to our Affairs."[75] These earnest disclaimers notwithstanding, it was clear to all readers of "Cato" that the authors had followed the line of attack proposed by Swift in 1710, when he had recommended an "expedient, frequently practised with great safety and success by satirical writers: which is, that of looking into history for some character bearing a resemblance to the person we would describe"; and, he adds, "with the absolute power of altering, adding or suppressing what circumstances we please, I conceive we must have very bad luck, or very little skill to fail."[76] The same strategy was adopted by the authors of the *Craftsman*, founded in December 1726 by Bolingbroke and his confederates with the purpose of undermining Walpole's ministry at every turn.

The first issue seems to have been supervised by one Nicholas Amherst, described by a contemporary as "full of Latin and Greek and fuller of himself than of either."[77] Throughout its history the journal was to employ classical *exempla* as a principal means of attacking Walpole and his government. The issue of 17 February 1727 was devoted to the evils of popularity attained by unjust means, and the example of classical government is brought forward in defense of rigorous and vigilant scrutiny of public officials. Consistent with the political orientation they shared with "Cato," the authors portray the people as honest and honorable, wishing only to be left in peace, encumbered with as few taxes as possible, but by virtue of their very good nature "liable to be imposed upon by false Shews, and artful Pretences." Popularity, therefore, is not necessarily to be regarded as a badge of patriotism, as it is all too often attained by sinister methods for pernicious purposes. It was in accord with this principle, the authors argue, that in the best-constituted governments of antiquity, it was made a crime "to affect uncommon *Popularity*," and it is for this reason that ancient history affords so many examples of outstanding patriots who were banished solely for rendering themselves unduly loved. The *Craftsman* is well aware that the ancient states have often been reproached for this habit—clearly Athenian ostracism is intended—but the authors find the conduct of antiquity prudent and praiseworthy in this regard, for these governments, they argue, judged rightly of human nature, knowing how "*Popularity* is apt to turn the wisest Heads, and corrupt the purest Hearts."[78]

The authors involved in the invective of the *Craftsman*—whose printer Walpole went so far as to have arrested—identified with Demosthenes and complained of "those modern, Philippick Statesmen, who have endeavoured to destroy the Liberty of the Press."[79] Most of all, however, they identified with the Athenian poets and comic dramatists, whom they billed repeatedly as the ancient equivalent of the free press, and they saw in the Athenians' joyous reception of jests upon their statesmen the hallmark of a free and vital people. Although the theme is touched upon in a variety of essays, it is developed most fully in a piece published in August 1730 consisting primarily of protracted citations from a recent work by the eccentric malcontent and future suicide Eustace Budgell. At Athens, Budgell had written, a bad minister "was sure to be mawled by the Wits and Poets . . . and his *Vices* and *Blunders* expos'd upon the publick Stage." So far from participating in the traditional outcry against the ingratitude of the Athenians, Budgell rejoiced that in Athens, "tho' a Man had done his Country the most important Service, his *Vices* or *ill Actions* were not spared," and he cites with approval both the fate of Themistocles and the revilement of Cleon and Alcibiades by the comic dramatists. The bulk of the argument, however, concerns the attacks of the poets and comedians on the arbitrary and profligate administration of Pericles. Citing the verses of Teleclides, Cratinus, Hermippus, and others, Budgell concludes with satisfaction that for all Pericles' tyranny, the one liberty of which he dared not deprive the Athenians was freedom of speech; for all his autocracy, "he never durst proceed to the last Degree of Tyranny, and attempt the laying a Restraint upon their *Pens.*"[80] The sins of Pericles provide a frequent theme for the writers of the *Craftsman*, and the message of their attacks is clear: for "Pericles," read "Walpole."

The grounds of the attack on Pericles are several: he undermined the venerable Council of the Areopagus because he was ineligible for admission, not having served as archon; he contradicted himself in the assembly in order to remain on the popular side of any issue; he regularly betrayed his friends; but, most of all, he was venal and corrupt, and the bulk of the allegations against him concern money in some way, shape, or form. The *Craftsman* was not alone in alleging that Walpole misused funds regularly, and additional suspicion attached to anyone involved in the disastrous South Sea Company debacle. Though Walpole had originally opposed the government's financial dealings with the South Sea Company and had worked with discretion and diplomacy to control the damage when the stock crashed, he himself had profited handsomely from South Sea stock, selling out the shares he had bought in 1720 at a profit of 1,000 percent. With this sum he began amassing his famous art collection at his estate at Houghton, and in November of 1730 the *Craftsman* claimed that the housekeeping bills at Houghton amounted to £1,500 a week. The *Craftsman* viewed Pericles as Walpole's administrative ancestor. Pericles' "licentious Distribution of *Bribes* and *Bounties* amongst the People" (i.e., state pay for state service) introduced luxury to all ranks and made even members of the most distinguished families unashamed to become his "known Pensioners." To bolster Athens's position abroad, the authors argue, Pericles had recourse to similar strategems and "back'd all his foreign Transactions with the Offers of a round Sum of Money." Taking advantage of the confusion surrounding diplomatic negotiations between Athens and Sparta and their various allies in the 430s to "fleece the People," Pericles ultimately pushed through "a Proposal for allowing Him *ten Talents* for *Secret-Service-Money,*" an act that constituted "a publick Sanction to *Corruption.*" Their chronology leaving something to be desired, the authors go on to complain that Pericles next confiscated the treasury at Delos. Any attempt to appoint overseers to examine Pericles' books, they maintain, "was opposed with the old Cant of distrusting so *virtuous an Administration.*" (For "old," read "new.") Finally, to deflect any possible further attempts at holding him accountable for the vast sums he was spending, Pericles brought on the Peloponnesian War. Thus, the authors conclude, the corrupt ambition of a single man ruined the most flourishing state in the world; and history provides numerous examples to demonstrate that parallel conduct will produce the same consequences "in all Ages and all Nations." But though Pericles in their view ultimately destroyed Athens, the authors are quick to point out the valiant efforts made to save her by the poets and comedians, who "endeavour'd to open the Eyes of their Countrymen, and animate Them against *Pericles*, by exposing his Conduct in satirical Poems and Invectives."[81]

. . . . .

The pious preference for a just monarchy that characterized Elizabethans who took time to write about Greek government encouraged a view of Athens that stressed the vulgarity and volatility of the Athenian demos, and in France at the same time the influential Bodin condemned the Athenian state on precisely the same grounds. For Bodin, as for Thomas Floyd, the demos, whether in Florence or Athens, was a beast with many heads, beyond the reach of justice or reason. Where Italians rejected Athens in favor of a stable mixed polity, on the whole English and French intellectuals rejected it in favor of monarchy. Morality and religion also affected British thinking about Athens: Poynet discounted the Athenians as heathens. Religion would play a role in shaping seventeenth-century attitudes as well, for Filmer insisted that God intended for kings to rule and to rule absolutely.

Though Filmer certainly resisted the seductions of the classical republicanism that so exercised Hobbes, others did not, and the ideals of mixed government that had been so cherished by Italians searching for stability produced a more open exploration of the Athenian system in seventeenth-century England. By and large rejected by Harrington, Athens was put forward as a positive example by Nedham, who heaped adulation on an Athens that had no more reality than the vulgar hydra of Floyd and Bodin, and by Sidney, who ignored the demotion of the Council of the Areopagus and looked ahead to the concerns of the next generation in his praise of the Athenian system of accountability. The use of classical *exempla* by Swift and others in the furor over the abortive impeachment of the Whig ministers at the turn of the century continued the pattern of writing about Greek history solely for the purpose of illuminating contemporary problems. No narrative histories of Greece appeared before 1729, when the French schoolmaster Charles Rollin published his *Ancient History*; the Englishman Temple Stanyan produced his history of Greece shortly afterward. But the first decades of the century saw Greek history relegated to the status of ammunition in political debates.

These debates, however, called forth considerable creativity and imagination in the use of Athenian models.[82] Through attacks on Pericles, first the *London Journal* and then the *Craftsman* not only lambasted what they saw as the venal and corrupt government of Walpole but also affirmed the merits of the Athenian political system. So far from viewing the purported excesses of Pericles as rooted in the Athenian ethos, the opposition journals saw in them the proof that the vigilant suspicion with which the Athenians regarded their statesmen was in fact warranted, and in it they saw a constructive model for modern Britain. And not only that: the careers of men like Pericles validated their belief in the crying need for a press that was both sleepless and ruthless. It is impossible to know whether Hobbes was correct in viewing ancient texts as breeding grounds for sedition; what is clear is that classical history could be used to advantage in the lively and sometimes bitter disputes that racked Britain from the beginning of the Stuart era. Though it continued be to be conducted with more petulance and stridency than twentieth-century readers are likely to associate with intellectual integrity, the debate over Athens that began in cliché at the dawn of classical studies in Britain early in the sixteenth century turned by the end of the seventeenth into a forum for vibrant and vigorous political discussion.

Chapter Eight

THE DEBATE OVER ATHENS AND SPARTA

> Can I forget that it was in the very lap of Greece that was seen to
> arise the City equally famed for its happy ignorance and for the
> wisdom of its Laws, that Republic of demi-Gods rather than of
> men, so much superior to humanity did their virtues appear?
> O Sparta! eternal shame to vain teaching!
> —Jean-Jacques Rousseau, *First Discourse*

I N THE SEVENTEENTH and early eighteenth centuries Athens provided a heartening model to many English republicans seeking instructive
analogues for increasing the accountability and moral tone of government
in their own day. Writers who did not share these concerns, however, generally found Athenian democracy distasteful. Though the study of antiquity was
frequently dragged down by insipid moralizing, interest in classical politics and
history intensified during the Enlightenment era. At the same time, however,
the appearance for the first time of narrative histories of Greece nurtured a
view of Athens that conceived its history as an unbroken line leading to the
defeat at Chaeronea. In both Europe and America, eighteenth-century writing
about the ancient world was frequently motivated by the desire to isolate the
cause of classical civilization's collapse so as to protect modern civilization
from a similar fate, and the tone of this inquiry was generally more anxious
than analytical.

The bulk of what was written about Athens in the eighteenth century was
produced in England and France. Whereas the work of English writers working after 1735 rarely rose from the level of cliché, French thinkers were significantly more imaginative.[1] Though the French must be credited with some of
the most tedious examples of sententious anti-Athenian moralizing, during
the second half of the century the work of French social scientists offered a
variety of new perspectives on Greek history. French views of Athens during
the later eighteenth century varied considerably from one author to the next,
and this diversity points to a level of ferment that was productive and promising of more serious intellectual work yet to come.

Although to some degree the history of Greece continued to serve as a field
to be mined for convenient object lessons easily transplantable from one culture to another, now in the eighteenth century it began if not to be valued in
its own right then at least to be examined more closely than had been the case

in earlier eras. To be sure, Rome continued to claim the lion's share of attention. Arnaldo Momigliano in his essay "Ancient History and the Antiquarian" has assembled a bibliography of over thirty eighteenth-century studies of Italy during the pre-Roman period alone.[2] Though Roman beginnings excited a certain antiquarian interest, however, it was ultimately the fall of Rome that gripped the eighteenth-century imagination. In 1734 Montesquieu brought out his *Considerations on the Greatness and the Decadence of the Romans*, and it was on 15 October 1764 that it first entered the head of Edward Gibbon, as he sat musing among the ruins of the Capitol, to write the work that would immortalize his name.

Greek history was never to unseat Roman as the predominant field of ancient historical study, either in the eighteenth century or in any other. Still, the study of Greece began nosing forward shortly after 1700 as at least a respectable contender for scholars' attention. Already in 1697 as Échard was bringing his *Roman History* down to the time of Augustus, Potter was compiling his ponderous *Greek Antiquities*, which were to serve as a common source for Greek history on both sides of the Atlantic. At the same time Bayle was wrangling zestfully with ancient and modern sources in the production of the impressive Greek entries in his *Dictionnaire*. Shortly afterward, Temple Stanyan produced his *Grecian History*, and by the time he completed the work in the 1740s he was able to draw on the detailed *Ancient History* composed by the schoolmaster Charles Rollin in France. Undertaken when Rollin was himself fairly ancient, his history appeared in 1729 with an imprimatur advertising its utility in the "improvement of young minds." How effectively it served this end is uncertain; there was wisdom in Stanyan's observation that Rollin's reflections, "tho they are generally just, are too frequent and too tedious, too trite and obvious, and too juvenile."[3]

In 1774, Oliver Goldsmith brought out his own history of Greece. It would be an understatement to say that Goldsmith drew deeply on the writings of Rollin and Stanyan; had the three authors published during the twentieth century, Goldsmith and his publishers would have been haled into court in short order. Still, the appearance of the work betokened a continuing interest in Greek antiquity. Meanwhile in France, the quasi-socialist Gabriel Bonnot de Mably published his *Observations on the Greeks* in 1749, two years before his *Observations on the Romans*, and his sententious *Conversations of Phocion, Concerning the Connection between Government and Morality* appeared in 1763. Mably's writings were to have considerable influence on the French revolutionaries and on the American colonists, about whom he would later write his *Observations on the Government and Laws of the United States of America*. On the very eve of the revolution appeared Barthélemy's *Travels of Anacharsis the Younger in Greece*, a historical novel in many volumes that served as a vehicle for extended commentary on Greek civilization, and De Pauw's *Philosophical*

Researches on the Greeks. Greek history also claimed the attention of eighteenth-century luminaries such as Condillac and Rousseau in France, Burke and Montagu in England, and Hume and Ferguson in Scotland, as well as a host of less familiar figures.

DEMOCRACY AND DECADENCE

The anti-Athenian tradition that characterized the first half of the eighteenth century was tiresome and monotonous. Allegations of the natural giddiness of the Athenians and their relentless fickleness and ingratitude continued to tumble pell-mell off the pen as one writer after another offered loose paraphrases of the strictures of classical thinkers, most particularly Plutarch, who enjoyed a popularity matched by no other author.[4] (In eighteenth-century America the only volume in more homes than Plutarch was the Bible.) Decade after decade, eager moralists wrung minor variations on a handful of favorite themes. Some of these topoi, such as the superiority of Lycurgus to Solon, were concerned with early Athenian history and the origins of the democracy, but most focused on the decline of the city throughout the course of the fifth and fourth centuries—the evils of Athenian imperialism; the disgraceful undermining of the Council of the Areopagus; the corruption of the Athenian demos by Pericles' bribery of the masses with jobs, spectacles, and pay for state service; the shamelessness of the demagogues who succeeded Pericles and the licentiousness of the people; the sorry state of fourth-century Athens (as of fourth-century Greece as a whole, where even Sparta had begun to decline from its pristine valor); and, uniting all these separate strands, the ill effects of luxury and its attendant vice, effeminacy. At times the virtues of Sparta are cited to set off the vices of the Athenians; on other occasions Athens is accused of having dragged down even noble Sparta in her train.[5]

Crusading journalists aside, eighteenth-century writers generally took a dim view of the evolution of the Athenian constitution and the attendant march of democracy. According to Stanyan, though Solon in his wisdom had created the Council of Four Hundred as a check on the "giddy unthinking multitude," still the difference between the laws of Lycurgus and those of Solon was "easily accounted for, from the Temper of the Athenians, which was too delicate, and capricious to be brought to those grave and regular Austerities."[6] Stanyan would not be the only writer of his day to associate the weaknesses of Athenian government with those of the national character. Goldsmith found Solon's laws "neither so striking nor yet so well authorized as those of Lycurgus."[7] The real villain of Athenian democracy, however, was generally taken by eighteenth-century writers to be Pericles, and those who were not English crusaders for accountability found him to be not only the perverter of the democratic system but its creature as well. The fiery Josiah Tucker, whose

1781 *Treatise Concerning Civil Government* was inspired in part by revulsion for the revolution in America, offers an interesting contrast to the views of the earlier republican pamphleteers. Pericles, he maintained, though "the Idol of the Athenians," nonetheless "laid the foundation of their Ruin, and deserved Banishment an hundred Times"—and he adds in a footnote that the instance of Walpole demonstrates that popularity need not correlate with worth; for Walpole, he writes, though one of the most unpopular statesmen in England, was "the best commercial Minister this country ever had, and the greatest Promoter of its real Interests."[8] Goldsmith, though he has some admiration for Pericles, stresses that the beautification of Athens was founded on Pericles' misappropriation of league funds, and Stanyan, paraphrasing a passage from Tourreil's preface to his edition of Demosthenes, asserted that the Athenians "thought, since they had delivered the Grecian cities from the Insults of the Barbarians, they had a right to oppress them in their turn" and "roughly treated the Grecian cities, of which they called themselves the Protectors."[9] David Hume observed that the so-called democracy of Periclean Athens excluded women, slaves, metics, and imperial subjects.[10] Mably ranked Pericles' imperialism high among his sins, while the philosopher Condillac labeled him "eloquent, scheming and deceitful," claiming that Pericles' zeal for the public good was only a mask that he removed when his position was secure.[11] When Pericles sought to rival Cimon by squandering public moneys to pay citizens to attend shows and trials, Condillac argues, the Athenians became preoccupied with these spectacles and left all authority in his hands.[12] A still more impassioned attack on Pericles was mounted by Rousseau, who proclaimed, plumbing the depths of praeterition: "I will not waste my time reviewing the secret causes of the Peloponnesian war which ruined the Republic; I will not inquire whether Alcibiades' advice was well- or ill-founded; whether Pericles was justly or unjustly accused of embezzlement." No, Rousseau will simply ask, like Socrates in the *Gorgias*, whether there was any single individual at Athens, slave or free, even among Pericles' own children, who was ennobled by Pericles' ascendancy.[13] Stanyan for his part saw Pericles as initiating not only the demotion of the Areopagite Council but its decadence as well, maintaining that "his Contempt of them serv'd to lessen their Dignity; and from that time the same Excesses and Vices, which were practis'd in the City, crept in among the Areopagites themselves."[14] Even Pericles' supporters Rollin and Goldsmith stressed his ambition and manipulativeness.[15]

In 424 Aristophanes' *Knights* had pilloried Cleon without mercy, and it was in this play that the word *demagogos* made its first appearance in extant literature. The *demagogoi* who succeeded Pericles were uniformly censured in the eighteenth century—so uniformly indeed that Goldsmith in writing that Cleon was "rash, arrogant and obstinate, contentious, envious and malicious, covetous and corrupt" was reproducing Stanyan's text word for word.[16] Thomas Hearne, in his 1714 *Ductor Historicus: or, A Short System of Universal*

History, had attributed the Athenians' unwillingness to make peace with Sparta after their successes in the Hellespont to "the Demagogues of the City . . . a sort of Men, who were very fierce, given to Change, and factious to the utmost of their Power."[17] Cleophon he named as "the most pestilent of these Demagogues," while Rollin pegs Hyperbolus as a "very wicked man" who was "hardened in evil" and "insensible to infamy."[18] Mably is particularly ruthless, labeling Pericles' successors a "petty and untalented swarm, morally and spiritually bankrupt."[19]

For Stanyan, it was the pernicious antagonism between demagogues and generals in the fourth century that spelled the ruin of Athens, whereas Rollin traced the decline of Demosthenes' Athens back to the self-serving policies of Pericles.[20] Citing Tourreil's discussion of Athens's decline, Rollin maintains that in the age of Demosthenes the "manly and vigorous policy" of earlier times had given way to the love of ease and pleasure, a degeneracy of which Pericles was the first author.[21] Rollin, Stanyan, and Goldsmith each offer a stock passage taken from the grafting of Justin onto Plutarch in which they lament the decadence of Athens after the death of Epaminondas. At that juncture, so the story goes, the Athenians gave themselves over to an endless succession of amusements, spending more on producing the plays of Sophocles and Euripides than had been expended on the entire war with Persia.[22] Rousseau made a parallel claim.[23] The degradation of fourth-century Athens was regularly compared to the heroism she had shown during the Persian Wars. Stanyan pointedly extended the contrast to the Greeks as a whole, opposing "the plain, hardy and untainted age" to the era that sought foreign conquests—conquests that in turn led to an increasingly cosmopolitan society in which "quicker degrees of Knowledge and Politeness" made the Greeks "more luxurious and effeminate."[24] Goldsmith at times seems to extend the decadence back into the fifth century, alleging that their successes against the Persians were "not more flattering to the Greeks, than in the end prejudicial to them," since the resulting influx of wealth produced a corruption in manners at all levels of society.[25] Rousseau had devoted his prizewinning essay to demonstrating the corruption attendant on the development of the arts and sciences, and Condillac admonished his reader that "the administration of Pericles is the epoch of the decadence of Athens; and, the more you study history, the more you will have occasion to remark that the excesses to which luxury conduces are always the forerunner of the fall of empires."[26]

The movement from manly vigor to effeminate luxury forms the theme of a rather strange essay published in 1759 and generally ascribed to the eccentric Edward Wortley Montagu, whose renowned mother Lady Mary Wortley Montagu (the celebrated letter-writer) thought so well of him that she left him in her will the sum of one guinea. *Reflections on the Rise and Fall of the Antient Republics, Adapted to the Present State of Great Britain* smacks of a schoolboy rhetorical exercise, though it appeared when its supposed author was forty-six.

In it Montagu fulminates on the impending collapse of civilization should Britain not change its course. In ancient Athens and Rome he saw ominous warnings for eighteenth-century England, for, he complains, the resemblance in manners between contemporary Britain and the ancient states in their periods of degeneracy is so great that "any well-meaning reader . . . would be apt to treat the descriptions of these periods, which he may frequently meet with, as licentious, undistinguishing satire upon the present age."[27]

Nothing in Montagu's research, he reports, gave him so much pleasure as the study of ancient history, because it made him so keenly sensible of the superiority of the British constitution. Nonetheless, he warns, it is necessary for Britons to be on guard against decadence, lest what happened to the free states of antiquity prove their ruin as well—a serious danger "when we reflect, that the same causes, which contributed to their ruin, operate at this time so very strongly amongst us."[28] These causes appear to be luxury and faction, in both of which regards Montagu sees Britain perilously mimicking the example of classical Athens, where virtue-engendering athletic contests gave way to virtue-eroding literary competitions and eventually to complete decadence. He includes in his diatribe the stock passages in which Plutarch pilloried fourth-century Athenians for spending more on dramatic productions than on the entire Persian wars, and he inquires whether if Plutarch was shocked by the Athenians' wasting so much time on the "chaste and manly" scenes of Sophocles and Euripides, "what must he have thought of the strange Shakespearomania . . . which prevailed so lately, and so universally among all ranks and all ages?" There follows a vehement attack on *Romeo and Juliet*, and Montagu goes on to speculate about how Plutarch would respond to seeing the upper classes who should be the bulwark of the nation "attentive only to the unmanning trills of an Opera; a degree of effeminacy which would have disgraced even the women of Greece, in times of greatest degeneracy." A preoccupation with manliness and its dread opposite, effeminacy, operates as an unrelenting leitmotiv throughout Montagu's essay. By her fall, Montagu warns, Athens "has left us some instructions highly useful for our present conduct," for her fate demonstrates that the best way for a minister to tame the spirit of a free people and melt them down to slavery is "to promote luxury, and encourage and diffuse a taste for public diversions . . . the never-failing forerunners of universal idleness, effeminacy and corruption."[29]

Montagu's shrill tirade is not carefully developed, and the connection between Athenian democracy and Athenian decadence is left unclear. The genesis and workings of faction remain fuzzier still. While Montagu was fulminating in England, more coherent arguments concerning the parallels between ancient and modern civilization were being shaped across the channel that were to have a great impact on historical thinking in Europe and America. In 1749 Mably published his *Observations on the Greeks*, and at the same time Jean-Jacques Rousseau submitted his prizewinning essay to the Academy of

Dijon concerning the effect of the arts and sciences on contemporary civilization.

In his general treatises on political theory, Mably advocated a state similar in many ways to classical republics—more oligarchic than Athens, less exclusive than Rome, and democratic in a way that Sparta only pretended to be. Less charmed by the ineffable virtues of the mixed state than Montesquieu or the English republicans, Mably wished a weak executive and a strong legislative branch. Those who wished to participate in the state, however, would be required to submit certain credentials, including the possession of property and proof of a secure income. In Mably's ideal state, acquisitiveness was unknown, principles of sharing were promulgated, simplicity and frugality would reign, and the state would be responsible for the poor. Poor and property there would be, however; Mably saw the prelapsarian world of shared goods, the world before private property, as gone forever. Mably's dislike of the concentration of power in the hands of a wealthy elite did not lead him to support a government in which the poor participated on an equal footing. Rather, he wished to minimize both poverty and wealth.

Predictably Mably preferred Sparta to Athens by a good bit. For other detractors of Athens, Solon had gone too far, but for Mably Solon's reforms had been altogether too timid. Prudent, xenophobic, nonacquisitive, hostile to the arts, egalitarian within their elite, the Spartans were everything the Athenians were not, and if the helots were cast as frugal rustics and the Peloponnesian League deemed nonimperialistic, the system could be seen as perfect. In Athens, by contrast, lust for power and riches promoted unacceptable inequalities and, in time, inevitably, decadence. For Mably, harmony meant uniformity, and though by the standards of today's multiethnic nations classical Athens was eminently homogeneous, until recently neither her admirers nor her detractors viewed her population in this way: it was the Athenian tolerance for diversity that Pericles had exalted in his funeral oration.[30]

Mably's *Observations* lambasted popular government in general and Athenian democracy in particular. Like all multitudes, Mably maintained, the Athenian people was blind, moved by passion, vice, and caprice. In Mably's view, the Athenians offered only the most dramatic instance of the failings of the ancient Greeks in general, who were as a lot divisive and prone to faction. In stark contrast to Trenchard and Gordon, who had stressed the gratefulness of citizens in a republic, Mably argued that monarchies are better at forgetting injuries than republics because a prince can impress his character on people, whereas magistrates are powerless to resist the force of public opinion. If one republic is incapable of reform, he reflects, imagine how dreadful things must have been in Greece, where there were as many republics as there were cities.

Mably also offers invidious comparisons between Athens's polity and that of Sparta. Though Mably's avowed belief in the abolition of property and in money as the root of all evil had not moved him to oppose monarchy in his

own day, it fostered a predictable preference for Lycurgan "equality" over Solonic timocracy. The pseudoegalitarian Spartans, moreover, stayed strictly
away from real democracy, which was, in Mably's view, to their credit.
Though Mably ascribes Sparta's preference for aristocracy in her allies to the
fact that experience had shown the Spartans the unreliability of popular sovereignty, he suggests two possible explanations for Athens's preference for
democracies in the Delian league: Athens preferred democracies either because she herself had one, or, alternatively, out of sheer perversity.[31] Though
in the end, Mably maintains, the rivalry between Athens and Sparta led the
two hegemons to support various factions in allied cities, at first factional
disputes did little harm to Greece since Sparta, occupied with her "obligations," intervened only to reconcile hostile parties and to foster equity—and
Athens, for her part, was so occupied with her own revolution that she neglected the affairs of her allies.[32] Whereas the Athenians were remiss, in other
words, the Spartans were merely busy—and, in a pinch, not even too busy to
serve justice.

Just after Mably published his *Observations*, the most famous of Sparta's
admirers was awarded the prize of the Academy of Dijon for his essay
"Whether the Restoration of the Sciences and Arts has contributed to the
purification of morals." In his award-winning entry Rousseau maintained that
"the progress of the Arts, the disintegration of morals, and the Macedonian's
yoke closely followed one another."[33] To the degeneracy of refined Athens he
pointedly contrasted Sparta, a "City equally famed for its happy ignorance and
for the wisdom of its laws, that Republic of demi-Gods rather than of men."[34]
Rousseau gives free rein to his theatrical bent in this passage, crying out, "O
Sparta! eternal shame to vain teaching!" At the same time, he writes, that
"the vices, led by the fine Arts, together insinuated themselves into Athens,
while a Tyrant was there so carefully assembling the works of the Prince of
Poets, you expelled the Arts and Artists, the Sciences and Scientists from your
walls."[35] Rousseau must date the corruption of Athens by its arts very early, as
the Tyrant who was "so carefully assembling the works of the Prince of Poets"
can only be Peisistratus, busy with his recension of Homer.

For all Rousseau's passion, however, the precise ways in which the arts and
sciences undid the Athenians are poorly articulated in this essay. Rousseau
clarifies his position in his *Discourse on the Origin and Foundations of Inequality
among Men*, submitted as an unsuccessful entry in the Dijon contest of 1754.
In this anthropological piece he ascribes the decline of Athens in part to the
Athenians' system of allowing new laws to be proposed promiscuously at any
time and by any citizen.[36] He condemns a government in which the people
retained the execution of the law in their own hands, maintaining that this
was one of the vices that ruined Athens. Such, he claims, "must have been the
rude constitution of the first governments arising immediately from the state
of Nature."[37] But if this primitive democracy was a short step from the state of

nature, it cannot have been the product of an advanced society corrupted by arts and sciences, and so Rousseau's contention that Athens fell by her very cultivation remains unconvincing. Altogether Athens seems to function for Rousseau more as a foil to virtuous Sparta than as a subject for sincere inquiry, for a serious examination of the Athenian state would inevitably lead to dissonance between the decadence he despises and the egalitarianism he admires.

It remained for Mably to take another stab at diagnosing the corruption of Athens in his *Conversations of Phocion, concerning the Connection between Morality and Government*, published in 1763. These conversations, which Mably purported to have been preserved for posterity by Phocion's friend Nicocles, served as a vehicle for Mably to exhort his contemporaries to stem the tide of decay in eighteenth-century France. Phocion's conversations amount to a searing attack on the moral decline of Athens during his day and offer stern admonitions about the consequences of laxity in morals at any time. The past, Phocion warns his friend Aristias, "is an image, or rather a forecast, of the future," and experience alone will not prove a sufficient guide to action; rather, it is in the study of the happy and unhappy events of history that one can acquire certain knowledge.[38] Mably promises that these conversations will demonstrate that *la politique* can work effectively for the good of society only when attached to rules of strictest morality—for Phocion had shown that it was a lack of virtue that caused the weakness of his Athenian contemporaries.

It is to a decline in morality, indeed, that Phocion traces the sorry state of fourth-century Greece as a whole. In his lifetime, Phocion complains, Philip has given asylum to the fugitive virtues that were abandoning the Greeks, while Greek orators were selling themselves to Macedon.[39] (Just how the noble Philip could retain his virtue while making these purchases is left unclear.) The decay, Phocion laments, has already spread beyond Attica, for Sparta has renounced the ancient virtues of Lycurgus and taken up Athenian ways.[40] Mably is inconsistent, however, about just when it was that Sparta began to stray from the paths laid out by Lycurgus, attributing this departure at times to the aftermath of the Persian Wars and on another occasion to the luxuries introduced at the end of the Peloponnesian War by Lysander.[41] A similar inconsistency marks his treatment of Athens, as he assigns the decline variously to the period right after the Persian Wars, the ascendancy of Pericles, or the restoration of the democracy in 403—though on one occasion he isolates a brief era in the fifth century when the tribute from the Delian League had strengthened Athens and rot had not yet set in.[42] Foreign conquests, Mably maintains, can lead to wealth and luxury, which soften a nation and make it vulnerable to attack, and a moral tone underlies Phocion's contention that Athens was destroyed by her imperialism.[43] To Mably, the quasi-Socialist economy of Sparta offered a far more promising field for the production of virtuous citizens than the acquisitive environment of commercial Athens, which fostered selfishness. In a footnote he cites Plato (in Latin) on the evils of the luxurious state.[44]

It is in the third of the *Conversations* that Mably makes clear just how it is that luxury corrupts the state: where there is luxury, there is need of artisans, and where artisans—that is, men who hold no land—determine what happens in the assembly, then power passes into the hands of people who have no heritage, and out of the hands of men who "alone truly have a fatherland."[45] Is it any wonder, Phocion asks, that Athens's fortunes have fallen while her government is in the hands of workmen? What sort of miracle could impart justice, prudence, and magnanimity to an assembly of artisans?[46] Such men—as even the republican Harrington had stressed—know only their particular interests and not those of the republic.[47] All Athens's greatest statesmen, Mably maintained, favored aristocracy with the exception of Aristides, whose opening up of the franchise to men who did not meet a minimum income requirement "was without doubt one of the principal causes of the enormous mistakes made by the republic and of the misfortunes she experienced after the death of Pericles, for the inquietude and insolence of the people knew no bounds."[48] (Similar observations were made in 1767 by the Scot Adam Ferguson, who expressed alarm about popular assemblies "composed of men whose dispositions are sordid, and whose ordinary applications are illiberal," as was the case in Athens, where the indigent brought to politics jealous minds intent upon profit and eager "to banish from the state whomsoever was respectable and eminent in the superior order of citizens."[49])

Mably's admiration for Sparta was tempered by his preoccupation with luxury and the decline that followed in its wake—at Sparta as elsewhere. His friend Rousseau was less temperate in his laconophilia, and in his attack on the arts and sciences he cites Sparta as the triumphant refutation of the proponents of cultivation and refinement. "My adversaries' discomfiture is evident," he writes, "whenever they have to speak about Sparta. What would they not give for this fatal Sparta never to have existed; and how dearly would those who contend that great deeds are good for nothing but to be celebrated, wish that Sparta's great deeds had never been celebrated?"[50] Imagine, he writes, the speech a Spartan might have delivered to his compatriots had he been swayed by the force of such arguments. "Citizens," he would say,

> open your eyes and behold what you have been blind to. I am pained to see you laboring solely in order to acquire virtue, to exercise your courage, and to preserve your liberty; yet you forget the more important duty of providing amusement for the idle of future generations. Tell me; what good is virtue if it does not cause a stir in the world? What will it have profited you to have been good men if no one will talk about you? What will it matter to later centuries that at Thermopylae you sacrificed your lives to save the Athenians, if you do not, like they, [sic] leave [behind] systems of Philosophy, or poems, or comedies, or statues? Hasten to give up, then, laws that are good for nothing but to make you happy; think only of being much talked about when you will be no longer; and never forget that if great men were not celebrated it would be useless to be one"[51]

In exalting Sparta at the expense of Athens, Rousseau was only going where hundreds of gentler men had gone before. Who, then, were these putative critics who had censured him for his stance?

THE REPUBLIC OF DEMI-GODS

The truth is that Rousseau was only the most flamboyant of a long line of laconophiles. As is well known, Athenian aristocrats from Cimon to Critias admired Sparta enormously. Xenophon's enthusiasm for Sparta knew few bounds; Plato and Aristotle both esteemed the city on the Eurotas highly, though neither was blind to its weaknesses. Affection for Sparta was more subdued among the Romans, whose chauvinism made it difficult for them to develop much enthusiasm for any civilization that had gone before—though Valerius Maximus judged that the Spartans, of all ancient peoples, approached most closely to Roman *gravitas*.[52] During the Italian Renaissance, however, Sparta was idolized by political theorists in search of stability at any price. In Florence, Machiavelli, Guicciardini, and Giannotti contrasted Spartan solidity with Athenian anarchy and chaos, and Venetians like Paolo Paruta agreed that Sparta realized in a singular way the much-touted ideal of the *governo misto*. In this regard Renaissance writers regularly paired Sparta with Venice. The same coupling is apparent in English thought, and the British enthusiasm for mixed government reached obsessive proportions among the classical republicans of the seventeenth century. Harrington denied that a commonwealth of artisans like the Athenian could compare with Rome, Sparta, and Venice, "plumed with their Aristocracies."[53] Like Mably he saw great merit in the equal distribution of land at Sparta, believing as he did that it was politically disastrous for too much property to be in the hands of too few citizens. Sidney liked Sparta, and it attests to the vigor of the pro-Spartan tradition that even the author of *Areopagitica* could in another work have described Sparta as an excellently ordered state.[54] Walter Moyle observed in 1698 that he found it agreeable to contemplate how many millions of people "lived happily and died quietly" throughout seven centuries of Spartan history, and he judged the separation of powers to have worked more effectively in Sparta than in England.[55]

In France, some discordant notes were struck. Bayle in his 1697 *Dictionnaire* had passed severe judgment not only on the Spartan king Agesilaus, whose dishonesty and appetite for warfare had earned him the criticism even of Xenophon, but also on the reformers Lycurgus and Agis IV, and the prelate Fénelon in the *Dialogue des morts* he composed early in the eighteenth century found the Spartans cruel, idle, and excessively warlike.[56] By Rousseau's time, however, these squalls had passed, and the prevailing tone about Sparta was admiring. The Genevan legist Burlamaqui carried forward the notion of

Sparta as a mixed state to be linked with England, and, most dramatically, Montesquieu's *Spirit of the Laws* brought a somewhat idealized Sparta before the public eye.[57] Montesquieu's belief that republics were founded on the virtue of their citizens led him to esteem greatly the ordinances of Lycurgus. In his appetite for the Lycurgan system, Montesquieu followed in the train of earlier civic humanists—in Italy, for example—whose concern for public virtue drew them to Spartan *agoge*, and Montesquieu writes approvingly of the Spartans' respect for age and for authority as well as of their self-discipline and frugality.[58]

Though Rousseau's fascination with Sparta exceeded that of his contemporaries, then, his portrait of himself crying out the laconic virtues alone in the wilderness arose more from rhetoric than from reality. The attack on Sparta's champions in Chastellux's tract *On Public Happiness* is probably a more reliable guide to traditional eighteenth-century attitudes to Sparta. In the introduction to this moving and elaborate plea for serious social engineering to relieve public miseries of many kinds, Chastellux raises his voice against the use of stock examples from antiquity to support simplistic solutions to modern problems, complaining of those who adduce the Scythians and Spartans as models by which the opulent commercial nations of his day should reform themselves.[59] Chastellux is aware that in his criticism of Sparta he is voicing a minority opinion: "Already," he reports, "I seem to hear many voices raised against me, and opposing to my observations the power, and the duration of this republic."[60] Chastellux denies the merits of the Lycurgan system, and in a burst of anticlericalism he compares the Spartans to "bold, intriguing monks, who, having overthrown provinces, and even whole states, perceive themselves compelled to retire again within their cloisters, where, in silent indignation, they bend beneath the laws of obedience and austerity."[61] Chastellux's writing conveys a powerful sense of outrage. In describing the Spartans' secret police, he reports that revulsion leads him to drop the pen from his hand; but his indignation, he continues, is directed less against the Spartans themselves than against the authors "who have, coldly, transmitted to us, the details of these execrable facts, and complaisantly, expatiated on the praises of the barbarous people who committed them."[62]

The Spartans' (wavering) popularity is also attested by the horror the Abbé Goguet expressed at the traditional view of them in his treatise on *The Origin of Laws, Arts, and Sciences, and their Progress among the Most Ancient Nations*. It was Goguet's belief that Lycurgus's strictures against virtually any form of activity had pretty well legislated life out of existence at Sparta and that the Spartans, though brave, were also imperious, deceitful, and perfidious. Like Chastellux, Goguet chastised other writers for holding up Sparta as a model of wisdom and virtue.[63] A similar frustration with rampant laconomania is evident in Voltaire. Distrustful generally of the adulation of antiquity fashionable in his day, Voltaire in his *Notebooks* cried out against people who acted as if one should conduct oneself at Paris as if it were Sparta, and in his article on luxury in the *Dictionnaire philosophique*, he asks what good Sparta ever did for Greece. Did she ever produce "any Demostheneses, any Sophocleses, any Appelleses, or any Phidiases?" (The plurals, of course, are more euphonious in French.) "The luxury of Athens," he argues, "made great men in all areas," while Sparta had only a handful of captains.[64]

Not all who rejected Sparta embraced Athens. Chastellux, in fact, pointedly rejected the Athenian model as equally unsuitable. He urges his readers to put aside not only romantic ideas about the Spartans but any similar notions they may have harbored about Athens as well. On close examination, he warns, the Athenians were frivolous, jealous, and ambitious, incapable of forming policy and plagued by an idle eloquence that led them to abandon the substance of argument for the form of rhetoric; in the last analysis they were "unjust to their allies, ungrateful to their chiefs and cruel to their enemies."[65] In vain, Chastellux laments, did learning and the arts settle in Athens, for the harshness of the Athenians toward the people of Mytilene and Sicyon "are such monuments of cruelty, as sufficiently prove the superiority of our modern philosophy, over that which could accommodate itself to such abominations."[66] (He plainly means here not Sicyon but Scione; the Athenians were believed to have maltreated not the Sicyonians in the Peloponnese but rather the people of Scione in northern Greece, who defected to the Spartans during the Peloponnesian War.) Like Rousseau, Chastellux sees Athens as raising unsettling questions about what relation the progress of the mind bears to the increase of public happiness. What has been termed the glorious age of Greece, he concludes, was in reality "a scene of torture, and punishment, inflicted on humanity."[67] It is a melancholy truth, he maintains, that intellectual progress in Athens did not benefit the people.[68]

The Rise of the Liberal Tradition

Though Chastellux followed tradition in condemning the Athenian state, his work is notable for its iconoclastic approach to Greek civilization, and he concedes some anxieties about "the displeasure of some eminent literati, whose respect for antiquity may be unlimited."[69] Although he is savage toward the Athenians, what he said about the Spartans would play an important role in the eventual debunking of the Spartan myth, a phenomenon that would lead in some instances to a reevaluation of Athenian government and society.

That some thinkers were beginning to reconsider the eighteenth-century condemnation of Athens is demonstrated by Goguet's caveat that "we commonly view the Athenians on their favorable and advantageous side."[70] To be sure, he goes on to undermine this enthusiasm, arguing that to explain the Athenian constitution is to make known its defects, since every state in which decision-making is in the hands of the people is "essentially vitious."[71] The Athenians' habits of "inconstancy, impatience and precipitation," he argues, were "defects, inseparable from the constitution of their government," and he summons Aristophanes, Cicero, Plato, and Valerius Maximus as witnesses to the depravity of Athenian democracy.[72]

At the same time, however, he has much good to say about Athens. No easy dichotomy can be posited to explain his position as one favoring Athenian "culture" while condemning Athenian "government," for as his ascription of flaws in the Athenian character to their form of government suggests, Goguet considers the two inseparable, and in fact he acknowledges that the Athenians' virtues were often reflected in their laws. A thousand proofs, he says, might be cited that generosity and greatness of soul "formed the general and predominant character of the Athenians," but he will content himself with mentioning only one, the law that ordained that anyone who had lost his way should be conducted to the right road; later on he supports his contention that humanity was the cardinal principle of the Athenians by reference to the law providing that those who had been maimed in wars should be maintained at the expense of the state.[73] Comparing Spartan and Athenian mores, he contends that mildness was the ruling propensity of the Athenians just as cruelty was of the Spartans, and he illustrates the contrast by the greater lenity with which he supposes the Athenians treated their slaves, whose condition, he maintains, "was infinitely more gentle at Athens than in any other city of Greece."[74] Most striking of all Goguet's departures from customary thinking about antiquity is his praise of Solon over Lycurgus. Lycurgus, he had argued, condemned the Spartans to lives of idleness, while Solon, a more enlightened man, had, on the contrary, "been sensible, that sloth and too much leisure are more to be feared than all the vices that can reign in a state."[75]

The ambivalence of Goguet was shared by the Encyclopedists, but on the whole the liberal tradition about Athens prevailed in the Encyclopédie—though nowhere are the inconsistencies of the Encyclopédie plainer than in the treatment accorded there to Athens by Jaucourt. In the article on Athens under the rubric "République," he portrays Athens as declining almost immediately after the Persian Wars, her citizens the helpless pawns of manipulative orators, and he cites with approval the famous passage of Justin regarding the complete disintegration of Athens following Epaminondas's death.[76] In his essay on Sparta, he had written: "I feel myself in every way a Lacedaemonian. Lycurgus satisfies me in everything; I need neither Solon nor Athens."[77] As Jaucourt's American editors point out, already here he has forgotten the condemnation of war in his article "Guerre" and the attack on helotry in his "Esclavage."[78] In Jaucourt's "Démocratie," however, probably written a good bit later than the entry for Sparta, Athens shines brightly. Here the Solon for whom he had no use in his article on Sparta is a hero. Jaucourt even manages to cite Plato as a source for the masterful way in which Athenian government succeeded in combining natural equality with proper deference to the wise and capable. He sees it as significant that democracies boast of being nurses to great men, and as evidence for the way democracy lifts the spirits he cites the manner in which Athens and Rome were elevated to empire "by virtue of their constitution." Does his reader question that the people are capable of choosing leaders? The continually excellent choices of leaders made by the Greeks and Romans should dispel these doubts.

Although he had little opportunity to discuss Greek government in his contributions to the *Encyclopédie* itself, Voltaire's other writings make clear his preference for Athens over Sparta. As we have seen, his essay on "Luxe" in the *Dictionnaire Philosophique* attacked the austere Spartans for having produced no notable artists, statesmen, or intellectuals and contrasted Sparta with the thriving commercial state of Athens, which fostered all manner of greatness. Following the lead of J. F. Melon, whose 1734 *Essai politique sur le commerce* had attempted to divorce the questions of affluence and decadence, Voltaire in his 1736 poem *Le Mondain* and his subsequent *Défense du Mondain* had sought to debunk myths of ancient modesty and sobriety, and his entry for "Democracy" in the *Philosophical Dictionary* afforded a further opportunity to refute contemporary views of the ancient world.[79] Taking as his point of departure the attack on democracy in general and Athenian democracy in particular that Bayle had mounted in his dictionary in the entry for "Pericles," Voltaire was quick to insist that Athenian justice was no worse than that dispensed by the supposedly enlightened countries of modern Europe, and he suggests that Bayle may have been unduly influenced by discontent with contemporary Holland when he judged Athens so harshly. Over a period of two centuries, Voltaire maintains, Athens's popular government was "stained only by five or six acts of judicial iniquity," and he is favorably impressed by reports that the Athenians had requested posthumous pardon of Socrates, Phocion, and the victors of Arginusae—a habit most writers before and after him have viewed as the product of a singularly repellent fickleness. Paralleling the anticlerical analogies of Chastellux, Voltaire finds democratic communities measuring up very well indeed against modern religious organizations: a democracy, he concedes, will make many mistakes, but only because it will be composed of men; though discord will prevail as in a convent of monks, still "there will be no St. Bartholemews there, no Irish massacre, no Sicilian vespers, no Inquisition, no condemnation to the galleys for having taken water from the ocean without paying for it." Voltaire's final judgment about Athens in this essay is unequivocal, as he proclaims

That the Athenians were warriors like the Swiss, and as polite as the Parisians were under Louis XIV; that they excelled in every art requiring genius or execution, like the Florentine in time of the Medici; that they were the masters of the Romans in eloquence, even in the days of Cicero; that this same people, insignificant in number, who scarcely possessed anything of territory, and who, at the present day, consist only of a band of ignorant slaves . . . yet bear away the palm from Roman power, by their ancient reputation, which triumphs at once over time and degradation.[80]

The most dramatic praise of Athens in eighteenth-century France, however, was reserved for the very eve of the Revolution. In 1788 two important French works on Greece appeared, one noteworthy for its immense popularity and the other for its startling originality. Published in the same year, Jean Jacques Barthélemy's interminable historical novel *The Travels of Anacharsis the Younger in Greece* and Cornelius De Pauw's *Philosophical Researches on the Greeks* are diametrically opposed in their perspectives and their conclusions. The work of Barthélemy reproduces the familiar clichés of the anti-Athenian tradition, while a striking open-mindedness and independence of thought is evident in that of De Pauw (who also published his researches on the Germans, the American Indians, the Egyptians and the Chinese).

Like the "docu-dramas" of our own age, *Anacharsis* offered its audience a view of ancient Greece that, while rich and detailed, was nonetheless palatable and entertaining, and it was repeatedly cited as a principal source in works of nineteenth-century scholarship.[81] It appeared in literally dozens of editions, including abridgments for schools and translations into Spanish, Italian, German, Greek, and English. An atlas to the voyages was also published, along with a companion volume of maps, plans, and coins. Barthélemy was a child of his age down to his adulation of Xenophon over Plato, complaining in a footnote that the Platonic Socrates lacked the "gravity" of Xenophon's.[82] The nature of Barthélemy's interests is indicated by another footnote that treats the topic of melons, as Barthélemy wrestles with tricky horticultural niceties, ultimately finding himself constrained to refer readers to various modern critics in view of his inability to determine whether the Greeks were acquainted with melons and considered them a species of cucumber.[83] When not concerned over the details of Hellenic flora or fauna, Barthélemy rehearses all the customary complaints about the Athenian multitude's "natural licentiousness of manners," the primacy of demagogues, and the obsession with games and festivals that led ultimately to the Macedonian conquest.[84]

De Pauw's line of thinking was entirely different. A Protestant polymath whose curiosity knew no bounds, De Pauw was originally a German and served as the ambassador to the city of Liège. His nephew was Anacharsis Cloots, who would be executed under the Terror.[85] De Pauw combined strong passions with bold iconoclasm, and he comes magnificently alive in the pages of his several anthropological treatises. Though he is little read today, he helped shape the thinking of Joseph de Maistre, Benjamin Constant, and Pierre-Charles Lévesque, the historian of Russia and China who also translated Thucydides.

De Pauw's treatment of Athens was as innovative as Barthélemy's was traditional. His intense frustration with modern writing about Greece is splashed liberally across his two-volume *Researches*. De Pauw sharply censures both his contemporaries and their predecessors for their mindless parroting of received wisdom in general and their repeated exaltation of Sparta over Athens in particular.[86] Montesquieu, De Pauw claims, was never more wretched than when he undertook to speak of the Greeks, whose language he did not know; and most particularly he had no understanding of the republic of Athens, about which he made appalling factual errors.[87] Rousseau he dismisses as "the most inconsequent thinker who has ever appeared."[88] De Pauw is savage toward the Spartans, who, he claims, contributed nothing to the progress of art or knowledge and were the professed enemies of repose, counting peace among public calamities, and he expresses the hope that his observations will produce a revolution in the thinking of those "who have admired this people with enthusiasm bordering on blindness."[89]

The degree to which De Pauw departs from tradition in his treatment of Athenian government is astonishing. Just as some peoples were naturally disposed to trouble and anarchy, he writes—like the Poles and the Slavs—so the Athenians had "an inner penchant for order and legislation," and everything in Athens was done with reflection and measure. De Pauw sees the Athenians' changeability not as a vice but as a virtue. For De Pauw, the frequency with which the Athenians overturned one law and replaced it with another pointed to assiduousness in the pursuit of equity rather than fickleness or volatility.[90] It is Athens, De Pauw writes, to which one looks for laws to build a new state just as one looks to Sweden for wood to build a ship; even ostracism is agreeable to De Pauw for its effectiveness in preventing political convulsions.[91] Athens, he claims, is wrongly censured for being bellicose, for had she not been, she would have fallen to Persia or Sparta, both developments that would have marked the end of learning and culture.[92] He is also quick to point out that many of the shortcomings of the Athenians were universal and not particular to them alone: why, he asks bitingly, should Pericles and Socrates be censured in Europe for the inadequacy of their offspring when the European nobility regularly produced such discreditable heirs?[93]

De Pauw's judgments about Athens and Sparta were intertwined, for one of the most unusual and dramatic of his departures from tradition is his decision to blame Sparta rather than Athens for the Macedonian conquest of Greece. Demosthenes, he maintains, exaggerated greatly the Athenians' slowness to furnish money for a campaign; for Philip himself was astonished at the promptness with which the Athenians sent out so many infantry, and they could hardly have done it without money. The real causes of the defeat at Chaeronea, De Pauw argues, were two. First, the Athenians were in too much of a hurry; second, and most decisively, the Spartans did not help. No people on earth, De Pauw writes, ever committed a fault so great or more irreparable than the Spartans who sat still while Philip conquered the Athenians. Furthermore, he adds, if the collapse of Greece is traceable to the failure of the confederative principle, to what is this very failure traceable if not to the uncooperativeness of the Spartans?[94]

Withal De Pauw finds Athens a grand state, superior in many respects to those of modern Europe.[95] His remarks look ahead to the despair Victorian essayists were to express so amusingly over the habit of attacking Athens by particularizing the universal, and they look back as well to the *Philosophical Dictionary* and Voltaire's insistence that the Athenians' inequities were no worse, and in some cases less bad, than those of modern Europeans. Altogether De Pauw and Voltaire were probably the most pointed exponents of the liberal view of Athens.

. . . . .

The appearance of the narrative histories of Rollin, Stanyan, and Goldsmith drew considerable attention to the history of ancient Greece, though the chronological format inevitably focused interest on the ultimate collapse of Athenian power, especially in the minds of readers worried about decadence—laxity in morals and luxury in commerce. In both France and Britain, Pericles was viewed harshly and frequently castigated for setting the Athenians on the road to decline. In a somewhat earlier period British crusaders for accountability had conceived an opposition between Pericles, the self-seeking minister, and the vigilant Athenian people alert to his transgressions. As the century wore on, however, the conduct of Pericles came to be portrayed as emblematic of everything that was wrong at Athens, the creature of the democracy rather than its traducer. On the whole, English thinkers took a dim view of Athens, and the strictures of Stanyan and Goldsmith would be echoed in the Greek histories penned later in the century during the revolutions in France and America by John Gillies, William Young, and William Mitford.

French thinking about Athens was less uniform. In France during the latter half of the eighteenth century there existed fundamentally three traditions about the Greek city-states. The austere virtues of the Spartans were applauded and Athenian decadence decried by those who although eccentric in some respects (Mably in his socialist leanings, Rousseau in pretty much everything) were nonetheless traditionalists where things Greek were concerned. Rousseau's association of cultivation and decadence ultimately trumped his preoccupation with equality and the involvement of citizens in government and led him to reject Athens for its refinements rather than embrace it for its egalitarianism. Iconoclastic liberals like Goguet and Chastellux deplored the inhumanity of Athens and Sparta alike. Eager proponents of the modern commercial state like De Pauw and Voltaire rejected Sparta and celebrated Athens. Whereas in England dissidents who opposed the government's involvement in finance and agonized over conspicuous consumption had lauded Athens for the strict accountability to which she held her officials and called for a return to the ancient virtues of simplicity, in France Athens was more likely to be popular with those who defended modern economic development and mocked the call for a return to the modesty and sobriety of the ancients.

On the whole the approach of French eighteenth-century thinkers to Greek government was oblique, as Athens and Sparta got caught up in the acrimonious debate over "le luxe," and the quality of life and the formation of character came to replacement constitutional questions as the focus of concern. The structure of government attracted interest primarily in its connection with social and economic institutions, as French writers employed antiquity to debate the prospects for public and private morality in a complex commercial state. A return to Athenian or Spartan government was not on the whole advocated, and in fact Voltaire stated openly that he would not endorse the resurrection of Athenian democracy.[96] Like the civil wars of seventeenth-century England, however, the revolutions soon to come in France and America would focus closer attention on actual questions of classical government.

Chapter Nine

ATHENIAN DEMOCRACY IN THE
AGE OF REVOLUTIONS

Interaction with men will teach you how to deal with them, but do
not hope that your experience alone will be able to provide you
with all the guidance you will need. If you do not understand what
you have seen, you will feel the constant weight of your ignorance,
unless some extreme presumption deceive you. No, it is in studying
in history the causes of fortunate outcomes that you will acquire
certain knowledge. The past is an image or rather a forecast of the
future. Add up the virtues and vices of a people; and like Jupiter,
who, according to the poets, weighed the destinies of republics and
empires in his golden scales, you will learn the advantages and
disadvantages that can be expected.
—Gabriel Bonnot de Mably, *Conversations of Phocion*

Is it not the glory of the people of America that, whilst they have
paid a decent regard to the opinions of former times and other
nations, they have not suffered a blind veneration of antiquity, for
custom, and for names, to overrule the suggestions of their own
good sense, the knowledge of their own situation,
and the lessons of their own experience?
—James Madison, *Federalist 14*

SINCE THE FOUNDATION of British colonies in the new world,
curiosity about the possible relevance of the Athenian experiment to
American experience has waxed and waned across the centuries and
throughout different decades of the same century. Anxiety over the state of
popular involvement in government and the withdrawal of energies from civic
concerns has prompted many American thinkers in recent years to reopen the
study of Athenian democracy and to ask once again whether the achievements of the Athenians might contain valuable lessons and might, *mutatis
mutandis*, provide a positive model in at least some areas. This belief contrasts
strikingly with the conviction of America's founders that what little Athens
had to teach was entirely of the negative variety. Reading the past backward
in the narrative histories of the eighteenth century—Rollin made his way into
many colonial libraries, and Jefferson excerpted Stanyan in his commonplace

book—for the framers of the American constitution the story of Athens was the story of failure, and the weaknesses of the democracy were held responsible for everything from the tyranny of the Thirty in 403 to the defeat by Macedonia in 338. Often, moreover, the Athenians were rejected along with the rest of the ancients as un-Christian slaveholders who channeled excessive energy into military pursuits and valued glory above virtue.

Writers in early America did not share the leisure of their educated French and English contemporaries in the Old World, and writing about ancient civilization in depth did not catch on until well after the founding of the republic. Indeed, the very utility of classical education was hotly debated. The colonists' hesitance to devote great chunks of time to the study of antiquity is easy to understand. To be sure, for men—and sometimes women—cut loose from the mother ship on a strange new continent, such allusions offered vital grounding in a past that bound the colonists not only to heroes and heroines long dead but to more recent generations in England who had agonized over the same texts as they themselves were growing up. In the new world, how-ever, a classical education did not seem justifiable on sentimental or ornamen-tal grounds alone. Rather, it stood or fell on its civic value. Eighteenth-cen-tury Americans asked hard questions concerning the relevance of Greek and Roman civilization to the challenges facing the colonists, and the answers to these questions reveal a strong conviction that the history of the tiny republics of antiquity had little of a positive nature to teach modern individuals who were the beneficiaries not only of a whole new range of experience but of a new science of politics as well.[1]

The Debate over Classical Learning

Because of the limited supply of books and the greater demands of life in the New World, educated people probably knew a little less about the ancient world than their European counterparts, but a determination to cultivate Old World roots and the comparative lack of grinding poverty in America led even the humblest to learn a little about the world of Greece and Rome, and, as Meyer Reinhold has pointed out, though eighteenth-century Americans knew much less about the ancient world than twentieth-century Americans, still "the learning they acquired, circumscribed though it was, affected their thought and action more," rooting them as it did in a venerable tradition that afforded them a yearned-for continuity with the thread of civilization in Eu-rope.[2] At the same time, the exigencies of life in the New World led some to question the value of the classics. In part, this questioning focused on the study of dead languages, a pastime that eighteenth-century Americans sub-jected to precisely the same scrutiny as do their modern descendants. Appeal-ing to arguments parallel to those of Priestley in England and Diderot in

France, many Americans called for a more obviously utilitarian education than could be found in the traditional classical curriculum. Quakers in general opposed classical learning, and William Penn decried the oppressing of American children with a "strange tongue or two, that it is ten to one may never be useful to them."[3] At the same time, the content of classical texts was lambasted; in 1769, John Wilson resigned his position at the Friends Academy in Philadelphia because of his belief that the reading of classical authors promoted "Ignorance, Lewdness & Profanity" in America's youth, and four years later the Tory Jonathan Boucher complained that exclusive devotion to the classics had created men who preferred the "darkness and filth of Heathenism" to "Christian verity and purity."[4] The physician Benjamin Rush was concerned that the close study of classical texts was tedious and time-consuming and that emphasis on dead languages excluded women from higher education; he also worried that preoccupation with the classics promoted not only ancient heathen immorality but modern European class-consciousness, asking, "Do not men use Latin and Greek as the scuttlefish emit their ink, on purpose to conceal themselves from an intercourse with the common people?"[5] If antiquity was sometimes taken to task for inspiring allegiance to an undesirable code of morality, it could also be rejected on grounds of irrelevance. Benjamin Franklin criticized his countrymen for seeking political wisdom in the classical world rather than in themselves and for spending too much time pondering the defunct republics of antiquity; he also groused that it was "better to bring back from Italian travel a receipt for Parmesan cheese than copies of ancient historical inscriptions."[6] Others cited the differences between American and classical states to demonstrate the irrelevance of ancient history. Madison in *Federalist* 14 pointed up the dangers of adulating the ancients, and around the time of the constitutional convention, William Vans Murray of Maryland criticized arguments "derived from the falsely imagined character of antiquity." The resemblance between the American states and the ancient republics, he argued, was so minor that Americans could gain little from the study of Greek and Roman history beyond "the contagion of enthusiasm." Problems in the analogy between the classical republics and modern America were also put forward by anti-Federalists who wished to demonstrate that small republics were not necessarily unstable; "Agrippa" (probably James Winthrop of Cambridge) contended in 1788 that the faults of classical republics would not plague the Americans since they were the consequence of widespread slavery.[7] Three years later a similar observation was put forward by Israel Evans, who denied that the slaveholding ancients could have been acquainted with principles of either liberty or humanity.[8] On other occasions, however, ancient history appeared in a different light. Even Franklin in his younger days affirmed that the study of Greek and Roman history would tend "to fix in the minds of youth deep impressions of the beauty and usefulness of virtue of all kinds."[9] In 1772 John Adams expressed the wish that Americans emulate the mixed governments of antiquity; in 1780 Jonathan Mason advocated the study of Greece and Rome to teach the lesson that the waning of patriotic virtue would ruin a state, and John Gardiner made the same point five years later.[10]

Certainly the participants in the Federal Convention of 1787 expected that references to antiquity would lend weight and dignity to their arguments. The notes of William Pierce show one delegate warning on 1 June that a plural executive would "probably produce a tyranny as bad as the thirty Tyrants of Athens, or as the Decemvirs of Rome."[11] On 6 June Madison appealed to the states of classical antiquity as evidence that "where a majority are united by a common interest or passion, the rights of the minority are in danger."[12] A similar stand was taken by Hamilton (who showed his opposition to popular government by his adoption of the pseudonym of Phocion.) On 18 June in his review of elements of government he cited Demosthenes on the duration of Greek hegemonies, and in arguing that jealousy of commerce begets war as well as jealousy of power, he adduced the examples of Sparta, Athens, Thebes, Rome, Carthage, Venice, and the Hanseatic League; Holland and Athens were put forward as examples to show that republics are "liable to foreign corruption and intrigue."[13] In maintaining ten days later that large states in a union were more likely to quarrel among themselves than to join in the op-pression of smaller ones, Madison contended that it was the rivalries and not the cooperation of Sparta, Athens, and Thebes that proved fatal to the smaller members of the Amphictyonic League.[14] According to the notes of Robert Yates, Madison also cited the rivalries of antiquity in defense of his argument that major powers were more likely to quarrel than to ally.[15] Later the same day Luther Martin apparently cited Charles Rollin on the system of represen-tation in the Council of the Amphictyonic League.[16]

Though some of these classical citations reflect the founders' need to legiti-mize their daring enterprise by grounding it firmly in the study of history, the conviction that the ancient world had something to teach modern Americans hung on until the end of the century and in some cases longer. Even Benjamin Rush, a notorious enemy of the ancient languages, conceded in 1795 that ancient historians contained "much useful knowledge."[17] Although Hamilton declared in the sixth *Continentalist* that it was "as ridiculous to seek models in the simple ages of Greece and Rome, as it would be to go in quest of them among the Hottentots and Laplanders," nonetheless both in his other *Conti-nentalist* and *Federalist* papers he recurred repeatedly to the examples of classi-cal history.[18] Writing in 1798, David Tappan echoed the assertion of Jonathan Mason and John Gardiner that the need for moral behavior and public spirit was borne out by ancient history, which is "peculiarly instructive to the people of America," since the prosperity, decline, and ruin of those states "experi-mentally show that virtue is the soul of republican freedom" and that "luxury tends to extinguish both sound morality and piety."[19]

Greek history afforded both positive and negative examples. Thomas Welch could adduce the Greeks' successful defense against Persia in support of his call for a militia, while the anonymous New Hampshire author of "The People the Best Governors" attributed the victory to the internal union of Athens; but Jonathan Maxcy viewed Xerxes' sack of Athens and near conquest of Greece as a whole as evidence of the need for union of a larger order. Underscoring the necessity for the study of ancient history in the new republic, he asks if it is not prudent to profit by the errors as well as the wisdom of days gone by: "Is it not the part of folly, in the present advanced state of the science of government, to admit an idea which the example of all the ancient independent republics reprobates, as the fruitful source of division, violence, and destruction?"[20] Benjamin Church and others disagreed with Alexander Hamilton about the merits of the Amphictyonic League, and although the independence of Greek colonies was often compared favorably with the dependence of Roman ones, the equal participation of Roman colonies in government was also cited.[21] Praise of Greek and Roman government in general was frequent, and the lukewarm republicanism of the oligarchically inclined Romans held considerable appeal; and yet the more closely the colonists examined the government of the ancient Athenians, the less they liked it.

AMERICA AND ATHENS

What Americans heard about classical Athens would inevitably carry a special valence, for unlike eighteenth-century Europeans concerned about the possible decadence of their large nation-states, Americans shared with the inhabitants of Renaissance Italy a real opportunity to resurrect the classical polis. They decided against it. There was no lack of glowing generalizations about ancient states in eighteenth-century America. William Smith maintained that the history of Greece and Rome might justly be called "the History of Heroism, Virtue and Patriotism"; John Adams insisted that the best governments of the world had all been mixed and cited Greece, Rome, and Carthage as examples.[22] Levi Hart praised the "public spirited, patriotic men whose hearts glowed with the love of liberty" to whom the great states of classical antiquity owed their stature.[23] Under scrutiny, however, the eventual collapse of all the ancient states was alleged against them, most particularly in Greece, and still more particularly in Athens.

To be sure, some eighteenth-century Americans had a kind word or two for Athenian government. The anonymous T. Q. and J., in an untitled piece written at Boston in 1763, stressed the need for a check on excessive power in the hands of one man, and the Athenians are presumably meant when the authors praise the Greeks for keeping "their good men from growing formidably great." These Greeks, they go on, "were a wise people, and all governments would do well in this particular to imitate their example."[24] Predictably, a dramatic defense of Athens appears in the anonymous 1776 New Hampshire pamphlet entitled "The People the Best Governors." God, the author maintains, "made every man equal to his neighbour, and has virtually enjoined them, to govern themselves by their own laws. . . . The people," he goes on, "best know their own wants and necessities, and therefore, are best able to rule themselves." In support of this he points out that "tent makers, cobblers and common tradesmen, composed the legislature at Athens." He argues further that any American representative council should lack veto power but rather serve in a merely probouleutic capacity, and again he cites the example of the Athenian *boule* (which he describes as consisting of four hundred people, a number valid only before Cleisthenes). Finally, and rather bizarrely, he enrolls Athens as a positive example in his argument that there should be no property qualification whatsoever for American representatives, advocating instead the ancient system whereby the best leaders were often in very needy circumstances—men, he explains, like "the Athenians, Cimon [!] and Aristides."[25]

The best-known praise of Athens surviving from eighteenth-century America came from the pen of Tom Paine, who claimed in 1792 that "what Athens was in miniature, America will be in magnitude," for "the one was the wonder of the ancient world; the other is becoming the admiration, the model of the present."[26] It did not go without saying, however, that the model of ancient Athens was applicable to modern America, and although Paine's joyous boast certainly reflects tremendous warmth for the Athenian experiment, he was quick to explain that the American system would benefit no end from "representation ingrafted upon Democracy." Representation, he claimed, was preferable to pure democracy even in small territories, and Athens itself would by representation "have outrivalled her own Democracy."[27]

Others took harsher views both of Athens in itself and of Athens as an example for moderns. Already in 1645 the New England divine John Cotton had written that "a democratical government might do well in Athens, a city fruitful of pregnant wits, but will soon degenerate to an *Anarchia* (a popular tumult) amongst rude common people."[28] In the eighteenth century, Athenian democracy was rarely considered suitable even for Athens, and such notions continued throughout the generation that followed the revolution. In his "Oration on the Anniversary of the Independence of the United States of America" delivered at Worcester in 1802, Zephaniah Swift Moore used the example of ancient Athens to support his argument that "vice is to the body politic, what a gangrene is to the natural body," and he sums up the tradition of the previous century in contrasting the heroism of early Athens with later days, when corruption and faction set in, as a result of which the Athenians, he claims, found themselves "enfeebled and enslaved, reduced to the lowest state of savage stupidity and ignorance, and became an easy prey to their enemies."[29] Similarly Mercy Warren, one of the few women from the early republic to leave behind written opinions about classical antiquity, decried the corruption, luxury, and faction that destroyed Athens, "wasted and lost by the intrigues of its own ambitious citizens."[30] Numerous American orators excoriated Athens for what writers of the Enlightenment in both England and America were fond of calling "licentiousness."

By and large, the Athenian example was one from which the founding fathers wished to dissociate themselves. Thus for instance Madison made a point of distinguishing the American republics from "the turbulent democracies of ancient Greece and modern Italy."[31] This allusion to the instability of Renaissance governments makes plain the continuing role of Florence in thinking about the Athenian past. In the representative principle he saw the remedy for the inherent turbulence of democracy, which, he argued, was a bad thing in ancient Athens. "In all very numerous assemblies," he insisted, "of whatever characters composed, passion never fails to wrest the scepter from reason. Had every Athenian citizen been a Socrates," he maintained, "every Athenian assembly would still have been a mob."[32] (It is important to distinguish these concerns about group psychology from the class prejudice that rejected popular assemblies on other grounds, though there is often some overlap.) It was probably also Madison who in *Federalist* 63 appealed to his audience to recognize the need for a well-constructed Senate to protect the people at moments when, "stimulated by some irregular passion, or some illicit advantage, or misled by the artful misrepresentations of interested men," they "may call for measures which they themselves will afterwards be the most ready to lament and condemn," and he cited Athens once more as a negative example: "What bitter anguish would not the people of Athens have often escaped if their government had contained so provident a safeguard against the tyranny of their own passions? Popular liberty might then have escaped the indelible reproach of decreeing to the same citizens the hemlock on one day and statues on the next."[33] Similar arguments were put forward by Hamilton.[34] Like Madison, he coupled the chaos of ancient Greece with that of Renaissance Italy, writing in *Federalist* 9 that he found it "impossible to read the history of the petty republics of Greece and Italy without feeling sensations of horror and disgust at the distractions with which they were continually agitated, and at the rapid succession of revolutions by which they were kept in a state of perpetual vibration between the extremes of tyranny and anarchy."[35] Like Madison, too, he stressed the misunderstandings willfully engendered by monarchists who have deliberately confounded republics with democracies in order to bring disrepute on all forms of free government. In truth, he himself stands well within the tradition of those who confused the stable democracy of Athens with the various fluctuating regimes of strife-torn Florence.[36] As time went on, the conviction that representation would resolve the problems of ancient democracies continued, and what Hamilton praised in *Federalist* 9 as the new "science of politics" could be appealed to in order to demonstrate the obsolescence of classical models. Writing in 1794, Samuel Williams of New England contended that governments founded, like the American, on representation, did not admit of what the ancients called democracy any more than they admitted of monarchy or aristocracy.[37] Over a generation later the former president James Monroe made similar observations in his treatise *The People the Sovereigns; being a comparison of the government of the United States with those of the republics which have existed before, with the causes of their decadence and fall.* Published in its unfinished form in 1831, the tract bears witness to the continuing preoccupation with the potential weakness of republican government and the need citizens—indeed, presidents—of the new republic felt to respond to criticisms based on classical parallels. That Monroe should have felt impelled to assemble such a document reveals much about the survival of traditional classical concerns in the first part of the nineteenth century. It is impossible to imagine any twentieth-century president thinking such a subject worthy of attention—not even Woodrow Wilson, who had taught ancient history and would have been perfectly capable of putting together a book of this kind. A deep chasm divides *The People the Sovereigns* from *Profiles in Courage.*

The aversion of the Founding Fathers to Athenian government is articulated nowhere more fully than in the writings of John Adams, which make plain that Adams had a large amount of enthusiasm for a small amount of democracy. If there is one lesson that leaps from the pages of history, Adams argued, it is the necessity for a separation of powers. Thucydides, Adams claimed, would have been more optimistic about the potential for stability in human governance had he known about the separation of powers; and recollection of the miseries of Greece would lead citizens of the eighteenth century to prize the checks and balances of free government and even of contemporary aristocracies.[38] Like others before him, Adams connected the sins of the Athenians with those of the Florentines, to whose sad history, "full of lessons of wisdom, extremely to our purpose," he devoted a sizable chunk of his long treatise on government, *The Defence of the Constitutions of the United States* (1787).[39] Like Athens, Florence demonstrated to Adams the pitfalls of inadequately mixed constitutions, what he called "All Authority in one Centre." Adams considered democratic governments to be the most turbulent and unstable of all unmixed constitutions, and he viewed the reforms of Solon— about which he made a number of factual errors—to be the first step in the destruction of Athens.[40] Solon, Adams wrote, "put all power into hands the least capable of properly using it."[41] Though Solon meant well and intended the *boule* and the Council of the Areopagus as checks on the democracy, nonetheless "factious demagogues" often encouraged the demos to headstrong self-assertion, and the subsequent development of the government of Athens led Adams to inquire, in a sentence borrowed from Rollin that stands alone as a paragraph,

"Is this government, or the waves of the sea?"[42]

Adams dismissed Cleisthenes as a man of no particular talent and censured Aristides for throwing open the archonship to the poor.[43] Not surprisingly, he had no use for ostracism.[44]

Adams's strictures on Aristides appear in his prolonged and vitriolic attack (in his *Defence of the Constitutions of the United States*) on Marchamont Nedham, of all people, whose defense of free governments in *The Excellencie of a Free State* had particularly aroused Adams's spleen. Adams devoted many pages to refuting Nedham's theories about government in general and Athens in particular, considering Nedham's confidence in the people seriously misplaced and seeing in popular sovereignty an alarming threat to the sanctity of property. Property, Adams maintained, "is surely a right of mankind as really as liberty," and consequently majority rule had to be rejected as it would entail "the eight or nine millions who have no property . . . usurping over the rights of the one or two millions who have." Debts, he claims,

> would be abolished first; taxes laid heavy on the rich, and not at all on the others; and at last a downright equal division of every thing be demanded, and voted. What would be the consequence of this? The idle, the vicious, the intemperate, would rush into the utmost extravagance of debauchery, sell and spend all their share, and then demand a new division of those who purchased from them. The moment the idea is admitted into society, that property is not as sacred as the laws of God, and that there is not a force of law and public justice to protect it, anarchy and tyranny commence.[45]

Adams's eye was caught by Nedham's unusual claim that Athenian democratic leaders were "adorned with such governors as gave themselves up to a serious, abstemious, and severe course of life." No democracy, Adams maintains, is conspicuous for these qualities, least of all Athens, where "on the contrary, from the first to the last moment of her democratical constitution, *levity, gayety, inconstancy, dissipation, intemperance, debauchery,* and a *dissolution of manners,* were the prevailing character of the whole nation."[46]

Adams's most dramatic indictment of the Athenian state, however, comes in his treatment of the Thirty Tyrants, for he argues that what undid the Thirty was the quintessentially Athenian nature of their power, which was unchecked. Where other authors have contrasted the bloody executions of the Thirty with the comparatively peaceful conduct of the democracy as a whole, Adams contrasts them rather with the conduct of the Spartans, who, he claims, put to death fewer Athenians in a war of thirty years than the Thirty did in eight months of peace, and sees in them not a stark contrast with the democracy but rather its natural outgrowth. Historians, he contends, are wrong to be taken aback at the conduct of the Thirty, when in truth every

unchecked assembly in Athens had been equally tyrannical. The astonishment, he concludes, "ought to be that there is one sensible man left in the
world who can still entertain an esteem, or any other sentiment than abhorrence, for a government in a single assembly."[47] The conviction of Plato and
Aristotle that tyranny and democracy were intimately connected also appeared in Adams's interpretation of Florentine history, where he contended
that the abuses of Walter, the Duke of Athens, during his rule over Florence
were "as wild, cruel and mad as all other tyrannies have been which were
created on the ruins of a republic." The Florentines, he argued, had no constitution to protect their rights, no rule by law, but "were slaves to every freak
and passion, every party and faction, every aspiring or disappointed noble."[48]
He was probably right about Florence, but this did not make him right about
Athens.

Adams spoke for most of his countrymen when he urged the principles of
representation and of the separation of powers. Americans of both the eighteenth and the nineteenth centuries took a great deal of pleasure in Aristotle's
Politics, which served for many decades as sacred writings in the cult of mixed
government.[49] John Corbin maintained in a backward glance at eighteenth-
century ideology that "the theory of our Constitution derives from Aristotle,
and was put into successful practice in ancient Rome, in eighteenth-century
England, and in our early state constitutions, before it was given its most
perfect embodiment by the Convention of 1787."[50] Auxiliary texts from antiquity were provided by Cicero and Polybius, whose preference for mixed
government over democracy informed their political writings, and altogether
founders as different in outlook as Hamilton and Madison found their concerns foreshadowed in classical writers and agreed that by the use of representation and the institution of checks and balances America could avoid the
mistakes of the Athenians. Similar ideas, of course, had been derived from
more recent texts such as Montesquieu's revered *Spirit of Laws*, whose influence in America was enormous.[51]

Altogether America's founders were deeply ambivalent about the utility of
classical history in general and Athenian history in particular. In the end, not
a single Greek institution was incorporated into the Constitution drawn up by
the Federal Convention of 1787. The Romans fared somewhat better, most
obviously in the shaping—and naming—of the Senate and in the adoption of
Roman mottos and catchwords such as *E pluribus unum* and *Novus Ordo
Saeclorum*; in view of the oligarchic bent of republicanism in ancient Italy,
this is no surprise. Despite the rejection of Athenian-style democracy, the
classical ideal of republican government served as an important legitimizing
tool for American constitutionalists seeking to demonstrate the ancient pedigree of accountable and nonmonarchic governments. Even Adams himself
included a paean to the animating force of classical republicanism in a letter

he wrote from Holland to Lafayette in 1782. "I have the honor and consola-
tion," he declared,

> to be a republican on principle; that is to say, I esteem that form of government the
> best of which human nature is capable. Almost every thing that is estimable in
> civil life has originated under such governments. Two republican powers, Athens
> and Rome, have done more honor to our species than all the rest of it. A
> new country can be planted only by such a government. America would at this
> moment have been a howling wilderness inhabited only by bears and savages, with-
> out such forms of government; and it would again become a wilderness under any
> other.[52]

(He goes on to underline his veneration for the French monarch and to stress
that he is "not a king-killer, king-hater or king-despiser.") Skepticism about
the value of classical history except as a source of admonitory counterexamples
continued after the adoption of the constitution, however, and Jefferson,
though an ardent champion of the classics and the author of a letter advising
a young man that the Greek and Roman historians were eminently worthy of
study in the original languages, in time concluded that classical history had
little to teach modern Americans.[53] In this dichotomy he echoed the ambivalence of Franklin, who had seen moral value in the study of the classics in
general but judged the study of ancient history in particular at worst distracting and at best irrelevant. Perhaps the most striking example of the distinction
in usefulness between classical ideals and ancient history is to be found in the
correspondence of Washington's friend Robert Morris. A proud citizen of the
eighteenth century, Morris's correspondent General Charles Lee proclaimed,
"I have ever from the first time I read Plutarch, been an Enthusiastick for . . .
liberty in a republican garb," for indeed, he goes on, it is natural for a young
person "whose chief companions are the Greek and Roman Historians and
Orators to be dazzled with the splendid picture." Alas, however, the perfect
liberty of antiquity depended on a degree of virtue lacking in modern individuals, a "public and patriotick spirit reigning in the breast of evry [sic] individual superseding all private considerations," for it was this spirit alone that
preserved the classical states, and emphatically not their constitutions, which
were hopelessly inadequate. Not surprisingly, he cites Montesquieu later in his
letter. Classical governments, he concludes, were "defective to absurdity—it
was virtue alone that supported 'em."[54] The unpopularity of the Athenian
democracy in eighteenth-century America is revealed as well in the striking
failure of the anti-Federalists to appeal to the Athenian example. Though on
the whole they were much more democratically inclined than their Federalist
opponents—the writer known as "Philadelphiensis" contending that "America under [a government] purely democratical, would be rendered the happiest
and most powerful nation in the universe"—still the handful of references
they made to classical Athens were either negative or neutral.[55]

The suspicion that the tiny, factious republics of Greece had little to teach modern Americans gathered force as the new nation prospered. Whereas some contrasted the merit of classical ideals with the irrelevance of ancient history, others rejected classical ideology itself, and the gloomy prognostications of John Wilson and Jonathan Boucher about the moral bankruptcy of the classics found a somewhat later analogue in the *Advice to the Privileged Orders* of Joel Barlow, author of the American epic the *Columbiad*. Writing in 1792, Barlow commended his fellow-citizens for a commitment to egalitarian principles inconceivable in ancient—or modern—Europe. Equality, he wrote, is so fundamentally alien to most people's ways of thinking that Europeans of the revolutionary era had been astonished at Washington's willingness to lay down his arms once the crisis had passed; remembering the classical examples of Rome and of Athens as well as the modern example of Cromwell, they had failed to understand that no American would have dared do otherwise. The habits of egalitarian thinking, he contended, "are deep-rooted ones," which "almost change the moral nature of man"; and they are "principles as much unknown to the ancient republics as to the modern monarchies of Europe."[56]

The American foundation would radically alter the connotations of democracy. Three very different men—Hamilton, Adams, and Madison—recoiled with force from the Athenian example and from the notion of direct democracy with which it was inextricably associated. By co-opting republican principles for liberal ends, Madison sought to detach the democratic impulses from republicanism; but he also engineered in his writings a deliberate redefinition of terms whereby an aristocratic theory of politics was couched in sufficiently democratic language that the founders would soon be claimed as the authors of American democracy by men whose beliefs were very different.[57] In 1816 Jefferson was able to proclaim, "We in America are self-consciously . . . democrats."[58] This new and more comfortable thinking about democracy had been made possible by the frequent reiteration in the *Federalist* of the alternatively destructive or irrelevant nature of the Athenian experiment; in turn it would make possible the far more enthusiastic picture of Athenian democracy that emerged in the nineteenth century in both Europe and America. In the 1930s, by which time democracy had firmly entrenched itself in American ideology (and propaganda), John Dewey identified the utility of historical knowledge as its capacity to provide us with "a lever for moving the present into a certain kind of future."[59] The future into which Madison and his cohorts moved their present was indeed in significant part facilitated by the ways in which they understood and deployed the Athenian example, but I suspect Dewey had something rather different in mind. The misinterpretation of history can be as profitable as its more thoughtful understanding, but Dewey seems to have posited the possibility of gaining true knowledge of the past.

There is no reason to believe that Americans confronting a frontier situation with the intellectual equipment of Englishmen formed their ideas about politics from reading about ancient Greece. The bulk of their thinking was surely a product of their own life experiences and the traditions they had absorbed from European writers. One such writer was Locke, who had ignored classical antiquity. Another was Hume, who decried Athenian slaveholding and imperialism and labeled Athenian democracy "such a tumultuary government as we can scarce form a notion of in the present age."[60] A third was Montesquieu, who saw the little republics of antiquity as grounded in virtue and was convinced that a large, modern, commercial republic was a contradiction in terms. Nonetheless, classical analogies could be, and were, used to legitimize just about anything. The energy men like Hamilton, Adams, and Madison devoted to reiterating the inadequacy of direct democracy was remarkable in view of the fact that no nation had tried it for over two thousand years—and in view of the belief frequently expressed by Hamilton and Madison that a new political science had redefined parameters so as to render classical schemata obsolete. Though they admired Montesquieu in many respects, it was crucial to refute him in the matter of the workability of large republics, and appeals to improvements in the science of politics could do just that. Where Jonathan Maxcy argued that, a fortiori, men fortified by "the present advanced state of the science of government" should find it easy to reject an idea that even "the example of all the ancient independent republics reprobates, as the fruitful source of division, violence, and destruction," Madison went further and contended that this new science made it possible to reject the outmoded formulas of earlier days.[61] As Sheldon Wolin has observed, Madison managed to "historicize democracy" as the product of a particular age now gone by, and by presenting the dynamics of representative government in "abstract, quasi-scientific language" to elevate Federalist notions about central powers "to an objective plane where The Federalist's teaching about them could appear axiomatic rather than contestable."[62] The same pretensions to science and objectivity, I would suggest, had characterized the most influential detractors of Athenian government, Plato and Aristotle, who chose to discuss democracy in the abstract while living in the most vibrant democracy in existence.

By eighteenth-century standards, Madison, at least, was no snob. Yet he concurred with Adams and Hamilton in their resounding rejection of direct popular control of government policy. In part, his beliefs seem plainly to have been derived from Montesquieu and the English republicans, who believed that a separation of powers offered the people an indispensable check on its own passions; and his contention that an assembly would still be a mob even were every individual voter a Socrates argues against class prejudice as the source of his concern. He writes at length about the psychology of factions in a way that does not plainly identify the poor as more likely than the rich to play the villains.[63] In part, however, his orientation must be traced to his experience of uneducated men in the Virginia legislature, where he served from 1784 to 1787, and to his preoccupation with the sanctity of private property, which he defends earnestly in his *Federalist* 10 against the potential attacks of democratic leaders.

The relentless insistence that the government of Athens offered no salutary example for the eighteenth century was noticeable on both sides of the Atlantic as well as on both sides of the channel, but the tone of America's founders was decidedly different from that of their European contemporaries. What concerned Athens's European detractors from Rousseau to Mably to Jean-Jacques Barthélemy to Edward Wortley Montagu to William Young was the supposed decadence that attended on the fervid growth of commercial ambition. Some decried the element of selfish competitiveness while others lamented the corrupting effects of luxury. Altogether Athens was judged to have been wanting in that backbone of the state, civic virtue. The picture Americans had of classical Athens was similar, but they focused on different issues. Though civic virtue still held interest, it was approached with a little more sophistication, a development inevitable in a civilization that, while still greatly dependent on agriculture, nonetheless was heavily invested (in every sense) in commerce. A good number of Americans who were concerned that government was becoming too big and European decadence oozing across the Atlantic did not belong to the literate class anyhow. Sparta was rarely held up as a viable model; though Hamilton in the first *Continentalist* had found it less repulsive than other Greek states, in *Federalist* 6 he labeled it "little better than a well-regulated camp."[64] On the whole eighteenth-century Americans were less drawn to the familiar European clichés about Spartan virtue versus Athenian vice (though they were not without concern about heathen ignorance versus Christian wisdom); where luxurious Athens was censured, as by Zephaniah Moore and Mercy Warren, frugal Sparta was not dragged in as a foil. For the kinds of late eighteenth-century Americans who left writings behind them, the issues seem to have been promoting stability, limiting faction, and putting the brakes on agitation for agrarian reform. Such agitation was precisely the sort of activity people of property associated with mobs.

The fear of the mob in American politics no doubt had something to do with the painful experience of Shays's Rebellion, which boasted some nine thousand men in arms seeking to close down courthouses in western Massachusetts to enable poor farmers to escape paying their debts, and with the intermittent cries for relief coming from debtors elsewhere. It is important to notice that Madison's exhortation to representative institutions in *Federalist* 10 was supported by intimations that direct democracy might lead to the implementation of "wicked" projects such as a "rage for paper money, for an abolition of debts, for an equal division of property."[65] These farmers' concerns were not entirely different from those of their ancient counterparts; in particular they were associated with seditious agrarian reformers at Rome, where the Gracchi had worked for the breakup of huge landed estates and the rebels whom Cicero put to death in 63 B.C. had wanted cancellation of debts. Solon had in truth altered the currency at Athens to facilitate trade, and, more famously, had canceled debts. He had most emphatically, however, not redistributed land as his more indigent supporters had hoped he might, and in reality Athenian jurors had regularly to swear that they would not tamper with private property. Despite this important Athenian principle, however—and no doubt because of some nasty verdicts in fourth-century trials in which the jury was swayed by the prospect of getting hold of the accused's wealth for the state—America's founders tumbled comfortably into the tradition that billed the Athenian demos as the enemy of property and of proper repayment of debt. In truth, not only were Athenians of the fifth and fourth centuries averse to redistributing land and canceling debts; the fact was that no such political movement in Europe or America had achieved the slightest success. Even the English Levellers of the seventeenth century, associated by their enemies with precisely such programs, in actuality limited their aims to political, not economic, equality. The redistribution of land would have to wait for the Communist revolutions of the twentieth century.

Despite all this, a mixture of recent and long-standing anxieties drew the founders comfortably into the venerable European tradition that discounted the Athenian achievement and focused instead on the shortcomings of majority rule—some real, some invented. Though the Athenians could be productively paraded as warnings to sensible men, however, Americans' concerns were plainly rooted in more recent developments. In part they arose from the immediate past—the issues they saw underlying Shays's rebellion, for example—and in part in the intermediate past: the turbulence of Renaissance Italy, for instance, and the rights of Englishmen.[66] There is reason to believe that Jefferson, absent from the Constitutional Convention, devoted some of his time in Paris to damage control, busily writing home that the rebellion of Shays had not drawn much attention in Europe and had not damaged the republican cause in European eyes: J. S. McClelland in his study of crowd theory has suggested that one of Jefferson's motives for playing the rebellion down was that he thought that the rebellion was being "played up for the benefit of the Founding Fathers at Philadelphia."[67] The propaganda value of history is not limited to *exempla* from antiquity.

Much can be learned about what political science meant to America's founders and framers from what they did not discuss when they wrote about Athens. Two crucial aspects of Athenian democracy were routinely ignored in eighteenth-century America: universal adult male suffrage among citizens, and the important extrapolitical structures that gave Athenian democracy much of its vitality and indeed made it possible.

To explain the unwisdom of distributing the franchise among all citizens would raise awkward questions that many American political theorists preferred to avoid discussing in a public forum. Instead, therefore, when direct democracy formed the subject of discussion, the emphasis was on "direct" and not on "democracy," with the result that democracy could be billed not as majority rule but as chaos, and tricky questions about what made men of property better decision-makers than the landless could be avoided.[68] Because direct political power had not been gathered in the hands of (male) citizens since classical times, people of property tended to assume that the impotent rage of disfranchised crowds would be only more dangerous should the ballot be placed in such scruffy fingers. The idea that the crowd would be less turbulent were it permitted to debate and legislate rarely surfaced, and when it did, the notion of the "turbulence" of Athenian democracy could be trotted out as proof of the impossibility of enfranchising the masses. Americans of the late eighteenth century actually did have evidence that chaos and violence were not the inevitable hallmark of popular bodies; though some recoiled from both the legislative decisions of broadly based state legislatures and from the Cleonesque manners of some elected representatives, meetings were plainly not of the order of riots and tumults. But ideas firmly held in a long tradition are not easily dislodged, and so on top of the accusations of imprudence constantly lodged against the Athenians there had come a new preoccupation with instability. It is important to notice that observers of Greek politics like Thucydides, Xenophon, the Old Oligarch and Isocrates focused on the crassness of the ordinary citizen and his incapacity for prudent decision making; the notion of the instability of democracy derived in large part first from the high-flown theoretical constructs of Plato and Aristotle (and to some extent from the Aristotelian *Athenaion Politeia* with its supposed eleven constitutions) and next from conflation with Renaissance Florence. It was primarily in the sixteenth century that instability became a key element in the hostile assessment of Athenian democracy rather than just one drawback among many. Inevitably, however, the connection between democracy and disorder was intensified in people's minds by the developments that followed shortly in France.

The same revolution, however, that would send Britons scurrying to books on Greek history that might assist them in belaboring the sins of democracy also focused attention on the role of the civic festival as an important building block of solidarity, virtue, and patriotism among citizens. Within a generation, Macaulay would exalt the education that civic life afforded in classical Athens and Hegel would stress the importance of Athenian festivals in fostering communal values. This concern was conspicuously lacking in writing about Athens in eighteenth-century America, as it had been missing from such writing during the centuries that had gone before. Its absence is more significant, however, in the special context in which the founders were examining the Athenian state—as a potential model for a daring enterprise of their own, a model whose rejection they needed to justify and explain. Given their passionate concern with the welfare of their fledgling nation, the indifference to the kind of civic education offered by everyday life in classical Athens takes on special meaning. To the condemnation of the demos and its fickleness in Thucydides and Plutarch, to the antidemocratic constructs of Plato and Aristotle, to the carping of the Old Oligarch and the disturbing story of Socrates' death, the founders in their search for a useful picture of Athenian democracy would have needed to add the writings of the tragedians and the astonishing story of how these remarkable national treasures functioned as a shared civic heritage—how ordinary citizens (men and to some degree women as well) had the patience and motivation to engage the most painful issues of human existence, and how this engagement contributed to their competence as judges and framers of policy. On the whole, however, the founders showed little interest in extraconstitutional civic structures in general or in Attic tragedy in particular, and the new political "science" mislaid art. This is not entirely surprising in light of the positions taken by Plato and Aristotle, the founders' ancestors in scientific political inquiry. Plato had banished the poets from the *Republic*; Aristotle in the *Poetics* had ignored the democratic roots of tragedy or its role in fostering community and dialogue of a high caliber, and his *Politics* had identified two different kinds of *mousike*, a challenging one for the class of serious political men and one for the lower orders of society that was merely entertaining and not designed to inculcate growth. The founders' writings show no curiosity about the extraordinary training for political decision-making that was afforded in the nature of civic life at Athens. Americans of the late eighteenth century were not indifferent to education. They took pride in the fact that literacy was high among whites in the American colonies at the time of the revolution—perhaps as high in some areas as 90 percent among adult males—and writers such as Benjamin Franklin, Noah Webster, Thomas Jefferson, and Benjamin Rush were all committed to education as one of the bulwarks of the new nation. Its connection with free political institutions was not ignored. Noah Webster proclaimed that "while *property* is considered as the *basis* of the freedom of the American yeomanry, there are other auxiliary supports; among which is the *information of the people*. In no country is education so general—in no country, have the body of the people such a knowledge of the rights of man and of the principles of government. This knowledge," he proclaimed, "joined with a keen sense of liberty and a watchful jealousy, will guard our institutions."[69] But the leap to understanding what had made Athens work was not made; and it could be argued too that "knowledge" is something quite different from what participation in the assemblies and the theatrical festivals gave the Athenians. Much can be learned about late eighteenth-century American thinking about education from Samuel Knox's 1799 prizewinning essay on education for Americans. Presumably because of its reputation for cultivation and its role as a university city in the

Hellenistic and Roman periods, Knox inferred that Athens provided public education to its citizens, something that the evidence suggests is not true. What Athens did provide was an extraordinarily active civic life that included attendance at extremely demanding tragic dramas that examined the most difficult questions facing humans. But Knox dismissed tragedy in his treatise on education; after encouraging the reading of Rollin's insipid *Ancient History* and the uninspired *Antiquities* of Potter—both common items in early American libraries—and of some Virgil, Theocritus, Hesiod, Anacreon, Pindar, and Horace, he suggests that "in order also to be acquainted with the state of dramatic poetry among the ancients, one or two of the most celebrated performances in each language might be read, but it does not appear that a long attention to that species of composition would be either proper or improving."[70]

Much of the Americans' difficulties with the Athenians lay in their inability to distance themselves from the question whether Athenian democracy should be resurrected *in toto* in the New World. To dwell constantly on this concern inevitably interfered with a thoughtful examination of the Athenian democracy. Even within the parameters inside which they were operating, however, Americans of the founding era asked limited questions of Greek history. They did not ask how best they might emulate the civilization that had produced the plays of Sophocles or the Zeus of Phidias, because the intensity of their fears stood in the way of their seeing a dynamic connection between Athenian democracy and Athenian creativity; they did not read the history of Greece by Lysias or Demosthenes' essays on government, for no such texts had been written. What they found in their reading was a composite picture built up over the centuries into which little critical or creative thought had been put, and the end product rendered by this tedious process taught the vices of Greek democracy alongside the virtues of a sort of bland, generic republicanism. The first group to enjoy the benefit of the moralizing narrative histories of antiquity composed in eighteenth-century Britain and France, America's founders chose not to question the account of Athens' history they found there and looked to the end of the "story" for an assessment of the Athenian achievement. Examining the past with an eye to the present, they did not examine it very much at all. It would be many generations before Americans could explore classical history in a context at least partially set apart from the challenges of their own day. Monroe's ponderous monograph on ancient governments focused obsessively on the superiority of the constitution of the United States to those of the classical republics, and the Greek portions of Thomas Dew's 1853 *Digest of the Laws, Customs, Manners, and Institutions of the Ancient and Modern Nations* frequently took the form of object lessons for modern Americans. Ironically, indeed, the most positive reaction to classical Athens in America made its appearance in an exceedingly presentist context: the greatest excitement generated by the history of Athens in America prior to the twentieth century came when Dew joined others like Calhoun, Holmes, and Fitzhugh in adducing the Athenian example in support of the merits of slavery.

Revolution and Nostalgia

Americans could, and did, hark back to the autonomy of Greek colonies and the victory of the Greek republics over the Persian monarchy, but the relevance of Greek history to revolutionary France was less clear, and on the whole the classically minded among the French revolutionaries recurred rather to republican Rome, home of Cato and the Bruti and the seat of resistance to tyranny. In comparisons with classical Athens, the French had both more and less to fear than the Americans. The loosely federated republics that fought together against England were more nervous about taking on the instability and vulnerability to foreign aggression that seemed to them to mark the ancient Greek city-states, but the French were more sensitive about the imputation of the chaos, violence, and popular tyranny that had come to be associated with classical democracies. Predictably, some French revolutionaries looked back nostalgically to the eager civic preoccupations of the Athenians, but most rejected the Athenian model and were careful to avoid associating modern France with ancient Athens. Just as predictably, enemies of the revolution were quick to throw cold water on enthusiasm for ancient republicanism and let no opportunity slip for exposing what they believed had been the true nature of political life in the anarchic states of antiquity.[71]

The French revolutionaries shared with their American counterparts a desire to ground their bold new venture in classical precedent, and calls for the resurrection of ancient virtue were commonplace. Robespierre identified the Greeks as men whose republican virtues "had raised them at times above humanity" and praised the "political virtue which accomplished so many prodigies in Greece and in Rome, and which ought to produce far more astonishing ones in republican France" as the essential principle of a democratic and popular government.[72] Saint Just proclaimed that his program offered not the happiness of Persepolis but rather that of Athens and Sparta, a universe in which "the people make the republic by the simplicity of their manners and morals."[73] Certain personality types are always especially vulnerable to the values propounded by texts read in youth, and both Buzot and his companion Jeanne-Marie Roland attributed their republicanism to their childhood education in the classics. Buzot reported in his memoirs that his head and heart had been filled from an early age with Greek and Roman history and its heroes, on whose virtues he nourished himself.[74] Roland's 1793 *Mémoires* tell how thirty years before, when she was nine years old, she had carried her Plutarch to church in place of a prayer book.[75] Brissot, filled from earliest youth with a desire to emulate Phocion, recalls in his *Mémoires* how he hid his light from his disapproving father when he stayed up through the darkness to improve his Latin.[76] The popularity of the craze for the classics is attested by the laments of the critics, such as the conservative Regnaud de Saint-Angély's complaint of his contemporaries' mindless admiration for antiquity and the scorn the professor Volney heaped on the revolutionaries' enthusiasm for the ancients.[77] The Marquis de Bouille also complained of the seditious effects of the high school study of classical civilization on the revolutionary generation.[78] The concerns of these men are evocative of the earlier condemnation of the study of classical authors by Hobbes, who had targeted them as a prime source for the evolution of dangerous republican ideals. The American scholar Harold Parker has astutely uncovered a note to a 1771 school text of Nepos in which the French editor warned his readers against Nepos's wrongheaded republicanism and cautioned them that Miltiades had sinned in plotting to preserve Greek liberty by betraying his employer, Darius.[79] It seems likely that most of the early, prerevolutionary attachment to classical antiquity took the form of wistful identification with republican heroes who operated in a universe in which renown could be achieved even by men born outside a limited circle of nobility. (Madame Roland apparently imagined that it could be achieved in antiquity by women as well, but that is another story.[80]) Robespierre looked back in nostalgia to the ancient republics in which talent even without birth might lead to glory, and Marat contrasted his own day, which witnessed the rewarding of various mercenaries and sycophants by mere money, with Greece, where men like Miltiades and Thrasybulus were honored with statues, trophies, and crowns.[81] Warmth for classical republicanism continued in many cases well into the revolution; Rabaut de Saint-Étienne reported with satisfaction in 1793 that his fellow-citizens took pleasure in recollecting the laws of the ancient republics and hoped that the Convention would find a means of overhauling France on "these happy models."[82]

The extent to which it was either possible or desirable actually to resurrect ancient institutions in modern France was the topic of considerable disagreement among the revolutionaries, and individual thinkers often changed their mind from one week to the next. Jacobins on the whole enjoyed setting up Sparta as a model; Billaud-Varenne contrasted the solidity of Sparta under the Lycurgan system with the disastrous effects of the weak and trusting Solon on Athens. Girondists sometimes rejected both Athens and Sparta, though it was the militaristic oppressor of the helots and enemy of commerce who generally bore the brunt of the attack: Vergniaud in 1793 cautioned his fellow revolutionaries against the dangers of resurrecting either Athenian softness or (*a fortiori*) Spartan austerity.[83] In many circles, however, a sentimental attachment to classical antiquity persisted, especially in Paris, where babies began to carry names like Solon, Lycurgus, Phocion, Aristides, Socrates, and—most of all—Brutus.[84] The popularity of Brutus serves as a reminder of the revolutionaries' essentially Roman focus. Parker has assembled a catalog of citations to classical authors among the revolutionaries that makes plain the far larger role played by Roman authors than Greek in their education.[85] The Roman orientation is particularly evident in the writings of the singularly humorless and puritanical Saint Just. Nonetheless, Saint Just's plans for overhauling French education offer striking parallels to the Spartan system, and many of the revolutionaries found the selfless and ascetic patriotism of Sparta inspirational.[86] Madame Roland's tearful wish that she had been born a Spartan is notorious. This sort of enthusiasm had been fostered by youthful reading in Plutarch and Rousseau. Others gravitated toward Athens, a gracious society more reminiscent of the blandishments of the French capital. Comparisons of the merits of Lycurgus and of Solon were frequent, and it was in the writings of the republican journalist Camille Desmoulins that Athens figured most prominently in the revolutionary vision of France.

The belief of Marat and Robespierre that antiquity would have afforded greater scope to their talents was shared a fortiori by Desmoulins, and by and large it was Athens on which Desmoulins's wistful eyes turned in his search for a better world. In the Athens of Desmoulins's imagining, as Parker has written, where liberty "meant rewards for the talented" and was not at odds with gracious living, Desmoulins's "wish for a career, a good time, and domestic joy would have been gratified."[87] In his journal the Vieux Cordelier Desmoulins makes a point of mentioning that Solon's (purported) enthusiasm for wine, women [sic], and song did not detract from the esteem he was accorded as a wise legislator.[88] In his fourth issue Desmoulins set up Thrasybulus as his hero and capped his call for clemency and compassion with an appeal to Athens, home of an altar to mercy and of "the most democratic people which has ever existed."[89] Plainly these are words of praise. The next issue reprised the same theme.[90] Attacking Brissot in the sixth issue for his championship of Sparta, Desmoulins maintained that Spartan equality amounted only to equal deprivation, reassuring those who feared that republicanism would establish that Spartan austerity so dear to the likes of Mably and Rousseau that the prosperity of Athens offered clear proof that "there is nothing like republican government to foster the wealth of nations."[91] In Number Seven (and in a disjointed fragment evidently attached to Number Six) Desmoulins paints France as the modern picture of Athens but for the absolute freedom of the Athenian press, of which the impunity of Aristophanes was the unmistakable proof. It was not freedom of the press, Desmoulins insists, that killed Socrates, but rather the calumnies of Anytus and Meletus. Except for the absence of this freedom, Desmoulins sees the France of his day as a true resurrection of ancient Athens:

read the three-thousand-year-old comedies of Aristophanes, he advises his readers, and you will find that across the centuries the French and the Athenians are soulmates and, indeed, contemporaries.[92]

But Desmoulins was not representative of his compatriots, and it was not as an exemplar of liberality and gentility that Athens found her niche in revolutionary literature but rather as the site of numerous inspirational martyrdoms. Desmoulins's hero had been Thrasybulus, but his contemporaries gravitated instead to Aristides, Socrates, and Phocion. Naturally the exiles and executions of such men reflected badly on the Athenian state, and identification with these heroes implied no endorsement of Athenian government. Robespierre cast himself as one of those unappreciated statesmen who, like Phocion, measured the degree of their virtue by that of their persecution, and he was quick to identify himself with Aristides as well.[93] Predictably, Girondists and other imminent victims of the guillotine awaiting their fate in jail positively wallowed in identification with classical republican martyrs. Le Bon, writing from prison to his wife, suggested that she "read ancient history and see how all the useful men were, one after the other, repaid with ingratitude," and he consoled himself with the belief that such a death "is the most glorious which man can desire."[94] Others were more specific: Buzot identified himself and his friends with Socrates, Aristides, Phocion, Demosthenes, and Themistocles; Brissot congratulated himself on sharing the fate of Phocion; Gensonne and Dufriche-Valazé appealed to the models of Phocion and Socrates; and Lasource on hearing himself condemned to death quoted Phocion's parting shot—that he was dying when the people had lost their reason, but his attackers would die when they recovered it.[95] The preoccupation with dying well goes some way to explain the revolutionaries' enthusiasm for Sparta and Rome. Chateaubriand, visiting the ruins of Greece in 1806, expressed the wish to have died with Leonidas and lived with Pericles; for those to whom a martyred death was a priority, only disaffected and ultimately antidemocratic Athenians could serve as role models.[96] Nobody yearned to die like Pericles.

The romantic glorification of Athenian martyrs by their Girondist counterparts was not the only possible perspective on the misfortunes of Athens's great men. Those who were not republicans placed more emphasis on the injustice and incompetence of the people than on the heroism of their victims. Arguing in 1789 that liberty depended on the continuation of the monarchy, Mounier adduced the governments of antiquity as evidence that the liberty of republics was illusory. The tyranny of a multitude, he argued, is more pernicious than that of an individual precisely in its failure to inspire the same heroic resistance. What ancient states enjoyed was the anarchy of license, not the blessings of liberty. Neither Greece nor Rome knew the essential principles of the separation of powers or of representation. (Because of its incorporation of the representative principle Mounier found the Unites States to be the best constituted of the ancient and modern republics.) Despite all the "sophisms of those who adulate the Greeks and Romans," Mounier concluded, the real state of affairs in antiquity was pitiful.[97] In February of 1790, Montlosier, arguing that what the French needed was "liberty, a constitution and a king," complained of the leveling tendency at Athens, where no house and no individual were permitted to be more glorious than any other, and decried the exile, proscription, and death with which Athens rewarded her benefactors.[98]

The reactionary Cazalès adopted a similar line of argument the following summer in opposing the election of judges by the people. Admonishing his audience that "the past is the school of the present," Cazalès cited the examples of Socrates, Lycurgus, Aristides, and Solon [sic], all of whom were "immolated by the people," in warning his compatriots of the "errors and violence" of the masses and the "inconveniences that attend on popular government."[99] A few days later Count Clermont-Tonnerre recurred to the theme of the sophistries that defended the policies of ancient states. Arguing that the right of making war and peace should remain with the King, Clermont-Tonnerre identified "sophism" as the guiding principle in decisions of war and peace in republican Rome and sought an equitable system to prevent France from "falling into democracy." Among ancient and modern republics that suffered reverses as a result of having decisions of war and peace deliberated in open assembly, he gave pride of place to the Athenians' failure to mobilize against Macedon.[100]

Athens, then, served as a negative example to French conservatives and was largely avoided by staunch republicans except as the instrument of the martyrdom of their heroes; most republicans who wished to be transported back to Athens wished it so that they might glory in being mistreated. For all Desmoulins's dreamy nostalgia, Athenian institutions were not resurrected; Rouzet, a representative of the Haute-Garonne, wanted an areopagite council and ostracism (as well as ephors), but nobody listened; in his history of Greece the distinguished twentieth-century historian Gustave Glotz made implicit comparisons with the creation of Departments in France during the revolution with the demes, trittyes, and tribes of Cleisthenes but, as Vidal-Naquet has pointed out, the analogy seems to have escaped the revolutionaries themselves, who had little knowledge of Cleisthenes or his work.[101]

• • • • •

In the intellectual and political tumult that surrounded the revolution in France, every possible opinion about antiquity was voiced at some time, often with considerable passion. In the last analysis, however, what appealed to those who advocated the emulation of antiquity was not classical government per se but rather the outlook on life and the societal and educational institutions that had made ancient governments workable. In the vast literature on education produced during the revolutionary era, for example, much care was taken to determine what festivals, competitions, and other communal experiences might best transplant ancient virtues to modern France.[102] In this respect the French revolutionaries differed from the American founding fathers, a far more peaceable and harmonious lot who had the leisure to frame a constitution under more auspicious conditions than their French successors were to enjoy, and whose disputes over questions of government were by comparison relaxed and amicable. For the Americans, the constitution was the primary issue in the examination of the ancient republics, while the French revolutionaries were more concerned with the regeneration of ancient virtue. It is interesting to notice that the revolution in America had not on the whole persuaded the French of the viability of classical models of government. Rather, the employment of both the federative and, most dramatically, the representative principle had pointed up the weaknesses of ancient governments and opened up a bright new future for republicanism. It had been the belief of Montesquieu that although ancient republicanism had fostered, and been fostered by, the virtue of citizens, nonetheless republican government was impossible in a large state. Now, France was a very large state. Followers of Montesquieu's principles, therefore—and there were many—had yearned for the simple virtues of the ancients without wishing to transplant any of the organs of ancient government. But the revolution in America had suggested that it might be possible to have the same virtues with new and improved organs. Far from causing the stock of the ancient states to rise, the founding of the American republic prompted invidious comparisons between the successful new republic across the Atlantic and the defunct ones in ancient Europe. To be sure, some, like Chastellux, praised the Americans by comparing them to the Greeks and Romans; but Brissot promptly took Chastellux to task for failing to see that the Americans had in fact succeeded where the ancients had fallen short, and Condorcet concluded that the American state was far superior to the classical republics.[103] The revolution in France, following upon that in America, did much to blunt the reformers' nostalgia for antiquity, refuting as it did the belief that modern life offered no scope to men (and women) of talent and conviction. Already in 1790 Desmoulins compared the French revolutionaries favorably with the Greeks and the Romans, concluding that nothing in past history had so honored any people as the revolution had honored its authors.[104] Even those who, like Jeanne-Marie Roland, avoided invidious comparisons reported that they no longer had any reason to envy the ancient republics, as they were being "enlightened by a purer day."[105]

The far greater promise afforded by the modern world in comparison with antiquity was also developed in scholarly and pedagogical circles. The most vehement champion of contemporary France over Greece and Rome was the polymath and orientalist Volney, who forcefully denounced the desire to recast the modern world according to classical specifications.[106] In his history lectures delivered at the École Normale and published in 1795, Volney complained bitterly of his contemporaries' excessive reverence for antiquity. "We scold Jews," he wrote, "for their superstitious worship, yet we are fallen into a no less superstitious worship of the Romans and the Greeks; where our ancestors swore by Jerusalem and the Bible, we swear by Athens and Livy."[107] What Volney finds astonishing about this new religion is that its apostles have so little understanding of the creed they are preaching and do not recognize that the ancient states provided no admirable model of liberty. He expatiates at length on the brutality of Greek slavery in general and helotry in particular. For Volney, oppression and butchery abroad and tyranny and faction at home characterized the glory that was Greece. Volney dismisses the Greek states as models for France on grounds of both irrelevance and turpitude. The size of France, he argues, should alone preclude meaningful comparison with the Greek world. Nor is any analogy possible between the French, for whom fifteen centuries of friction have only produced increasing unity, and the divided savages and bandits of Greece.

Volney goes on, however, to reject the Greek models on other grounds as well, complaining that his contemporaries, seduced by Athens's artistic achievements, have lost sight of the key role played by her great monuments in her eventual collapse. These very temples and public buildings, he argues, were the first cause of Athens's ruin and the first symptom of her decadence, as the rapine and extortion that had made them possible sparked the defection of her allies and the jealousy and cupidity of her enemies. Volney compares the needless luxury entailed in Athens's building programs with the Louvre, Versailles, and other construction projects in contemporary France that forced the increase of taxes and placed an alarming strain on the treasury. Learning, Volney concluded, is the prerequisite of progress, and by teaching the moral, spiritual, and political bankruptcy of Greece he hoped to liberate his countrymen from the adulation of antiquity and encourage them to see that their own age—an age that had discovered, among other things, the principle of representation—had the opportunity for a future far more glorious than the Greek past.

Not surprisingly, French conservatives such as the ultraroyalists who despised republicanism ancient and modern were not converted to its cause by the abolition of the monarchy in France, a development that served only to intensify the hostility of such men to Athens. One of the fiercest and most eloquent of the ultraroyalists, Count de Bonald, included in his *Theories of Political and Religious Power in Civil Society, Demonstrated through Reason and through History* a sweeping attack on the Greeks in general (whom he labeled "degenerate Egyptians") and Athens in particular.[108] In ancient Greece, a terrible place where the separation of powers was unknown, the absence of a general will led to the ascendancy of the individual wills of particular legislators and fostered a multiplicity of godless and fluctuating ambitions that made any concerted effort impossible. De Bonald reproaches the wrongheaded writers who have failed to see that the republican Greeks defeated the monarchic Persians only because of superior military discipline and the desperate determination to survive.[109] Like Filmer and assorted thinkers of the Renaissance, De Bonald identifies monarchy with the eternal and republicanism with the ephemeral. In republics, he contends, the present is all, everything that is eternal is called into question, doubted, and the very existence of God denied, whereas "monarchy, like religion, eternalizes everything." An examination of human history, De Bonald concludes, has demonstrated to him the truth that atheism, materialism, and republicanism all go hand in hand.[110]

THE BRITISH BACKLASH

The revolutions in America and France also inspired monarchists of other nationalities to warn their countrymen against trying the experiment at home. The anxiety was most keenly felt in England, and the reaction was discernible soon after the first shots were fired at Lexington and Concord. In his 1778 edition of Lysias and Isocrates, John Gillies, the Scottish historian to the king, warned dissidents who, ignoring the sad history of Greece, wished to "set on foot a republican confederacy" to tremble "at the prospect of those calamities, which, should their designs be carried into execution, they must both inflict and suffer."[111] Gillies's 1786 *History of Ancient Greece* also served as a vehicle to convey to readers the evils of nonmonarchic government. Greek history, Gillies announced in his dedicatory epistle to the king, by "describing the incurable evils inherent in every form of Republican policy," evinces the inestimable benefits to liberty from the "lawful dominion of hereditary Kings," and therefore may with singular propriety be offered to George III as sovereign of the most free nation on earth.

Not surprisingly, Gillies presents the story of Athens as the history of "a wild and capricious democracy" in which an unbridled mob interacted with a series of worthless demagogues from Ephialtes to Eubulus.[112] Gillies is not content to let his readers draw their own conclusions about the evils of democratic government; he states plainly that democracy in general is "a fierce and licentious form of government" with "incurable defects" and a "tyrannical spirit."[113] Frequent references to the character flaws of the poor with their "gross appetites" make plain the source of Gillies's objection to popular sovereignty.[114] In ancient times, he explains, as in modern, "the corrupt taste of the licentious vulgar was ever at variance with the discerning judgment of the wise and virtuous."[115]

Developments in America also led Josiah Tucker to crystallize his thinking about government in his 1781 *Treatise concerning Civil Government*, but the nature of Tucker's revulsion for Athens was different from Gillies's. Though Tucker resembled Gillies in his desire to rouse in "every true Friend to Liberty an Abhorrence of the Idea of an Athenian Common-wealth," he alternately censured Athens for being a flagrant democracy and mocked her as a closet aristocracy.[116] An attack on the principles of Locke and their recent application in America, Tucker's treatise warns potential republicans in England that "this very Argument of *unalienable Rights*, weak and trifling as it is, may nevertheless become a formidable Weapon, in the Hands of desperate *Catalinarian* Men, for establishing a real and cruel Tyranny of their own (according to the Example which the *American* Rebels have already set) instead of that harmless, imaginary Tyranny, of which they so bitterly complain at present."[117] Though Tucker censures all forms of unmixed government—absolute monarchy, hereditary aristocracy, and democracy—he is particularly concerned to caution his readers about government by the "Caprice and Humour of the giddy Populace."[118] Tucker makes clear that it was experience rather than scholarship that led him to reject democracy. In a footnote to his section on comparative government he reports that he is sorry to say that in his fifty years as an observer of government, he "hardly ever knew an unpopular Measure to be in itself a bad one, or a popular one to be truly salutary," and he lists numerous helpful measures for the development of commerce that were universally opposed by the English people.[119] Scant indeed, he laments, "must the Pittance of Power be, which results from the Union of 40, 50 or even 100 Savages, issuing forth from their Dens and Caverns, and assembled together *for the first Time*, in order to constitute a *Body Politic*" in the form of an "Insect Commonwealth," that "Grub of a free, equal and Sovereign Republic" that is "a reptile, democratical Institution."

It is noteworthy that Tucker felt some need to assure his readers that he was not, in fact, attacking classical governments. Some admirers of antiquity, he conjectures, will say, "What? Do you compare the famous republics of *Greece* and *Rome* to Insects, Grubs, and Reptiles?" To this "smart Objection" Tucker has "the following Reply to make: that in ancient republics by far the majority of the populace was excluded from political privilege, so that one cannot in fairness call them democracies"; insofar as they were democratic, however, they were indeed to be excoriated.[120] As we will have occasion to observe later on, Tucker takes a harsh view of ancient slavery—and modern. Tucker regarded Athenian exclusivity concerning citizenship as both impolitic and uncharitable, and he saw the restriction of citizenship working with imperialism and slavery to create a de facto hereditary aristocracy. Athens, in short, was bad insofar as she was democratic and worse insofar as she wasn't.

It was the revolution across the channel, however, that sparked the greatest anxiety and provoked the most energetic counterattacks in England. Two powerful essays appearing in the 1790s linked Athens and France in obloquy—William Young's *The British Constitution of Government Compared with that of a Democratic Republic* (1793) and Robert Bisset's *Sketch of Democracy* (1796). Both tracts were designed to counter suggestions that republican reforms would profit contemporary England—suggestions that Young attributes to "no very friendly advisers" and that Bisset ascribes to the London Corresponding Society and "hireling lecturers."[121]

For Young, the hallmark of democracy was constant contention, since under a democracy men will constantly compete for preferment. At the same time that individuals and parties of the people contend with one another, the people at large contest with other nations, stirred up by demagogues who have a private interest in fomenting troubles that may make them indispensable to the people. He supports this allegation by reference to the story that Pericles brought on the Peloponnesian War to avoid having to render his accounts to the Athenians.[122] All the traditional accusations against Athens are reprised in Young's complaint that demagogues in a democracy support the tyranny of the many poor over the few rich and bribe the electorate on the pretext of remunerating public duties. Athenian democracy for him consists of a licentious "bargain of a demagogue on one part, and of the people on the other—for rights to do wrong."[123] Like his contemporary John Adams, Young compares the excesses of democrats in Athens to those of their counterparts in Italy.[124] Young also sees ancient Athens as the forerunner of modern France, in all its "wretched anarchy"; for although the Athenians ostracized simply for unpopularity, without any specific charge, still the climax of popular tyranny remained to be realized in the massacres of revolutionary France.[125] The revolution in France, Young concludes, is no example to England, for while the French had nothing in their old government worth clinging to, the English with their excellent British constitution had "every thing to fight for."[126]

Young considered himself particularly qualified to hold forth on the weaknesses of Athenian democracy as he had published in 1777 the first edition of his *History of Athens*, at once an impassioned encomium on the *patrios politeia* of Solon and Cleisthenes and a savage indictment of the "leveling" that began with Aristides' extension of the franchise and led to the demagogy of Pericles and Ephialtes. But Young was not the only Englishman to draw the French and the Athenians together in a comprehensive attack on the violence of democratic government. A similar spirit informs the *Sketch of Democracy* penned by a Chelsea schoolmaster, Robert Bisset. The stated purpose of Bisset's work was to remove "erroneous notions from those who had listened to modern lecturers and demagogues," and Bisset expresses the hope that his essay will succeed in showing those of his countrymen who are "deluded by democratic theories, or enamored of fanciful innovations, that the happiest of all lands is"—and this in all capital letters—"THE LAND WE LIVE IN." His argument, he contends, will deal as little as possible in abstraction, since "many of those who have embraced democratical opinions, are probably men not much accustomed to abstract reasoning."[127]

Bisset, in fact, reads the sins of democracy back into the earliest days of Greece, billing Thersites as a "seditious demagogue" and Achilles as a self-interested whig—for, he explains, "the same cause often makes that subject a whig, who if a king would be a tyrant impatient of controul."[128] Greek history, he maintains, is the story of the substitution of democracy for limited monarchy, a subversion that converted Greece to a scene of wicked license wherein Athens was especially notorious. Attacking the sophists, "a set of pretended philosophers" who abetted the multitude in its licentiousness, he posits a natural connection between the presence of democracy and the absence of religion, since "those who will submit to no human authority, however salutary, come by no very different transition to disavow divine."[129] Democracy, moreover, is strikingly volatile and labile, and in another reference to the revolution in France Bisset cites Aristotle's observation that "mutability is one striking feature in democracy," arguing that Aristotle saw in the history of Greek democracies and inferred from human nature "what every man now sees in the awful monuments of recent facts."[130]

Bisset confronts directly the connection between domestic and foreign affairs in Athens. Even the guarded Americans had posited a connection if only of the most general kind between Greek republicanism and the defeat of Persia; but Bisset takes an opposite stand. Friends to democracy, he complains, affect to impute the Athenians' gallant conduct in the Persian war to their democratic constitution; but he points out that nondemocratic countries have done just as well, citing the heroism of William Wallace's band in Scotland and of the English navy against Spain. In fact, he argues, it was the choice to make Miltiades sole commander in the first war and Aristides and Themistocles "really princes" in the second that accounted for the Athenians' success, with the result that the Athenians' famous victories, so far from arising from their democratic form of government, in reality were due to a "temporary departure from its spirit."[131] It was indeed the Athenians' form of government, however, and the "imbecility" of the "mob" to which Bisset attributed the Athenian failure in Sicily, though he concedes that the Athenians, although wise in wanting to change from their democracy in 411, simply raised four hundred of the mob above the others, gaining "no more by the change, than did the French by their change from the club and mob government in the time of Petion, Brissot, and Condorcet, to that of the junto of Danton, Marat and Robespierre." Even Aristophanes' comedies are for Bisset "the comedies of democracy," and their vulgarity was predictable in view of the characteristic coarseness of democratic sensibilities.[132] Throughout Athenian history, Bisset concludes, it is plain that the Athenians' "misfortunes were chiefly owing to the nature of their government, their successes to a temporary deviation from that government."[133]

Bisset died in 1805, and his writings, which included a couple of novels and a book on George III, attracted little attention; somewhat more has been paid to the works of Young, and more still to Gillies's *History*. Though Gillies's work was well received, however, in the end it was Mitford's ten volumes that caught the public eye and superseded Rollin's history. Mitford had traveled a good deal in France, where he reported finding enormous admiration for the balance of the English constitution. To this admiration he was conspicuously receptive. When he returned to England and became a colonel in the South Hampshire militia, he found Edward Gibbon serving in the same company. It was apparently Gibbon who suggested to Mitford that he write a history of Greece, and the first of Mitford's ten volumes appeared in 1784.

Mitford's profound commitment to monarchy manifested itself in an orientation to Greek history that even some of his Tory associates found peculiar. He judged the Persians to be quite delightful and considered Persian rule over Greece perfectly thinkable. His consistent defense of Philip of Macedon bordered on hysteria, as when he insisted that Philip had never abridged the "civil rights" of the "Macedonian people," or when he maintained that the Athenian prisoners who requested from Philip clothes in which to return home gave proof thereby of the "arrogance and levity of the Athenian Many in that age." (Mitford also discounted the story of a reproof administered to Philip on the part of Demades the orator, arguing that this tale, if true, would give partial credit to the Athenian democracy with molding the character of a man as great as Philip.)[134] Not surprisingly, Mitford is intensely preoccupied with the dangerous example the Athenian democracy had set for modern Europe—one England had, to its credit, largely ignored. A perfectly executed history of Greece, he maintains, should offer education in political science to all nations, and in so claiming he seeks to justify some rather protracted digressions in his middle volumes on the superiority of the English government to all other systems.

Mitford makes a point of conceding that there is some difficulty in translating political terms from one culture to another. Nonetheless, he lapses frequently into comparisons between Athens and England, comparisons that are invariably favorable to his own country. Life, liberty, and property, he warns, had not been as secure in Athens as in England—England, where the democratic element was "more wisely given, and more wisely bounded, notwithstanding some defects, than in any other government that ever existed."[135] Only at the local democratic level did England resemble Athens—Athens, where all shared the "burthensome, disgraceful and mischievous office" of flattering the multitude, and where freedom of speech was frequently denied.[136] Nothing in modern Europe, Mitford contends, has so much resembled the constant Athenian canvas for popular favor as the contest for the representation of a county in England, Middlesex in particular.[137] Athenian political life, he writes, "strange as it may appear to those who have had no experience of a democratical mixture in government, cannot appear strange among ourselves, where county meetings, too frequently, and the common hall of London, continually exhibit perfect examples of that tyranny of a multitude."[138]

If democracy was appalling in England, so much worse was it in France. Trying to find some silver lining for the cloud that was the late revolution, Mitford in his second edition pointed out that at least the disgraceful proceedings in France served to make Greek political life credible to the English, who under the security of their own excellent constitution might otherwise have found it utterly inconceivable. Greek and French politics cast light on one another, Mitford maintains, and show that neither state is alone in atrocity. Although the parallel Mitford draws between the tribunal of the Committee of Public Welfare in Paris and the Thirty Tyrants at Athens might seem at first to cast no shadow over the Athenian democracy, in fact Mitford (like John Adams and like Paolo Paruta) blames the democracy for the rise of the Thirty and sees Critias himself as the inevitable product of democratic excess. Not surprisingly, however, Mitford reached his conclusions about the evils of Athenian democracy prior to the revolution in France. Aware that readers might suppose his work to be influenced by the revolution, Mitford takes pains to assure them that his aversion to Athens is based entirely on the ancient evidence. In discussing the Peloponnesian War, he attributes it to the "apprehension excited, among the oligarchical states, by the growing preponderance of the Athenian democracy, rendered terrible by its spirit of conquest, its spirit of tyranny, and its particular disposition to overthrow and oppress the oligarchal [sic] interest"; but in a footnote to this paragraph he insists that this passage predated the revolution: "The alarm spred over Europe by a similar spirit . . . in the French democracy, may possibly be supposed to have furnished this idea; but it was derived purely from the Grecian cotemporary [sic] historian, and indeed the passage was written before the spirit of conquest and tyranny among the French had given the lie direct to their pretension of peaceful and equitable principles."[139]

What appears to have frightened Mitford most powerfully about democracy was the attendant insecurity of property. "The satisfaction . . . of an Englishman in considering his house and his field more securely his own, under the protection of the law, than a castle defended by its own garrison, or a kingdom by its armies," he writes, was unknown in Athens, where, after the Solonic constitution was overthrown, the nobility were forced to "cringe" to the rabble in order to protect their property.[140] He praises the clandestine Athenian oligarchic clubs, the *synomosiai*, as counterweights to the despotism the democracy exercised over the rich in a society in which both life and property were incomparably less secure than under the mild firmness of British government.[141]

That the concern over property was hardly idiosyncratic to Mitford is made clear by the prominence of the theme in the writings of Young and Bisset in Britain and the founding fathers in America. Both Bisset and Young praised Solon's refusal to redistribute land, and Bisset saw Solon's program sharing with English law the goal of preserving property. Bisset also cited Peisistratus as an example of a demagogue to whom men of "sense and property" were opposed; Adams, it must be remembered, attacked Marchamont Nedham for separating power and property.[142] Young saw many of Athens's problems arising out of the unseating of the landed aristocracy by the new aristocracy of trade. In his history of Athens he portrayed post-Cleisthenic Athens as declining into a democracy in which the corruption at the core was concealed by the *"ruddy and rich superficies which ever covers the diseases of a commercial state,"* and later in his comparison of Britain with democratic republics Young warned that political theorists must take men as they are, not shepherds of Arcadia but rather "men who follow trade and commerce . . . who abuse, or are ready to abuse, both power and wealth."[143] Young's enthusiasm for early Athens is matched only by his revulsion from Athens at its most democratic, and his growing anxiety about the impact of democracy on a commercial state is made plain by the changes the title of his book underwent from the first edition of 1777 to the second of 1786 and the third of 1804. The original edition was entitled *The Spirit of Athens. Being a political and philosophical investigation of the history of that republic*; the next, *The History of Athens politically and philosophically considered with the view to an investigation of the immediate causes of elevation and decline, operative in a free and commercial state*; and the 1804 edition, *The History of Athens, including a commentary on the principles, policy and practice of republican government, and on the causes of elevation and decline, which operate in every free and commercial state.*[144]

•   •   •   •   •

By the close of the eighteenth century, the longing to resurrect ancient virtue had by and large been replaced by a more forward-thinking mentality that saw the solution to society's problems in the future rather than in the past. Abandoning the search for a route by which to return to the prelapsarian world of antiquity, monarchists and republicans alike sought governments that would best protect the bustling and diverse commercial world of the present. Though the more democratically inclined focused their energies on protecting the aspirations of the little man while more conservative thinkers devoted theirs to protecting the acquisitions of the big one, they shared a fundamental interest in serving the needs of the present. The new concerns that agitated citizens of the nineteenth century, however—and of the late eighteenth century in Germany—were to raise new questions about the relationship of the modern world to the ancient.

What Desmoulins cherished about Athens was the life-style of democracy, where graciousness, prosperity, and freedom of the press were important building blocks of a comfortable existence. Where the ponderous search for stability that exercised the framers of the American constitution had led to a negative valuation of Athens that looked back to the preoccupations of the Renaissance, an interest in how people were to live projected Desmoulins into the intellectual universe of the next century, when Hegel would point to Athenian festivals as emblematic of the vitality of the civilization and Macaulay would identify the life of the city as the best education in civics. Wrapped up in their cherished science of politics, the framers of the American constitution paid scant attention to the extraconstitutional structures that made a civilization what it was. Already before the revolutions in America and France, Winckelmann had published the study of Greek art in which he identified a connection between democracy at Athens and the extraordinary flowering of Athenian culture, and nineteenth-century thinkers in Germany and Britain would soon articulate these ideas at some length. Asking new questions of precisely the same evidence was to produce radically new constructs that differed sharply from what had gone before.

Chapter Ten

A SHIFT IN THE SANDS

Sage, wo ist Athen?
[Tell me, where is Athens?]
—Friedrich Hölderlin, "Der Archepelagus"

B Y THE MIDDLE of the nineteenth century, Mitford's place on the shelf had been usurped by a Greek history of a very different stamp. Today students of Greece are not likely to go back any farther than Grote's *History* in their secondary research; Mitford's work is not found in many libraries, and where it is, its several volumes sit quietly for the most part and gather dust on the shelf, consulted more often by historiographers than by historians. There is no question that a pronounced shift in political currents in England was the proximate cause of Grote's new perspective—on Athens in particular—and of its warm reception. At the same time, however, important political currents outside the British Isles contributed to Grote's enthusiasm for Athenian government, while in Britain itself, though Mitford's work was quite popular in some circles, Grote was hardly the first to cry foul.

For all Mitford's energy, and for all his scholarship, his *History of Greece* was a work whose time was passing even as it was being painstakingly turned out volume after volume. Many factors contributed to this development besides the changing political climate in England. To begin with, each successive year undermined the belief that the American experiment was doomed to end in anarchy. Because of its bad—and Athenian—associations, the word "democracy" had been avoided by eighteenth-century egalitarians, but it was used early in the 1790s by Thomas Paine, and by 1816 Thomas Jefferson was comfortable writing that "we in America are self-consciously . . . democrats."[1] In Europe, a shift in the connotations of the word was perceptible around 1800. The later eighteenth century, moreover, had seen a surge of enthusiasm in Germany for the Greek aesthetic ideal, and this increased appetite for Greek literature and sculpture inevitably suggested that the Athenians had perhaps possessed some important virtues that the Spartans, for instance, had lacked: the holistic approach to culture that marked many German thinkers made it difficult to compartmentalize art and government in such a way as to facilitate an easy division between the aesthetic and political spheres. In France, the old enthusiasm for Sparta was slowly being replaced by a new appreciation of Athens; and revolution was still in the air—not only in France and America, where the dust had begun to settle, but in Greece itself. For Hellas captured the hearts of many Europeans and Americans in the war of independence it began from Turkey in 1821, the war that sparked a furor of philhellenism whose most famous product was Byron's encomium "The Isles of Greece."

The first attested use of the term *democracy* in a positive context may have been in France during the 1730s, when d'Argenson circulated secretly his *Considerations on the Government of France*; but though the word appeared repeatedly in d'Argenson's manuscript, it did not catch on among republicans.[2] The sorts of revolutionary Americans who left writings behind them did not call themselves democrats, but the word crops up in France in 1789, perhaps coined by Dutch revolutionaries in the 1780s. Tom Paine was in France when he began work on *The Rights of Man*, in which he used the word *democracy* frequently. Two years later democracy was praised, once more by name and repeatedly, in Robespierre's speech to the Convention in February of 1794, where it was proclaimed that "democracy is the only form of state which all the individuals composing it can truly call their country, and which can therefore count on as many interested defenders as it has citizens."[3] Peter Ochs of Basel wrote in the constitution penned for the Helvetic Republic in 1798 that the government of the republic should at all times be a representative democracy. Democracy was also used in a favorable sense during the very last years of the eighteenth century, as the future Pope Pius VII in a curious 1797 Christmas homily assured his diocese repeatedly that Christianity was not necessarily incompatible with democracy. Times were changing, and with them the meanings of words; for at least a handful, democracy had come to betoken a broad power base rather than anarchy and chaos.

THE BIRTH OF GERMAN HELLENISM

At the same time that the notion of democracy was slowly inching toward respectability in Western thought, a remarkable Hellenic revival was taking shape in the least likely of quarters. Classical studies had flourished briefly in Germany in the sixteenth century, but this efflorescence was short-lived and was followed around 1700 by a rejection of all that was not Christian. The primary credit for initiating the German classical revival probably belongs to Johann Matthias Gesner. Schoolmaster successively at Weimar, Ansbach, and Leipzig, Gesner was summoned in 1734 to the new university at Göttingen, where he was given the position of Professor of Eloquence. It was Gesner who took the crucial initiative in directing the steps of German Hellenism not back to the Old Humanism that had entailed the formal and verbal imitation of Latin models but rather toward what came to be called New Humanism, which sought through the reading of both Greek and Latin texts to reenter the minds and recapture the spirit of the ancients. Both Gesner and his successor at Leipzig, Christian Gottlob Heyne, exemplified a broad and holistic approach to ancient civilization that contrasted sharply with the stale classicism of sixteenth-century Germany.[4]

The year 1755 witnessed the appearance of Winckelmann's *Gedanken über die Nachahmung der Griechen in der Malerei und Bildhauerkunst* (Reflections on the imitation of the Greeks in painting and sculpture). A cobbler's son who walked eighty miles in order to purchase classical texts, Winckelmann was a remarkable individual. His work on ancient art made him an overnight sensation, and the second half of the eighteenth century was so conspicuous for its German neo-Hellenism as to have sparked in this century Eliza Butler's book entitled *The Tyranny of Greece over Germany*.[5] Political concerns were generally far from the minds of German phil-Hellenes, and by far the bulk of the Germans' interest in Greek antiquity focused on the Greek aesthetic ideal and its expression in the arts; but because Athens was viewed as the cradle of Greek sculpture, philosophy, and drama, her stock rose dramatically, and some thinkers connected the flourishing of the arts in Athens directly with her democratic government.[6]

Winckelmann's attribution of the glorious era of Athenian art to Athens's democratic constitution is cited with approval by Herder in his *Outlines of a Philosophy of the History of Man*, which appeared in 1791.[7] In Athens, Herder argues, democratic government fostered the growth of architecture since it called for numerous public structures for government, religion, exercise, and entertainment. He argues too that it was the investment of the Athenian people in everything that carried their name that accounted for the splendid temples to the gods. In the Greek city-states, Herder maintained, "grandeur and magnificence were not so divided as in modern times, but concentrated in whatever pertained to the state." Pericles, consequently, did more for the arts "than ten kings of Athens would have done." Besides, he goes on, statesmen in democracies need to please the public, and what better avenue "than such kinds of expense, as, while they tended to propitiate the tutelary deities, were calculated to gratify the eyes of the people, and afford subsistence to many?" The oppression of the allies and other similar wrongs Herder sees as justified by the adornment of the city, particularly with temples.[8]

Herder has high praise for Greek government in general, and he stands squarely apart from the tradition that viewed the city-states as faction-torn centers of endless squabbling. In general, he maintains, "All the mistakes and errours of the governments of Greece are to be considered as the essays of youth, which commonly learns to be wise only from misfortune."[9] Once again here he awards the palm to Athens, and it is the political institutions of Athens that he singles out for analysis.[10] For, he writes, "if enlightening the people with regard to those things, in which they are most concerned, ought to be the object of a political establishment, Athens was unquestionably the most enlightened city throughout the whole World," with which no ancient or modern city can compete.[11] Dissociating himself from the tradition eager to condemn Athens for the execution of Socrates, Herder maintains that without Athens, even the virtues of Socrates and his disciples would have failed to bloom, "for Socrates was no more than a citizen of Athens, and all his wisdom was only the wisdom of an Athenian citizen."[12] Herder also departs from conventional wisdom in his defense of Athenian oratory and drama, questioning the prudence of inferring public morality from the stage and eloquently praising the political engagement of the Athenians in words that foreshadow the work of George Grote and Edward Freeman. For all the rashness of the Athenian assembly, he contended, daily experience in deliberation "opened even the ears of the unruly mob, and gave them that enlightened mind, that propensity to political conversation, with which all the asiatic nations were unacquainted."[13]

Sharing in the cultural relativism of Voltaire and Ferguson—Herder had read Ferguson's History of Civil Society—Herder insisted on taking the ancients on their own terms and refused to judge them as failed moderns. This outlook combined with his view of history as the study of communities rather than as that of the exploits of famous men to produce an account of Greece significantly different from those composed early in the century. Like Vico in Italy, Goguet and Montesquieu in France, and Hume and Ferguson in Scotland, Herder abandoned the traditional emphasis on the doings of powerful politicians and military men. His focus on the dynamics of the Athenian community fostered a view of Athens that liberated it significantly from its previous image as the persecutor of martyred statesmen.[14]

In 1795 Schiller published his letters On the Aesthetic Education of Man. His goal in the letters was to formulate a program for the education of mankind for a life of freedom. The French revolution, Schiller believed, had failed because the moral education of the revolutionaries had not equipped them with the sensibilities necessary to build new structures to replace the ones they had destroyed. Schiller's construct for the overhauling of mankind involved some kind of return to the wholeness and integration that marked the ancient Greek individual and the ancient Greek state, although he was well aware of the obstacles to this regeneration.[15] The alienation that marked modern civilization, he argued, arose because man had become fragmented, with his senses and his reason divided and set against each other. If one compares the ancient Greek state to the modern state, Schiller maintained, the modern will rival the ancient; but if we compare the ancient Greek individual to the modern individual, the modern is a fragment. Schiller attributes the fragmentation of man in large part to the division of labor and sees the happy era of integration lying in Greece as it was before this division developed. "The zoophyte condition of the Grecian states," he writes, where each individual enjoyed an independent life, and could, in case of necessity, become a separate whole and unit in himself, gave way to an ingenious mechanism, when from the splitting up into numberless parts, there results a mechanical life in the combination. Then there was a rupture between the state and the church, between laws and customs; enjoyment was separated from labour, the means from the end, the effort from the reward. Man himself, eternally chained down to a little fragment of the whole, only forms a kind of fragment; having nothing in his ears but the monotonous sound of the perpetually revolving wheel, he never develops the harmony of his being.[16]

Schiller has a clear sense of where the Greek ideal was most visibly realized: it was in Athens. "Who among the moderns," he asks, "could step forth, man against man, and strive with an Athenian for the prize of higher humanity?"[17]

Schiller's preference for Athens among the Greek states was developed more fully in his essay on *The Legislation of Lycurgus and Solon*. It is with vehemence that Schiller rejects the Spartan system, which, he argues, was appropriately designed for an inappropriate end. Though the laws of Lycurgus were well calculated to preserve a self-sufficient and stable system, that very stability was posited on the complete absence of the aesthetic, intellectual, and spiritual growth that is in fact the end of human existence. The institutions of Lycurgus dulled human feeling and treated human beings as means rather than ends. To the Lycurgan program, that of Solon presents a dramatic contrast. Though he disapproves of the degree to which Solon placed power in the hands of the multitude, Schiller sees the Solonic legislation as fundamentally dynamic, flexible, and conducive to growth; for Schiller some of the most dramatic evidence for the stark difference between the approach of Solon and that of Lycurgus lies in Solon's instructions for his laws to remain in force for a hundred years. Solon, Schiller believed, had seen farther than Lycurgus, for Solon "understood that laws are only the maidservants of a culture, that nations in their manhood require a different kind of guidance from what they needed in their childhood."[18] Time, Schiller concludes, is a correct judge of merit, and he sets himself conspicuously apart from the laconophiles in denying that Lycurgus's institutions in truth endured the test of time; all Lycurgus accomplished, he claimed, was to eternalize the spiritual infancy of the Spartans.

How humankind was to restore the ideals of Solon is unclear. Neither hard labor nor leisured contemplation, Schiller argues, is conducive to Hellenic wholeness. In *Naive and Sentimental Poetry*, Schiller distinguishes between *Arbeit*, labor, which is exhausting and distracting, and *Tätigkeit*, activity, which is energizing and positive. Although Schiller seems to have associated social hierarchy with the fragmentation and alienation he sought to eliminate, it is hard to imagine a universe in which more than a minority could arrange their lives in happy *Tätigkeit*, freed from the draining demands of *Arbeit*, and in time

Schiller himself came to question whether attempts to resurrect the Hellenic ideal were not perhaps a bad use of energy. Before abandoning his hopes for the restoration of a Greek-style wholeness in human life, however, Schiller had imparted his enthusiasm for the Hellenic ideal to his wildly sensitive protégé Friedrich Hölderlin.

For Hölderlin, Greece represented a lost paradise in which man was "one with all," and Hölderlin was to play an important part in the romanticizing of ancient Greece in general and Athens in particular.[19] The search for the Greek past forms the theme of Hölderlin's cloyingly sentimental novel *Hyperion*, composed between 1797 and 1799. The plot, such as it is, concerns the longings of Hölderlin's hero Hyperion, a contemporary Greek, for Greek antiquity and for a world that contrasts not only with the decadence of contemporary Greece but with the sad state of contemporary Germany as well. It is the quest for this Greek paradise that unites Hyperion with his (male) companion Alabanda, another Greek, in a passionate bond that Hölderlin couches in the form of a betrothal. (The lines in which Hölderlin describes this connection make Antigone's attachment to her brother Polyneices appear chaste and temperate by comparison. Hölderlin published a free rendition of *Antigone* in 1804.[20]) The friendship of Hyperion and Alabanda is compared to that of Harmodius and Aristogeiton, particularly when they join together in the Greek uprising against Turkey in 1760, the year of Hölderlin's birth. Hyperion also develops a consuming passion for a Greek girl, whom he names Diotima. Diotima was not only the name of the high priestess of love in Plato's *Symposium* to whom Socrates attributed his knowledge of the subject; it was also the name Hyperion had given to Susette Gontard, the (evidently Platonic) lover whom he met when her husband engaged him as tutor for their children and to whom he remained devoted throughout his life. It is Diotima who "teaches" Hyperion that the agony he experiences upon a rift with Alabanda arises from his identification of Alabanda with the lost world of ancient Greece. "It was no man that you wanted," she says in an echo of the original Diotima's speech on love and beauty; "believe me, you wanted a world. The loss of all golden centuries crowded together, as you felt them, in one happy moment, the spirit of all spirits of a better time."[21]

Though on the whole it is a generalized picture of ancient Greece that fires Hyperion's mind, Athens is singled out for praise and contrasted to its advantage with Sparta. A long discussion of Athens takes place as Hyperion and his friends approach the city. Sparta, Hyperion explains, excelled Athens in its "exuberant vigor" and for that reason required the Lycurgan discipline; but the very result of that discipline was that "every excellence was laboriously conquered, bought at the price of conscious effort," with the result that the "Spartans forever remained a fragment." On the Athenians, however, Hyperion bestows praise evocative of the "praise of cities" genre that had generated the Panathenaic orations of Isocrates and of Aelius Aristides as well as Bruni's panegyric to Florence. Drawing also on Thucydides' account of early Greek history, he explains that the Athenians grew to manhood "freer from ruthless interference than any other people on earth," and he praises too the moderation with which Athens had been granted the bounties of nature, receiving "neither poverty nor superfluity." Dwelling on the earliest periods in their history, Hyperion is able to boast that the Athenians were intoxicated by no success in war and were urged on by no rash wisdom. Again evoking the *Symposium* of Plato, he maintains that the "first child of divine Beauty is art," and so it was among the Athenians, in whom beauty of mind and spirit "inevitably produced the indispensable sense of freedom." He goes on to make invidious comparisons between the Athenians on the one hand and the Egyptians and the "sons of the North" on the other.[22]

Athens, then, for Hölderlin, stands as an emblem for the greatest cultural attainments of the Greeks, and he ascribes the freedom of Athens to her aesthetic excellence. By dwelling on the earliest days of Athenian history, he is able to avoid a number of potentially awkward topics. It is significant that Schiller also focused his attention on the early period of Athenian history and seems to imagine that the unhappy division of labor did not develop until sometime in the fifth century. For writers as different as the sober intellectual Herder, the nostalgic Schiller, and the borderline hysteric Hölderlin, Athens appeared to be the focal point of Hellenic excellence; what for Hölderlin was a sentimental attachment to the cradle of the arts was emphatically for Herder, as for Winckelmann and to some degree for Schiller, a rational and articulated belief in the integrity of Greek civilization in general and Athenian civilization in particular, an integrity that linked Athens's government indissolubly with her achievements in the visual and literary arts.

HEGEL AND ATHENS

Hölderlin died insane. His discovery that his mentor Schiller had led him down the garden path of nostalgic Hellenism only to abandon the attempt to resurrect the Greek ideal may have been a contributing cause of his decline.[23] Constructs about the relationship of the decay of civilization to the collapse of the integrated Greek worldview continued to be made, however, by one of Hölderlin's closest friends, a thinker more hardheaded and analytical than any of the German neo-Hellenists (except perhaps Herder) who had gone before.[24] In his early essay *The Positivity of the Christian Religion*, Hegel decried the feebleness of a faith that had "emptied Valhalla, felled the sacred groves," and "extirpated the national imagery as a shameful superstition." Lamenting the lack of meaningful national heroes in specifically Athenian terms, he asks: "Who could be our Theseus, who founded a state and was its legislator? Where are our Harmodius and Aristogiton to whom we could sing scolia as the liberators of our land?" To modern, Christian Germany with its divorce between religion and nationalism, classical Athens presented a stark contrast, its joyous national festivals answering a need left unsatisfied by wearisome recitations of the Augsburg Confession.[25] The massive *Phenomenology* of 1807 also contrasted the exuberance of the Olympian outlook with the poverty and fear of the Judeo-Christian worldview and its humbling of humanity before an awesome and distant authority. There Hegel expressed nostalgia for the simple moral universe of the earlier Athenians and the mentality personified by Antigone, in whose unquestioning obedience to a comforting and familiar ethical code Hegel saw the last gasp of the integrated worldview before it was torn asunder by the unavoidable tensions that divided Antigone and Creon, male and female, religion and government, family and state.

The roughly contemporaneous *Lectures on the History of Philosophy* and *Lectures on the Philosophy of History* also reveal a deep yearning for what was good in the Athenian way of life and the polis that made these things possible. Hegel shared Schiller's view of Sparta as narrow and limited, distorted by the regular subordination of individual consciousness. Athens, on the other hand, avoided this imbalance. For Hegel, Athens's achievements were tied closely to her democratic form of government. Athens, he maintained, owed her primacy in the arts and sciences to the character both of her constitution and of its spirit as a whole. Athens shared with Sparta the substantial unity of the consciousness of the citizens with the laws of the state, but it was a "purer democracy" than Sparta—whatever that means—and differed dramatically from Sparta in giving free rein to the individual mind. (Hegel did see one important similarity between the two states, for he believed that the work of daily life was done in Athens by slaves. It was slavery, he contended, that enabled the Athenians to enjoy participating in government, celebrating festivals, and coming together to exercise[26]).

In the *Philosophy of History* Hegel articulates the contrast between Athens and Sparta in detail.[27] Athens and Sparta, Hegel maintains, both enjoyed political virtue, but only in Athens did this virtue develop itself to a work of art, that is, Free Individuality.[28] As in the *Lectures on the History of Philosophy*, Hegel makes clear in the *Philosophy of History* that for him the democratic spirit represents what is most characteristically and positively Greek. He praises not only Solon and Cleisthenes but also Pericles and the weakening of the Areopagus. As a general principle, he writes, "the Democratic constitution affords the widest scope for the development of great political characters; for it excels all others in virtue of the fact that it not only *allows of* the display of their powers on the part of individuals, but *summons* them to use those powers for the general weal. At the same time, no member of the community can obtain influence unless he has the power of satisfying the intellect and judgment, as well as the passions and volatility of a cultivated people."[29] From the Athenians, Hegel maintains, sprang a band of men whose genius would become classical for all centuries, and he has kind words even for Aristophanes, whom he views as a patriot and a deeply serious man. We recognize in the Athenians, Hegel wrote, not only enormous industry and élan but also "the development of individuality within the sphere of Spirit conditioned by the morality of Custom," and he ascribes the censure of the Athenians found in Plato and Xenophon (probably the pseudo-Xenophontic author of the Constitution of the Athenians) to the period of the decline of democracy; for the true verdict of the ancients on political life at Athens he commends readers rather to Athenian statesman such as Pericles—the "Zeus of the human Pantheon of Athens." He goes on to quote at length from the funeral oration.[30]

The democratic principle, however, was safe in Hegel's view only when it was naive and spontaneous; once reflection and self-consciousness set in, corruption was inevitable. Both in the Philosophy of History and in the Lectures on the History of Philosophy Hegel stresses the role of Socrates in the decline of Athens. In the History of Philosophy, Hegel argues that for all its freedom, Athenian democracy was dependent on an unreflective virtue (Sittlichkeit) that could not last. Once Socrates transformed the Athenian universe by the introduction of reflective virtue (Moralität), the Athenian mind became vulnerable to a second transformation into an individualism that ultimately starved the state rather than feeding it. In the earlier days of the democracy, Hegel maintained, the Athenians had been virtuous spontaneously, and, like Antigone, did what they instinctively knew to be right. Socrates, however, advocated reflection to make that virtue self-conscious, the product of deliberate and deliberative moral philosophy. Hegel found the Athenians' reaction to Socrates perfectly reasonable, as the Greek world of Socrates' day "could not yet bear the principle of subjective reflection," essential as this development is in the developing consciousness of the self.[31] Because the principle of individual determination of right and wrong was "not yet identified with the constitution of the people," Athenian life became weak, and the State powerless, as its spirit was hopelessly divided within itself.[32]

Hegel in his depiction of the decline of Athenian democracy works variations on several familiar themes. Some of his arguments are the traditional ones. He reflects concern about the "new doctrine that each man should act according to his own conviction," a doctrine that inevitably entails "a subjective independent Freedom, in which the individual finds himself in a position to bring everything to the test of his own conscience." Even Thucydides, he writes, notices this decay in observing that everyone believed things were going badly when he had no role in their management. But Thucydides was in many ways profoundly antidemocratic, and here Hegel echoes the Athenians' complaints about their own form of government. In portraying the Athenian democracy as a rather squawky form of government in which everyone was a critic, Hegel echoes not only Thucydides but Thucydides' own enemy Cleon, who in the Mytilenean debate complained of the Athenians' habit of scrutinizing and improving their laws at every turn and opposed to it the anti-democratic notion that bad laws that stay the same are better than good laws that change. Hegel also reiterates the complaint familiar in ancient and modern times about the persistent envy and leveling equality in Athens, arguing that "confidence in Great Men" is antagonistic to "a state of things in which every one presumes to have a judgment of his own," and he reflects some nostalgia for the authoritarianism of the past when he maintains that in the days when Solon and Lycurgus had overhauled the governments of their respective poleis, it was "evidently not supposed that the people in general think they know best what is politically right."[33]

In casting aspersions on the moral fiber of the sophists Hegel certainly stands within a long tradition. He sets himself distinctly apart, however, in including Socrates' teachings about the worthlessness of the unexamined life as a principal factor in the decline of Athens, which he viewed as integrally bound up with Socrates' exaltation of questioning and self-examination. It was in a direct line, Hegel maintained, that Socrates led citizens to secede from practical and political life and dwell instead in a world of thought. When Socrates wishes to induce reflection, Hegel points out, his discourse "has always a negative tone" as he brings his interlocutors to recognize that they do not know what is right. Even in its decay, however, the spirit of Athens remains majestic since it "manifests itself as the free, the liberal. . . . Amiable and cheerful even in the midst of tragedy is the light-heartedness and nonchalance with which the Athenians accompanied their national morality to its grave."[34]

No one had ever called the Spartans amiable or cheerful.

Hegel's arguments about the decline of Athens are problematic, for the agitation of Socrates was only one turning point he identified in the collapse of unquestioned values; there was also the matter of Antigone. Like Hölderlin, Hegel was fascinated by Sophocles' *Antigone*. For Hegel, moreover, Antigone's gender adds an additional dimension to her rebellion against Creon, which he discusses in both the *Phenomenology* and the later *Philosophy of Right* and treats as if it were a historical event of the mid–fifth century. Hegel in the *Phenomenology* had defined womankind as the internal enemy of the state, and at one level this belief system conduces to a view of Antigone's action as disruptive; wrapped up in family concerns, she is by her female nature unable to achieve transcendence. He would later write in *The Philosophy of Right* that whereas man "has his actual substantive life in the state, in learning and so forth . . . woman, on the other hand, has her substantive destiny in the family and to be imbued with family piety is her ethical frame of mind." This construct fosters a view of Antigone as a prisoner of her female nature, trapped within the ideology of the family, a slave to emotion, and unable to ask the hard questions necessary for transcendence. And yet, of course, Antigone's imprisonment ultimately takes place at the hand of Creon, whose vision is in some ways narrower than hers, and Hegel in the *Philosophy of Right* recognizes the conflict between the king and his niece as "the supreme opposition in ethics and therefore in tragedy, . . . individualized in the same play as the opposing natures of man and woman." Problems are raised, in other words, by Hegel's characterization of Antigone's family piety in *The Philosophy of Right* "as principally the law of the woman, as the law of substantiality, at once subjective and on the plane of feeling, the law of the inward life, a life which has not yet attained its full actualisation, as the law of the ancient gods, 'the gods of the underworld,' as 'an everlasting law, and no man knows at what time it was put forth.'"[35] For insofar as Antigone is reconciled to the religious order and at one with it, she represents for Hegel a positive force, but insofar as she is out of joint with the civil order, she is disruptive. It is Creon, of course, who has created this dissonance, but Hegel's enthusiasm for the civil state as the guarantor of freedom puts him in an awkward position where Creon is concerned, and altogether he manifests a striking ambivalence: is Antigone to be applauded for her adherence to the values of the good old days when people knew instinctively what was right—the happy *Sittlichkeit* of early Athens—or censured for her failure to reconcile with the new, improved order of civil society? Hegel's ambivalence about the value of these ancient and divine laws inevitably colors his view of Antigone's actions. As Joanna Hodge has pointed out, for Hegel "the opposition between woman as bearer of the ethical order of the family and man as legal person in civil society, cannot be sustained as absolute, since for Hegel these two incomplete parts—ethical life and legality—must be reunified in the state. Hegel seeks to show that just as women and men are two parts of a single unity, which is brought into being through marriage, so ethical life and legality are two parts of a single unity, which is brought into being in particular states."[36] If it is the goal of the state to integrate the competing claims of family and government, religious and civil law, both Creon and Antigone are at fault, but if it is the state's function to transcend the lesser, more circumscribed interests of women, whose thought patterns are confined by the limiting parameters of family, then Antigone alone is to be blamed; and Hegel cannot seem to make up his mind.

Hegel's notion, then, that Antigone's worldview reflected a happy and unreflective time in the development of Athenian civilization is undercut by much of his own logic, and altogether it remains unclear how, in his construct, her rebellion fits into the disintegration of which Socrates' advocacy of analytical reflection was the next step. What is plain, however, is that for Hegel the dissonances revealed in the conflict between Creon and Antigone and in the intellectual questing of Socrates marked the predictable but poignant collapse of a secure and comforting moral universe, consistent, cohesive and predictable. Hegel sought to console himself for what was irretrievably lost by the notion that the subjective freedom that had destroyed Greek civilization could be contained in modern society and that some elements of the Greek worldview could be incorporated into the modern world despite the alienation and estrangement that he saw around him. As Philip Kain has put it, according to Hegel "the greatness of modern society is that it combines subjective freedom with the organization and stability of the whole, the philosophy of right." Whereas in Greece the interests of the state were those of the citizens, because reflection, subjectivity, and private interest had not yet developed and the state "was not abstract," the modern state "stands above its citizens."[37]

Predictably, however, Hegel saw no future for democracy based on the Athenian model. The breakdown of the unity that had characterized the Greek polis at its best and the divorce of subjective and objective wills precluded the resurrection of the Greek ideal, and Hegel did not share Schiller's optimism that the Greek ideal could be resurrected and reconstituted *mutatis mutandis* to suit modern conditions (though he was hopeful at times that Christianity might serve to forge a new fusion of will and psyche that would be superior even to that known to the Greeks).[38] At a more mundane level, modern states were simply too large, their populations too diverse; they lacked that "unity of opinion" that can be accomplished only by oral persuasion rather than in the "abstract, lifeless" mode of writing. Even the tabulation of referenda would be insufficient to outweigh the deadness of such a system— hence the failure of the French convention. A political entity of this kind, Hegel maintains, "is destitute of life, and the world is IPSO FACTO broken into fragments and dissipated into a mere Paper-world." In France, consequently, democracy was never realized, but rather despotism in the guise of freedom and equality. Hegel's arguments against an Athenian-style state, however, go far beyond this, for in his view the justification of democracy rests on the "still immanent Objective Morality," and for the "modern conceptions of Democracy this justification cannot be pleaded." The success of a system based on thoroughgoing popular involvement in government is posited on the notion that the interests of the state are the interests of its individual members, but "the essential condition in regard to various phases of democracy is: WHAT IS THE CHARACTER of these individual members?" For they are "authorized to assume their position, only in so far as their will is still OBJECTIVE WILL—not one that wishes this or that, not mere 'good' will," for good will rests on the conviction and subjective feeling of individuals that "constitutes the principle and determines the peculiar form of freedom in OUR world."[39]

J. Glenn Gray in his study of *Hegel and Greek Thought* has observed that whereas Herder and Hölderlin were inclined to see Greek values in the light of a new Germany, stressing the likeness of the two peoples and upholding the possibility of a new Periclean age, Hegel's interpretation of Greece arose "not out of a sense of its likeness to his own age, but out of a sharp sense of antithesis. The classic world was dead, palingenesis impossible."[40] Similar ideas would soon be voiced by Marx. But though the various German thinkers who wrestled with the question of the resurrection of Greek ideals came to different conclusions, there was a consensus that Greece represented a prelapsarian universe of some kind in which man had not yet become fragmented within himself and alienated from the structures around him. It was at Athens, so it was believed, that the individual Greek had most fully attained wholeness within himself and integration into society and the state. The intense preoccupation with the Greek aesthetic ideal, moreover, worked to the inevitable detriment of Sparta, whose self-immolating patriotism appeared impoverished in comparison.

ANCIENTS AND MODERNS RECONSIDERED

It was no coincidence that among the German thinkers the one who was least optimistic about resurrecting the Greek universe also came last. Predictably, an increasing awareness of the complexities of modern life undermined the happy congruence that had been perceived between Greece and Germany by those who in the full bloom of the adolescence of classicism and romanticism alike had come upon the Hellenic ideal and surrendered themselves to it with all the customary passion of youth—and all the unquestioning obedience Hegel had associated with prelapsarian Athens. At the same time, similar questions about the relationship of the ancient world to the modern were being asked in France, where fallout from the revolution had allowed antiquity to be approached with rather more perspective than had been possible in the tumult of the revolution itself.

Radically different interpretations of the relationship of antiquity to contemporary Europe were offered in Chateaubriand's *Historical, Political, and Moral Essay on Revolutions Ancient and Modern* and Benjamin Constant's essay *On the Liberty of the Ancients Compared with That of the Moderns*. The twenty-two years that separated the two works placed them not only in different generations but in different centuries. No two intellects, moreover, could have been less similar than those of Chateaubriand and Constant. For Chateaubriand, the similarities between Athens and France were paramount, whereas for Constant the differences were crucial; yet, for all that, Constant hoped for a synthesis of ancient and modern civic values whereas Chateaubriand despaired of the regeneration of ancient virtue.

If a foolish consistency is the hobgoblin of little minds, then Chateaubriand may have enjoyed a very capacious mind indeed. The *Essay*, which he later disowned but did not suppress, ranged over the whole spectrum of ancient and modern history with the idea of demonstrating patterns in revolutions. Though some of Chateaubriand's parallels are facile and unpersuasive, he does allow for some important differences between cultures—stressing, for example, the way in which the opening up of communications had transformed the modern world and made contemporary France significantly different from ancient Greece. By and large he avoids simplistic determinism. Nonetheless, he plainly sees history repeating itself in the republican revolution in France, which he compares with the upheaval that overthrew monarchies throughout Greece and established the rudiments of democracy at Athens. Persia is Germany, the Persian Wars and the Delian League the French wars of the 1790s. Chateaubriand views the parties of Solon's day as parallel to those of his own, matching the parties he calls the Mountain, Valley, and Coast with the Jacobins, aristocrats, and modérés, respectively (though elsewhere he follows his contemporaries in casting the Jacobins as Spartans). None of these parallels surprises him, as he sees the Athenians and the French sharing a deeply ingrained national character: unsteady in prosperity, firm in adversity, gifted in the arts, exceedingly genteel in times of domestic tranquility, brutal in times of civil strife, "floating like a vessel without ballast at the will of their impetuous passion," ambitious, fond of novelty, "charming in their own country, insupportable everywhere else"—such, Chateaubriand concludes, "were the Athenians formerly, and such are the French now!"[41] (A British perspective on the same question was offered a few years later in the *Quarterly Review*, where an essay on an English translation of Aristophanes contended that in Athens people were "credulous, not like Englishmen, from an unsuspecting honesty, but like Frenchmen, to whom their character is very similar, from vanity and self-conceit."[42])

In one respect, however, Chateaubriand sees an unbridgeable gap between classical Athens and contemporary France, and that is in the area of morality. Unlike those who perceived the revolution as opening up bright new vistas and replacing the limited polis of antiquity with a broad representative system that floated on the wave of the future, Chateaubriand viewed the principal difference between the system of his own day and that of ancient Athens as a sheer and precipitous moral decline that boded no good for the future. Solon and the French reformers, he writes, were in virtually identical situations, with many voices clamoring for an equal division of land; but whereas Solon refused to confiscate the property of the rich, the national assemblies of France were less squeamish. Chateaubriand takes this comparison as a point of departure for a general contrast between morality at Athens, where women were pure and no man of depraved morals would presume to serve as a legislator or judge, and France, where wantonness and decadence were the order of the day. Some of this difference he ascribes to the replacement of Athenian piety with French atheism. The French, in Chateaubriand's construct, though fanatical in their admiration of antiquity, had borrowed all its vices and none of its virtues.[43] Though Chateaubriand reflects a great deal of anxiety about popular government, nonetheless he praises the Athenians for having possessed in reality the democratic constitution to which contemporary France only pretended.[44] Where his contemporaries have gone wrong, Chateaubriand suggests, is in modeling themselves not after their soulmates, the Athenians, but after the cruel and rigid Spartans—a topic to which he devotes an entire chapter. The "total subversion," he argues, that the Jacobins tried to effect in the manners of France "by assassinating the men of property, transferring estates, changing the customs, usages, and even worship of the country is only an imitation of what Lycurgus did in Lacedaemon."[45] In Chateaubriand's construct, then, two obstacles had hampered the resurrection of Greek virtue in modern France. First, morality had declined so sharply that the French would not tolerate a return to the rectitude of ancient days. Second, the revolutionaries had sought their model not in genteel Athens but in barbaric Sparta.

Chateaubriand's mother was apparently upset by the *Essay*, and her distress may explain why he subsequently disowned it. Around the same time as the *Essay* appeared, the question of the relevance of ancient values to modern France was exercising vastly keener and more responsible minds. Many of the ideas in Benjamin Constant's 1819 essay *On the Liberty of the Ancients Compared to That of the Moderns* were surely derived in conjunction with Madame de Staël, by whose 1798 *Circonstances actuelles qui peuvent terminer la Révolution* they were plainly adumbrated. (What role Constant played in shaping the 1798 essay is unclear.) Like Chateaubriand, Constant and de Staël traced many of the problems of their own day to the misguided attempt to resurrect the ancient polis in modern France. Constant also shared Chateaubriand's concern that the mantle of Greek republicanism was being used to pass off as democracy something that was in fact very different. Constant set himself sharply apart from his contemporaries, however—Chateaubriand included— by his refusal to pine for the polis. In Constant's view, the problem in returning to the political universe of the Greeks lay not in the irreversible moral decline that had intervened but rather in the ethically neutral march of historical change. Seen in this light, attempts to revive ancient virtues and ancient liberty revealed an inadequate understanding of the nature of history.

Ancient liberty, in Constant's view, consisted of the right not only to have input into government but to exercise that input directly and immediately. Constant views the right to a say in government as fundamental to a satisfying existence, but he sees direct participation of all citizens in government as incompatible with fulfillment in private life in general and in commercial life in particular. Both the ancient and the modern state, he argues, worked on the premise of a trade-off. Citizens of ancient states were able to participate directly in government. This participation was made possible by the comparatively small size of ancient states and by slavery, which afforded citizens of classical states leisure for frequent deliberations. On the other hand, the closed system of the polis empowered the group at the expense of the individual. Privacy and freedom of religion were essentially unknown. The universe of the polis encouraged uniformity among its citizens; the primary focus of ancient energies was war, which ties the citizenry together, whereas in the modern world it is commerce, which sets people apart. Warfare, moreover, was seasonal and afforded breaks for deliberation, while commerce demands constant attention. Constant sees Athens as the most modern of the ancient states because of its intense involvement in trade. Even in Athens, however, the harmony of the state was founded not so much on the integration of its diverse elements as on the fundamental homogeneity of its members.

As a consequence of the satisfaction afforded them by direct and constant participation in government, ancient citizens did not need the same freedoms modern ones require. Individuals of Constant's day, compelled by the size of modern nations to delegate political power to representatives, find their satisfaction in private endeavors, chiefly in the sphere of commerce; and in order to protect their private opportunities, they require new liberties—not only majority rule and trial by jury, as in Athens, but also freedom of speech and of religion, and a system of checks and balances in government.

Because of these essential differences between the needs of ancient and modern citizens, Constant saw the attempt to restore classical political ideals as destructive, founded as it was on an anachronism that offended his strong historical sense. Though Constant applauded the determination of ancient citizens to exercise political responsibility vigilantly and directly, he saw no virtue in romantic nostalgia for a closed society that would not accommodate pluralism or individuality. Constant did not view the champions of ancient values as entirely innocent in their misguidedness. Rather he believed that ancient republicanism was invoked in the most calculated manner to justify tyranny and oppression—not, as so many of his contemporaries feared, on the part of the majority but rather on the part of various minorities. Stephen Holmes in his impassioned study of Constant has denied that Constant's liberalism was in any sense antidemocratic. He calls attention to Constant's 1829 observation that all tyrannies in France in his lifetime have been tyrannies of various minorities. "The majority," Constant wrote the following year, "never oppresses. One confiscates its name, using against it the weapons it has furnished."[46] Constant viewed the invocation of ancient liberty as an incantation with which authoritarians from Mably and Rousseau to Robespierre and beyond sought to legitimize the empowerment of the state over the individual.

Among the ancient states, Constant did not hesitate to choose Athens over Sparta. Though he often expressed admiration for Rousseau, he was revolted by Rousseau's philolaconism, and he observed trenchantly that Mably, who had the deepest disdain for Athens, "detested individual liberty as one detests a personal enemy."[47] But it is not only the preference for Sparta over Athens that Constant censures; he also abhors the resurrection of anachronistic Athenian usages in the service of tyranny but the guise of democracy. In 1802, he reports, an attempt was made to introduce ostracism into France, and a steady stream of orators invoked the name of Athenian liberty to give legitimacy to the brutal project. Predictably, he recoils from this attempt to exile citizens under the pretext of protecting the public welfare, and he takes the occasion to launch into a long contrast between the assumptions of the ancient polis, founded as it was on the right to participate in government but not the right to be left undisturbed by government, and those of the modern state, in which citizens have renounced the right to participate directly in government in exchange for the right to pursue their private interests unhindered. A deep passion underlies Constant's plea for the freedom of citizens to live their lives unmolested, and it is difficult not to imagine that he foresaw himself as a likely winner in any Athenian-style unpopularity contest: No one, he writes (with what was exceptional fervor even for him), "has the right to snatch the citizen from his fatherland, the landowner from his holdings, the merchant from his trade, the husband from his wife, the father from his children, the writer from his contemplations, the old man from his daily routine."[48]

Constant was also repelled by the use men like Robespierre made of the classical tradition of the all-knowing lawgiver and by their insistence that the state take the lead in the moral formation of citizens. A Protestant in Catholic France, educated at the University of Edinburgh during the Scottish Enlightenment, Constant was vitriolically anticlerical and intensely engaged for the last decade and a half of his life in combatting the attempts of the ultraroyalists (often led by De Bonald) to impose their will on others by censoring the press, making divorce illegal, and ensuring Catholic control of education. Here his line of argument is diametrically opposed to that of Chateaubriand, who discarded government intervention in morality along classical lines only because he considered his countrymen beyond redemption. So far from wanting to maximize the role of government in the lives of citizens so as to bind them together in the happy harmony of the ancient polis, he sought a government that would leave citizens free to maximize their individual potential. As Holmes has put it, "Unlike the ancient *politeia*, [Constant's] modern constitutional order was not meant to generate or contain all valuable human possibilities. Its principal task was to protect chances in life produced by extrapolitical institutions."[49]

◆   ◆   ◆   ◆   ◆

The birth of German Hellenism had a dramatic impact on perceptions of the Athenian state. The militaristic uniformity of Spartan virtue lost much of its charm once primacy was given to questions of aesthetics. Formerly viewed as productive only of decline and decay, in the light of the new enthusiasm for Greek aesthetic ideals the Athenian democracy came to be perceived as the seedbed of great art. Winckelmann and Herder were convinced of the connection between Athenian art and Athenian democracy, and Schiller identified the once-idealized stability of the Spartan state with the absence of the aesthetic and spiritual aspiration that is the true goal of human existence. Hegel praised both Pericles and democracy, though he saw little hope of resurrecting Athenian ideals in his own day.

In both France and Germany, indeed, the postrevolutionary generation reinforced the fundamental judgment of the eighteenth century that the modern world was very different from the ancient and that the gap that divided the two worlds could not ultimately be bridged. A liberal like Constant who saw the Revolution as a vital step in the dismantling of age-old privilege was nonetheless alienated by what he saw as the exploitation of reverence for the past to pass authoritarianism off as classical republicanism, whereas Chateaubriand, to whose fluctuating ideology it would be impossible to assign a label, saw his own age standing on the near side of an irreversible decline. While Frenchmen reacted to the Revolution, Germans became disillusioned with the first bloom of the Hellenic revival, and by the time Hegel died he had come to share Constant's view that the gulf that divided the ancient world from the modern called for new ideals, though unlike Constant he saw the hope of the future in the replacement of the objective morality of old with a subjective morality that would find its expression in Christianity. Sharing Constant's conviction that the size and diversity of modern states obviated any Athenian-style democracy, which depended for its success on oral persuasion of a homogeneous populace, Hegel also saw the need to formulate a new ideal that would define the relationship of the individual to the state. The various ideals with which he toyed, however, were dramatically different from Constant's. Hegel saw no future in the individualism Constant was so eager to protect.

The mania for antiquity had a longer history in France than in Germany and had been put into practice during the Revolution with quite dramatic effects; this along with a radically different temperament led Constant to reject straight off what Hegel only turned away from when it became clear that no amount of wishing would revive the prelapsarian world of unreflective virtue, of *Sittlichkeit*. In the end, though, both men agreed that the attempt to resuscitate classical republicanism was a waste of time. For both men, as for Chateaubriand, it was Athens that was the greatest temptation. Constant indeed did not fully reject Athens. Though her use of ostracism made clear that she conformed in essentials to the ancient construct for the state, one that asserted its unlimited power over individuals, still in the hustle and bustle of her commercial life—combined with majority rule, jury trials, and at least a modicum of free speech—Constant saw some overlap in Athens with the modern state. And it was Periclean Athens that for Hegel embodied the lost paradise (though *Antigone* was produced in 441, which limits the golden age to only a few years). Despite the burst of laconism in France in the generation that preceded the Revolution, in France as in Germany it was ultimately Athens that triumphed. But the enthusiasm for Athens, although it certainly fostered the higher valuation of Athenian democracy that was to come later in the century, did not in all cases amount in itself to endorsement of Athenian government. It was not on the whole the Athens of Aristophanes or of Plato, not the Athens of Nicias or Alcibiades and certainly not the Athens of Demosthenes that appealed. Herder and Constant had genuine affection for Athens. But Schiller, Hegel, and Chateaubriand fixed their admiration on an early period in Athens's history. Schiller ascribed the collapse of the Greek ideal to the development of economic specialization—a development so early that one has trouble imagining just when he conceived the glorious days of Athens to have been. For Hegel, all was lost when Socrates began making waves. Chateaubriand saw the victory over Persia and the attendant lust for conquest as the point from which decline can be traced.

It would not be in France or Germany that Athens would first be exalted in the full flower of democracy and empire. While Constant and Hegel were busy penning alternate ideals for modern times, English intellectuals were wondering once again whether Athens might not offer an example to be followed rather than a negative role model to be rejected at all costs.

PART THREE

MODERN TRANSFORMATIONS

Chapter Eleven

THE TURNING OF THE TIDE

> The battle of Marathon, even as an event in English history,
> is more important than the battle of Hastings.
> —John Stuart Mill, "Grote's History of Greece [I]"

M ANY ASPECTS of classical Athenian culture persuaded Victorians of either its timelessness or its modernity or both. Thomas Arnold was convinced that, far from being mired in a remote past, in truth writers like Aristotle, Plato, Thucydides, and Cicero were "virtually our own countrymen and contemporaries," and in his edition of Thucydides he declared that fifth-century Athens belonged more properly to modern than to ancient history; his son Matthew in his 1857 address "On the Modern Element in Literature" praised the modernity of the Athenians in invidious contrast to the antiquated customs of the Elizabethans.[1] (Citizens of the late twentieth century will be amused to note Arnold's contention that the absence of crime is a basic requirement for modernity.) Arguing along similar lines, the Irish Hellenist John Pentland Mahaffy claimed in 1874 that an educated man of his own culture transported to Periclean Athens "would find life and manners strangely like our own, strangely modern, as he might term it," for, he maintained, the classical Greeks were "men of like culture with ourselves, who argue with the same logic, who reflect with kindred feelings," and are, in a word, "thoroughly modern, more modern than the epochs quite proximate to our own."[2]

The work that went into Gibbon's *Decline and Fall* and the enthusiasm with which it was received reflected the primacy of Roman studies over Greek in the eighteenth century, but in the Victorian era Greece at last came to contend with Rome for the attention of the British reading public. Travel to Greece had begun in the latter half of the eighteenth century, and by the middle of the nineteenth a variety of Englishmen had seen Byron's "land of lost gods" with their own eyes. At the same time—as Frank Turner has pointed out in his valuable study *The Greek Heritage in Victorian Britain*—the humanistic tradition that had begun as early as the sixteenth century with humanists like Colet and More came to serve as an essential conduit not only for the transmission of Greek culture but also for the transformation of Hellenic traditions into recognizably Victorian ideals.[3] For at least the first half-century of the Victorian era, the conviction that the lessons of Greek antiquity could be applied more or less directly to modern Britain ran both wide and deep.

Charmed by what they perceived as the happy cohesiveness of the Greek state and alarmed by the rise of particularist concerns in their own, many Victorians turned with special interest to Greek art and literature, for the notion that unifying civic values prevailed in the Hellenic state in general and the Athenian in particular drew great strength from Greek aesthetics—in part from the unities of time, place, and action associated with Aristotle's *Poetics*, but in part too from the role Greek art and architecture was believed to have played in the life of the polis. Grounded in shared civic values, Greek sculpture, it was thought, not only achieved a pleasing blend of sensuality and restraint and a paradoxical resolution of motion and rest; it also reflected the communal interests of society—interests in whose triumph over individual and particularist impulses many reflective Victorians saw the hope of the future. (Then as now, belief in the delightfully stark simplicity of Greek sculpture was enhanced by the fact that the gaudy paint that once adorned statues in classical Greece had long since eroded, leaving the sparkling marble that all moderns associate with classical antiquity.[4]) Throughout the century men and women were drawn to the idealism of Greek art that exalted the general over the specific. Already in his *Discourses* presented to the Royal Academy of Art in the 1770s and 1780s, Sir Joshua Reynolds combined an appeal to represent the general rather than the particular with the hope that the effects of such art "may extend themselves imperceptibly into public benefits," and a century later Jane Ellen Harrison in her *Introductory Studies in Greek Art* claimed that Greek sculpture manifested "that instinct for generalization, that rising from the particular to the universal, which for the Greek issued ultimately in the highest idealism" and attributed this phenomenon in part to the "democratic instinct" among the Greeks that resented the preeminence of individuals.[5] Shortly afterward Percy Gardner's *Grammar of Greek Art* proclaimed that Hellenic idealism was "not individual, but social," belonging "to the nation, the city, or the school, rather than to this or that artist."[6] Travel abroad had encouraged such notions; already during the previous century James Stuart and Nicholas Revett had fostered the British enthusiasm for Greek architecture after their return from Greece with the publication in 1762 of their *Antiquities of Athens* and the construction of Greek-style buildings: the Doric temple James Stuart designed at Hagley Park in 1758 was the first piece of Greek revival architecture in modern Europe. Stuart and Revett had seen a gratifying affinity between modern and classical Athenians and had suggested a bustling republicanism at its core, writing that their Athenian contemporaries "want not for artful speakers and busy Politicians," and observing that "the coffee house where such men gathered stood within the ancient Poikile."[7] Though for some Victorians Athens appeared as a hotbed of precisely the sort of faction and divisiveness that the idealism of their beloved Plato sought to combat, many preferred to downplay the conflict between Plato and his fellow Athenians and focus instead on what the ideology of the polis shared with that of its sternest critic. Unity of a pan-Hellenic nature, moreover—a rare departure from the ancient norm—was highlighted by the modern Greek efforts to throw off the dominion of the Turkish despots who so readily evoked the Persian autocrats of yore.

THE WAR IN THE JOURNALS

A good bit of the earliest Victorian debate over the merits of Athenian democracy found a forum in the ferocious combat that broke out over Mitford's *History* in the newly founded review journals of the nineteenth century. While liberal French thinkers were suggesting that cosmopolitan Athens replace xenophobic Sparta as a model of the best Greece had to offer and German writers were putting Athens forward as the embodiment of the Hellenic aesthetic ideal, Englishmen, in the witty formulation of Richard Jenkyns, fought over Mitford and the Athenians in the reviews "like Greeks and Trojans over the body of Patroclus."[8] The debate was not entirely academic. The political orientations of the two journals in which the debate was principally conducted were well known, and when a new Greek history was finally written to supplant Mitford, it was the product not only of prodigious scholarship but of profound political commitment as well.

The publication of Mitford's later volumes coincided with the foundation of several lively review journals. The last chapters of Mitford's *History* appeared in 1810. The *Edinburgh Review* began publishing in 1802, the *Quarterly Review* in 1809, and the *Westminster Review*, Bentham's journal, somewhat later, in 1824. It was primarily in the *Quarterly* and the *Westminster* that the debate about Mitford and Athens was aired, although a long review of Mitford appeared in the *Edinburgh* in 1808, and it was *Knight's Quarterly* that published Macaulay's review of Mitford in 1824. At the same time a sharp controversy broke out in the journals over Greek rhetoric, touching on many of the same issues as the Mitford debate. The essay on "Panegyrical Oratory of Greece" published by the *Quarterly Review* in 1822 initiated a memorable repartee on the subject of Athens between the *Quarterly* and the *Westminster*. Though conducted with genuine acrimony—Charles Austin labeling one article in the opposing journal "monstrous in stupid malignity"—portions of these debates are liable to dissolve twentieth-century readers in paroxysms of laughter, at least some of which was plainly intended.[9]

High seriousness characterized the *Quarterly Review* essay, which took as its point of departure a Greek and French edition of Demosthenes and Aeschines.[10] The reviewer found Greek praises of democracy composed "in such a transcendant style of excellence, that to translate them with spirit might cost half the sovereigns of Europe their crowns," a catastrophe the reviewer was eager to avert by laying bare the moral bankruptcy and shameless mendacity of Athenian thinkers, voters, and statesmen.[11] Panegyrical oratory in Athens, the reviewer maintained, consisted of conscious, calculating prodemocratic fictions. Many of these concerned the Athenian empire, an autocratic venture that orators sought to cloak in fair-sounding words. The sophists are the particular object of the reviewer's spleen, a "pestilent" lot whose exercises he took quite literally, expressing pained concern for the undermining of female morals in Gorgias's speech in praise of Helen. The reviewer clinches his case against the sophists by citing Bishop Burnet's observations on "the learning of the Popish doctors," which he considered parallel in its speciousness.[12]

Athenian rhetoricians, then—both native and adoptive—were branded as "Popish" liars and corruptors of women. Thus far the *Quarterly* reviewer. The attacks on the Athenian ethos in this earnest essay were answered blow for blow in two hilarious articles in the new *Westminster Review*. The January issue placed the debate about Athens squarely within the context of the contemporary conflicts between conservatives and liberals, monarchists and republicans, Catholics and Protestants, and mocked the anxious concerns of the contemporary enemies of Athens—men, as the author saw them, who subscribed to "the great article of orthodoxy, viz., that whatever is in the nineteenth century is good, and could only be made better by being brought back to the standards of the twelfth." Every second issue of the *Quarterly*, the writer maintains, has attacked the Athenians by a "predatory system of warfare," because "even the charity of the *Quarterly Review*, which can pardon much, cannot pardon free discussion." The citizen of a republic, the reviewer claims, whether an Athenian or an American, is a miscreant placed by the *Quarterly* "out of the pale of social intercourse."[13] There exists an unexpected similarity, he contends, between "the stoutly orthodox and the fine lady"; in the same way as the latter is bound to quiver at the mention of blood or the death of a fly, so the former must necessarily become agitated at the notion of liberty or the idea of free discussion. Just as it is frequently difficult to get an overwrought child to calm down sufficiently to explain the cause of his terror, the reviewer goes on, so it is with the *Quarterly* reviewer: in response to his mother's inquiry as to what is causing his alarm,

> He runs to tell Mamma of Lysias, and tells his tale in these words;
> "Lysias, a man who, with all the graces of language upon his tongue, had all the fury of a republican in his heart, and in whose writings may be traced all the wishes, feelings, and politics of the mob, from the inmost workings of the thoughts, to the desperate and atrocious deeds, which gave to those thoughts vitality and effect"—
> In the midst of all this blubbering, being asked, "What has he done to you, what has he done to Mamma's Pet?"—After much sobbing, and much rubbing his eyes

with his dirty knuckles, it turns out, that the chubby simpleton has been terrified out of his wits, by a phrase, used to denote "the majority of you," or some such notion equally innocent. . . . —"To the sovereign multitude." This favourite expression of Lysias, signifies your Manyship, or your Mobship. He might as well have said, it means, "Down with Reviews! Reviewers à la Lanterne! Christianos ad Leonem! A certain field is not as noble as that of Marathon itself!" or any thing else likely to inspire terror.[14]

Not even the Church escaped the *Westminster* writer's tongue as he took the occasion of the *Quarterly*'s concern about Gorgias's praise of Helen to attack the interference of the various Christian establishments in marriage.[15] The essay ends, in fact, with a long passage translated from an anticlerical dialogue of Erasmus. But the principal concern of the *Westminster* writer is the faulty logic of the *Quarterly* reviewer who sought to blacken the Athenian character by treating the common frailties of human nature as peculiar to Athenians alone. In this he echoes the concerns voiced by De Pauw in his *Philosophical Researches*.[16] It may be true, the *Westminster* reviewer concedes, that the Greek litigant sought to "strain the laws to his own feelings," but surely other litigants have behaved similarly:

> We might as well blame the men of Athens for permitting the tooth-ache to torture their argumentative mouths, and allege in accusation, that when any of these detestable democrats, who was not accustomed to the sea, went on board ship, he basely suffered himself to be afflicted with a most distressing sickness; the countryman of Pericles turned pale and lost his appetite, and the hateful slave of the worst of tyrannies, a mobocrasy, . . . was thoroughly uncomfortable.[17]

It is by a parallel line of argument that the *Westminster* reviewer portrays the Athenian empire as no better or worse than the next imperialistic venture; for violence, he contends, has always been the arbiter of power, and where the empire was concerned, Britain herself did not disdain to vie with other colonial powers in misgovernment and oppression.[18]

The July review that appeared in the same year in the *Westminster* followed an identical line of approach, once more accusing the *Quarterly* of particularizing the general in its attack on Athens and citing examples from contemporary sectarian acrimony.[19] The *Quarterly* struck back the following year with "Greek Courts of Justice," a review of several works—vol. 10 of the Greek and French edition of the orators, vol. 2 of Mitchell's Aristophanes, and Rev. H. F. Cary's edition of *The Birds*. Taking the accusations Greek orators hurled at one another in deadly earnest and showing little sensitivity to the ironies of the genre, the reviewer took these slurs as solemn indictments of the entire Greek legal profession. He cites with approval Mitford's contempt for the Athenian legal system and, judging Greek courts to have been disgraceful affairs that made a pitiful contrast with their English counterparts, concludes that "we should consider it a proof of a very indifferent taste to bring the pure ermine of a British judge into any close contact with the dirty cloak of an Athenian dicast."[20] Not surprisingly, the French revolution and the papacy were also dragged in to fortify the reviewer's case. Quoting Edmund Burke's complaint that the French National Assembly had sat too uninterruptedly to avoid exhaustion, he complains that the Greek courts sat even more unremittingly, giving rise to the "carelessness, and indifference which sometimes crept into their proceedings." He stresses, moreover, the papal deference the democracy demanded: scarcely, he writes, "did the Pope in his utmost plenitude of power exact for the crosier staff a deference more profound, than Democracy did for the staff or sceptre which the Athenian dicast bore as the emblem of his office."[21] Plainly the papal analogy was designed to spark revulsion and terror in readers.

It was in this climate that the battle was engaged over Mitford. Because Mitford's scholarship so plainly surpassed that of his predecessors in its thoroughness, his work represented in many ways a dramatic step forward in the study of Greek history; it was richer (though in some respects less thoughtful) than the briefer history of Gillies, and *a fortiori* it was an improvement over the shallow moralizing of Goldsmith and Stanyan. On the whole, it was eagerly received by the reading public—a development that men like Macaulay and Grote took as a sorry commentary on the state of classical scholarship in Britain.

Still, there was plainly enough revulsion from Mitford's unrelenting snipes at republicanism for the *Edinburgh* writer of 1808 to have published a review that sought to mediate between Mitford's admirers and his enemies. At first glance the review appears to be enthusiastic, and at the outset the author handles Mitford tenderly, taking pains to identify the improvements he had made on the work of those who had gone before and admiring his superior discrimination in his use of sources. The praise begins to ring a little hollow, however, when the reviewer proceeds to the core of his essay, an exposition of the weaknesses in Mitford's treatment of the contest between Athens and Macedon—weaknesses that arose because "Mr. Mitford hates democracy."[22] Mitford, it is suggested, cannot have read the sources dealing with the rise of Macedonia "with his accustomed care."[23] In the end, Mitford walks away with a mixed review: upon the whole, the reviewer concludes, though Mitford's work was undermined by hostility to republicanism, still it represented an improvement on what had gone before, and even those who do not share his politics "must still acknowledge their obligations to the clearness and fullness of his narrative."[24]

Thomas Babington Macaulay felt no such obligation. Macaulay's review of Mitford appeared in *Knight's Quarterly* in November of 1824, but three months earlier he had published a bold essay on the Athenian orators that in many respects set the stage for his attack on Mitford. The essay is an example of cultural relativism in the mode of Herder, as Macaulay insisted that the fundamentally oral civilization of the Athenians needed to be understood on principles very different from those of modern European culture, which depended on printing. Taking as a point of departure Samuel Johnson's insistence that the audience of Demosthenes must have been a mass of brutes, as they did not read, Macaulay isolated a serious flaw in Johnson's reasoning. Johnson, he conceded, was an astute but narrow-minded observer of mankind who confused people's general nature with their particular circumstances. The truth about the Athenians, Macaulay imagined, was very different. There was, he argued, "every reason to believe that, in general intelligence, the Athenian populace far surpassed the lower orders of any community that has ever existed. Books were, indeed, few; but they were excellent; and they were accurately known." But it was not, in the end, books that educated an Athenian citizen, but rather the energizing nature of public life in the city itself: "We enter the public space; there is a ring of youths, all leaning forward, with sparkling eyes, and gestures of expectation. Socrates is pitted against the famous atheist of Ionia, and has just brought him to a contradiction in terms. . . . Pericles is mounting the stand. Then for a play of Sophocles; and away to sup with Aspasia. I know of no modern university which has so excellent a system of education."[25] How Macaulay imagined impoverished farmers and potters dropping in on Aspasia at dinnertime is rather mysterious.

The notion that Athens must be understood and judged (if at all) on its own terms also underlies Macaulay's review of Mitford published three months later. Macaulay acknowledges grudgingly that the work of Mitford might serve as a corrective to the undue romanticizing of Greece in earlier authors; French and English writers, he complains, have been too eager to inhale the sentimental paeans to ancient liberty in the writings of men who, like Plutarch and Diodorus, misapplied to the little republics of Greece lessons they had learned through studying the sprawling empire of Rome. Such people, he argues, knowing nothing of liberty, nonetheless ranted about it "from the same cause which leads monks to talk more ardently than other men about love and women." The wise man, Macaulay maintains, values liberty because of the benefits it confers—because it functions as a check on ministers, because it fosters arts and sciences and industry and conduces to the comforts of all classes. But the writers of whom he complains considered it not as a means but as an end and canonized those who for the mere name of freedom sacrificed the prosperity, the security, and the justice from which liberty derived its value. Like Constant, in other words, Macaulay inveighed against the romanticizing of ancient liberty, and for this sentimentality he concedes that even the most dismal portions of Mitford's work may serve as a useful corrective.

Ultimately, however, he sees the problem with Mitford's view of Greece as its ahistorical approach to both education and politics. A good government, Macaulay argues,

> like a good coat, is that which fits the body for which it is designed. A man who, upon abstract principles, pronounces a constitution to be good, without an exact knowledge of the people who are to be governed by it, judges as absurdly as a tailor who should measure the Belvidere Apollo for the clothes of all his customers. The demagogues who wished to see Portugal a republic, and the wise critics who revile the Virginians for not having instituted a peerage, appear equally ridiculous to all men of sense and candor.[26]

Despite these impassioned caveats, Macaulay is comfortable pronouncing a few pages later that "the happiest state of society is that in which supreme power resides in the whole body of a well-informed people," and he proclaims cheerfully that "he alone deserves the name of a great statesman whose principle it is to extend the power of the people in proportion to the extent of their knowledge, and to give them every facility for obtaining such a degree of knowledge as may render it safe to trust them with absolute power." Because Mitford's preference for oligarchy has made popular a preference for Sparta over Athens, Macaulay writes, and because this preference is so misguided, he feels called upon to compare the two at some length. Macaulay misreads Mitford here. In reality Mitford had been highly critical of Sparta and emphatic in his condemnation of helotry; besides, the British preference for Athens over Sparta was evident well before the appearance of Mitford's volumes. Macaulay's misperception, however, was felicitous in giving rise to a memorable commentary on Sparta in particular and oligarchy in general. In Sparta, Macaulay observes, there was "little to admire and less to approve," because oligarchy owes its very stability to its weakness: "It has a sort of valetudinarian longevity; . . . it takes no exercise, it exposes itself to no accident; it is seized with an hypochondriac alarm at every new sensation; it trembles at every breath; it lets blood for every inflammation: and thus, without ever enjoying a day of health or pleasure, drags on its existence to a doting and debilitated old age."[27] Macaulay is quick to contrast the perpetual senescence of Sparta with the eternal youth of Athens, where children were not snatched from their mothers, adults were not starved into thievery, no government told people what to think or to say, and altogether "freedom produced excellence."[28] Where Mitford went wrong, Macaulay argues, was not simply in imparting his political biases to his historical work—"Is this a history, or a party pamphlet?" he asks (as others would soon ask about Grote's project)—but also in neglecting literature and the arts so thoroughly as to fail to see what democracy had accomplished in Athens.[29] Wherever a few outstanding minds have taken a stand for freedom and rationality against violence and fraud, he proclaims, "the spirit of Athens has been in the midst of them; inspiring, encouraging, consoling;—by the lonely lamp of Erasmus; by the restless bed of Pascal; in the tribune of Mirabeau; in the cell of Galileo; on the scaffold of Sidney. . . . Wherever literature consoles sorrow or assuages pain, wherever it brings gladness to eyes which fail with wakefulness and tears, and ache for the dark house and the long sleep, there is exhibited, in its noblest form, the immortal influence of Athens."[30]

In Macaulay's view, Mitford had erred in trying to set up a single political standard for all times and places. Democracy, Macaulay suggested, simply happened to be best for Athens because of the singularly high level of education of the Athenian demos. But of course he also ascribed that high level of education—education both in information and in sensibility—to the democracy itself. Though it was Macaulay's ostensible wish to withdraw Athens from the debate over government raging in contemporary Britain, his true goal appears to have been to purloin the Athenian example for the reformers. In view of the terror of the Athenian state reinforced in English hearts not only by Mitford but by Gillies, Young, and Bisset as well, Macaulay could not afford to advertise this appropriation too blatantly—hence the pious disclaimers; subsequently during the debate in the House of Commons over the Reform Bill Macaulay insisted that the bill would not establish an Athenian-style democracy.[31] But the sonorous conclusion of his essay is plainly at odds with his insistence that ancient Athens carried no implications whatsoever for modern Britain.

The banker and utilitarian essayist George Grote published his review of Mitford in the *Westminster Review* a year and a half later. Finding Mitford bigoted, illogical, inconsistent and devoid of analytical capacity, Grote, who had been at work on his history of Greece since 1823, made no bones about his own view of Greek government, proclaiming at the outset that "democracies were by far the best among all the Grecian governments" and arguing that "it is to democracy alone (and to that sort of open aristocracy which is, practically, very similar to it), that we owe that unparalleled brilliancy and diversity of individual talent which constitutes the charm and glory of Grecian history."[32] Mitford, he maintains, was fundamentally a misanthrope who had no respect for the bulk of mankind and partook of the strong tendency in the human mind to worship power—a tendency that, Grote complains, "everything in English education tends to nourish, to strengthen, to perpetuate." In Mitford's mind, Grote argues—"a mind priding itself on adherence to everything English"—this bent shaded into idolatry, with the result that Mitford was devoted to monarchy "not only with preference, but even with passion and bigotry."[33] In his inconsistency, Grote asserts, Mitford cannot seem to decide whether the Athenians are to be dismissed as poor working folk or condemned as idle; whether they are restless or lazy; all-powerful or impotent. When Athenian commanders are active in the Aegean, they are pirates, but when they are put on trial for the very conduct Mitford has portrayed as habitual, then the historian's tone changes, and he depicts them as innocent victims of popular ingratitude and democratic jealousy. There is no way, Grote writes, to count up the innumerable disparaging epithets with which Mitford refers to the Athenian people. Mitford is particularly fond of "sovereign beggars," and Grote takes the occasion of this oxymoron to observe that "had this phrase proceeded from any other writer, we should have regarded it as a disguised compliment to the Athenian many; for we believe they would be the first sovereigns on earth who ever consented to remain beggars while they had rich men for their subjects."[34] Mitford, moreover, is illogical in arguing that "the sovereignty passes into the hands of the poor, when no political privileges are allowed to the rich." This, Grote maintains, "is as absurd as to say, that if the tall men in the community are not permitted to possess peculiar privileges, the government must necessarily be in the hands of the short men."[35] (Mitford's argument here, of course, reproduces that of the Old Oligarch.)

The antidemocratic bias of Mitford, Grote maintains, is evident throughout the whole of his *History* but particularly in the portions written subsequent to the French revolution. Grote denies that the political concerns of modern Europe are comparable to those of ancient Greece. Withal, Grote judges Mitford's work a disaster, and he takes its popularity as evidence of the superficiality of interest in Greece in contemporary Britain. Should Greek history ever be rewritten, he concluded, "with care and fidelity, we venture to predict that Mr. Mitford's reputation, for these as for other desirable qualities, will be prodigiously lowered."[36]

GROTE'S HISTORY OF GREECE

In his strictures on Mitford Grote was beating a distinctly moribund horse, and rather hard at that. The stock of Mitford had already fallen considerably; Thomas Keightley in his (fundamentally anti-Athenian) *History of Greece* published in 1839 maintained that Mitford's prejudices were well known and that he had not a single follower on the continent, while in Britain it fell still further when Grote's friend Connop Thirlwall began publishing his careful if unexciting Greek history in 1835.[37] What gave Grote's own volumes their place in the history of historiography was not their "care and fidelity," for Thirlwall had certainly shown these, but rather a deeply seated commitment to liberal ideals that spurred him to question received wisdom in a way that transformed the way Greek history would be approached by future historians even when the ideals those historians cherished were dramatically different from the ones that informed Grote's work. A contemporary nineteenth-century observer might have predicted that the language of the first great nineteenth-century history of Greece would be German. Particularly in philology, by the middle of the nineteenth century the Germans' primacy in classical studies was undisputed; aspiring American classicists dreamed of studying at Göttingen, and the *Quarterly Review* maintained rather extravagantly that in the study of Greek and Latin the Germans had "gained such a decided ascendancy, that their neighbours appear to have given up all hope of rivalling them, and are satisfied to follow as mere servile imitators of their triumphant career."[38] Grote himself observed in his review of Mitford that a comparison of Mitford's so-called scholarship and that of Niebuhr had made him "painfully sensible of the difference between the real knowledge of the ancient world possessed or inquired for by a German public, and the appearance of knowledge which suffices here."[39] Certainly Britain had not produced works as meticulous as Böckh's *Public Economy of the Athenians* (1817) or Meier and Schömann's *Attische Prozess* (1824), and no English author writing on Greece had rivaled Niebuhr in intellectual energy. But most German scholars found Mitford's orientation to antiquity fundamentally congenial. Very late indeed leaving the gate, German scholarship on Greece had advanced rapidly and overtaken both the English and the French. Whereas on the whole Germans who were not professional Greek historians expressed a great deal of enthusiasm for Athens and did not hesitate to prefer her to Sparta, hard-nosed academic specialists saw things differently. Böckh in his *Public Economy*, Wachsmuth in his *Historical Antiquities of the Greeks*, and Hermann in his *Manual of the Political Antiquities of the Greeks* all delivered stinging indictments of the Athenian state.[40] But it was not in Germany that the seminal nineteenth-century history of Greece was to be produced but in Britain, and when the epoch-making volumes appeared, they came not from the pen of a German professor but from that of an English banker. They were written by George Grote, who had a solid grounding in German scholarship but was deeply dyed in Benthamite utilitarian ideals. Following the lead not of the uncritical Wachsmuth but of the reflective Niebuhr—whose exasperated strictures on those who took Xenophon and Plutarch seriously as historians looked ahead to Grote's own outbursts—Grote turned out, volume by volume, the earliest history of Greece that is still consulted by modern scholars.[41] Throughout, Grote's *History* reveals a simmering frustration that evokes that of his liberal predecessors De Pauw and Constant, and the advancement of scholarship—and of history—made it possible for him to detail the inadequacy of traditional views with more elaborate documentation than earlier writers and to marshal more effective ammunition against them.

In an interesting passage in his otherwise rather plodding biography of Grote, M. L. Clarke speculates on the turn Grote's life might have taken had his father valued education more highly. Had the elder Grote been of a more intellectual bent and less determined to have his son's assistance in the family business, Clarke suggests sensibly, the bright young man would probably have wound up in Trinity College, Cambridge; his headmaster at Charterhouse, Matthew Raine, had graduated from Trinity and had blessed (or burdened) it with a number of Grote's classmates. There Grote would have distinguished himself and quite possibly taken holy orders, ending up as a liberal clergyman like his brother John. Most important, he would never have met James Mill.[42]

But Grote did meet Mill. Whether or not Grote would have slid comfortably into a clerical existence had the circumstances of his life been different is uncertain, but it is clear that his development was affected profoundly by his relationship with James Mill, whom he met in 1819 when he was twenty-five. Mill filled the void left in Grote's life by his own father's lack of imagination. A further wedge had been driven between Grote and his father by the elder Grote's opposition to his son's marriage to the intellectual Harriet Lewin, and Henry Reeve was probably quite correct when he wrote in the *Edinburgh Review* that Grote's lifelong opposition to authority and authoritarianism derived some of its force from the suffering he had experienced at his father's hands.[43] (The austere evangelism of his mother may have fostered this bent as well.) Mill soon became Grote's mentor, and Grote found Mill's ideas immensely congenial, at least as regarded utilitarianism and attendant political reform; the idea of abandoning his religious faith sat less comfortably, but after a short struggle he submitted to the skepticism of the Benthamites. Through Mill he met Bentham, but it was Mill himself whose ideas guided him, and he once observed that Mill's *Logic* was "the best book in my library."[44]

Grote's earliest publications attacked religion and advocated political reform. His 1822 *Analysis of the Influence of Natural Religion on the Temporal Happiness of Mankind*, written at Bentham's request from four volumes of notes Bentham himself had compiled, was so provocative that it was published under a pseudonym and printed by a man who was already in jail. By 1823 Grote was hard at work on his history of Greece, and it occupied much of the time left over from the family bank until liberation came in the form of his father's death in 1830. That same year the success of the July revolution in Paris that replaced the Bourbon Charles X with the more liberal regime of Louis Philippe lent additional force to the reform movement that had been gathering strength among the English, and Mill urged Grote to focus his energy on his *Essentials of Parliamentary Reform*. (Grote himself had dedicated £500 to the cause of the French reformers.) Not daring to propose universal suffrage, in the *Essentials* Grote nonetheless recommended extending the franchise to create an electorate of one million; he also argued for an attendant extension of the British educational system.[45] In May of 1832 the First Reform Bill passed; in June Grote announced his candidacy for Parliament. At the election the following December he won his seat by a wide margin, and for the next nine years he devoted himself to the cause of reform. He then returned to the Greek history, publishing the article on Mitford in the *Westminster* in 1843. The first volume of Grote's *History* appeared in 1846, the last in 1856. He then turned his attention to Plato. Like his *History of Greece*, Grote's work on the Platonic dialogues is still being consulted over a hundred years later.

The passionate nature of Grote's commitment to utilitarian ideals underlay all that he said and did, whether as a political activist or as a student of Greek texts. In the 1830s John Stuart Mill wrote that Grote's utilitarian conviction amounted to "a belief . . . most deep and conscientious, for which he chiefly lives, and for which he would die."[46] Some of Grote's fellow Philosophical Radicals were in truth neither quite so philosophical as he nor quite so radical, and his uncompromising idealism cost him some friends and some votes. Because of Grote's profound commitment to liberal ideals, the regeneration of the much-maligned Athenian democracy formed an important part of his agenda. Greek democracy, Grote maintained, sparked a rare energy and eager patriotism in citizens, a vital force dramatically different from the passivity inevitably fostered by oligarchy. Among the Athenians, he argued, "it produced a strength and unanimity of positive political sentiment, such as has rarely been seen in the history of mankind."[47] Most previous scholars had seen the sophists as a singularly pestilent crew whose vices were precisely those that Plato in the *Gorgias* had ascribed to the Athenian democracy; Grote defended the sophists against time-honored allegations of shallowness, superficiality, and self-interested charlatanry, viewing the bad press they had customarily received as the product of the same uncritical reading of sources responsible for the hostility to the democracy. Where other historians had largely ignored Cleisthenes, Grote saw his determination to break down the particularist interests of the aristocrats and to dismantle geographically based coalitions as pivotal in the history of the democracy.[48] So far from viewing the coup of the Four Hundred as promising some kind of relief from the chaotic pseudopolicy of the democracy, Grote construes the episode as clear evidence that the enemies against which the likes of Cleon and Hyperbolus inveighed "were not fictitious but dangerously real" and proof that in reality the demagogues "formed the vital movement of all that was tutelary and public-spirited in democracy."[49]

Arguing along the same lines, Grote defends ostracism as a necessary check on politicians, and he is resolute in refuting the charges leveled for centuries against the Athenians for their treatment of their leaders, arguing that it was crucial in a Greek state to watch over the conduct of military officers since the real danger in Greece lay not in insufficient gratitude to victorious soldiers but rather in excessive adulation. Predictably, Grote defends the impeachments of Miltiades, of Alcibiades—who he claims was plainly guilty of profaning the mysteries—and of Thucydides.[50] He is singularly exasperated at attempts to exculpate Thucydides (and his colleague Eucles) for the loss of Amphipolis. "Had they," he asks, "a difficult position to defend? Were they overwhelmed by a superior force? Were they distracted by simultaneous revolts in different places, or assailed by enemies unknown or unforeseen? Not one of these grounds for acquittal can be pleaded."[51] Grote blames Sparta and Corinth for the Peloponnesian War and contends that the loss of the war is not to be assigned to lower-class upstarts like Cleon and Cleophon (who were actually members of the middle class) but rather must be laid at the door of the supremely respectable Nicias.[52] What Grote finds noteworthy in past historians' treatment of Nicias is not simply their refusal to hold him accountable for the Sicilian debacle but rather their failure to see that what really destroyed Athens was not the fickleness of the demos but in truth its fanatical loyalty to a patent incompetent. From the case of Nicias, Grote writes, we can learn

> that the habitual defects of the Athenian character were very different from what historians commonly impute to them. Instead of being fickle, we find them tenacious in the extreme of confidence once bestowed and of schemes once embarked upon: instead of ingratitude for services actually rendered, we find credit given for services which an officer ought to have rendered, but has not: instead of angry captiousness, we discover an indulgence not merely generous, but even culpable.[53]

Grote expatiates at great length on the inadequacy of Nicias, and he does so because the dangers posed to Athens by the demos's adulation of great men justified in his eyes the so-called demagogy of Cleon and his ilk. Performing in essence the functions of a constitutional opposition, the demagogues' "accusatory eloquence" had the potential to serve as a corrective to the damage that could be done by "decorous and pious incompetence, when aided by wealth and family advantages." In Grote's view, Athens lost the war not because of rampant demagogy but because of insufficient leadership, and in the last analysis the man who ended by destroying the Athenian endeavor abroad was "not a leather-seller of impudent and abusive eloquence, but a man of ancient family and hereditary wealth—munificent and affable, having credit not merely for the largesses which he bestowed, but also for all the insolences which as a rich man he might have committed but did not commit."[54] The message for his own time is unmistakable; Grote's Benthamite radicalism left no room in Britain for the deference traditionally paid to birth and wealth. In Grote's view a straight and dangerous line had led from Athenian class prejudice and the overvaluation of the elite to the bloody slaughter of the Athenian forces as they drank from the Assinarus River in Sicily. It had not been good for Athens, and it had not been good for England.

Athens's reputation has suffered, Grote stated baldly, because "democracy happens to be unpalatable to most modern readers."[55] In his attempt to redeem that reputation, Grote enlisted elaborate critical apparatus, but though his notes referred readers to appropriate passages in classical authors, these on the whole could not be counted on to help his case, since classical writers were generally antidemocratic. Nor was his argument going to be appreciably strengthened by his frequent citations of other authors, since he so often cited them (Mitford, for example, and Wachsmuth) in order to disagree. What fortified Grote's case was a steady stream of modern analogies generally designed to demonstrate that the Athenian democracy, so far from being the most irrational and inhumane of governments, had in fact conducted itself as well as any government in modern Europe—and in many cases better. (In the deployment of modern analogies, Grote plainly had one set of rules for himself and another for Mitford.)

Much of the comparative material Grote introduces is used casually and in passing, and the weight of these examples is more cumulative in total than it is decisive in any one case. Some of Grote's modern *exempla* are concrete, others hypothetical. ("What do you suppose would happen today if . . . ?") Grote points out, for example, that the critics of ostracism do not consider it any extravagant injustice that pretenders to the throne are excluded from modern countries—in his own day the Duke of Bordeaux, after 1815 Napoleon, and Charles Edward in the eighteenth century—even though the overthrowing of the Athenian government would have involved much more pervasive transformation than a mere change in dynasties.[56] He notes that the terrible strains of the plague did not prompt the Athenians either to offer up human sacrifice such as those performed at Carthage during parallel times of pestilence or to undertake persecutions against imaginary authors of the disease, such as happened in Milan in 1630.[57] Were Cleon's invectives against Pericles, he asks, necessarily any fiercer than those against Walpole with which Chatham initiated his career?[58] Were the mistakes of the overconfident Athenians in sending away the envoys who came to them after the victory at Sphacteria really singular to democracy—or are they the same mistakes made by Napoleon or by the British aristocracy? Grote quotes Burke himself on the similar effect early victories against the American rebels had on Englishmen.[59] Again, Napoleon and the British are invoked in a hypothetical example to question whether the Athenians' harshness to Thucydides after the loss of Amphipolis had the slightest connection with the democratic form of their government. If, he asks, Napoleon or the Duke of Wellington had lost a crucial post to a tiny enemy force, would either man be content to hear from the officer in command, "Having no idea that the enemy would attempt any surprise, I thought that I might keep my force half a day's journey off from the post exposed, at another post which it was physically impossible for the enemy to reach . . . ?"[60]

Grote takes the occasion of Mitford's attack on Athenian courts to deliver an encomium on the jury system in general and Athenian juries in particular (though he certainly sees particular defects in the system at Athens, as in the system in England). Athenian dicasteries, he finds, compare favorably to the best juries in the world—those in the United States, and those in England after 1688. Although Grote is aware of certain disadvantages that attend on the absence of judges in Athenian courts, he sees the presence of such individuals as potentially pernicious. In England prior to 1688, he points out, jurors who found a verdict contrary to the dictation of the judge were liable to a fine, and even in modern times the influence of the judge "has always been such as to overrule the natural play of [the jurors'] feelings and judgment as men and citizens," whereas in Athens jurors were "free, self-judging persons—unassisted by the schooling, but at the same time untrammeled by the awe-striking ascendancy, of a professional judge." It is probable, he ultimately concludes, that an Athenian defendant would have had greater hopes of a fair trial in Athens than he could have expected anywhere in the modern world except England or the United States, and better than he would have had in England down to the seventeenth century. Grote's enthusiasm for the jury system was so great that he allowed himself page after page of footnotes to modern sources on the topic—including one note that went onto a third page and incorporated a long panegyric on jury trials cited from the American author of the penal code for the state of Louisiana.[61]

Grote musters a formidable arsenal of comparative material in his defense of the Athenians against the many accusations that had been leveled against them concerning the crisis of 415 (the profanation of the mysteries and the mutilation of the Hermae)—so formidable, indeed, that had he been at work today, he would surely have been urged by his friends to publish his discussion of the crisis as an article, or at least to inflict it on a scholarly audience at an appropriate conference, without requiring the world to wait for the appearance of the opus to read it. (Once the opus was accepted for publication, however, an editor would probably have suggested that he excise the entire business as extraneous popularizing.) Grote argues that the depth and sincerity of the Athenians' conviction that the well-being of the state hung on the protection of the gods easily explains the panic that attended the discovery of the impieties of 415 and the attendant conviction that the state was in the gravest danger.[62] (Grote is very close to his material here; his response contrasts dramatically with that of Niebuhr, who had confessed candidly in his lectures on Greek history that he had difficulty imagining how the mutilation of the herms could have persuaded people there was a conspiracy to overthrow the government. There are questions, Niebuhr concluded rather endearingly, "which I cannot explain to myself."[63]) Grote's friend Thirlwall had drawn a parallel between the crisis of 415 and the so-called Popish Plot in England in 1678–79, and Grote reiterates the analogy in a footnote of about a thousand words, arguing that in a comparison with the English—a comparison Grote was as fond of making as was Mitford—the Athenians come out ahead in all respects, since the Athenians were far more scrupulous in their methods of gathering evidence, and since the profanation of the mysteries and the mutilation of the herms, whatever its political significance or lack thereof, had in fact taken place, whereas the Popish Plot was a mendacious lie.[64]

Other parallels are adduced as well. Those baffled by the Athenians' strong response in the affair of the herms, Grote writes, may be reminded of an analogous event of modern times, to wit, the condemnation in France in 1766 of two young men for having injured a wooden crucifix that stood on the bridge in the town of Abbeville and sung indecent songs to boot. Despite "exceedingly doubtful" evidence, the youths were condemned to have their tongues cut out by the roots, to have their right hands severed, and then to be tied to a post and burnt by a slow fire. One youth escaped; the other was actually executed according to the procedure specified, though it was decided he might be decapitated before he was burnt—but not before he was put to torture to disclose his accomplices. This sentence, Grote observes pointedly, was passed "not by the people, nor by any popular judicature, but by a limited court of professional judges, sitting at Abbeville, and afterwards confirmed by the Parlement de Paris, the first tribunal of professional judges in France."[65] Grote also recurs to the analog of the *Untori* of Milan already raised for the first time in the discussion of the plague. In Milan in 1630 the strains of plague had sparked accusations against suspects named *Untori*, the "anointers," who were commonly believed to be spreading the pestilence by ointments they applied to the doors of houses. Manzoni in his *Storia della Colonna Infame* recounts how the government of Milan tortured and executed the supposed perpetrators, tearing down the house of one of them and setting up the "infamous column" of Manzoni's title to commemorate the deed. The lesson in this? That the Athenians, despite their acute and understandable alarm in their hour of crisis, should be commended for resisting the temptation to apply torture—something that, Grote points out, would not have been totally alien to them, since they did torture slaves to obtain testimony. (Throughout his *History*, Grote the great liberal manifested no distress at the Athenians' slaveholding. He also sympathized with the southern states in the American civil war.) From Manzoni's narrative, Grote argues, readers "will understand . . . the degree to which public excitement and alarm can operate to poison and barbarise the course of justice in a Christian city, without a taint of democracy, and with professional lawyers and judges to guide the whole procedure secretly—as compared with a pagan city, ultra-democratical, where judicial procedure as well as decision was all oral, public and multitudinous."[66]

It is no coincidence that Grote saw the hand of religion not only in the hysteria that attended on the mutilation of the herms but also in the trial of Socrates and in that of the victors of Arginusae. His Benthamite skepticism, in other words, enabled him to blame the conduct for which the Athenians were customarily excoriated not on excessive differences between Athenian and modern society but in fact on excessive similarities; the Athenians, he suggests, would have done better had they been less pious, not more so. Better than modern Christians, they could have been more excellent still had they cast aside superstitions left over from the more primitive period of their history and adopted an even more rational outlook than they did. Grote plainly had a deep personal investment in his Athenians; Momigliano has contrasted Grote's orientation with that of his friend Thirlwall by sagely observing that while Thirlwall really loved Germany, Grote loved Athens, but he goes on to maintain that Grote in fact "loved Athens without any romantic nostalgia as a state which was formed for the sake of the good life."[67] It is probably going too far to deny that Grote had any romantic attachment to the Athenians, but it is certainly true that he laid the blame for the final debacle squarely at the Athenians' door.

The conquest of Greece by Philip in 338 has traditionally assured Athens's detractors of the fundamental rottenness of the Athenian system, but it has always presented a problem for her admirers. De Pauw had taken a distinctly maverick position in blaming Chaeronea on the inactivity of the Spartans; in his 1877 Democracy in Europe Sir Thomas Erskine May would ascribe it to the overwhelming military superiority of Macedon.[68] Grote does not offer a very cogent explanation of Chaeronea at all, reverting, as Frank Turner has pointed out, to "an extended organic metaphor" that conceived the Athenian of Demosthenes' era as having grown old; quiet and "home-keeping," the Athenians of the mid–fourth century had, in Grote's view, redefined civic life in terms of bureaucratic obligations and religious festivals rather than war and peace.[69] This construct in fact explains very little, for, like others concerned with the question of decline at Athens, Grote gives no fully adequate account of how this erosion of public spirit came about. But he does connect it with the undercurrent that had always existed in Athens of private interests and religious piety, two phenomena that the democracy had been only partially successful in eradicating.

REPLIES AND ECHOES

Grote's work was well received by two to contributors the Edinburgh Review. The liberal cabinet minister George Cornewall Lewis published his review of Grote's fifth and sixth volumes—ending with the Peace of Nicias—in January of 1850.[70] Like Grote, Lewis was steeped in German scholarship on Greece. He had translated Böckh's Public Economy in 1828 and Karl Ottfried Müller's Historical Antiquities of the Doric Race in 1830; early in the 1840s his translations of the first volumes of Müller's History of the Literature of Ancient Greece appeared. Lewis's estimate of Grote's work was enthusiastic, although while forcefully concurring with Grote's positive assessment of the Delian League he did question Grote's assertion that Athens's governance of it could match the excellences of Britain's administration of her own empire. But though Lewis regarded Grote's work favorably, it is unlikely that any man alive was more relieved to see Mitford superseded by Grote than John Stuart Mill, whose father had placed Mitford's work in his son's hands faute de mieux accompanied by warnings against Mitford's "Tory prejudices," "perversions of facts for the whitewashing of despots," and "blackening of popular institutions." In reading Mitford, Mill reported, his "sympathies were always on the contrary side to those of the author."[71] It was with great satisfaction that Mill in his adult life found himself reviewing Grote's work for the *Edinburgh*. (The *Edinburgh* reviews of Grote's *History* smack of clubbiness among the eager liberals; both Mill and Lewis were good friends of the author.) In his 1846 review of Grote's first two volumes, Mill had affirmed the relevance of Greek history to his countrymen in the strongest possible terms, proclaiming that because the true ancestors of the European nations were those from whom they derived the most valuable portion of their heritage, consequently "the battle of Marathon, even as an event in English history, is more important than the battle of Hastings"; for had the issue of that day been different, "the Britons and the Saxons might still have been wandering in the woods."[72] Like Grote, Mill saw Athens as having approached more closely than most states to the Benthamite ideal of a state unified in defense of the common good, overriding the divisive selfishness of particularist interests more than the governments of modern Europe had been able to do. In his autobiography Mill suggested that this had been easier to do in antiquity: the whole course of the institutions of his own day, he wrote, fostered the "deep-rooted selfishness which forms the general character of the existing state of society"—in modern society in some respects more than in ancient, since the occasions on which individuals were called upon for unpaid public service were far less frequent in the modern world than they had been in the classical republics.[73] Mill was an enthusiastic champion of the Grotean view of Athens. In his review of Grote's later volumes he was vehement and determined in his defense of the Athenian empire, and he followed Grote in choosing the Athenians over the Spartans—"those hereditary Tories and Conservatives of Greece," he labeled them, peculiarly petty and selfish, "objects of exaggerated admiration to the moralists and philosophers of the far nobler as well as greater and wiser Athens."[74] The Spartan ethos, Mill alleged, was capable of providing stability but not of fostering progress. To this the Athenian system provided a dramatic contrast: of other Greek democracies, Mill writes, "not one enjoyed the Eunomia, the unimpeded authority of law, and freedom from factious violence, which were quite as characteristic of Athens as either her liberty or her genius; and which, making life and property more secure than in any other part of the Grecian world, afforded the mental tranquillity which is also one of the conditions of high intellectual or imaginative achievement."[75] Implicit here is a slap in the face to the Mitfordian tradition that had harped on the very insecurity of life and property under a democracy, and that had been indifferent to the connection between the Athenian system of government and the unique cultural explosion that had marked classical Athens.

A third English liberal, Edward Freeman, gave Grote an equally favorable review. Like that of George Cornewall Lewis, his enthusiasm was tempered by some minor reservations about Grote's historical parallels, and he was inclined to suspect that Grote's own experience in modern politics had skewed his vision of Athens somewhat. Despite these concerns, however, Freeman eagerly embraces Grote's view of Athens as a whole. The Athenian democracy, Freeman maintains, "was the first great instance which the world ever saw of the substitution of law for force." Citing Macaulay's contention in his *History of England* that an assembly tends by its very size to become a mob, Freeman gladly concedes that the supreme executive council of Athens was indeed a mob—not the mob of five or six hundred Macaulay feared in England, but a mob of many thousands; and, he goes on in a passage that has since become famous,

> a fair examination of Grecian history will assuredly lead us to the conclusion that this mob clothed with executive functions made one of the best governments which the world ever saw. It did not work impossibilities; it did not change earth into paradise nor men into angels; it did not forestall every improvement which has since appeared in the world; still less did it forestall all the improvements which we may trust are yet in store for mankind. But that government cannot be called a bad one which is better than any other government of its own time. And surely that government must be called a good one which is a marked improvement upon every government which has gone before it.[76]

Ironically, in censuring Grote for failing to distinguish between the political structures of his own age and those of classical Athens, Freeman criticizes him for an error similar to those of Mitford, who, he claims, made undue extrapolations to the society of Athens from the world in which he himself lived. Mitford, Freeman argues, had been right in his low opinion of the political capacities of groups of Englishmen with no formal education; but he had been wrong in extending this opinion to the Athenian assembly. "Certainly," Freeman concedes, "squires and farmers alike, gathered together at times few and far between under some political excitement, are utterly incapable of really entertaining a political question." But, he insists, "we must not thence infer that the Ekklesia of Athens presented a scene equally deplorable." He goes on to cite with approval Macaulay's contention that the daily life of an Athenian was itself the best possible political education, comparing Athens favorably with Florence and reporting that "we suspect that the average Athenian citizen was, in political intelligence, above the average English Member of Parliament."[77]

Grote's volumes had a forceful impact in America, where John Adams's grandson Charles Francis Adams brought out an edition of his grandfather's works amending a number of his conclusions in the light of Grote's *History*.[78] They were also well received across the Channel. In a series of reviews in the *Revue des Deux Mondes* that appeared in several installments as Grote's own volumes were turned out, the politician and man of letters Prosper Mérimée gave Grote's *History* his enthusiastic approval, offering his congratulations not only to Grote himself but to "his fortunate fatherland, which possesses so many readers for such a sober and substantial work."[79] Although Mérimée considers Grote too lenient in his judgment on the empire, he finds this regrettable lapse easy to understand in view of what he identifies as the perilous seductiveness of the Athenians, those great respecters of individual liberty.[80] The impact of Grote's history in France can be gauged by the footnote Victor Duruy attached to the second edition of his *Histoire Grecque*, published at Paris in 1856. Duruy—a professor who went on to serve as minister of education in the 1860s—reported in this note that his preference for Athens over Sparta in his first edition of 1851 had called forth a severe dressing-down from the administration of his university on the topic of his "temerities"; but since the publication a year later of Grote's assessment, he writes, his outlook has achieved respectability.[81]

Grote's work was not fused in a vacuum. The outbursts of Macaulay revealed a very similar orientation, and Grote's friends Mill and Thirlwall had been thinking along analogous lines. All were influenced by German schools of thought. Mill, an admirer of Herder, was impatient with the traditional view of Athens, and many of Grote's central themes were adumbrated in Thirlwall's *History of Greece*—so much so that Grote reported in his preface that, had he not progressed so far in his own project, he would have abandoned his own *History* when Thirlwall's work appeared. Duruy's first edition was filled with references to Thirlwall. But Thirlwall lacked Grote's spark, and so it was ultimately the name of Grote that came to be attached to the new valuation of Athenian government and society. John Pentland Mahaffy, for example, in his introduction to the 1889–90 English translation of Duruy's *History* by M. M. Ripley, devoted considerable attention to Grote, while the page on Thirlwall bore the marginal rubrics, "his merits; his coldness; his fairness and accuracy; but without enthusiasm."[82] Thirlwall's work did not provoke loss of temper; Grote's did. Grote's critical reading of Thucydides in general and his attempt to rehabilitate Cleon in particular sparked Richard Shilleto's pamphlet "Thucydides or Grote?"—a squawky piece that in turn spawned a still wordier and equally carping pamphlet by Grote's brother John, a professor of moral philosophy at Cambridge.[83] Much can be learned about the intense engagement of Victorian males with classical Athens from this ponderous philological equivalent of a schoolyard brawl in which John pulls no punches in avenging himself upon the bully who has dared impugn his brother's honor.

Grote's *History* also served as a point of departure for numerous English histories. One of the most dramatic examples of Grotean influence is afforded by George William Cox in his 1874 *History of Greece*, which showed embarrassingly heavy dependence on Grote and referred to him every few pages. Though he is careful to disagree with Grote from time to time, Cox's departures from Grotean wisdom often appear forced and sometimes seem designed to justify the originality of his own work. Despite his own caveat that "comparisons are often dangerous," Cox, like Grote, fleshed out his *History* with numerous modern parallels, parallels designed on the whole to place the conduct of the Athenian democracy in a flattering light.[84] The Renaissance is now long past; it is an index of a shift in the temper of the times that when Cox compares the Spartan ephors to the Venetian Council of Ten, the comparison is meant to be unflattering, even sinister.[85] Whereas Grote had seen in Athens what Britain could be, moreover, Cox saw in her what Britain actually was: if the picture painted by Pericles was substantially accurate, Cox writes,

> we shall find it difficult to avoid the conclusion that distinctions of time and place go for little indeed. All the special characteristics of the English polity—its freedom of speech, the right of the people to govern themselves, the supremacy of the ordinary courts of law over all functionaries without exception, the practical restriction of state interference to the protection of person and property, the free play given to the tastes, fancies, prejudices, and caprices of individual citizens—may be seen in equal development in the polity of Athens.[86]

The force of the new liberal tradition was equally evident in both the text and the annotations of Sir Thomas Erskine May's *Democracy in Europe*, which appeared in 1877; Grote and Cox often appear in the notes, and one long footnote on the glories of Athens includes quotations from Macaulay, Mill, and Freeman. Though he censured the Athenians for what he considered a fundamental ethic of selfishness—one that expressed itself in the phenomenon of slavery—and voiced some concern about the godless and "turbulent leaders of democracy and communism" in his own day, on the whole May fairly glowed on the topic of Athenian government and society.[87] Citing Grote on Sparta, he condemns the Spartans in the harshest terms he knows, comparing them in their xenophobia and immobility to Asians, always with May a term of the severest disapprobation.[88] Athens's fall, he claims, was due neither to internal dissent nor to the failure of its democratic institutions but rather to the overpowering strength of Macedonia.[89] He defends Athens in the matter of Socrates, inquiring where else Socrates would have been able to ply his pesky trade as long as he did and concluding that "there was far more toleration in Pagan Athens, than in Christian Spain."[90]

The impact of Grote's work was also felt in Germany, where a translation was published at Leipzig beginning already in 1850. Although Athens had benefited enormously from the German enthusiasm for the Greek aesthetic ideal, the attitude toward Athens evident in the German scholarly community had been more skeptical. The first half of the nineteenth century had witnessed the rise of serious classical philology in German universities. There was some truth, however, in George Cornewall Lewis's contention that German thinking about ancient government suffered from the closeted, academic nature of scholarship conducted by ivory tower academic specialists disengaged from the political life of their own day.[91] The most prominent students of Athenian government, Augustus Böckh and Wilhelm Wachsmuth, had taken a dim view of Athenian democracy. Böckh had set out his opinions at considerable length in his 1817 treatise *The Public Economy of Athens*, which was translated into English by George Cornewall Lewis himself. For Böckh, all Greek states carried within them the seeds of destruction, since the polis system itself was doomed to be replaced—and blessedly so—by large monarchies; besides, the Greeks suffered morally as a result of having lived before the advent of Christianity.[92] Athens in particular was doomed by her decision to pay citizens for state service, for, Böckh had argued, "it is a condition requisite for good government, that all who wish to partake in the ruling power should support themselves upon their own property."[93] Wachsmuth stressed the role of bad character in the failure of the Athenian democracy, identifying credulity and irascibility as the most prominent features of the Athenian character.[94] These defects, he contended, were predictable in republican governments, of which backbiting and slander "have ever been the mainstay."[95]

The orientation of Böckh and Wachsmuth never died out in Germany. Just a few years after the publication of Grote's volumes on Athens, Ludwig Herbst in his 1855 monograph on the battle of Arginusae reiterated the traditional view in the face of Grote's revisionism; the picture of Athenian government and society set forth in Burckhardt's cultural history of Greece was nothing less than devastating; and Eduard Meyer continued the tradition into the twentieth century, where it continued to thrive.[96] The work of the English liberals, however, sparked a competing school of thought among German scholars, and the multivolume Greek histories of both Ernst Curtius (1857–67) and Adolph Holm (1886–94) were both indebted in some degree to the British revisionists—Holm more than Curtius. Curtius, who often cited Grote, frequently used "demagogue" in a nonpejorative sense, preferred the Athenians to the languid, unimaginative Spartans, defended Athenian imperialism, considered the democrats less dangerous than the oligarchic conspirators, admired leaders like Pericles and Demosthenes, and expressed a vague and general enthusiasm for Athenian civilization.[97] His warmth for Athens, however, faded sometime after Pericles' death; he supported Herbst's refutation of Grote in the matter of the victors of Arginusae, saw nothing worthwhile in the fourth century, and opposed the sophists unrelentingly. The spirit of Holm's work was very different. Holm not only defended fifth-century Athens—Cleon, empire and all—but devoted considerable energy to debunking the "alleged degeneracy of the Athenians" after the death of Pericles, arguing in his text that "the decline of Athens, of which we hear so much, is little better than a fable" and taking on Curtius by name in a number of footnotes, one of them over two pages long.[98] What the history of Athens during the century before Chaeronea demonstrates, Holm argues, is that "whenever a distinctly perceptible elevation of moral tone appears, it is due to the democrats."[99] In Athens, he insists, democracy, so far from fostering decay, was in reality "a factor in the moral preservation of the city."[100] Finally, Holm denies that the defeat at Chaeronea should be ascribed to anything resembling moral decline at Athens, stressing the peaceability of life in the city once the fifth-century tensions between democrats and oligarchs had eased.[101] In fourth-century Athens, he contends, "violence has disappeared. The democracy is thoroughly disciplined; it commits no excesses; riots never occur; the people remain collected, cool and dignified in the most difficult situations; there is no trace of mob-rule."[102] Times have indeed changed; Holm compares the excesses of the French revolutionaries not with those of the Athenian democrats but rather with those of the Thirty, likening Critias specifically to Robespierre and casting Theramenes as a victim parallel to Danton.[103]

. . . . .

The liberal students of Greece were for a long time convinced that the sun would never set on the new day that had dawned. Happy at last, they merrily reviewed one another's works in the journals and rejoiced to think the reputation of Athens had been saved. The long night was over. Athens was redeemed; but not only that. Many continued unshaken in their faith in the essential modernity and profound relevance of classical Athens. The collection of Edward Freeman's *Historical Essays* that appeared in 1873 carried as its epigram Thomas Arnold's contention (set forth in his edition of Thucydides) that "the history of Greece and Rome is not an idle inquiry about remote ages and forgotten institutions, but a living picture of things present, fitted not so much for the curiosity of the scholar, as the instruction of the statesman and the citizen"; Sir Thomas Erskine in his 1877 *Democracy in Europe* cited the identical passage.[104]

Other ways of reading history, however, survived, as they always do. The march of democracy was not greeted with enthusiasm in all quarters; and belief in the identification of Victorian Britain with Periclean Athens did not necessarily imply enthusiasm for either. Just as eighteenth-century thinkers like Montagu had viewed the slide to Chaeronea as the clear harbinger of the collapse of their own civilization, so some writers of the nineteenth saw in the sins of the Athenian democrats the precursor of the problems of their own age, expressing the fear that Britain would be done in by the "dagger of democracy"; the essay on the *Outlines of History* published in the *Quarterly* in 1831 identified the two cultures precisely in respect to the danger democratic tendencies posed in both. In every human community, the reviewer argues, the majority are "at all times hostile to *Law*." The only means to stability, he maintains, is an unremitting effort on the part of the governing party acting in concert with "the wise and good of every class" to uphold "the sanctity of law, and the inviolability of right"; for the history of both Rome and Athens demonstrated that it is "the violated rights of the privileged orders" that brings republics down. The lesson of classical antiquity, he contends,

> is neither local nor temporary; the facts are only exemplifications of the great princi-
> ple which governs human affairs, that in every state there must exist a conservative
> and [an] innovating party; a party in possession of power, and a party bent on attain-
> ing it. . . . If then the party which should naturally be conservative, yields on princi-
> ple at every summons, an endless series of precipitate changes, with all their atten-
> dant horrors, must be the inevitable result; if they relax their efforts for an instant,
> they must be swept away by the resistless torrent of innovation.

Like numerous eighteenth-century Britons, the reviewer concludes that the greatest safeguard to liberty lies in an aristocratic government such as exists in England. The author's distaste for democracy is not surprising in view of the journal in which his essay appeared, but what is striking is the unwavering conviction he shared with Grote and his liberal ilk that antiquity provided a living lesson for the present. The conviction that classical Athens was a useful laboratory in which to study the problems that beset Victorian Britain is re-flected in the author's term for the members of the Delian League: for him they are Athens's "colonies."[105]

Concerns about the dangers of democracy remained vigorous throughout the century. Although the ability of the Americans to preserve a stable polity without the ministrations of a monarch served at first to defuse some of the apprehension Europeans felt about republicanism in general and even in some instances democracy in particular, as time passed many Europeans found themselves disturbed by the gap in refinement they saw dividing them from Americans, and some were inclined to associate American democratization with what Matthew Arnold termed "low ideals and want of culture." This concern made it necessary to explain away the indisputable cultural achieve-ments of the seeming democracy of the Athenians. Though Arnold conceded that Athens was "not an aristocracy, leavening with its own high spirit the multitude which it wields, but leaving it the unformed multitude still," he also denied that it was "a democracy, acute and energetic, but tasteless, narrow-minded, and ignoble." Rather it was an extraordinary universe in which the middle and lower classes, having attained the highest development of human-ity to which such classes had been able to aspire, found themselves satisfied with nothing less than the highest monuments of intellectual and artistic achievement. Sharing the concerns of many other Victorians that individual-istic and particularist impulses would destroy the fabric of society, Arnold appealed to the pronounced friends of progress to turn an eye to the past and emulate the Athenians. For, he maintains, the course taken over the next half-century by the British middle classes would be decisive in its history; and, he argues, if these classes continue "exaggerating their spirit of individualism" and remain resentful of government action, "they may succeed in a brief ascendancy in government, but they will, alas, *Americanise* it" by bringing culture down to their own dismal level.[106] Far better the Athenian example, then, than the American. The arguments of the jurist and historian Sir Henry Maine were similar. Concerned about the debasement of society under a democratic regime, he concluded that the achievements of the Athenians precluded the possibility that Athenian government could actually have been democratic. Athens, he contended, had in reality been an aristocracy. Claiming that it is in fact aristocracy alone that preserves and advances civilization, he cites the example of Athens, whose supposed democracy was in reality "only an aristocracy which rose on the ruins of one much narrower," as the glories of Athenian culture were dependent on the harsh taxation of subject cities and the widespread use of slaves.[107]

The philhellenism sparked by the revolt against Turkey in the 1820s and the apparent success of the bold American endeavor in republicanism both contributed to the rise in Athens's fortunes during the nineteenth century, as did the resurrection of Greek aesthetic ideals in Germany. It is curious that the period during which this dramatic shift in thinking about Athenian democracy took shape coincides precisely with the years Martin Bernal identifies as those that witnessed another important transformation in thinking about antiquity. Bernal contends that these very decades saw the replacement of what he calls the "Ancient Model" of Greek civilization with a romantic and racist approach that denied the African and Asian roots that had previously been accepted as important elements in what became Hellenic civilization.[108] Broad trends may have been at work here, and if Bernal is right, the two developments may be linked by the growing idealism that affected thinking about ancient Greece. The chief catalyst responsible for rehabilitating the Athenians, however, was the reaction provoked by the long-standing British concern with property and hierarchy, what Matthew Arnold was to call the characteristically English "religion of inequality."[109] When men like Mill and Bentham decided they had had enough, and when traditional snobbery was reiterated in a multivolume history of the Greek world by a man of idiosyncratic spelling and equally eccentric notions about the civil rights of the Macedonian people, the response of men like Macaulay and Grote was foreseeable. Historians could have predicted that a Mitford would spawn a Grote; what they could not have predicted was that a Mitford would arise in the first place. Had Greek history of the eighteenth century stopped with Gillies's comparatively innocuous antidemocratic volumes, it is unclear whether it would have drawn the interest of Macaulay and Grote. In some ways the modern view of Athens owes more to Mitford's squeakiness than to Grote's eloquence.

Even more than Athens's Florentine critics and the crusaders for accountability in early eighteenth-century Britain, the English liberals of Grote's generation manifested the "group prejudice" W. H. Walsh discussed in his *Intro-*

duction to Philosophy of History. Convinced that the society they envisioned for Britain had to a substantial degree been realized in the past, they delighted in uncovering a model that could function as what Dewey would soon praise as a lever for moving the present into a particular kind of future.[110] Education, they were confident, would make a broadened franchise workable, and in the energized civic life of classical Athens they believed that the education of the average working person had been accomplished. Macaulay let himself imagine that ordinary Athenian voters had more leisure for lingering in the agora than is realistically possible in any society, while Grote chose not to know that many, many working people in Athens were slaves. Where America's founders had focused on constitutional issues and questions of stability, asking where Athens had failed, the liberals of Victorian Britain focused on education and civic life, asking how Athens had succeeded. Using precisely the same texts as the founders—to which must be added Mitford's several volumes—Macaulay and his successors came to radically different conclusions because they asked radically different questions. Whereas the founders had considered it useful to distance themselves from the unpopular Athenian example and were genuinely afraid of the instability that they associated with popular government (in Renaissance Florence, for example), the English liberals found it profitable to reconstruct an idyllic cohesive Athens that could serve as an inspiration for modern Britain.

Chapter Twelve

ATHENIANS AND OTHERS

> Marriage is too much like slavery not to be involved in its fate.
> —George Fitzhugh, *Sociology for the South*

LREADY IN ANTIQUITY it was occasionally suggested that the Athenian state could have done better by those groups that stood outside the democracy—women, slaves, metics, and allies. Particularly among the sophists, several thinkers seem to have questioned the legitimacy of slavery. The haughty Callicles, speaking in Plato's *Gorgias*, suggested that "natural justice" was violated by slavery; the sophist Antiphon questioned the validity of distinctions between noble and commoner, Greek and barbarian, arguing that all grew *homoios*, "alike," by nature; and Gorgias's pupil Alcidamas claimed that "God left everyone free; nature made nobody a slave."[1] Aristotle in his defense of slavery in *Politics* 1.2–7 (1252a–55b) refers directly to an abolitionist movement. Herodotus in his *Histories* alerted the Athenians to models of gender relations different from those known in Greece; several of the tragedies of Sophocles and Euripides raised questions about the denigration and seclusion of women; and the appearance of Aristophanes' *Congresswomen* so close to the date of composition of Plato's *Republic* strongly suggests that the appropriateness of disfranchising women was a lively topic of conversation at the beginning of the fourth century. Some contemporaries also opposed Athenian imperialism. Scholars will never agree on the position the historian Thucydides took regarding the empire, but it does seem that his relative, Thucydides the son of Melesias, headed a political party that painted it as exploitive and unbecoming. Though the motive of the alleged anti-imperialists may have been simply to undermine Pericles, their plan could have had no prospects for success had not at least some Athenians had reservations about the empire. The tone of the "Old Oligarch" is always difficult to assess, but his contention (1.14) that the Athenians supported the lower classes in the subject states by disfranchising, fining, exile, and killing the *chrestoi* does not seem kindly meant, and he connected the empire to the Athenians' democratic form of government in citing the utility of imperial revenue in financing state pay for state service (1.16). Tremendous amounts of ink have been spilt by twentieth-century scholars trying to determine how popular the empire was with Athens's allies. What is certain is that it was not popular with her enemies, and the Spartans were able to allege the oppressive character of the empire as propaganda before and during the Peloponnesian War.

Increasingly during the twentieth century, writing about antiquity has come to stress the limited parameters within which the so-called democracy of the Athenians operated. This is particularly true of textbooks and other works designed for general audiences.[2] At times these observations amount to simple cautions, issued with or without attendant moral condemnation and allegations of hypocrisy. Some thinkers, however—chiefly those working during the last third of the century—have viewed the exclusion of these several categories of "others" as part and parcel of the Athenian system and have posited intimate connections between Athenian exclusivity and Athenian democracy. These connections are frequently accompanied by criticism of the Athenian system and sometimes by strenuous moral condemnation. In part as a result of new perspectives offered by Marxism and feminism, some critics have also placed the dynamics of Athenian democracy in the context of what they view as a long history of exploitation and abuse. While the articulation of this phenomenon represents the distinctive contribution of the twentieth century to the anti-Athenian tradition, in reality the exclusivity of the Athenians has attracted interest for hundreds of years.

IMPERIALISM AND DEMOCRACY

Whereas pacifically minded egalitarians of the twentieth century are made nervous by the juxtaposition of imperialism and democracy, earlier thinkers, who on the whole disliked democracy, saw no contradiction between the two and in fact believed that the tyranny of the mob abroad could easily have been predicted from the tyranny of the mob at home. Forceful attacks on Athenian imperialism burst forth at the end of the eighteenth century. For William Young, the problem with imperialism had lain in the encouragement it gave to luxury, but Mitford and Bisset eagerly compared the bloody expansionism of the Athenians to that of the French, and both associated it with democracy.

"Striking features in democrats," Bisset wrote in 1798, "have been the desire of conquest, and oppressive cruelty to the conquered." This, he maintained, was particularly noticeable in the Athenians, whose behavior in Greece, he reported, confirmed his belief that the cruelty of democracy exceeded that of "any other system of despotism"; Melos in particular showed "the moral creed of conquering democrats." Such, he concludes, "is the ambition, the injustice, the barbarity of democracy."[3] Bisset went to great lengths to argue that the Athenians' success against the Persians was due not to the strength of their constitution, to which friends of democracy imputed the victories at Marathon and Salamis, but rather to the "temporary departure" from democratic principles that led Athens to elevate men like Miltiades, Aristides, and Themistocles to the status of "princes."[4] He saw their mistreatment of their fellow Greeks, however, as a direct consequence of their form of government. Democracy, in other words, cannot account for anything Bisset admires, but it can explain what he deplores. In Bisset's view, moreover, the frequency with which democracies undertake wars can be ascribed not only to the inherent bloodthirstiness of democrats but also to the fact that their insolence and caprice (which surpassed that of bashaws and janissaries) provoke their neighbors to wars more frequently than the actions of autocratic rulers.[5] Similar views were put forward by Mitford, who was also fond of comparing Athenian democrats to Turkish despots.[6] Meanwhile in France Volney saw a negative model for his country in the Athenians' willingness to oppress allies to raise money for beautifying their city.[7]

When Grote came to displace Mitford on the shelves and English liberals joyfully recognized the ancient Athenians as their long-lost ancestors, the tide turned not only on the Athenian democracy but on the empire as well. Thenceforth the relationship between imperialism and democracy would be couched in different terms. Grote was hardly the first to place a positive construction on the empire. In 1840 Karl Ottfried Müller's *History of the Literature of Ancient Greece* was published in England in the translation of George Cornewall Lewis. Müller was eager to point out that the purpose of the empire was not to minister to the wants of an elite of thousands but rather to enable the allies to share with the Athenians in the Panathenaic and Dionysiac festivals. In a footnote he maintained that there were many grounds for believing the festivals were established "expressly for the allies, who attended them in large numbers."[8] A.H.J. Greenidge in his 1896 *Handbook of Greek Constitutional History* contended that even Periclean exclusivity in matters of citizenship "was tempered by the nobler aim of asserting individual liberty by the spread of the democratic ideal, and of raising the subject classes of Athens's subject states by freeing them from the government of restricted oligarchies."[9] He went on to argue that the blessings of democracy inevitably flowed over into Athens's dependencies and cited Cleon's complaint that a democracy could not govern an empire (Thucydides 3.37) as evidence of the Athenians' extreme leniency with their allies.

The appearance of Grote's work entrenched this sort of thinking about the empire, and the enthusiasm of many Britons survived not only into Victoria's later years but into the Edwardian era and beyond. The lecture delivered by the historian John Cramb on the Boer War in May of 1900 soared to dizzying heights in comparing the imperialism of Britain with that of Athens. Claiming that the Athens of Plato and of Sophocles demonstrated the compatibility of militarism and cultivation, Cramb saw an Athenian antecedent for Britain's transfiguration by the imperial democratic ideal of bringing "the larger freedom and the higher justice" to subject peoples. As in Periclean Athens, he maintained, "in the present conflict a democracy, at once imperial, self-governing and warlike, and actuated by the loftiest ideals, confronts the world." Quoting apprehensively from what he called the "embittered wisdom" of Aeschylus and Sophocles, he expressed concern that a defeat in South Africa would be still more devastating to human welfare than the Athenian debacle at Syracuse.[10] Cramb finished putting his lectures together for publication just before his death in 1913; Pickard-Cambridge's *Demosthenes and the Last Days of Greek Freedom* was published the following year. There British imperialism was portrayed as broader in conception than that of the Athenians, but even so it was Athens that moved the author to observe that it is not "an absurd contention that the life of the individual is . . . ennobled by membership of an imperial nation." As reservations about the ethics of imperialism deepened, so inevitably people began viewing the Athenian empire differently. So for example the British poet and Hellenist Louis MacNeice, writing in the 1930s, reflected with regret that England had been "like fifth-century Athens, able to maintain free speech and a comparatively high standard of living, but only on the basis of gagged and impoverished subject peoples."[11] The progress of British revulsion from imperialism can be gauged from a comparison of successive editions of J. C. Stobart's popular *The Glory That Was Greece*. Writing in 1911, Stobart, a lecturer at Trinity College (Cambridge)—who fell somewhere between a conventional academic and an educated amateur—impressed the reading public with a lively cultural history decked out with numerous plates. He sternly warned his readers never to "forget the thousands of slaves whose cruel toil in mine and factory rendered this brilliant society possible at such an early stage in history." Greek "liberty and communism," he maintained, was essentially that of an aristocracy.[12] The march of sensitivity throughout the twentieth century is signaled by the addition that was made by a later editor. In the introduction to his 1964 edition of Stobart's successful book, R. J. Hopper observed that since 1911 "horizons [had] widened" and "some of the views expressed in the original version rest on attitudes and values different from those of the present day." And in fact when it came time to revise the passage in question Hopper expanded the first sentence, adding to the caveat about slavery another concerning imperialism. "We must never forget," the sentence now reads, "the thousands of slaves whose cruel toil in mine and factory rendered this brilliant society possible at such an early stage in history, *nor that it was aided by the revenues of an empire*" (italics mine).[13]

As imperialist fantasies migrated from England to the United States, British pride began to give way to American squeamishness. To be sure, two World Wars inspired in both British subjects and American citizens a legitimizing identification with classical Athens. In England placards on buses during World War I displayed selections from Pericles' funeral oration, and in America journalists and scholars vied to produce the pithiest wartime analogies.[14] As time passed, a dichotomy became visible dividing scholars, who disputed the connection between democracy and empire, from journalists, who, taking a more sentimental tack, tended to assume that Athens's imperialism constituted betrayal of democratic ideals. Some academics certainly considered the empire justified by the high level of culture it enabled the Athenians to attain at home. For the Canadian William Scott Ferguson of Harvard, the contrast between Thucydides on the one hand and Plato and Aristotle on the other pointed up the "loss of power for sustained historical thinking which Greece suffered when men of genius were no longer enriched by the experience which came through living in a state like the imperial democracy."[15] Half a century later, Tom Jones's 1969 survey text *From the Tigris to the Tiber* suggested to students that though it was the Athenian navy that turned back the Persians, it was that same navy, transformed into the tool of imperial greed, that soon deprived many Greek city-states of their freedom and "subjected them to a ruthless exploitation more direct and comprehensive than any the Persians might have imposed."[16] The nineteenth-century enthusiasm for democracy-and-culture-through-empire, moreover, still lived on in North American scholars like the late Malcolm MacGregor of the University of British Columbia, whose book *The Athenians and Their Empire*, written for a general audience, appeared in 1987. MacGregor defended the empire, insisting that the Persian menace, so far from an Athenian public relations ploy, was all too real, and contended that "it would be folly to deny connexions among government, Empire and the culture that we associate with the Liberal Arts." MacGregor recommends that his readers turn to Pericles' funeral oration in order fully to grasp the culture that empire made possible.[17] But MacGregor, who enjoyed his reputation as a crotchety conservative, made plain that he sensed that in the matter of the Athenian empire—as elsewhere—he was engaged in an uphill fight, reporting the "regrettable fact that since the Second World War the very words 'empire' and 'imperialism' have acquired unpleasant connotations."[18] Clear thinking, he contended, was inhibited by "a vulgar prejudice against Empire, which is made somehow to seem immoral."[19]

Among journalists, on the other hand, the strains of life in the bipolar universe of the Cold War focused attention on the Peloponnesian War in a way that made the failures of Athens seem to cry out warnings that Americans would ignore only at their peril. In the 1950s *Life* magazine ran a series of articles cautioning Americans about the disasters that might attend on ignoring the lessons of the Greek past. Robert Campbell's piece "How a Democracy Died" was designed for high drama, beginning with an account of deadly powers facing one another across the 38th parallel, only to reveal a bit later on that the author is describing fifth-century Greece and not the endangered universe of his own era. Despite its democratic pretensions, Campbell complained, Athens ultimately failed to grasp the most basic principles about the free association of states and instead substituted the rule of force for the bond of principle.[20] Athens, in other words, fell because of a failure to extend democratic egalitarianism and fairness beyond the home front. Similar ideas were expressed in "Hope and History," an earnest plea for America to avoid the mistakes of her democratic predecessor penned in 1953 by Buell Gallagher, the Congregational minister who had just been appointed president of the College of the City of New York, and published in the *Saturday Review*.[21] Gallagher contended that Athens had ultimately fallen because of her refusal to follow her professed democratic principles to their logical conclusions, dooming herself by her imperialism and by her refusal to extend citizenship to allies.

The war in Vietnam prompted parallels with ancient imperialism in general and the Sicilian expedition in particular among teachers, scholars, journalists, and many other Americans who had studied classical history or read Thucydides in school. The role of classical analogies in the college classroom is underlined by Walter Karp, a contributing editor to *Harper's*, in a piece entitled "The Two Thousand Years' War: Thucydides in the Cold War" that appeared in *Harper's* in March 1981. Reminiscing about his college days in the early 1950s, when his Humanities 1 professor suggested that the students might get more out of Thucydides if they compared the struggle between Athens and Sparta to the recently named "Cold War," Karp reports that analogies "fell at our feet like ripe apples," with authoritarian Sparta evoking the Soviet Union and democratic Athens America.[22] Returning to Thucydides a generation later, Karp was struck by the deepening of the parallel between fifth-century Athens and the United States of his own day, and he perceived analogies with the Athenians' overconfidence after the Spartan surrender at Sphacteria not only in Truman's attempt to conquer North Korea after MacArthur's sweeping victory at Inchon but also in Kennedy's ripeness for a war in Vietnam after his triumph in the Cuban missile crisis.

What all these articles shared in common was a conviction that the United States resembled Athens both in its democratic ethos and in its foreign policy—and that the latter was disturbing precisely because the former was so laudable. None of the authors suggests Americans would do better to emulate the Spartans, and all agree that the American way of life is worth preserving for much the same reasons as was the Athenian. The reaction of scholars, however, has been somewhat different, for increasingly during the twentieth-century people who have thought hard and unhurriedly about the ancient world have come to wonder whether the imperialism of the Athenians, far from being an embarrassing blot on an otherwise exemplary civilization, may not have been one reflection of a tendency toward exclusivity that was intimately bound up with the democratic ethos itself. Practical connections between empire and democracy had long been noticed; the empire, it has often been maintained, made democracy possible both by generating the revenues to finance state pay for state service and by fostering a level of cultural development that favored the growth of an educated citizenry. Recently, however, scholars have begun to suggest that from a psychological standpoint the egalitarianism of the Athenians was made possible only by the existence of highly visible categories of "others" to whom citizens could feel superior. These arguments are rarely made about imperialism alone; rather they tie together the empire, slavery, and the status of women.[23]

THE OUTSIDERS WITHIN: SLAVES AND WOMEN IN A PATRIARCHAL DEMOCRACY

On the whole, European and American intellectuals have disliked slavery. Those who also opposed democracy found themselves in a fairly comfortable position in writing about the coexistence of the two. Hume, who frequently characterized Athenian government as a tumultuous and arbitrary despotism of the demos, looked ahead in his 1752 essay "On the Populousness of Ancient Nations" to the concerns of the postrevolutionary generation, voicing distress that many "passionate admirers of the ancients, and zealous partizans of civil liberty" are willing to endorse slavery because of their failure to see that the hardships it imposed made life far more painful in antiquity than did the most arbitrary of European governments in modern times.[24] The monarchist Josiah Tucker pounced with glee on Athenian slaveholding, while Mitford for his part contended that only a tenth of the inhabitants at Athens were citizens and reported astonishment at the proportion of slave to free "in a commonwealth so boastful of liberty as its darling passion."[25] Recoiling from democracy because of his distrust of the poor, Mitford (at times) saw slavery as intensifying the intrinsic civic uselessness of the lower classes, arguing that the existence of slavery aggravated the ills of democracy by rupturing the customary bonds between the laboring poor on the one hand and the rich whom they served on the other; with work in the hands of slaves, he maintained, all hope of common interests between classes evaporated.[26]

Those who have disliked slavery but admired Athens have resorted to a variety of stratagems to explain away the seeming contradiction between egalitarian professions and the ultimate in social stratification. Some argue that the Athenians did the best they could in view of the pandemic myopia of their day, while others have stressed the comparative leniency of Athenian slaveowners. It has long been a commonplace—though it may not be true—that the treatment of slaves in Athens was on the whole mild and compares favorably with that of slaves in other societies such as Rome, the American South, or the Caribbean: from Potter's seventeenth-century *Antiquities* to Clarkson's 1785 *Essay on the Slavery and the Commerce of the Human Species* to the writings of eager Victorians like Lowes Dickinson and the Australian professor T. G. Tucker, the supposed leniency of Athenians to their slaves has been underlined with relentless regularity.[27] Still others have sought to minimize the role played by slavery in Athenian civilization. The continuing controversy about the ratio of slave to free in the ancient world that has been handed down dutifully from generation to generation owes its vigor not simply to intellectual curiosity but also to the intense anxiety generated by the coexistence in antiquity of slavery and republicanism—a fortiori in the case of Athens, where the issue is not simply generic republicanism but something that called itself "demokratia"—to its Greek proponents, the shared rule of free males, but sounding to moderns much like its cognate "democracy."[28]

The most popular argument in defense of Athenian slavery has focused on the role it played in making possible the full florescence of Athenian culture. In the nineteenth century this argument was particularly popular in Germany and in the American South. Schiller's friend Wilhelm von Humboldt, who in his 1792 Limits of State Action had spoken of slavery as an erroneous decision to sacrifice a segment of the human race to "an unjust and barbarous system," a year later referred cheerfully to the important role of slavery in fostering a "liberal spirit" among the Greeks and the reign in Greece of "noble" attitudes genuinely worthy of free men.[29] It was the labor of slaves, von Humboldt argued, that enabled citizens to participate freely in athletics, learning, and politics. Not long afterward the Göttingen professor Arnold Heeren suggested that the cultural achievements of the Greeks would have been impossible without slavery; that these achievements had been enormously important for civilization; and that consequently "we may at least be permitted to doubt, whether they were purchased too dearly by the introduction of slavery."[30] Predictably, Nietzsche gloried in proclaiming that the cultural achievements of the Greeks demonstrated the "cruel sounding truth, that slavery is of the essence of Culture." Who, he asks, "can avoid this verdict if he honestly asks himself about the causes of the never-equalled Greek art-perfection?"[31] The prophet of German unification Heinrich von Treitschke was marginally more delicate in his formulation, labeling the introduction of slavery as a "saving act of civilization" and arguing that "the price paid by [slaves'] suffering for the tragedies of Sophocles and Phidias's statue of Zeus was not too high."[32] Similar ideas about ancient Greece in general and Athens in particular were put forth in the United States to justify the enslavement of Africans. These arguments, of course, differed from those put forward in Europe (except, perhaps, by Nietzsche) in that they did not consider the utility of slavery to be by any means unique to classical Athens.

As southern slavery came increasingly under attack from abolitionists, its proponents forged a variety of arguments that cast it as at worst a necessary evil and at best a positive good. For those who wished to stress the benefits slavery might confer on society, the classical example did double duty, for it could be used to demonstrate not only the role of slavery in promoting equality and liberty among citizens but also the cultural achievements that slavery facilitated. Thomas Dew, president of the College of William and Mary, maintained that slaves outnumbered citizens in the classical states, "where the spirit of liberty glowed with most intensity," and suggested that American slavery also conduced to the spirit of both freedom and equality, since division among citizens was removed by relegating menial labor to blacks.[33] Classical slavery, moreover, fostered culture, and the peroration of Dew's *Review of the Debate in the Virginia Legislature of 1831 and 1832* was focused on the classical example, as Dew reminded his audience that the slaveholding societies of antiquity produced the achievements of Lycurgus, Demosthenes, and Cicero "without for *one moment* loosing the ties between master and slave."[34]

Dew died at forty-three, but his crusade lived on in the person of his fellow Virginian George Fitzhugh, described by the American historian Eugene Genovese as "a man who wrote too much and read too little."[35] Fitzhugh took it upon himself to save the world in general and the American South in particular from what he viewed as a short-term aberration from the customary decency of humankind, to wit, the free society found in his day in Europe and the northern United States. It was slavery and serfdom, he maintained, that formed the natural condition of society; but in his own lifetime greedy capitalists had fostered the enormity of free labor for their own selfish motives. All Fitzhugh's writing was dominated by the contrast he saw between self-involved, elitist, shortsighted abolitionists on the one hand and generous, civic-minded, positively visionary slaveholders on the other. It was to slavery, he argued, that ancient states "were indebted for their great prosperity and high civilization" and for a level of culture never equaled in later times.[36] As to the modern world, it was his passionate belief that American slavery saw to it that poor whites were not at "the bottom of society as at the North" but privileged persons, "like Greek and Roman citizens, with a numerous class far beneath them."[37] It is not likely to be a coincidence that the heyday of neo-Hellenic architecture in the American South coincided with precisely those decades when the Greek example was put forward in reinforcing the positive good argument for slavery—the thirty years prior to the outbreak of the Civil War. For it was Athens above all that provided the most dramatic evidence that slavery and culture mixed well, and the proud white columns that adorned the facades of antebellum mansions worked nicely to proclaim that the inhabitants of such edifices believed in both.[38]

At the same time, the popular outcry against black slavery in both America and Europe prompted some to compare Athenian slavery favorably with its modern counterpart. T. G. Tucker's *Life in Ancient Athens* appeared in the Handbooks of Archaeology and Antiquities series published in England and was reprinted over a dozen times. Tucker stressed the importance of distinguishing between the "mutual confidences and even affection" that developed between slaves and their owners in Athens and the mistreatment of blacks by the Simon Legrees of the American South. The only people, Tucker maintained, whose humanity to slaves exceeded that of the Athenians may have been the Jews.[39] (Compare the views of Cicero, who described the Jews as a people "born for slavery" [*De Provinciis Consularibus* 10]) The continuing mistreatment of American blacks in the twentieth century also fostered comparisons with Athens in which the ancients came out ahead. In his widely read Penguin paperback *The Greeks*, the Englishman H.D.F. Kitto combined the suggestion that slavery was a necessary price for the glory that was Greece with the allegation that, comparatively speaking, it was not on the whole such a disagreeable thing to be a slave at Athens. Athenian slaves, he assured his many readers, were not only happier than black slaves in the antebellum South but also possessed far more legal protection than the enfranchised American blacks of his own day. Kitto—who was also one of the best-known twentieth-century apologists for the status of women at Athens—compared the misery of slaves in the Athenian silver mines with the deaths of randomly selected Britons in auto accidents, arguing that just as Athenians exploited slave labor, so the English "kill 4,000 citizens annually on the roads because [their] present way of life could not otherwise continue." Kitto concludes that to "understand is not necessarily to pardon, but there is no harm in trying to understand," but he certainly seems to me to be pardoning, and rather graciously, too.[40]

For every defender of Athenian slavery, there has probably been at least one detractor. Bodin was horrified by ancient slavery and devoted a chapter of his *Six Books* (1.5) to its condemnation and to wrangling with those who cite the antiquity of slavery as a justification for it. Some have come at the subject from more than one angle: Mitford, for example, alternately censured the Athenians for their slaveholding and expressed relief that at least the existence of slaves at Athens had seen to it that the truly impoverished were excluded from the franchise.[41] The revolutions in France and America had focused a good deal of attention on the ideals of the classical republics. Americans were ambivalent about the value of Hellenic models, but many in France believed that their country could benefit from the resurrection of Athenian and Spartan institutions in their midst. In the years that followed, a new enthusiasm for Greece developed in the southern United States as the need arose for a model of "liberty-equality-and-culture-through-slavery," but in France the opposite phenomenon was visible as Volney and Constant recoiled from what they saw as the oversimplifications of the revolutionaries.[42] In his attack on the modern priests of the cult of antiquity, Volney maintained that slaves outnumbered free citizens at Athens by a ratio of four to one and contended that there was not one Athenian home wherein a despotism was not practiced worthy of the American colonies—or of Greek tyrants: and all this by "these make-believe democrats." So much for the classical republicanism of the revolutionaries.[43]

A generation later Constant would include slavery in his discussion of classi-cal ideals of liberty and their limitations.[44] The new sensitivity to the problems posed by ancient slavery to those who wished to resurrect classical ideals was also evident in other parts of Europe. Shortly after Mitford's death in 1827, his brother Lord Redesdale composed (for a new edition of the *History of Greece*) an apology for his brother's work that was just that: in his "Short Account of the Author, and of his Pursuits in Life, With an Apology for Some Parts of his Work," Redesdale recurred again and again to the evils of slavery ancient and modern and stressed repeatedly that his brother's rejection of Greek democ-racy was based on its slaveholding. It was because of its exclusivity and the narrowness of its franchise (i.e., rather than because of any revulsion from republicanism), Redesdale insisted, that his brother had decried those who wished to resurrect Greek republican ideals in the modern world.[45] In the *Holy Family* of 1845, moreover, Marx and Engels contended that the colossal and fatal error of Robespierre and his cohorts had lain in their failure to under-stand the crucial role of slavery in ancient states; hence the erroneous belief that classical political ideals could be compatible with modern bourgeois soci-ety. "Robespierre, Saint-Just and their party fell," they maintained,

> because they confused the ancient, *realistic-democratic commonweal* based on *real slavery* with the *modern spiritualistic-democratic representative state*, which is based on *emancipated slavery, bourgeois society*. What a terrible illusion it is to have to recog-nise and sanction in the *rights of man* modern bourgeois society, the society of indus-try, of universal competition, of private interest freely pursuing its aims, of anarchy, of self-estranged natural and spiritual individuality, and at the same time to want afterwards to annul the *manifestations of the life* of this society in particular individu-als and simultaneously to want to model the *political head* of that society in the manner of *antiquity*![46]

Similar observations were made in 1895 by Gustave Le Bon in his famous monograph on crowds, where he accused the revolutionaries of anachronism in their attempt to revive the institutions and the rhetoric of the so-called free states of the classical world. "What resemblance," he asked, "can possibly exist between the institutions of the Greeks and those designated to-day by corre-sponding words? A republic at that epoch was an essentially aristocratic insti-tution, formed of a union of petty despots ruling over a crowd of slaves kept in the most absolute subjection. These communal aristocracies, based on slavery, could not have existed for a moment without it."[47]

In 1847, the year before slavery was abolished in the French colonies, Henri Wallon published his massive history of slavery in antiquity. He was able to incorporate the 1848 abolition law, for whose passing he was partially respon-sible, into the second edition of 1879. Wallon viewed slavery as not only immoral but antithetical to progress, a belief shared by numerous nineteenth-century authors—by John Elliott Cairnes, for example, in his 1862 study *The Slave Power: Its Character, Career, & Probable Designs*, and by Marx. Floating on a wave of abolitionist fervor, Wallon's polemical *Histoire de l'esclavage dans l'antiquité* contended that the flourishing of a thoroughgoing slave labor system was not evident until the period of Athens's "decline" after the Peloponnesian War.[48] The reaction continued as the century wore on. In 1864 Numa Denis Fustel de Coulanges published *The Ancient City*, which was translated into several languages and often reprinted; it is still widely read today and is available in English translation in paperback. Like Volney and Constant, Fustel was intensely exercised about the determination of the revolutionaries and some of their successors to emulate ancient ideals and their failure to understand the inadequacies of classical governments. Fustel was also convinced that slavery had been intensely harmful to the ancient state, encouraging as it did indolence on the part of citizens.

This line of thinking was by no means unique to Fustel de Coulanges. What political scientist Ellen Wood has called "The Myth of the Idle Mob"—the belief that Athenian citizens fundamentally did not work, and that the existence of a slave population encouraged bad thinking and bad living—has a long history.[49] The association of hard work with slavery, some have felt, encouraged free Athenians to despise labor in theory, while the availability of slaves enabled them to avoid it in practice. The notion that slavery freed Athenian voters from the need to work is of uncertain origin. Contemporary literature makes plain that the average Athenian actually did work for a living; the only text that would call this patent reality into question is Aristophanes' *Wasps*, which suggests in a comic vein that some people chose to live on jury pay alone. Outside of this, the entire corpus of Athenian literature paints a portrait of working citizens, and if Plato and Aristotle recoiled from a state in which the franchise was entrusted to those whose minds were deadened by "banausic" labor, their revulsion only confirms the reality with which they were confronted in the world around them. Athenians were not freed from working for a living by the existence of slavery any more than plumbers or waitresses or college professors are freed from working by the existence of automobiles, washer-dryers, and computers. For several centuries, however, the peculiar conviction that slavery joined with pay for jury duty and minor public offices to free the average citizen for a life of leisure has enjoyed enormous popularity. For some, this notion has fostered a glorious image of a perfect universe in which the responsible business of living like a gentleman could be shared more or less equally among a gracious elite. Others have followed Plato and Aristotle in stressing the impossibility of intellectual development on the part of people who need to work. Still others have excoriated the idleness and technological stagnation that might result from slave-owning. Many have been determined to have it both ways, lambasting the Athenians for empowering the laboring classes while at the same time censuring classical Athens as a hotbed of state-supported indolence where government pay for civic service made possible a gracious life without "real" work.

Shortly before the revolutions in France and America, slavery became an issue in a debate between two Swiss, J.-F. Deluc of Geneva and the Bernese scientist Haller. In his correspondence with Haller, Deluc had adduced the ancient Athenians as evidence that ordinary citizens were qualified to make political decisions. When Haller countered with the contention that in fact Greek democracies often made very bad decisions, Deluc responded by underlining the differences between the slave-owning states of antiquity and modern Geneva. In Geneva, he argued, slaveless citizens needed to work for a living, unlike the ancient Athenians, who lived idly on the labor of others; hence the worst aspects of Athenian government could be avoided there.[50] In 1793, while serving in the French Convention, Lenoir-Laroche, warning against facile identifications of modern France with Athens and Rome, contended that in these states real work was left to slaves, freeing citizens to spend their lives in the business of government.[51] In the monarchist *Sketch of Democracy* penned by Robert Bisset in 1798, Athenian citizens were portrayed as living off slaves, a phenomenon to which Bisset ascribed the prominence of idleness in the Athenian "national character."[52] The author of a mysterious essay published at Edinburgh in 1828 saw it as a great advantage in Athens that "menial and agricultural labour was performed by slaves," which afforded citizens the leisure to participate in government and warfare.[53] Two better-known writers, Condorcet and Constant, stressed the crucial conjunction of slavery and smallness as conditions for the development of Athenian democracy, and Condorcet in the *Sketch* of human progress he penned while imprisoned by the Jacobins contended that slavery was essential for Greek political development because the education that was such a crucial building block of the system was practicable only in societies in which the really arduous work in crafts and agriculture was carried out by slaves.[54] Hegel also stressed the centrality of education in the Athenian system, viewing slavery as an essential condition of an "aesthetic democracy" in which citizens were required to participate in government, the celebration of festivals, and exercises in the Gymnasia. Athenian citizens, he maintained, were liberated from handicraft occupations because the work of daily life was done by slaves.[55]

"Nobility" is a word that often turns up in such discussions. The German historian Arnold Heeren cited Aristotle with some frequency in his discussion of slavery, maintaining that it "served to raise the class of citizens to a sort of nobility" and praising the application that the "noblest" of the Greek slaveholders made of their leisure.[56] Later in the century the Victorian W. Warde Fowler would write of nobility and appeal to Aristotle in maintaining that it was difficult to grudge Athens its slaves since they seemed to be necessary to enable an elite to develop the glory that was Greece. The sweet reasonableness of the Athenian democracy, Fowler argued, forged a more comfortable material environment for slaves at Athens than anywhere else in the ancient world; Aristotelian ideology may well have underlain his contention that nowhere ("perhaps") were slaves "so exclusively drawn, not from Greek, but from foreign and semi-civilized peoples." (The latter phenomenon seems to carry for Fowler powerful moral valence of a positive kind.) And not only this; "all things considered," Fowler wrote, "it is hard to grudge Athens her 100,000 slaves, if they really were, as I think we must believe, essential to the realisation of the 'good life' of the free minority which has left such an invaluable legacy to modern civilisation. . . . In Aristotle's view, the *raison d'être* of slavery was to make a noble life possible for the master; and where the master actually lived such a life, and at the same time did his duty by his slaves, the institution might be justified."[57]

The imagined idleness of a citizen in a slaveholding state has made possible the belief that the lack of mutual dependence fostered constant tension between rich and poor at Athens. This idea may first have been articulated by Mitford. Although relieved that the phenomenon of slavery cut the very lowest element in society off from participation in politics, Mitford was nonetheless concerned that the use of slave labor on the part of the rich eliminated an essential basis of common interest between upper and lower classes. Mitford was too well read to have failed to notice that in reality the Athenian riffraff held jobs and led structured lives; he complains in fact of the low trades that characterized the men who controlled policy and praises the "high discipline" that marked the Athenian armed forces in a state "whose men were all soldiers and seamen." But when the mood strikes him, he nonetheless laments the ways in which slavery displaced the poor from their natural place as the suppliers of goods and services to the rich.[58]

Writing a generation later, Böckh stressed the pernicious interplay of slavery and state pay. For him, this deadly interaction in fact interfered with the practice of "nobility." Slavery, he argued, fostered indolence, which in turn prompted citizens to pressure the government into supporting them, a support that took the form not only of pay but also of the division of property wantonly confiscated from the rich by demagogues. These pressures diverted Athenian resources from "noble" objects, and Böckh was forced to conclude that even among the Athenians, one of the "noblest" races of Greece, "depravity and moral corruption were prevalent throughout the whole people."[59] He concludes that any successful government must require those who wish to participate to support themselves and must refrain strictly from remunerating state service.

Like Mitford, however, Böckh makes clear throughout his widely read book that Athenians did in fact work for a living, and states baldly that the lower classes in fact "were as much reduced to the necessity of manual labor as the poor aliens and slaves."[60] A similar inconsistency marks the work of Böckh's contemporary and countryman Arnold Heeren, who in his discussion of slavery contended that it created a leisured citizen "nobility" but nonetheless questioned the wisdom of Greek democratic lawgivers who failed to see that "to intrust ... unlimited power to the commons, was not much less than to pave the way for the rule of the populace, if we include under that name the mass of indigent citizens."[61]

Fustel's conviction that slavery fostered an unhealthy attitude to work that in turn prompted Athenian citizens to live off the state was echoed in the history of Greek culture published by the Swiss Jacob Burckhardt a generation later in 1898. There Burckhardt caricatured the Athenians as a people who lived by graft and greed, perjury and sycophancy, confiscations and political trials. This depravity he traced in part to slavery, which deprived the majority of Athenians of the soothing effect provided by daily labor. In words very similar to Fustel's, Burckhardt complained that the poor man learned to use his vote to get hold of the property of others, getting himself paid for participation in politics, selling his vote, decreeing liturgies and masterminding confiscations of property, which lost all its sanctity.[62] These words evoke the arguments of Fustel: from the refusal to make an honest living, Fustel had maintained, came pressure placed upon the government to remunerate citizens for participation in state business, as well as a system that taxed the rich mercilessly, and in time the indolent poor "began to use their right of suffrage either to decree an abolition of debts, or a grand confiscation, and a general subversion." For Fustel, then, and for Burckhardt, slavery contained within it the seeds of disaster, for it led in turn to that great bugaboo of the eighteenth and nineteenth centuries alike, the failure to respect "the superior principle that consecrates the right of property."[63] For Burckhardt, as for Fustel, the degeneration of Athenian government into the rule of a petulant, impudent mob evoked more recent developments in France. What had been lost in the Athenians' movement into democracy, Burckhardt believed, was nobility.

Belief in the idleness of the Athenian citizenry survives into the twentieth century. A popular government textbook of the 1920s set the ratio of slave to free at three to one and maintained that free citizens "did no disagreeable work but devoted their time to government, fine arts, and refinements of life." The *National Geographic* for December 1922 assured readers that there were four slaves at Athens to every one citizen. A ratio of five or six to one was propounded to young people in Van Loon's 1921 *Story of Mankind*, which portrayed citizens spending all their time and energy discussing war and peace in the assembly or viewing tragedies in the theater, while work was the exclusive province of slaves.[64] Some have rejoiced in the belief that slavery facilitated a gracious life for citizens, convinced that the cultural and political achievements of the Athenians had not been bought too dearly; others more squeamish hesitated to come down on the side of Athenian slavery but did brace themselves to raise the question whether possibly the ends might have justified the means; still others excoriated the leisure of free citizens, viewing it not as the stepping stone to pithy ideas and stately temples but rather as a breeding ground for idleness and indolence.

The notion that Athenian citizens on the whole enjoyed lives of leisure while the disagreeable aspects of existence were relegated to slaves does not fit well with the evidence, but it does suit the needs of Marxists invested in demonstrating the role of oppression in history.[65] Marx himself shared a good deal of the nostalgia for Greece evident in Schiller and Hegel. Some of his yearnings were directed at early Greece—the age of epic heroes as it emerged from the mists of myth—and, like many thinkers of the early nineteenth century in Germany and France, he located much of the appeal of ancient Greece in the impossibility of returning to the conditions that fostered its development. Why, he asks, "should not the historic childhood of humanity, its most beautiful unfolding, as a stage never to return, exercise an eternal charm?"[66] He was also drawn, however, to the democratic state of the classical era, by which he can only mean Athens, and here his pessimism about the possibility of return was tempered by hopes of restoring egalitarian ideals. In a letter written in 1843 he wrote of his fellow Germans that "freedom, the feeling of man's dignity, will have to be awakened again in these men. Only this feeling, which disappeared from the world with the Greeks and with Christianity vanished into the blue mist of heaven, can again transform society into a community of men to achieve their highest purposes, a democratic state."[67] Despite this paean to the Greeks' attachment to freedom, however, his characterization of ancient society as based on slavery in the *Holy Family* penned with Engels two years later was to have a profound effect on his followers.[68]

Marxists of various stamps have played a crucial role in the development of thinking about Greek slavery over the past century. Despite the powerful emotions involved in debates between Marxists and anti-Marxists, and despite the many areas of disagreement among the Marxists themselves, it is to a considerable degree the Marxists who are responsible for moving the discussion of Athenian slavery from a posture of indignant moralizing to a scholarly plane. To be sure, the Marxists' critics have accused them of exaggerating the importance of slavery in the ancient world in order to underline the prominence of economic injustice in history, while the Marxists, because of their preoccupation with the evils of social stratification, have alternately condemned slavery or welcomed it as one of the five stages in the progression toward the liberation of humanity. The principal consequence of the rise of Marxist history for Athenian slavery, however, has been a closer examination of the precise function of slavery in the Athenian state, and many of those who today identify slavery as crucial to ancient society are not Marxists at all.[69]

The very different histories of antiquity by Diakov and Kovalev on the one hand and Korovkin on the other demonstrate something of the range of response to Athenian democracy in the Soviet Union.[70] The *History of Antiquity* assembled evidently in the 1950s under the direction of Diakov and Kovalev is aimed at the educated general reader, whereas Korovkin's *History of the Ancient World*, published in 1981, appears to be designed for adolescents. The authors working under Diakov and Kovalev stress repeatedly the centrality of slavery in Athenian civilization and make clear that Athenian citizens were a minority living off the thankless toil of the enslaved masses; Pericles is billed as the protector of the slave-owning class. On the whole, "slave-owner" is the authors' standard expression for those whom Western historians have traditionally termed "citizens." Like Western historians, the authors suggest a contradiction between Athens's democratic pretensions and Athenian imperialism, which they portray as designed to acquire new slaves. Although both Athenian slaveholding and the imperialism they believe it occasioned are condemned as vitiating democratic principles, however, the authors applaud these principles in their essence and show considerable enthusiasm for Athens as a "progressive" improvement over Greek aristocracies and oriental despotisms.[71] The cultural and intellectual achievements of the Greeks, they argue, retain their value in the modern world and in fact influenced the founders of Marxism-Leninism.[72]

The school text of Korovkin, which sought to call attention to the centrality of class struggle in history, contains numerous large-type headings and drawings designed to illustrate the prominence and hardships of slavery in Greece. It paints a different picture of Athens. The title of chapter 8, on the rise of the polis, is entitled "The Establishment of the Slave-Owning System and the Rise of the Greek City-States in the 8th–6th Centuries BC," and its first section is labeled "Formation of the Athens [sic] Slave-Owning State." The next chapter bears the title "The Development of Slavery in Greece and the Rise of Athens in the Fifth Century BC," and within this chapter the section on Athenian government is labeled "The Athenian Slave-Owning Democracy."[73] (In the section in that chapter on the influx of slaves into Greece, lip service is paid to the inclusion of women among the class of slaves, but except in the sentences that so indicate, Korovkin assumes that slaves are male.) Korovkin's view of the relationship of slaves to slave-owners makes a radical contrast with that of Western historians. "The slaves," he writes (making liberal use of italics, unless these were introduced by the English translator), "did everything they could to bring harm to the slave-owners: they *broke* the implements, *injured* the cattle, and *sought to work as badly as they could.* Often slaves attempted to *escape* from their masters although they knew that they would be punished harshly if caught. Not rarely they *killed* the most cruel slave-owners. Frequently there were *uprisings* of slaves. *This was a class struggle—the struggle waged by the slaves against the slave-owners.*"[74] In the conclusion to his book—a conclusion devoted almost entirely to the issue of slavery—Korovkin concedes that slavery made a civilization to which future generations are indebted and that it was an important step forward from the primitivism of earlier times, but in his discussion of Athens he presents it as an unmitigated evil.

In a well-known article published in 1959 entitled "Was Greek Civilization Based on Slave Labour?" Sir Moses Finley, approaching the question from a somewhat Marxist standpoint, alleged a correlation between democracy and slavery both in Athens and in democratic Chios and argued more broadly that "the more advanced the Greek city-state, the more it will be found to have true slavery. . . . More bluntly put, the cities in which individual freedom reached its highest expression—most obviously Athens—were cities in which chattel slavery flourished." Chattel slavery, Finley argued, played little role in pre-Greek civilizations of the ancient near east, for it was fundamentally a Greek discovery. In short, Finley concludes, one aspect of Greek history "is the advance, hand in hand, of freedom *and* slavery."[75]

This connection has been drawn again and again in the late twentieth century. In the survey text *The World of Athens* put out in Cambridge (England) by the Joint Association of Classical Teachers the authors contend that "in the final analysis it was the growth of slavery that permitted the growth of citizen freedom and democracy at Athens."[76] The conjunction of freedom and slavery has a long pedigree. In the antebellum South of the United States, the role of black slavery in fostering white freedom formed an important part of proslavery rhetoric. At the same time similar ideas were put forward in Europe, where the essay published at Edinburgh in 1828 praised the merits of Athenian civilizaion by listing back to back in a single sentence the Athenians' "unconquerable love of freedom" and the fact that at Athens "menial and agricultural labour was performed by slaves."[77] The importance of the link between freedom and slavery in proslavery ideology is indicated by the titles of works on American slavery such as Edmund Morgan's presidential address to the Organization of American Historians entitled "Slavery and Freedom: The American Paradox" and James Oakes's *Slavery and Freedom: An Interpretation of the Old South* (New York, 1990).[78] Increasingly the interdependence of freedom and slavery at Athens has formed the focus of scholarly concern, and with it the ways in which the Athenian democrats attempted to define themselves in terms of the privileges they denied to women, allies, and other outsiders. In the generation since the appearance of Finley's article, a number of scholars working in areas such as philosophy, literary criticism, psychology, and anthropology have framed new constructs to accommodate the Athenian treatment of those who belonged to various out-groups. Many of them French or influenced by modern schools of thought that have their roots in France, these scholars have examined the ways in which the Athenian democrats' definition of themselves was bound up with the distinctions they made between themselves and others, and have seen the Athenians' egalitarian ethos as dependent on the domination of outsiders not simply in a practical manner (e.g., obtaining leisure for political debate or salaries with which to pay jurors and officials) but also in a fundamental ideological sense. In the construct of these thinkers, egalitarianism among Athenian citizens was made in effect psychologically bearable only by channeling aggression into the abuse of those who had been excluded from the 'club.'[79]

The most recent thinker to explore in depth the role of slavery in developing the free male Athenians' concept of themselves is the Harvard sociologist Orlando Patterson. The Athenian portions of Patterson's sweeping diachronic study *Freedom* (1991) are premised on the notion that it was slavery that moved rich and poor Athenians to see themselves as united in a shared enterprise, as "kinsmen, kith and kin against a world of unfree barbarians."[80] Unlike most people who have written extensively about ancient Athens, Orlando Patterson is black. A deeply personal interest in questions of slavery and freedom moved him to write a book with a strong ideological agenda that has attracted considerable attention. Published by Basic Books, *Freedom* stresses the role of women in the development of the ideal of liberty and often draws connections between the condition of the female and that of the slave. Pointing to the frequency with which the heroines of Attic tragedy were also slaves, Patterson explores the imagery of slavery in *Antigone* and other dramas and cites with approval the words of Vidal-Naquet written ten years earlier about the linking of women and slaves in Greek thought: "In Greek myth, Greek life, and Greek drama, we find not only that 'servile power and female power are linked' but also that the two are linked with the strong desire for, and dangers of, personal freedom."[81]

Patterson's book is informed by a positive valuation of freedom for all people and by a dislike of both slavery and patriarchy. Ironically, however, the notion of democratic Athens as an elite culture built on the deprivations of outsiders was first developed by thinkers who saw in such a system everything to commend and nothing to condemn. One of the great unsolved mysteries in the history of proslavery thought in the American South is the relationship of George Fitzhugh's thinking to that of Marx and of the French Socialists. Fitzhugh insisted his familiarity with contemporary European social and political thought extended only as far as reviews, and on the whole Socialism was a dirty word in his vocabulary. In many respects, however, his thought parallels that of much more educated intellectuals in Europe.[82] What is most intriguing about Fitzhugh's arguments is their place in the development of social and economic constructs linking slaveholding and the subjugation of women. Fitzhugh was convinced that the same sorts of seditious individuals who advocated abolition also championed the rights of women, and in this he was not entirely mistaken. In fact, a number of important nineteenth-century reformers were motivated by a double agenda that opposed not only slavery but patriarchy as well. Many of the champions of women's rights in America such as the Grimké sisters as well as the Englishwomen Fanny Wright and Harriet

Martineau were also ardent abolitionists, and their convictions were shared by men like William Lloyd Garrison. Dew in his *Review of the Debate in the Virginia Legislature* complained of women's disposition to "embrace with eagerness even the wildest and most unjust schemes of emancipation."[83]

Fitzhugh's sense that the fortunes of feminism were somehow linked to those of abolitionism not only in his own society but in the Western tradition more broadly was in fact rather astute. The connection, of course, was not universal; the feminists of Aristophanes' *Congresswomen*—a work of considerable interest to Fitzhugh—make plain that their intention was not to abolish slavery but rather to exploit the institution for their own ends. Broadly speaking, however, Fitzhugh was right to see that the fabric of the society he wished to see preserved was in fact interwoven with patriarchy and hierarchy (though of course he would have identified slavery as making possible the *absence* of hierarchy in free society), and he was correct in believing that these concerns had been shared by a number of Greeks. Both Plato and Aristotle had made frequent linkings between women and slaves. Often, as in Aristotle's *Politics*, children formed the closing part of a tricolon that joined together various out-groups who, though in many respects plainly sharing in the humanity of citizen males, nonetheless could not begin to match them in rational capacity. Elsewhere animals supply the third part of the triangle: Plato in the *Laws* contends that the Muses would never make the mistake of giving a feminine melody or gestures to verses designed for males or assign the rhythm of slaves to a melody and gestures of free men, and he goes on to insist that along the same lines the Muses would never combine the sounds of humans and animals in a single piece (669C). Aristotle linked women with slaves in the *Poetics*, arguing that "goodness can be manifest even in a slave or a woman, though the woman is perhaps an inferior creature and the slave entirely worthless" (1454a [15.20–22]), and he also expressed concern in the *Politics* about overindulgence toward slaves and women (1269b [2.9.7ff.]) and about the way in which laxness toward women and slaves was characteristic of democracy and opened the door to tyranny (1313b [5.11.11–12]).[84] Most European writers who condemned the Athenians for their treatment of women and their slaveholding were plainly convinced that these transgressions set the Athenians off from men of their own era who, by contrast, recoiled from slavery and treated women with respect. Some, however, saw slavery as an extreme form of social stratification, a phenomenon they could not fail to recognize in their own societies, and perceived the denigration of women as a fundamental building block of Western civilization. Though the majority of nineteenth- (and twentieth-) century Englishmen were confident that women were treated quite well enough in their own day, even in Britain dissenting voices were heard, as (on top of the complaints of John Stuart Mill) George Cox foreshadowed the savage attack mounted against the patriarchal tradition by Engels in 1884 in *The Origins of the Family, Private Property, and the State*. The holistic approach of Marxist scholars has combined with the schemata of structuralists to suggest important similarities between the roles played by slaves and by women in the psychology of those privileged by the franchise. The notion popular in late twentieth century America that women and persons of color are joined by common bonds forged by parallel strains is not, as some have imagined, simply a product of the trendy rhetoric of victimization and oppression; rather it has roots reaching back at least as far as the nineteenth century and in some respects much farther.

The history of attitudes toward the relationship between democracy and the status of women is similar to that of attitudes toward the relationship between democracy and slavery. Prior to the twentieth century, the relationship was viewed from a number of different angles. During the earlier part of the century, it was common to consider the perceived denigration of women at Athens as an embarrassing anomaly that in some degree vitiated the claims of the Athenians to a democratic way of life. Thus for example in 1911 the British historian of Greece Alfred Zimmern, who wrote with powerful anguish about the division of women at Athens into housewives and courtesans, saw this unfortunate fragmentation—the result of the Athenian men's refusal to accord citizen status to the children of non-Athenian women—as a regrettable departure from liberal and democratic principles (which he considered synonymous.) "Thus," he concluded, "did the liberal-minded democracy of Athens, by one of those odd freaks of blindness which afflict great peoples, check the progress of a powerful movement toward the consolidation of city life upon a broader and better basis."[85] In the past quarter-century, it has become more common to view the discounting of women and the democratic ethos as intimately intertwined. Scholars of the most recent generation have provided a variety of constructs concerning the connections between the status of women in classical Athens and such -isms as urbanism, militarism, ethnocentrism, narcissism, phallocentrism, and capitalism. Current work on the connection between democracy and the way Athenian men regarded citizen women has been influenced by a new openness to confronting the sexual and romantic element in bonding among Athenian voters, who were always male. Building on the recognition of an entire sexual universe in which all participants were also voting members of the democracy, scholars such as Sir Kenneth Dover in England, Michel Foucault in France, and David Halperin in the United States have formulated new scenarios for the connection between sex and politics. But the ways in which modern thinkers have explained the dynamics of this connection owe much to a willingness to set aside the sentimental democratic platitudes of the first half of the century and carry forward the work begun by pioneers of earlier eras. In reality, the intriguing relationship between the egalitarian ethos of Athenian males and their treatment of women has been the object of debate for fully two centuries.

One important difference, of course, separates the question of the Athenians' slaveholding from their mistreatment of women: there can be no question that Athenian society included thousands of slaves, but there has been considerable disagreement over whether Athenian women were in actuality denigrated, ignored, or abused. In fact the status of women in classical Athens has been hotly debated for some time. Scholars have disagreed deeply over whether, how, and in what degree Athenian women were accorded low status. In part, the disagreement derives from a lack of consensus both about the criteria for determining status and about the proper role of women in society. (There is no reason to believe that all or most critics of the status of women in Athens have supported the equality of the sexes. Few people in any century have done so, and among those who have, there has been little agreement about what this equality means or how it might be implemented.) Disagreements about the status of Athenian women have also been fostered by what appear to be puzzling contradictions in the evidence. Athenian prose authors paint a picture of citizen females largely confined to the women's quarters of their homes, discouraged from the slightest individuality or initiative. Bonds between males appear to have been exceptionally close, and countless texts suggest that they were considered more significant and substantial than bonds between spouses. Because the Periclean citizenship laws of the mid–fifth century disfranchised the children of unions with non-Athenian women, Athenian men who wanted legitimate heirs—as nearly all did—were compelled to marry Athenian women in order to produce sons who would enjoy civic rights at Athens. Since citizen women received little education, however, Athenian men seeking stimulating associations often turned elsewhere for companionship and frequently consorted with non-Athenian mistresses (the so-called *hetairai*, or "companions," sometimes Latinized as *hetaerae*) while they were married to Athenian wives; it is possible that only by such an arrangement could a man both enjoy the company of a scintillating woman and also produce fully lawful male heirs. These *hetairai* ranged from common-law wives to well-educated courtesans to hard-working prostitutes, and they seem to have formed an integral part of the social life of many Athenian men of the middle and upper classes. It is easy to see how uneducated, sheltered citizen wives would find it difficult to compete with cultivated citizen men and foreign women for their husbands' attention and affection.

Other evidence, however, conveys a different impression. Attic drama regularly portrayed women as forceful and assertive. The cast of characters that paraded across the Attic stage included not only the melodramatic Clytemnestra, Antigone, and Medea but also the spunky, resourceful citizen women of Aristophanes' comedies. The males in Aristophanes' plays appear henpecked, and they seem quite apprehensive about displeasing their wives. Some gravestones, moreover, suggest considerable tenderness between spouses, and it was not unheard of for husbands to boast of their marital fidelity.

These seeming contradictions have made it possible for a wide variety of theories to be put forward concerning the status of women in Athens and the relationship of this status to the democratic ethos. No author has maintained that Athenian women were able to vote, but nearly every other conceivable interpretation of the evidence has been put forward at some time. Like reservations about slavery, reservations about the status of women originated in Athens itself. We know of no Athenian male who seriously proposed the enfranchisement of Athenian females. We do know, however, that Plato advocated full participation of females in the government of his ideal state, and it is highly probable that several of the plays of Sophocles and Euripides— *Antigone* and *The Trachiniai*, for example, as well as *Medea*, *Hippolytus*, and *The Trojan Women*—were intended to raise questions about the limits Athenian men placed on women's dignity and freedom. (In his own day, Euripides was evidently regarded as a misogynist, but it seems likely that this rests on a misunderstanding of his interest in women of powerful passions.) When the issue was engaged once more at the end of the eighteenth century, opinions were found to differ sharply. Criticism of Athenian exclusivity often formed part of the antidemocratic rhetorical agenda, and dislike of democracy has not prevented European thinkers from denigrating the Athenians by denying that they really enjoyed one. In this argument the disfranchisement of women is often cited, frequently by men who made no signs of wanting to share voting privileges with women in their own states. Hume, for example, who found Athenian democracy "such a tumultuary government, as we can scarce form a notion of in the present age," also attacked Athens on the grounds that the disfranchisement of women, slaves, and metics resulted in measures being voted on by a small fraction of those who were bound to obey them.[86] Not long afterward Josiah Tucker sniped at Athenian men for disfranchising women as he had carped at them for their slaveholding, and the Scottish historian of Greece John Gillies—who had been indifferent to slavery at Athens—remarked on the "miserable degradation of women" there.[87] A few years later, Gillies's successor Mitford insisted in his *History* that the status of women was exceptionally low in the Athenian democracy. Mitford ascribed this phenomenon to democracy itself. Arguing that the natural turbulence and distastefulness of life under a democratic government "made it often unsafe, or at least unpleasant for them to go abroad," he contended that Athenian women, withdrawing indoors in fear for their lives and in order "to avoid a society which their fathers and husbands could not avoid," soon found themselves "equally of uninstructed minds, and unformed manners."[88] Aristocratic Greece of an earlier era, he maintained, had posed no such difficulties, and in fact the status of women had been higher in previous centuries.

Mitford's opinion was attacked vigorously by an indignant reviewer for the *Westminster* who denied that it was possible for women to be less free in a responsible republic than under an unbridled monarchy, and the anonymous author of the Edinburgh essay praised the men of Athens for their fine treatment of women, ascribing it to their excellent constitution: citing the high status of (noncitizen) courtesans such as Phryne and Aspasia, the Edinburgh writer insisted that the democratic Athenians afforded proof that "wherever man has been barbarous, worthless, or depraved, it has been woman's lot to suffer and obey," whereas "wherever his mind has been generous and enlightened, she has assumed her proper empire, as if, scorning the dominion of the savage and the slave, she sought only to rule the hearts of the brave and the free."[89] A very different sort of connection was posited between women and the democratic ethos by J. A. St. John in his 1842 *Manners and Customs of Ancient Greece*. St. John shared Mitford's dislike for democracy, but he disagreed about the treatment of women in Athens. Suspecting that Athenian men might have been too lenient to women, he followed Aristotle in maintaining that it was a customary evil in democracy that it conferred undue influence on females. St. John does not explain the dynamics of this, but he sees the profligacy of Athenian wives and daughters as a major cause of Athens's eventual collapse. It was by women, he claimed, that "the springs of education were poisoned" at Athens "and the seeds sown of those inordinate artificial desires which convulse and overthrow states."[90]

The twentieth-century conjunction of warmth for democracy with at least lip service to the dignity of women has produced constructs that resemble those of the more sentimental Victorians in their desire to show that women were well treated in Athens. These arguments, however, can be distinguished from earlier ones by their defensive tone, for after 1900 the notion that the democratic Athenians treated their female relations shabbily became sufficiently commonplace that thinkers who wished to speak well of the treatment of women at Athens have been compelled to wrangle with the opposing view. In the 1920s the prominent English Hellenist A. W. Gomme ransacked Victorian literature for examples demonstrating that Athenian women enjoyed every bit as much equality as women in the exemplary society of nineteenth-century Britain.[91] Some years later Gomme's tactics provided a model for the learned popularizer H.D.F. Kitto. In the same successful paperback in which he had spoken so cheerfully of Athenian slavery, Kitto cited Gomme's essay with approval and carried his line of argument still farther. Kitto drew on the mores of his own era in suggesting that the division of women at Athens into wives and courtesans was characteristic of Western civilization and (therefore) fundamentally harmless. Even in his own society, he writes, "it is not unknown that a girl who lives alone in a small flat and takes her meals out may have a more active social life than the married woman. These hetaerae were adventuresses who had said No to the serious business of life. Of course they amused men—'But, my dear fellow, one doesn't *marry* a woman like that.'"[92] For Gomme and for Kitto, it was sufficient to cite parallels from modern society in order to demonstrate that there was nothing fundamentally rotten in the Athenian system. This was a comfortable posture for them since they were not alienated from their own heritage. For others less approving of the status quo, the situation of women in classical Athens was tied up with the deeply problematic legacy of the Western tradition itself. Some thinkers in all eras, moreover, have been able to distance themselves from questions of right and wrong, healthy and unhealthy, and, as in the case of slavery, to ask simply how a phenomenon fits into a larger system. In the category of alienated thinkers, George Cox, John Stuart Mill, and Friedrich Engels questioned the broad traditions that governed Western society, while in the class of historical analysts John Pentland Mahaffy speculated about how the low status of women in classical Athens might fit in with the development of the democracy as a whole.

Kitto had introduced his discussion of the status of women at Athens by an analogy with a detective. In mystery stories, he wrote, there often comes a point at which the detective, being in possession of all the facts, sees unmistakably that they all lead to one conclusion; but since ten chapters of the book remain, the detective is troubled by a vague unease. Kitto went on to confess that he felt rather like such a detective, for he could not accept the picture of the Athenian man that was implied in the mistreatment of the Athenian woman. Something was wrong. Curious and humane, Athenian men could not have treated half their own race with indifference and contempt.[93] Kitto concluded that the two could not be reconciled, so he decided the notion of the denigration of women at Athens would have to be cast overboard. The Irish classicist John Pentland Mahaffy had posed the same question, but he had answered it very differently. How, he had asked, could it be that Athens, "the home of the arts and of literature . . . this Athens, which had thoroughly solved the problem of the extension of privileges to all citizens" had nonetheless "retrograded" where women were concerned and "if not in practice, yet certainly in theory, denied them that reasonable liberty which all the older Greek literature shows them to have possessed?"[94] The framing of the question itself suggests a historical perspective lacking in Kitto, and Mahaffy provided a historical answer. Though he shared Mill's belief both in Athenian government and in the dignity of women, and shared too his regret that the two had not coexisted, he agreed with Mitford that the advance of democracy in fact contributed to the seclusion of women. Where he disagreed with Mitford was in the nature of the dynamics he saw at work. In this regard, Mahaffy was an important forerunner of the holistic approach to Athenian civilization that was to mature during the century that followed his death. Mahaffy isolated three strands tying Athenian civilization of the classical era to a decline in the liberty of women—the movement from the country, where a wife had a certain status as mistress of an estate, into the city; the "Asiatic jealousy" that may have been introduced through contact with Ionia; and the advance of democracy. When the aristocratic tone of life gave way before democracy, Mahaffy argued,

> The result of this equality upon the position of woman is obvious. . . . A common man, with an actual vote, would become of more importance than an Alcmaeonid

lady, who might possibly of old have swayed her ruling husband; and so with the development of political interests, gradually absorbing all the life of every Athenian, there came, in that deeply selfish society, a gradual lowering in the scale of all such elements as possessed no political power. Old age and weaker sex were pushed aside to make way for the politician—the man of action—the man who carried arms, and exercised civic rights.[95]

At the same time, thinkers in Europe and America who were alienated from the values of patriarchal society began to apply historical perspectives of a somewhat different nature. Fitzhugh, of course, was alienated not from the Western tradition as a whole but from what he saw as departures in his own day from long-standing norms. Throughout history, he believed, society had been governed by a patriarchal system predicated on subordinate females and servile labor. "Marriage," Fitzhugh wrote in *Sociology for the South*, "is too much like slavery not to be involved in its fate."[96] Much of Fitzhugh's praise for Aristotle's worldview turned on Aristotle's support of the patriarchal family, the topic with which the *Politics* had begun. Throughout his work Fitzhugh contrasted Aristotle's views with those of Plato, who, he insisted, proposed, like the reformers Fourier, Owen, Greeley, and (of all people) Protagoras, to abolish not only slavery but indeed the family itself. In truth, Greeley opposed women's suffrage, but Fitzhugh still included him on a list of seditious reformers who he suspects might have stolen their doctrines from Aristophanes' *Ecclesiazusae*, "a satire upon the women's rights, and other agrarian and socialistic doctrines then prevalent in Athens." "May not," Fitzhugh asks in his review of a translation of the *Ecclesiazusae*, "Athenian corruption and effeminacy have grown out of the Greelyite isms inculcated by Plato . . . ?"[97]

Convinced that northern reformers sought to undermine the entire fabric of patriarchal society, Fitzhugh proclaimed in *Cannibals All* that "the family is threatened, and all men North or South who love and revere it, should be up and a-doing."[98] (That the linkage of slavery and the subjugation of women was not limited to the South is made plain by an editorial that appeared in the New York *Herald* in 1852 explaining that woman had become subject to man "by her nature, her sex, just as the negro is and always will be, to the end of time, inferior to the white race, and, therefore, doomed to subjection."[99]) Further connections between slavery and the family were drawn by southern moralists who sought to counter the allegations of northern reformers that easy access to black women undermined the fidelity of slave-owning husbands. William Gilmore Simms wrote a protracted response to Harriet Martineau's abolitionist *Morals of Slavery*, complaining among other things of "her wild chapter about the 'Rights of Women,' her groans and invectives because of their exclusion from the offices of state, the right of suffrage, the exercise of political authority."[100] Simms contended that in truth sexual access to slaves functioned as a safety valve in protecting the virtue of white women as well as the integrity of white marriages. Chancellor Harper of South Carolina explained at length how the morals of white women were protected by the existence of slavery, as the well-known unchastity of black females reacted upon white women (as if by some law of physics) to produce a higher degree of virtue among southern ladies than could be found in the free society of the north.[101] Someday, perhaps, Harper muses, England herself may be "overrun by some Northern horde—sunk into an ignoble and anarchical democracy, or subdued to the dominion of some Caesar,—demagogue and despot." Then, he concludes, "in southern regions, there may be found many republics, triumphing in Grecian arts and civilization, and worthy of British descent and Roman institutions." A footnote explains his meaning here: "I do not use the word democracy in the Athenian sense, but to describe the government in which the slave and his master have an equal voice in public affairs."[102] In the view of Harper, Simms, and Fitzhugh, an Athenian-style society could produce culture for citizens by creating a class of noncitizen slaves and a class of noncitizen mistresses. Male citizens would then enjoy equality of political rights and access to sexual satisfaction without having to endure hard labor or compromise the chastity of citizen women.

In his review of Grote's *History of Greece* John Stuart Mill had linked slavery and the denigration of women as blots on Greek civilization, and his belief (expressed there and elsewhere) that women were inexcusably devalued in his own society is well known. It remained for later thinkers, however, to develop constructs similar to those of antebellum Americans connecting slavery and the subjugation of women. George Cox's *General History of Greece* is a strange document, with its polemical digressions condemning the homosexuality of James VI.[103] Cox also vented his spleen concerning patriarchy. Pericles, he maintained, was driven to his irregular union with the *hetaira* Aspasia by "the working of a disease which has its root in the first principles of Aryan civilisation,—in other words, in the absolute subjection of the members of a household to the father of the family, as its priest and its king." From this root, Cox argued, "sprang the institutions of caste and of slavery, and the subservience, if not the degradation, of women."[104]

The case against patriarchy was stated still more forcefully in 1884 by Engels in *The Origins of the Family, Private Property and the State*, published in the light of Lewis Morgan's work. There Engels contended that the downfall of Athens was caused not, as "lickspittle historians assert to flatter their princes," by democracy but rather by slavery, which, he maintained, "banned the labor of free citizens." Identifying the overthrow of mother-right as the "world historic defeat of the female sex," moreover, he deplored in the strongest terms the consequent degradation of women to instruments for breeding, a degradation he saw as still operational in his own day.[105] According to Engels, the first class antagonism discernible in history was that between man and woman in monogamous marriage and the first class oppression that of the female sex by the male. Engels strenuously condemned the division of women at Athens into wives and *hetairai*, and in writing of his own day he maintained that "the more the old traditional hetaerism is changed in our day by capitalistic commodity production and adapted to it . . . the more demoralising are its effects." This system of gender relations, he contended, "degrades the character of the entire male world."[106]

Like the proslavery writers of the American South, in other words, both Cox and Engels linked slavery and the subjugation of women as related aspects of patriarchy, and, like them, they considered patriarchy to be the cornerstone of Western civilization; where they differed was in the moral valence they ascribed to patriarchal institutions. The thinking of Cox and Engels contrasts markedly with scenarios that lament the mistreatment of women at Athens as an intrusion of primitive thinking into a society that had served as a forerunner of the enlightened moral universe of the modern world. For Cox and Engels, fundamental and enduring principles explained what they perceived as unhealthy dynamics between the sexes in Athens, just as such principles had explained to the proslavery men the desirability of guaranteeing the stability of the privileged order by maintaining sexual and laboring fringe groups. Similar notions underlie two important twentieth-century books on Greece written in the United States, Philip Slater's 1968 *The Glory of Hera* and Eva Keuls's *The Reign of the Phallus: Sexual Politics in Ancient Athens* (1985). Slater in fact derived his theory of family dynamics in Athens from those he perceived in the American middle class of his own day. The question Slater sought to answer was how Attic tragedians could have portrayed so many forceful, articulate females if Athenian women were really, as popularly believed, sequestered, poorly educated, and kept in constant subjection to husbands, fathers, and brothers. Drawing on an analogy with his own culture, Slater posited that the foreseeable rage of Athenian women was likely to have been taken out on their male infants and toddlers, whose early childhood memories then provided the materials for the dramas they wrote as adults. The consequences of Greek women's frustrations, he maintained, was narcissism both in the mother and in the male children she raised. Slater deplored the persistence of these same dynamics in his own society, for he viewed narcissism as a grave threat to the survival of the race. For Slater, a direct line led from the suppression of women's talents to nuclear conflagration, for in his view, in a world in which, as in Athens and America, the educated female is underemployed and her talents underutilized, the male child will be "the logical vehicle for these frustrated aspirations, as well as the logical scapegoat for her resentment," and these dynamics go far to explain why the world of the mid–twentieth century was engaged in "constant infantilism in international relations." Slater cited the inability of the American State Department and the North Vietnamese to agree on a site for peace talks as evidence of this infantilism and claimed that "buried beneath every Western man is a Greek—

western man is nothing but Alcibiades with a bad conscience, disguised as a plumber."[107]

Eva Keuls of the University of Minnesota shares Slater's belief that Athenian sexual dynamics, so far from being an obsolete product of a mentality long since passed away, are in fact part of a continuing tradition. She also agrees with Slater in viewing these dynamics as pernicious. Keuls's *Reign of the Phallus: Sexual Politics in Ancient Athens* may well be the most forceful indictment of Athenian society ever crafted. Connecting what she perceived as the persistent denigration of females by Athenian men with "rampant saber-rattling," Keuls expresses the wish that her book may prove useful to those "who feel that phallocracy remains a problem in modern, more subtle forms." Classical Athens, Keuls argues, "is a kind of concave mirror in which we can see our own foibles and institutions magnified and distorted."[108]

Like Cox and Engels, neither Slater nor Keuls connects the unhealthy dynamic they perceive in Athens specifically with its democratic constitution. Along the same lines as these earlier thinkers, however, their work is important in this connection because of the fact that they view the denigration of women in Athens as characteristic of Western civilization rather than as an embarrassing anomaly. Engels had a profound influence on Marylin Arthur of Wesleyan University in Connecticut, who in her article entitled "Early Greece: The Origins of the Western Attitude to Women" utilized a Marxist construct and quoted Engels in her footnotes. Where the aristocracy had ensured a leisured life for itself by concentrating all economic and social privilege in its hands, Arthur argued, "the democracies of ancient Greece secured liberty for all its [sic] citizens by inventing a system of private property which required women to legitimate it and slaves to work it." In discussing Solon's social legislation, Arthur maintained that the reiteration of the distinction between public and private that underlay much of Solon's legislation had important ramifications for women. For

> Insofar as women continued to be associated with the private side of life alone, they now appear as a sub-species of humanity. That is to say, women had before been conceived of as an aspect of life in general; now they are seen as an aspect of man's existence. The difference is an important one, for it means that the inferiority of women, their subservience to men, has to be explicitly recognized. . . . Now, the social and legal structure of the state specifically endorses and prescribes the subservience of women to men.[109]

Other scholars have taken different tacks. In her book *Sowing the Body*, for example, Page duBois of the University of California at San Diego offers a new twist on Mahaffy's argument regarding the role of the move to an urban culture in lowering the status of women at Athens. DuBois argues that because women were associated with land in a variety of persistent metaphors by virtue of their fertility and imagined passivity, the movement away from an aristocratic social hierarchy based on the amount of land one possessed also served to devalue women.[110]

A new disposition to validate the sexual element in male bonding at Athens has also played an imortant role in construing connections between sexuality and politics there. Writing in 1777, William Young expressed indignation that anyone could suppose that relations between Greek men "were ever sullied with immorality; and that mere custom, in a word, could give the most horrid and disgustful vice a preference over the dearest and most necessary instinct of nature."[111] Two hundred years later, the Oxfordian Sir Kenneth Dover wrote with his customary frankness that "it was taken for granted in the Classical period that a man was sexually attracted by a good-looking younger male, and no Greek who said he was 'in love' would have taken it amiss if his hearers assumed without further inquiry that he was in love with a boy and that he desired more than anything to ejaculate in or on the boy's body."[112] Along with Michel Foucault, Dover and Keuls have argued that for Athenian men homosexual bonding was an important way of participating in society—of exercising, in effect, their rights of citizenship. To play a passive role in a sexual act, Dover contends, was perhaps acceptable for a boy, who could not yet participate in the democracy, just as it was for a woman; but it was not acceptable for a man. Dover has maintained that partial limitations were placed upon acquiescence for a courted teenage boy, whose behavior was circumscribed by the fact that he would someday vote and should not therefore give in fully to his lover.[113] Dover connects the excitement attached to pederastic relationships with the sense of self-worth that came from being accepted by a partner who was one's equal in a way that no slave or woman (i.e., nonvoter) could ever be.

Dover's analysis of sexual and political dynamics in Athens in some ways anticipated that of Foucault. Not technically a structuralist but profoundly influenced by structuralism, Foucault saw important political underpinnings in Greek sexual ethics, claiming that what an Athenian man achieved by adherence to the prevailing ethical code regarding appropriate sexual behavior was precisely the validation of his civic privileges and his right to the leadership of the polis. This line of approach enables Foucault to explain several apparent inconsistencies in Greek thinking about male sexual conduct. It throws light, for example, on the ambivalence of the sources about the need for sexual fidelity on the part of husbands. Foucault argues that there was indeed a model of a faithful husband in Athens, but that the rationales for husbandly and wifely fidelity were different, for the fidelity of a wife was occasioned by her husband's control over her, whereas the fidelity of a husband was prompted by a man's control over himself: it was only because a man "exercised authority and because he was expected to exhibit self-mastery in the use of this authority, that he needed to limit his sexual options. . . . For the husband, having sexual relations only with his wife was the most elegant way of exercising his control."[114] Though the day would come, Foucault writes, when the paradigm most commonly used for illustrating sexual virtue would be the chaste female, for the Greeks "a more representative model of the virtue of moderation . . . was that of the man, the *leader* [italics mine], the master who was capable of curbing his own appetite even when his power over others allowed him to indulge it as he pleased."[115] Foucault also believed that the marriage of sex and politics explained another inconsistency in the sources, that concerning the acceptability of male homosexual acts. For an Athenian, Foucault argued, sex was tied indissolubly to constructs of dominance and submission. Each sexual act mandated one active individual, a free and privileged person, and one passive individual ultimately lacking in dignity and independence. For the passive partner to be another male citizen was therefore problematic, for the division of sexual partners into the one who counted and the one who did not count inevitably made sex between citizen males a source of anxiety—hence, Foucault argues, the enigmatic oscillation concerning the "natural" or "unnatural" character of male romantic love.

Foucault's central thesis concerning the marked asymmetry of Greek sexual ethics is profoundly political, for he maintains that though women in Greece—by which he clearly means Athens—were subject to strict constraints, yet this ethics was not addressed to women and did not concern their behavior but rather was an ethics "thought, written, and taught by men, and addressed to men—to free men, obviously" and was designed "to give form to *their* behavior." The most political aspect of Foucault's construct is his view of Greek sexual ethics as more prescriptive than prohibitive, more active than passive. The Greek sexual ethic, he wrote, spoke to men "concerning precisely those conducts in which they were called upon to exercise their rights, their power, their authority, and their liberty."[116] Though Foucault's book *The Uses of Pleasure* appears at first sight to be entirely about men, then, in fact through the perspective of male homosexual bonding in Athens he has synthesized a long tradition of speculation about the connection between the exercise of political freedom and the discounting of women. Both Cox and Engels, who saw the denigration of women deeply rooted in Western civilization, had accompanied this contention with powerful condemnation of Greek homosexuality and had believed that it was fostered by the degradation of women, but it remained for twentieth-century thinkers who were not hostile to homosexual relations to conceptualize the sexual dynamics of democratic Athens in political terms.

In 1989 and 1990 Routledge published two books dealing with Greek sexuality in their series "The New Ancient World." *The Constraints of Desire* was written by Jack Winkler of Stanford, a distinguished gay scholar who had received the American Philological Association's Goodwin Award of Merit in 1988; *One Hundred Years of Homosexuality and Other Essays on Greek Love* was the work of David Halperin, a gay activist who was head of the literature faculty in the School of Humanities and Social Sciences at M.I.T. Drawing on the work of Dover, Keuls, and Foucault, Halperin in a chapter entitled "The Democratic Body" engaged the question of the loss of civic rights with which Athenian law punished men convicted of prostituting themselves. Why, Halperin asks, should this be? What is "more 'private' and less 'civic' than sex?" Exploring the "cultural poetics of manhood" that Athenian democratic ideology "at once took for granted and mobilized in its own support," Halperin concludes that the inviolability of the voter's body against both violent assault and sexual penetration was an integral part of the ethos of Athenian democracy, contending that

> one of the first tasks of the radical democrats at Athens, who brought into being a form of government based (in theory at least) on universal male suffrage, was to enable every citizen to participate on equal terms in the corporate body of the community and to share in its rule. The transition to a radical democracy therefore required a series of measures designed to uphold the dignity and autonomy—the social viability in short—of every (male) citizen, whatever his economic circumstances.

Though the elimination of economic inequality was considered neither practical nor, ultimately, desirable, nonetheless Halperin argues, "a limit could be set to the political and social consequences of such inequities, a zone marked out where their influence might not extend. The body of the male citizen constituted that zone." Similarly, Halperin contends, to violate the sanctity of a citizen's body in nonsexual ways "was not only to insult him personally but to assault the corporate integrity of the citizen body as a whole and to offend its fiercely egalitarian spirit."[117] The new disposition to ground homosexual bonds in the body politic is indexed by the five-page discussion of pederasty in Paul Rahe's Republics Ancient and Modern: Classical Republicanism and the American Revolution (Chapel Hill, 1992), possibly the first work of scholarship to discuss classical sexuality alongside the chaster passions of Hume, Descartes, and James Madison.[118]

A slightly different perspective appears in Centaurs and Amazons, Page duBois's study of Greek self-definition. DuBois also stressed the need of male citizens in Greek states to define themselves in contradistinction to what they were not. Early attempts to define heroism, she argued, "involved a consideration of humanness, maleness, Greekness in terms of opposition," and in Athenian sculpture of the classical period the myth of the Amazons "became the property of the city of Athens, to be used again and again . . . to present a discourse on the differentiation of kinds. How are human beings different from animals? How are women different from men? How are Greeks different from barbarians?"[119] DuBois places the concept of isonomia in a new context, stressing the meaning of isos not as "equal" but as "same" and makes it possible to see isonomia as "just"-ice for people who are "just" like us.[120] She provides, in other words, a *political* context for the common view that Athenian males viewed women as "other." Similar ideas are expressed by Sarah Pomeroy of Hunter College, whose book on women in antiquity, *Goddesses, Whores, Wives, and Slaves* brought her considerable fame when it was published in 1975. It may be suggested, Pomeroy wrote, that "after the class stratification that separated individual men according to such criteria as noble descent and wealth was eliminated, the ensuing ideal of equality among male citizens was intolerable. The will to dominate was such that they then had to separate themselves as a group and claim to be superior to all non-members: foreigners, slaves, and women."[121]

. . . . .

Popular twentieth-century schools of thought such as Marxism, feminism, and structuralism have encouraged students of Athens to think in increasingly holistic terms. In this they are following in tracks laid down in previous centuries by a variety of thinkers who perceived connections between democracy and such phenomena as imperialism, slaveholding, and the denigration of women. In the eighteenth century, it was generally the opponents of egalitarianism who portrayed the Athenians as greedy expansionists or dehumanized slave-owners, and there was no consensus (as there still is not) that women were mistreated. Dissident voices, however, were heard, as reformers like Chastellux cried out for a better world. During the nineteenth-century, enthusiasm for the achievements of the Athenians combined with British involvement in their own imperialism to encourage many people writing about the ancient world to gloss over possible embarrassments; the role of imperialism and slavery in forging the glory that was Greece was often stressed, and the denigration of women indignantly denied. (Neither women nor slaves were visible in Grote's happily imperialistic Athens.) Dissenting voices, however, grew increasingly loud. Again, antiegalitarian thinkers used ancient slavery to smear classical ideals, and social critics like Mill, Cox, and Engels saw the Athenians' failure to apply democratic principles to the human community at large as in varying ways emblematic of underlying problems in Western civilization throughout history. Debunking the myth of Sparta, Victor Duruy cried out against those who had failed to notice that the entire system was dependent on massive slavery: no helot, no Spartiate, he shouted to the world.

Similarly holistic lines of thought continued to be pursued during the second half of the twentieth century. Despite the hopes voiced by Boston Red Sox fans that their city might, by victory in the 1986 World Series, become not only the Athens of the North but its Sparta as well, it is no longer as fashionable as once it was to yearn like the men and women of the Renaissance or the Enlightenment for a society filled with Athenian sculpture and Spartan virtue, Athenian drama and Spartan discipline; few have echoed d'Alembert's dream of joining "the prudence of Lacedaemon to the urbanity of Athens."[122] Belief in the cohesive nature of society, moreover, has ultimately reinforced the preference for Athens over Sparta. Toward the beginning of the nineteenth century, the revulsion in France and elsewhere in Europe from classical slavery tended for a time to link the two city-states in infamy, and it was popularly believed that Athenian citizens, like their Spartan counterparts, were greatly outnumbered by their exploited slaves. As time passed, however, what Nicole Loraux and Pierre Vidal-Naquet have called the myth of "bourgeois Athens" took shape, and moderns began to find the city of commerce, family, ambition, and private property to be eminently more congenial than the armed camp in the Peloponnesus, with its communal living and discouragement of trade. It was not only in France that the perceived bourgeois values of the Athenians led the city of Pericles to seem more modern in its relevance than that of Lycurgus, but in the rest of Europe and in America as well. Twentieth-century concerns about the limitations of bourgeois values, however, have in turn fostered the formulation of schemata wherein the concept of "otherness" is seen as an integral part of the democratic ethos, as scholars of the later part of the century have sought to substitute a cohesive view of social psychology for the *apologiae* of earlier decades. Hegel had seen that communities need to define themselves in contradistinction to other communities; twentieth-century thinkers like William Connolly have developed this notion as it operates within subgroups of the same community, writing that "identity requires difference in order to be, and it converts difference into otherness in order to secure its own self-certainty." What is defined as other will inevitably suffer, for "to establish an identity is to create social and conceptual space for it to be in ways that impinge on the spaces available to other possibilities."[123] Precisely because of its perceived modernity, moreover, classical Athens is subjected to closer scrutiny and held to higher standards than ancient Sparta, which has come itself to be viewed as "other": in 1979 an American classicist recovering from a stroke used her diminished vocabulary to indicate Sparta with the words "the other place" while Athens for its part was "our place."

Not all thinkers who have wrangled with the complexities of Athenian democratic ideology have chosen to stand in judgment on the Athenian system from the standpoint of either practicality or ethics. Some, of course, have passed judgment, and loudly at that; others who have declined to do so have nonetheless provided perspectives that have facilitated the formulation of condemnatory constructs on the part of those who are inclined to make them. (A world of difference separates the denunciations of Hume and Mitford, of Slater and Keuls, from the clinical analysis of Foucault or Halperin.) On the whole the criticism directed at Athenian imperialism and slaveholding has entailed moral condemnation, but to describe the Athenian ethos as contingent upon delimiting categories of "others" is not necessarily to claim that it

was wicked or that it did not work, nor does stress on the importance of homoerotic ties among Athenian voters imply resentment of the discounting of
women—or even belief in it. In the egalitarian climate of the twentieth century, however, to suggest that the Athenian system was able to function only
by an overriding "us/them" dichotomy is inevitably to suggest a deficiency of
a serious order, and it is fair to say that the formulation of this construct in
many ways represents the twentieth-century contribution to the anti-Athenian tradition.

Chapter Thirteen

EPILOGUE

THE OLD AND THE NEW

> Nothing new can be said about an acknowledged folly.
> —Alcibiades, speaking in the pages of Thucydides

> No book can ever be finished.
> —Karl Popper, *The Open Society and Its Enemies*

SPARTA HAS FALLEN, and fallen hard. The thud was most audible in France, where Rousseau and many of the revolutionaries had sought so conspicuously to revive Spartan virtues in the modern world. French textbooks of the later nineteenth century such as those of Dussieux, Ducoudray, and Bachelet regularly attacked the Spartans for their militarism, their indifference to intellectual life, and their exploitation of the helots.[1] Like Fustel de Coulanges, Dussieux censured Rousseau for seeing equality in what was in reality an aristocracy built on slavery.[2] Revulsion from Sparta did not in all cases imply enthusiasm for Athens; Dussieux and Bachelet were often critical of the Athenian state, and Fustel de Coulanges echoed Constant in his conviction that Athenian liberty was not what the admirers of antiquity had made it seem. As in the second half of the eighteenth century, however, the strictures of French thinkers of the nineteenth on the presumed virtues of the Spartans fostered a more generous view of Athens in many quarters, and when in the twentieth-century totalitarian states arose in Europe and Asia that seemed in many respects to evoke the Spartan ethos, the Athenians came to be valued even more highly than had been the case in Victorian Britain.

The exaltation of Athens over Sparta has been particularly dramatic in the English-speaking world. For severity, few can match the Englishman Ronald Latham, who in his 1946 book *In Quest of Civilization* pictured the Spartiates as "warrior ants of a human ant-hill, finding in their joyless isolation a stern and disciplined joy."[3] For humor, the palm should probably be awarded to the American journalist Elmer Davis, who in 1926 appealed for the defeat of prohibition in the United States by decrying the Spartan example of cloistered virtue. Lining up Lycurgus with Lenin, Mussolini, Carrie Nation, and the Ku Klux Klan, Davis insisted that whereas Athens was the great and glorious producer of culture, the "paradise of prohibition" in the Peloponnese was a place where "a helot had no more rights . . . than a conservative in Russia or a pedestrian in the United States."[4] Invidious comparisons have continued to abound in all decades and on both sides of the Atlantic.[5] In the second volume of the massive *Story of Civilization* he produced in conjunction with his wife Ariel, the American Will Durant offered a typical twentieth-century anglophone opposition between the "selfishness, coldness, and cruelty of the Spartan character" and the civilization of the Athenians, "broad in scope and yet intense in action, open to every new idea and eager for intercourse with the world."[6]

It is hard to predict what future happenings might restore Sparta to its pristine glory. Only time will show whether the collapse of the Soviet system will discredit Socialist and Communist dreams once and for all or will work in an opposite way to remove the aura of terror associated with such projects in Western minds and open the way to a more sympathetic view of noncapitalist economic institutions. But though the about-face in valuation of both Sparta and Athens during the middle decades of the nineteenth century was dramatic and undeniable, nonetheless many scholars have continued to press the traditional charges against the Athenian democracy. Allegations of instability, fickleness, irrationality, and ingratitude have persisted in some quarters; many continue to blame democracy for both the loss of the Peloponnesian War and the Macedonian conquest. At the same time, the changing political orientation that had played an important part in the shifting of the balance between Athens and Sparta led to redoubled accusations of hypocrisy in the Athenians' supposed egalitarianism. And though the development of representative democracy has in some respects enhanced the reputation of Athens by making popular government respectable, it has also afforded citizens of the modern era a vantage point from which to look down their noses at the Athenians, who knew no system more complex than referendum and plebiscite; who never developed—so it is said—a representative system; who, it was argued, knew nothing of checks and balances, and whose most brilliant political theorists could imagine no civic universe broader than the city-state.

In France the familiar allegations not only persisted but were deployed in the interests of anti-Semitism; in response, Jewish outrage lined up the Athenian oligarchs with the Vichy government. Through rightists associated with the agenda of Action Française, the French backlash against the revolution and its aftermath was carried straight from the organization's hero Fustel de Coulanges into the twentieth century; Charles Maurras, who founded the movement in 1899, died only in 1952. (There is no reason, of course, to believe that Fustel would have endorsed Maurras's agenda.[7]) In 1909 the literary critic Pierre Lasserre published a pamphlet denouncing the enthusiastic account of the Athenian democracy that had been given by the historian Alfred Croiset, and the booklet's introduction was provided by none other than Maurras.[8] There he attacked in one breath what he termed the *morbus democraticus* in both ancient Athens and the modern world, complaining, to be sure, of America, but most of all of his beloved France, whose difficulties he blamed on democracy and its attendant "metics." Customarily an entirely neutral and descriptive term, the word "metic" in Maurras's hands was used to designate unwelcome interlopers and specifically Jews.[9] Maurras, who supported the Vichy government, was eventually sentenced to life imprisonment for collaboration with the Germans. A predictable reaction followed. The twentieth-century French Marxist Bertrand Hemmerdinger has labeled Maurras an Athenian oligarch arrived twenty-three centuries late; the parallel struck earlier Frenchmen as well, and in 1942 Jules Isaac took the occasion of the puppet government at Vichy to resurrect discussion of the collapse of Athens. Writing like a good patriot under the pseudonym "Julius," Isaac published a little book entitled *Les Oligarques. Essai d'histoire partiale*. Aimed at the Vichy government, the book identified the fall of Athens as the work of similar sympathizers with the enemy, laying blame for the loss of the Peloponnesian War squarely at the door of pro-Spartan Athenians.

A lively anti-Athenian tradition also persisted in Germany, where Grote's work had received decidedly mixed reviews. The liberal leader Johann Jacoby made extracts from Grote for purposes of political propaganda, and the scholar Hermann Müller-Strübing, then living in Grote's own London, wrote a lengthy work defending him against his German critics; but critics there were, from the distinguished historian Eduard Meyer, who discounted much of Grote's work as hopelessly partisan, to the quasi-Marxist Robert von Pöhlmann, who found Grote's view of the unity of the Athenian democracy sadly out of keeping with the historical reality of class struggle and sought to provide a wider historical context identifying the failings of democracy not only in classical Athens but in modern Europe and America as well.[10] Where Macaulay had embraced the Athenians' democracy while recoiling from their empire, the great German philologist Ulrich von Wilamowitz-Möllendorff rejected the democracy but advocated the empire as a good model for Germany.[11]

Admiration for imperial monarchies also fostered in many German thinkers a respect for Philip that often worked to undermine any incipient enthusiasm for Athenian democracy. (Often, but not always; Adolph Holm wrote warmly of the Athenian system but championed Philip as well.) Already during the eighteenth century Frederick of Prussia had been proudly compared to Philip—a man later described by the famous German historian Karl Julius Beloch as the greatest monarch ever to grace a throne. (Beloch is often viewed as a disciple of Grote who looked warmly on Athens. This is simply not true.) The comparison may actually have begun with the Scottish monarchist and historian of Greece John Gillies, who published in 1789 his *View of the Reign of Frederick II of Prussia with a Parallel between That Prince and Philip II of Macedon*. Whatever the origins of the analogy, Philip became a Prussian hero, and the adulation of the Macedonian king brought in its train a concomitant contempt for the pathetic political network he so mercifully put out of its misery. Droysen, the former pupil of Hegel who became a renowned scholar in his own right, found Philip heroic and forward-thinking, Demosthenes piteous and deluded.[12] Beloch identified Demosthenes' aggressive stance as the principal cause of the defeat at Chaeronea; the most savage attack on Demosthenes appeared in Drerup's 1917 book *Aus einer alten Advokatenrepublik (Demosthenes und seine Zeit)*. Rather as Mitford had credited the misdeeds of the French revolutionaries with making the excesses of the Athenian democrats credible for the first time, so Drerup in his preface credited the contemporary world war "into which half the world was plunged by the rancor and lies of Paris and London lawyer-politicians" with tearing the mask from the face of that chauvinistic demagogue Demosthenes, who, he contends, "now is shown to be the worthy forerunner and soulmate of Asquith and Lloyd George, of Poincaré and Briand, of Venizelos and Jonescu, not to mention the classic Land of Broken Faith."[13] Examples could be multiplied at length; instances of this kind of thinking during the late nineteenth and earlier twentieth century have been collected by John Knipfing in an article published in the *American Historical Review* in 1921.[14]

Within Nazi Germany, political developments of the twentieth century tended to reinforce identification with Sparta. Otto Strasser, an early Nazi party activist who later broke with Hitler, recalled the Führer's expressing his hope that all other nations would become "helots" for the German warrior caste.[15] The Nazi regime exhorted Teutonic youths to identify with the Spartans, and beginning during World War II, Simonides' epitaph for the dead at Thermopylae attained, in the words of Roderick Watt of the University of Glasgow, "the status of a leitmotif and literary commonplace"; in an article in the *Modern Language Review* for 1985, Watt argues that liberal use was made of the Simonides epitaph in Nazi propaganda in order to cast the disastrous defeat at Stalingrad in 1943 as a successful sacrificial holding action much like that of Leonidas and his men, who gave their lives, so Greek tradition had it, to buy time for the coordinated amphibious forces marshaled against the invading Persian hordes. (Schiller's 1795 poem "Der Spaziergang" was the most popular German translation of the famous epitaph *O xein, angellein Lakedaimoniois hoti tede keimetha tois keinon rhemasi peithomenoi* ["O stranger, tell the Spartans that we lie here obedient to their commands"]). In Watt's view, the use of the Thermopylae motif was "an attempt to rationalize a military blunder and then to glorify it as such a heroic defeat as to be almost a moral victory."[16]

Outside Nazi circles, however, the rise of totalitarian ideologies in the twentieth century has served to enhance Athens's reputation considerably. The identification of Germany with Macedon had done little good to the reputation of either state in non-Teutonic circles—in Britain, Demosthenes remained a hero and his works were employed for training in civics—and Nazi militarism and eugenics gave a bad name to Athens's other enemy, the Spartans. Whereas many in Hitler's camp sought to identify Germany with Sparta, Germany's enemies, picking up on the analogy, tended to ally themselves with Athens instead. In France, Jules Isaac blamed pro-Spartan sympathizers for the loss of the Peloponnesian War, and in Britain one of the most dramatic defenses of the Athenian ethos came from the pen of Sir Karl Popper. A native of Austria, Popper was driven by his experience of Nazi totalitarianism to formulate one of the most savage attacks ever mounted against what he called "the Spell of Plato."[17] In the first volume of The Open Society and Its Enemies, Popper marshaled a formidable intellectual arsenal in an impassioned and deeply felt plea to his readers to abandon the traditional reverence for Plato and see him for the ruthless totalitarian he believed him to be. Popper's bold book, which presented the Athenian democracy in a favorable light, won him many friends and many enemies, and it remains the focus of lively controversy.[18]

On the whole, American and English thinkers—along with refugees from Hitler's Europe—have taken pride in identifying themselves with Athenian cultivation against German militarism. When the time came to seek classical analogies for the phenomenon of Nazism, they were by and large prepared to line up the Third Reich with both the Spartans and the Macedonians. In the United States, for example, Mars Westington of Hanover College in Indiana gave an address to the Classical Association of the Midwest and South in which no effort was spared in pointing up potential analogies between the militarism, eugenics and all-around evil of the Nazis with that of the Spartans.[19] Westington's analogy between the krypteia and the Gestapo was paralleled in Britain by the schoolmaster Cyril E. Robinson (who also proclaimed in his postwar history of Greece that though historical parallels were dangerous, still "Hitler leaps to the eye" in Philip).[20] Despite the frequency with which English-speaking writers decried Nazism, however, when Americans decided to become classical scholars, it was still to the Germans that they went for both education and inspiration—not quite as uniformly as in the nineteenth century, but with considerable frequency nonetheless. The earliest American classicists like Edward Everett and George Bancroft had traveled dutifully to Göttingen to import its scholarly wares to their intellectually underdeveloped homeland, and the phenomenon continued throughout the century. Ironically, between the wars Jewish classicists often saw a better chance of doing successful graduate work in Germany than in the United States. The thought of Germany cast a powerful spell on the work of American academics, and though it encouraged at least the posturings of sober Wissenschaftlichkeit, it also could foster an anti-Athenian political orientation. Thus for example William Kelly Prentice of Princeton, who dedicated his 1940 book The Ancient Greeks to Eduard Meyer, was comfortable with easy references to the "vanity and greed of the masses" and of "the common man" in Athens—as elsewhere. Prentice had a very low opinion indeed of the ordinary Athenian citizen, writing that the triumph of democracy at Athens "meant the unrestricted power of the largest class of voters, the most thoughtless, the most bigoted, and the most irresponsible."[21] In his portrait of the corruption of selfish citizens by equally selfish politicians he cites the distinguished philologist Ulrich von Wilamowitz-Möllendorff, another German (still more famous than Meyer) who, though he saw the Athenian empire as a good model for that of Germany, had little use for Athenian democracy.[22] Numerous footnotes to Meyer's works dot Prentice's text. The frequency with which Nazis were lined up pejoratively with both the militaristic eugenics of Sparta and the imperialism of Macedon did not prevent postwar Americans from retaining considerable admiration for German scholarship. German classicists are still prized commodities in the American job market, and though proficiency in both French and German is usually required of graduate students in ancient history in the United States, study abroad is far more likely to take place in Göttingen or Munich or Berlin than anywhere in France.[23]

Though Popper's attack on what he perceived as Plato's totalitarianism met with mixed reviews, the new willingness to reject the value systems of classical authors has not extended to all quarters.[24] One ancient author has remained remarkably immune from criticism. It is one thing to mount defenses against the elitism of the affable Plutarch, his vision skewed by the Roman glasses through which he saw classical Athens, or Xenophon the squire, with his embarrassing Spartan sympathies; it is apparently quite another to call into question the wisdom of the historian's historian—the son of Olorus, whose piercing eye is still accorded a reverence long since withdrawn from his fellows.[25] It is extremely difficult to find any printed text that speaks less than glowingly of Thucydides—Thucydides, of whom his translator Thomas Hobbes boasted that he never digressed "to read a lecture, moral or political, upon his own text, nor enter into men's hearts further than the acts themselves evidently guide him."[26] One generation after another, moreover, has been convinced he was speaking about their age above all past ages. John Adams wrote to his wife in 1777 that he sometimes felt inclined to write the history of the American revolution in imitation of Thucydides, since he saw "a striking Resemblance, in several particulars, between the Peloponnesian and the American War." (The parallel he had identified had to do with the causes of the wars; British jealousy of American power, he believed, caused the latter war as Spartan jealousy of the Athenians had caused the former.)[27] At the same time, the Abbé Mably observed that while reading Thucydides he perceived among the passions of the Greeks "the portraiture of those which agitate the present states of Europe, and which will cast us into wretched servitude, as they enslaved the Grecian Republics, if, at some future period, another Philip of Macedon should rise against us."[28] Withal, Thucydides' wisdom is considered to stand confirmed by the unfolding of history; did not his analysis of the civil war on Corcyra look ahead with chilling accuracy to the violence of the French revolutionaries? Mitford saw in Thucydides' account of Athenian imperialism a clear parallel to French expansionism, while his contemporary in France Pierre-Charles Lévesque reported in the preface to his 1795 translation of Thucydides that a distinguished English member of Parliament claimed there was no question with which he was compelled to deal in debate on which Thucydides did not afford guidance. Thomas Arnold in his edition of Thucydides contended that the era of the Peloponnesian War belonged more properly to modern than to ancient history, and the distinguished Johns Hopkins classicist Basil Gildersleeve, the founder of the American classical profession, composed a famous essay on the American Civil War published in 1897 and entitled "A Southerner in the Peloponnesian War."[29] To many twentieth-century thinkers Thucydides has appeared to warn against violating the neutrality of Belgium and committing American troops to either Vietnam or the Persian Gulf.

It is difficult to find anyone who will question the magnificence of Thucydides' work for accuracy, integrity, and import. To be sure, occasional voices of protest have been raised—most conspicuously by Mabel Lang of Bryn Mawr College in Pennsylvania and by her pupil Virginia Hunter of York University in Ontario.[30] In North America, women scholars are overrepresented among Thucydides' few serious detractors. The Marxist Margaret Wason has labeled Thucydides' account of the Peloponnesian War "a record of trivialities unworthy of the dignity of history" and his political judgment "ruined by extreme bias."[31] Such departures from orthodoxy, however, have not been received graciously by the scholarly establishment—in part, perhaps, because they have so often come from women, whose challenges in the areas of warfare and diplomacy may seem easy for men to discount; although the percentage of female classicists and historians has increased dramatically during the second half of the twentieth century, female scholars almost never choose to write about Athenian military and political history, which remain largely a male preserve. Altogether, the reputation of Thucydides remains untarnished, and his judgments about the Athenian assembly retain their authority in academe.

Journalists of the twentieth century (almost invariably male) have taken particular delight in the opportunity Thucydides affords them for combining hardheaded political analysis with a measure of erudition. The Thucydides of American journalists has not in general been perceived as an enemy of democratic Athenian government, for journalists find it unthinkable that their hero could truly have disliked democracy; rather they view him as a voice crying out against the errors democracy is particularly prone to make—errors he surely must have wanted democracies to avoid so that they might live in a world made safe for democracy. Thucydides' popularity, however, has led many enthusiasts of democracy to judge Athens harshly where foreign policy is concerned. The use American journalists throughout the century have made of Thucydidean material has reflected a basic identification of Athenian with American democracy but has shown too a marked fear that the Americans might, by errors in foreign policy, go the way of the Athenians in not conducting their (fundamentally laudable) government quite well enough. Norman Cousins in the *Saturday Review* during the 1940s and Robert Campbell in *Life* magazine in the 1950s decried the sins of imperialism. In 1941, echoing his contributing editor Elmer Davis, Cousins labeled Thucydides "Required Reading" for those who want to know "why it was that Athens lost [the Peloponnesian War] and democracy died," whereas Campbell's Cold War piece "How a Democracy Died." was decked out with ominous line drawings of Greeks doing one another dirt and contended that Americans could learn much from discovering how an earlier democracy had destroyed itself.[32] At times, this concern has been extended to domestic policy as well. Thus for example Gerald Johnson writing in the *New Republic* in 1961 identified Cleon with Joseph McCarthy and the impeachment of Alcibiades as the work of a House Committee on un-Athenian activities.[33]

Coming from American journalists, dire warnings about the perils threatening the United States always take as their point of departure the axiom that the system is eminently worth fighting for. Though academics are generally less facile in their judgments and less sentimental in their attachments, it remains true that particularly among English-speaking scholars, the last quarter of the twentieth century has on the whole been kind to the Athenians. This orientation arises in part from uncritical assumptions that continue to connect democracy with liberalism and the open society; in part it can be traced to an entirely opposite phenomenon: the growing influence of relativist anthropological perspectives that encourage scholars to measure societies in terms of the way in which they sought to fulfill their goals rather than focusing on the merits of the goals themselves. In part it is probably due to a still-increasing sensitivity to the biases of the primary sources. Among scholars whose particular interests do not lie in slavery or gender relations, a puzzling rise in the popularity of the Athenian system has been evident since 1980. To be sure, a number of well-known scholars who think well of Greek democracy produced important work earlier. Sir Moses Finley gave the lectures that issued in his *Democracy Ancient and Modern* in the United States in 1972. There he argued that under its democratic constitution "Athens managed for nearly two hundred years to be the most prosperous, most powerful, most peaceful internally, and culturally by far the richest state in all the Greek world. The system," he concluded, "worked, insofar as that is a useful judgment about any form of government."[34] Prosperous, powerful, culturally rich—these things had often been said about Athens; but it was a new intellectual universe that credited the Athenians with internal peacefulness. The rise in the valuation of Athens, however, has been most dramatic since 1985. The later 1980s and early 1990s witnessed the appearance of a spate of books that take a strikingly positive view of Athenian government. Cynthia Farrar's *Origins of Democratic*

Thinking (Cambridge, 1988), which seeks to recover the beginnings of democratic thought in Greece, is deeply sympathetic to the premises of the Athenian system. Farrar is also a contributor to John Dunn's *Democracy: The Unfinished Journey 508BC to AD1993* (Oxford, 1992), a collection of essays on the history of democracy imbued with admiration for the Athenian model. David Stockton's book *The Classical Athenian Democracy* paints an enthusiastic picture of Athenian government (and discounts the exploitation of out-groups in a single footnote on the very last page).[35] Josiah Ober's 1989 *Mass and Elite in Democratic Athens* is informed by the belief that, in Ober's words, "the Athenian example has a good deal to tell the modern world about the nature and potential of democracy as a form of social and political organization." The Athenian democracy, Ober contends, can serve as a "tool for political analysis and action by those who are, or would be, citizens of democratic states."[36] Ober's book received the American Philological Association's Goodwin Award of Merit, an honor rarely accorded to a scholar under forty years of age.

While still teaching at Montana State University in the 1980s, Ober began working with Charles Hedrick (then at Buffalo, now at Santa Cruz) on a project funded by the National Endowment for the Humanities and the American School of Classical Studies at Athens to commemorate the twenty-five hundredth anniversary of the "founding" of Athenian democracy by Cleisthenes. In part, of course, the significance of Cleisthenes has been put forward for strategic reasons: who could get funding to commemorate the 2,453d anniversary of the reforms of Ephialtes? In part, however, the stress on Cleisthenes derives from a late twentieth-century belief in the importance of the participatory element in Athenian democracy. In 1985, two book-length studies of the demes by British scholars appeared when no such work had been written for fully a century—Robin Osborne's *Demos: The Discovery of Classical Attica* [Cambridge] and David Whitehead's *The Demes of Attika* [Princeton]; in 1988 Cambridge University Press published *Democracy and Participation in Athens* by R. K. Sinclair of the University of Sydney. The nature of Athenian citizens' participation in government has also been the focus of the ongoing work of the Danish scholar Mogens Herman Hansen. The commemorative events for the twenty-five hundredth anniversary included a conference in Athens in December 1992, a second conference in Washington, D.C., in April 1993 (punctuated by a memorable staging of Euripides' *Suppliants* provided by the drama department of Stanford University), and an exhibit at the National Archives in Washington, which agreed to devote the June 1993 issue of its magazine *Prologue* to the topic of democracy. Charles Hedrick also received NEH funding on a separate project, a summer institute on Athenian democracy at the University of California at Santa Cruz given in 1992 and co-directed by his colleague J. Peter Euben. At the same time, Euben, Ober, and John Wallach of Hunter College are editing a collection of essays for Cornell University Press entitled *Educating Democracy* and premised on the conviction that the Athenian example has much to teach an America plagued by apathy and imperiled by the dangers of technocracy. The educative civic function of Attic tragedy has also attracted considerable attention in these last decades of the century. Two books published by Princeton, Euben's *The Tragedy of Political Theory: The Road Not Taken* (1990) and the collection of essays edited by Jack Winkler and Froma Zeitlin entitled *Nothing to Do with Dionysos: Athenian Drama in Its Social Context* (also 1990) stress the central role of tragic drama as a forum for discussion of issues crucial to a democracy; much is revealed in the title of Justina Gregory's *Euripides and the Instruction of the Athenians* (Ann Arbor, 1991).

The absence of historical perspective makes it impossible to understand fully why the celebration of Athenian democracy has become so chic in the United States at the end of the millennium, and in a few years the phenomenon may have burned itself out. Recent attacks on classics as an antiquated and elitist discipline may go part way to explain the interest of American classicists in affirming the viability of the Athenian democratic model; some have connected the current advocacy of Athens with an academic reaction against the erosion of liberalism. Certainly several of Athens's American champions are motivated in part by the desire to provide a counterweight to the alternative model of Greek politics cherished by followers of the University of Chicago political philosopher Leo Strauss—by Allan Bloom, for example, who died as this book was going into production; because of his provocative book *The Closing of the American Mind*, Bloom's name is far more familiar to the general public than is that of Strauss, whose fame is largely confined to academe. A beloved teacher and mentor, Strauss shared Plato's belief that important ideas could be appreciated only by a small number, and he wrote an obscure prose likely to be understood only by members of his circle—a habit Bloom analyzes in the touching account he wrote of Strauss's life and work just after Strauss's death.[37] Many American political theorists who specialize in ancient Greece are members of the Straussian school. Reaction against the Straussian perspective on Greece—a perspective that focuses on the brilliance of Plato and Aristotle—has moved a number of thinkers to bring a different Athens before the American public and to stress instead the energizing aspects of Athenian democracy and its capacity to engage large numbers in meaningful political activity. Shortly after the appearance of Bloom's book in 1987, moreover, a direct challenge to the value of Athenian democracy was offered in the work of Yale political scientist Robert Dahl, whose highly articulate *Democracy and Its Critics* brought before the general public once again the notion that the participatory nature of Athenian democracy made it an impossible model for a large modern state. It is this challenge that Ober, Euben, Hedrick, and Wallach seek to meet in their current projects. (I think it would be dishonest of me not to identify my own points of involvement here: I was a speaker at both the Santa Cruz Institute [1992] and the Washington conference [1993], I authored one of the pieces in the June 1993 issue of *Prologue*, and I will have an essay in the Cornell collection.)

The battle has also been engaged on the fringes of the academy in the popular press. In 1991 Basic Books published *The Honey and the Hemlock: Democracy and Paranoia in Ancient Athens and Modern America* by Eli Sagan, a lecturer at the New School for Social Research in New York who has written on a variety of topics including Freud and women. Sagan argued passionately in favor of an egalitarian and peaceful America, stressing the strengths and weaknesses of the Athenians in achieving the kind of society he would like to see in the United States and in the world. In Sagan's view, the Athenians were good in their ability to envision a more democratic universe than their contemporaries and predecessors could conceive, but bad in their noninclusive view of the community. More attention has been paid to another popular book with a more famous author. In 1988 Little, Brown published *The Trial of Socrates* by the celebrated journalist and free speech activist I. F. Stone. The egalitarian Athenians, in Stone's formulation, were speaking out for "Greek" values in standing up to Socrates, whose autocratic ethos and social snobbery were at odds with the way "Greeks" looked at the world. Stone made a lot of odd assumptions about the historical Socrates and the egalitarianism of the average Greek, but the book made quite a splash.

Stone had hoped that his study of free speech—the project that led him to the trial of Socrates—would not only help to preserve freedom of expression where it existed but also help beleaguered dissidents in the Communist world find their way to what he labeled "a liberating synthesis of Marx and Jefferson."[38] In fact the belief that egalitarianism was more fundamental to the Greek ethos than elitism also crops up in Marxist thinkers and their forerunners. Much of what Engels set out to do in *The Origins of the Family, Private Property, and the State* built on the researches of the American anthropologist Lewis H. Morgan, whose *Ancient Society: or, Researches in the Lines of Human Progress from Savagery, through Barbarism* appeared in 1877. Morgan found himself drawn to the egalitarianism of the Iroquois, of whose gens he maintained that "liberty, equality, and fraternity, though never formulated, were cardinal principles," and he was convinced that it was safe to extrapolate from the experience of the Iroquois to that of all other civilizations.[39] Though Morgan treated Grote's work with respect, he disagreed with Grote's contention that the primitive Greek government was essentially monarchical, alleging that even Grote was a victim of the phenomenon whereby modern ideas had been "moulded by writers accustomed to monarchical government and privileged classes, who were perhaps glad to appeal to the earliest known governments of the Grecian tribes for a sanction of this form of government, as at once natural, essential and primitive." The truth, he maintains, "as it seems to an American, is precisely the reverse of Mr. Grote's; namely, that the primitive Grecian government was essentially democratical, reposing on gentes, phratries and tribes, organized as self-governing bodies, and on the principles of liberty, equality and fraternity."[40] Democratic ideas, Morgan contended, had existed in Athens for years before the development of the classical democracy and needed only to rise once more to the surface to overcome the "false element" of aristocracy. It was to the high degree to which the Athenians developed their democracy that Morgan ascribed their becoming "the most intellectual and most accomplished race of men the entire human family has yet produced."[41]

Similar ideas were expressed in different ways in 1975 by Robert Padgug, a classicist then at Rutgers University. In the 1960s the first issue of the journal *Arethusa* was published at the State University of New York at Buffalo, at that time a hotbed of avant-garde thinking of various kinds. *Arethusa* devoted its 1975 issue to Marxism and the classics and its 1983 issue to articles on women in the ancient world. The issue on Marxism included Padgug's essay "Classes and Society in Classical Greece." Padgug saw fifth- and fourth-century Athens as a restored commune created on the ruins of an earlier, purer commune. In the restored commune, reconstituted after an "aristocratic interlude," political equality and an emphasis on civic rights replaced the earlier economic equality. Slavery and imperialism, however, were needed to enable all members of the commune to live on a minimally acceptable level and to help compensate for the relatively small amount of land available in Attica. The restored commune consequently "was in fact an artificial attempt to recreate and preserve" the equality of the earlier commune "using political means."[42] The system, Padgug maintains, worked well in the fifth century, but the precarious balance on which it depended led to its disintegration after the loss of the Peloponnesian War, for the city's economic dependence on outsiders (slaves, metics, allies) inevitably opened the door to the fragmentation of society and the breakdown of communal values, developments that did in fact occur when the city's material resources were significantly diminished.

Other Marxist thinkers have formulated the collapse of Athens differently. The Englishman Geoffrey de Ste. Croix of Oxford, for example, followed his own contribution to the *Arethusa* issue with a long book, *The Class Struggle in the Ancient Greek World*, published in 1981. There he broke with a long Western tradition in ascribing the selfishness that brought down antiquity not to the demos but to the elite. A certain amount can also be learned about twentieth-century Marxist views of Athens from the pages of the Marxist journal *Quaderni di Storia*, published at Bari. There selected passages have been reprinted (with commentary) from saints and sinners of earlier eras: Volney's indictment of the cult of antiquity, with its condemnation of inequality and slavery, and Maurras's anti-Semitic attack on democratic Athens as a forerunner of Jew-ridden France. No exculpation of any kind is provided for Maurras; Volney's capacity to transcend the compulsive classicism of his heritage is ascribed by Bertrand Hemmerdinger of Paris (who was responsible for reprinting both Volney and Maurras) to the illumination provided by his experience with the class struggle during the revolution. Praising Volney for his "admirable realism," Hemmerdinger identifies the image of happy antiquity Volney sought to expunge not only as a product of eighteenth century bourgeois myths but as the hallmark of twentieth-century mythology as well, and contends that such thinking continues to shape writing about Greece and Rome. Marx himself was torn between a conviction that classical states were dependent on slavery, which he condemned, and a dreamy nostalgia for the egalitarian ideals of Greek democracy. The inequity of slavery and the injustice of social stratification remain just as crucial to Marxist thinking about Athens as enthusiasm for the Athenians' professed democratic ideals.[43]

Questions of class and class struggle also have bearing on non-Marxist twentieth-century approaches to Athenian democracy. In his enthusiastic popular book *The Emergence of Greek Democracy* the British classicist George Forrest has argued that the "partisan views" of the ancient sources—views he considers "more or less totally false"—have held appeal for twentieth-century scholars in part because "modern historians too have not been men of the lower-class."[44] Nobody who has read Peter Novick's study of the American historical profession, *That Noble Dream* (Cambridge, 1988), or heard Joan Scott's address at the plenary session of the American Historical Association in Cincinnati in 1988 can remain ignorant of the resounding elitism of the historical "establishment" in the United States or fail to be struck by the prestige and power enjoyed even after the Second World War by historians of overtly racist, sexist, and anti-Semitic views. It would be eminently gratifying to demonstrate a dramatic shift in the valuation of Athens with the entry into the historical profession of scholars whose backgrounds probably would have disqualified them from exercising political rights in an aristocratic government—to discover that this demographic shift has intensified general enthusiasm for the Athenian ethos while still focusing attention on the element of exclusivity. The truth, of course, is far more complex, but it is plain that not all people currently conducting scholarship on the ancient world are affluent, white Christian males; many fail to check out on all counts. An intensive examination of classical Athens appears in a powerful book driven by ideology but forged in careful scholarship, Orlando Patterson's 1991 *Freedom*, the work of a black Harvard professor. Jewish scholars raised in an era of anti-Semitism account for a number of Athens's most enthusiastic defenders, from Sir Moses Finley, possibly the most distinguished Greek historian of the twentieth century, to the Lithuanian-born Donald Kagan, the celebrated historian of the Peloponnesian War.[45] To be sure, in English-speaking countries (unlike, for example, France) female historians have rarely chosen to make classical Athens the focus of their research—a fact that is quite interesting in itself, since anglophone women write regularly on Athenian art and literature and have begun to write quite a bit on Greek political theory. Still, the entry into the profession of women in significant numbers, combined with the rise of the feminist movement in the late twentieth century, has contributed to broadening perspectives on the Athenians.

On the whole a more positive valuation of Athens has been perceptible concomitant with the increasing professionalization of historical writing, and this is no coincidence. As the use of history for the moral formation of statesmen and citizens has yielded to a desire to understand the past and an increased patience with evidence that does not yield pat paradigms, so the preoccupation with uplifting *exempla* has abided. The school of historical writing that has regarded the past as a series of cautionary tales providing a storehouse of virtues to emulate and vices to avoid was never favorable to the Athenians; as French revolutionaries discovered, Spartans and Romans made far better heroes. There was a time when the only Athenians who really fired people's minds were Solon, who could easily be dissociated from the radical democracy of the fifth and fourth centuries, and those martyrs to the demos Phocion and Socrates. As Vidal-Naquet has pointed out, the classical heroes of the revolution implied antiheroes.[46] In Athens, sadly devoid of Tarquins and Caesars, the only antihero was the democracy itself. It was impossible to revere Lycurgus and Cato without some admiration for the ethical systems with which they were associated; it was difficult to cherish Phocion or Socrates without implicitly condemning the government that put them to death. Pericles never became a schoolboy's role model. The Athenians' reputation has also profited from the rise of scholarship in America, where little original thinking about the classical past was discernible prior to the twentieth century but where warm associations have congregated around the amorphous notion that is "democracy." To be sure, the establishment of the democratic American republic encouraged some to abandon the study of classical states; Jefferson claimed that the new principle of representative democracy had made it pointless to seek guidance on government from the ancients, and de Tocqueville found the differences between America and classical antiquity so dramatic that he reacted to attempts to judge America in terms of Greece and Rome by threatening to burn his classical books. Still, the stability of the American experiment did much to neutralize the volatile democratic discourse of early modern Europe and to make democracy significantly more palatable on both sides of the Atlantic.

The new political and diplomatic problems of the past century and a half, moreover, have brought with them a host of new uses for Athenian democracy. To be sure, the rise of a substantial class of professionally trained historians and the general public's decreased interest in the distant past has meant that Athenian government is now far more likely to be studied for its own sake than for its instantaneous applicability to contemporary dilemmas. (It has also meant the evolution of a new intellectual universe in which no one would dream of seeking knowledge about antiquity by consulting Bodin, or of citing

Rollin as an authority for classical government.) A marked decrease in the degree to which direct inferences are made from ancient to modern history is noticeable around the middle of the nineteenth century. This drop becomes more striking still toward 1900 with the takeover of historical writing by academic historians who have often been more clinicians than politicians. Concerned for the survival of both their values and their paychecks, however, classical historians in the age of twentieth-century technology have come to recur rather nervously to the theme of relevance, and have felt a certain triumph—not to mention relief—in being able to draw convincing parallels between, say, the Athenian expedition to Sicily and the American expedition to Vietnam or the Persian Gulf. Thus though sober scholarly articles on the reforms of Ephialtes or the Peace of Antalcidas continue sedulously to eschew any appearance of "popularizing," many students of the past recognize that the people who might buy their books or read them in libraries may be different from the people who subscribe to the *Journal of Hellenic Studies* or *Symbolae Osloenses*, and modern analogies may be made to illuminate, entertain, or simply seduce. These analogies can be counted on to multiply exponentially in classroom situations. They are also dear to the hearts of journalists, who so far from fleeing facile parallels are in fact likely to discuss ancient politics only when they are in a mood to point timely morals. Consequently, although a lighter touch has replaced a rather heavy-handed approach to modern analogy that most twentieth-century readers would find overbearing, the practice has survived sufficiently to give some sense of the uses to which Athenian democracy has been put by historians and politicians of the past half-century or so—to contrast England with Germany and America with the Soviet Union, to warn of the perils of McCarthyism and imperialism, to intone insistently that eternal vigilance is the price of liberty.

♦　♦　♦　♦　♦

The American feminist Marilyn Skinner has categorized "postclassicism" as a mode of relating to antiquity marked by "its denial of the *classicality* of the ancient cultural product, its refusal to champion Greco-Roman ideas, institutions and artistic works as elite terrain, universally authoritative and culturally transcendent, and therefore capable of only one privileged meaning." Instead, Skinner goes on, postclassicism subscribes to the notion "of all cultural artifacts and systems as broadly accessible 'texts' open to multiple and even conflicting readings."[47] It is these "conflicting readings" that have provided the subject matter for this book.

By and large, these conflicts have arisen because of differences in value systems across cultures and among assorted thinkers produced by the same or similar cultures, rather than from the discovery of new evidence that produces a "text" that is objectively "different." In some instances, perceptions have remained constant while values have changed. Will Durant's paean to the Athenians, for example, sounds rather as if he were drafting a personal ad on their behalf: he bills them as "tolerant, varied, complex, luxurious, innovating, skeptical, imaginative, poetical, turbulent, free. . . ."[48] Eighteenth-century intellectuals concurred that the Athenians were luxurious and turbulent, but the valence they attached to these characteristics was radically different. Durant's description of the Athenians contained little if anything with which Madison or Montagu or Mably would have disagreed; all four men entertained similar notions of what had happened but dramatically discrepant views of what it all meant. During the nineteenth century, Engels, decrying slavery and patriarchy, condemned Athens in the strongest language, while across the Atlantic, Fitzhugh and his cohorts, seeing a very similar picture of Athens, acclaimed Athenian civilization as a legitimizing exemplar.

In other instances, however, different readers of Athenian democracy have plainly imagined different "texts" before them. For Samuel Johnson and Lord Brougham, Athenian voters were crassly ignorant. Johnson maintained that Demosthenes spoke to a people of brutes, and Brougham described Athenian citizens as "only half educated" and "wholly incapable of thinking for themselves."[49] Brougham's contemporaries Mahaffy and Freeman, on the other hand, contended that Athenian citizens were "more highly educated than any general public" in their own day.[50] For Rollin and Mitford, the *ekklesia* was packed full of ignorant tradesmen; but Ferguson in 1913 would write admiringly of the high level of political expertise in an assembly in which such a large proportion of members had held public positions.[51] Nineteenth-century Germans like Böckh and Burckhardt, for whom belief in the idleness of the Athenian citizenry was practically a matter of religious conviction, would have been astonished to see their twentieth-century countryman Christian Meier proclaim in 1980 that "the Attic *demos* was undoubtedly hardworking"; eighteenth-century Britons brought back to life would be mystified to hear Sir Kenneth Dover referring casually and in passing to the "extraordinary stability of fourth-century democracy" and contending that the apparent absence of any demand for redistribution of property suggests a fundamental consensus among the city's economic groups.[52] In 1972 Sir Moses Finley described Athens as not only the richest culturally of all the Greek states—something even the Florentines would have conceded—but also the stablest and most internally peaceful.[53] Many historians of the later twentieth century agree: Josiah Ober and his collaborator Barry Strauss of Cornell, both still in college when Finley penned these words, wrote in 1990 that "Athenian political society was remarkably stable."[54] The leveling tendency of democratic culture in general and Athenian culture in particular has often been cited against it—by Hegel, for example, and by Matthew Arnold. These allegations were contested as the Victorian era drew to a close by A.H.J. Greenidge, who in his *Handbook of Greek Constitutional History* maintained that "if democracy be taken to imply the levelling of individual eminence, that of Athens was a failure," for "few states have ever been more completely under the sway of great personalities." It is oligarchy, Greenidge contended, that is "the true leveller of merit," whereas it is "one of the oldest lessons in history that . . . a democracy brings with it a hero-worship generally of an extravagant kind."[55] The debate over leveling has also focused on economics. For Mitford, as for John Adams, one of the principal sins of the Athenians was their lack of respect for private property; for Engels, the Greek, and specifically the Athenian, state "sanctified the private property formerly so little valued, and declared this sanctification to be the highest purpose of all human society."[56] Mitford recurred frequently to the topos of the violence of democracy, a constant threat to the security of Athenian streets for both sexes; De Pauw, on the other hand, maintained that it was the Athenians' success in the area of public safety that did most honor to their moral character and taste for civilization. In four hundred years in Athens, he contended, there was less violence than in twenty-four hours between London and Greenwich.[57] These disagreements cannot always be ascribed to the altered perspective of a new day; Mitford and De Pauw were born only five years apart.

The different readings of the Athenian ethos are not simply matters of likes and dislikes, whether it is good or bad to have poor people hold office, whether it is useful or destructive to attach a high degree of accountability to government, whether individual ownership of land is ethical or not, whether ostracism helps or hinders statesmanship, whether slavery is acceptable sometimes or never. The Athens of Mitford is simply not the Athens of De Pauw; the Athens of Adams is not the Athens of Finley. With some minor exceptions— the discovery of the Aristotelian *Athenaion Politeia*, for example, and the development of a sounder chronology for the years leading up to the outbreak of the Peloponnesian War—precious little new evidence has surfaced since antiquity that could explain the dramatic differences in the way assorted thinkers have approached Athenian democracy. Why, then, such divergent perceptions of the same phenomenon?

Hobbes, we know, fretted that the reading of classical texts promoted dangerous disrespect for authority and prompted all manner of seditious republicanism. It did not have that effect on him, however, nor on Bodin or Filmer, and I know of not a single monarch whose classical education prompted him to lay aside his crown and make *De Officiis* and the *Parallel Lives* required reading throughout the realm.[58] (The study of the classics has been blamed for inculcating an extraordinarily wide range of sentiments; in his biography of Lenin, Trotsky identified the study of classics as an instrument of torture that paved the way for the acceptance of czarist ideology.[59]) The warm embrace in which English liberals enfolded the dead Athenians might seem to suggest that the opposite is true—that it is contemporary experience that shapes response to classical reading rather than the other way around. Were this demonstrable in an immediate and predictable way, it would be possible to see the anti-Athenian texts that sprouted in the wake of the revolutions in France and America as the clear by-products of these unsettling challenges to tradition. In fact, however, the dominant view about Athens on the eve of the revolutions was already predominantly hostile. The truth is that a complex undulation marks the interplay between life experience, the legacy of the immediate past in the form of tales told by parents and grandparents, and reading about the far away and long ago. Responses to Athenian democracy have often been determined by an intricate interaction of snobbery, recent experience, false analogy, uncritical use of sources, failure to ask hard questions, and fear. The sociology of ancient literacy and literature has rarely been taken into consideration in the evaluation of written sources for ancient history and government, nor has much scrutiny been applied to the practice (dictated by necessity) of recovering an intensely oral culture from written texts. Coming themselves from an elite, moderns writing about history have inevitably continued to play a role in the perpetuation of upper-class mythology. As David Carr has pointed out, citing Dilthey and Vico, "we are historical beings first, before we are observers of history," and "he who studies history is the same as he who makes it."[60] Though an increasing number of twentieth-century academics come from non-elite backgrounds, writing about the classical past still remains largely the preserve of an upper crust; very few underprivileged young men decide to make Greek history their life's work, and very few women of any social class. In his provocative *Black Athena*, Martin Bernal of Cornell has made a case for the role played by racism in distorting the development of Greek civilization as a whole.[61] Certainly the bulk of classical scholarship has been produced by whites. It is significant that historians have so often dismissed Herodotus as a lovable raconteur while embracing Thucydides as one of their own; two of the characteristics that make Thucydides more "professional" than Herodotus are his upper-class perspective and his blind faith in his own intellectual superiority.

It would be gratifying to demonstrate decisively that journalists and moralists have experienced classical Athens very differently from professional historians. It would be nice to develop some criterion for what makes a historian a "professional." (If making a living at history is the standard, we are all in trouble.) And it would be a great deal of fun to surprise expectation by demonstrating that in reality there is no difference at all in the way in which Athens has been perceived by *Life* magazine on the one hand and by *Museum Helveticum* on the other. Alas, none of these things is possible. In reality people whose principal focus is the past rather than the present do see things rather differently from those whose orientation to antiquity is as a storehouse of cautionary tales; they are more patient and more open-minded, less presentist and less judgmental. But no matter how much historians would like to delude themselves, these differences are frequently matters of degree rather than of kind. Monarchists and republicans, slaveholders and abolitionists, feminists and traditionalists—we all have our axes to grind, though some of us grind them more gracefully than others. The French created bourgeois Athens; the Germans made of all Greece a prelapsarian wish-fulfillment; the Victorians imagined an Athens that was the best of London and a London that was the best of Athens; twentieth-century social critics see an exclusive club founded on the denigration and exploitation of nonmembers. All this is true of scholars and journalists, researchers and romantics.

Predictably, thinking about Athenian government and society has been shaped by shifting perceptions not only about the desirability of democracy but about the nature of the beast itself. Already in 1885 Sir Henry Maine observed that there was no word "about which a denser mist of vague language, and a larger heap of loose metaphors, has collected."[62] Greek in its origins, the word has undergone a remarkable variety of transformations in meaning, ranging from mob rule to the embodiment of human dignity to anti-Communism to Communism itself. Democracy has been excoriated as the bedfellow of atheism and adulated as Christianity in action. As has been pointed out by Richard Wollheim of University College, London, the word itself is problematic when compared with words like plutocracy or theocracy: how really "can the people rule in the way in which the rich or the priests clearly can? For surely there are too many of them for it to be a practical possibility. And secondly, if the people rule, who is there left to be ruled?"[63] The truth is that the semantics of democracy have dissolved into pablum. In the twentieth century, democracy is synonymous with fairness and accountability and all-around decency.[64] In the conclusion to *Democracy: The Unfinished Journey*, John Dunn has pointed out that it is democratic ideals that today ground the legitimacy of the modern state—the very state that was invented by thinkers like Bodin and Hobbes "for the express purpose of denying that any given population, any people, had either the capacity or the right to act together for themselves."[65] Today everyone is a democrat, as Third World dictators vie with erstwhile Soviet Communists and American capitalists to demonstrate that they champion a democracy more pure and absolute than that of their neighbors. Consider the following definition of democracy: "The meaning of democracy is precisely that the people, from time to time, should be called upon to judge the achievements and acts of a government, to judge whether the program of the government is of any use or whether the men are of any use who take it upon themselves to execute that program." Consider the author: Adolf Hitler. Hitler's words were cited in a 1956 assemblage of glosses on democracy collected by a UNESCO ideology research team.[66] Chronology prevented the UNESCO people from including the following words on democracy that issued from the mouth of Leibole Muchnik, a Miami hot-dog vendor, during the visit of Queen Elizabeth in 1991: "To me this is democracy. Over here you've got protesters against the Queen. Over there you've got people who love her. Me, I've got business from both."[67]

Inevitably, democracy meant something different to citizens of the Italian Renaissance who were convinced it entailed constant tumult, to eighteenth-century moralists who viewed it as the erosion of virtue by decadence, to the American founders who believed it encouraged the equalization of property, and to citizens of the late twentieth century, to some of whom it apparently has come to mean freedom to sell your frankfurters to all comers. It would be too simple, however, to assume that people throughout history have made facile assumptions that the virtues or vices of what their own era perceived as democracy were the same as the strengths and weaknesses of classical Athenian government. To be sure, there are instances of such confusion. Looking back in horror at the recent history of Florence, Italian political theorists ignored vital differences between stable Athens and the volatile banking city on the Arno where class conflict stood ready to tear the state apart at any time. Another example is afforded by the assumption Macaulay ascribed to Samuel Johnson about the ignorance of the average Athenian citizen, a confusion that arose, Macaulay believed, from mistaken identification of classical Athens with Augustan Britain: in reality the world of the Athenians was so much smaller and the level of interaction among citizens so high that probably the degree of informedness of the average voter would have compared favorably to that of any voting body in Johnson's age or today. But when John Adams said that he did not like Athenian democracy, he really meant it; he did not mean that he disliked Athens simply because of what he knew about democracy in his own era. (Actually, he could have known nothing about modern democracy, as there was none to know.) John Adams was not confused about what Athenian democracy had been because of the negative associations that had congregated around the word *democracy* in his own day. If Adams was confused, it was because of a long anti-Athenian tradition that was based on a genuine conviction that the Athenians had deployed a singularly unstable and unjust form of government. If he was confused, his error lay in unquestioning acceptance of traditional wisdom and traditional priorities. In his belief that Athenian democrats had violated private property, he was largely mistaken; no doubt individual defendants were sometimes wrongly convicted in court so that their property might be confiscated, but the Athenian poor never did rise up and demand redistribution of land. Despite all this, however, Adams's plainly stated conviction that power should follow property was in reality violated by Athenian law (though not always by Athenian practice). If John Adams thought he would dislike sharing power with landless men, he was right to think he would not have wanted to live in Athens.

It is an interesting exercise to ponder whether the course of Western politics and political theory might have been different had Lysias or Demosthenes,

Pericles or Sophocles bequeathed us histories of their times or treatises on political theory to place beside those of Thucydides and Xenophon, Plato and Aristotle. It is important, however, to notice the conspiracy of silence that has surrounded works favorable to the democracy such as Aristides' speech *On the Four*, Drake's *History of the Last Parliament*, the pertinent portions of *Cato's Letters* or the *Craftsman*, the iconoclastic researches of De Pauw. Aristides' oration has been available in several editions since the sixteenth century; Drake's pamphlet wended its way into a good number of libraries; both the *Craftsman* and *Cato's Letters* enjoyed a considerable readership not only in Europe but in the American colonies and formed an important part of the Whig heritage across the Atlantic. Readers chose, however, to embrace the generic republican ideals championed in British opposition literature while passing over the praise of Athenian accountability frequently found there. And De Pauw has never been much read. To a remarkable degree, people free to pick and choose among their sources have chosen to discount ideology that deviated from the dominant tradition.

That tradition was devoted to demonstrating the inadequacies of Athenian democracy with a passion that often bordered on obsession. Though some of the small Italian states flirted with democracy during the late Middle Ages and early in the Renaissance, the truth is that Athenian-style government had never been tried since the fourth-century B.C. When the *vox populi* made itself heard, it was usually in the form of the kinds of agitated uprisings that develop only when the disfranchised mobilize to vent their frustration; and even these were often not as frightening as defenders of the established order made out. The seventeenth-century Levellers, for example, had limited their demands to political equality, not economic parity; and although the more radical Diggers did indeed advocate a communistic agrarian society, there were probably fewer than a hundred of them all told, and they could not afford to threaten violence. There was some recognizable popular government among state legislatures in the American colonies and the early republic; but of Madison's three fears—paper money, abolition of debts, and redistribution of land—only the first was realized or even attempted, and a system of tumult and intimidation never did replace the ballot. But the conviction that the demos was the beast Plato and Bodin had painted in such vivid colors died hard and still lives on today, particularly as countries such as the United States are undergoing dramatic demographic shifts that have produced masses that are multicolored in a way far more literal than either Plato or Bodin could have imagined, and the classical clichés about the monster of many heads have won a permanent place in political theory. Droysen's observation that the evidence can only answer the questions that are put to it points up the choices that were made in the examination of Athens.[68] Much can be learned from the questions that were rarely raised. What kind of civilization produces a Phidias or a Plato, an *Antigone* or a Parthenon? What connections can be drawn between politics and art? What prompts people to break out of the hereditary mold and institute a system of orderly elections? How did life in Athens foster a level of informedness among its citizens that made selection by lot for public office a workable plan? What value system encouraged the belief that ordinary people could make responsible decisions? Over a lifetime Plato devoted considerable energy to the question, Who shall rule? In this project he was succeeded by countless others. The more sophisticated question might be how a system could be devised in which the notion of rulers and ruled was obsolete—a question that came to be asked, of course, by Marx and his cohorts. Inevitably, the discounting of women and slaves gravely compromises the Athenian system in twentieth-century eyes, as the existence of a (male) elite in the recently deceased Soviet Union vitiated the Marxists' claim to a classless society. Still, the notion has a potential that the tradition has chosen to discount.

By the standards of the late twentieth century, the Athenians were not very nice people. They had no concept of the brotherhood of man, much less of the siblinghood of humankind. They thought nothing of affirming their control over policy by executing a general whose only crime was that he had ceased to represent the wishes of his constituency; they sent dedicated public servants into ten-year exiles for no other reason than that they seemed a bit too big for their britches. They had no organized bodies of concerned citizens lobbying for the trampled rights of animals destined for sacrifice, of slaves marked for the mines, or of brotherless girls about to be married off to mean, boring relatives in order to keep land in the family. No Geneva convention prevented anyone from doing what he liked with Spartan prisoners of war, and no Athenian convict grew old on death row awaiting the outcome of his lawyers' machinations on his behalf; by the time his countrymen were sorry about Socrates, he was quite thoroughly dead. But the Athenians did devise a government remarkable for its time and forge a civilization that created amazing works of art, literature, and philosophy, and neither the Athenian democratic system nor the study of history has benefited from an approach that posits the connection between democracy and military defeat while ignoring the connection between the democratic ethos and the dizzying heights of creative achievement that are both associated with classical Athens, and instead asks only where the Athenians went wrong—why they executed the victors of Arginusae, lost the war with Sparta, executed Socrates, and were conquered by Macedon. Dubious in journalists and politicians, this strategy is of no value at all to historians. Surely we can find more useful things to do with our time and energy than stealthily stalking ancient cultures, waiting for them to slip up so that we may pounce with glee and kill them all over again.

That Athenian freedom and democracy ultimate fell before Macedon is indisputable. For those who incline to the view of W. B. Gallie that history "is a species of the genus Story," the entire story line has often been defined in terms of its ending, which came to be cast as its "direction."[69] When principles of colligation are combined with a disposition to read the past backward, a glum assessment of Athens follows naturally. (The modern celebrants of Athens tend to eschew a narrative, chronological approach.) The impulse to view history as a series of stories—with the potential to be integrated into a rich epic with subplots ("Western Civilization"?)—has shaped perceptions of Athenian democracy in immeasurable but profound ways. Solon's advice to Croesus to count no man happy while he was still alive has been taken closely to heart by Athens's critics, who have seen in the defeats at Aegospotami and Chaeronea clear proof of the inadequacy of the system. History has amply fulfilled Socrates' prophecy that there would come upon the Athenians after his death critics yet sterner than he.

Where passions are deeply felt, the temptation to use the example of the Athenians' defeats to cry out against wrong reason and warn of impending collapse has been powerful. The issues around which the battle has been engaged have varied from one era to the next. Some, I have suggested, were false issues—the issue of instability, for example. Others seem to have been engaged with peculiar intensity: it is testimony to the legitimizing value of classical examples (and perhaps to the blandishments of egalitarianism) that intellectuals drawing up blueprints for large modern nations should have felt the need to recur again and again to the difficulties of direct democracy. But the indignation of Marxist and feminist critics of the Athenian system serve as a reminder that not all readers of the "text" of classical Athens have viewed its civilization as in any sense dead. Whereas America's founders put on the coroner's coat and deployed all the instruments of their reason to determine the cause of the ancient republics' demise, what many critics are crying out against is the survival into their own day of a hardy system of pernicious values that have hung on tenaciously since well before Pericles. For some of Athens's admirers, her role as the origin of much that is distinctive about Western civilization has been cause for celebration, whether this distinction is perceived—as by Edward Freeman, for example—to lie in the development of egalitarian institutions or, as Fitzhugh believed, in the facilitation of high culture through the relegation of physical labor to a disfranchised class. For others, the ability of moderns to improve on Athenian institutions was paramount; Tom Paine rejoiced that the representative principle would enable America to outshine even Athens. Still others have been inclined to think things have gotten worse; thus Thomas Erskine May contended that there had been far more toleration in pagan Athens than in Christian Spain. The question of Christianity exercised Athens's detractors as well; for Böckh, the advent of Christianity accounted for a supposed improvement in the moral tone of European life, while its absence explained much that had been wrong with Athens. Yet other critics have seen the Athenian democracy as the seedbed of modern vices. Where the champions of private property asked what might happen were Athenian democracy to be resurrected, Marxists, feminists, and many other social critics have come during the past century or so to suggest that in reality the unhealthy structures they perceive in Athens have been the emblematic abuses of Western civilization throughout its history. Eva Keuls speaks for a large body of the Athenians' critics in suggesting that Athens provides us with "a kind of concave mirror in which we can see our own foibles and institutions magnified and distorted" since the dynamics she identifies in Athens still remain a problem "in modern, more subtle forms."[70]

In the introduction to his book *The Political Unconscious: Narrative as a Socially Symbolic Act*, the American Marxist Fredric Jameson contends that "we never really confront a text immediately, in all its freshness as a thing-in-itself. Rather, texts come before us as the always-already-read; we apprehend them through sedimented layers of previous interpretations, or—if the text is brand-new—through the sedimented reading habits and categories developed by those inherited interpretive traditions." These sedimented habits and categories have formed the subject matter of this book. It is these habits and categories that have made possible a wide variety of interpretations of an extraordinarily vibrant civilization and a surprisingly bold experiment in government. The various elements that make up what Jameson called "the essential *mystery* of the cultural past" can, he argues, "recover their original urgency for us only if they are retold within the unity of a single great collective story."[71] But not everyone has found the same unity, or the same story. I have told my own story about the hi-story of an idea; other stories could be told about the same idea using the material I included—and excluded. Philosophers of history cannot agree on whether there is such a thing as an untold story: if it is untold, some ask, how can it be a story? I hesitate consequently to speculate about the "untold stories" concerning Athens that may yet come to birth; but it is safe to say that new stories will be told in the future. Fortunately, however, I am a historian only of the past.

NOTES

CHAPTER ONE

1. J. S. McClelland, *The Crowd and the Mob: From Plato to Canetti* (London and Boston, 1989), 1–2.

2. Throughout this work I cite the *Politics* in the translation of Ernest Barker (Oxford, 1946).

3. Citations to the Aristotelian *Constitution of the Athenians* are modified from the Loeb Classical Library translation by H. Rackham, *Aristotle: The Athenian Constitution, The Eudemian Ethics, On Virtues and Vices* (London and Cambridge, Mass., 1935).

4. R. A. Dahl, *Democracy and Its Critics* (New Haven and London, 1989), 2.

5. Jean Bodin, *Six Livres de la République*, translated as *Six Bookes of a Commonwealth* (1606), 702.

6. R. Filmer, *Patriarca*, in *Patriarca and Other Political Works*, ed. Peter Laslett (Oxford, 1949), 86–89.

7. Thomas Hobbes, *Leviathan* 2.29.

8. James Harrington, *The Commonwealth of Oceana*, reprinted in *The Political Works of James Harrington*, ed. J.G.A. Pocock (Cambridge, 1977).

9. Rendered in English as *The Ancient History of the Egyptians, Carthaginians, Assyrians, Babylonians, Medes and Persians, Grecians and Macedonians* (Edinburgh and London, 1861), 1.16.

10. Rollin, *Ancient History* 1.184–85.

11. L'Abbé J. Barthélemy, *Voyage du jeune Anacharsis en Grèce dans le milieu du quatrième siècle avant l'ère vulgaire* (Paris, 1782), translated as *Travels of Anacharsis the Younger in Greece*, 7 vols. (1794), 1.184–85.

12. Robert Bisset, *Sketch of Democracy* (London, 1796), xxv.

13. Victor Duruy, *Histoire Grecque*, 2d ed. (Paris, 1856), 3.613–14.

14. A. Zimmern, *The Greek Commonwealth: Politics and Economics in Fifth-Century Athens* (1911; 5th ed., 1931; reprint, New York and Oxford, 1961), 367n.

15. T. Jones, *From the Tigris to the Tiber* (3d ed., 1969; (new ed., Homewood, Ill., 1983), 175, 174.

16. In *The Closing of the American Mind* (New York, 1987), 377.

17. S. Lakoff, *Equality in Political Philosophy* (Cambridge, Mass., 1964), 16.

18. In *Between Philosophy and History: The Resurrection of Speculative Philosophy of History within the Analytical Tradition* (Princeton, 1970), 117.

19. W. Dray, *On History and Philosophers of History* (Leiden, 1989), 164.

20. A. Nevins, *The Gateway to History* (New York, 1938), cited in E. Nagel, "Some Issues in the Logic of Historical Analysis," in *Theories of History*, ed. P. Gardiner (New York and London, 1959), 377.

21. For White's arguments, see most recently the essays collected in *The Content of the Form: Narrative Discourse and Historical Representation* (Baltimore, 1987).

22. In *Historical Understanding*, ed. B. Fay, E. Golob, and R. Vann (Ithaca and London, 1987), 186.

23. D. Carr, *Time, Narrative, and History* (Bloomington, 1986), 46, 61.

24. W. Dray, On History and Philosophers of History, 157.

25. W. H. Walsh, "The Intelligibility of History," Philosophy 17 (1942); 128–43, and "Colligatory Concepts of History," in Studies in the Nature and Teaching of History, ed. W. H. Burston and D. Thompson (London, 1967), 65–87.

26. D. Giannotti, Discorso intorno alla Forma della Repubblica di Firenze, in his Opere Politiche e Letterarie, ed. F.-L. Polidori (Florence, 1850), 1.17.

27. W. Brown, Manhood and Politics: A Feminist Reading in Political Theory (Totowa, N.J., 1988), ix–x.

28. On pp. 61–62 and 187.

29. E. Nagel, "Some Issues in the Logic of Historical Analysis," in Theories of History, 373–86.

30. J. H. Hexter, "History, the Social Sciences, and Quantification," Proceedings of the XIIIth International Congress of Historical Sciences (Moscow, 1970), 32.

31. Richard Jenkyns, The Victorians and Ancient Greece (Cambridge, Mass., 1980), 13.

CHAPTER TWO

1. The bibliographical citations offered in the notes to this chapter are designed to provide additional background for modernists unfamiliar with the history and government of classical Athens. Because it is a central tenet of this book that there is no such thing as objective history, I present these suggested readings with some hesitation. I do not mean for a moment to imply that with the dawning of the twentieth century quaint eccentricities were miraculously replaced by scientific scholarship in which readers may place unqualified trust. It is to be hoped that the biases represented hereunder may to some degree cancel one another out.

In addition to the readings listed in these notes, readers are referred to numerous entries in the Pauly-Wissowa Realencyclopädie der klassischen Altertumswissenschaft (Stuttgart, 1894–1980) under the names of important individuals and of various organs of Athenian government. Somewhat briefer notices appear in C. Daremberg and E. Saglio, eds., Dictionnaire des antiquités grecques et romaines (Paris, 1877–1919) and briefer ones still in the Oxford Classical Dictionary (Oxford, 1970). The principal bibliography of scholarship on classical antiquity appears annually in L'Année philologique, which follows listings for individual classical authors with listings for categories such as "Histoire grecque" and "Civilisation grecque," where books and articles on Athenian government and society can be found. Abbreviations for scholarly journals cited in these notes follow the precedents set in L'Année.

2. On the Athenian constitution and its development, see U. von Wilamowitz-Möllendorff, Aristoteles und Athen, 2 vols. (Berlin, 1893); G. Busolt and H. Swoboda, Griechische Staatskunde (Munich, 1920–26); R. Bonner and G. Smith, The Administration of Justice from Homer to Aristotle, 2 vols. (Chicago, 1930–38); C. Hignett, A History of the Athenian Constitution to the End of the Fifth Century B.C. (Oxford, 1952); J. Day and M. Chambers, Aristotle's History of Athenian Democracy (Berkeley and Los Angeles, 1962); W. G. Forrest, The Emergence of Greek Democracy (New York and Toronto, 1966); and P. J. Rhodes, A Commentary on the Aristotelian "Athenaion Politeia" (Oxford, 1981). Conflicting modern assessments of Athenian democracy appear in P. Cloché,

La démocratie athénienne (Paris, 1951); V. Ehrenberg, *From Solon to Socrates: Greek History and Civilisation during the Sixth and Fifth Centuries B.C.* (London, 1968); C. Mossé, *Histoire d'une démocratie, Athènes, des origines a la conquête Macédonienne* (Paris, 1971); T. Tarkiainen, *Die athenische Demokratie* (Munich, 1972); J. K. Davies, *Democracy and Classical Greece* (London, 1978); J. Bleicken, *Die athenische Demokratie* (Paderborn, 1985); M. Ostwald, *From Popular Sovereignty to the Sovereignty of Law: Law, Society, and Politics in Fifth-Century Athens* (Berkeley and Los Angeles, 1986); R. Sealey, *The Athenian Republic: Democracy or the Rule of Law?* (University Park, Pa., and London, 1987); J. Ober, *Mass and Elite in Democratic Athens* (Princeton, 1989); and D. Stockton, *The Classical Athenian Democracy* (Oxford, 1990). See also the works of M. Hansen cited in n. 6 here and Hansen's *The Athenian Democracy in the Age of Demosthenes: Structure, Principles, and Ideology* (Oxford, 1991). Particularly full and up-to-date bibliography can be found throughout Ostwald, *From Popular Sovereignty*, and in Hansen, *The Athenian Democracy* (which also includes a valuable glossary).

3. Solon's reforms are treated in the works cited in n. 2 and in I. M. Linforth, *Solon the Athenian*, University of California Publications in Classical Philology No. 6 (Berkeley, 1919); K. Freeman, *The Work and Life of Solon* (Oxford, 1926); W. J. Woodhouse, *Solon the Liberator: A Study of the Agrarian Problem in Attika in the Seventh Century* (Oxford, 1938); and A. Masaracchia, *Solone* (Florence, 1958).

4. The purpose and results of Cleisthenes' reforms are discussed in the works cited in n. 2 and in J. Headlam, *Election by Lot at Athens*, 2d ed., revised by D. MacGregor (Cambridge, 1933); H. T. Wade-Gery, "Studies in the Structure of Attic Society: II. The Laws of Kleisthenes," *CQ* 27 (1933): 17–29; P. Levêque and P. Vidal-Naquet, *Clisthène l'Athénien* (Paris, 1964); D. M. Lewis, "Cleisthenes and Attica," *Historia* 12 (1963): 22–40; H. W. Pleket, "Isonomia and Cleisthenes: A Note," *Talanta* 4 (1972): 63–81; J. Martin, "Von Kleisthenes zu Ephialtes: Zur Entstehung der athenischen Demokratie," *Chiron* 4 (1974): 5–42; A. Andrewes, "Kleisthenes' Reform Bill," *CQ* 27 (1977): 241–48; and C. Meier, "Cleisthenes and the Institutionalizing of the Civic Presence in Athens," now chap. 4 of *The Greek Discovery of Politics*, trans. D. McLintock (Cambridge, Mass., 1990), 53–81 and 235–46.

The late twentieth century has witnessed an explosion of interest in demes a hundred years after the appearance of Bernard Haussoullier's *La vie municipale en Attique* in 1884: see R. Osborne, *Demos: The Discovery of Classical Attika* (Cambridge, 1985) and D. Whitehead, *The Demes of Attica, 508/7–ca. 250 B.C.: A Political and Social Study* (Princeton, 1985).

5. The fullest treatment of the *boule* appears in P. J. Rhodes, *The Athenian Boule* (Oxford, 1972), which includes pertinent bibliography. See also R. de Laix, *Probouleusis at Athens: A Study of Decision Making*, University of California Publications in History no. 83 (Berkeley, 1973); and W. R. Connor, "The Athenian Council: Method and Focus in Some Recent Scholarship," *CJ* 70 (1974): 32–50.

6. A series of close studies of the *ekklesia* by M. H. Hansen has been published in the two volumes of his *The Athenian Ecclesia* (Copenhagen, 1983 and 1989). See also the bibliography assembled there as well as in Hansen's *The Athenian Assembly* (London, 1987) and his *The Athenian Democracy in the Age of Demosthenes*.

7. Considerable controversy still surrounds the precise nature and extent of Ephialtes' reforms. Bibliography on Ephialtes prior to 1966 is compiled in E. Ruschenbusch,

"Ephialtes," *Historia* 15 (1966): 369–76; see also R. Sealey, "Ephialtes," *CP* 59 (1964): 11–21; J. R. Cole, "Cimon's Dismissal, Ephialtes' Revolution, and the Peloponnesian Wars," *GRBS* 15 (1974): 369–85; R. Wallace, "Ephialtes and the Areopagus," *GRBS* 15 (1974): 259–69 and *The Areopagos Council to 307 b.c.* (Baltimore, 1985); and G. Audring, "Ephialtes stürtz den Areopag," *Altertum* 23 (1977): 234–38. I have not yet been able to consult C. Meier, "Der Umbruch zur Demokratie in Athen (462/61 c Chr.)" in R. Herzog and R. Koselleck, eds., *Epochenschwelle und Epochenbewusstsein*, vol. *Poetik und Hermeneutik*, vol. 12 (Munich, 1987), 353ff.

8. On this bizarre Athenian institution see R. Bonner, "The Minimum Vote in Ostracism," *CP* 8 (1913): 223–25; J. Carcopino, *L'ostracisme athénien* (Paris, 1935); A. E. Raubitschek, "Athenian Ostracism," *CJ* 48 (1952–53): 113–22 and "The Origin of Ostracism," *AJA* 55 (1961): 221–29; A. R. Hands, "Ostraka and the Law of Ostracism: Some Possibilities and Assumptions," *JHS* 79 (1959): 69–79; D. Kagan, "The Origin and Purposes of Ostracism," *Hesperia* 30 (1961): 393–401; E. Vanderpool, *Ostracism at Athens: Lectures in Memory of Louise Taft Semple* (Cincinnati, 1970); R. Thomsen, *The Origin of Ostracism: A Synthesis* (Copenhagen, 1972); Podlecki, *Life of Themistocles* (Montreal and London, 1975): 185–94; and J. T. Roberts, *Accountability in Athenian Government* (Madison, Wis., 1982), 142–53. On the possible role of Cleisthenes in instituting ostracism see C. A. Robinson, "Cleisthenes and Ostracism," *AJA* (1952): 23–26; and P. Karavites, "Cleisthenes and Ostracism Again," *Athenaeum* 52 (1974): 326–36.

Several books on Themistocles have appeared in the past two decades: A. J. Podlecki, *The Life of Themistocles: A Critical Survey of the Literary and Archaeological Evidence*; R. J. Lenardon, *The Saga of Themistocles* (London, 1978); and F. J. Frost, *Plutarch's Themistocles: A Historical Commentary* (Princeton, 1980).

9. The history of attitudes toward Sparta is analyzed in E. N. Tigerstedt, *The Legend of Sparta in Classical Antiquity* (Stockholm, 1965), and E. Rawson, *The Spartan Tradition in European Thought* (Oxford, 1969).

10. Recent overviews of the history of Greece from the Persian Wars to the Macedonian conquest may be found in N.G.L. Hammond, *A History of Greece to 322 b.c.* (Oxford, 1967); R. Sealey, *A History of the Greek City-States, 700–338 b.c.* (Berkeley and Los Angeles, 1976); J.V.A. Fine, *The Ancient Greeks: A Critical History* (Cambridge, Mass., 1983); and S. Hornblower, *The Greek World 479–323 b.c.* (London and New York, 1983). Readers may also wish to consult the revision of the Victorian J. B. Bury's 1900 *History of Greece to the Death of Alexander the Great* by Russell Meiggs (New York, 1975).

11. On the Athenian empire see B. D. Meritt, H. T. Wade-Gery, and M. F. Mac-Gregor, *The Athenian Tribute Lists*, 4 vols., vol. 1 (Cambridge, Mass., 1939) and vols. 2–4 (Princeton, 1949–53); R. Meiggs, *The Athenian Empire* (Oxford, 1972); W. Schuller, *Die Herrschaft der Athener im Ersten Attischen Seebund* (Berlin and New York, 1974); and most recently M. F. MacGregor, *The Athenians and Their Empire* (Vancouver, B.C., 1987).

12. Responses to the exclusivity of the Athenian democracy are discussed in detail in chap. 12.

13. On the politicians who succeeded Pericles see M. I. Finley, "The Athenian Demagogues," *Past and Present* 21 (1962): 3–24, and W. R. Connor, *The New Politicians of Fifth-Century Athens* (Princeton, 1971).

14. For a discussion of this period in Athenian history and an ample bibliography of scholarship down to 1982, see P. Krentz, *The Thirty at Athens* (Ithaca and London, 1982).

15. Two scholars have re-created very engaging debates between Athenian democrats and detractors of the democracy—Kurt Raaflaub of the Center for Hellenic Studies in "Contemporary Perceptions of Democracy in Fifth-Century Athens," *Classica et Medievalia* 40 (1989): 33–70; and Robert Dahl of Yale in *Democracy and Its Critics*, published by Yale University Press the same year.

16. These fragments and quotations are collected in H. Diels and W. Kranz, *Fragmente der Vorsokratiker*, 10th ed. (Berlin, 1960–61), Greek text with German translation. An English translation appears in Kathleen Freeman, *Ancilla to the Pre-Socratics* (Cambridge, Mass., 1962). Commentary is available in Freeman's *Companion to the Pre-Socratics* (Oxford, 1946). Selected texts and commentary appear in G. S. Kirk and J. E. Raven, *The Presocratic Philosophers* (Cambridge, 1957).

17. Good discussions of the *nomos-physis* controversy appear in F. Heinimann, *Nomos und Physis: Herkunft und Bedeutung einer Antithese im griechischen Denken des 5. Jahrhunderts* (Basel, 1945; reprint, 1965); Eric A. Havelock, *The Liberal Temper in Greek Politics* (New Haven and London, 1957; reprint, 1964); W.K.C. Guthrie, *The Sophists* (Cambridge, England, 1971), chap. 4; G. B. Kerferd, *The Sophistic Movement* (Cambridge and New York, 1981); and H. D. Rankin, *Sophists, Socratics, and Cynics* (London and Totowa, N.J., 1983), chap. 4. See also the chapter on the sophists in W. Jaeger, *Paideia: The Ideals of Greek Culture*, trans. Gilbert Highet (New York, 1939; orig. German ed., 1933), 1.286–331.

18. The reconstruction of democratic theory among the sophists has been attempted by scholars such as Alban Winspear in *The Genesis of Plato's Thought* (New York, 1940), chap. 5, and Eric Havelock in *The Liberal Temper in Greek Politics*, chap. 7. Although both efforts are heroic and enlightening, both Winspear and Havelock push the evidence as far as it will go if not farther. One is reminded of the opening scene of Woody Allen's *Sleeper*, in which doctors are planning to reconstruct the late party leader based on the cells in the one part of his body that survives, his nose. The analogy, though bizarre, seems nonetheless apt. The political philosopher Leo Strauss offers a detailed critique of Havelock's book in "The Liberalism of Classical Political Philosophy" (chap. 3 in his *Liberalism Ancient and Modern* [Ithaca, 1968], 26–64).

19. Xenophon's authorship of the first treatise (discussed in chap. 3, here) was widely accepted until the nineteenth century; the Aristotelian tract was uncovered only in 1880 and published for the first time in 1891, and its attribution to Aristotle is still debated (see chap. 3).

20. Works on the authenticity of the debate published prior to 1957 are listed in H. Apffel's 1957 Erlangen dissertation *Die Verfassungsdebatte bei Herodot (3, 80–82)* (reprint, New York, 1979). Subsequent studies have appeared in M. Ostwald, *Nomos and the Beginnings of Athenian Democracy* (Oxford, 1969), 107–16; R. Sealey, "The Origins of *Demokratia*," *California Studies in Classical Antiquity* 6 (1973): 272–77; and D. Lateiner, "Herodotus' Historical Patterning: 'The Constitutional Debate,'" *QS* 20 (1984): 257–84. Additional citations appear in R. Kranskopf, W. Marg, and W. Nicolai, "Literaturverzeichnis," in W. Marg, ed., *Herodot: Eine Auswahl aus der neueren Forschung* (Darmstadt, 1982), 759ff.

The threefold classification of states also appears in somewhat different form in Pindar's Second Pythian Ode, composed probably in the 470s but certainly no later than 467. The Pindaric reference to what was apparently a current idea is discussed by Ostwald (*Nomos*, 30–31) and Sealey ("Origins," 273).

21. The appearance of *isonomos* as early as the drinking songs that celebrated the murder of the tyrant Hipparchus in 514 and the comparatively late appearance of *demokratia*, used only infrequently before the death of Pericles, have led scholars to speculate that *isonomia* was simply the original word for what was later called *demokratia*; that it began as an aristocratic catchword meaning the equality of noblemen as against the singularity of tyranny, but later came to mean democracy; or that it never meant democracy per se and referred throughout its existence to all constitutional governments. The quantity of ink spilt on this topic is equaled only by the quality of the minds that have applied themselves to the problem: V. Ehrenberg, "Isonomia," *RE* Supplementband 7, "Eunomia," *Charisteria Alois Reich* (Reichenberg, 1930), revised and translated into English in *Aspects of the Ancient World* (Oxford, 1946), and also "Origins of Democracy," *Historia* 1 (1950): 515–48; A. Debrunner, "Demokratia," *Festschrift für E. Tieche* (Bern, 1947), 11–24; J.A.O. Larsen, "Cleisthenes and the Development of the Theory of Democracy at Athens," in M. Konvitz and A. Murphy, eds., *Essays in Political Theory Presented to George H. Sabine* (Ithaca, 1948), 1–16; G. Vlastos, "Isonomia," *AJP* 74 (1953): 337–66 and "ISONOMIA POLITIKE," in J. Mau and E. G. Schmidt, *Isonomia: Studien zur Glecheitsvorstellung (sic) im griechischen Denken* (Berlin, 1964), 1–35, reprinted in G. Vlastos, *Platonic Studies*, 2d. ed. (Princeton, 1981), 164–203. I have nothing to add to the dialogue beyond the observation that unwitting tribute to the loss of sleep that the *isonomia* problem evidently occasioned these scholars is paid in Donald Kagan's *The Great Dialogue: History of Greek Political Thought from Homer to Polybius* (New York and London, 1965), in which a printer's error coined the appropriate conflation "insonomia" (77).

22. On Herodotus's political thought in general see K. Wüst, *Politisches Denken bei Herodot* (Ph.D. disseration, University of Munich 1933; reprint, N.Y., 1979); H.-F. Bornitz, *Herodot-Studien* (Berlin, 1968); J. Cobet, *Herodots Exkurse und die Frage der Einheit seines Werkes. Historia Einzelschrift 17* (Wiesbaden, 1971); C. Fornara, *Herodotus: An Interpretive Essay* (Oxford, 1971); W. Nikolai, *Versuch über Herodots Geschichtsphilosophie* (Heidelberg, 1986); K. Raaflaub, "Herodotus, Political Thought, and the Meaning of History," *Arethusa* 20 (1987): 221–48; and B. Shimron, *Politics and Belief in Herodotus* (Stuttgart, 1989). The traditional view that Herodotus was a supporter of the Athenian (i.e., Periclean) democracy of his own day has been attacked by H. Strasburger, "Herodot und das Perikleische Athen," *Historia* 4 (1955): 1–25. See, however, the brief response of F. D. Harvey, "The Political Sympathies of Herodotus," *Historia* 15 (1966): 254–55.

23. Translated by Freeman in the *Ancilla* as 265 and 251. Cf. also Freeman, 252, 253, and 262. The long discussion of Democritus's political and social ideology offered in chap. 6 of C. Farrar, *The Origins of Democratic Thinking: The Invention of Politics in Classical Athens* (Cambridge, England, 1988) is useful though it often stretches the evidence farther than it can reasonably be asked to go. See the alternative argument in G. Aalders, "The Political Faith of Democritus," *Mnemosyne*, 4th ser., 3 (1950): 302–13, who cites fragments 49, 75, 254, 266, and 267. A certain amount hangs on whether

a Democritean origin can be assigned to a fragment of the late fifth-/early fourth-century writer known as the Anonymus Iamblichi; this question is discussed in the context of the relationship between the thinking of Plato, Protagoras, and Democritus by A. T. Cole, "The Anonymus Iamblichi and His Place in Greek Political Theory," *Harvard Studies in Classical Philology* 65 (1961): 127–63.

The connection between scientific speculation and political principle is central to Havelock's *Liberal Temper*, in which chap. 6 is devoted to Democritus. A helpful discussion also appears in Winspear, *The Genesis of Plato's Thought*, 147–60.

24. On the political opinions of Aeschylus see the relevant entries in n. 26. The climax of the trilogy in the matricide Orestes' acquittal at the hand of an Athenian court also points to the essentially masculine value system of Greek democracy: not only is Orestes acquitted of his mother's murder on the grounds that mothers have no genetic input into fetuses and are hence less important than fathers, but it is determined that the emotional and vindictive female Furies who have pursued him across Greece must bow to the wishes of Athenian juries. A detailed twentieth-century reading of the sexual politics of the *Oresteia* appears in F. Zeitlin, "The Dynamics of Misogyny: Myth and Mythmaking in the *Oresteia*," in J. Peradotto and J. P. Sullivan, eds., *Women in the Ancient World: The ARETHUSA Papers* (Albany, 1984), 159–94.

25. Cited in the translation of F. W. Jones in D. Grene and R. Lattimore, eds., *The Complete Greek Tragedies*, vol. 4 (Chicago, 1958). I have made one small emendation; at the suggestion of Kurt Raaflaub, I have changed the translation of *isaiteron* in line 441 from "fair" to "equal," because this more adequately reflects what I perceive to be Euripides' political agenda here.

26. The subtlety with which the question of democracy was treated in Attic tragedy lies largely outside the scope of this book, because these subtleties, being subtleties, have not on the whole played a large role in the shaping of modern thinking about Athenian democracy. Indeed a case could be made that the significance of the entire phenomenon of tragedy for the development of the skills necessary in a democracy has been noticed only in the late twentieth century. Still, the subject is fascinating, and readers are referred to G. Thomson, *Aeschylus and Athens* (London, 1941); V. Ehrenberg, *Sophocles and Pericles* (Oxford, 1954); G. Zuntz, *The Political Plays of Euripides* (Manchester, 1955); M. Jameson, "Politics and the *Philoctetes*," *CP* 51 (1956): 217–27; K. J. Dover, "The Political Aspect of the *Eumenides*," *JHS* 77 (1957): 230–37; R. Y. Hathorn, "Sophocles' *Antigone*: Eros in Politics," *CJ* 54 (1958–59): 109–15; E. R. Dodds, "Morals and Politics in the *Oresteia*," *Ancient Concept of Progress and Other Essays* [Oxford, 1973], 45–63); A. J. Podlecki, *The Political Background of Aeschylean Tragedy* (Ann Arbor, Mich., 1966); W. M. Calder III, "Sophokles' Political Tragedy: *Antigone*," *GRBS* 9 (1968): 389–407; C. Meier, "Aeschylus' *Eumenides* and the Rise of the Political" in *The Greek Discovery of Politics* (London and Cambridge, Mass., 1990), 82–139; D. K. Nichols, "Aeschylus' *Oresteia* and the Origins of Political Life," *Interpretation* 9 (1980): 83–91; C. W. Macleod, "Politics and the Oresteia," *JHS* 102 (1982): 124–44; B.M.W. Knox, "Sophocles and the *Polis*," *Entretiens sur l'antiquité (Fondation Hardt)* 29 (1983): 1–17; P. Burian, "*Logos* and *Pathos*: The Politics of the *Suppliant Women*," in his *Directions in Euripidean Criticism: A Collection of Essays* (Durham, 1985); S. Goldhill, *Reading Greek Tragedy* (Cambridge, England, 1986); J. P. Euben, ed., *Greek Tragedy and Political Theory* (Berkeley and Los Angeles, 1986), and Euben's

The Tragedy of Political Theory: The Road Not Taken (Princeton, 1990); Christian Meier, *Die politische Kunst der griechischen Tragödie* (Munich, 1988); and Farrar, *Origins*, 30–38.

27. English editions of Protagoras include W.K.C. Guthrie, *Plato, Protagoras, and Meno* (Harmondsworth, 1956); G. Vlastos, ed., *Plato, Protagoras: Jowett's Translation Revised by Martin Ostwald* (Indianapolis and New York, 1956); and C.C.W. Taylor, *Plato: Protagoras* (Oxford, 1976.) See also L. Goldberg, *A Commentary on Plato's Protagoras* (New York, 1983); and P. Coby, *Socrates and the Sophistic Enlightenment: A Commentary on Plato's "Protagoras"* (Lewisburg, Pa., London, and Toronto, 1987). Discussions of the political theory in the dialogue appear in A. Levi, "The Ethical and Social Thought of Protagoras," *Mind* n.s. 44 (1940): 284–302; J. S. Morrison, "The Place of Protagoras in Athenian Public Life," *CQ* 35 (1941): 1–16; G. B. Kerferd, "*Protagoras* of Plato," *JHS* 73 (1953): 442–45; A.W.H. Adkins, "Arete, Techne, Democracy, and Sophists: *Protagoras* 316b–328d," *JHS* 93 (1973): 3–12; E. and N. Wood, *Class Ideology and Ancient Political Theory* (Oxford, 1978), 128–37; P. P. Nicholson, "Protagoras and the Justification of Athenian Democracy," *Polis* 3 (1980–81): 14–24; and Farrar, *Origins*, chap. 3; see also Gregory Vlastos's introduction to Ostwald's revision of Jowett. Bibliography on the dialogue is collected in the Taylor edition and in Farrar, *Origins*. I have not yet been able to consult D. Loenen, *Protagoras and the Greek Community* (Amsterdam, 1941).

28. Bibliographical guides to the debate over the origins of the Platonic Protagoras are provided in E. Havelock, *The Liberal Temper*, 407–9 and W.K.C. Guthrie, *The Sophists*, 64n. See also J. P. Maguire, "Protagoras—or Plato?" *Phronesis* 18 (1973): 115–38, and 22 (1977): 103–22; and Farrar, *Origins*.

Withal it is curious that Protagoras, a citizen of Abdera, uses Athenian mores to bolster his view of the world while simultaneously using his worldview to justify the Athenians, who are Socrates' compatriots and whom he mentions several times by name.

29. A prodigious amount of scholarship has been devoted to the question of the authenticity of the speeches in Thucydides' history. A massive bibliography on the topic was compiled by William C. West III for Philip Stadter's *The Speeches in Thucydides* (Chapel Hill, N.C., 1973) and includes 351 separate entries not counting book reviews; much could now be added to this by consulting entries under Thucydides' name in *L'Année philologique* since 1972.

30. A detailed study of democratic ideology and the genre of the funeral oration appears in N. Loraux, *The Invention of Athens: The Funeral Oration in the Classical City* (Cambridge, Mass., and London, 1986). J. Moravcsik contrasts the view of freedom articulated in Pericles' oration with that held by Plato in "Plato and Pericles on Freedom and Politics," in F. Pelletier and J. King-Farlow, eds., *New Essays on Plato* (Guelph, Ontario, 1983), 1–17. On the democratic ideology of liberty, see K. Raaflaub, *Die Entdeckung der Freiheit* (Munich, 1985), 258–312. Orlando Patterson in his *Freedom*, vol. 1: *Freedom in the Making of Western Culture* (New York, 1991) devotes a great deal of space (47–180) to the development of the concept of freedom in preclassical and classical Greece.

31. My work in progress on the gender of democracy will take note of its masculinity in Aeschylus; Pericles' defense of it against charges of effeminacy; allegations of effeminacy in the eighteenth century; and insistence on the masculinity of republicanism

among America's founding fathers and in Victorian Britain. Questions of gender and Athenian democracy are discussed in chap. 12 and in D. Halperin, *One Hundred Years of Homosexuality and Other Essays on Greek Love* (New York and London, 1990). A variety of perspectives on related issues in eighteenth- and nineteenth-century France are offered in L. Hunt, ed., *Eroticism and the Body Politic* (Baltimore, 1990).

32. The notion that the word *demokratia* may originally have been coined by the enemies of democracy is supported in R. Hirzel, *Themis, Dike und Verwandtes* (Leipzig, 1907), 263n.; V. Ehrenberg, "Isonomia," *RE* Supplementband 7, 297; and Larsen, *Essays in Political Theory Presented to George H. Sabine*, 13. Gomme (*A Historical Commentary on Thucydides*, vol. 2 [Oxford, 1956], 110) dismisses the idea, claiming that demos was "a very respectable word in all manner of states, including Sparta," but I think he is mistaken about the significance of this respectability (respectability that I grant). Demos and *demokratia* are different words. On the way in which the usage of words for political programs evolved and changed in classical Athens see in its entirety Sealey's long and witty essay "Origins." It is often difficult for outsiders to understand the nuances of political terminology. American feminists will be the first to proclaim themselves believers in women's liberation, but no feminist calls herself—or himself—a "libber." The epithet is heard exclusively on the lips of outsiders (who frequently have no idea that the use of the word labels them as such). Subtle distinctions are powerful (cf. feminine, feminist, effeminate).

33. Cited in the Loeb Classical Library translation of J. H. Vince, *Demosthenes against Meidias, Androtion, Aristocrates, Timocrates, Aristogeiton* (Cambridge, Mass., and London, 1935).

34. [*Lysias*] 2.18–19, cited in the Loeb Classical Library translation of W.R.M. Lamb (Cambridge, Mass., 1930.)

35. As Kurt Raaflaub has pointed out, tyranny, though obsolete in mainland Greece during the fifth century, nonetheless retained its "prominence in political thought on democracy because it served the useful function of representing a system that radically denied all the values and achievements of democracy. By refuting the negative features of tyranny, it was possible to emphasize through a stark contrast some of the positive aspects of democracy" ("Democracy, Oligarchy, and the Concept of the 'Free Citizen' in Late Fifth-Century Athens," *Political Theory* 11 [1983]: 522–23.) On the use of antityrannical rhetoric in antidemocratic authors see B. Gentili, "Polemica antitirannica," *Quaderni Urbinati di Cultura Classica* n.s. 1 30 (1979): 153–56; and V. Rosivach, "The Tyrant in Athenian Democracy," *Quaderni Urbinati di Cultural Classica* n.s. 30 (1988): 56–57.

CHAPTER THREE

1. The idea that power and prestige were the prerogatives of people from a few families that had possessed wealth for as long as anyone could remember was deeply ingrained in Greek thinking. Greek elitism is studied in R. Seager, "Elitism and Democracy in Classical Athens," in F. C. Jaher, ed., *The Rich, the Well-Born, and the Powerful: Elites and Upper Classes in History* (Urbana, Ill., 1973), 7–26; M.T.W. Arnheim, *Aristocracy in Greek Society* (London, 1977); W. Donlan, *The Aristocratic Ideal in Ancient Greece: Attitudes of Superiority from Homer to the End of the Fifth Century* B.C. (Lawrence, Kans., 1980); and J. Ober, *Mass and Elite in Democratic Athens: Rheto-*

ric, Ideology, and the Power of the People (Princeton, 1989). Although many scholars (myself included) will find his ideas about Socrates odd, I. F. Stone has provided a readable account of Greek elitism for popular audiences in his book on *The Trial of Socrates* (Boston, 1988).

2. Cited in the translation of Richmond Lattimore (Chicago, 1951). Homer's own views are more complex; see for example K. Raaflaub, "Homer and the Beginning of Political Thought in Greece," *Boston Area Colloquium in Ancient Philosophy* 4 (1988): 1–33, with a reply by L. Edmunds.

3. See, e.g., A. R. Burn, *The Pelican History of Greece* (Harmondsworth, 1966), 122; and, in more detail, M. I. Finley, *Early Greece: The Bronze and Archaic Ages* (New York, 1970), 104.

4. Raphael Sealey has suggested that "Angry Young Man" might be a better term than "Old Oligarch" ("The Origins of *Demokratia*," *California Studies in Classical Antiquity* 6 [1973]: 262). Other discussions of the pseudo-Xenophontic *Constitution* appear in H. Frisch, *The Constitution of the Athenians: A Philological-Historical Analysis of Pseudo-Xenophon's Treatise de re publica Atheniensium* (Copenhagen, 1942); J. M. Moore, ed., *Aristotle and Xenophon on Democracy and Oligarchy* (London, 1975); C. G. Starr, "Thucydides on Sea Power," *Mnemosyne* 31 (1978): 343–50; the essay appended to Luciano Canfora's Italian translation of the text that bears the pointed title, *La democrazia come violenza*, published at Palermo in 1982; and A. Fuks, "The Old Oligarch," in his *Social Conflict in Ancient Greece* (Jerusalem and Leiden, 1984).

5. I cite the text in the translation that appears at the beginning of H. Frisch, *The Constitution of the Athenians*.

6. Herodotus has Megabyzus express similar ideas at 3.81 in the constitutional debate, but they are formulated much less analytically.

7. In *Time, Narrative, and History* (Bloomington, 1986), David Carr distinguishes between the narrative of the radio announcer, who, performing the functions of "chronicler," offers a live description of a baseball game in progress ("'There's the pitch ... the batter swings ... line drive to center field!' etc.") and that of the person who, after the game is over, will tell the "*story* of the game ... in full knowledge of who won," mentioning only "the most important events, especially those that contributed to scoring points and thus to the outcome" (59). Looked at in this way, it is difficult for anyone who has read Thucydides to class him with the radio announcer rather than with the postgame narrative interpreter. Not surprisingly, even the so-called "Separatist" critics concede, as W. R. Connor has pointed out (*Thucydides*, [Princeton, 1984]), that "whatever the stages of composition" of Thucydides' narrative, "the work is likely to have taken its present form amid the disputes and recriminations that followed the Athenian defeat" (10).

8. Because Thucydides' work does not deal directly with constitutional questions, not a great deal has been written on his views of Athenian democracy. Mary Lefkowitz of Wellesley College is one among several scholars who have observed that Thucydides "describes the Athenian demos behaving as if it were an individual person rather than a collection of many different people"—hardly a promising approach to domestic politics. (Her remarks appear in her review of Eli Sagan's *The Honey and the Hemlock* in the *New York Times Book Review* [3 May 1992]: 35.) Attempts to uncover Thucydides' opinions about the government of his native city include J. H. Finley, *Thucydides* (Cambridge, Mass., 1942); A. W. Gomme, A. Andrewes, and K. J. Dover, *A Historical*

Commentary on Thucydides, 5 vols. (Oxford, 1945–81); M. F. MacGregor, "The Politics of the Historian Thucydides," Phoenix 10 (1956): 93–102; the chapter on Thucydides in D. Kagan, The Great Dialogue: A History of Greek Political Thought from Homer to Polybius (New York and London, 1965); W. R. Connor, Thucydides, 24–230; S. Hornblower, Thucydides (Baltimore, 1987); and C. Farrar, The Origins of Democratic Thinking (Cambridge, 1988) (where an interpretation strikingly different from my own is offered). Scholarly twentieth-century studies of Thucydides range from the conservative G. Grundy, Thucydides and the History of his Age (1911; 2d ed., Oxford, 1948), who endorses all Thucydides' strictures on democracy, to the iconoclastic study of V. Hunter, Thucydides: The Artful Reporter (Toronto, 1973). Thucydides has also been extremely popular in the twentieth century with journalists, particularly those writing in the United States. On the significance of modern estimates of Thucydides' work, see chap. 13, pp. 296–98.

The thoughtful article of Maurice Pope in Historia 37 (1988): "Thucydides and Democracy" (276–96) stresses the complexity of Thucydides' views and argues that antidemocrats have been wrong to assume him as a legitimizing ancestor for their own opinions. Pope's article is important not only for its close reading of Thucydides but for the emphasis it places on Thucydides' co-optation into the antidemocratic tradition. As Pope observes in his first sentence, "Thucydides is often used to torpedo the cause of democracy."

9. On ostracism see chapter 2, n. 8.

10. See, e.g., A. Fuks, The Ancestral Constitution: Four Studies in Athenian Party Politics at the end of the Fifth Century B.C. (London, 1953), 52. Speculation about the way in which late fifth- and fourth-century Athenians chose to interpret and/or recast their earlier constitutional history also appears in E. Ruschenbusch, "PATRIOS POLITEIA: Theseus, Drakon, Solon und Kleisthenes in Publistik und Geschichtsschreibung des 5. und 4. Jahrhunderts v. Chr." Historia 7 (1958): 398–424; and L. Boffo, "L'intervento di Efialte di Sofonide sull'Areopago nell'interpretazione del IV secolo," Rendiconti della Classe di Scienze morali, storiche e filologiche dell'Accademia dei Lincei 31 (1976): 435–50. See also the relevant portions of P. J. Rhodes's Commentary on the Aristotelian Athenaion Politeia (Oxford, 1981) and the long chapter on the "Patrios Politeia" in Ostwald, From Popular Sovereignty to the Sovereignty of Law: Law, Society, and Politics in Fifth-Century Athens (Berkeley and Los Angeles, 1986), 337–411.

11. On the political opinions of Isocrates, see (in addition to the works cited in n. 14 here) R. von Pöhlmann, Isokrates und das Problem der Demokratie (Munich, 1913); G. Mathieu, Les idées politiques d'Isocrate (Paris, 1925); M.L.W. Laistner's introduction to his Isocrates: De Pace and Philippus, Cornell Studies in Classical Philology no. 22 (New York and London, 1927), 15–24; K. Bringmann, Studien zur den politischen Ideen des Isokrates, Hypomnemata Heft 14 (Göttingen, 1965), esp. 75–95; two recent articles, I. Labriola, "Terminologia politica isocratea I: oligarchia, aristocrazia, democrazia," QS 4, no. 7 (1978): 147–68, and M. Silvestrini, "Terminologia politica isocratea, 2: L'Areopagitico o dell' ambiguità isocratea," QS 4, no. 7 (1978): 169–83; and A. Fuks, "Isocrates and the Social-Economic Situation in Greece," in Social Conflict in Ancient Greece, 52–79.

I have not yet been able to see the unpublished Ph.D. dissertation of Allan Bloom, "The Political Philosophy of Isokrates" (University of Chicago, 1955).

12. On the Panegyricus in its historical context see E. Buchner, Der Panegyrikos des

Isokrates: Eine Historisch-Philologische Untersuchung, Historia, suppl. 2 (Wiesbaden, 1958).

13. For a Roman version of the notion that people in the old days competed only to outdo one another in public spirit see Sallust, *De Bello Jugurthino* 4.6–7.

14. The key passages in which Isocrates denigrates the Athenian government of his day in *On the Peace* and the *Areopagiticus* are collected by J. Kessler, *Isokrates und die panhellenische Idee, Studien zur Geschichte und Kultur des Altertums* 4.3 (Paderborn, 1911), 30–32. See also P. Harding, "The Purpose of Isokrates' *Archidamos* and *On the Peace,*" *California Studies in Classical Antiquity* 6 (1973): 137–49.

15. The text of Isocrates is cited with minor variations from G. Norlin and L. Van Hook, *Isocrates,* 3 vols. (London and Cambridge, Mass., 1928–45).

16. Cf. Aristotle, *Politics,* 1294b, 18ff.

17. Isocrates' failure to use the expression *patrios politeia* escaped my notice in reading; it was kindly pointed out to me by Martin Ostwald.

CHAPTER FOUR

1. Because of the key role of Plato and Aristotle in shaping the anti-Athenian orientation of Western thought, I have chosen to include rather more bibliographical references in this chapter than elsewhere. I hope the reader will find these more useful than burdensome.

Impressive work on the political thought of Plato and Aristotle began already in the nineteenth century with George Grote's work on Plato (*Plato and the Other Companions of Socrates,* 3 vols.) and continued into the twentieth at the hands of thinkers as different as Sir Ernest Barker (*Political Thought of Plato and Aristotle* [London, 1906] and *Greek Political Theory: Plato and His Predecessors* [London, 1918]) and Leo Strauss (*The City and Man* [Charlottesville, Va., 1964]). Interesting thought has continued to unfold throughout the twentieth century.

Helpful modern works on Plato include G. C. Field, *Plato and His Contemporaries* (London, 1930; reprint, 1967); W. Fite, *The Platonic Legend* (New York, 1934); Karl R. Popper, *The Open Society and Its Enemies,* vol. 1: *The Spell of Plato* (London, 1945; reprint, New York and Evanston, 1962, with additions and a response to the attack in Ronald Levinson, *In Defense of Plato* [Cambridge, Mass., 1953]; on Popper see also see also R. Bambrough, ed., *Plato, Popper, and Politics* [Cambridge, 1967]); John Wild, *Plato's Modern Enemies and the Theory of Natural Law* (Chicago, 1953); Eric A. Havelock, *The Liberal Temper in Greek Politics* (London, 1957; reprint, New Haven and London, 1964); J. Luccioni, *La pensée politique de Platon* (Paris, 1958); H. D. Rankin, *Plato and the Individual* (London and New York, 1964); W.K.C. Guthrie, *A History of Greek Philosophy,* vol. 4: *Plato: The Man and His Dialogues: Earlier Period* (Cambridge, 1975); Alvin Gouldner, *Enter Plato: Classical Greece and the Origins of Social Theory* (New York, 1965; reprint, New York, 1971); Terence Irwin, *Plato's Moral Theory* (Oxford, 1977); R. W. Hall, *Plato* (London, 1981); and G. Klosko, *The Development of Plato's Political Theory* (New York, 1986). See also the collection of Gregory Vlastos's essays on Plato in Vlastos, *Platonic Studies,* 2d ed., with corrections (Princeton, 1981). How Plato might have viewed modern cultures is explored in R.H.S. Crossman's *Plato Today* (1937; reprint, New York, 1959). Excerpts from Crossman, Popper, Wild, John Hallowell, Leo Strauss, and Bertrand Russell appear in Thomas L. Thorson, ed., *Plato:*

Totalitarian or Democrat? (Englewood Cliffs, N.J., 1963). Additional responses to Popper appear in R. Robinson, "Dr. Popper's Defence of Democracy" (1951, reprinted in Robinson's *Essays in Greek Philosophy* [Oxford, 1969]) and in Jordan, "The Revolt against Philosophy: The Spell of Popper," included in John Wild, ed., *The Return to Reason* (Chicago, 1953). Popper and Levinson are both analyzed in J. Neu, "Plato's Analogy of the State and Individual: *The Republic* and the Organic Theory of the State," *Philosophy* 46 (1971): 238–54. T. Gomperz, *The Greek Thinkers*, 4 vols., English translation by L. Magnus and C. G. Berry (London, 1901–12) remains a valuable work, as does Werner Jaeger's *Paedeia* (1933): English translation by Gilbert Highet, 3 vols. (Oxford, 1939–45). The iconoclastic book of Ellen M. and Neal Wood, *Class Ideology and Ancient Political Theory: Socrates, Plato, and Aristotle in Social Context* (Oxford and New York, 1978) argues that the criticisms made of Athens by these three seminal thinkers are traceable to class bias and are not in fact valid. In this the authors follow the neglected side of Plato so carefully delineated in A. Winspear, *The Genesis of Plato's Thought* (New York, 1940).

Bibliography of work on Plato appears in *Lustrum* 4 (1959) and 5 (1960) for 1950–57, *Lustrum* 20 (1977) for 1958–75, *Lustrum* 25 (1983) for 1975–80, and *Lustrum* 30 (1988) for 1980–85. A good working bibliography appears at the end of Robert W. Hall's *Plato* (in the Geraint Parry "Political Thinkers" series [London, 1981]). Hall's last chapter, on Plato in modern thought, is very useful. More recent work is listed in *l'Année philologique*.

2. The reliability of Xenophon's *Memorabilia* and *Oeconomicus* as sources for the opinions of the historical Socrates has been variously estimated by scholars. I think both dialogues reflect primarily the views of Xenophon. As Barker has pointed out, "The Athenians would not have put to death the Socrates depicted by Xenophon" (*Greek Political Theory*, 107). The most intensive treatment of the question is probably that of A.-H. Chroust, *Socrates, Man, and Myth: The Two Socratic Apologies of Xenophon* (Notre Dame, Ind., 1957), but see also G. Vlastos, "The Paradox of Socrates" in G. Vlastos, ed., *The Philosophy of Socrates* (New York, 1971), 1–21, and the response of D. Morrison, "On Professor Vlastos' Xenophon," *Ancient Philosophy* 7 (1987): 9–22.

3. T. A. Sinclair observes wittily that it was natural for his contemporaries to think Socrates' professed ignorance was "a sham and a pose" in view of his devotion to the quest for knowledge by the method of question and answer, since "one cannot help observing that if to the end of his days Socrates still knew nothing, the method cannot have been very effective" (*A History of Greek Political Thought* [1951; reprint, New York, 1968], 87).

4. A thorough bibliography of work on *Crito* down to 1983 appears in R. Kraut, *Socrates and the State* (Princeton, 1984).

5. An impassioned argument in favor of Socrates' support for Athenian democracy appears in Popper, *The Open Society*, 128–29 and 189–91. The nature of Popper's agenda is revealed by the terms in which he couches his argument. As a critic of Athens and her democratic institutions, Popper writes, Socrates

> may have borne a superficial resemblance to some of the leaders of the reaction against the open society. But there is no need for a man who criticizes democracy and democratic institutions to be their enemy, although both the democrats he criticizes, and the totalitarians who hope to profit from any disunion in the demo-

cratic camp, are likely to brand him as such. There is a fundamental difference between a democratic and a totalitarian criticism of democracy. Socrates' criticism was a democratic one, and indeed of the kind that is the very life of democracy. (Democrats who do not see the difference between a friendly and a hostile criticism of democracy are themselves imbued with the totalitarian spirit). (189)

Popper is answered directly by Kraut in the section on "Popper's Socrates" on pp. 203–7 of *Socrates and the State*. The search for the historical Socrates is the subject of Alban Winspear and Tom Silverberg, *Who Was Socrates?* (New York, 1939). The authors conclude that from an early position as a liberal student of the sciences Socrates developed into a hardened conservative. Combining the evidence of Plato and Xenophon (see n. 2), Wood and Wood in *Class Ideology* (esp. in chap. 3) see Socrates as a class-conscious critic of the Athenian system.

The evidence concerning Chaerephon and Lysias is forcefully presented in G. Vlastos, "The Historical Socrates and Athenian Democracy," *Political Theory* 11 (1983): 495–516, but just as cogently refuted by E. and N. Wood in "Socrates and Democracy: A Reply to Gregory Vlastos" in *Political Theory* 14 (1986): 55–82. On the political ambiguities of Socrates' positions, see F. S. Whelan, "Socrates and the 'Meddlesomeness' of the Athenians," *History of Political Thought* 4 (1983): 1–27. I cannot agree with Whelan that Plato never portrays Socrates as condemning Athenian imperialism. The question of Plato's attitude toward the Athenian empire is extremely complex. An important article with valuable bibliography is S. Dusanic, "Plato's Atlantis," *L'Antiquité Classique* 51 (1982): 25–52.

6. Useful twentieth-century editions of the *Gorgias* are that of Dodds, a revised Greek text with introduction and commentary (*Plato Gorgias* [Oxford, 1959]) and, more recently, of Terence Irwin, *Plato Gorgias*, translated into English with notes (Oxford, 1979). On political life and *Gorgias* see A. Saxonhouse, "An Unspoken Theme in Plato's *Gorgias*: War," *Interpretation* 11 (1983): 139–69, and B. Calvert, "The Politicians of Athens in the Gorgias and Meno," *History of Political Thought* (Exeter), vol. 5 (1984): 1–15.

7. I have profited enormously from conversations about *Gorgias* with a number of colleagues, most particularly Stephen Carter, Elaine Fantham, Andrew Ford, Barry Goldfarb, Michael Miller, C. Jan Swearingen, and Peter Euben, who was kind enough to provide me with a copy of some work in progress.

8. Editions of Plato's *Laws* include E. B. England, ed., *The Laws of Plato*, 2 vols. (Manchester, 1921), and R. G. Bury, ed. and trans., *The Laws*, 2 vols. (London and Cambridge, Mass., 1926) (Loeb Classical Library, with facing English translation; this is the translation I have cited in the text. The Budé edition by E. Des Places and A. Dies with Greek text and French translation includes important commentary. *The Laws* have been translated into English by T. Saunders (Harmondsworth, 1970) and Thomas Pangle (New York, 1980, with interpretive essay). Studies of the *Laws* appear in Glenn Morrow, *Plato's Cretan City: A Historical Interpretation of the Laws* (Princeton, 1960); Leo Strauss, *The Argument and Action of Plato's Laws* (Chicago, 1975); and R. F. Stalley, *An Introduction to Plato's Laws* (Indianapolis, 1983). A useful review of Morrow is by C. Hahn, *Journal of the History of Ideas* 22 (1961): 418–24.

Bibliography up to 1975 on the *Laws* was compiled by T. Saunders, *Bibliography on Plato's Laws* (New York, 1976).

9. On Greek attitudes toward naval power see Momigliano's "Sea Power in Greek Thought," *Classical Review* 58 (1944): 1–7. Momigliano suggests that Thucydides was familiar with the pamphlet of the Old Oligarch and that Pericles' last speech (2.60–64) was directed at its arguments about naval power, and argues that Thucydides 4.85.4 is a rejoinder to the Old Oligarch's 2.5. Aristotle, Momigliano contends, was more positive about sea power. "A famous passage of the *Politics* (VIII. 3, p. 1327a II)," he writes, "obviously aimed at the *Laws*, waters down Platonic intransigence into typical Aristotelian compromise" (5).

10. Editions of the *Republic* include J. Adam, ed. *The Republic of Plato*, 2 vols. (Cambridge, 1902); D. J. Allan, ed., *Plato, The Republic Book I* (London, 1940; reprint, London, 1953); and Paul Shorey, ed. and trans., *The Republic of Plato*, 2 vols. (London, 1930) (Loeb Classical Library, with facing English translation). Helpful English translations include F. Cornford, *The Republic of Plato* (Oxford, 1941), and the very different rendition of A. Bloom, *The Republic of Plato* (New York, 1968).

A great deal has been written on the *Republic*. The best and most important works for the purposes of studying Plato's attitude toward Athenian government are Barker, *Greek Political Theory*, 168–313; T. A. Sinclair, *A History of Greek Political Thought*, chap. 8; H. Rankin, *Plato and the Individual*; J. Neu, "Plato's Analogy of the State and Individual," *Philosophy* 46 (1971): 238–54; J. Annas, *An Introduction to Plato's Republic* (Oxford, 1981); and M. Nichols, *Socrates and the Political Community: An Ancient Debate* (Albany, 1987). See also C.D.C. Reeve, *Philosopher-Kings: The Argument of Plato's "Republic"* (Princeton, 1988), and S. Benardete, *Socrates' Second Sailing: On Plato's Republic* (Chicago and London, 1989), 189–213.

11. On Plato's eugenics and the noble lie, see H. Rankin, *Plato and the Individual*, chaps. 3–4. J. Faris, "Is Plato's a Caste State?" *CQ* 44 (1950): 38–43, takes issue with Popper's contention (with which I agree) that citizens born into the wrong class by mistake may be moved down but not up.

12. My translations from the *Republic* are taken from Cornford, *The Republic of Plato*.

13. Opinions about whether or not Plato intended to describe Athens in his portrait of the democratic state range from Barker's contention "that Athens is the basis of his sketch of democracy is obvious" (*Greek Political Theory*, 290) to Wild's insistence that "no safe conclusion concerning Plato's attitude toward his mother city can be drawn from the formalistic discussions of Book VIII of the *Republic*" (Thorson, 106). (Living two generations before Wild, Barker could not have been expected to heed his caveat.) The best discussion to my mind is that of Julia Annas in *The Republic of Plato*, 299–305. Although most of my own conclusions were reached independently, still the similarity of my own line of thinking to that of Annas is evident in the text. On Plato and the historical Athens see also Field, 128–29; Popper, 189ff. and 294; Winspear, *Genesis*, 168–70; and Fite, *Platonic Legend*, 152. I have not yet been able to consult S. Dusanic, "Platon et Athènes," *Ziva Antike* (Skopje), vol. 31 (1981): 135–56, where it is apparently argued that Plato's attitude to Athens is not fundamentally negative.

14. On the controversy over the status of women in classical Athens, see chap. 12.

15. These possible historical foundations for Plato's reasoning here are explored in Morrow, *Plato's Cretan City*.

16. The wise judgment of Sinclair on Plato comes to mind: "His talents were altogether remarkable. . . . What indeed in the intellectual or artistic sphere could he not

have been, except a historian?" ("For Plato," he goes on, "historical truth hardly deserved the name") (*History of Greek Political Thought*, 121–22).

17. I have chosen to omit the discussion of Athenian democracy in Plato's *Menexenus* because of the tremendously vexed question of the dialogue's genre: strong arguments can be made out in favor of both straightforwardness and parody. The difficulties standing in the way of determining Plato's purpose here seem to me overwhelming. The *Menexenus* is treated at length in Nicole Loraux's *The Invention of Athens: The Funeral Oration in the Classical City* (orig. French ed., 1981; English trans. by A. Sheridan, Cambridge, Mass., 1986).

18. Bibliography on the controversy over the authority of the seventh letter appears in H. Tarrant, "Middle Platonism and the *Seventh Epistle*," *Phronesis* 28, no. 1 (1983): 92–93.

19. J. Moravcsik argues that many of Plato's social and political views represented "a conscious attempt to contrast with Periclean conceptions of freedom and democracy a new point of view" ("Plato and Pericles on Freedom and Politics," in F. Pelletier and J. King-Farlow, *New Essays on Plato* [Guelph, Ontario, 1983], 1). On the connection between freedom and democracy, see K. Raaflaub, "Democracy, Oligarchy, and the Concept of the 'Free Citizen' in Late Fifth-Century Athens," *Political Theory* 11 (1983): 517–44.

20. On the political thought of Xenophon see J. Luccioni, *Les Idées politiques et sociales de Xenophon* (Paris, 1948), and W. Higgins, *Xenophon the Athenian* (Albany, 1977).

21. Despite his enormous influence on European thought, considerably less has been written on the political work of Aristotle. Helpful works include C. I. McIlwain, *The Growth of Political Thought in the West* (London, 1932); A. E. Taylor, *Aristotle* (rev. ed., London, 1943); M. Hamburger, *Morals and Law: The Growth of Aristotle's Legal Theory* (New Haven, 1951); E. Vögelin, *Order and Society*, vol. 3: *Plato and Aristotle* (Baton Rouge, 1957); D. J. Allan, *The Philosophy of Aristotle* (London, Oxford, and New York, 1970); A.-H. Chroust, *Aristotle: New Light on His Life and on Some of His Lost Works*, 2 vols. (London, 1973); John B. Morrall, *Aristotle*, in the Geraint Parry "Political Thinkers" series (London, 1977); R. G. Mulgan, *Aristotle's Political Theory: An Introduction for Students of Political Theory* (Oxford, 1977); C. Lord, *Education and Culture in the Political Thought of Aristotle* (Ithaca and London, 1982); W. von Leyden, *Aristotle on Equality and Justice: His Political Argument* (New York, 1985); S. Salkever, *Finding the Mean: Theory and Practice in Aristotelian Political Philosophy* (Princeton, 1990); and M. Nichols, *Citizens and Statesmen: A Study of Aristotle's Politics* (Savage, Md., 1992).

A number of articles on the *Politics* are collected in *La Politique d'Aristote*, Entretiens sur l'antiquité classique XI (Geneva, 1965). Other useful articles include M. Wheeler, "Aristotle's Analysis of the Nature of the Political Struggle," *AJP* 72 (1951): 145–61; J. de Romilly, "Le Classement des constitutions d'Herodote a Aristote," *REG* 72 (1959): 81–99; G. Morrow, "Aristotle's Comments on Plato's *Laws*," in I. Düring and G. E. Owen, eds., *Aristotle and Plato in the Mid–Fourth Century* (Göteborg, 1960), 145–62; M. Chambers, "Aristotle's 'Forms of Democracy,'" *TAPA* 92 (1961): 20–36; W. T. Bluhm, "The Place of the Policy in Aristotle's Theory of the Ideal State," *Journal of Politics* 24 (1962): 743–53; R. G. Mulgan, "Aristotle and the Democratic Conception of Freedom," in B. Harris, ed., *Auckland Classical Essays* (Auckland and Oxford, 1970), 95–111; S. Cashdollar, "Aristotle's Politics of Morals," *Journal of the History of Philosophy* 11 (1973): 145–60; R. Brandt, "Untersuchungen zur politischen Philosophie des Aristoteles," *Hermes* 102 (1974): 191–96; F. Rosen, "The Political Context of Aristotle's Categories of Justice," *Phronesis* 20 (1975): 228–40; D. Dobbs, "Aristotle's Anticommunism," *American Journal of Political Science* 29, no. 1 (1985): 40–41; G. Huxley, "On Aristotle's Best State," *History of Political Thought* 6 (1985): 139–49; and L. Rubin, "Aristotle's Criticism of Socratic Political Unity in Plato's *Republic*," in *Politikos* (Selected Papers of the North American Chapter of the Society for Greek Political Thought), vol. 1 (Pittsburgh, 1989), 93–121. Bibliography on Aristotle's political theory appears in Mulgan, *Aristotle's Political Theory*, 139–52; subsequent work is listed in *L'Année philologique*.

22. The fascination that peasants held for conservative Greek thinkers is treated wittily by L. B. Carter in *The Quiet Athenian* (Oxford and New York, 1986).

23. I cite the *Politics* in the translation of Ernest Barker (Oxford, 1946). Other translations into English include those of Sinclair (rev. T. Saunders, Harmondsworth, 1981); C. Lord (Chicago, 1984); and S. Everson (Cambridge, 1988).

24. Aristotle's equivocation about the role of the *banausoi* in the ideal *politeia* is discussed in C. Johnson, "Who Is Aristotle's Citizen?" *Phronesis* 29, no. 1 (1984): 73–90, esp. 84–86. On the whole, Johnson takes a different view of Aristotle's position from the one I do, grounding it in the inconsistencies of citizenship rights among the various existing Greek constitutions.

25. On Aristotle's response to the *Laws* in particular, see G. R. Morrow, "Aristotle's Comments on Plato's *Laws*," in I. Düring and G.E.L. Owen, eds., *Aristotle and Plato in the Mid–Fourth Century*, 147–62. Morrow may well be right in suggesting that Aristotle had access to an earlier draft of the *Laws* that differed in some respects from the one available today. Aristotle's response to Plato in the matter of political theory is discussed in Nichols, *Socrates and the Political Community*, 153–80.

26. On the different kinds of equality (with particular reference to Aristotle) see D. Keyt, "Distributive Justice in Aristotle's Ethics and Politics," *Topoi* 4 (1985): 23–45, and chap. 3, "Justifiable Inequality and the Different Kinds of Civic Excellence," in W. von Leyden, *Aristotle on Equality and Justice: His Political Argument* (New York, 1985).

27. On Aristotle and democracy, see D. H. Frank, "Aristotle on Freedom in the Politics," *Prudentia* 15 (1983): 109–16, and Barry Strauss, "On Aristotle's Critique of Athenian Democracy," in C. Lord and D. O'Connor, eds., *Essays on the Foundations of Aristotelian Political Science* (Berkeley and Los Angeles, 1991). I have not yet been able to consult M. Bastit, "Aristote et la démocratie," *Cahiers de philosophie politique et juridique* (Caen University), no. 2, (1982): 7–9. Conflicting modern views of this subject are discussed by Nichols in *Socrates and the Political Community*, 1–6.

28. On Aristotle's equivocation concerning citizenship see C. Johnson (cited in n. 24) as well as H. von Arnim, *Zur Entstehungsgeschichte der Aristotelischen Politik* (Vienna, 1924), 35–37; C. Mossé, "La Conception du citoyen dans la Politique d'Aristote," *Eirene* 6 (1957): 17–21; E. Braun, *Das Dritte Buch der Aristotelischen "Politik"* (Vienna, 1965); E. Levy, "Cité et citoyen dans la Politique d'Aristote," *Ktema* 5 (1980) 223–48; P. Gauthier, "La citoyenneté en Grèce et Rome," *Ktema* 6 (1981): 167–79; and most recently L. Bescond, "Remarques sur la conception aristotelicienne de la

citoyenneté," *Cahiers de philosophie politique et juridique* (Caen University), no. 4 (1983), 23–24.

29. On the different kinds of *mousike* suited to people with and without capacity for growth, see C. Lord, *Education and Culture in the Political Thought of Aristotle* (Ithaca and London, 1982), 138–46.

30. I cite the *Ethics* in the translation of J.A.K. Thomson, *The Ethics of Aristotle* (1953; reprint, Harmondsworth, 1973).

31. Aristotle's unsystematic use of evidence is treated in G.J.D. Aalders, "Die Mischverfassung und ihre historische Dokumentation in den Politica des Aristoteles," *La Politique d'Aristote*, 219–37. See also G. Huxley, "On Aristotle's Historical Methods," *GRBS* 13 (1972): 157–69; R. Weil, *Aristote et l'histoire* (Paris, 1960); and K. Adshead, "Aristotle, Politics v. 2. 7 (1302B34–1303A11)," *Historia* 35 (1986) 372–77. The relationship of Aristotle's dicta on democracy and his thinking about Athens itself is discussed in B. Strauss, "On Aristotle's Critique of Athenian Democracy."

CHAPTER FIVE

1. On the Roman view of the comparative antiquity of the Roman republic and classical Athens see e.g., Cicero, *Brutus* 10.39–41.

2. Greek attitudes toward Romans throughout the republic and empire are discussed in Bettie Forte, *Rome and the Romans as the Greeks Saw Them*, Papers and Monographs of the American Academy in Rome, vol. 24 (Rome, 1972); on Roman attitudes toward Greeks see chap. 3.1 of J.P.V.S. Balsdon, *Romans and Aliens* (London, 1979).

3. I cite the *Aeneid* from Allen Mandelbaum's translation (New York, 1961), 6.1129–37 (lines 6.837–53 of the original).

4. Early points of contact between Greeks and Romans have been traced in Forte, *Rome and the Romans as the Greeks Saw Them*, 5–93; N. Petrochilos, *Roman Attitudes to the Greeks* (Athens, 1974), 15; and Erich Gruen, *The Hellenistic World and the Coming of Rome*, 2 vols. (Berkeley and Los Angeles, 1984), 1.253–55. The unfolding of relations between Greeks and Romans is treated in R. Syme, "The Greeks under Roman Rule," in his *Roman Papers*, ed. E. Badian (Oxford, 1979), 566–81. A modern perspective with particular reference to the interaction of ethnic groups in South Africa is provided in T. J. Haarhoff, *The Stranger at the Gate: Aspects of Exclusiveness and Co-Operation in Ancient Greece and Rome, with Some Reference to Modern Times* (London and New York, 1938).

5. W. W. Tarn (*Alexander the Great*, vol. 2 [Cambridge, 1948], 21–26) offers a strong argument against the historicity of the embassy. Discussion of the problem along with comprehensive bibliography appears in Piero Treves, *Il mito di Alessandro e la Roma d'Augusto* (Milan and Naples, 1953), 27–29.

6. Examples are attested in Forte, *Rome and the Romans as the Greeks Saw Them*, 9–11.

7. See *Mostellaria*, 20–24, 64–65, 958–60; *Bacchides*, 742–43, 812–13; *Truculentus*, 86–87; *Poenulus*, 600–603.

8. Cicero *De Oratore* 2.4, 1.82, 1.102, 1.105, cited by Gruen, *The Hellenistic World* 2.264.

9. As Gruen points out (*The Hellenistic World*, 257). Cato's position on Greek studies has been difficult for scholars to pin down. A recent discussion and bibliography

appears in Alan Astin, *Cato the Censor* (Oxford, 1978), chap. 8, "Cato and the Greeks."

10. *Pro Flacco*, 62. I cite the oration in the translation of L. Lord in the Loeb Classical Library's Cicero, *In Catilinam, Pro Flacco, Pro Murena, Pro Sulla* (Cambridge, Mass., and London, 1978). Praise of Athens as the flower of Greece, mother of eloquence, the arts, and intellectual cultivation in general also appear at, e.g., *De Natura Deorum* 3.82; *De Legibus* 2.36; *Brutus* 26, 39, 50, and 332; *De Oratore* 1.13; *De Optimo Genere Oratorum* 7.

On the background of the trial see T.B.L. Webster, ed., *M. Tulli Ciceronis Pro L. Flacco Oratio* (Oxford, 1931).

11. It was inevitable that as anxious and complex a Roman as Cicero should have suffered from painful ambivalence about the Greeks. A tremendous number of valuable citations on this topic are collected in the doctoral thesis of Sister M. A. Trouard, O. P., "Cicero's Attitude towards the Greeks" (Chicago, 1942). See also the thoughtful article by the same name by H. Guite in *Greece and Rome*, 2d ser., 9 (1962): 142–59, especially the last page, on which Guite describes Cicero as a "novus homo, forever looking over his shoulder."

12. *Contiones* and their relationship to the Roman political process are discussed in L. R. Taylor, *Roman Voting Assemblies* (Ann Arbor, 1966), 15–33; appendix A to the Loeb edition cited in n. 10; and in F. Metaxaki-Mitrou, "Violence in the *Contio* during the Ciceronian Age," *L'Antiquité Classique* 54 (1985): 180–87.

13. Cicero's references to Themistocles are listed s.v. "Themistocles" in I. C. Orelius and I. G. Baiterus, *Onomasticon Tullianum* (Hildesheim, 1965); see also H. Berthold, "Die Gestalt des Themistokles bei M. Tullius Cicero," *Klio* 43–45 (1965): 38–48; and A. Podlecki, *The Life of Themistocles*, 115–17.

14. I cite *De Republica* in the Loeb Classical Library translation of C. W. Keyes (London and Cambridge, Mass., 1928).

15. The careful schema of the six constitutions, which Polybius sees as a cycle rather than as the progressive decline suggested by Plato, may in fact have been developed without knowledge of Aristotle. Kurt von Fritz in his important study of *The Theory of the Mixed Constitution in Antiquity: A Critical Analysis of Polybius' Political Ideas* (New York, 1954) argues that Polybius, though influenced by Plato's *Republic*, had not read the *Politics*, and that the cyclical concept originated in any event with Polybius.

16. On the lost historians of classical Greece, see n. 22.

17. I suspect Wardman (*Rome's Debt to Greece* [London, 1976], 79) is a little hard on Nepos in arguing that his "apparent tolerance for Greek ways" is essentially a stratagem designed to facilitate flattering comparisons with Rome. Wardman is probably correct, however, in ascribing the general indifference to Greek political history among Nepos's contemporaries to the Romans' conviction that Greeks were liars anyhow (*Rome's Debt to Greece*, chaps. 1, 4); why would such notoriously eloquent characters confine themselves to the truth in recounting the exploits of their own people? Sallust was not alone in suggesting (*Bellum Catilinae* 2.2) that the glories of Greek history had gained a good bit in the telling.

18. For a later allusion to Solon's purported exile, see chap. 6, p. 340, n. 12.

19. Cf. Cicero's Scipio in *De Republica* 1.35.55 on the differing motivation of aristocrats and democrats (p. 103).

20. A detailed discussion of Aristides' relationship to his sources in the Panathenaic oration appears in J. W. Day, *The Glory of Athens: The Popular Tradition as Reflected in the Panathenaicus of Aelius Aristides* (Chicago, 1980).

21. The speeches of Aristides are cited in the translation of C. A. Behr, *P. Aelius Aristides: The Complete Works*, vol. 1 (Leiden, 1986).

22. The theory that Plutarch followed primarily a single Hellenistic source that served as a transmitter of earlier sources was advocated in 1899 by Eduard Meyer ("Die Biographie Kimons," *Forschungen zur alten Geschichte*, vol. 2 [Halle], 1–87) and enjoyed respectability for a while because of Meyer's distinguished reputation, but it does not seem likely to me, and it has been rejected by several twentieth-century scholars including F. Frost (*Plutarch's Themistocles* [Princeton, 1980]).

Good recent discussions of Plutarch's sources (now lost) for Athenian politics appear in A. J. Podlecki, *The Life of Themistocles: A Critical Survey of the Literary and Archaeological Evidence*, and P. Stadter, *A Commentary on Plutarch's Pericles* (Chapel Hill and London, 1989); see also G. L. Barber, *The Historian Ephorus* (Cambridge, 1935); F. Jacoby, *Atthis* (Oxford, 1949); and W. R. Connor, *Theopompus and Fifth-Century Athens* (Cambridge, Mass., 1968).

23. On Plutarch and Plato see R. M. Jones, *The Platonism of Plutarch* (New York, 1916); and A. Wardman, *Plutarch's Lives* (Berkeley and Los Angeles, 1974), 203–11.

24. The political opinions of Plutarch are discussed in R. Hirzel, *Plutarch* (Leipzig, 1912); R. H. Barrow, *Plutarch and His Times* (London, 1967); C. P. Jones, *Plutarch and Rome* (Oxford, 1971); and Wardman, *Plutarch's Lives*, 197–220. A good recent discussion of Plutarch's connections between Greek democracy and Roman political life appears in C.B.R. Pelling, "Plutarch and Roman Politics," *Past Perspectives* (Cambridge, 1986), 159–87.

25. *Pericles* 1–2. With the exception of the life of Phocion, from which I have made my own translations, citations from Plutarch's lives of Athenian statesmen are cited in this chapter from the translation of I. Scott-Kilvert, *Plutarch: The Rise and Fall of Athens: Nine Greek Lives* (London, 1960).

26. On Themistocles and Plutarch see the studies of Podlecki and Frost cited in n. 22.

27. On Plutarch and Pericles see A. Podlecki, *Plutarch: Life of Pericles* (Bristol, 1987); and Stadter, *Commentary*.

28. The silence of Thucydides, the absence of harsh verdicts on Athenian generals prior to Paches' trial, and the rarity of suicide in fifth-century Athens cast considerable doubt on Plutarch's melodramatic account of this development.

29. Ephialtes, he alleges (citing Plato) had "poured out neat a full draught of freedom for the people and made them unmanageable, so that they nibbled at Euboea and trampled on the islands, like a horse which can no longer bear to obey the rein" (*Pericles* 7.6, citing Plato, *Republic* 562c). He ascribes the demotion of the Areopagus from its original position of prestige to the people's breaking loose from all control while Cimon was away, and Cimon's subsequent ostracism he attributes to demagogues trying to stir up the populace against him by reviving old scandals. Pericles in his earlier demagogic days was ready to give way to the people's caprices "which were shifting and changeable as the winds" (*Pericles* 15.2). Cleon, he maintains (citing the comic poets), bought the favor of the multitude and made "the basest and most unsound element of the people his associates against the best" (*Praecepta Rei Publicae Aerendae* 806E–F. I cite the *Precepts of Statecraft* in the Loeb Classical Library transla-

tion of H. N. Fowler, *Plutarch's Moralia* [14 vols.], vol. 10 [Cambridge and London, 1936]).

30. To be sure, it is not always possible to peg the Athenians as the particular object of Plutarch's censure when he is discussing democracy—when, for example he writes that "the masses always smile upon him who gives to them and does them favours, granting him an ephemeral and uncertain reputation" (*Praecepta* 821F) or that an *ochlos* "is not a simple and easy thing for any chance person" to control but rather one "must be satisfied if the multitude accept authority without shying, like a suspicious and capricious beast, at face or voice," or that there is "in every democracy a spirit of malice and fault-finding directed against men in public life" (813A). Still, it is no coincidence that it is the Athenian comic dramatists whom he quotes when he is lambasting democracies for their choice of leaders (e.g., 801A–B).

31. Petrochilos (*Roman Attitudes to the Greeks*) offers some particularly sensitive remarks about this phenomenon on pp. 197–200. Certainly the orator and historian Dionysius of Halicarnassus, who wrote a long history of Rome in twenty books around the time of the birth of Christ, used Greek history chiefly for rhetorical effect, to flatter the Romans by comparison. An admirer of Rome for the longevity of its imperial sway, Dionysius was quick to point out the short-lived nature of both the Athenian and the Spartan empires (1.3.2–3). A contextual treatment of Dionysius and the Greeks appears in H. Hill, "Dionysius of Halicarnassus and the Origins of Rome," *Journal of Roman Studies* 51 (1961): 88–93.

32. Frank Frost writes eloquently that the *Lives* "became the plaything of an intellectual *haut monde* that shared Plutarch's preoccupation with virtue and his interest in man as a moral animal" and ascribes his popularity to the fact that "Plutarch is unique in his ability to be inoffensive without being dull. His strictures against inhumanity and abuse of privilege have warmed liberal spirits to a degree comfortably below the point of combustion while his obvious preference for enlightened autocracy has found him a favored position in the libraries of the most unenlightened despots" (*Plutarch's Themistocles*, 40–41).

CHAPTER SIX

1. Portions of this chapter appeared in *Medievalia et Humanistica*, n.s. 15 (1987): 25–41, although the conclusions I have reached here are somewhat different.

2. On the state of Greek in the Western empire during the Middle Ages, see J. E. Sandys, *A History of Classical Scholarship from the Sixth Century b.c. to the End of the Middle Ages*, vol. 1 (Cambridge, 1906), 458–68; as well as L. D. Reynolds and N. G. Wilson, *Scribes and Scholars* (Oxford, 1968.)

3. A general survey of medieval writings about ancient history is offered in E. M. Sanford, "The Study of Ancient History in the Middle Ages," *Journal of the History of Ideas* 5 (1944): 21–43. For *demokratia* as chaos in the streets, see G. I. Bratianu, "Empire et 'Démocratie' a Byzance," *Byzantinische Zeitschrift* 37 (1937): 86–111, esp. 86–91, followed by A. Cameron, *Circus Factions: Blues and Greens at Rome and Byzantium* (Oxford, 1976), 305–6. The new meanings of demos and its derivatives at Byzantium are discussed in Cameron, 34–44.

4. 2.16–26. The text was edited by Hofmeister and appears in the *Scriptores Rerum Germanicarum in usum scholarum* (Hanover and Leipzig, 1912.) It has been translated into English with notes and introduction by C. C. Mierow as *The Two Cities: A Chron-*

icle of Universal History to the Year 1146 A.D. by Otto, Bishop of Freising (New York, 1928). Mierow calls attention to Otto's difficulties with Orosius (171n–73n).

5. J. Sandys, *History of Classical Scholarship*, vol. 2 (Cambridge, 1908), 20.

6. On the discovery of the Greek world during the Italian Renaissance, see R. Weiss, *The Renaissance Discovery of Classical Antiquity*, 2d ed. (Oxford, 1988), 131–44.

7. *De Institutione Reipublicae Libri IX, ad Senatum Populumque Senensem Scripti* (ca. 1460) and *De Regno et Regis Institutione Libri IX, ad Alphonsum Aragonium inclytum ac celeberrimum Calabriae Ducem Scripti* (ca. 1485): reprinted together in 1608.

8. *De Institutione* 62, 369.

9. Ibid., 43.

10. Ibid., 268.

11. *De Regno*, 306–7.

12. Ibid., 17–18, 430.

13. These rallying cries of antiquity are examined in such works as M. Pohlenz, *Griechische Freiheit* (Heidelberg, 1955); E. Bickerman, "Autonomia," *Revue Internationale des Droits de l'Antiquité* 5 (1958): 313–44; C. Wirszubski, *Libertas as a Political Idea at Rome during the Late Republic and Early Principate* (Cambridge, 1960); J. Bleicken, *Staatliche Ordnung und Freiheit in der Römischen Republik* (Kallmünz, 1972); M. Ostwald, *Autonomia: Its Genesis and Early History*, (Chico, Calif., 1983); and K. Raaflaub, *Die Entdeckung der Freiheit* (Munich, 1985). On the use of *libertas* by Bruni and Salutati, see R. G. Witt, *Coluccio Salutati and the Public Letters* (Geneva, 1976).

14. Elizabeth Rawson (*The Spartan Tradition in European Thought* [Oxford, 1969]) sees medieval chronicles as unwittingly paving the way for this parallel by crediting Athens alone with the victory over the Persians, but she cites no sources.

15. From the *Responsiva*, reprinted in D. Moreni's edition of the *Invectiva Lini Colucci Salutati in Antonium Luschum Vicentinum* (Florence, 1826), 246–47.

16. Editions of the *Laudatio* appear in *Studi medievali*, 3d ser., 8 (1967): 529–54; and H. Baron, *From Petrarch to Leonardo Bruni* (Chicago, 1968), 217–65. An English translation can be found in *The Earthly Republic: Italian Humanists on Government and Society*, ed. B. Kohl, R. Witt, and E. Welles (Philadelphia, 1978), 135–75. Bruni's use of Aristides is discussed at length by Baron in *The Crisis of the Early Italian Renaissance* (Princeton, 1955), chap. 9. A good bibliographical background to the *Laudatio* has been assembled by Witt in *The Earthly Republic*, 121–33.

17. Reprinted in E. Baluze and G. Manzi, *Miscellanea novo ordine digesta et . . . aucta* (Lucca, 1761–64), 4.2–7.

18. *Il Paradiso degli Alberti*, ed. A. Lanza (Rome, 1975), esp. 43–44.

19. The essay of Alamanno Rinuccini is translated by Reneé Neu Watkins in her anthology *Humanism and Liberty: Writings on Freedom from Fifteenth-Century Florence* (Columbia, S.C., 1979), 186–224. Corsi's depiction of Florence as "Athenae alterae" appears in the dedication to his life of Ficino, reprinted in P. Villani, *Liber de Civitatis Famosis Civibus ex codice mediceo laurentiano nunc primum editus et fr Florentinorum litteratura principes fere Synchroni scriptores*, ed. Gustavus Galletti (Florence, 1847), 189.

20. See, e.g., Baron, *Humanistic and Political Literature in Florence and Venice* (Cambridge, Mass., 1955), 5; Robert Lopez, *The Three Ages of the Italian Renaissance* (Charlottesville, 1970), 72; James Cleugh, *The Medici: A Tale of Fifteen Generations* (Garden City, N.J., 1975), 1.

21. Reprinted in Florence, 1529.

22. N. Machiavelli, *Discorsi sopra la prima deca di Tito Livio*, cited in the edition of S. Bertelli, *Il Principe e Discorsi* (Milan, 1960), 3.6. Machiavelli also imagines (*Discorsi* 3.31) that the Persian king with whom Themistocles sought refuge was Darius rather than Artaxerxes.

Long passages from Machiavelli's *Discorsi* cited in English are from the translation of Luigi Ricci, revised by E.R.P. Vincent, in *The Prince and the Discourses* (New York, 1950), with the exception of the epigram to this chapter, which is translated by Allan Gilbert in *Machiavelli: The Chief Works and Others* (Durham, 1965).

The literature on Machiavelli is vast. In addition to the works cited below, I have drawn particular profit from J.G.A. Pocock's *The Machiavellian Moment: Florentine Political Thought and the Atlantic Republican Tradition* (Princeton, 1975). The *Discorsi* are discussed there on pp. 183–218, but see also the discussion of *Il Principe*, 156–82.

23. Did Machiavelli know Greek? The answer is uncertain and hangs in part on the availability in Latin of book 6 of Polybius and of Plutarch's *Praecepta regendae reipublicae*.

24. *Discorsi* 1.2; Ricci, 110. Machiavelli also mentions the alleged eight-century duration of Lycurgus's unchanged system earlier in this same chapter (129–30).

25. *Discorsi* 1.2; Ricci, 115.

26. Incisive remarks concerning this ambivalence appear throughout Mark Hulliung's *Citizen Machiavelli* (Princeton, 1983) (see n. 33) and in Philip Ralph, *The Renaissance in Perspective* (New York, 1973), 57–58.

27. *Discorsi* 2.2; Ricci, 282, and *Discorsi* 1.58; Ricci, 264.

28. *Discorsi*, 2.59; Ricci, 268.

29. *Discorsi*, 2.53; Ricci, 249–50.

30. *Discorsi*, 1.2; Ricci, 115.

31. *The Machiavellian Moment*, 54, 53.

32. For all his iconoclasm, Machiavelli in reality embodied in many ways what Pocock identifies as the late medieval and Renaissance tendency to find the particular "less intelligible and less rational than the universal" (*The Machiavellian Moment*, 4).

33. Mark Hulliung, *Citizen Machiavelli*, 47–48.

34. Praise of Pericles appears, for example, in the *Discorso di Logrogno* (in the *Opere Inedite*, ed. P. and L. Guicciardini [Florence, 1958], the edition to which further citations to Guicciardini refer), 287; in the *Dialogo del Reggimento di Firenze*, 434; in the *Oratio Consolatoria*, 494; in the *Oratio Defensoria*, 576; and in the *Considerazioni sui Discorsi del Machiavelli*, 666.

35. *Dialogo del Reggimento di Firenze*, 402. On this work, see Pocock, *The Machiavellian Moment*, 219–71, and the more general discussion of Guicciardini, 114–55.

36. *Opere Inedite*, 258–59.

37. The evils of popular trials are discussed ibid., 621.

38. Ibid., 258–59.

39. Ibid., 295, 625, 443.

40. Giannotti's remarks appear in his *Discorso intorno alla Forma della Repubblica di Firenze* in his *Opere Politiche e Letterarie*, ed. F.-L. Polidori (Florence, 1850), 1.137–38.

41. In the *Opere* 1.200.

42. Reprinted ibid., vol. 2.

43. Zera Fink, *The Classical Republicans: An Essay in the Recovery of a Pattern of Thought in Seventeenth-Century England* (Evanston, 1945), 33.

44. On the truly astonishing proportions that the myth of Venice attained in the Renaissance, see, for example, the chapter "The Most Serene Republic" in Fink, *Classical Republicans*; "Venice and the Political Education of Europe," in William Bouwsma's *Venice and the Defense of Republican Liberty* (Berkeley and Los Angeles, 1968); Oliver Logan, "The Mythology of Venice," in *Culture and Society in Venice, 1470–1790: The Renaissance and Its Heritage* (New York, 1972); Myron Gilmore, "Myth and Reality in Venetian Political Theory," in J. R. Hale, ed., *Venice* (Totowa, N.J., 1973); and Pocock, *The Machiavellian Moment*, 272–330.

45. Gasparo Contarini, *De Republica Venetorum libri V* (1543); Trajano Boccalini, *Ragguagli di Parnaso* and *Pietra del paragone Politico*, both published in 1613 when Boccalini was dead and translated into English in 1626 as *The new-found politicke, wherein the governments, greatnesse and power of the most notable kingdomes and common-wealths of the world are discovered and censured.*

46. The treatise *Della perfettione della Vita Politica Libri Tre, Ne' quali si ragiona delle virtù Morali, e di tutto ciò, che s'apartiene alla Felicità civile* was published in 1579; the *Discorsi Politici*, in 1599.

47. I cite from the Venice, 1586, edition of the *Perfettione* and from the Venice, 1629, edition of the *Discorsi*. References to the virtues of Sparta: *Perfettione*, 439, *Discorsi*, 13, 25, 156, 209.

48. *Discorsi*, 439.

49. Ibid., 19.

50. Ibid., 26.

51. *Perfettione*, 70; *Discorsi*, 211, 229.

52. *Discorsi*, 118–20.

53. *Trattato*, 74.

54. Cited in Lauro Martines, *Power and Imagination: City States in Renaissance Italy* (New York, 1980), 195. On humanists and history, see the observations of Paul Kristeller in *Renaissance Thought II: Papers on Humanism and the Arts* (New York, 1965), especially pp. 27 and 65.

55. On Machiavelli's classical sources, see Leslie J. Walker, S.J., *The Discourses of Niccolò Machiavelli* (New Haven, 1950; new ed., London, 1975). Vital information concerning the availability and use of historical texts is gathered in Peter Burke, "A Survey of the Popularity of Ancient Historians, 1450–1700," *History and Theory* 5 (1966): 135–52; on Plutarch in particular, see Burke, 142–43, and R. Hirzel, *Plutarch* (Leipzig, 1912).

56. Philip Ralph, *The Renaissance in Perspective*, 57.

57. Benedetto Croce comments on "the difficulty that philologists and critics [during the Renaissance] experienced in persuading themselves that the Greek and Roman writers had perhaps been able to deceive themselves, to lie, to falsify, to be led astray by passions and blinded by ignorance, in the same way as those of the Middle Ages" (*History: Its Theory and Practice* [1915], trans. D. Ainslee [New York, 1960], 227).

58. *Opere*, vol. 1, 17.

59. Figures are cited in Martines, *Power and Imagination*, 148; see also F. Gilbert, *Machiavelli and Guicciardini* (Princeton, 1965), 20.

60. Fink, *The Classical Republicans*, 12. I wonder whether it is to this calculated oversimplification as well that we should trace not only Machiavelli's failure to con-

sider the helots—which may be interpreted more simply as an attempt to give the Spartans a better press—but also his repeated contention in the *Discorsi* that the Spartans had only one king, than which he had every reason to know better.

61. Instructive illustrations of the Renaissance reduction of history to anecdote are collected and analyzed in Paul Grendler, "Francesco Sansovino and Italian Popular History, 1560–1600," *Studies in the Renaissance* 16 (1969): 139–80.

62. Felix Gilbert, "The Renaissance Interest in History," in C. Singleton, *Art, Science, and History in the Renaissance* (Baltimore, 1967), 373; Paul Grendler, "Francesco Sansovino," 176.

63. L. *Bruni Epistolarum libri VIII*, e.g., 1.5, 2.1.

64. C. C. Bayley, *War and Society in Renaissance Florence* (Toronto, 1961), 396.

65. The passage is cited in translation by E. Emerton in *Humanism and Tyranny* (Cambridge, Mass., 1925), 47. The comparative indifference of many of Bruni's contemporaries to the fine points of Hellenic history may perhaps be indexed by Matteo Palmieri's reference to Epaminondas—the Lacedaemonian! (*Della Vita Civile* [1st extant ed., Florence, 1529], 46). But none of these lapses should blind us to the significant improvement in the understanding of Hellenic civilization ushered in by the discovery of the Greek language—and by the translation of Greek texts into Latin: the lapses of fifteenth- and sixteenth-century scholars do not on the whole compare to the fourteenth. Witness, for example, the opening of Salutati's essay *De Tyranno*, in which the word is derived from the Greek *tyros*, meaning brave, and, according to Salutati, was used by the early Greeks and Italians to signify their kings, coming to have a pejorative connotation only as kings came to rule oppressively (cited by Emerson, 74–75).

66. Eric Cochrane, *Historians and Historiography in the Italian Renaissance* (Chicago, 1981), 7.

67. *Historiarum florentini populi libri xii* (reprint, Florence, 1855–1860), 3.8.

68. *De Regno*, 96.

CHAPTER SEVEN

1. The origins of classical studies in Britain are traced in M. Creighton, *The Early Renaissance in England* (Cambridge, 1895), and in Sandys's *History of Classical Scholarship* 2.219–50.

2. *The Governor* 1.10 (p. 28 in S. E. Lehmberg's modernized Everyman edition) (London and New York, 1962).

3. Ibid., 1.2 (Everyman ed., 6).

4. Ibid., (Everyman ed., 10).

5. Ibid., 1.14 (Everyman ed., 56).

6. *De Republica Anglorum* 1.3. I cite the tract in the 1970 Scolar Press facsimile reprint (Menston, England) of the first published edition of 1583.

7. Ibid., 1.4.

8. On the perceived value of Greek studies in sixteenth-century England, see Sandys, *History* 2.230, 235. Elizabeth, Ascham reports, never missed a day in her Greek studies, working on Demosthenes and Isocrates and using Ascham's method of daily translation.

9. Starnes maintains that what Floyd did not garner from Elyot was pirated from Nicholas Ling's *Politeuphuia, Wits Commonwealth* (1597) ("The Picture of a Perfit

Common Wealth" [1600]: Studies in English, no. 11, *University of Texas Bulletin* 3133 [1 September 1931]: 32–41).

10. Floyd, 15.

11. Ibid., 19.

12. Ibid., 83–84 and 120. Floyd may be confusing Solon's voluntary travel with the involuntary travel of exile and ostracism; see chap. 5, p. 106, here, on Valerius Maximus's description of Solon as dying in Cyprus *profugus*. He makes a more conspicuous error at p. 292 where he cites Plutarch as maintaining that Antiphon, when asked by Dionysius the tyrant what the best kind of copper was, replied that "in his opinion that was the most excellent, whereof the Athenians had made the pictures of the two tyraunts, Armodius and Aristogiton." The reference is to the life of Antiphon in the *Lives of the Ten Orators* (probably not by Plutarch), 833B, where of course Harmodius and Aristogiton are not called tyrants. Perhaps "tyraunts" replaced "tyrannicides" at the hands of a distracted copyist.

13. I cite the *Methodus* in the translation of Beatrice Reynolds, *Method for the Easy Comprehension of History* (New York, 1945). All page references are to the Reynolds translation. On the political thought of Bodin in its context, see J. H. Franklin, *Jean Bodin and the Rise of Absolutist Theory* (Cambridge, 1973); and N. Keohane, *Philosophy and the State in France: The Renaissance to the Enlightenment* (Princeton, 1980) (with comprehensive bibliography).

14. *Method*, 267.

15. Ibid.

16. Ibid., 187. Bodin's independence of mind, it should be noted, did not prevent him from falling from time to time into errors of a factual nature. Confusing the historian Thucydides, son of Olorus, with the conservative politician Thucydides, son of Melesias, he was surprised to find the author of the history of the Peloponnesian War so charitable toward Pericles, who was responsible for his exile (ibid., 56; *Six Books*, 430. I cite the *Six Books* in K. D. McRae's 1962 facsimile edition of Richard Knolles's 1601 translation [Cambridge, Mass.]). More surprisingly, he writes that "Hipparchus and Hippias, the sons of Peisistratus, maintained their rule by force for seventy years, as Aristotle wrote, until one was killed. The other having died, popular power was first established by Solon" (*Method*, 237).

17. Ibid., 218.

18. Ibid., 218–19.

19. *Six Books*, 430.

20. *Method*, 248–49.

21. *Six Books*, 531–32.

22. Ibid., 530–31.

23. Ibid., 423.

24. Ibid., 424.

25. Ibid., 544; cf. "the seditious declamations of Ephialtis" (392).

26. *History*, 265. Page numbers for the *History* refer to the text that appears in vol. 5 of *The Works of Sir Walter Ralegh* (Oxford, 1829).

27. Ibid., 156, 185, 180.

28. Ibid., 178.

29. Ibid., 185, 188.

30. *Leviathan* 2, 21; similarly thirty years later in *Behemoth*.

31. "Of the Life and History of Thucydides," in *Hobbes' Thucydides*, ed. and with an intro. by Richard Schlatter (New Brunswick, 1975), 13.

32. In his edition of *Patriarca and Other Political Works* (Oxford, 1949).

33. In *Directions for Obedience to Government in Dangerous or Doubtful Times*, in Laslett, *Patriarca*, 231.

34. *The Machiavellian Moment*, 54.

35. *Patriarca*, 86. The intensity of Filmer's opposition to popular participation in government is attested by his insistence that the Romans should not have expelled Tarquin the Proud for his son's rape of the matron Lucretia: "To say truth," Filmer writes of this famous turning point in Roman history, "we find no other cause of the expulsion of Tarquin, than the wantonness and licentiousness of the people of Rome" (*Observations Touching Forms of Government*, in Laslett, *Patriarca*, 210).

36. In *The Art of Lawgiving*, in *The Political Works of James Harrington*, ed. J.G.A. Pocock (Cambridge, 1977), 676. Pocock also discusses Harrington and *Oceana* in *The Machiavellian Moment: Florentine Political Thought and the Atlantic Republican Tradition* (Princeton, 1975), 383–400.

37. *Oceana* (in *Political Works*), 343.

38. Ibid., 257, 259.

39. Ibid., 268.

40. Ibid., 324.

41. *Excellencie*, 38. I cite from the London, 1767, edition. On Nedham, see J. Frank, *The Beginnings of the English Newspaper* (Cambridge, Mass., 1961); and Pocock, *The Machiavellian Moment*, 381–83.

42. *Excellencie*, 55, 50.

43. See for example ibid., 72, 80–81; 132–33.

44. Ibid., 80.

45. Ibid., 23.

46. Ibid., 40.

47. Algernon Sidney, *Discourses* (reprint, New York, 1805) 2.311–12.

48. Ibid., 2.155.

49. Ibid.

50. Ibid., 2.158.

51. Ibid., 3. 289, 319, 357.

52. *Paradise Regained* 4.268–69. Milton also prefaced to the *Areopagitica* his own rendition of lines 436–41 of Euripides' *Suppliants* (Theseus's paean to Athenian political principles; see above pp. 38–39). Unquestionably inspired by classical republicanism in its most generic form, Milton seems not to have thought very hard about what Athens in particular had or had not achieved; on his involvement with classical republicanism in general, see Z. Fink, *The Classical Republicans: An Essay in the Recovery of a Pattern of Thought in Seventeenth-Century England* (Evanston, 1945).

53. Swift's essay appears in Jonathan Swift, *A Discourse of the Contests and Dissentions between the Nobles and the Commons in Athens and Rome with the Consequences They Had upon Both Those States*, ed. Frank H. Ellis (Oxford, 1967), along with elaborate background material and the other contemporary works discussed in the following material.

54. W. Scott, *The Works of Jonathan Swift* (1883): 3.196; Ellis, 135.

55. Ellis, 97.

56. Ibid.,125. So far from suggesting that Britons are likely to do a better job of popular government than the Athenians, he concedes, while granting the Athenians grudging praise for their recall of Aristides during the invasion of Xerxes, that "it must be still confessed on behalf of the Athenian People, that they never conceived themselves perfectly infallible, nor arrived to the Heights of modern Assemblies, to make Obstinacy confirm what sudden heat and temerity began" (ibid., 94).

57. The pertinent portions of Drake's *History of the Last Parliament* (1702) are reprinted in Ellis.

58. Ellis, 216.

59. Ibid., 218–19.

60. Ibid., 220.

61. Also reprinted ibid.

62. Ibid., 229, 231.

63. Ibid., 244.

64. Ibid., 234–35.

65. On opposition to Walpole in the British press see C. B. Realey, *The London Journal and Its Authors 1720–1723*, Bulletin of the University of Kansas, Humanistic Studies 5.3 (Lawrence, 1935); W. Laprade, *Public Opinion and Politics in Eighteenth-Century England to the Fall of Walpole* (New York, 1936); L. Hanson, *Government and the Press, 1695–1763* (Oxford, 1936); C. Robbins, *The Eighteenth-Century Commonwealthman: Studies in the Transmission, Development, and Circumstance of English Liberal Thought from the Restoration of Charles II until the War with the Thirteen Colonies* (Cambridge, Mass., 1959); and the introduction to D. L. Jacobson, ed., *The English Libertarian Heritage from the Writings of John Trenchard and Thomas Gordon in "The Independent Whig" and "Cato's Letters"* (Indianapolis, New York, and Kansas City, 1965).

66. On Trenchard and Gordon, see, in addition to the references cited in n. 65, the entry s.v. Trenchard in the *Dictionary of National Biography*. I have cited *Cato's Letters* in the London, 1755, edition (reprint, New York, 1969, 4 vols. in 2) *Cato's Letters; or, Essays on Liberty, Civil and Religious, and Other Important Subjects*.

67. *London Journal*, 3 December 1721.

68. *Cato's Letters* 4.63; cf. 3.317 and 4. 117. The letters are discussed in Pocock, *The Machiavellian Moment*, 467–77.

69. *Cato's Letters* 4.104–17.

70. Ibid., 4.104.

71. Ibid., 4.105.

72. Ibid., 4.109.

73. Ibid., 4.112.

74. Ibid., 4.113–14; similarly at 1.72.

75. Ibid., preface, 1.xxvi–xxvii.

76. Swift, in *The Examiner* (3 November–30 November 1710), in *The Prose Works of Jonathan Swift, D.D.* (London, 1902), 9.101–2.

77. Cited in C. R. Realey's University of Pennsylvania thesis "The Early Opposition to Sir Robert Walpole, 1720–1727" (Philadelphia, 1931), 200.

78. *Craftsman* (17 February 1727): 21–22.

79. Ibid., no. 201, (9 May 1730): 21; cf. vol. 221 (16 September 1730): 41.

80. Ibid., no. 216, (22 August 1730): 279–83.

81. Ibid., nos. 325 and 326 (23 and 30 September 1732): 242–52.

82. Roman history could also be very useful in British politics: see Frank Turner's "British Politics and the Demise of the Roman Republic 1700–1939," *Historical Journal* 29 (1986): 577–99.

CHAPTER EIGHT

1. An engaging collection of passages illustrating the spectrum of views about the value of the classics in eighteenth-century Britain appears in P. Crutwell, "The Eighteenth Century: A Classical Age?" *Arion* 7 (1968): 110–32; a detailed study of vacillating French attitudes toward Athens and Sparta is offered in L. Guerci, *Libertà degli antichi e libertà dei moderni: Sparta, Atene e i "philosophes" nella Francia del Settecento* (Naples, 1979).

2. In *Studies in Historiography* (New York, 1966), 28–30.

3. Cited from the preface to vol. 2 of *The Grecian History* (1739 ed.).

4. On Plutarch in the eighteenth century, see M. W. Howard, *The Influence of Plutarch in the Major European Literatures of the Eighteenth Century* (Chapel Hill, 1970).

5. On the debate over decadence in France as it affected perceptions of Greek antiquity see Guerci, *Libertà degli antichi*, 167–92.

6. Stanyan, *Grecian History* 1.180.

7. Goldsmith, *The Grecian History from the Earliest State, to the Death of Alexander the Great*, cited from the 13th ed. (London, 1820), 1.54.

8. Tucker, *A Treatise Concerning Civil Government* (reprint, New York, 1967), 222.

9. Goldsmith, 1.193; Stanyan, 1.328. An English translation of Tourreil's *Several Orations of Demosthenes* appeared in 1702.

10. Hume, "Essay X, Of Some Remarkable Customs," in *Essays, Moral, Political, and Literary* (1742): 498.

11. Mably, *Observations sur l'Histoire de la Grèce*, 72–89. On Mably see n. 30.

12. Condillac, *Histoire Ancienne*, reprinted in *Oeuvres Complètes de Condillac*, vol. 7 (Paris, 1821), 190–91. On Condillac's views of classical Greek states see Guerci, *Libertà degli antichi*, 205–12.

13. In the *Last Reply* to the critics of his *First Discourse*, translated in V. Gourevitch, ed., J.-J. Rousseau, *The First and Second Discourses Together with the Replies to Critics and Essay on the Origin of Languages* (New York, 1986), 78, par. 46.

Of the enormous literature on Rousseau, works most pertinent to Rousseau's orientation to Greece include J. N. Shklar, *Men and Citizens: A Study of Rousseau's Social Theory* (Cambridge, 1969); R. Masters, *The Political Philosophy of Rousseau* (Princeton, 1968); D. Leduc-Fayette, *J. J. Rousseau et le mythe de l'antiquité* (Paris, 1974); L. Lehmann, *Mably und Rousseau: Eine Studie über die Grenzen der Emanzipation im Ancien Regime* (Frankfurt, 1975); S. Ellenburg, *Rousseau's Political Philosophy: An Interpretation from Within* (Ithaca, 1976); R. A. Leigh, "Jean-Jacques Rousseau and the Myth of Antiquity in the Eighteenth Century," in R. R. Bolgar, ed., *Classical Influences on Western Thought A.D. 1650–1870* (Cambridge, 1979), 155–68; and J. Miller, *Rousseau: Dreamer of Democracy* (New Haven, 1984).

14. Stanyan 1.136.

15. Rollin, *The Ancient History*, cited in the English translation of 1861, 1.366; Goldsmith, 1.187.

16. Goldsmith 1.224; Stanyan 1.379.

17. Hearne, 320.

18. Ibid.; Rollin, 2.410.

19. *Observations*, 88.

20. Stanyan 2.226; Rollin 1.586.

21. Rollin, ibid.

22. Ibid., 1.587; Stanyan 2.204; Goldsmith 1.410.

23. Rousseau, in his *Letter to Grimm* responding to Gautier's refutation of his *First Discourse* in Gourevitch, 82, par. 57.

24. Stanyan 1.69.

25. Goldsmith 1.168.

26. Condillac, 212. Condillac seems to lean at times to the English republican view of a decent Athens oppressed by a self-seeking Pericles. The more one admired Periclean Athens, Condillac maintained, the more one praised Pericles. Consequently, as the Athenians were more eloquent and articulate than other peoples, Pericles' name had passed on to posterity along with the praises his fellow citizens had bestowed on him, "and the historians, who have reiterated these praises, have not examined whether he merited them." One would understand eras such as those of Pericles better "if the noise made by those who celebrate them allowed the moans of the people to be heard."

27. Montagu, cited from the 3d ed. of 1769, 8.

28. Ibid., 12.

29. Ibid., 132–33, 144.

30. A good treatment of Mably's political ideals and their relationship to his views of classical states appears in T. Schleich, "Mably e le Antiche Costituzioni," *QS* 23 (1986): 173–97.

On Mably's life and work see E. Whitfield, *Gabriel Bonnot de Mably* (1930, reprint, New York, 1969); Aldo Maffey, *Il pensiero politico del Mably* (Torino, 1968); Brigitte Coste, *Mably: pour une utopie du bon sens* (Paris, 1975); L. Guerci, *Libertà degli antichi*, 105–39; and a variety of articles cited on p. 391 of P. Vidal-Naquet, *La démocratie grecque vue d'ailleurs* (Paris, 1990).

31. Mably, *Observations*, 127.

32. Ibid., 128.

33. Rousseau, *Restoration of the Sciences and Arts*, in Gourevitch, 8, par. 18.

34. Ibid., 10, par. 24.

35. Ibid.

36. Rousseau, *Epistle Dedicatory to Inequality*, in Gourevitch, 121–22, par. 9.

37. Ibid., 122, par. 10.

38. Mably, *Entretiens de Phocion*, cited from the 1804 edition, 236.

39. Ibid., 133.

40. Ibid., 12, 13, 76, 168.

41. Ibid., 167–68, 77.

42. Ibid., 94, 167–68, 72–73, 12–13, 186.

43. Ibid., 94.

44. Ibid., 72.

45. Ibid., 125.

46. Ibid., 120.

47. Ibid., 119.

48. Ibid., 122.

49. Ferguson, *An Essay on the History of Civil Society* (Edinburgh, 1767), 286.

50. Rousseau, *Last Reply* to the critics of his *First Discourse*, in Gourevitch, 76, par. 41.

51. Ibid., 78, par. 46.

52. *Valerius Maximus* 2.6.

53. From *Oceana*, in J.G.A. Pocock, ed., *The Political Works of John Harrington* (Cambridge, 1977), 259.

54. *Defensio Secunda* (1654), in *Works* (New York, 1931–38), 8.49.

55. Cited from his *Essay on the Roman, and on the Lacedaemonian, Governments* (without page reference) in Rawson, *The Spartan Tradition in European Thought* (Oxford, 1969), 201.

56. *Dialogues des morts*, vii, xvii.

57. J. J. Burlamaqui, *Principes du droit politique* 2.2.24–36, available in the English translation of Thomas Nugent (Cambridge, 1807).

58. The influence of Montesquieu outside France was enormous. See, for example, on England L. Landi, *L'Inghilterra e il pensiero politico di Montesquieu* (Padua, 1981); and on America P. Spurlin, *Montesquieu in America* (University, La., 1940), and S. Wolin, "Montesquieu and Publius: The Crisis of Reason and *The Federalist Papers*," in Wolin's *The Presence of the Past: Essays on the State and the Constitution* (Baltimore and London, 1989), 100–119.

59. Cited from the London 1774 translation of *An Essay on Public Happiness* (reprint, New York, 1969), 1.xviii. Chastellux's orientation to classical Greek states is discussed in Guerci, *Libertà degli antichi*, 205–12.

60. *On Public Happiness* 1.69.

61. Ibid., 1.73.

62. Ibid., 1.75.

63. Goguet, cited from the English translation published at Edinburgh in 1761, *The Origin of Laws, Arts, and Sciences and Their Progress among the most Ancient Nations*, vol. 3: *From the Establishment of Monarchy among the Israelites, to Their Return from the Babylonish Captivity*, 222–23.

64. *Dictionnaire*, 291–92. Voltaire's notes to Chastellux's essay on public happiness express frequent frustration with his rejection of Athens (Guerci, *Libertà degli Antichi*, 214–15).

65. Chastellux, 1.66.

66. Ibid., 1.76.

67. Ibid., 1.77.

68. Ibid., 1.93.

69. Ibid.

70. Goguet 3.37.

71. Ibid., 3.36.

72. Ibid., 3.180.

73. Ibid., 3.38, 180.

74. Ibid., 3.231.

75. Ibid., 3.224.

76. The *Encyclopédie* was reprinted in Stuttgart in 1966.

77. Cited from the translation of Nelly S. Hoyt and Thomas Cassirer in *Encyclopedia: Selections* (Indianapolis, 1965), 161.

78. Ibid., 160.

79. On *Le Mondain*, the *Défense du Mondain* and Voltaire's treatment of antiquity in the context of the debate over "le luxe," see A. Morize, *L'apologie du luxe au dix-huitième siècle et "Le Mondain" de Voltaire: étude critique sur "Le Mondain" et ses sources* (1909; reprint, Geneva, 1980); and Ellen Ross, "Mandeville, Melon, and Voltaire: the Origins of the Luxury Controversy in France," in Theodore Besterman, ed., *Studies on Voltaire and the Eighteenth Century*, vol. 155 (Oxford, 1976), 1897–1912.

80. *Philosophical Dictionary*, in *The Works of Voltaire: A Contemporary Version* (Paris, London, New York, and Chicago, 1901), 8.75–83.

On Voltaire and Greek government see Michele Mat-Hasquin, *Voltaire et L'Antiquité Grecque*, *Studies on Voltaire*, vol. 197 (Oxford, 1981), 237–46; and Guerci, *Libertà degli Antichi*, 212–20.

81. Twentieth-century thinkers are less generous toward what George Steiner has termed a "pedagogic fantasy" that was "one of the major works in the history of European taste" (in *Antigones* [New York and Oxford, 1984], 7).

82. Cited in the English translation of 1794, 4.483. On *Anacharsis* in its context, see Maurice Badolle, *L'Abbé Jean-Jacques Barthélemy (1716–1795) et l'Hellenisme en France dans la Seconde Moitié du XVIIIe Siècle* (Paris, 1927).

83. *Anacharsis* 4.479.

84. Ibid., 1.184; 2.253, 258, 263; 1.436–37, 443.

85. On De Pauw, see Michaud, *Biographie universelle*, 2d ed., vol. 32 (Paris, 1861), 321–22. Largely ignored by modern scholars, his important work is discussed in Guerci, *Libertà degli antichi*, 263–72.

86. *Philosophical Researches* 1.xv; 2.36, 169–70, 192.

87. Ibid., 2.169–70. At heart a *patrios politeia* man, Montesquieu throughout his work evinced enthusiasm for a certain generic republicanism along with revulsion from a system that allowed the poor to hold office. On Montesquieu and Athens, see Mossé, *L'Antiquité dans la Révolution française* (Paris, 1989), 55–61.

88. *Philosophical Researches*, 2.167.

89. Ibid., 1.iv, xv.

90. Ibid., 2.3, 165.

91. Ibid., 2.3, 12–13.

92. Ibid., 2.162.

93. Ibid., 2.141–46.

94. Ibid., 2.179.

95. Ibid., 2.141–46.

96. From the *Correspondence*, cited with bibliography on Voltaire and the masses in Mat-Hasquin, *Voltaire et l'Antiquité Grecque*, 242; see also Guerci, *Libertà degli Antichi*, 216–20.

CHAPTER NINE

1. The study of the founding fathers' attitudes toward classical civilization would be far more arduous than it is were it not for the labors of numerous painstaking scholars working during the second half of the twentieth century. The most useful book for classicists is Meyer Reinhold's *Classica Americana: The Greek and Roman Heritage in the United States* (Detroit, 1984). Valuable studies also appear in Richard Gummere, *The American Colonial Mind and the Classical Tradition: Essays in Comparative Culture* (Cam-

bridge, Mass., 1963); Trevor Colbourn, *The Lamp of Experience: Whig History and the Origins of the American Revolution* (Chapel Hill, N.C., 1965); and Paul Rahe, *Republics Ancient and Modern: Classical Republicanism and the American Tradition* (Chapel Hill, N.C., 1992). I have also profited a great deal from Richard Johnson's essay "Hellas and Hesperia: Ancient Greece and Early America," in Carol Thomas, ed., *Paths from Ancient Greece* (Leiden, 1988), 140–67. On the question of the founders' relationship to classical history and politics specifically, see Charles F. Mullett, "Ancient Historians and 'Enlightened' Reviewers," *Review of Politics* 21 (1959): 550–65; Richard Gummere, "The Classical Ancestry of the United States Constitution," *American Quarterly* 14 (1962): 3–18; William Gribbin, "Rollin's Histories and American Republicanism," *William and Mary Quarterly*, 3d ser., 29 (1972): 611–22; and Edwin A. Miles, "The Young American Nation and the Classical World," *Journal of the History of Ideas* 35 (1974): 259–74. Much valuable insight is also to be gleaned from the introductory material in Bernard Bailyn's *Pamphlets of the American Revolution 1750–1776* (Cambridge, Mass., 1965.) Useful collections of primary sources in addition to Bailyn's *Pamphlets* include H. Niles, *Principles and Acts of the Revolution in America* (reprint, New York, Chicago, and New Orleans, 1876); M. Farrand, ed., *The Records of the Federal Convention of 1787* (New Haven and London, 1937); and C. Hyneman and D. Lutz, eds., *American Political Writing during the Founding Era* (Indianapolis, 1983). More general background concerning the intellectual heritage of the revolutionary period can be found in Bailyn's *Intellectual Origins of the American Revolution* (Cambridge, Mass., 1967); in F. MacDonald, *Novus Ordo Seclorum: The Intellectual Origins of the Constitution* (Lawrence, Kans., 1985); and in T. Pangle, *The Spirit of Modern Republicanism: The Moral Vision of the American Founders and the Philosophy of Locke* (Chicago and London, 1988).

This chapter also owes much to Angelo and Sofia Tsakopoulos, who generously funded a conference on the Greek heritage of the American constitution in 1987, and to the organizer of the conference, Theodore Brunner.

2. *Classica Americana*, 24.

3. Originally 1693, cited from *The Fruits of Solitude and Other Writings* (London, 1915), 28.

4. Both cited by Reinhold in *Classica Americana*, 157–58. It is interesting to note, however, that as Richard Johnson has pointed out ("Hellas in Hesperia," 150), colonial American enthusiasts of antiquity did not, like their European counterparts, deploy the classics and their pagan associations in any broad campaign against the church and never sought to enthrone classicism as "an alternative to Christian belief."

5. In a letter to John Adams cited in R. Johnson, "Hellas and Hesperia," 160.

6. Cited by Gummere, *The American Colonial Mind*, 128. Despite his periodic dismissal of ancient history, Franklin's investment in craftsmanship owed much to the ideals of fifth-century Athens, which he recognized were not separable from the democratic system. I very much hope that the late Michael Shute's manuscript exploring these connections in Franklin's thought will be published posthumously.

7. Murray, *Political Sketches* (London, 1787), also published in *American Museum* 2 (September, 1787): 228–35; "Agrippa," in two different letters, one of 23 November 1787 and another of 14 January 1788, reprinted in H. Storing, ed., *The Complete Anti-Federalist* (Chicago, 1981), 4.6.6 and 4.6.49.

8. Cited in Rahe, *Republics Ancient and Modern*, 568, and 1047, n. 96.

9. "Proposals Relating to the Education of Youth in Pennsylvania," in Thomas Woody, *The Educational Views of Benjamin Franklin* (New York, 1931), 167.

10. Cited by Reinhold in *Classica Americana*, 156, 41.

11. Farrand, *Records* 1.74.

12. Ibid., 1.135.

13. Ibid., 1.310.

14. Ibid., 1.448.

15. Ibid., 1.456.

16. Ibid., 1.459. As the summer wore on, Mason adduced the "dangerous insurrections of the slaves in Greece and Sicily" as proof of the inherent perils in the slave system, while Charles Pinckney maintained that "if slavery be wrong, it is justified by the example of all the world," and he cited the cases of Greece, Rome, and other ancient states as well as "the sanction given by France, England, Holland & other modern States" (ibid., 2.370–71. These remarks are preserved in the notes of Madison). Gouverneur Morris on 15 August argued for a veto power in the executive as one way of guarding against "encroachments of the popular branch of the Government" such as that of the ephors at Sparta, who became "in the end absolute" (ibid., 2.299).

17. Cited by Harry S. Good in *Benjamin Rush and His Services to American Education* (Berne, Ind., 1918), 236.

18. Reprinted in Hamilton's *Papers*, ed. H. Syrett, vol. 3 (New York, 1962), 103.

19. *A discourse delivered to the Religious Society in Brattle Street, Boston*, 2d ed. (Boston, 1798), 18–19.

20. Welch, "Oration delivered at Boston, March 5, 1783," in Niles, *Principles and Acts*, 76; the anonymous New Hampshire pamphleteer, in Hyneman and Lutz, *American Political Writing*, 391; Maxcy, "An Oration," in Hyneman and Lutz, *American Political Writing*, 1047.

21. On the debate at the Continental Congress over the efficacy of the Amphictyonic League, see Gummere, *American Colonial Mind*, chap. 6, "Colonies Ancient and Modern," 97–119.

22. Smith, *A General Idea of the College of Mirania* (New York, 1753), cited by Reinhold in *Classica Americana*, 38; Adams in his *Diary and Autobiography*, ed. L. H. Butterfield (Cambridge, Mass., 1962), 2.58.

23. "Liberty Described and Recommended: in a Sermon Preached to the Corporation of Freemen in Farmington" (Hartford, 1775), in Hyneman and Lutz, *American Political Writing*, 307.

24. Hyneman and Lutz, *American Political Writing*, 21.

25. Ibid., 397.

26. In *The Rights of Man, Part II* (1792; reprint, London, 1915), 176.

27. Ibid., 177.

28. In *The Way of the Churches of Christ in New England* (London, 1645), cited by Richard Gummere in "Church, State and Classics: The Cotton-Williams Debate," *CJ* 54 (1959): 175–83.

29. "An Oration on the Anniversary of the Independence of the United States of America" (Worcester, 1802), in Hyneman and Lutz, *American Political Writing*, 1212.

30. From her *History of the Rise, Progress and Termination of the American Revolution* (1805), in H. Storing, *The Complete Anti-Federalist* 6.14.122 and 6.14.135.

31. *Federalist* 14, in *The Federalist Papers*, ed. C. Rossiter (New York and Scarborough, Ontario, 1961), 100.

32. Ibid., 342.

33. Ibid., 384.

34. In Syrett, ed., *Papers*, vol. 2 (New York, 1961), 657. In the *Continentalist* no. 1 of 1781 Hamilton compares the history of the Greek states (except Sparta)—a history that "no friend to order or to rational liberty can read without pain and disgust"—with the bright future of an America that had discovered such phenomena as checks and balances and popular representation.

35. Rossiter, *Federalist Papers*, 71.

36. John Dickinson in the fifth of his "Letters of Fabius" moved swiftly from antiquity to Florence in his excoriation of the "encroachments of the people" that destroy states (reprinted in P. L. Ford, ed., *Pamphlets on the Constitution of the United States Published during Its Discussion by the People 1787–1788* [1888], 190).

37. "The Natural and Civil History of Vermont" (Walpole, N.H., 1794), chap. 15, reprinted in Hyneman and Lutz, *American Political Writing*, 963.

38. C. F. Adams, ed., *The Works of John Adams, Second President of the United States* (Boston, 1850–56), 4.285.

39. Ibid., 5.9.

40. Charles Francis Adams later felt the need to emend his grandfather's works in the light of Grote's *History*; see chap. 11, p. 248.

41. *Works* 4.479.

42. Ibid., 4.480–85.

43. Ibid., 4.486; 6.101.

44. Ibid., 4.490.

45. Ibid., 6.9.

46. Ibid., 6.100.

47. Ibid., 6.102.

48. Ibid., 5.37.

49. To be sure, Adams censures Aristotle for the limitations he placed on the franchise, but his position seems to derive from a major misunderstanding of the sociology of ancient society and the assumption that Aristotle would exclude practically everyone (ibid., 4.526).

50. Cited in Gummere's chapter "The Classical Ancestry of the Constitution," in *The American Colonial Mind*, 176.

51. The holdings of colonial libraries are discussed in Colbourn, *The Lamp of Experience*, 199–232. Inevitably views of Athens were also colored for the Americans by recent works on ancient history such as Potter's *Antiquities* and Rollin's *Ancient History*. *Cato's Letters* appeared regularly in American libraries, though the discordant opinions voiced there about classical Athens went unremarked; the same is true of the *Craftsman*. On Rollin in early America see W. Gribbin, "Rollin's Histories and American Republicanism," 611–22; Montesquieu's influence in the United States is discussed in P. Spurlin, *Montesquieu in America* (University, La., 1940). Though in time Jefferson developed a revulsion for what he considered Montesquieu's elitism, on the whole the shapers of the constitution found his views eminently congenial.

52. 21 May 1782, in *Works* 7.593.

53. The 1786 letter appears in Jefferson's *Papers*, ed. J. Boyd (Princeton, 1950–), 10.305–9.

54. In J. Catanzariti and E. J. Ferguson, eds., *The Papers of Robert Morris* (Pittsburgh, 1973), 6.213.

55. For Philadelphiensis, see Storing, *The Complete Anti-Federalist* 3.9.76; other references can be collected from the excellent index. Significantly, some of the negative observations of the Athenians concern insufficient rather than excessive democracy; George Clinton of New York looked ahead to the strictures of George Grote (see chap. 11) in complaining not of the Athenians' excessive readiness to impeach their officials but rather of their "unbounded confidence in their statesmen and rulers," which he contended "caused the ruin of Athens" (2.6.48).

56. Reprinted in *Political Writings of Joel Barlow* (New York, 1971), 63–64, 27.

57. I owe much in these observations to the suggestions of Ellen Wood and J. Peter Euben, who read the manuscript for Princeton University Press.

58. In a letter to Dupont de Nemours written on 24 April.

59. In "Historical Judgments," cited from *Logic: The Theory of Inquiry*, in W. Dray, *On History and Philosophers of History* (Leiden, 1989), 177–78.

60. Hume, essay 10, "Of Some Remarkable Customs," in *Essays* (1742): 403, 498.

61. See n. 20. Some anti-Federalists questioned the validity of any such new "science"; cutting references appear to "axioms in the science of politics . . . as irrefragable as any in Euclid" in George Clinton's letters of "Cato" (Storing 2.6.13) and the "Maryland Farmer" cited at 5.1.21 who contended that "there is no *new* discovery in this most important of all sciences, for ten centuries back."

62. In *The Presence of the Past* (Baltimore, 1989), 72, 96–97.

63. In *Federalist* 10, for example.

64. In Rossiter, *Federalist Papers*, 57; see n. 31.

65. Federalist 10, in ibid., 84. A good discussion of Madison's critique of democratic government and his preference for republican institutions appears in M. White, *Philosophy, "The Federalist," and the Constitution* (New York and Oxford, 1987), 136–45.

66. Some of the issues involved in near vs. far history are explored in the section "Reason, Long Experience, and Short Experience," in White, *Philosophy*, 45–49.

Not everyone was comfortable generalizing about mobs and their vices; Robert Coram in his 1791 "Political Inquiries: to which is Added, a Plan for the General Establishment of Schools Throughout the United States" distinguished between European and American mobs, contending that in reality "the mob that burnt the tea at Boston, and even that under Shays, was a regular and orderly body, when compared with that of Lord George Gordon or any of the late mobs in France. We know of no such outrages committed in America" (reprinted in F. Rudolph, ed., *Essays on Education in the Early Republic* [Cambridge, Mass., 1975], 124–25).

67. J. S. McClelland, *The Crowd and the Mob: From Plato to Canetti* (London and Boston, 1989), 100.

68. On Adams and property see p. 183 here.

69. From "Leading Principles of the Federal Constitution, etc." in Ford *Pamphlets*, 57–58.

70. "An Essay on the Best System of Liberal Education, Adapted to the Genius of the Government of the United States," reprinted ibid., 304, 342.

71. To Harold Parker's learned study of classical antiquity in the French Revolution, *The Cult of Antiquity and the French Revolutionaries: A Study in the Development of the Revolutionary Spirit* (Chicago, 1937), should now be added Claude Mossé's lively book *L'Antiquité dans la Révolution française* (Paris, 1989). The chapter on the Revolution in Rawson, *The Spartan Tradition* is also extremely valuable, and Rawson is more

sensitive than Parker to the hostility of many of the revolutionaries to Sparta. See also F. Díaz-Plaja, *Griegos y Romanos en la revolución francesa* (Madrid, 1960); Pierre Vidal-Naquet, "Tradition de la Démocratie Grecque," published as the introduction to Monique Alexander's translation of M. I. Finley, *Démocratie antique et démocratie moderne* (Paris, 1976), 7–44, esp. 15–35; Nicole Loraux and Pierre Vidal-Naquet, "La Formation de l'Athènes Bourgeoise: Essai d'Historiographie 1750–1850," in R. R. Bolgar, ed., *Classical Influences on Western Thought* A.D. *1650–1870* (Cambridge, 1979), 169–222, esp. 183–98; and the chapters "La Place de la Grèce dans l'Imaginaire des Hommes de la Révolution" and "Paris-Athènes et Retour" in P. Vidal-Naquet, *La Démocratie Grecque Vue D'Ailleurs* (Paris, 1990), where "La Formation de l'Athènes Bourgeoise" is reprinted.

72. Cited in Parker, *The Cult of Antiquity*, 162, 166.

73. Ibid., 167.

74. Buzot, *Mémoires sur la Révolution Française*, ed. and with an intro. by M. Guadet (Paris, 1823), 23.

75. Jeanne-Marie Phlipon Roland de la Platière, *Mémoires de Madame Roland écrits durant sa captivité*, ed. C. Perroud (Paris, 1905), 2.22.

76. Brissot's *Mémoires (1754–1790)*, ed. C. Perroud (Paris, 1911), contain several references to the author's identification with Phocion (e.g., 1.9–10, 1.42, 2.227).

77. Regnaud de Saint-Angély's remark is cited in Parker, *The Cult of Antiquity*, 2; Volney's attack on the emulation of antiquity runs throughout his *Leçons d'Histoire* (discussed here on pp. 198–99).

78. In *Souvenirs et fragments* (Paris, 1906), 1.17.

79. Parker, *The Cult of Antiquity*, 30.

80. Surely misogyny lies at the root of some of the condescension with which Madame Roland has been treated in modern literature. Although her enthusiasm for antiquity may have been tied up with immaturity, neurosis, and a personal agenda, of what male revolutionary is the same not true?

81. Cited in Parker, *The Cult of Antiquity*, 48.

82. *Chronique de Paris* 6 (6 January 1793): 22.

83. The remarks of Billaud-Varenne and Vergniaud are both cited in Mossé, *L'Antiquité dans la Révolution française*, 92–93.

84. E. Lévy, *Le Manuel des prénoms* (Paris, 1922).

85. Parker, *The Cult of Antiquity*, 17–21.

86. On the debate among the revolutionaries as to the desirability of a Spartan-style *agoge*, see Rawson, 278–84.

87. Parker, *The Cult of Antiquity*, 75–76.

88. *Le Vieux Cordelier*, ed. Henri Calvet (Paris, 1936), no. 7, 232.

89. Ibid., no. 4, 124.

90. Ibid., no. 5, 148–49.

91. Ibid., no. 6, 188–91.

92. Ibid., no. 7, 230; cf. similar remarks in the *Discours de la Lanterne Aux Parisiens*, reprinted in M. Jules Claretie, ed. *Oeuvres de Camille Desmoulins* (Paris, 1874), 1. 174.

93. M. Robespierre, *Le Défenseur de la Constitution* (1792): reprinted in G. Laurent, ed., *Oeuvres Complètes de Robespierre*, vol. 4 (Paris, 1939), 36, 117.

94. Cited by Parker, *The Cult of Antiquity*, 177.

95. Buzot, *Mémoires sur la Révolution Française*, 45–46; Parker, *The Cult of Antiquity*, 175–76.

96. Chateaubriand, *Itineraire de Paris à Jerusalem et de Jerusalem à Paris, en allant par la Grèce, et revenant par l'Egypte, la Barbarie et l'Espagne*, 3 vols. (1811): 1.169.

97. *Archives Parlementaires de 1787 à 1860; recueil complet des débats legislatifs et politiques des chambres françaises*, 1st ser., 1787–99 (Paris, 1862–93), vol. 8 (12 August 1789), 407–10.

98. Ibid., vol. 11 (23 February 1790), 684.

99. Ibid., vol. 15 (7 May 1790), 419.

100. Ibid., (18 May 1790), 560–62.

101. I owe both the reference to Rouzet's suggestion and the citation of Glotz's observation to Vidal-Naquet, *La démocratie grecque vue d'ailleurs*, 220–21; Rouzet's efforts are discussed at greater length in Mossé, *L'Antiquité dans la Révolution française*, 100–101.

102. The most detailed study of the role of festivals in the ideology of the revolution remains M. Ozouf, *La fête révolutionnaire (1789–1799)* (Paris, 1976).

103. Parker, 67.

104. Discussed ibid., 97.

105. 18 July 1790 (*Lettres* 2.107–8).

106. Volney in his relationship to antiquity is discussed by the Italian Marxist Luciano Canfora in *Ideologie del Classicismo* (Turin, 1980).

107. Volney, *Leçons d'Histoire Prononcées a l'École Normale, en l'An III de la République française* (1795): in *Oeuvres Complètes* 6 (Paris, 1821), 124.

108. L. de Bonald, *Théorie du Pouvoir Politique et Religieux dans la Societé Civile, Demonstrée par le Raisonnement et par l'Histoire* (1796; reprint, Paris, 1843), 1.125, 128.

109. Ibid., 1.166.

110. Ibid., 1.200, 199.

111. J. Gillies, ed., *The "Orations" of Lysias and Isocrates* (1778): lxii–lxiii.

112. Gillies, *The History of Ancient Greece, Its Colonies, and Conquests, Part the first; from the earliest accounts till the Division of the Macedonian Empire in the East*, 6th ed., 4 vols. (London, 1820), 2.1.64, 121–22, 126; 3.1.473.

113. Gillies, ibid., 3.1.13, 4.1.174. Were Gillies's text on disk, a word search on "licentious" would generate a long list.

114. Ibid., 2.283; Gillies writes comfortably of the "natural malignity" and "tumultuous passions" of the "vulgar" (2.1.150, 283; 3.1.79).

115. Ibid., 3.1.474.

116. Tucker, *A Treatise* (reprint, New York, 1967), 226.

117. Ibid., 237–38.

118. Ibid., 207. Tucker's introductory paragraph about Athens concerns the evils of ostracism, than which nothing "could have been better calculated for gratifying the Caprice and Licentiousness of a Mob" (220).

119. Ibid., 212.

120. Ibid., 215–16.

121. Young, *British Constitution*, 3; Bisset, *Sketch of Democracy*, 20.

122. Young, *British Constitution*, 8–10.

123. Ibid., 10–12.

124. Ibid., 53.

125. Ibid., 53, 44.

126. Ibid., 62.

127. Bisset, *Sketch*, 127–28 and 33.

128. Ibid., 24, 27.

129. Ibid., 95.

130. Ibid., 119.

131. Ibid., 73.

132. Ibid., 127.

133. Ibid., 144.

134. Mitford expatiates on the excellences of Philip in *The History of Greece* (1822 ed.), 8.458–73.

135. Ibid., 5.219 and 1.278.

136. Ibid., 5.337–38, 373.

137. Ibid., 5.373.

138. Ibid., 9.74.

139. Ibid., 4.353–54.

France continued to be drawn into the debate about Athens for some time after the publication of Mitford's *History*; for the discussion of Mitford in the *Quarterly Review*'s essay on Étienne Clavier's *Histoire des premiers Temps de la Grèce*, see p. 358, n. 21 here.

140. Mitford, *History of Greece* 5.31, 34; 3.4.

141. Ibid., 5.219.

142. Bisset, *Sketch of Democracy*, 59.

143. Young, *History of Athens*, 66.

144. On the importance of property in the ideology of the English Country Party, see H. T. Dickinson, *Liberty and Property: Political Ideology in Eighteenth-Century Britain* (New York, 1977). French thinkers of the same era approached the question of property rather differently; see for example chap. 9, "Equality and Property," in K. Martin, *The Rise of French Liberal Thought: A Study of Political Ideas from Bayle to Condorcet* (New York, 1929).

CHAPTER TEN

1. In a letter to Dupont de Nemours written on 24 April.

2. Although it would be flattering to have the reader think otherwise, the fact is that (nearly all) the observations in this paragraph are derived from R. R. Palmer, "Notes on the Use of the word 'Democracy' 1789–1799," *Political Science Quarterly* 68 (1953): 203–26.

A rich collection of passages reflecting different notions of democracy has been assembled in A. Naess, J. Christophersen, and K. Kjell, *Democracy, Ideology, and Objectivity: Studies in the Semantics and Cognitive Analysis of Ideological Controversy*, the product of a Unesco ideology research project (Oslo, 1956).

3. Cited in Palmer, "Notes on the Use," 215.

4. On the origins of classical scholarship and the Hellenic revival in Germany, see Sandys, *History*, 3.1–101; G. P. Gooch, *History and Historians in the Nineteenth Century* (1893; reprint, Boston, 1959), 24–38; U. von Wilamowitz-Möllendorff, *History of Classical Scholarship*, trans. A. Harris (London, 1982, from the German ed. of 1921), 92–117; H. Trevelyan, *Goethe and the Greeks* (Cambridge, 1941), 1–14; the biography of

Heyne by his son-in-law Heeren (*Christian Gottlob Heyne, biographisch dargestellt* [1813]); and the long discussion in C. Bursian, *Geschichte der classischen Philologie in Deutschland von den Anfängen bis zur Gegenwart* (1883).

5. Cambridge, 1935.

6. See for example Winckelmann's *Geschichte der Kunst des Alterthums (1764)*, translated by G. Henry Lodge, M.D., as *The History of Ancient Art* (Boston, 1872), 2.10, 14.

7. The relationship of Herder's thought to that of Winckelmann is discussed in chap. 3, "Due giudizi su Winckelmann," in M. Pavan, *Antichità Classica e Pensiero Moderno* (Florence, 1977), 57–80. On Herder and Greece more broadly see the chapter "Weimar Theories of Culture" in W. H. Bruford, *Culture and Society in Classical Weimar 1775–1806* (Cambridge, 1962), and F. M. Barnard, *Herder's Social and Political Thought: From Enlightenment to Nationalism* (Oxford, 1965).

8. I cite Herder's *Outlines of a Philosophy of the History of Man* (*Ideen zur Philosophie der Geschichte der Menschheit*) in the 1800 translation of T. Churchill (reprint, New York [Bergman], n.d.), 368.

9. Ibid., 373.

10. Ibid., 376.

11. Ibid., 375.

12. Ibid., 376.

13. Ibid.

14. On Herder's pluralism and cultural relativism and on his relationship to other eighteenth-century thinkers, see I. Berlin, *Vico and Herder: Two Studies in the History of Ideas* (London, 1970).

15. Schiller's orientation to the Greek state is discussed in P. Kain, *Schiller, Hegel, and Marx* (Kingston and Montreal, 1982), 13–33.

16. Letter 6, cited from Nathan H. Dole, ed., *Aesthetical and Philosophical Essays* (Boston, 1902), 1.19.

17. Ibid., 1.18.

18. *Die Gesetzgebung des Lykurg und Solon* (1790; reprint, Vaduz, 1956), 82.

19. On the cultural context of Hölderlin's hopes of reviving ancient Greek ideals in Germany, see D. Constantine, *Early Greek Travellers and the Hellenic Ideal* (Cambridge, 1984).

20. On Hölderlin's *Antigone* see George Steiner's *Antigones* (New York and Oxford, 1984), 66–103, and accompanying bibliography.

21. *Hyperion*, 70. References to Hyperion are to *Hyperion, or the Hermit in Greece*, trans. Willard Trask (New York, 1959). On the context of Hyperion in Hölderlin's work, see C.C.T. Litzmann, *F. Hölderlins Leben* (1890), J. Claverio, *La Jeunesse d'Hölderlin jusqu'au roman d'Hyperion* (1922), and M. Montgomery, *Hölderlin and the German Neo-Hellenist Movement* (Oxford, 1923). The treatment of Hölderlin in Butler's *Tyranny of Greece over Germany* is perceptive. See also Franz G. Nauen, *Revolution, Idealism, and Human Freedom: Schelling, Hölderlin, and Hegel and the Crisis of Early German Idealism* (The Hague, 1971), esp. chaps. 3–5.

22. *Hyperion*, 92.

23. Hölderlin's foster father apparently ascribed his madness to his "enthusiasm for those blasted heathens" (cited by Butler in *The Tyranny of Greece over Germany*, 239).

24. A particularly full treatment of Hegel and the Greek state appears in Kain, *Schiller, Hegel, and Marx*, 34–74. See also J. Hoffmeister, *Hegel und Hölderlin* (Tübingen, 1931); M. Foster, *The Political Philosophies of Plato and Hegel* (Oxford, 1935); Martin Heidegger, "Hegel und die Griechen," in Dieter Henrich, ed., *Die Gegenwart: Der Griechen im Neueren Denken, Festschrift für Hans-Georg Gadamer zum 60. Geburtstag* (Tübingen, 1960); J. Glenn Gray, *Hegel and Greek Thought* (New York, 1941; reprint, New York and Evanston, Ill., 1968); J. d'Hondt, ed., *Hegel et la pensée grecque* (Paris, 1974); D. Janicaud, *Hegel et le destin de la Grèce* (Paris, 1975); Judith Shklar, *Freedom and Independence: A Study of the Political Ideas of Hegel's Phenomenology of Mind* (Cambridge, 1976), esp. 69–95; Merold Westphal, *History and Truth in Hegel's Phenomenology* (Atlantic Highlands, N.J., 1979), esp. 30–36, 138–60; and George McCarthy, *Marx and the Ancients: Classical Ethics, Social Justice, and Nineteenth-Century Political Economy* (Savage, Md., 1990), 123–68 and notes. On Hegel's political universe more generally, see George Armstrong Kelly, *Idealism, Politics, and History: Sources of Hegelian Thought* (Cambridge, 1969), and Nauen, *Revolution, Idealism and Human Freedom*, esp. 69–97.

25. Cited in the translation of T. M. Knox in Hegel's *Early Theological Writings* (Chicago, 1948), 146–47.

26. In *Lectures on The Philosophy of History*, trans. J. Sibree (reprint, New York, 1956), 254–55; see chap. 12 here, p. 268.

27. See, for example, 262–65.

28. Ibid., 258.

29. Ibid., 260.

30. Ibid., 261.

31. *History of Philosophy*, cited in the 1892 translation of E. S. Haldane and F. Simson (reprint, Atlantic Highlands, N.J., 1955), 1.444, 445.

32. Ibid., 448. Similarly Hegel distinguished (265) between the happy era of Objective morality (*Sittlichkeit*), which he isolates during the fifty-year period between the Persian and the Peloponnesian wars, and the subsequent era of decay, the era of Subjective morality (*Moralität*), brought on by the questioning of Socrates and the sophists, when the principle of subjective morality introduced during the Peloponnesian Wars became "the germ of corruption" at Athens.

33. *Philosophy of History*, 253.

34. *Philosophy of History*, 269–71.

35. *The Philosophy of Right*, trans. T. M. Knox (Oxford, 1952), 114, 263, 116.

36. J. Hodge, "Women and the Hegelian State," in *Women in Western Political Philosophy: Kant to Nietzsche*, ed. E. Kennedy and S. Mendus (New York, 1987), 152. In my discussion of Hegel and Antigone I have drawn deeply on Hodge's insights; I also owe a great debt to Juliet Floyd, my colleague at the City College of New York, who took time to discuss these matters with me but is in no way responsible for the arguments I have put forward here. For other perspectives on this crux, see Shklar, *Freedom and Independence*, esp. 82–86, and J. Loewenberg, *Hegel's Phenomenology: Dialogues on the Life of the Mind* (La Salle, Ill., 1965), esp. 190–201, 326–33.

37. P. Kain, *Schiller, Hegel, and Marx*, 67, 71, 72.

38. The evolution of Hegel's attitude to Christianity is discussed in Kain, ibid., 34–54.

39. *Philosophy of History*, 255–56, 252.

40. J. G. Gray, *Hegel and Greek Thought*, 41.

41. Cited from the London 1815 translation, 59–61.

42. In the *Quarterly Review* for March 1813, 144.

43. *Essay*, 28.

44. Ibid., 24, 26.

45. Ibid., 40; cf. 54.

46. Cited in Holmes's *Benjamin Constant and the Making of Modern Liberalism* (New Haven and London, 1984), 25. I am greatly indebted to Holmes's eloquent and persuasive book. Most of what I have said about Constant has also said by Holmes, and he has said it better. Like many thinkers cited in this book as secondary sources, Holmes also published his own opinions about Greece; see, for example, "Aristippus in and out of Athens," *American Political Science Review* 73 (1979): 113–28.

47. Henri Benjamin Constant de Rebecque, *De la Liberté des Anciens Comparée a Celle des Modernes*, in *Cours de Politique Constitutionelle ou Collection des Ouvrages Publiés sur le Gouvernement Représentatif*, ed. M. Edouard Laboulaye (Paris, 1861), 2.550.

48. *De la Liberté*, 553.

49. *Benjamin Constant*, 193.

CHAPTER ELEVEN

1. A. P. Stanley, *The Life of Thomas Arnold*, D.D. (1844), 1.129; T. Arnold, *The History of the Peloponnesian War by Thucydides*, 4th ed. (1857), 3.xiv. "On the Modern Element in Literature," Matthew Arnold's inaugural address as professor of poetry at Oxford, was published in 1869 and can be found in R. H. Super, ed., *On the Classical Tradition* (Ann Arbor, 1960), 18–37.

2. J. P. Mahaffy, *Social Life in Greece from Homer to Menander* (1874), 1–3; cf. the parallels drawn by Jowett in his edition of the *Dialogues of Plato* (see 1.xxv in the 3d ed. [5 vols., New York, 1892]).

3. *The Greek Heritage in Victorian Britain* (New Haven, 1981), 15. Those who have read Turner's book will recognize my enormous debt to it throughout this chapter; those who have not will certainly want to do so. Much of the material in pp. 229–30 above came to my attention in the course of my reading of Turner's work.

4. The selectivity with which the literature of ancient Greece was preserved by subsequent generations has fostered a vaguely analogous development in the verbal arts. As Richard Jenkyns has pointed out, only the nature and extent of the tiny surviving corpus made possible the beliefs of thinkers like Virginia Woolf, who could contend that Greek was an "impersonal literature," a "literature of masterpieces" in which "there are no schools; no forerunners; no heirs." (*The Victorians and Ancient Greece* [Cambridge, Mass., 1980], 78). This chapter owes a great deal to my reading of Jenkyns's work.

Thoughtful reviews of Jenkyns and Turner by classicists include ones by Peter Green in the *Times Literary Supplement*, reprinted in *Classical Bearings* (New York, 1989), 31–44, and by Bernard Knox, in the *New York Review of Books*, reprinted in his *Essays Ancient and Modern* (Baltimore, 1989), 149–61.

5. J. Reynolds, *Discourses Delivered to the Students of the Royal Academy*, ed. R. Fry (London, 1905), 264; J. E. Harrison, *Introductory Studies in Greek Art* (1885), 189.

6. P. Gardner, *Grammar of Greek Art* (New York, 1905), 14.

7. *The Antiquities of Athens*, vol. 1 (1762), x. On Stuart and Revett and the Greek revival, see R. Stoneman, *Land of Lost Gods: The Search for Classical Greece* (Norman, Okla., and London, 1987), 120–30. Stoneman's book offers a lively account of the modern attempt to recapture Greek antiquity in Greece itself.

8. R. Jenkyns, *The Victorians and Ancient Greece*, 14.

9. C. Austin, *Westminster Review* 7 (January 1827): 258.

10. "Panegyrical Oratory of Greece," a review of *Oeuvres complètes de Démosthène et d'Eschine, en Grec et en Français. Traduction de l'Abbé Auger*, new ed., J. Planche, vols. 1–4, *Quarterly Review* 27, no. 54 (1822): 382–404.

11. "Panegyrical Oratory," 392.

12. Ibid., 385–86; cf. the observations on Isocrates, 394–95.

13. Response to "Quarterly Review—Articles on Greek Literature," *Westminster Review* 3 (January 1825): 233, 235.

14. Ibid., 3.242.

15. Is marriage so exclusively the province of the Church, the *Westminster* writer asks, "that to write even about old Helen (or rather, to have written full two thousand years before the martyrdom of Archbishop Laud) is apt to bring it into hazard? The papal government long disturbed the happiness of mankind, and defiled the purity of religion, by the exercise of this jurisdiction, and the Protestant church succeeded to it nearly entire." Following this train of thought, the *Westminster* reviewer takes the *Quarterly* writer to task for the way he blamed Athens for discounting the importance of Egypt in history. The Athenians, the *Quarterly* reviewer had complained, often forgot Egypt as the ambitious man may forget the ladder he kicks out from beneath him once it has served his purpose of rising in the world. Surely, the *Westminster* reviewer observed, "The Church of Rome gained the power, which the reformed Church adopted, and then called her mother bad names, and scarlet names; surely this was kicking the ladder, and kicking it rather hard too?" (259–60).

16. See chap. 8, p. 172 and n. 93.

17. *Westminster Review* 3.241.

18. Ibid., 3.257.

19. The example here cited is the devious use—so the reviewer maintains—the theologian Conyers Middleton had made of early customs regarding the use of incense in church in his attempt "to make the Protestants detest the Roman Catholics, and to widen more and more the breach between them." This parallel is developed at some length, as the reviewer lambasts "the hot zealot, who cries 'let us not wash our bodies; for thus did the publicans and the harlots': and the sour protestant, whose commands are, 'Comb not; for the idolaters, and after them the church of Rome, used the comb.'" These misrepresentations on the part of Middleton concerning the use of incense, the reviewer contends, are "an apt illustration of the proceedings of the Quarterly-reviewer." The *Westminster* writer also attacks Thomas Mitchell, whose approach to Aristophanes the *Quarterly* reviewer had approved, for citing the words of Martin Joseph Routh, president of Magdalen College at Oxford, who had claimed that the Greek sophists infected people with a "puerile appetite for disputing": "The schoolmen

of the middle age were Catholics," the *Westminster* writer summarizes derisively, "and erroneous Sophists, but Martin Joseph Routh, is a protestant, and seems to hint, with admirable self-complacency, that he is the true philosopher: they erred in discoursing about every thing, he will avoid this error by discoursing of nothing" (*Westminster Review* 4 [1825 July: 235–37, 248).

20. "Greek Courts of Justice," *Quarterly Review* 33 no. 66 (1826): 335–36, 344, 355.

21. "Greek Courts of Justice," 338, 355. For a French perspective on Mitford, Athens, and the evils of the revolution in France, see a review of Étienne Clavier's *Histoire des premiers Temps de la Grèce* in the *Quarterly Review* 5, no. 9 (1811): 30–33.

22. "Mitford's *History of Greece*," *Edinburgh Review* 12 (July 1808): 491.

23. Ibid., 505–6.

24. Ibid., 517.

25. T. B. Macaulay, "On the Athenian Orators," cited from the *Complete Works of Lord Macaulay*, ed. Trevelyan (New York and London, n.d.), vol. 8, 153–55.

26. "On Mitford's History of Greece," reprinted from the November 1824 issue of *Knight's Quarterly* in Trevelyan, ed., *Complete Works of Lord Macaulay*, vol. 3, 183–86.

27. "On Mitford's History," 190–91.

28. Ibid., 194.

29. Ibid., 202. Paeans to the glorious achievements of democratic Athens appear in this same essay on pp. 196 and 208–9.

30. Ibid., 208–9.

31. Cited in Turner, *Greek Heritage*, 206.

32. G. Grote, "Institutions of Ancient Greece," *Westminster Review* 5 (April 1826): 278–80. Ostensibly a review of Fynes Clinton's *Fasti Hellenici*, the essay's chief subject matter was in fact Mitford's work in particular and Greek government in general.

33. "Institutions," 282.

34. Ibid., 285–86.

35. Ibid., 292.

36. Ibid., 330.

37. T. Keightley, *History of Greece* (1839): 395.

38. *Quarterly Review* 51.144.

On classical education in Britain during the first half of the nineteenth century see J. W. Donaldson, *Classical Scholarship and Classical Learning* (Cambridge and London, 1856).

39. "Institutions," 281.

40. On Böckh and Wachsmuth, see p. 251 here.

41. Niebuhr's complaints appear in the notes for his *Lectures on Ancient History* (translated into English by L. Schmitz in 1852), 2.216, 299.

42. M. L. Clarke, *George Grote: A Biography* (London, 1962), 22.

43. *Edinburgh Review* 138 (1873): 221, cited in Clarke, *George Grote*, 21.

44. A. Bain, *John Stuart Mill* (1882): 83.

45. The outlines of Grote's argument here were the traditional Benthamite ones; the question of "The English Utilitarians and Athenian Democracy" is discussed in a general way by H. O. Pappé in R. R. Bolgar, ed., *Classical Influences on Western Thought 1650–1870* (Cambridge, 1979), 295–307.

46. H. Elliott, ed., *Letters of John Stuart Mill* (London and New York, 1910), 1.58.

47. G. Grote, A *History of Greece from the Earliest Period to the Close of the Generation Contemporary with Alexander the Great*, orig. 1846–1856, cited in the ten-volume edition of 1907, 3.395.

48. As Pierre Vidal-Naquet has pointed out, the traditional view that Grote was the first to notice the importance of Cleisthenes in the evolution of the Athenian state is somewhat exaggerated; Cleisthenes was also singled out by Thirlwall and by a number of Germans—Niebuhr (1811), Hermann (1831), and Droysen (1847). Vidal-Naquet's remarks appear in his introduction to the French edition of Sir Moses Finley's *Democracy Ancient and Modern* (Paris, 1976), 38.

49. *History* 7.271.

50. Ibid., 7.46–48 (Alcibiades).

51. Ibid., 5.330.

52. Ibid., 5.19.

53. Ibid., 7.116.

54. Ibid., 7.184.

55. Ibid., 3.396.

56. Ibid., 3.378.

57. See p. 245 and n. 66 here.

58. *History*, 4.168.

59. Ibid., 5.247–48.

60. Ibid., 5.332–3.

61. Ibid., 3.469–79.

62. Ibid., 6.7.

63. B. Niebuhr, *Lectures*, 2.115.

64. *History* 7.49–50.

65. Ibid., 6.12.

66. Ibid., 6.37.

67. "George Grote and The Study of Greek History," delivered at University College, London, in 1952 and reprinted in Momigliano's *Studies in Historiography* (New York, 1966), 62. Thirlwall's orientation to Greece is discussed in his biography by John Connop Thirlwall, *Connop Thirlwall: Historian and Theologian* (London, 1936).

68. See p. 250 and n. 87 here.

69. Turner, *Greek Heritage*, 232.

70. G. C. Lewis, "Grote's *History of Greece*," *Edinburgh Review* 91 (1850): 118–52.

71. *Autobiography*, drafted in 1853–54 and published posthumously, cited in the New York, 1924, edition with a preface by J. Coss, 8–9.

72. J. S. Mill, "Early Greek History and Legend: A Review of the First Two Volumes of 'Grote's History of Greece,'" reprinted from the October 1846 issue of the *Edinburgh Review*, vol. 84, in Mill's *Dissertations and Discussions* and cited from *Essays on Philosophy and the Classics* in vol. 11 of his *Collected Works* (Toronto, 1978) as "Grote's History of Greece [I]," 273.

73. *Autobiography*, 163.

74. From Mill's review of Grote's later volumes, which appeared in the *Edinburgh Review* for October 1853 (vol. 98), reprinted as "Grote's History of Greece [II]" in *Essays on Philosophy and the Classics*, 316, 302–3.

75. Ibid., 316.

76. E. Freeman, "The Athenian Democracy: A *History of Greece*. By George Grote,"

reprinted in *Historical Essays*, 2d ser. (1873): 136–37. Freeman also concedes in his review of Curtius that Grote had "political bias" and "a certain love of novelty for its own sake," but he maintains that "such a tendency on his particular subject does much more good than harm" (reprinted in *Historical Essays*, 155).

77. "The Athenian Democracy," 131.

78. Cited p. 349, n. 38 here.

79. P. Mérimée, "De l'Histoire ancienne de la Grèce: History of Greece by G. Grote," *Revue des Deux Mondes*, n.s., 6, no. 2 (1850): 846.

80. Ibid., 854.

81. V. Duruy, *Histoire Grecque*, 2d ed. (1856): 3.613–14, also cited in chap. 1, p. 12 and n. 13, here.

82. J. P. Mahaffy in the introduction to V. Duruy, *History of Greece, and of the Greek People, from the Earliest Times to the Roman Conquest*, trans. M. M. Ripley (1890). Much can be learned about both the impact of Grote's work and political currents in late nineteenth-century Britain from the pessimism Mahaffy expressed about persuading his fellows of the weaknesses of democracy. "The love of political liberty," he wrote, "and the importance attached to political independence, are so strong in the minds of Saxon nations that it is not likely I or any one else will persuade them, against the splendid advocacy of Grote, that there may be such losses and mischiefs in a democracy as to justify a return to a stronger executive and a greater restriction of public speech" (73). In his own day, he maintained, "To utter anything against Demosthenes . . . is almost as bad as to say a word in old Athenian days against the battle of Marathon" (69).

83. J. Grote, "A Few Remarks on a Pamphlet by Mr. Shilleto Entitled 'Thucydides or Grote'" (1851).

84. G. W. Cox, *A General History of Greece from the Earliest Period to the Death of Alexander the Great*, 2 vols. (1874): 1.448.

85. Ibid., 2.229.

86. Ibid., 1.184. On occasion Cox's desire to illuminate Athenian society by placing it in the fabric of European history as a whole gets the better of him, and on at least one occasion he appears transported into another world entirely. The foresight of Hippias and Hipparchus, he writes, "failed to guard them against dangers arising from their pleasant vices; and Hipparchos in an evil hour sought to form with the beautiful Harmodios the shameful intimacy into which James VI. wished, it would seem, to decoy Alexander Ruthven and which disgraced his relations with Ramsay and Carr." Thus far the text: but Cox goes on to express himself more forcefully and at considerable length in the footnote attached. "The only difference between these cases," he writes,

> is that by his attempt Hipparchos brought about his own death, while James, to hide his own guilt, wrought the death of his victim. That the whole of King James' story on the subject of the so-called Gowrie conspiracy is a tissue of falsehoods and contradictions, is undeniable. It is enough to say that his tale was altogether disbelieved by archbishop Spottiswoode and Robert Bruce of Kinnairs; but less than this could not in fairness be said on a subject in which historians are still content to wrong the memory of the two boys in order to save the credit of one of the worst tyrants that ever disgraced a throne." (1. 213, 262)

All this, it must be remembered, in a history of ancient Greece.

The prolific Reverend Cox also wrote widely on a variety of other subjects ranging from the history of the crusades to the shoeing of horses.

87. T. May, *Democracy in Europe: A History* (1877): lxii–lxiii.

88. Ibid., 63–64.

89. Ibid., 93.

90. Ibid., 106; cf. 98.

Grote's influence was also plain in the most popular one-volume Greek history text of the second half of the century, William Smith's 1855 *History of Greece from the Earliest Times to the Roman Conquest.*

91. Lewis, "Grote's *History of Greece,*" 122.

92. A. Böckh, *The Public Economy of Athens*, trans. G. C. Lewis, 2d ed. (1842): 613, 194.

93. Ibid., 226; for other criticisms, see, e.g., 193–94, 271, 603–4.

94. I cite from the 1837 English translation of E. Woolrych, *The Historical Antiquities of the Greeks, with Reference to Their Political Institutions* 2.201.

95. Ibid., 2.198. Other flaws of the Athenians (including an "immoderate desire" for self-government) are cited at 2.28–29, 201, 456, 353, 82, 200, and 196.

A similar orientation had characterized G. F. Schömann's *Dissertations on the Assemblies of the Athenians*, which appeared in Latin in 1819 and was translated into English in 1838. After Pericles' institution of state pay for jurors, Schömann argued, the republic once so well constituted by Solon degenerated into "an abominable democracy" (17). Schömann also attributed Athens's decline to the unsavory types with whom naval commerce had filled the city—merchants, innkeepers, sailors, and others who lived by "haunting the ports and marketplaces," a crew that was by its very nature "naturally fickle, seditious and idle" (17–18).

96. On Burckhardt, Meyer, and the survival of the anti-Athenian tradition in Germany, see chapters 12 (Burckhardt) and 13 (Meyer), here.

97. E. Curtius, *Griechische Geschichte* (1857–67). For Freeman's review of Curtius see n. 76.

98. Cited in the English translation *The History of Greece from its Commencement to the Close of the Independence of the Greek Nation* (London and New York, 1900), 3.194–97.

99. Ibid., 3.196.

100. Ibid., 3.197.

101. Ibid.

102. Ibid., 3.197–98.

103. Ibid., 2.530.

104. *Democracy in Europe*, 1.42.

105. "Subversion of Ancient Governments," *Quarterly Review* 45 (June 1831): 468–70, 454.

106. M. Arnold, "Democracy," reprinted in *Mixed Essays, Irish Essays, and Others* (New York, 1883), 29–30. On Arnold, democracy, and America, see J. Roper, *Democracy and Its Critics: Anglo-American Democratic Thought in the Nineteenth Century* (London, 1989), 156–66.

107. H. Maine, *Popular Government: Four Essays* (1885; cited from the New York, 1886, ed.), 42–43.

108. Bernal's arguments are presented in his controversial *Black Athena: The Af-*

roasiatic Roots of Classical Civilization, vol. 1: *The Fabrication of Ancient Greece 1785–1985* (New Brunswick, 1987).

109. M. Arnold, "Equality," reprinted in *Mixed Essays*, 65.

110. John Dewey, *Logic: The Theory of Inquiry*, excerpted in H. Meyerhoff, ed., *The Philosophy of History in Our Time* (Garden City, 1959), 171.

CHAPTER TWELVE

1. These and other citations are assembled in Gregory Vlastos's article "Slavery in Plato's Thought," *Philosophical Review* 50 (1941): 289–304 (esp. p. 294).

2. See, for example, the contention of Robert MacIver that "the limited democracy had an anti-democratic base" and that under these circumstances "the principle of democracy could never find its true expression or its true justification" (from *The Web of Government* [published first in 1947 when MacIver taught at Columbia, cited from the New York, 1965, edition], 134). It is easy to assemble a collection of similar formulations. In his study of Greek culture, *The Will of Zeus* (Philadelphia and New York, 1961), Stringfellow Barr of Rutgers extended the principle of exclusion even to indigent citizens, warning that at Athens "the dream of equal freedom under law was far from realized: the poor man, the man who was not well-fathered, the slave, the woman, the metic were all in varying degrees shut out" (125). Textbooks are particularly prone to this sort of disclaimer. In 1954 Philip Ralph of Lake Erie College in Ohio cautioned readers of his survey text *The Story of Our Civilization* that in the premodern world democracy at its best, in Athens, was "coupled with an arbitrary discrimination between the sexes, condoned slavery, and was soon tarnished by imperialistic ambitions." Even the democratic Athenians, Ralph alleged, operated within "the confines of a callow provincialism." (*The Story of Our Civilization* [New York, 1954], 119, 51). (For Ralph's observations on Machiavelli, see chap. 6, p. 131, here). For more recent texts, see Frank Frost of the University of California at Santa Barbara in *Greek Society* (Lexington, Mass., and Toronto, 1987), 86; and William H. McNeill, onetime president of the American Historical Association, in his *History of the Human Community* (Englewood Cliffs, N.J., 1987), 134, the outgrowth of a long series of texts on Western and world history.

3. R. Bisset, *Sketch of Democracy*, 104, 107.

4. Ibid., 73.

5. Ibid., 117–18.

6. Mitford 5.31, 7.336ff.; see also chapter 9, pp. 204–5, here.

7. *Leçons*, 131; see pp. 198–99, here.

8. Reprinted Port Washington and London (Kennikat Press, 1962), 1.374.

9. See, for example, Greenidge's *Handbook of Greek Constitutional History* (1896): 203.

10. J. Cramb, *The Origins and Destiny of Imperial Britain* (published posthumously in London in 1915), 95–97, 110.

11. I owe the citations to Pickard-Cambridge and MacNeice to Jenkyns, *The Victorians and Ancient Greece* (Cambridge, Mass., 1980), 335–36. Jenkyns also quotes from Cramb.

12. *The Glory That Was Greece* (London, 1911), 145.

13. Hopper's remarks appear on p. viii of the preface, and the revised sentence is on p. 139 (*The Glory That Was Greece*, 4th ed. [London, 1964]).

14. The appearance of the placards is cited in F. Turner, *The Greek Heritage in Victorian Britain* (New Haven, 1981), 187, from Graham Wallas, *Our Social Heritage* (New Haven, 1921), 166.

At times it was the Athens of Pericles that modern anglophones sought to emulate, preserving democratic values against the likes of totalitarian Sparta; at times it was the Athens of Demosthenes, holding the line against Philip redivivus in the guise of Hitler. For the Oxford classicist and man of letters Gilbert Murray, it was both. Seeing a parallel between the plight of his own nation facing a German threat and the Athenians' situation before the might of Macedon, he compared Demosthenes' *Philippics* to Churchill's "Arms and the League" speeches; but the confrontation with Sparta also seemed pertinent. "Just as in 1914 or 1939," he wrote of the Peloponnesian War,

> a rich democratic sea power with a naval empire, full of interest in all forms of social, artistic, and intellectual life, was pitted against a reactionary militarist land power, which had sacrificed most of its earlier culture to stark efficiency in war. The broad similarity is obvious, and it leads to similarities in detail which are at times almost fantastic. At one time, for example, the Spartans, their blockade baffled by the Athenian command of the sea, decided to sink at sight every ship they found afloat, of whatever nationality. Admiral Tirpitz' "unrestricted submarine campaign" was evidently not entirely his own invention.

(The citation is from *Greek Studies* [Oxford, 1946], 200–202.) The German analogy can work both ways, since Athens was the more obviously imperial power among the two Greek hegemons. Illustrative parallels scattered throughout the English scholar N.G.L. Hammond's study of *The Classical Age of Greece* (London, 1975) line the Germans up alternately with Athens and with its enemies (70, 110, 123–24, 140–41, 153, 157). For the analysis of the World War I parallel by a German scholar, see E. Bethe, "Athen und der Peloponnesische Krieg im Spiegel des Weltkrieges," *Neue Jahrbücher für das Klassische Altertum, Geschichte und Deutsche Literatur* 20 (1917): 73–87; a Swiss perspective is offered in W. Déonna, "L'éternel present: Guerre du Péloponnèse (431–404) et Guerre Mondiale (1914–1918)," *Revue des Études Grecques* 35 (1922): 1–62. I have not been able to consult Déonna's apparently longer work by the same title published in Paris in 1923. In a chapter entitled "The World War of 431–404," Prentice of Princeton portrayed Athens as resembling England in its democratic politics, commercial basis, and naval empire but similar to Germany in the public perception of the menace it presented to the prosperity and independence of other nations (though Prentice makes plain that he believes this perception was misguided) (*The Ancient Greeks: Studies towards a Better Understanding of the Ancient World* [Princeton, 1940], 153).

15. *Greek Imperialism* (Boston and New York, 1913), 77. Others questioned the dependence of the democracy on imperial revenue, adducing the fact that the democracy outlived the empire; see for example the British scholar T.B.L. Webster (then teaching at Stanford) in *Athenian Culture and Society* (Berkeley and Los Angeles, 1973), 16.

16. Jones, *From the Tigris to the Tiber* (1969; reprint, Homewood, Ill., 1983), 157.

17. MacGregor, *The Athenians and Their Empire* (Vancouver, British Columbia, 1987), 176–77.

18. Ibid., 166.

19. Ibid., 175.

20. R. Campbell, "How a Democracy Died," *Life* 30 (1 January 1951): 96.

21. B. Gallagher, "Hope and History," *Saturday Review* 36 (4 July 1953): 24–25.

22. W. Karp, "The Two Thousand Years' War," *Harper's* 262 (March 1981): 80.

Some, of course, have approved of imperialism without approving of democracy. During the course of the eighteenth and nineteenth centuries a school sprang up in Germany that identified Frederick of Prussia and later Otto von Bismarck with Philip of Macedon, and the comparisons were intended to flatter all parties. A number of enthusiasts for imperialism ancient and modern were decidedly lacking in sympathy for Athens. Though Curtius, for example, had little use for Greek democracy, he saw no problem with the Athenian empire. He complains of the unreasonableness of the subject cities, who, "incapable of real independence," were nevertheless "unwilling to obey the stronger," and of the ingratitude of the Hellenes who were willing to set aside the services of the Athenians and undertake the Peloponnesian War to bring their empire to an end (*Griechische Geschichte* 3.37; cf. 3.517, where similar ideas are expressed). Wilamowitz in his 1921 history of classical scholarship praised the Athenian empire as a model for the German empire of his own era, though he had little sympathy with Athenian democracy (cited on p. xviii of Hugh Lloyd-Jones's introduction to A. Harris's translation of the *History of Classical Scholarship* [London, 1982]). In Britain, on the other hand, one of Athenian democracy's most impassioned defenders decried the Athenian empire in the strongest of terms. Macaulay, the soaring eloquence of whose paean to Athens at the end of his review of Mitford in *Knight's Quarterly* has never been equaled, nonetheless in his essay on the Athenian orators complained that the Athenians, once the deliverers of Greece, "became its plunderers and oppressors": the Athenian sword, he maintained, "unpeopled whole islands in a day," and the Athenian plough swept over the ruins of once renowned cities ("Athenian Orators," in Trevelyan, ed., *Complete Works of Lord Macaulay* [New York and London, n.d.], 8.161). Most frequently, however, fans of the democracy were, if not fans of the empire, at least its apologists.

23. On the whole the treatment of metics at Athens has escaped censure; after all, metics were free to leave or to become affluent and respected if they stayed. An exception to the trend is Michael Walzer of the Institute for Advanced Study at Princeton, who has recently condemned the Athenians for their exploitation of metics as "live-in servants" and compares them in this respect to women in many societies (*Spheres of Justice: A Defense of Pluralism and Equality* [New York, 1983], 53–55).

24. In T. H. Green and T. H. Grose, eds., *David Hume: The Philosophical Works*, vol. 3 (London, 1882; reprint, 1964), 385.

25. Tucker, *Treatise*, 214ff.; Mitford 1.404. A similar indictment appears in the radical *Vindication of Natural Society* evidently penned in 1756 by (*mirabile dictu*) the young Edmund Burke. There Burke billed the history of Athens as "but one Tissue of Rashness, Folly, Ingratitude, Injustice, Tumult, Violence, and Tyranny," and he pointed up the hypocrisy of including slaveholding societies under the rubric of free states: since, he claimed, the freemen in these states were "never the twentieth Part of

the People," the truth is that the so-called free states of antiquity were "no better than pitiful and oppressive Oligarchies" (reprint, F. Pagano, ed. [Indianapolis, 1982]), 65). I accept Burke's indignation as sincere, though some have viewed the *Vindication* as satire.

26. Mitford 1.270.

27. This allegation appears regularly in works for the general reader, textbooks, and scholarly writings—most strikingly, perhaps, in those published in Great Britain, but widely in works appearing in other countries as well. The comparatively gentle treatment of slaves in Athens was remarked as early as 1697 by Potter, who roundly condemned ancient slavery and rejoiced that Christianity had arrived to produce kinder masters. "Slaves," Potter wrote, "were treated with more humanity at Athens than in other places," and though their lot was "in itself deplorable enough, yet, if compared with that of their fellow-sufferers in other cities, seems very easy, at least tolerable, and not to be repined at" (*Antiquities of Greece*, 2 vols., [reprint, Edinburgh, 1813], 66–67, 76, 79, 82). The popular notion that Christianity improved attitudes toward slavery is attacked fiercely by the twentieth-century English Marxist Geoffrey de Ste. Croix, *The Class Struggle in the Ancient Greek World* (London, 1981), 419. Antislavers in England encouraged a literary competition at Cambridge in 1785 on the subject of slavery, and the prize was taken by Thomas Clarkson's *Essay on the Slavery and Commerce of the Human Species, Particularly the African*; Clarkson duly contended that slaves were better treated in Athenian society than in any other ancient state (*Essay*, 1785 [published 1788], 10). Not surprisingly, much of the literature produced on the crest of Victorian euphoria over Athens found slavery there to be mild in comparison with parallel servitude elsewhere and considered it in any event a small price to pay for the creation of the glory that was Greece. (Some, like Grote, dealt with it by glossing over it with remarkable thoroughness. Grote leaned toward the South in the American Civil War.) In 1896 G. Lowes Dickinson published his glowing paean to *The Greek Way of Life*—a way of life that, among other things, accorded a tolerance to homoerotic attachments between men that would have made his personal psyche more at home than in his own repressive era. Lowes Dickinson argued that "the freedom and individuality that was characteristic of the Athenian citizen, appears to have reacted favourably on the position of the slaves," who, he maintains, were "allowed a license of bearing and costume which would not have been tolerated in any other state." Taking in deadly earnest the complaint of the Old Oligarch about the license of slaves at Athens and the impossibility of distinguishing them on the street from citizens, he cites this same writer as an authority for the fact that it was open to Athenian slaves "to acquire a fortune and live in ease and luxury." Slavery at best, he concludes, "is an undemocratic [i.e., wicked] institution; but in Athens it appears to have been made as democratic [i.e., nonwicked] as its nature would admit" (*The Greek Way of Life* [reprint, Ann Arbor, Mich., 1958, with a preface by E. M. Forster], 119). The belief that slaves in Athens were treated better than in other ancient states survives into the twentieth century but has been questioned by the American feminist Eva Keuls, who maintains that in fact Athenian slaves were singularly abused (*The Reign of the Phallus: Sexual Politics in Ancient Athens* [New York, 1985]).

28. Beginning at least as early as Hume, the debate over the proportion of slave to free at Athens and the role of slavery in the Athenian state has continued well into the twentieth century; much of the bibliography of work done during the first half of this

century is summarized in the exchange that appeared in the *Journal of Economic History* in the late 1950s between Chester Starr, an ancient historian then at the University of Illinois, and Carl Degler, an Americanist then at Vassar College in upstate New York. For Starr, who made analogies with black slavery in America, both nineteenth-century humanitarianism and twentieth-century Marxism had led to an overestimation of the role of slavery in antiquity. From Degler's perspective, Starr's American analogy sank his case, since, in Degler's view, slavery was in fact integral to the economy of the antebellum South. Notions about the role of slavery in the Athenian state have been closely bound up with the question of the Greek attitude toward labor and with the relationship of slavery to the lack of significant technological progress in the ancient world as a whole. See Starr, "An Overdose of Slavery," *Journal of Economic History* 18 (1958): 17–32; Degler, "Starr on Slavery," *Journal of Economic History* 19 (1959): 271–77.

The answer to these questions has been of more than academic interest, for Athens's claims to the kinds of achievement for which it has been admired have seemed to many to be vitiated by the possible dependence of Athenian civilization on slave labor. The more slaves there were in Athens, the more the Athenians are suspected of having "cheated" in their quest for excellence. In one of the few doctoral dissertations on Athens written by women in the 1920s, Rachel Sargent, a student at the University of Illinois, accumulated an amusing number of passages in which the ratio of slave to free at Athens was calculated variously at three, four, and five and a half, and the inference drawn that citizens did not work. H. M. Hyndman's *Evolution of Revolution* (London, 1920) proposed a ratio of fourteen slaves to one adult citizen (Sargent, *The Size of the Slave Population at Athens during the Fifth and Fourth Centuries before Christ* [Ph.D. dissertation, University of Illinois, 1923; Westport, Conn., 1924], 9–11). Writing in 1840, De Tocqueville in his *Democracy in America* claimed that Athens boasted only 20,000 citizens for 350,000 inhabitants, and Engels in 1884 pegged the ratio at eighteen slaves to every adult male citizen (De Tocqueville, *Democracy in America*, reprinted in the "Classics of Conservatism" series, trans. H. Reeve [New Rochelle, N.Y., n.d.], 2.64; F. Engels, *The Origins of the Family, Private Property, and the State, in the Light of the Researches of Lewis H. Morgan*, translated for International Publishers [New York, 1942], 107).

29. From *The Limits of State Action*, ed. J. W. Burrow (Cambridge, 1969), 28; and *Gesammelte Schriften*, vol. 1 (*Schriften zur Anthropologie und Bildungslehre*, ed. A. Flitner [Düsseldorf and Munich, 1956]), 271.

30. A. Heeren, *Ancient Greece*, trans. George Bancroft (London, 1841), 127.

31. In *The Complete Works of Friedrich Nietzsche*, ed. O. Levy, vol. 2 (trans. M. A. Muegge), 7, 15.

32. Cited from Treitschke's *Der Socialismus und seine Gönner* (Berlin, 1875), 10, 17, 40, in Thomas Wiedemann's translation of Joseph Vogt's *Ancient Slavery and the Ideal of Man* (Cambridge, Mass., 1975), 208. Despite pious disclaimers, Vogt himself is plainly sympathetic to the notion that slavery was an acceptable price for the Greek achievement. Discussion of the evolution of attitudes to ancient slavery appear in Vogt; in Finley's *Ancient Slavery and Modern Ideology* (London and New York, 1980); and in G. Cambiano, "Dalla polis senza schiavi agli schiavi senza polis," *Opus* 1 (1981): 11–32.

33. *Review on the Debate in the Virginia Legislature of 1831 and 1832* (reprint, Westport, Conn., 1970), 112.

34. Ibid., 130.

35. E. Genovese, *The World the Slaveholders Made: Two Essays in Interpretation* (New York, 1969), 128. The second of the two long essays concerns Fitzhugh. On Fitzhugh see also the biography by H. Wish, *George Fitzhugh: Propagandist of the Old South* (Baton Rouge, 1943); and C. Vann Woodward's introduction to his edition of *Cannibals All! Or Slaves without Masters* (Cambridge, Mass., 1960).

36. *Slavery Justified, by a Southerner* (1850): 8.

37. *Cannibals All*, ed. Woodward, 220.

38. On the importance of Greek models to the rhetoric of proslavery ideology see (as well as pp. 274–76, here) V. Parrington, *Main Currents in American Thought*, vol. 2 (Norman, Okla., 1927); S. F. Wiltshire, "Jefferson, Calhoun, and the Slavery Debate: The Classics and the Two Minds of the South," *Southern Humanities Review* 11 (special issue, 1977): 33–40; H. Temperley, "Capitalism, Slavery, and Ideology," *Past and Present* 75 (1977): 94–118; J. D. Harrington, "Classical Antiquity and the Proslavery Argument," *Slavery and Abolition* 10 (1989): 60–72; and L. Tise, *Proslavery: A History of the Defense of Slavery in America, 1701–1840* (Athens, Ga., 1988). A discussion of classical ideology and antebellum architecture appears in R. Gamble, "The White-Column Tradition: Classical Architecture and the Southern Mystique," *Southern Humanities Review* 11 (1977): 40ff.

39. *Life in Ancient Athens* (London, 1906): 43–45.

40. Originally published in 1951 (reprint, Harmondsworth, 1981), 132.

41. At 1.270, for example (moral condemnation of slavery), and 1.406 (practical advantages of slavery).

42. Some revolutionaries, of course, had expressed concern about slavery. See, for example, Vidal-Naquet, *La democratie grecque vue d'ailleurs* (Paris, 1990), 223.

43. Volney, *Leçons d'Histoire*, 125–26.

44. Constant, "De la Liberté des Anciens comparée a Celle des Modernes" (1819): in *Cours de Politique Constitutionelle, ou Collection des Ouvrages publiés sur la Gouvernement Représentatif*, ed. E. Laboulaye, vol. 2 (1861): 545.

45. Reprinted in the new 1829 eight-volume edition, 1.vi–xlii, esp. pp. xv–xxii.

46. Marx-Engels, *The Holy Family, or Critique of Critical Criticism, against Bruno Bauer and Company* (1845): English translation published by Progress Publishers (Moscow, 1975), 151. On Marx's reaction against the late eighteenth-century idealization of antiquity in France see F. Furet, *Marx et la Revolution Française* (Paris, 1986). Furet (24, 33) is followed by Vidal-Naquet (*La Democratie Grecque, Vue d'Ailleurs*, 212) in his conviction that Marx was strongly influenced by Constant.

47. Gustave Le Bon, *The Crowd: A Study in the Popular Mind* (English translation reprinted New York, 1960), 104.

48. Wallon, *Histoire de l'esclavage dans l'antiquité*, 1.61. Similar arguments were put forward by abolitionists on the other side of the Atlantic. Adam Gurowski, writing in 1860, saw slavery as deeply at odds with the Athenian democracy. For him, both slaves and slave-owners stood outside the democratic system, since the slaves could not vote, and the slave-owners, he contended, were disloyal oligarchs. Despite the prevalence of slavery, Gurowski writes, on the eve of the Peloponnesian War "democracy still pre-

vailed. The oligarchs, proud of their slaves, mines, plantations and estates, scorned the democracy of Athens." It was the increase in the proportion of slaves, Gurowski argues, after the death of Pericles that ultimately accounted for the Macedonian conquest (*Slavery in History* [New York, 1960], 117–19).

49. E. Wood, *Peasant-Citizen and Slave: The Foundations of Athenian Democracy* (London and New York, 1988; paperback, 1989), 5–41.

50. Letters between J.-F. Deluc and Baron Albrecht von Haller, MSS. Haller xxv, Burgerbibliothek, Berne, cited in R. Leigh, "J.-J. Rousseau and the Myth of Antiquity in the Eighteenth Century," in R. R. Bolgar, ed., *Classical Influences on Western Thought, 1650–1870* (Cambridge, 1979), 163–64.

51. Cited in C. Mossé, *L'Antiquité dans la Révolution française* (Paris, 1989), 102.

52. Bisset, 132.

53. *Rejected Essay*, 33–34.

54. Condorcet, *Esquisse d'un Tableau Historique des Progrès de l'Esprit Humain* (1793; reprint, Paris, 1970), ed. O. H. Prior and Y. Belaval, 59.

55. In *Lectures on The Philosophy of History*, trans. J. Sibree (reprint, New York, 1956), 254.

56. Heeren, *Ancient Greece*, 127.

57. W. Warde Fowler, *The City-State of the Greeks and Romans* (1893; reprint, London, 1966), 178–79.

The appeal to Aristotle was particularly common in nineteenth-century America, especially in the work of George Frederick Holmes and George Fitzhugh; and Aristotle had received high marks from Calhoun (cited and discussed in Wiltshire, "Jefferson, Calhoun, and the Slavery Debate," 35ff.). In a rambling piece published in the proslavery journal *De Bow's Review* in 1857, Fitzhugh pointed up the similarities in thought between Calhoun and Aristotle and recommended that the classical economists such as Adam Smith be replaced with Aristotle in the American curriculum. Censuring the fundamentally Platonic cast of the "wild and profane political philosophy" that had lately been working its wiles in Europe and lamenting that "the minds of Franklin, Jefferson, Paine and probably many others who gave tone and direction to public opinion" around the time of the revolution "were tinctured with this rash philosophy," he was greatly relieved to come to Aristotle, who "took human nature as he found it" and tried to adapt government to man rather than the other way around ("The Politics and Economics of Aristotle and Mr. Calhoun," vol. 23 [1857], 164). After extensive praise of Aristotle, Fitzhugh proceeded to Calhoun, who, he claimed, had in his *Disquisition on Government* maintained "much of the doctrines of Aristotle" (169).

Fitzhugh's friend Holmes, who taught at the University of Virginia for forty years, not only made frequent appeal to the authority of Aristotle in his defenses of slavery but composed a long article that appeared in the 1850 issue of the *Southern Literary Messenger* entitled "Observations on a Passage in the Politics of Aristotle Relative to Slavery." There he set out at length Aristotle's views regarding slavery, concluding that it was a "necessary consequence of social organization" and "consonant with the laws of nature" (196).

58. Mitford, *History of Greece* 4.1–2, 1.270.

59. Böckh, *The Public Economy of the Athenians* (1842 ed.), 614.

60. Ibid., 45.

61. Heeren, *Ancient Greece*, 127, 112.

62. J. Burckhardt, *Griechische Kulturgeschichte*, ed. R. Marx (Leipzig, 1929), 1.254–55. On Burckhardt and Greek slavery see Wood, *Peasant-Citizen*, esp. p. 26.

63. N. D. Fustel de Coulanges, *The Ancient City: A Study on the Religion, Laws, and Institutions of Greece and Rome* (1864; English translation, Baltimore, 1980), 330.

64. These and other examples are collected in R. Sargent, *The Size of the Slave Population*, 9–11.

65. Herself often employing Marxist approaches, Wood is critical of the Marxists' preoccupation with the importance of slavery in the Athenian economy.

66. From the *Grundrisse: Foundations of the Critique of Political Economy (Rough Draft)*, trans. M. Nicolaus (London, 1973), 111. A later period of antiquity could provoke nostalgia as well; in the *Grundrisse* Marx comments on the moral tenor of ancient economic debates, observing that in the ancient world wealth is not identified as aim of production, but rather "the question is always which mode of property creates the best citizens." The old view, he contends, in which "the human being appears as the aim of production" is in many respects loftier than the modern construct in which "production appears as the aim of mankind and wealth the sum of production."

67. Cited from the *Writings of the Young Karl Marx on Philosophy and Society*, trans. L. Easton and K. Guddat (Garden City, N.Y., 1967), 206.

68. Above, p. 266. Despite the similarity of his thinking to that of Schiller and Hegel, Marx mentions Greece much less often than they, and Athens almost never. For all Aristotle's disdain for banausic labor, however, Marx admired his work and drew deeply on it. On Marx and the Greeks, see Kain, *Schiller, Hegel, and Marx* (Kingston and Montreal, 1982), 75–158; and G. McCarthy, *Marx and the Ancients* (Savage, Md., 1990), with ample bibliography. I have not yet been able to consult McCarthy's collection of essays *Marx and Aristotle* (Savage, Md., 1992).

69. M. I. Finley is right, of course, that Marxists and anti-Marxists have spent considerable time in affirming or denying the premise that ancient society was based on slave labor and that "the question which is most promising for systematic investigation is not whether slavery was the basic element, or whether it caused this or that, but how it functioned," but I think he underestimates the degree to which, despite all the distracting polemics, the intrusion of Marxism into classical studies actually did contribute to a focus on the function of slavery in ancient society ("Was Greek Civilization Based on Slave Labour?" Historia 8 [1959]: 69).

The role of Marxism in the study of Greek slavery is examined in the introduction to Yvon Garlan, *Slavery in Ancient Greece* (French ed., Paris, 1982), trans. Janet Lloyd (Ithaca, 1988). A discussion of Marxist approaches to Athens and a bibliography of works written in Russian appears in E. Frolov, "Griechische Geschichte bis zum Zeitalter des Hellenismus," in H. Heinen, ed., *Die Geschichte des Altertums im Spiegel der sowjetischen Forschung* (Darmstadt, 1980), 69–123, esp. pp. 111–17. See also Padelis Lekas, *Marx on Classical Antiquity: Problems of Historical Methodology* (Sussex and New York, 1988), 86–129 and notes. Marxist approaches to classical history in general are discussed in H. F. Graham, "The Significant Role of the Study of Ancient History in the Soviet Union," *Classical World* 61 (1967): 85–97; R. I. Frank, "Marxism and Ancient History," *Arethusa* 8 (1975): 43–58; G.E.M. de Sainte Croix, "Karl Marx and the History of Classical Antiquity," *Arethusa* 8 (1975): 7–41; D. Lanza and M. Vegetti, "L'ideologia della città," *QS* 1, no. 2 (1975): 1–37; M. Mazza, "Marxismo e storia antica," *Studi Storici* 17 (1976): 95–124; and L. Canfora, "Antiquisants et marxisme,"

Dialogues d'Histoire Ancienne 7 (1981): 429–36. A bibliography down to 1975 appears in R. Padgug, "Select Bibliography on Marxism and the Study of Antiquity," *Arethusa* 8 (1975): 201–25.

I have not been able to consult R. Sannwald, *Marx und die Antike* (*Staatswissenschlaftliche Studien*, N. F. 27; Zurich, 1957), or D. Lanza et al., *L'ideologia della città* (Naples, 1977).

70. I have consulted only the French translation, *Histoire de l'Antiquité*, Editions en Langues Etrangères (Moscow, n.d. [but apparently 1959]). The work was assembled under the direction of V. Diakov and S. Kovalev, with the sections on Greece evidently done by A. Berguer, A. Dekonski, D. Noudelman, and O. Rotberg. F. Korovkin's *History of the Ancient World* originally appeared in 1981; the English translation was published in Moscow in 1985.

A bibliography on Soviet work concerning Greek slavery appears in Garlan, *Slavery in Ancient Greece*, 8.

71. This paradox too, of course, has shaped much Western twentieth-century thinking as well.

72. The authors' footnotes by and large restrict themselves to Lenin, Marx, and in particular Engels (primarily *The Origins of Private Property, the Family, and the State*).

73. In discussing intellectual life in ancient Greece, Korovkin writes that "Democritus' teaching which destroyed the belief in the gods and the immortal human soul provoked the anger of many Greek slave-owners" (171).

74. Pp. 149–50.

Ellen Wood has reminded me that not all scholars working in what has until recently been the communist world stress the centrality of slavery in Athens; see, for example, the downplaying of slavery in Athenian production in two articles in the East German journal *Klio*: Gert Audring, "Grenzen der Konzentration von Grundeigentum in Attika während des 4. Jh. v. u. Z.," *Klio* 56 (1974): 445–46; and Lea Gluskina, "Zur Spezifik der klassischen griechschen Polis im Zusammenhang mit dem Problem ihrer Krise," *Klio* 57 (1975): 415–31. Cf. also V. N. Andreyev, "Some Aspects of Agrarian Conditions in Attica in the Fifth to Third Centuries BC," *Eirene* 12 (1974): 5–46.

75. "Was Greek Civilization Based on Slave Labour?" 72.

76. *The World of Athens: An Introduction to Classical Athenian Culture* (Cambridge, 1984), 187–88.

77. *Rejected Essay* (pp. 268, 277–79 here), 33–34.

78. Morgan's essay has been reprinted in S. Katz and J. Murrin, eds., *Colonial America: Essays in Political and Social Development* (3d ed., New York, 1983), 527–96. The first chapters of Oakes's book, which explores the nature of slave status, is entitled "Outsiders."

79. Although the notion of a "men's club" is associated with Pierre Vidal-Naquet and reflects twentieth-century sensibilities, the idea of a club had itself been articulated by a number of earlier thinkers and appeared, for example, Barker's 1918 *Greek Political Theory* (16) and in Van Loon's 1921 *Story of Mankind*, where students could read that "ancient Athens resembles a modern club" (66). Vidal-Naquet contends that "the Greek city in its classical form was marked by a double exclusion: the exclusion of women, which made it a 'men's club'; and the exclusion of slaves, which made it a 'citizens' club'" (*The Black Hunter: Forms of Thought and Forms of Society in the Greek World*, [trans. A Szegedy-Maszak [1981; reprint, Baltimore, 1986], 207).

80. Patterson, *Freedom*, volume 1: *Freedom in the Making of Western Culture* (New York, 1991), 99.

81. Ibid., 110. Vidal-Naquet's words appear in *The Black Hunter*, 211.

82. Whether Fitzhugh had actually read Marx has been sharply contended. His biographer, Harvey Wish, was convinced that he had (*George Fitzhugh: Propagandist*, 182–83), whereas Genovese (*The World the Slaveholders Made*, 182 [sic]) insists he had not.

83. *Review of the Debate in the Virginia Legislature*, 116.

84. In his thoughtful book *Finding the Mean: Theory and Practice in Aristotelian Political Philosophy* (Princeton, 1990), Stephen Salkever questions traditional notions of Aristotle's misogyny and stresses Aristotle's concern to distinguish between slaves and women in the role they played in the lives of free men; he also sees Aristotle (and Plato) as championing a complex of virtues that is more a blend of traditional masculine and traditional feminine merits than the more "macho" ideology of his contemporaries (chap. 4). I am more persuaded by the arguments of Wendy Brown in *Manhood and Politics: A Feminist Reading in Political Theory* (Totowa, N.J., 1988), who emphasizes Aristotle's role in a long tradition that saw politics as intimately bound up with masculinity.

85. A. Zimmern, *The Greek Commonwealth: Politics and Economics in Fifth-Century Athens* (Oxford, 1911), 333. The shift in thinking over the past century is indexed by the insistence of Paul Rahe of the University of Tulsa in 1992 that Athens' exclusivity was intrinsic to its ethos and that "Athens was not a liberal democracy occasionally subject to fits of aberrant behavior" (*Republics Ancient and Modern: Classical Republicanism and the American Revolution* [Chapel Hill, N.C., 1992], 197).

86. Hume, Essay X, "Of Some Remarkable Customs," in *Essays* (1742): 403, 498. "The republic of ATHENS," Hume wrote, "was, I believe, the most extensive democracy, which we read of in history: Yet if we make the requisite allowances for the women, the slaves, and the strangers, we shall find, that that establishment was not, at first, made, nor any law ever voted, by a tenth part of those who were bound to pay obedience to it. Not to mention the islands and foreign dominions, which the ATHENIANS claimed as theirs by right of conquest."

87. Tucker, *Treatise*, 214 ("why the adult *Females* should be excluded, is impossible to say"); Gillies, *The History of Ancient Greece* (1820 ed.), 2.1.155.

88. Mitford, *History of Greece* 3.3–5. A different perspective on women and democracy is offered in chaps. 9 through 12 of the third book of De Tocqueville's *Democracy in America*.

89. "Quarterly Review.—Articles on Greek Literature," *Westminster Review* 4 (1825): 249. "How," he asks, "could a people be great and excellent, who despised, and who had reason to despise, their mothers, their sisters, and their wives?" But of course Mitford did not consider the Athenians great and excellent. Similar observations were made half a century later by James Donaldson of the University of St. Andrews, who wrote that "the student of the history of women is continually reminded of the fact that when men lose their dignity and eminence, woman disappears from the scene, but when they rise into worth, she again comes on the stage in all her power and tenderness" (in "The Position and Influence of Women in Ancient Greece" [1878], reprinted in *Woman: Her Position and Influence in Ancient Greece and Rome, and among the Early Christians* [New York, 1973], 35). The same level of generalization was evident in Sir

372 NOTES TO CHAPTER TWELVE

Thomas Erskine May's *Democracy in Europe*. For May, the Greeks' reverence for women attested their superiority to the Asiatic races, for, he contended, "Respect for women has ever been the characteristic of free races, and contempt for them the mark of a lower civilization, and of slavery" (*Democracy in Europe* [London, 1877], 48).

90. St. John, *Manners and Customs of Ancient Greece* (1842): 2.39–40. St. John's impassioned introduction suggests that his concern for the character of women lay in a certain preoccupation with mothers. The "great sources of a nation's happiness," he maintains, "must always lie about the domestic hearth," for "men are everywhere exactly what their mothers make them" (1.xv). Writing of Athenian patriotism later in this same introduction, he maintains that because the Athenians believed that they had sprung "from the bosom of the earth" of their city, "it stood, therefore to them in the dearest of all relations, being, to sum up everything holy in one word,—their MOTHER" (1.xx).

91. A. W. Gomme, "The Position of Women in Classical Athens in the Fifth and Fourth Centuries," *CP* 20 (1925): 1–25.

92. *The Greeks*, 235.

93. Ibid., 222.

94. J. P. Mahaffy, *Social Life in Greece from Homer to Menander*, 139.

95. Ibid., 137.

96. G. Fitzhugh, *Sociology for the South*, 205; cf. "Southern Thought Again," *De Bow's Review* 23 (1857): 449–62.

97. G. Fitzhugh, "Black Republicanism in Athens," *De Bow's Review* 23 (1857): 27.

98. *Cannibals All!* 198.

99. 12 September 1852.

100. W. G. Simms, *Morals of Slavery*, in *The Pro-Slavery Argument; as Maintained by the Most Distinguished Writers of the Southern States* (1852): 248.

101. *Slavery in the Light of Social Ethics*, in E. N. Elliott, ed., *Cotton is King, and Pro-Slavery Arguments* (1860): 601.

102. Harper, *Slavery in the Light of Social Ethics*, 605.

103. See chap. 11, n. 86, here.

104. G. Cox, *General History of Greece* 2.100–101.

105. F. Engels, *Origins of the Family, Private Property, and the State* (1884): English translation for International Publishers (New York, 1942), 107, 58. The belief in the primary role of slavery in the collapse of Athenian society has been affirmed by numerous Marxists of the twentieth century, such as the Englishman George Thomson, who contended in 1955 that slavery, by replacing the old nobleman/commoner tensions with a sharper conflict between slave-owners and slaves, "destroyed democracy" (*Studies in Ancient Greek Society*, vol. 2: *The First Philosophers* [London, 1955], 227).

106. Engels, *Origins*, 69–72.

107. P. Slater, *The Glory of Hera: Greek Mythology and the Greek Family* (Boston, 1968), chap. 1 and 450–51.

On the whole Slater's work was not received well by classicists. See, for example, the review by Helene Foley of Barnard (then at Stanford), in *Diacritics* 5, no. 4 (1975): 31–36.

108. *The Reign of the Phallus: Sexual Politics in Ancient Athens* (New York, 1985), 1, 12.

109. Reprinted in *Women in the Ancient World: The Arethusa Papers* (Albany, 1984), 37, 36.

110. DuBois, *Sowing the Body: Psychoanalysis and Ancient Representations of Women* (Chicago, 1988), especially chap. 3.

111. Young, *History of Athens* 1.70.

112. "Classical Greek Attitudes to Sexual Behaviour," *Women in the Ancient World: The Arethusa Papers*, 149.

113. "Classical Greek Attitudes," 143–57; see also Dover's *Greek Homosexuality* (Cambridge, Mass., 1978). Specifically, Dover argues that a boy could offer his lover a variety of means of gratification but was not to allow himself to be penetrated anally, on pain of forfeiting citizenship rights in the future.

114. *L'Usage des plaisirs* (1984): cited in the English translation of Robert Hurley, *The Use of Pleasure* (New York, 1985), 151.

115. Ibid., 82.

116. Ibid., 22–23.

117. D. Halperin, *One Hundred Years of Homosexuality and Other Essays on Greek Love* (New York and London, 1990), 95–96.

118. Pp. 128–33.

119. *Centaurs and Amazons: Women and the Pre-History of the Great Chain of Being* (Ann Arbor, Mich., 1982), 60–61.

Notions parallel to those of duBois crop up in a variety of places. Yvon Garlan in *Slavery in Ancient Greece* contends that slavery in Athens and elsewhere in Greece was "the necessary element" for Greek society to "affirm its identity" (144); Edith Hall's study of Athenian tragedy, *Inventing the Barbarian* (Oxford, 1989), portrays the notion of the barbarian as formulated not in contrast to what is Greek but specifically as a foil to the Athenian democracy of the fifth century and hence as a crucial building block of the rhetoric of tragedy. Hall's subtitle is *Greek Self-Definition through Tragedy*.

120. The pun on "just," though suggested by duBois' argument on p. 123 and throughout, is my own.

121. *Goddesses, Whores, Wives, and Slaves: Women in Classical Antiquity* (New York, 1975), 78. The new thinking about Athens has even crept into works intended for a general or undergraduate audience; a construct similar to that of Pomeroy only with the emphasis on slavery appears in the *Economic and Social History of Ancient Greece: An Introduction* of Pierre Vidal-Naquet and Michel Austin. The preface to the 1977 English edition identifies the book as "aimed in the first place at an undergraduate audience, though it is hoped that it will also be of interest to a wider, non-specialist readership interested in the history and civilization of ancient Greece." The authors make much of the crucial role played by outsiders in the insiders' quest for both self-definition and economic success. Slavery, they argue, made Greek society possible "by guaranteeing the freedom of the citizen." The growth of democracy at Athens, they maintain, made it particularly important for members of the egalitarian community to define themselves in contradistinction to those who did not belong (*Economic and Social History of Ancient Greece* [original French edition, 1972; trans., Berkeley and Los Angeles, 1977], xii, 23, 94).

122. Cited by Rousseau in "J.-J. Rousseau, Citizen of Geneva to Monsieur d'Alembert," in J.-J. Rousseau, *Politics and the Arts*, trans. Allan Bloom (Ithaca, 1973), 16.

123. W. Connolly, *Identity/Difference* (Ithaca, 1991), 64, 160.

CHAPTER THIRTEEN

1. Ducoudray, *Cours d'études a l'usage de l'enseignement secondaire moderne, Histoire de l'ancien Orient et de la Grèce, Classe de sixième, conforme aux programmes de 1891*, 223, 235; L. Dussieux, *Histoire Ancienne: La Grèce* (Paris, 1877), 37–39; T. Bachelet, *Cours d'histoire a l'usage des établissements d'Instruction Publique, Histoire Grecque (Classe de cinquième)* (cited from the 5th ed., of 1881), 177.

2. N. D. Fustel de Coulanges, *The Ancient City: A Study on the Religion, Laws, and Institutions of Greece and Rome* (English trans. Baltimore, 1980), 213. Fustel was also distressed by the outlook of Plutarch.

3. R. Latham, *In Quest of Civilization* (London and New York, 1946), 197.

4. E. Davis, "Remarks on the Perfect State," *Harper's Monthly Magazine* 153 (1 November 1926): 695, 686–87, 694.

5. See, e.g., Simon Hornblower's *The Greek World, 479–323 BC* (London, 1983), 183, 104–5.

6. W. Durant, *The Life of Greece, The Story of Civilization*, part 2 (New York, 1939), 87.

7. On the adulation of Fustel by l'Action Française, see Jane Herrick's Catholic University dissertation, "The Historical Thought of Fustel de Coulanges" (Washington, D.C., 1954), 106–112.

8. The Italian Marxists have reprinted Maurras's piece in "L'Action Française et la démocratie athénienne" in their journal *Quaderni di Storia*, 2, no. 4 (1976), with a preface by Bertrand Hemmerdinger of Paris (pp. 7–18); see pp. 302–3 here.

9. "L'Action Française," 7.

10. H. Müller-Strübing, *Aristophanes und die historische Kritik* (1873); E. Meyer, *Geschichte des Altertums* (1884–1902; reprint, Stuttgart, 1954), 3.228; R. von Pöhlmann, "Zur Beurteilung Georg Grotes und seiner Griechischen Geschichte" (*Deutsche Zeitschrift für Geschichtswissenschaft*, 1890), reprinted in *Aus Altertum und Gegenwart* (Munich, 1911), 315–42.

11. See chapter 12, n. 22, here.

12. J. G. Droysen, *Geschichte Alexanders des Grossen* (1833): esp. p. 13.

13. E. Drerup, *Aus einer alten Advokatenrepublik*, 189.

14. J. R. Knipfing, "German Historians and Macedonian Imperialism," *American Historical Review* 26 (1921): 657–71.

15. Cited from the 1940 American edition of Strasser's *Hitler and I*, trans. G. David and E. Mosbacher (Boston, 1940), 214–15.

16. R. Watt, "'Wanderer, kommst du nach Sparta': History through Propaganda into Literary Commonplace," *Modern Language Review* 80 (1985): 871–73. Watt also follows the motif through the German literature that unfolded for a generation after the war (877–83).

17. Popper's association of Plato's political thought with Nazism was not crazy; during the war, the expatriate Karl Lehmann-Hartleben of New York University described German classicists suddenly discovering under government pressure that "Greek education, for instance Plato's Laws, constituted a Bible of Nazi philosophy." Lehmann-Hartleben also contended that "while one professor of ancient history formerly had proved that Sparta had been great only in the archaic period, when it was not militaristic or reactionary, he now recanted and proved that Athens after all decayed because

of democracy, while Sparta developed the really great values of heroic Nazi-humanity" (K. Lehmann-Hartleben, "United Front of Humanism," *Classical Weekly* 36 [1943]: 173). On the study of ancient history in Nazi Germany, readers will want to consult V. Losemann, *Nationalsozialismus und Antike: Studien zur Entwicklung des Faches Alte Geschichte 1933–1945* (Hamburg, 1977), which I have not yet been able to obtain.

18. It is ironic that while Popper recoiled from the foreshadowing of Nazism in Plato, E. M. Blaiklock in the lecture "The Decline and Fall of Athenian Democracy" he gave in 1948 at Auckland University College in New Zealand pitted Plato on the side of the struggle against totalitarianism. Quoting from the *Republic* (485) Plato's rhetorical question whether the same nature can love both wisdom and falsehood, he glosses the response: "'Never!' Never! The word stands over Plato's work like the great NO marked in stone on the Greek hillside for the skies to see during the days of Nazi tyranny." (*The Decline and Fall of Athenian Democracy* [Auckland, 1949], 15).

19. M. Westington, "Nazi Germany and Ancient Sparta," expanded and published in *Education* magazine in November 1944, 152–64.

20. C. E. Robinson (not Brown University's more famous C. A. Robinson), *Hellas: A Short History of Greece* (Boston, 1948), 35–36, 123, 160.

21. W. K. Prentice, *The Ancient Greeks: Studies towards a Better Understanding of the Ancient World*, (Princeton 1940), 150, 151.

22. U. von Wilamowitz-Möllendorff, *Aus Kydathen* (1880): 6.

23. The influence of German scholarship on America (largely through German émigrés) is discussed in W. Calder, "Die Geschichte der klassischen Philologie in den Vereinigten Staaten" (1966): reprinted in Calder's *Studies in the Modern History of Classical Scholarship, Antiqua* 27 (Naples, 1984): 15–42.

24. In "Plato's Modern Friends and Enemies" (*Philosophy* 37 [1962]: 97–113), Renford Bambrough discusses some of the issues in what he labels the "Thirty Years' War" between the two camps; see also the works cited in n. 1 of chap. 4 here and L. Versenyi, "Plato and His Liberal Opponents," *Philosophy* 46 (1971): 222–37.

25. The debate over the utility of the past has not, of course, limited itself to classical authors; the perceived value of the recorded history of classical antiquity (such as it is) has waxed and waned with the passing of time. Heated debate has surrounded the question whether the fortunes of Athens afford useful instruction for modern times. Many thinkers of the Renaissance and eighteenth-century England and France were convinced that Athens provided powerful lessons in how not to do things. Germans writing around 1800 were troubled about the prospects of resurrecting Greek ideals in the modern world, but the happy liberals of Victorian England had no doubt that Athens provided a shining model of unity and generosity. Eighteenth-century Americans were deeply divided about whether the values of Greece and Rome were helpful, destructive, or simply passé, and as the revolution receded into the past, reservations about the perpetuation of the classical ethos increased. The learned Jefferson himself began to question the usefulness of ancient history, and the happy classicism of John Adams's *Defence of the Constitutions of the United States* was attacked by Jefferson's friend John Taylor in his *Inquiry into the Principles and Policy of the Government of the United States*, published in 1814 but begun a few years after the constitutional convention. Arguing that ancient history "is invariably treacherous in some degree, and comes, like an oracle, from a place into which light cannot penetrate," Taylor, who accused Adams of "diving after wisdom into the gloom of antiquity," exhorted his

fellow Americans not to be "intimidated by apparitions of departed time" (cited in Reinhold, *Classica Americana*, 7). Writing several generations later, Emerson addressed the American conflict about the desirability of preserving classical values by maintaining somewhat defensively that "our admiration of the Antique is not admiration of the old but of the natural," contending that "we admire the Greek in an American ploughboy often" (cited in Johnson, "Hellas in Hesperia," 164–65). Both the French Revolution and the First World War, however, ushered in eras in which questions were raised about the utility and relevance of classical values. After the revolution Volney decried the pretended egalitarianism of the ancients; Chateaubriand found the project of resurrecting classical virtues to be impossible in decadent France; Constant stressed the differences between ancient and modern liberty. In early twentieth-century Britain, the poet Louis MacNeice stressed the crushing weight of the differences that divided ancient from modern society. "It was all so unutterably different," he wrote, "and all so long ago."

26. In the introduction to his translation (1629).

27. On 20 August 1777, cited in L. H. Butterfield, ed., *Adams Family Correspondence*, vol. 2 (Cambridge, Mass., 1963), 320–21.

28. *Two Dialogues Concerning the Manner of Writing History* (English trans., 1783), 43.

29. Gildersleeeve's essay appeared in the *Atlantic* for September 1897 (80.330–42).

30. Citations of the sinning articles of Lang, as well as complaints about Hunter's book *Thucydides: The Artful Reporter* (Toronto, 1973), appear in Hunter Rawlings's more orthodox study *The Structure of Thucydides' History* (Princeton, 1981), 267–69.

31. M. Wason, *Class Struggles in Ancient Greece* (Rome, 1972), 137. It is interesting to compare Wason's strictures with those of a Victorian male, J. P. Mahaffy, who denied the significance of the war but reiterated the merit of the historian. The Peloponnesian war itself, he contended, "had little import in the world's history, even in its largest crisis," and he maintained that the fact that "the little raids and battles, the capture of a couple of hundred Spartans, or the defeat of twenty ships should still be studied with minuteness, and produce libraries of modern criticism, is due solely to the power of the historian and of the famous language in which he wrote his book." Mahaffy's remarks appear on p. 52 of his introduction to M. M. Ripley's English translation of Duruy's *History of Greece, and of the Greek People, from the Earliest Times to the Roman Conquest* (1890).

32. N. Cousins, "Still Required Reading," *Saturday Review* 24 (7 June 1941), 8; R. Campbell, "How a Democracy Died," *Life* magazine 30 (1 January 1951): 88–96 (see p. 260 here). Davis's original piece "Required Reading," advocating perusal of Thucydides as an aid in understanding both World War I and World War II, had appeared in the *Saturday Review* for 14 October 1939; Davis had also written about analogies with the Peloponnesian War in 1917.

33. G. Johnson, "God Was Bored," *New Republic* 145 (11 September 1961): 10. In their belief in the relevance of Thucydides' work to their own times journalists have been joined by academics whose chief focus is not classical antiquity. Thus for example in 1991 Westview Press published a collection of essays entitled *Hegemonic Warfare: From Thucydides to the Nuclear Age*, ed. by R. Ned Lebow and Barry Strauss. Strauss is a classicist, but his Cornell colleague Lebow is not, and the essays that appear represent a variety of nonclassicist perspectives.

34. *Democracy Ancient and Modern* (1973; reprint, London, 1985), 23.

35. D. Stockton, *The Classical Athenian Democracy* (Oxford and New York, 1990), 187.

36. J. Ober, *Mass and Elite in Democratic Athens: Rhetoric, Ideology, and the Power of the People* (Princeton, 1989), 9.

37. Reprinted in *Giants and Dwarfs, Essays 1960–1990* (New York, 1990), 235–55.

38. I. Stone, *The Trial of Socrates* (Boston, 1988), xi.

39. L. Morgan, *Ancient Society: or, Researches in the Lines of Human Progress From Savagery, through Barbarism* (1877): 85, vii.

40. Ibid., 247.

41. Ibid., 254.

42. R. Padgug, "Classes and Society in Classical Greece," *Arethusa* 8 (1975): 101–2.

43. B. Hemmerdinger, "L'esclavagisme antique vu par le thermidorien Volney," *QS* 1 (1975): 115–16, and "L'Action Française et la démocratie athénienne," *QS* 2, no. 4 (1976): 7–18.

44. W. G. Forrest, *The Emergence of Greek Democracy 800–400 B.C.* (New York and Toronto, 1966), 16.

45. The difficulties Finley experienced in his career extended well beyond anti-Semitism. He was dismissed from teaching positions in the United States during the McCarthy era because of suspected leftist leanings and because of his appeal to the fifth amendment in avoiding questions put to him by the U. S. Internal Security Committee. He then moved to England, where he spent most of his life until his death in 1986. After his dismissal from Rutgers was finally invalidated, he returned there in the 1970s to deliver the lectures that were then published as *Democracy Ancient and Modern*.

46. *La démocratie grecque, vue d'ailleurs* (Paris, 1990), 215.

47. Skinner's remarks appear in her introduction to *Rescuing Creusa: New Methodological Approaches to Women in Antiquity, Helios*, n.s. 13, no. 2 (1986): 4.

48. W. Durant, *The Life of Greece*, 87.

49. Johnson's remarks are cited by Macaulay in his "Athenian Orators," 153; Brougham's observations are from his *Political Philosophy*, part 2 (1843): 234.

50. Mahaffy in his introduction to Ripley's translation of Duruy's Greek history (1890): 63, makes this contention and cites Freeman's *History of Federal Government* as an authority.

51. Mitford and Rollin (see chaps. 8 and 9 here); Ferguson, *Greek Imperialism* (Boston and New York, 1913), 57.

52. C. Meier, *The Greek Discovery of Politics* (English trans. D. McLintock; London and Cambridge, Mass., 1990), 145; K. J. Dover, *Greek Popular Morality in the Time of Plato and Aristotle* (Berkeley and Los Angeles, 1974), 39–40.

53. M. I. Finley, *Democracy Ancient and Modern* (1973; 2d ed., New York, 1985), 23.

54. In J. Winkler and F. Zeitlin, eds., *Nothing to Do with Dionysos? Athenian Drama in Its Social Context* (Princeton, 1990), 243.

55. *Handbook of Greek Constitutional History* (reprint, London and New York, 1902), 179.

56. *The Origins of the Family, Private Property, and the State, in the Light of the Researches of Lewis H. Morgan*, translated for International Publishers (New York, 1942), 97. Engels conceded that Solon had attacked property and argued that some such attack had been intrinsic in all revolutions to date, contending that "from the first to

the last, all so-called political revolutions have been made to protect property—of *one* kind; and they have been carried out by confiscating, also called stealing, property—of *another* kind. The plain truth is that for two and a half thousand years it has been possible to preserve private property only by violating property" (103).

57. De Pauw, *Philosophical Researches* 2.141–46.

58. In *The Politics of History*, Howard Zinn cites the case of a priest on trial for burning draft board records who traced the genesis of his subversive tendencies to reading a book on the participation of Germany's practicing Catholics in the extermination of Jews. "I was trained in Rome," the priest related. "I was quite conservative, never broke a rule in seminary. Then I read a book" that "told how SS men went to mass, then went out to round up Jews. That book changed my life. I decided the church must never behave again as it did in the past; and that I must not." This line of development, Zinn observed, "is unusually clear," for "in most cases, where people turn in new directions, the causes are so complex, so subtle, that they are impossible to trace" (H. Zinn, *The Politics of History* [Boston, 1970], 35).

59. Cited in Luciano Canfora's *Ideologie del Classicismo* (Torino, 1980), 4.

60. In David Carr, *Time, Narrative, and History* (Bloomington, 1986), 4.

61. M. Bernal, *Black Athena: The Afroasiatic Roots of Classical Civilization*, vol. 1: *The Fabrication of Ancient Greece 1785–1985* (New Brunswick, 1987).

62. *Popular Government* (1885; reprint, Indianapolis, 1976), 79.

63. R. Wollheim, "Democracy," *Journal of the History of Ideas* 19 (1958): 233.

64. Around the middle of this century American sociologists and political scientists were positively tripping over themselves describing the psychological characteristics of the "democratic man" in glowing terms that would have no doubt have intrigued Plato, who first developed the notion. The democratic man, they explained, was characterized by all the traits one would generally associate with maturity and health. See, for example, Harold Lasswell's *Power and Personality* (New York, 1946), Seymour Lipset's *Political Man* (Garden City, N.Y., 1960) and the discussion of these works in G. Almond and S. Verba, *The Civic Culture: Political Attitudes and Democracy in Five Nations* (Princeton, 1963).

65. *Democracy: The Unfinished Journey*, 247. Dunn also discusses the universal appeal to the rhetoric of democracy at the opening of his *Western Political Theory in the Face of the Future* (Cambridge and New York, 1979).

66. The passage comes from Hitler's *Speeches* (London, 1942), 1.254, and is cited as Item 193 in A. Naess, J. Christophersen, and K. Kjell, eds., *Democracy, Ideology, and Objectivity: Studies in the Semantics and Cognitive Analysis of Ideological Controversy* (Oslo, 1956).

67. Cited as the Quotation of the Day in the *New York Times* for 22 May 1991.

68. Vidal-Naquet has observed in connection with the French revolutionaries' attitude to antiquity that "the Revolution invented nothing—but it did make choices" (*La démocratie grecque vue d'ailleurs* [Paris, 1990], 239).

69. W. B. Gallie, *Philosophy and the Historical Understanding* (London, 1964), 66.

70. E. Keuls, *The Reign of the Phallus: Sexual Politics in Ancient Athens* (New York, 1985), 12.

71. *The Political Unconscious: Narrative as a Socially Symbolic Act* (Ithaca, 1981), 9.

SELECTED BIBLIOGRAPHY

THIS bibliography is of necessity selective, and readers are urged to use the index to locate citations not found here. References to works on, say, Isocrates or Rousseau, for example, can be found easily enough by locating the discussion of Isocrates or Rousseau in the text. I have not on the whole repeated here the numerous works dealing with the evolution of Athenian democracy that were cited in the notes to chapter 2, or the extensive bibliography given in chapter 4 on the political ideas of Plato and Aristotle.

Works that are commonly known only by title are alphabetized by title.

A few works are included here from which I drew considerable benefit but that are not cited at any particular point in the text or notes. These are identified with asterisks.

The nature of this project has prompted me to include full names of authors where possible instead of initials, as I wished to take this occasion to underline the fact that each work cited hereunder was composed at a particular time by a real person. (I am also moved to do this by the tendency of students to say "It says in the book . . ." when they mean "In this book Forrest McDonald says . . .") Because of some of the issues raised in the later chapters of this work, I also thought it useful to provide some sense of how the authors cited break down with respect to gender.

Adams, John. *Diary and Autobiography.* Ed. L. H. Butterfield. Cambridge, Mass., 1962.
———. *The Works of John Adams, Second President of the United States.* Ed. Charles F. Adams. Boston, 1850–56.
Archives Parlementaires de 1787 à 1860; recueil complet des débats legislatifs et politiques des chambres françaises. 1st ser., 1787–99.
Aristides, Aelius. *P. Aelius Aristides: The Complete Works.* Ed. C. A. Behr. Leiden, 1986.
Aristotle. *Aristotle: The Athenian Constitution, The Eudemian Ethics, On Virtues and Vices.* London and Cambridge, Mass., 1935.
Aristotle, *Politics.* Trans. E. Barker. Oxford, 1946.
Arnheim, M.T.W. *Aristocracy in Greek Society.* London, 1977.
Arnold, Matthew. "Democracy" and "Equality." Reprinted in his *Mixed Essays, Irish Essays, and Others.* New York, 1883.
———. "On the Modern Element in Literature." 1869. In *On the Classical Tradition,* ed. R. H. Super. Ann Arbor, 1960.
Arthur, Marylin. "Early Greece: The Origins of the Western Attitude to Women." In *Women in the Ancient World: The Arethusa Papers,* ed. John Peradotto and John Sullivan. Albany, 1984.
Austin, Charles. "The Quarterly Review: 'Greek Courts of Justice.' No. 66." *Westminster Review* 7 (January 1827): 227ff.
Bailyn, Bernard. *Intellectual Origins of the American Revolution.* Cambridge, Mass., 1967.
———, ed. *Pamphlets of the American Revolution 1750–1776.* Cambridge, Mass., 1965.
Bambrough, Renford, ed. *Plato, Popper, and Politics.* Cambridge, 1967.
Barker, Ernest. *Greek Political Theory: Plato and His Predecessors.* London, 1918.
———. *Political Thought of Plato and Aristotle.* London, 1906.

Barnard, F. M. *Herder's Social and Political Thought: From Enlightenment to Nationalism.* Oxford, 1965.

Baron, Hans. *The Crisis of the Early Italian Renaissance.* Princeton, 1955.

———. *From Petrarch to Leonardo Bruni.* Chicago, 1968.

Barrow, R. H. *Plutarch and His Times.* London, 1967.

Barthélemy, J.-J. *Voyage du jeune Anacharsis en Grèce dans le milieu du quatrieme siècle avant l'ère vulgaire.* Paris, 1782. Trans. as *Travels of Anacharsis the Younger in Greece,* 7 vols. London, 1794.

Bernal, Martin. *Black Athena: The Afroasiatic Roots of Classical Civilization,* vol. 1 *The Fabrication of Ancient Greece 1785–1985.* New Brunswick, 1987.

Bethe, E. "Athen und der Peloponnesische Krieg im Spiegel des Weltkrieges." *Neue Jahrbücher für das Klassische Altertum, Geschichte und Deutsche Literatur* 20 (1917): 73–87.

Bisset, Robert. *Sketch of Democracy.* London, 1796.

Blaiklock, E. M. *The Decline and Fall of Athenian Democracy.* 1948. Auckland, 1949.

Bleicken, Jochen. *Die athenische Demokratie.* Paderborn, 1985.

Bodin, Jean. *Method for the Easy Comprehension of History.* Trans. Beatrice Reynolds. New York, 1945.

———. *Six Livres de la République.* Trans. Richard Knolles in 1606 as *Six Books of a Commonwealth.* Ed. K. D. McRae. Cambridge, Mass., 1962.

Böckh, Augustus. *The Public Economy of Athens.* 1817. Trans. George Cornewall Lewis. 2d ed., 1842.

Brissot de Warville, Jacques Pierre. *Mémoires (1754–1790).* Ed. C. Perroud. Paris, 1911.

Brown, Wendy. *Manhood and Politics: A Feminist Reading in Political Theory.* Totowa, NJ, 1988.

Burckhardt, J. *Griechische Kulturgeschichte.* Ed. R. Marx. Leipzig, 1929.

Bursian, Conrad. *Geschichte der classischen Philologie in Deutschland von den Anfängen bis zur Gegenwart.* 1883.

Bury, J. B. *History of Greece to the Death of Alexander the Great.* 1st ed., 1900. Rev. ed. by Russell Meiggs. New York, 1975.

Butler, Eliza. *The Tyranny of Greece over Germany.* Cambridge, 1935.

Buzot. *Mémoires sur la Révolution Française.* Ed. with an intro. by M. Guadet. Paris, 1823.

Calder, William. *Studies in the Modern History of Classical Scholarship.* Antiqua, vol. 27. Naples, 1984.

Canfora, Luciano, ed. *La democrazia come violenza.* Palermo, 1982.

———. *Ideologie del Classicismo.* Turin, 1980.

Carter, L. B. *The Quiet Athenian.* Oxford and New York, 1986.

*Cary, Max. "Athenian Democracy." *History,* n.s. 12 (1928): 206–14.

*Chambers, Mortimer, ed. *Georg Busolt: His Career in His Letters.* Mnemosyne, supplement 113. Leiden and New York, 1990.

———, and J. Day. *Aristotle's History of Athenian Democracy.* Berkeley and Los Angeles, 1962.

Chastellux, Francois Jean, Marquis de. *An Essay on Public Happiness.* 1772. English trans. London, 1774. Reprint, New York, 1969.

Chateaubriand, François René. *Historical, Political, and Moral Essay on Revolutions Ancient and Modern.* Trans. anonymously. 1815.

Cicero, Marcus Tullius. *De Republica*. Trans. C. W. Keyes. London and Cambridge, Mass., 1928.

———. *In Catilinam, Pro Flacco, Pro Murena, Pro Sulla*. Trans. Louis Lord. Reprint, London and Cambridge, Mass., 1978.

———. M. *Tulli Ciceronis Pro L. Flacco Oratio*. Oxford, 1931.

Clarke, M. L. *George Grote: A Biography*. London, 1962.

Cloché, Paul. *La démocratie athénienne*. Paris, 1951.

Colbourn, H. Trevor. *The Lamp of Experience: Whig History and the Origins of the American Revolution*. Chapel Hill, N.C., 1965.

Cole, A. Thomas. "The Anonymus Iamblichi and His Place in Greek Political Theory." *Harvard Studies in Classical Philology* 65 (1961): 127–63.

Condillac, Étienne Bonnot de. *Histoire Ancienne*. Reprinted in *Oeuvres Complètes de Condillac*, vol. 7. Paris, 1821.

Condorcet, Marie Jean Antoine Nicolas Caritat, Marquis de. *Esquisse d'un Tableau Historique des Progrès de l'Esprit Humain*. 1793. Ed. O. H. Prior and Y. Belaval. Paris, 1970.

Connor, W. Robert. *The New Politicians of Fifth-Century Athens*. Princeton, 1971.

Constant de Rebecque, Henri Benjamin. *De la Liberté des Anciens Comparée a Celle des Modernes*. 1819. In *Cours de Politique Constitutionelle ou Collection des Ouvrages Publiés sur le Gouvernement Représentativ*. Ed. Edouard Laboulaye. Paris, 1861.

Constantine, David. *Early Greek Travellers and the Hellenic Ideal*. Cambridge, 1984.

Cox, George. *A History of Greece*. 1874.

The Craftsman. 1727–32.

Cramb, John. *The Origins and Destiny of Imperial Britain*. London, 1915 (posthumous).

Crossman, R.H.S. *Plato Today*. 1937. New York, 1959.

Crutwell, P. "The Eighteenth Century: A Classical Age?" *Arion* 7 (1968): 110–32.

Curtius, Ernst. *Griechische Geschichte*. 1857–67.

Dahl, Robert. *Democracy and Its Critics*. New Haven and London, 1989.

Davies, John K. *Democracy and Classical Greece*. London, 1978.

Day, Joseph. *The Glory of Athens: The Popular Tradition as Reflected in the Panathenaicus of Aelius Aristides*. Chicago, 1980.

De Bonald, Louis. *Théorie du Pouvoir Politique et Religieux dans la Societé Civile, Demonstrée par le Raisonnement et par l'Histoire*. 1796. Reprint. Paris, 1843.

Degler, Carl. "Starr on Slavery." *Journal of Economic History* 19 (1959): 271–77.

Déonna, W. "L'éternel present: Guerre du Peloponnese (431–404) et Guerre Mondiale (1914–1918)." *Revue des Études Grecques* 35 (1922): 1–62.

De Pauw, Cornelius. *Recherches philosophiques sur les Grecs*. 1787? 1794 ed.

Desmoulins, Camille, ed. *Le Vieux Cordelier*. Modern ed. by Henri Calvet. Paris, 1936.

———. *Oeuvres de Camille Desmoulins*. Paris, 1874.

Dew, Thomas. *Review of the Debate in the Virginia Legislature of 1831 and 1832*. Reprint. Westport, Conn., 1970.

Diakov, V., and S. Kovalev, eds. *Histoire de l'Antiquité*. Moscow, n.d. (probably 1959).

Díaz-Plaja, F. *Griegos y Romanos en la revolución francesa*. Madrid, 1960.

Dickinson, G. Lowes. *The Greek Way of Life*. 1896. Reprint, with a preface by E. M. Forster. Ann Arbor, Mich., 1958.

Dickinson, H. T. *Liberty and Property: Political Ideology in Eighteenth-Century Britain*. New York, 1977.

Donlan, Walter. *The Aristocratic Ideal in Ancient Greece: Attitudes of Superiority from Homer to the End of the Fifth Century B.C.* Lawrence, Kans., 1980.

Dover, Sir Kenneth. "Classical Greek Attitudes to Sexual Behaviour." In *Women in the Ancient World: The Arethusa Papers*, ed. John Peradotto and John Sullivan. Albany, 1984.

———. *Greek Homosexuality.* Cambridge, Mass., 1978.

Dray, William. *On History and Philosophers of History.* Leiden, 1989.

duBois, Page. *Centaurs and Amazons: Women and the Pre-History of the Great Chain of Being.* Ann Arbor, Mich., 1982.

———. *Sowing the Body: Psychoanalysis and Ancient Representations of Women.* Chicago, 1988.

Dunn, John, ed. *Democracy: The Unfinished Journey 508BC to AD1993.* Oxford, 1992.

Duruy, Victor. *Histoire Grecque.* 2d ed. Paris, 1856.

Ehrenberg, Victor. *From Solon to Socrates: Greek History and Civilisation during the Sixth and Fifth Centuries B.C.* London, 1968.

Elliott, E. N., ed. *Cotton Is King, and Pro-Slavery Arguments.* 1860.

Elyot, Thomas. *The Book Named the Governor.* Ed. S. E. Lehmberg. London and New York, 1962.

Encyclopédie; ou, Dictionnaire raisonné des sciences, des arts, et des metiérs. Reprint, Stuttgart, 1966.

Engels, Friedrich. *The Origins of the Family, Private Property, and the State, in the Light of the Researches of Lewis H. Morgan.* 1884. Trans. for International Publishers. New York, 1942.

Euben, J. Peter. *The Tragedy of Political Theory: The Road Not Taken.* Princeton, 1990.

Farrand, Max. *The Records of the Federal Convention of 1787.* New Haven and London, 1937.

Farrar, Cynthia. *The Origins of Democratic Thinking: The Invention of Politics in Classical Athens.* Cambridge, 1988.

Filmer, Robert. *Patriarca and Other Political Works.* Ed. P. Laslett. Oxford, 1949.

Ferguson, Adam. *An Essay on the History of Civil Society.* 1767.

Ferguson, William Scott. *Greek Imperialism.* Boston and New York, 1913.

Fine, J.V.A. *The Ancient Greeks: A Critical History.* Cambridge, Mass., 1983.

Fink, Zera. *The Classical Republicans: An Essay in the Recovery of a Pattern of Thought in Seventeenth-Century England.* Evanston, Ill., 1945.

Finley, Moses. *Ancient Slavery and Modern Ideology.* Harmondsworth, 1980.

———. "The Athenian Demagogues." *Past and Present* 21 (1962): 3–24.

———. "Was Greek Civilization Based on Slave Labour?" *Historia* 8 (1959): 53–72.

Fitzhugh, George. "Black Republicanism in Athens." *De Bow's Review* 23 (1857): 20–26.

———. *Cannibals All! Or Slaves without Masters.* 1857. Reprint, with an introduction by C. Vann Woodward. Cambridge, Mass., 1960.

———. *Sociology for the South.* 1854. Reprinted in *Ante-Bellum: Writings of George Fitzhugh and Hinton Rowan Helper on Slavery*, ed. Harvey Wish. New York, 1960.

———. *Slavery Justified, by a Southerner.* 1850.

Floyd, Thomas. *The Picture of a perfit Commonwealth, describing aswell the offices of Princes and inferiour Magistrates ouer their subiects, as also the duties of subiects towards their Gouvernours.* 1600.

Ford, Paul L. *Pamphlets on the Constitution of the United States Published during Its Discussion by the People 1787–1788.* 1888.

Forrest, W. George. *The Emergence of Greek Democracy 800–400 BC.* New York and Toronto, 1966.

Forte, Bettie. *Rome and the Romans as the Greeks Saw Them.* Papers and Monographs of the American Academy in Rome, vol. 24. Rome, 1972.

Foster, Michael. *The Political Philosophies of Plato and Hegel.* Oxford, 1935.

Foucault, Michel. *L'Usage des plaisirs.* 1984. Trans. into English by Robert Hurley as *The Use of Pleasure.* New York, 1985.

Frank, Richard. "Marxism and Ancient History." *Arethusa* 8 (1975): 43–58.

Freeman, Edward. "The Athenian Democracy: A *History of Greece.* By George Grote." Reprinted in Freeman's *Historical Essays,* 2d ser. 1873.

Frisch, Hartvig. *The Constitution of the Athenians: A Philological-Historical Analysis of Pseudo-Xenophon's Treatise de re publica Atheniensium.* Copenhagen, 1942.

Frost, Frank. *Plutarch's Themistocles.* Princeton, 1980.

Fuks, A. *The Ancestral Constitution: Four Studies in Athenian Party Politics at the End of the Fifth Century B.C.* London, 1953.

Furet, F. *Marx et la Révolution Française.* Paris, 1986.

Fustel de Coulanges, Numa Denis. *The Ancient City: A Study on the Religion, Laws, and Institutions of Greece and Rome.* 1864. Baltimore, 1980.

Gardiner, Patrick, ed. *Theories of History.* New York and London, 1959.

Garlan, Yvon. *Slavery in Ancient Greece.* 1982. Trans. Janet Lloyd. Ithaca, 1988.

Giannotti, Donato. *Opere Politiche e Letterarie.* Ed. F.-L. Polidori. Florence, 1850.

Gildersleeve, Basil Lanneau. "A Southerner in the Peloponnesian War." *Atlantic* 80 (September 1897): 330–43.

Gillies, John. *The History of Ancient Greece, Its Colonies, and Conquests, Part the first; from the earliest accounts till the Division of the Macedonian Empire in the East.* 1786. 6th ed., London, 1820.

Goguet, Antoine Yves. *The Origin of Laws, Arts, and Sciences and their Progress among the most Ancient Nations, Vol. III, From the Establishment of Monarchy among the Israelites, to their Return from the Babylonish Captivity.* 1758. English trans., 1761.

Goldsmith, Oliver. *The Grecian History from the Earliest State, to the Death of Alexander the Great.* 13th ed., London, 1820.

Gomme, Arnold Wycombe. "The Position of Women in Classical Athens in the Fifth and Fourth Centuries." *Classical Philology* 20 (1925): 1–25.

———, Antony Andrewes, and Kenneth Dover. *A Historical Commentary on Thucydides.* 8 vols. Oxford, 1945–81.

Gordon, Thomas, and John Trenchard. *Cato's Letters; or, Essays on Liberty, Civil and Religious, and Other Important Subjects.* London, 1755. Reprint, New York, 1969.

Gouldner, Alvin. *Enter Plato: Classical Greece and the Origins of Social Theory.* New York, 1965. Reprint, New York, 1971.

Gray, J. Glenn. *Hegel and Greek Thought.* 1941. New York and Evanston, 1968.

"Greek Courts of Justice." *Quarterly Review* 33, no. 66 (1826): 332–56.

Greenidge, Abel Hendy Jones. *Handbook of Greek Constitutional Antiquities.* 1896.

Gribbin, W. "Rollin's Histories and American Republicanism." *William and Mary Quarterly,* 3d ser., 29 (1972): 611–22.

Grote, George. *A History of Greece from the Earliest Period to the Close of the Generation Contemporary with Alexander the Great*. 1846–56. Reprint, London, 1907.

———. "Institutions of Ancient Greece." *Westminster Review* 5 (April 1826): 278–80.

———. *Plato and the Other Companions of Socrates*. 3 vols. London, 1865.

Gruen, Erich. *The Hellenistic World and the Coming of Rome*. 2 vols. Berkeley, 1984.

Guerci, Luciano. *Libertà degli antichi e libertà dei moderni: Sparta, Atene e i "philosophes" nella Francia del Settecento*. Naples, 1979.

Guicciardini, Francesco. *Opere Inedite*. Ed. P. and L. Guicciardini. Florence, 1958.

Guite, H. "Cicero's Attitude towards the Greeks." *Greece and Rome*, 2d ser., 9 (1962): 142–59.

Gummere, Richard. *The American Colonial Mind and the Classical Tradition: Essays on Comparative Culture*. Cambridge, Mass., 1963.

Haarhoff, Theodore J. *The Stranger at the Gate: Aspects of Exclusiveness and Co-Operation in Ancient Greece and Rome, with Some Reference to Modern Times*. London and New York, 1938.

Hansen, Mogens. *The Athenian Assembly in the Age of Demosthenes: Structure, Principles, and Ideology*. Oxford, 1991.

———. "The Tradition of the Athenian Democracy A.D. 1750–1990." *Greece and Rome* 29 (1992): 14–30.

Halperin, David. *One Hundred Years of Homosexuality and Other Essays on Greek Love*. New York and London, 1990.

Hamilton, Alexander. *The Papers of Alexander Hamilton*, vol. 3. Ed. H. Syrett. New York, 1962.

———, John Jay, and James Madison, *The Federalist Papers*. Ed. Clinton Rossiter. New York and Scarborough, Ontario, 1961.

Hammond, Nicholas. *The Classical Age of Greece*. London, 1975.

Hanson, Russell. *The Democratic Imagination in America: Conversations with Our Past*. Princeton, 1985.

Harrington, J. Drew. "Classical Antiquity and the Proslavery Argument." *Slavery and Abolition* 10 (1989): 60–72.

Harrington, James. *The Political Works of James Harrington*. Ed. J.G.A. Pocock. Cambridge, 1977.

Havelock, Eric. *The Liberal Temper in Greek Politics*. 1957. Reprint, New Haven and London, 1964.

Heeren, Arnold. *Ancient Greece*. Trans. George Bancroft. London, 1841.

Hegel, G.W.F. *Early Theological Writings*. Trans. T. M. Knox. Chicago, 1948.

———. *Lectures on the History of Philosophy*. Trans. in 1892 by E. S. Haldane and F. Simson. Reprint, Atlantic Highlands, N.J., 1955.

———. *Lectures on the Philosophy of History*. Trans. J. Sibree. Reprint, New York, 1956.

Heidegger, Martin. "Hegel und die Griechen." In *Die Gegenwart: Der Griechen im Neueren Denken, Festschrift für Hans-Georg Gadamer zum 60. Geburtstag*, ed. Dieter Henrich. Tübingen, 1960.

Herder, Johann Gottlieb von. *Outlines of a Philosophy of the History of Man (Ideen zur Philosophie der Geschichte der Menschheit)*. Trans. in 1800 by T. Churchill. Reprint, New York, n.d. (probably 1966).

Hignett, Charles. *A History of the Athenian Constitution to the End of the Fifth Century B.C.* Oxford, 1952.

Hirzel, Rudolph. *Plutarch*. Leipzig, 1912.

Hobbes, Thomas. *Hobbes' Thucydides*. Ed. with an intro. by Richard Schlatter. New Brunswick, 1975.

Hölderlin, Friedrich. *Hyperion, or The Hermit in Greece*. Trans. Willard Trask. New York, 1959.

Holm, Adolph. *The History of Greece from Its Commencement to the Close of the Independence of the Greek Nation*. 1886–94. English trans., London and New York, 1900.

Holmes, Stephen. *Benjamin Constant and the Making of Modern Liberalism*. New Haven and London, 1984.

Hornblower, Simon. *The Greek World, 479–323 BC*. London, 1983.

—————. *Thucydides*. Baltimore, 1987.

Howard, Martha. *The Influence of Plutarch in the Major European Literatures of the Eighteenth Century*. Chapel Hill, N.C., 1970.

Hulliung, Mark. *Citizen Machiavelli*. Princeton, 1983.

Hume, David. *Essays, Moral, Political, and Literary*. 1742.

Hunter, Virginia. *Thucydides: The Artful Reporter*. Toronto, 1973.

Hyneman, Charles, and Donald Lutz, eds. *American Political Writing during the Founding Era*. Indianapolis, 1983.

Jaeger, Werner. *Paideia: The Ideals of Greek Culture*. 1933. English trans. by Gilbert Highet, New York, 1939.

Jenkyns, Richard. *The Victorians and Ancient Greece*. Cambridge, Mass., 1980.

Johnson, Richard. "Hellas and Hesperia: Ancient Greece and Early America." In *Paths from Ancient Greece*, ed. Carol Thomas. Leiden, 1988.

Jones, Christopher P. *Plutarch and Rome*. Oxford, 1971.

Jones, Tom. *From the Tigris to the Tiber*. 1969. 3d ed., Homewood, Ill., 1983.

Kagan, Donald. *The Great Dialogue: History of Greek Political Thought from Homer to Polybius*. New York and London, 1965.

Kain, Philip. *Schiller, Hegel, and Marx*. Kingston and Montreal, 1982.

Kelly, George A. *Idealism, Politics, and History: Sources of Hegelian Thought*. Cambridge, 1969.

Keohane, Nannerl. *Philosophy and the State in France: The Renaissance to the Enlightenment*. Princeton, 1980.

Keuls, Eva. *The Reign of the Phallus: Sexual Politics in Ancient Athens*. New York, 1985.

Kitto, Humphrey. D. F. *The Greeks*. 1951. Reprint, Harmondsworth, 1981.

Knipfing, John R. "German Historians and Macedonian Imperialism." *American Historical Review* 26 (1921): 657–71.

Korovkin, F. *History of the Ancient World*. 1981. English trans., Moscow, 1985.

Kraut, Richard. *Socrates and the State*. Princeton, 1984.

Leduc-Fayette, D. *J. J. Rousseau et le myth de l'antiquité*. Paris, 1974.

Lehmann, Lutz. *Mably und Rousseau: Eine Studie über die Grenzen der Emanzipation im Ancien Regime*. Frankfurt, 1975.

Leigh, R. A. "Jean-Jacques Rousseau and the Myth of Antiquity in the Eighteenth Century." In *Classical Influences on Western Thought A.D. 1650–1870*, ed. R. R. Bolgar. Cambridge, 1979.

Lekas, Padelis. *Marx on Classical Antiquity: Problems of Historical Methodology*. Sussex and New York, 1988.

Levinson, Ronald. *In Defense of Plato*. Cambridge, Mass., 1953.

Lewis, George Cornewall. "Grote's *History of Greece*." *Edinburgh Review* 91 (1850): 118–52.

*Lloyd-Jones, Hugh. *Blood for the Ghosts: Classical Influences in the Nineteenth and Twentieth Centuries*. London, 1982.

Loraux, Nicole. *The Invention of Athens: The Funeral Oration in the Classical City*. Trans. Alan Sheridan. Cambridge, Mass., and London, 1986.

————, and Pierre Vidal-Naquet. "La Formation de l'Athènes Bourgeoise: Essai d'Historiographie 1750–1850." In *Classical Influences on Western Thought* A.D. *1650–1870*, ed. R. R. Bolgar. Cambridge, 1979.

Mably, Gabriel Bonnot de. *Entretiens de Phocion*. 1763. Reprint, 1804.

————. *Observations sur l'Histoire de la Grèce, ou, Des causes de la prosperité des Grecs* (1766).

Macaulay, Thomas Babington. "On the Athenian Orators" and "On Mitford's History of Greece." In the *Complete Works of Lord Macaulay*, ed. Hannah Trevelyan. New York and London, n.d. (1873?).

McClelland, J. S. *The Crowd and the Mob: From Plato to Canetti*. London and Boston, 1989.

MacDonald, Forrest. *Novus Ordo Seclorum: The Intellectual Origins of the Constitution*. Lawrence, Kans., 1985.

MacGregor, Malcolm, *The Athenians and Their Empire*. Vancouver, B.C., 1987.

————. "The Politics of the Historian Thucydides." *Phoenix* 10 (1956): 93–102.

Machiavelli, Niccolò. *Discorsi sopra la prima deca di Tito Livio*. In *Il Principe e Discorsi*, ed. S. Bertelli. Milan, 1960.

————. *The Discourses of Niccolò Machiavelli*. Ed. Leslie J. Walker, S. J. 1950. New ed., London, 1975.

Mahaffy, John Pentland. *Social Life in Greece from Homer to Menander*. 1874.

Maine, Henry. *Popular Government: Four Essays*. 1885. Reprint, Indianapolis, 1976.

Mat-Hasquin, Michele. *Voltaire et l'Antiquité Grecque*. Studies on Voltaire, no. 197. Oxford, 1981.

Maurras, Charles. "L'Action Française et la démocratie athénienne." 1909. Reprinted with a preface by Bertrand Hemmerdinger in *Quaderni di Storia* 2, no. 4 (1976): 7–18.

May, Thomas Erskine. *Democracy in Europe: A History*. 1877.

Mill, John Stuart. *Autobiography*. 1853–54. With a preface by J. Coss. New York, 1924.

————. "Grote's History of Greece [I]" (1846) and "Grote's History of Greece [II]." In *Essays on Philosophy and the Classics*, vol. 11 of his *Collected Works*. Toronto, 1978.

Miller, Jim. *Rousseau: Dreamer of Democracy*. New Haven, 1984.

Mitford, William. *The History of Greece*. 1784–ca. 1790. Reprint, 1822.

"Mitford's History of Greece." *Edinburgh Review* 12 (July 1808): 478–517.

Momigliano, Arnaldo. *Studies in Historiography*. New York, 1966.

Montagu, Edward. *Reflections on the Rise and Fall of the Antient Republics. Adapted to the Present State of Great Britain*. 3d ed. 1769.

Moore, J. M., ed. *Aristotle and Xenophon on Democracy and Oligarchy*. London, 1975.

Morgan, Lewis. *Ancient Society: or, Researches in the Lines of Human Progress from Savagery, through Barbarism*. 1877.

Morrow, Glenn. "Aristotle's Comments on Plato's *Laws*." In *Aristotle and Plato in the Mid-Fourth Century*, ed. I. Duering and G. E. Owen, 145–62. Göteborg, 1960.

————. *Plato's Cretan City: A Historical Interpretation of The Laws.* Princeton, 1960.

Mossé, Claude. *L'antiquité dans la Révolution française.* Paris, 1989.

————. *Histoire d'une démocratie, Athènes, des origines a la conquête Macédonienne.* Paris, 1971.

Mulgan, R. G. *Aristotle's Political Theory: An Introduction for Students of Political Theory.* Oxford, 1977.

Murray, Gilbert. *Greek Studies.* Oxford, 1946.

Naess, A., J. Christophersen, and K. Kjell. *Democracy, Ideology, and Objectivity: Studies in the Semantics and Cognitive Analysis of Ideological Controversy.* Oslo, 1956.

Nichols, Mary. *Citizens and Statesmen: A Study of Aristotle's Politics.* Savage, Md., 1992.

Niles, Hezekiah. *Principles and Acts of the Revolution in America.* Reprint, New York, Chicago, and New Orleans, 1876.

Ober, Josiah. *Mass and Elite in Democratic Athens: Rhetoric, Ideology, and the Power of the People.* Princeton, 1989.

Ostwald, Martin. *From Popular Sovereignty to the Sovereignty of Law: Law, Society, and Politics in Fifth-Century Athens.* Berkeley and Los Angeles, 1986.

————. *Nomos and the Beginnings of Athenian Democracy.* Oxford, 1969.

Padgug, Robert. "Select Bibliography on Marxism and the Study of Antiquity." *Arethusa* 8 (1975): 201–25.

Paine, Thomas. *The Rights of Man, Part II.* 1792. Reprint, London, 1915.

Palmer, Robert R. "Notes on the Use of the Word 'Democracy' 1789–1799." *Political Science Quarterly* 68 (1953): 203–26.

"Panegyrical Oratory of Greece." *Quarterly Review* 27, no. 54 (1822): 382–404.

*Pangle, Thomas. *The Ennobling of Democracy: The Challenge of the Postmodern Age.* Baltimore, 1992.

————. *The Spirit of Modern Republicanism: The Moral Vision of the American Founders and the Philosophy of Locke.* Chicago and London, 1988.

Parker, Harold. *The Cult of Antiquity and the French Revolutionaries: A Study in the Development of the Revolutionary Spirit.* Chicago, 1937.

Paruta, Paolo. *Discorsi Politici.* 1599. Reprint, 1629.

————. *Della perfettione della Vita Politica Libri Tre, Ne' quali si ragiona delle virtù Morali, e di tutto ciò apartiene alla Felicità civile.* 1579. Reprint, 1586.

Patrizi, Francesco. *De Institutione Reipublicae Libri IX, ad Senatum Populumque Senensem Scripti.* 1460? Reprint, 1608.

————. *De Regno et Regis Institutione Libri IX, ad Alphonsum Aragonium inclytum ac celeberrimum Calabriae Ducem Scripti.* Ca. 1485. Reprint, 1608.

Patterson, Orlando. *Freedom in the Making of Western Culture.* New York, 1991.

Pauly, A., G. Wissowa, and W. Kroll, eds., *Realencyclopaedie der klassischen Altertumswissenschaft.* Stuttgart, 1894–1980.

Pavan, Massimiliano. *Antichità Classica e Pensiero Moderno.* Florence, 1977.

Pelling, C.B.R. "Plutarch and Roman Politics." In *Past Perspectives.* Cambridge, 1986.

Petrochilos, Nicholas. *Roman Attitudes to the Greeks.* Athens, 1974.

Plato. *The Laws.* Ed. and trans. R. G. Bury. 2 vols. London and Cambridge, Mass., 1926.

Plato. *The Republic of Plato.* Trans. Allan Bloom. New York, 1968.

Plato. *The Republic of Plato.* Trans. Francis Cornford. Oxford, 1941.

————. *The Republic of Plato.* Ed. and trans. Paul Shorey. London, 1930.

Plutarch. *Plutarch: The Rise and Fall of Athens: Nine Greek Lives*. London, 1960.

———. *Precepts of Statecraft*. Trans. H. N. Fowler in *Plutarch's Moralia*, vol. 10. Cambridge and London, 1936.

Pocock, John G. A. *The Machiavellian Moment: Florentine Political Thought and the Atlantic Republican Tradition*. Princeton, 1975.

Podlecki, Anthony. *The Life of Themistocles*. Montreal and London, 1975.

Pomeroy, Sarah. *Goddesses, Whores, Wives, and Slaves: Women in Antiquity*. New York, 1975.

Pope, Maurice. "Thucydides and Democracy." *Historia* 37 (1988): 276–96.

Popper, Karl. *The Open Society and Its Enemies*, vol. 2: *The Spell of Plato*. London, 1945. Reprint, New York and Evanston, 1962, with additions and a response to the attack in Levinson's *In Defense of Plato*.

Potter. *Antiquities of Greece*. 1697. Reprint, 1813.

Prentice, William Kelly. *The Ancient Greeks: Studies towards a Better Understanding of the Ancient World*. Princton, 1940.

The Pro-Slavery Argument; as Maintained by the Most Distinguished Writers of the Southern States. 1852.

Raaflaub, Kurt. "Contemporary Perceptions of Democracy in Fifth-Century Athens." *Classica et Medievalia* 40 (1989): 33–70.

———. "Democracy, Oligarchy, and the Concept of the 'Free Citizen' in Late Fifth-Century Athens." *Political Theory* 11 (1983): 517–44.

Rahe, Paul. *Republics Ancient and Modern: Classical Republicanism and the American Revolution*. Chapel Hill, N.C., 1992.

Ralegh, Walter. *History of the World*. Reprinted in *The Works of Sir Walter Ralegh*. Oxford, 1829.

Rawson, Elizabeth. *The Spartan Tradition in European Thought*. Oxford, 1969.

Reinhold, Meyer. *Classica Americana: The Greek and Roman Heritage in the United States*. Detroit, 1984.

A Rejected Essay. Published in Edinburgh, 1828.

Response to "Quarterly Review—Articles on Greek Literature." *Westminster Review* 3 (January 1825): 233ff.

Revett, Nicholas, and James Stuart. *The Antiquities of Athens*. 1762.

Reynolds, L. D., and N. G. Wilson. *Scribes and Scholars*. Oxford, 1968.

Rhodes, Peter J. *A Commentary on the Aristotelian Athenaion Politeia*. Oxford, 1981.

*Richard, Carl. *The Founders and the Classics: Greece, Rome, and the American Enlightenment*. Cambridge, Mass., 1994.

Rinuccini, Alamanno. "On Liberty." In *Humanism and Liberty: Writings on Freedom from Fifteenth-Century Florence*, ed. Renée Neu Watkins. Columbia, S.C., 1979.

Roberts, Jennifer. *Accountability in Athenian Government*. Madison, Wis., 1982.

Robinson, Cyril E. *Hellas: A Short History of Greece*. Boston, 1948.

Robinson, Richard. "Dr. Popper's Defence of Democracy." 1951. Reprinted in Robinson's *Essays in Greek Philosophy*. Oxford, 1969.

Roland de la Platière, Jeanne-Marie Phlipon. *Mémoires de Madame Roland écrits durant sa captivité*. Ed. C. Perroud. Paris, 1905.

Rollin, Charles. *The Ancient History of the Egyptians, Carthaginians, Assyrians, Babylonians, Medes and Persians, Grecians and Macedonians*. 1729. Reprint, Edinburgh and London, 1861.

Rousseau, Jean-Jacques. *The First and Second Discourses Together with the Replies to Critics and Essay on the Origin of Languages*. Ed. V. Gourevitch. New York, 1986.

Rudolph, F., ed. *Essays on Education in the Early Republic*. Cambridge, Mass., 1975.

St. John, J. A. *Manners and Customs of Ancient Greece*. 1842.

Ste. Croix, Geoffrey de. *The Class Struggle in the Ancient Greek World*. London, 1981.

Salkever, Stephen. *Finding the Mean: Theory and Practice in Aristotelian Political Philosophy*. Princeton, 1990.

Sandys, J. E. *A History of Classical Scholarship From the Sixth Century B.C. to the End of the Middle Ages*. Cambridge, 1903–8.

Sanford, Eva. "The Study of Ancient History in the Middle Ages." *Journal of the History of Ideas* 5 (1944): 21–43.

Saunders, Trevor. *Bibliography on Plato's Laws*. New York, 1976.

*Schieder, Theodor. "The Role of Historical Consciousness in Political Action." *History and Theory: Studies in the Philosophy of History*, Beiheft 17, *Historical Consciousness and Political Action*. Middletown, 1978.

Schiller, Friedrich von. *Aesthetical and Philosophical Essays*. Ed. Nathan H. Dole. Boston, 1902.

———. *Die Gezetzgebung des Lykurg und Solon*. 1790. Reprint, Vaduz, 1956.

Schleich, T. "Mably a le Antiche Costituzioni." *Quaderni di Storia* 23 (1986): 173–97.

Seager, Robin. "Elitism and Democracy in Classical Athens." In *The Rich, the Well-Born and the Powerful: Elites and Upper Classes in History*. Ed. F. C. Jaher. Urbana, Ill., 1973.

Sealey, Raphael. *The Athenian Republic: Democracy or the Rule of Law?* University Park, Pa., and London, 1987.

———. *A History of the Greek City-States, 700–338 B.C.* Berkeley and Los Angeles, 1976.

———. "The Origins of Demokratia." *California Studies in Classical Antiquity* 6 (1973): 272–77.

Shklar, Judith. *Freedom and Independence: A Study of the Political Ideas of Hegel's Phenomenology of Mind*. Cambridge, 1976.

———. *Men and Citizens: A Study of Rousseau's Social Theory*. Cambridge, 1969.

Sidney, Algernon. *Discourses*. 1698, posthumously; written probably 1680. Reprint, New York, 1805.

Sinclair, T. A. *A History of Greek Political Thought*. 1951. Cleveland and New York, 1968.

Slater, Philip. *The Glory of Hera: Greek Mythology and the Greek Family*. Boston, 1968.

Smith, Thomas. *De Republica Anglorum*. 1583. Menston, England, 1970.

Spurlin, Paul. *Montesquieu in America*. University, La., 1940.

Stadter, Philip. *A Commentary on Plutarch's Pericles*. Chapel Hill, N.C., and London, 1989.

Stalley, R. F. *An Introduction to Plato's Laws*. Indianapolis, 1983.

Stanyan, Temple. *The Grecian History*. 1739.

Starr, Chester. "An Overdose of Slavery." *Journal of Economic History* 18 (1958): 17–32.

Steiner, George. *Antigones*. New York and Oxford, 1984.

Stobart, John C. *The Glory that was Greece*. London, 1911.

Stobart, John C. *The Glory that Was Greece*. 4th ed., revised by Robert J. Hopper. London, 1964.

Stockton, David. *The Classical Athenian Democracy*. Oxford and New York, 1990.

Stone, Isidor F. *The Trial of Socrates*. Boston, 1988.

Stoneman, Richard. *Land of Lost Gods: The Search for Classical Greece*. Norman, Okla., and London, 1987.

Storing, Herbert, ed. *The Complete Anti-Federalist*. Chicago, 1981.

Strauss, Leo. *The Argument and Action of Plato's Laws*. Chicago, 1975.

———. *The City and Man*. Charlottesville, 1964.

———. *Liberalism Ancient and Modern*. Ithaca, 1968.

Swift, Jonathan. *A Discourse of the Contests and Dissentions between the Nobles and the Commons in Athens and Rome with the Consequences They Had upon Both Those States*. Ed. Frank Ellis. Oxford, 1967.

Syme, Ronald. "The Greeks under Roman Rule." In *Roman Papers*, ed. E. Badian. Oxford, 1979.

Tarrant, Harold. "Middle Platonism and the *Seventh Epistle*." *Phronesis* 28 (1983): 92–93.

Tigerstedt, Eugene N. *The Legend of Sparta in Classical Antiquity*. Stockholm, 1965.

Tocqueville, Alexis de. *Democracy in America*. 1840. English trans. by H. Reeve. New Rochelle, n.d.

Trouard, Sister M. A. *Cicero's Attitude towards the Greeks*. Chicago, 1942.

Tucker, Josiah. *A Treatise Concerning Civil Government*. 1781. Reprint, New York, 1967.

Tucker, Thomas G. *Life in Ancient Athens*. London, 1906.

Turner, Frank. "British Politics and the Demise of the Roman Republic." *Historical Journal* 29 (1986): 577–99.

———. *The Greek Heritage in Victorian Britain*. New Haven, 1981.

Vidal-Naquet, Pierre. *La démocratie grecque vue d'ailleurs*. Paris, 1990.

———. "Tradition de la Démocratie Grecque." Introduction to Monique Alexander's translation of M. I. Finley, *Démocratie antique et démocratie moderne*. Paris, 1976.

Vlastos, Gregory. "The Historical Socrates and Athenian Democracy." *Political Theory* 11 (1983): 495–516.

———. *Platonic Studies*. 2d ed. Princeton, 1981.

Vogt, Joseph. *Ancient Slavery and the Ideal of Man*. Trans. Thomas Wiedemann. Cambridge, Mass., 1975.

Volney, Constantin-Francois. *Leçons d'Histoire Prononcées a l'École Normale, en l'An III de la République française*. 1795. In *Oeuvres Complètes*, vol. 6. Paris, 1821.

von Fritz, Kurt. *The Theory of the Mixed Constitution in Antiquity: A Critical Analysis of Polybius' Political Ideas*. New York, 1954.

von Leyden, Wolfgang. *Aristotle on Equality and Justice: His Political Argument*. New York, 1985.

Wachsmuth, Wilhelm. *The Historical Antiquities of the Greeks, with Reference to Their Political Institutions*. Trans. E. Woolrych. 1837.

Wardman, Alan. *Rome's Debt to Greece*. London, 1976.

Wason, Margaret. *Class Struggles in Ancient Greece*. Rome, 1972.

Watt, Roderick. "'Wanderer, kommst du nach Sparta': History through Propaganda into Literary Commonplace." *Modern Language Review* 80 (1985): 871–83.

Weiss, Roberto. *The Renaissance Discovery of Classical Antiquity.* 2d ed., Oxford, 1988.

White, Morton. *Philosophy, the Federalist, and the Constitution.* New York and Oxford, 1987.

Wilamowitz-Möllendorff, Ulrich von. *Aristoteles und Athen.* Berlin, 1893.

———. *History of Classical Scholarship.* 1921. Trans. A. Harris with an intro. by Hugh Lloyd-Jones. London, 1982.

Wiltshire, Susan Ford. "Jefferson, Calhoun, and the Slavery Debate: The Classics and the Two Minds of the South." *Southern Humanities Review* 11 (special issue, 1977): 33–40.

Winckelmann, Wilhelm. *Geschichte der Kunst des Alterthums (1764).* Trans. G. Henry Lodge as *The History of Ancient Art.* Boston, 1872.

Winkler, John, and Froma Zeitlin, eds. *Nothing to Do with Dionysos? Athenian Drama in Its Social Context.* Princeton, 1990.

Winspear, Alban. *The Genesis of Plato's Thought.* New York, 1940.

Witt, Ronald. *Coluccio Salutati and the Public Letters.* Geneva, 1976.

Wolin, Sheldon. *The Presence of the Past.* Baltimore, 1989.

Wollheim, Richard. "Democracy." *Journal of the History of Ideas* 19 (1958): 232.

Wood, Ellen M. *Peasant-Citizen and Slave: The Foundations of Athenian Democracy.* London and New York, 1988.

———, and Neal Wood. *Class Ideology and Ancient Political Theory: Socrates, Plato, and Aristotle in Social Context.* Oxford and New York, 1978.

———. "Socrates and Democracy: A Reply to Gregory Vlastos." *Political Theory* 14 (1986): 55–82.

Young, William. *The British Constitution of Government Compared with That of a Democratic Republic.* 1793.

Zimmern, Alfred. *The Greek Commonwealth: Politics and Economics in Fifth-Century Athens.* 1911. 5th ed., 1931. Reprint, New York and Oxford, 1961.

INDEX

DATE DU